To: Edwina, Rachel and Rosie
Jackie, Erin and Aidan

Third Edition

CONTEMPORARY HUMAN RESOURCE MANAGEMENT
Text and Cases

Tom Redman

Adrian Wilkinson

 **FT** Prentice Hall
FINANCIAL TIMES

An imprint of **Pearson Education**
Harlow, England • London • New York • Boston • San Francisco • Toronto • Sydney • Singapore • Hong Kong
Tokyo • Seoul • Taipei • New Delhi • Cape Town • Madrid • Mexico City • Amsterdam • Munich • Paris • Milan

Peason Education Limited
Edinburgh Gate
Harlow
Essex CM20 2JE
England

and Associated Companies throughout the world

Visit us on the World Wide Web at:
www.pearsoned.co.uk

First published 2001
Second edition published 2006
Third edition published 2009

ISBN: 978-0-273-71633-4

British Library Cataloguing-in-Publication Data
A catalogue record for this book is available from the British Library

Library of Congress Cataloging-in-Publication Data
Contemporary human resource management : text and cases / [edited by]
Tom Redman, Adrian Wilkinson. – 3rd ed.
    p. cm.
 Includes bibliographical references and index.
 ISBN 978-0-273-71633-4 (pbk. : alk. paper)
 1. Personnel management. 2. Personnel management–Study and teaching. 3. Personnel management–Case studies. I. Redman, Tom, 1952- II. Wilkinson, Adrian, 1963-
 HF5549.15.C66 2009
 658.3–dc22

                                                                              2008036788

10 9 8 7 6 5 4 3 2 1
12 11 10 09

Typeset in 10pt Minion by 73
Printed and bound by Rotolito Lombarda, Italy

The publisher's policy is to use paper manufactured from sustainable forests.

CONTENTS

Supporting resources

Visit **www.pearsoned.co.uk/redman** to find valuable online resources

Companion Website for students
- Multiple choice questions to help test your learning
- An online glossary to explain key terms

For instructors
- An Instructor's Manual containing teaching notes to case studies
- PowerPoint slides that can be downloaded and used for presentations

Also: The Companion Website provides the following features:
- Search tool to help locate specific items of content
- E-mail results and profile tools to send results of quizzes to instructors
- Online help and support to assist with website usage and troubleshooting

For more information please contact your local Pearson Education sales representative or visit **www.pearsoned.co.uk/redman**

CASE STUDIES AND EXERCISES

EDITORS

Tom Redman is Professor of Human Resource Management and Director of Research at University of Durham Business School. His books include *Managing Managers* (1993) and *Managing through TQM: Theory and Practice* (1998). He is a Fellow of the Chartered Institute of Personnel and Development.

Adrian Wilkinson is Professor of Employment Relations at Griffith University and Director of the Centre for Work, Organisation and Wellbeing. He is also Visiting Professor at Loughborough University Business School. His books include *Making Quality Critical* (1995), *Managing Quality and Human Resource* (1997), *Managing through TQM: Theory and Practice* (1998), *Understanding Work and Employment: Industrial Relations in Transition* (2003) and *Human Resource Management at Work* (2008). He is a Fellow and Accredited Examiner of the Chartered Institute of Personnel and Development. He is Chief Editor of the *International Journal of Management Reviews* and Associate Editor of the *Human Resource Management Journal*.

CONTRIBUTORS

Peter Ackers	Professor of Employment Relations and Labour History, Loughborough University Business School
Stephen Ackroyd	Professor of Organisational Behaviour, University of Lancaster
Nicolas Bacon	Professor of Human Resource Management, Nottingham Business School
Michelle Barker	Professor of Management, Griffith Business School
Sara Branch	Research Fellow, Centre for Key Ethics, Law, Justice and Governance, Griffith University
Catherine Cassell	Professor of Organisational Behaviour, Manchester Business School
Alistair Cheyne	Senior Lecturer in Organisational Psychology, Loughborough University Business School
Allen Clabaugh	Lecturer in Human Resource Management, School of Management, Edith Cowan University
Laurie Cohen	Professor of Organisational Behaviour, Loughborough University Business School
David Collings	Lecturer, National University of Ireland, Galway
Graeme Currie	Professor of Organisational Behaviour, Nottingham Business School
Tony Dundon	Lecturer in Human Resource Management, Department of Management, National University of Ireland, Galway
Amal El-Sawad	Lecturer in Human Resource Management, Loughborough University Business School
Mark W. Gilman	Senior Lecturer in Industrial Relations and Human Resource Management, Kent Business School
Irena Grugulis	Professor of Human Resource Management, Management School, Bradford University
Philip Hancock	Lecturer in Organisational Behaviour, Warwick Business School
Gail Hebson	Lecturer in Human Resource Management, Manchester Business School
Donald Hislop	Lecturer in Organisational Behaviour, Loughborough University Business School
William Hunter	Senior Lecturer in HRM, University of Sunderland
Sue Hutchinson	Teaching Fellow, School of Management, University of Bath
Stewart Johnstone	Research Associate, Loughborough University
Nicholas Kinnie	Reader in Human Resource Management, School of Management, University of Bath
John Loan-Clarke	Senior Lecturer in Organisational Development, Loughborough University Business School
Anne McCormack	Lecturer, University of Strathclyde
Paula McDonald	Lecturer, Queensland University of Technology

Miral Metawie	Doctoral Student, Kent Business School
Stephen Procter	Alcan Professor of Management, School of Management, University of Newcastle
Alexandros Psychogios	Lecturer in Organisational Behaviour and HRM, City College, Greece
Sheryl Ramsay	Lecturer in Management, Griffith Business School
Douglas Renwick	Lecturer in Human Resource Management, University of Sheffield Management School
Bradley Saunders	Doctoral Student, Loughborough University
Dora Scholarios	Reader in HRM, Strathclyde University
Ed Snape	Professor, Department of Management, Hong Kong Polytechnic
Juani Swart	Senior Lecturer in Human Resource Management, School of Management, University of Bath
Leslie T. Szamosi	Senior Lecturer in HRM and Global Marketing, City College, Greece
David Thompson	Associate Professor, Department of Management, Hong Kong Polytechnic
Keith Townsend	Research Fellow, Centre for Work, Organisation and Wellbeing, Griffith University
Melissa Tyler	Senior Lecturer in Organisation Studies, Loughborough University Business School
Steven Vincent	Senior Lecturer in Industrial Relations and HRM, Leeds University Business School
Geoffrey Wood	Professor of Comparative Human Resource Management, University of Sheffield

ACKNOWLEDGEMENTS

As with any book, the list of acknowledgements is extensive. But these are the most important. Thanks to our editor Laura Dent and also to Matthew Walker. As usual, family and friends make the major contribution and Tom and Adrian are grateful to their families for their support while the book was being written. Jackie Wilkinson helped with some of the research material in the book. The authors and publishers wish to thank the following for permission to use copyright material: Blackwells, MCB University Press, Croners, International Thompson Business Press, Macmillan, Industrial Relations Service, Sage.

Thanks to Erin for her help in designing the cover.

We are grateful to the following for permission to reproduce copyright material:

Figure 16.1 reprinted with the permission of John Wiley & Sons, Inc; Figure 17.1 reproduced from 'Participation and Democracy at Work' edited by Jeff Hyman, Paul Thompson and Bill Harley ISBN PB 978-1-4039-0004-3. Reproduced by kind permission of Palgrave Macmillan; Figure 22.1 reproduced with the permission of Anton Hout of Overcome Bullying Canada; Figure 22.5 reproduced with the permission of Linda Shallcross of Workplace Mobbing Australia; Table 1.6 Caldwell, R. (2004) 'Rhetoric, facts and self-fulfilling prophecies: exploring practitioners' perceptions of progress in implementing HRM', Industrial Relations Journal, Vol.35, No.3, pp.196–215. Table reprinted by kind permission of Wiley-Blackwell Publishers © 2004; Table 3.2 Source: IDS HR Study 865, Competency Frameworks, March 2008 p.17. www.idshrstudies.com. Table reprinted by kind permission of Incomes Data Services; Table 6.1 Millward N, Bryson A and Forth J, 2000. All Change at Work. London: Routledge. Table reprinted by kind permission of Taylor and Francis © 2000; Table 8.2 based on Table 3.3 Trade union density and collective bargaining coverage in OECD countries, 1970–2000, OECD Employment Outlook: 2004 Edition; Table 8.3 from Hamann, K. and Kelly, J. (2008) 'Varieties of capitalism and industrial relations'. In P. Blyton, N. Bacon, J. Fiorito and E. Heery (Eds) The Sage Handbook of Industrial Relations. London: Sage, pp. 129–148. SAGE Publications Ltd © 2008; Table 13.2 adapted from 'Career Management interventions in organizations' from Arnold, J., Managing Careers into the Twenty-first Century, copyright © Sage Publications Ltd, 1997; Table 18.3 reproduced from Hislop, D. (2008). 'Conceptualizing Knowledge Work Utilizing Skill and Knowledge-Based Concepts: The Case of Some Consultants and Service Engineers'. Management Learning, forthcoming. SAGE Publications Ltd © 2008.

In some instances we have been unable to trace the owners of copyright material, and we would appreciate any information that would enable us to do so.

Part I

FUNDAMENTALS OF HUMAN RESOURCE MANAGEMENT

Chapter 1

HUMAN RESOURCE MANAGEMENT:
A CONTEMPORARY PERSPECTIVE

Tom Redman and Adrian Wilkinson

Introduction

This book is about human resource management and is concerned with the way in which organisations manage their people. In this introductory chapter we discuss our own approach to the study of HRM and the rationale underpinning the ordering and presentation of material in the book. Our aim is to chart some of the broad terrain of a rapidly developing field of study in order to prepare the reader for the more finely grained treatment of specific HRM topics to be found in the individual chapters. In particular, we examine the rise of HRM, the effects of the changing context of work on HRM, what it involves, and the strategic nature of HRM practice, its impact on organisational performance and the changing role of the HRM function. The chapter concludes with a consideration of our views on the audience at which the book is targeted and some thoughts on how it may best be used.

The development of HRM

The roots of HRM can be found in the emergence of industrial welfare work from the 1890s, as organisations driven by a mix of humanitarian, religious and business motives began to provide workplace amenities such as medical care, housing and libraries. In addition, employment offices were established to deal with hiring, payroll and record keeping. When scientific management emerged, the principles of science were also to be applied to the management of people as well as the management of production. We see here the shift from direct systems of management (personal supervision, traditional paternalism and simple piecework systems) to more technical systems of management and bureaucratic forms of employment (Gospel 2005). From here the HRM function came to life, responsible for establishing modern personnel methods (Kaufman 2007), and we have seen a growing professionalisation of the role. However, it has been often seen as largely administrative and dealing with the 'labour problem' rather then contributing to strategic goals. This is the backcloth for the rise of the new HRM.

The past 20 years or so have seen the rise of what has been called the human resource management (HRM) new orthodoxy (Guest 1998; Bacon 2003; Marchington and Wilkinson 2008; Boxall *et al.* 2007; Wilkinson *et al.* 2008). In the mid-1980s in the UK, and earlier in the US, the term 'HRM' became fashionable and started gradually to replace others such as 'personnel management', 'industrial relations' and 'labour relations'. The practitioners of people management are no longer personnel officers and trainers but are HR managers and human resource developers (and importantly, line managers). The 1990s saw the launch of new journals and the flourishing of university courses in HRM. The then Institute of Personnel Management, the main professional body for personnel practitioners, re-launched its journal *People Management,* but subtitled it *'the magazine for human resources professionals'.* The millennium has now witnessed the professional body receiving a Royal Charter to become the Chartered Institute of Personnel and Development. The new HRM bandwagon was well and truly rolling.

Early contributions on the implications of the rise of HRM were concerned to define it and to compare it with the more traditional British approach to personnel management (e.g. Guest 1987). HRM was in turn both heralded as 'a new era of humane people oriented employment management' (Keenoy 1990, p.375) and derided as a 'blunt instrument to bully workers' (Monks 1998), especially with the decline of collective bargaining and the reduced influence of trade unions (Wilkinson 2008). There has been considerable ambiguity in the use of the term, with various commentators using 'HRM' as simply a more modern label for traditional personnel management, as a 're-conceptualising and re-organising of personnel roles', or as a new and distinctive approach, attempting to develop and utilise the potential of human resources to the full in pursuit of the organisation's strategic objectives. It is the promise that is held by this latter view that has most excited practitioners and attracted the attention of management academics (Storey 2007; Marchington and Wilkinson 2008).

There has long been a debate over whether HRM is no more than a relabelling of person-nel management, the 'old wine in new bottles' critique, or something more fundamental (Legge 1995; Gennard and Kelly 1997). As we have noted, traditionally, personnel manage-ment is often characterised as having little focus on broader business links and being overly concentrated on the activities of personnel professionals, unions and a range of operational techniques. Thus personnel management was seen as a low-level record-keeping and 'people maintenance' function. The HRM stereotype, in contrast, is characterised as being much more concerned with business strategy, and linkages with HR strategy, taking the view that HR is a, if not *the,* most important organisational resource. Thus there has been much talk of an HRM 'revolution'.

The new HRM?

Storey conceptualises HRM as being about: beliefs and assumptions, strategic qualities, the critical role of managers and key levers (see Table 1.1). The definition of HRM by Storey emphasises a particular set of policies now identified with 'high-commitment management' or 'high-performance work systems':

> Human resource management is a distinctive approach to employment management which seeks to achieve competitive advantage through the strategic deployment of a highly committed and capable workforce, using an integrated array of cultural, structural and personnel techniques. (Storey 1995, p.5)

In contrast, a broader definition is provided by Boxall and Purcell:

> HRM includes anything and everything associated with the management of employment relationships in the firm. We do not associate HRM solely with a high-commitment model of labour management or with any particular ideology or style of management. (Boxall and Purcell 2000, p.184)

Bacon points out that if HRM is defined exclusively as high-commitment management then the subject marginalises itself to the discussion of a relatively small number of distinct companies since many organisations pursue a 'low wage path'. The above 'exclusive' definition thus identifies HRM in contrast to other forms of labour management (industrial relations

Table 1.1 The new HRM model

1. Beliefs and assumptions

- That it is the human resource which gives competitive edge.
- That the aim should not be mere compliance with rules, but employee commitment.
- That therefore employees should, for example, be very carefully selected and developed.

2. Strategic qualities

- Because of the above factors, HR decisions are of strategic importance.
- Top management involvement is necessary.
- HR policies should be integrated into the business strategy – stemming from it and even contributing to it.

3. Critical role of managers

- Because HR practice is critical to the core activities of the business, it is too important to be left to personnel specialists alone.
- Line managers are (or need to be) closely involved as both deliverers and drivers of the HR policies.
- Much greater attention is paid to the management of managers themselves.

4. Key levers

- Managing culture is more important than managing procedures and systems.
- Integrated action on selection, communication, training, reward and development.
- Restructuring and job redesign to allow devolved responsibility and empowerment.

Source: Storey 2007, p.9

or traditional personnel management), whereas the second inclusive definition covers all forms of labour management (Bacon 2003, p.73).

Slippage between these two differing definitions, the new HRM à la Storey and HRM as a more generic term, is the cause of considerable confusion, generating more heat than light in debates on HRM and its meaning. However, although evolution is less exciting than revolution, Torrington *et al.*'s (2002) view that HRM is merely the next stage in the development of personnel management is persuasive. Torrington (1993), a staunch defender of 'good' personnel management, has also suggested that much of what is now labelled 'HRM' may be seen much more simply as longstanding good people management practice, while what was less effective has been relegated to remain, rather unfairly it seems, with the 'personnel management' brand. Equally, Lewin (2007) defines HRM as the attraction, retention, utilisation, motivation, rewarding and disciplining of employees in organisations – in short, the management of people at work. This seems a good definition, which is broad and less subject to fashion. However, he also notes that HRM as a label conveys the shift in terms of a greater emphasis on people as a resource whose active management can positively contribute to organisational success. In this sense HRM has an aspirational quality.

The changing context of work

Things are happening in employment that are neither a cause nor an effect of HRM but which could have some impact on it. These include the intensification of work, the choices of work location provided by technology and the divisive nature of a society in which many are idle and impoverished while many others are seriously over-worked. (Guest 1998, p.51)

Even the more 'upbeat' HRM work such as that of Storey (1992) indicates that changes in the arena of HRM did not come from initiatives designed directly to do this. Change was driven by broader organisational initiatives and personnel specialists have not been seen as the key drivers of change. Similarly Wood's (1999) work on high-commitment practices suggests that innovations in HRM tend to accompany changes in production concepts and that innovations on humanistic grounds are unrealistic. Thus in part HRM can be seen as a consequence of managing in 'uncharted territory' with new rules governing the employment relationship (Beardwell 1998).

In the main, developments in HRM, as we argue above, have been driven by large-scale organisational changes as employers adjust to a much more competitive global economic environment. To meet some of the challenges posed by intense competition, organisations have been downsized, delayered and decentralised (Wilkinson 2004). Organisations are now less hierarchical in nature; have adopted more flexible forms; and have been subjected to continuing waves of organisational change programmes such as total quality management, business process re-engineering, performance management, lean production, learning organisations and a seemingly relentless series of culture change initiatives.

The type of staff employed and the way they are organised have also undergone considerable change in the new organisational form. Employees are often now more likely to be female, work part-time, away from the workplace (e.g. home working and mobile working) mediated by technology (e.g. hot desking, telework), and be subcontractors, consultants, temps and interims. The boundaries between work and home are much more blurred (Walsh 2008) and employment now has to be managed across organisational boundaries, public, private, partnerships, franchises, agencies and other forms of inter-firm contractual relations which have a major impact on work and employment (Marchington *et al.* 2004).

Such pressures have not been restricted to the private sector and we have seen the rise of the so-called 'new public management' with its emphasis on economy and efficiency (Exworthy and Halford 2002; Bach 2008). The public sector has undergone many similar changes, with new organisational forms emerging in wake of 'marketisation', compulsory competitive tendering and 'best value'. For example, the civil service has experienced delayering, market testing and citizens' charters as well as the creation of next-step agencies, and most recently has been targeted for major downsizing and restructuring. The NHS has seen the creation of internal markets and the introduction of performance league tables and patients' charters. The suggestion is that healthcare provision has changed from being a citizen's right to a customer service. The traditional NHS culture has moved from one based on professionalism to one imbued with the rhetoric of the market, with hospitals and clinics 'franchised' by the Department of Health to sell healthcare services (see Dent 1995).

Some of these changes are seen as facilitating more discretion for staff while at the same time retaining control of performance. Here the relevance of HRM comes to the fore; new forms of work and organisation demand new HRM strategies and practices. The new work context also brings new HRM challenges; not the least of these derives from the impact of such changes on the stresses and strains involved in working under such conditions. Here the growing literature on stress at work paints a rather disconcerting picture of organisational life in the new workplace. Typical of this work is the series of surveys of safety reps by the TUC (2007). These show that the number of workers suffering from stress has steadily increased over the series. The main reasons cited for stress are increased workloads, change at work, staff cuts, long hours, bullying and job insecurity. Interestingly, given the changes highlighted above, it is the public sector where the highest stress levels are found. The TUC surveys find nearly two-thirds (64 per cent) of public sector workers complained of stress at work, compared to less than half (48 per cent) in the private sector. Similarly, results from the Bristol Stress and Health at Work Study report 5 million workers in the UK as having very high levels of stress at work (Smith 2001).

It is perhaps thus hardly surprising that much research reports a decline in organisational commitment and employee engagement at work. Taylor (2003) notes a significant deterioration that has taken place among workers in having any sense of personal commitment to their company. Despite all the HRM rhetoric there is no widespread belief in any sense of obligation to the firms who employ them. Green's research (2005) shows a significant downturn in job satisfaction since the early 1990s, despite rising wage levels and a generally tight labour market. Green notes people receiving less control and autonomy, with more targets, rules and greater stress. High workload allied to little control over work is liable to cause stress.

While HRM practices (e.g. employee assistance programmes, workplace counselling schemes etc.) are used in some organisations to provide a more supportive environment and there is some evidence that these appear to have some potential to ease but not cure the impact of workplace stress, the general picture is rather bleak. Indeed, HRM practices may have added considerably to the stresses of modern worklife with the increased use of such practices as performance management systems, contingent pay and flexibilisation. For example, in relation to flexibility, reports from the Citizens' Advice Bureau find numerous accounts of worker exploitation, with unilateral changes in contracts and forced reduction in hours and pay. Recent times have also witnessed the growth of 'zero hours contracts', particularly in retailing, whereby employers do not guarantee that any work will be offered but should they require labour the employee is expected to be available. The impact of organisational change on employees has been so considerable that commentators now argue that there is a need to radically reconstruct the nature of the 'psychological contract' between employer and employee (Brotherton 2003; Guest 2007). The search is now on for new deals for new times (Herriot and Pemberton 1995).

Thus HRM is clearly not a simple panacea, and may even contribute directly to some of the above problems, but it is relatively safe to speculate that it looks likely to play an increasingly important role in the workplaces of the future. However, in this discussion we must also be careful not to overstate the case for HRM. There is a danger that accounts of change in organisations are always portrayed as major paradigm-shifting events when the reality is rather different. The rhetoric of organisational change often relies too heavily on hype from unrepresentative examples (Thompson and O'Connel Davidson 1995; Beynon *et al.* 2002). Managers, it seems, often perceive themselves to be in the midst of massive organisational change. Eccles and Nohira's (1992) historical account of post-Second World War management traces how it has been the norm rather than the exception for practitioners and writers to view their organisational environment as turbulent and characterised by transformative change or, as Sorge and van Witteloostuijn (2004) put it, the nature of the change hype changes regularly just as flu viruses mutate over time. Thus issues of continuity are in many respects overlooked in the brave new world of HRM (Noon and Blyton 2002). As we note above, poor people management practice is not just a product of old management systems, such as that attributed to personnel management by HRM advocates. It may be that many commentators have been rather blinded by the glossy nature of the new HRM vision, but we would suggest that talk of the end of traditional career jobs and the demise of trade unions and the like is somewhat premature (Taylor 2003). History generally has a fairly cruel way of treating such rash predictions.

In particular, the 'rose tinted' managerial accounts of HRM in practice have recently been tempered somewhat by a literature examining HRM 'from below'. Surprisingly, the voice of the worker in evaluating HRM's achievements has been relatively silent. In their review of the impact of HRM, Wall and Wood note that only three of the 25 studies examined use employee survey data. Thus there is a danger, apparent in much of the prescriptive literature in HRM (Armstrong 2004), of focusing almost exclusively on the initiatives of management and thereby seeing employees as essentially passive beings, whose attitudes and behaviour are there to be moulded by HR strategy in the pursuit of competitive advantage. The feasibility of a 'top-down' approach to the management of organisational culture has already been challenged by a number of authors (Grugulis and Wilkinson 2002). Employees too may respond to changes in the competitive environment, and this suggests that the effective implementation of HRM may be more than simply a matter of management will. However, there is some evidence that the employee experience of HRM is not always negative and exploitative. According to Guest (1999, p.23): 'it appears that workers like their experience of HRM. The more HR practices they are currently experiencing in their employment, the more satisfied they seem to be and the better their psychological contract.' Indeed, work by Guest and Conway (1999) found that management practices are more important than union membership in determining whether staff feel fairly treated. Interestingly, they argue that union leaders should overcome their natural scepticism and pressure management to adopt progressive HRM practices (see also Guest 2007).

Clearly more research is needed in this area. A strong central theme of HRM in these accounts is that of linking the people management practice to business strategy and we examine this in the next section of this chapter.

Strategy and HRM

More recently, the study of HRM has adopted a cross-functional approach and expanded its breadth of analysis beyond the staple concerns of selection, training, reward etc. In particular, one stream of research, strategic human resource management (SHRM), has emerged as being particularly influential in this respect. In essence SHRM theory posits that an organisation's human resource assets are potentially the sole source of sustainable competitive advantage. Much of the work in this area draws from the resource-based theory (RBT) of the firm (Barney 1991, 1995; Boxall and Purcell 2003; Allen and Wright 2007). Here RBT suggests that competitive advantage depends ultimately on an organisation having superior, valuable, rare, non-substitutable resources at its disposal and that such resources are not easily imitated by others. The non-imitable nature of resources is a key aspect, otherwise competitors would be able to replicate and the advantage would rapidly disappear.

The subtleties of the human resource value creation process, however, are extremely difficult for competitors to imitate. The ambiguities and complexities associated with even the 'strongest' of organisational cultures, and how HRM practices are related to culture, are considerable and cannot be easily teased out by would-be imitators. Equally, any competitive advantage located in a codified and explicit set of HRM practices is also much less likely to be non-imitable than one based on the complex interaction of HRM policies and an organisation's 'social architecture' (Mueller 1996). By social architecture Mueller is referring to skill formation activities, cooperative behaviour and the tacit knowledge that organisations possess. Thus the value creation process arising from HRM competencies does appear to meet the criteria set out by RBT and consequently a growing body of empirical and theoretical work has emerged on SHRM (see Boxall and Purcell 2003 for reviews of this literature). Thus RBT perhaps helps us explain some the contradictions in HRM, and provides answers to questions such as that posed by Guest and King (2001, p.11), namely, 'If good people management is self-evidently beneficial to organisations, why do not more of them adopt it?'

Nevertheless, our knowledge base of SHRM is still rather limited, not least by its somewhat fragmented nature, and there is, as yet, little consensus in the empirical findings. However, a particular concern in applying the RBT to HRM is that it lacks a theory of the employment relationship because it assumes that internal resources do not have interests which may conflict or require negotiated alignments (Bacon 2003, p.80). In the discussion below, we review some of the more influential debates and findings of SHRM research.

A classic early work by Kochan et al. examined the nature of 'strategic choice' in HRM and provides an example whereby changes in the competitive environment lead to business decisions which 'reverberate through the organisation and its industrial system' (1983, p.13).

While such a response is clearly connected with business changes, Miller (1987) is undoubtedly right to question whether, in such circumstances, strategy is an appropriate term. The strategic management of human resources must be more than a mere knock-on effect: most business decisions will have some effects on the management of people, but such effects are not necessarily strategic decisions. For Miller, operational linkages between the business strategy and the policy towards employees are the key, or in his words, the 'fit of HRM with the strategic thrust of the organisation'. This is clearly an important point, but Miller's definition of SHRM:

> those decisions and actions which concern the management of employees at all levels in the business and which are directed towards creating and sustaining competitive advantage (p.352),

while important in demanding that human resources be a corporate-level concern, has a significant weakness because of its concentration on linkages to the neglect of content.

If we return to the work of Porter (1985), from which Miller borrows, we find that competitive advantage can be achieved through *either* cost leadership or differentiation. Thus Miller's definition of SHRM would cover firms adopting either of these two approaches, as long as there was a 'fit' of HRM with the business policy followed. Yet these two approaches are likely to embody very different strategies for the management of human resources: one being based on seeing employees as a commodity, with the emphasis on cost control, while the other may emphasise differentiation in terms of quality, with employees as a resource to be developed.

A more useful approach might be to characterise SHRM as entailing strategic integration and a 'positive' approach to the management of employees with an emphasis on staff as a resource rather than a cost. Thus strategic integration is a necessary but not sufficient component of SHRM. The emphasis on staff as a resource would be likely to embody policies designed to achieve the goals. However, we would argue that an emphasis on staff as a resource without strategic integration is not SHRM either. For instance, the many customer care and employee involvement programmes owe much to the fact that other companies are doing them rather than relating to the business strategy of the organisation concerned. Thus in circumstances whereby HRM programmes become ends in themselves it is hard to credit them with being strategic. Equally, it clearly fails one of the tests of resource-based theory, namely being non-imitable. In contrast, an 'accounting' view of labour management may well be strategic in that it may be related to competitive advantage through cost leadership and as such strategically integrated, but this is not what SHRM is supposed to be about. Hence the latter approach sees the importance of staff in a 'negative' sense of not hindering existing business strategy as opposed to actively contributing towards it. Of course, many companies would fit neither category in that the management of staff may not be considered a strategic issue at all, and not integrated into the strategic planning process nor considered as a resource (see Table 1.2). Thus there is generally much academic criticism of failure of SHRM in practice but we must ask whether our expectations of what SHRM can deliver are rather too high.

Table 1.2 Strategic HRM

	Strategic	Non-strategic
People as resource	SHRM	Personnel management
People as cost	Cost-driven SHRM	Traditional management

One recurrent theme in the SHRM literature is that organisations need to 'match' their human resource strategies to their business strategies, so that the former contribute towards the successful implementation of the latter (Miller 1987; Lengnick-Hall and Lengnick-Hall 1988; Schuler and Jackson 1989; Boxall 1992). A number of sectoral and company-level studies have shown how organisations facing change in their competitive environment have responded with new business strategies, which in turn have required a transformation in the organisations' approach to the management of staff (see, for example, Snape *et al.* 1993; Boxall and Steenveld 1999).

This approach, the so-called 'matching model' by Boxall (1992), argues for a fit or match between business strategy and a human resource strategy, which fosters the required employee attitudes and behaviour. In this sense, human resource strategy flows from the initial choice of business strategy (Purcell 1989). Furthermore, to the extent that changes in the corporate environment evoke a particular business strategy response, human resource strategies can also be seen as being strongly influenced by environmental change (Hendry *et al.* 1988). As Sparrow and Hilltrop (1994, p.628) argue, 'HRM strategies are all about making business strategies work'. A closely related body of work has recently called for a *configurational* approach to SHRM. Here it is argued that it is the pattern of HRM practices that supports the achievement of organisational goals and that, in line with the contingency approach, fit with strategy is vital to explaining the HR–performance nexus. The configurational approach takes the best-fit view a step further in that it argues that there are a number of specific ideal types that provide both horizontal fit, between HR practices, and vertical fit, between HR practices and business strategy (Ferris *et al.* 1999). The configuration of practices which provides the tightest fit is then seen as being ideal for the particular strategy. Although this work is still in its infancy, there has been some theorising on the nature of the 'ideal types' of configurations for customer, operations, product etc. led organisations (Sheppeck and Militello 2000).

Nevertheless, there is an issue as to how far human resource strategies can simply be 'matched' with the requirements of a changing business strategy. As Boxall (1992, p.68) notes, much of the 'matching' literature has implicitly assumed that employee attitudes and behaviour can be moulded by management strategy in the pursuit of strategic fit. However, human resource outcomes cannot be taken for granted, and whatever the merits of the view that personnel managers must increasingly see themselves as 'business managers' (Tyson 1987, 1995), it is important to recognise that personnel management and industrial relations are about more than simply selecting the appropriate fit with a given business strategy. Thus the best-fit approach can be criticised for failing to acknowledge the importance of social norms and legal rules in the search for alignment (Paauwe and Boselie 2007). Indeed, the notion of fit is somewhat static and an inappropriate metaphor in a fast-changing corporate world.

A commonly expressed view is that since businesses exist to produce profit, not good HRM, and to the extent that such practices are essentially facilitative and not 'stand alone' activities but must flow from corporate strategy, it is inevitable that they are indeed second or third order (Boxall and Purcell 2003). However, the discussion on much of this debate has been relatively unhelpful because of the assumption that it is only first-order strategies that are really 'strategic', and other concerns relate essentially to operational considerations and are hence non-strategic. This is potentially misleading as it assumes that strategies are of one kind (partly stemming from the view that strategy relates to product market issues) and other matters are either strategic or non-strategic, whereas in fact it may be better to think of degrees of strategy. It is clear, for instance, that HR is downstream from the overall corporate mission, be it a return on assets or profits through business decisions. The common argument posed above is undoubtedly correct: businesses are not formed to create good HR practice. However, this is less than helpful in examining the significance of the relationship with business issues. What is being called for is that such matters should be considered within the overall business strategy of the organisation rather than separately from it. In other words, HR should not merely be affected in a knock-on manner, but be located much further up in the business strategy process. As Purcell notes, once strategy is recast, moving from outside the firm to inside to look at resources, processes and behaviour, the strategic potential of HRM is much more easily defined (Purcell 2001, p.74).

What appears to be demanded is integration at two levels: first at the level of implementation, where it is argued that much of the success of policy implementation depends on the effective management of human resources. Second, it is argued that this is not in itself adequate, that human resources should actually be considered further up the planning process, so that rather than just flowing from the business strategy, it should be part of it, in that the human resource dimension may constrain the type of business strategy adopted or provide opportunities. It is no good making a business decision (strategic) to relocate if the organisation finds it cannot recruit the workforce in the area. The existing skills of the workforce may well constrain business growth, etc. Either or both of these approaches would be consistent with SHRM. In other words, the first approach suggests that the human resource strategy should be consistent with business strategy and implementation should take account of human resource factors. The second approach demands rather more: that human resource factors not only be considered in the implementation of policy but actually influence which business strategy is adopted.

As Boxall and Purcell note (2003, p.197), inconsistent application of well-designed HR policies often undermines their desired impact. This is very evident in the work of Gratton *et al.* (1999) and their study of seven leading-edge UK organisations. Hence, according to Boxall and Purcell 'there is no such thing as *the* single HR practice of the firm. It is more accurate to imagine the HR practices of the firm as norms around which there is variation due to the idiosyncratic behaviour of line managers' (2003, p.198). Truss (2001) notes the importance of 'agency', thus we should not assume that simply having a particular human resource policy will necessarily lead to a desired outcome. Problems of implementation and interpretation occur alongside people's sometimes unpredictable responses and actions.

Performance and HRM

For years, HR professionals have yearned for evidence to show that people were really the most important asset a company had and that good HR practice delivered in terms of organisational performance. By the mid-1990s their prayers appeared to have been answered in that a growing number of studies appeared to demonstrate just that. For example, in research undertaken on behalf of the then Institute of Personnel and Development in the UK, the Sheffield Effectiveness Programme (based on 100 small and medium-sized enterprises (SMEs) in manufacturing) concluded that people management is not only critical to business performance but is also much more important than an emphasis on quality, technology, competitive strategy or R&D in terms of influence on the bottom line. Thus according to Patterson *et al.* (1998), this finding in one sense validates the oft-quoted claims of CEOs that people are the most important asset but is also paradoxical in that it is one aspect of business that is the most neglected:

> Overall, the results of this study clearly indicate the importance of people management practices in influencing company performance. The results are unique, since no similar study has been conducted, comparing the influence of different types of managerial practices upon performance. If managers wish to influence the performance of their companies, the results show that the most important area to emphasise is the management

of people. This is ironic, given that our research has also demonstrated that emphasis on HRM practices is one of the most neglected areas of managerial practice within organisations. (Patterson *et al.* 1998, p.21)

These findings have been replicated in the public sector. In a well-cited study of the NHS, UK, West *et al.* (2002) reported that practices associated with high-performance work systems (HPWS), particularly the extent and sophistication of appraisal systems, the extent of teamworking and the quality and sophistication of training, were associated with lower patient mortality. However, research studies sponsored by the Chartered Institute of Personnel Development (CIPD) have also underscored the broad scale of the implementation problems of 18 'high-commitment' practices in 237 UK companies. Only 1 per cent used more than three-quarters of the practices, 25 per cent used more than half and 20 per cent used fewer than a quarter (Guest 2000). These findings and others have become a source of increasing concern to both HR practitioners and academics (Caldwell 2004).

There are various terms used in these studies, for example high-performance management, high-commitment management, best practice HRM, high-involvement management, but a common message: the adoption of HRM practices pays in terms of where it matters most, the bottom line (Huselid 1995) (see Kinnie and Swart, Chapter 2 of this volume). An exhaustive review by Ichniowski *et al.* (1996, p.299) concluded that a 'collage of evidence suggests that innovative workplace practices can increase performance, primarily through the use of systems of related practices that enhance worker participation, make work design less rigid and decentralise managerial tasks'. They also note that individual work practices have no effect on economic performance but 'the adoption of a *coherent and integrated system* of innovative practices, including extensive recruiting and careful selection, flexible job definitions and problem-solving teams, gainsharing-type compensation plans, employment security and extensive labour–management communication, substantially improves productivity and quality outcomes'. The general argument is that piecemeal take-up of HR practices means that many managements miss out on the benefits to be gained from a more integrated approach (Marchington and Wilkinson 2008). Thus such collections of reinforcing HR practices have begun to be referred to as a 'bundle', and the task of HR managers is to identify and implement such HR systems.

However, this appears to be rather more easily prescribed than achieved. Many authors produce lists of HR practices which should be included in these bundles. Unfortunately, there is as yet little consistency and we still await a definitive prescription of the best 'bundle'. Boselie *et al.* (2005), Wall and Wood (2005) and Storey (1992) identified aspects such as integrated selection systems, performance-related pay, harmonisation, individual contracts, teamworking and learning companies. Pfeffer (1994, pp.30–59) provides a list of 16, which includes employment security, selectivity in recruitment, incentive pay, employee ownership, participation and empowerment, teamworking, training and skill development, wage compression and promotion from within. These are held together under an overarching philosophy with a long-term commitment and a willingness to engage in consistent measurement of whether or not high standards are being achieved. Dyer and Reeves (1995) counted 28 HR practices across four studies of the human resource–performance link, of which only one practice, formal training, was common to all. Similarly Becker and Gerhart (1996) found 27 practices, none of which was common across five studies of the human resource management–performance link. Delaney *et al.* (1989) identified 10 practices, Huselid (1995) 13, Wood (1999) 17, while Delery and Doty (1996) appear quite miserly in comparison in only identifying seven strategic practices. All this must seem at the very least confusing to the practitioner but, more than this, there appear to be some quite contradictory notions in the various lists (Wall and Wood 2005). For example, on the one hand formal grievance systems appear in some bundles as an indicator of best practice but are associated in others with trade unionism and thus seen as part of the bureaucratic 'personnel management' approach.

Aside from the inconsistencies in the HRM bundle, the best practice and universalistic approach has received considerable criticism. Purcell, for example, is wary of the claim for a universal application:

> The claim that the bundle of best practice HRM is universally applicable leads us into a utopian cul-de-sac and ignores the powerful and highly significant changes in work, employment and society visible inside organisations and in the wider community. The search for bundles of high commitment work practices is important, but so too is the search for understanding of the circumstances of where and when it is applied, why some organisations do and others do not adopt HCM, and how some firms seem to have more appropriate HR systems for their current and future needs than others. It is only one of many ways in which employees are managed, all of which must come within the bounds of HRM. (Purcell 1999, p.36)

Whitfield and Poole (1997, p.757) point out that there are unresolved issues of causality, problems of the narrow base of the work undertaken (largely manufacturing) and concerns that much of the data is self-reported by single management respondents, as well as doubts about measures of performance which are used. Even if the data does indicate a causal link, we lack understanding of the processes involved and the mechanisms by which practices translate into desired outcomes. Equally problematic is the implicit assumption that a particular bundle of practices is feasible for all organisations. Some organisational structures and cultures will provide major difficulties in implementing certain HRM practices, for example high-involvement practices in highly bureaucratic and formal organisations will be particularly problematic. The notion of a reinforcing bundle of practices also cannot be fully convincing given the variation in the bundles noted above. It cannot yet be dismissed that the different HR practices have a differential impact on firm performance. The best practice approach thus appears somewhat of a black box and many questions remain as yet unanswered. Why is there a linkage? What is it about having these practices that delivers performance? What is the process by which these outcomes have occurred? It is unlikely, say, that the very act of introducing practices X, Y and Z will deliver benefits directly. Much will depend on the context of its introduction, the way it is implemented, the support provided, etc.

As Pass notes,

> the mechanisms involved in the 'causal chain' are rarely specified and are, in general, based upon assumptions or beliefs in 'employee outcomes' of commitment, motivation and increased competence. As a result, a 'black box' has been created with organisations left wondering 'how it works' – they are, instead, prescribed to follow a make believe scenario whereby they borrow Dorothy's ruby slippers from the Wizard of Oz (the appropriate bundle of HR practices), click them together three time and then arrive at their destination (high organisational performance with happy workers). (Pass 2004, p.1)

Some writers (e.g. Godard 2004, p.371) argue that the conflicts embedded in the structure of the employment relation may limit the effectiveness of the high-performance paradigm for employers, and render it highly fragile, and it is this that may explain its variable adoption depending on workplace context. These same conflicts may also explain why high-performance practices are often implemented in ways that tend to have negative effects for workers and unions. In other words, it may be in the interests of only a minority of employers to adopt high-performance management and, even when it is adopted, it may not have positive implications for workers or their unions. Thus there is a need to recognise that there may not be a universal coincidence of interests here, in which what is good for employers is also always good for workers and their unions. Equally, others such as Lewin have suggested a dual theory of HRM – while some groups of employees are best managed through HCM or what he terms high-involvement management, others may be best managed via a low-involvement model. The former applies to core employees only (Lewin 2007). The key question he sees concerns the best balance of core and peripheral staff (an answer which is likely to differ by industry).

The changing role of HRM

Despite the growing recognition of the importance of effective people management for organisational success, discussed above, there are still a number of concerns about the future for HRM. At a surface level the HRM function seems to be in good health. The CIPD now claims over 130,000 members (CIPD 2008) and Workplace Employment Relations Survey (WERS) data shows that the proportion of workplaces with personnel specialists, defined as managers whose job titles contain personnel, HR or industrial, employee or staff relations and who spend at least a quarter of their time on such matters, has been rising. In 2004 the percentage of workplaces that employed a personnel specialist was up from 14 per cent in 1984 and 20 per cent in 1998 (Kersley *et al.* 2005; Cully *et al.* 1999). However, deeper worries about the effectiveness of the HR function linger on.

According to Peter Drucker, there has been a tendency in the past for the HR department to be seen as something of a 'trash can' function, a repository for all those tasks which do not fit neatly anywhere else:

> Personnel administration . . . is largely a collection of incidental techniques without much internal cohesion. As personnel administration conceives the job of managing worker and work, it is partly a file-clerk's job, partly a housekeeping job, partly a social worker's job and partly fire-fighting to head off union trouble or to settle it . . . the things the personnel administrator is typically responsible for . . . are necessary chores. I doubt though that they should be put together in one department for they are a hodge-podge . . . They are neither one function by kinship of skills required to carry out the activities, nor are they one function by being linked together in the work process, by forming a distinct stage in the work of the managers or in the process of the business. (Drucker 1961, pp.269–70; quoted in Legge 1995, p.6)

Table 1.3 lists some of the key functions that HR departments now provide. In part, Drucker's critique that the HR function lacks coherence has been moderated by some recent organisational changes. In particular, the practice of outsourcing during the 1980s and 1990s

Table 1.3 Functions performed by the HR department

Job analysis
Human resource planning
Recruitment and selection
Training and development
Pay and conditions of employment
Grievance and disciplinary procedures
Employee relations and communications
Administration of contracts of employment
Employee welfare and counselling
Equal opportunities policy and monitoring
Health and safety
Outplacement
Culture management
Knowledge management

saw many of the more peripheral HR responsibilities, such as catering arrangements and security, subcontracted to specialist firms. Equally, the practice of decentralising HR responsibility from corporate central departments to business-unit-level departments and further still to line management has seen much 'streamlining' of HR responsibilities. However, perhaps more worrying for the HR function is that these trends have also seen some traditional core personnel areas, such as recruitment, training and employee welfare management, also outsourced to HR consultants. In some accounts these trends have been seen as part of a 'crisis' as HR struggled for legitimacy and status in cost-conscious times and the function has been described as being 'under siege from external consultants' (Clark and Clark 1990). In Torrington's view this 'crisis' is nothing new and reflects an unreasonably high standard being applied as criteria of success:

> There is a crisis of confidence among personnel specialists, as there always has been. Their results are almost impossible to measure and their successes and failures are largely the successes and failures of other people. Furthermore, they operate in a field – how people behave – in which everyone else is an expert with a personal point of view from which they will not depart. The difficulty for personnel people is that they know how intractable some of the people problems really are. (Torrington 1998, p.36)

Others have interpreted the increasing use of consultants as reflecting a sign that HR is now seen as being much more important and thus merits additional investment. Management consultants are argued to be an important conduit along which new and more sophisticated HR practices flow between organisations. However, some recent trends suggest that a 'crisis' interpretation may be more in tune with the facts. In particular, the reduction of the HR domains appears to have been taken one step further and there is now a considerable debate on the benefits of outsourcing the entire HR function. In part, such changes have been driven by further cost pressures in a period of corporate downsizing, but more worrying for the HR function is that outsourcing may also have been fuelled by senior management concerns about the quality and responsiveness of in-house HR functions (Greer *et al.* 1999).

For example, from one of the CIPD's own studies of a survey of senior executives, non-HR managers rated the HR profession poorly, seeing it as 'bureaucratic' and 'isolated from the outside world' (Guest and King 2001). Perhaps more worrying is that this 'news' does not appear to be new to the HR profession. The survey canvassed the views of over 3,000 HR managers in the UK and found that:

- just a quarter think HR is respected by other managers, is seen as a key function of senior management, or has strong input at board level;

- 85 per cent agree that the profession 'struggles to get a voice at the highest level in organisations' and a similar number admit that it is 'often overlooked by executives'.

Yet, when asked to rate themselves and the contribution they make, the respondents have been more diametrically opposed:

- over 85 per cent of HR managers believe that HR will be vital to the continued success of an organisation;

- over 75 per cent of respondents believe HR has a strategic business focus and acts as internal consultant and enabler.

Thus there is a large gap between what HR professionals see as their role and how other managers in the organisation see it. Thus the rising recognition that HR issues are vitally important in organisations has, paradoxically, not been all good news for the HR department given its 'Cinderella' image. It seems that many senior managers may be of the view that people management is far too important to be left to the HR department. Thus in a *Fortune* article one commentator urged CEOs to 'Blow the sucker [HR] up' (Stewart 1996). While others have not been as forthright as this, the HR function appears to be at a dangerous cross-roads, with some suggesting ascendancy to a full 'business partner' while others predict a painful demise. On the one hand the ascendancy school sees the rise of HR following hard on the success of SHRM and the creation of competitive advantage for organisations. In contrast, the formula for demise often involves the failure of HR to understand the broader business agenda. The literature typically sees a need for the 'reinvention' of HR along such lines, and that HR must simply evolve or die. However, Ulrich (1997) has also warned that the literature is replete with premature death notices of the HR function.

What then is the 'formula' for HR success? First, in addressing this question there is a real danger in slipping into unrealistic, wishful thinking – of which there is already an ample supply in the prescriptive HR literature. Second, there is rather more consistency in the literature on what the future for HR should *not* be based on than that on what it should be. Thus Rucci (1997) has suggested that the worst-case scenario for HR survival is a department that does not promote change, does not identify leaders, does not understand the business, does not know customers, does not drive costs and does not emphasise values. According to Pfeffer (1998, p.195), 'if human resources is to have a future inside organisations, it is not by playing police person and enforcer of rules and policies, nor is it likely to be ensured by playing hand-maiden to finance'.

In contrast, there are a wide variety of suggestions for what the HR department should do in the future. The future agenda according to Brockbank (1997) is that a successful HR department needs to be involved in framing not only HR strategy but also business strategy, promoting growth rather than downsizing, and building more credible relationships with key shareholders and board members. Beer and Eisenstat (1996) emphasise the need for a comprehensive HR vision and that in the future HR managers will require coordination skills across functions, business units and borders following the increased globalisation of business, and general management, communication leadership, creativity and entrepreneurship competencies. Research by Eichinger and Ulrich (1995) on the top priorities that HR professionals believe need to be addressed in the future emphasises organisational redesign, attracting new leaders, customer focus, cost containment, rejecting fads, addressing diversity and becoming a more effective business partner with their line management customers. Ulrich (1998) also reports the results of survey research on the key competencies managers believe will be necessary for future success in HR roles – see Table 1.4. The ability to manage culture and change coupled with personal credibility is seen as critical.

According to Hamel, HR has to lead the way in making businesses more like communities and less bureaucratic in the quest for business resilience. HR is seen as having a historic opportunity to create organisations 'in which people can bring all their humanity to work every day'. This would involve breaking down traditional hierarchies and creating forums

Table 1.4   Key competencies of HR professionals

Relative importance to effectiveness	%
Understanding of business	14
Knowledge of HR practices	17
Ability to manage culture	19
Ability to manage change	22
Personal credibility	27

Source: Ulrich 1998, pp.20–1. Reprinted by permission of Harvard Business School Press. From *Human Resource Champions* by Ulrich, D., Boston, MA, 1998, pp.20–21. Copyright © 1998 by the Harvard Business School Publishing Corporation; all rights reserved.

where everyone can analyse where things have gone wrong, and offer '1,000 wacky ideas'. 'As long as it's mostly bureaucracy, there will be an upper limit on human effort,' he said. 'Resilience depends on initiative, creativity and passion.' However, HR would first have to get managers to 'escape the denial trap', and look at the world 'in the way it is, and not in the way we want it to be' (Millar 2004).

Thus a key theme in much of the work is that HR needs to earn its place at the top, i.e. senior management, table. One danger in these accounts is that the emphasis is very much on the strategic and business aspects of the HR role. In particular, the 'bread and butter' issues of effectively managing the recruitment, selection, appraisal, development, reward and involvement of staff have been rather pushed to the periphery. What is interesting about Table 1.4 is the relatively low rating of knowledge of HR practices. There is thus a real concern that HR managers could be neglecting 'the basics' in their search for legitimacy and status with senior managers. In short, HR could be accused of ignoring employees. Indeed, HR 'futurologists', it seems, need to be reminded of Giles and Williams' (1991) rejoinder to accept that the HR role is to serve their customers and not their egos. We feel that there is a danger that the senior management and shareholder customers will still be getting rather better service than the 'employee customer' in the HR department of the future. Such a view is shared by Francis and Keegan (2006), who note that the employee champion role is shrinking because HR professionals have been encouraged to aspire to the role of strategic or business partner.

Lewin (2007) argues that it is not just about being a business partner:

> There are many other roles and purposes that HR functions and those who lead these functions serve in modern business enterprises including complying with human resource/labor regulation (newer and older regulation), enforcing organizational and employment policies and practices, measuring employee performance, providing services and assistance to employees, maintaining employee personnel files, monitoring workplace safety, handling employee relocation. With this menu of potential duties and responsibilities, it is understandable that many HR functions in modern business enterprises are considered to be largely operational functions rather than strategic functions. But if the claim that business enterprises increasingly compete on the basis of their intellectual capital is at all valid, then the main challenge regarding HRM in the 21st Century is for HR functions and leaders to keep their eye on the prize of a strategic role in these enterprises while also performing the necessary operational role. (p.1)

Perceived from the perspective of HR practitioners, 'progress' in implementing HRM is an unfinished process. The six areas where practitioners believe most policy progress has been made are the areas they consider less important (Table 1.5). Caldwell (2004, p.211) argues that a plausible interpretation of this is to suggest that the idea of 'most progress' tends to correlate with the easier to deliver, softer and less high-level strategic aspects of HRM. Improvements in employee communications, for example, are achievable through the relatively low-level interventions associated with 'traditional' personnel management. In contrast, the areas where 'least progress' appears to have been made towards implementation seem to be associated with the more strategic aspects of HRM. For example, the shift towards treating people as assets, productivity improvements and competitiveness requires that HRM becomes an integral aspect of strategic decision making at the highest level.

Thus one of our aims in the presentation of material in this book has been to balance the discussion in terms of both employee expectations and management expectations of the HR function. For example, in accounts of topics such as downsizing, empowerment, performance management, reward, flexibility etc. the aim has been not only to examine critically HR's strategic role in the process but also to review the impact of these practices on employees. The last section of this chapter now discusses in more detail the layout of the book and some suggestions on its use.

Table 1.5 Policy importance and progress in implementing HRM

Most important, least progress

Managing people as assets which are fundamental to the competitive advantage of the organisation
Developing a close fit of personnel policies, procedures and systems with one another
Creating a flatter and more flexible organisation capable of responding more quickly to change
Encouraging team working and cooperation across internal organisational boundaries
Creating a strong customer-first philosophy throughout the organisation
Increasing line management responsibility for personnel management and HR policies

Least important, most progress

Improving employee involvement through better internal communication
Aligning HRM policies with business planning and corporate strategy
Empowering employees to manage their own self-development and learning
Developing reward strategies designed to support a performance-driven culture
Developing the facilitating role of managers as enablers
Building greater employee commitment to the organisation

Source: Caldwell 2004, p.200 (www.blackwell-synergy.com)

The book

This book has been written primarily as a text for students of business and management who are studying HRM. It aims to be critical but pragmatic: we are wary of quick fixes, slogans, prescriptive checklists and bullet points of 'best practice'. The authors are all prominent researchers and draw from a considerable depth of research in their field. Each chapter provides a critical review of the topic, bringing together theoretical and empirical material. The emphasis is on analysis and insight and areas of growing significance are also included in each chapter. At the same time we wish to look at the implications of HRM research and theory development for practice and to do so in a readable, accessible manner. The book does not assume prior knowledge on the part of the reader but seeks to locate issues in a wider theoretical framework. It is suitable for MBAs, and for undergraduates who these days may be doing business studies as well as degrees in engineering, humanities, social sciences etc. As such, this is appropriate for modular degree courses.

Each chapter is accompanied by a combination of case studies and/or exercises for students. The intention is that students should be actively involved in the study of HRM. We believe that in this sense the book is unique in the UK, where the trend has been for the publication of separate text and case books. Our aim in combining these elements in a single volume is to permit a smoother integration of the topic material and supporting cases and exercises. In all chapters the authors have provided both text and cases, although in some we also include additional material from other authors. The cases and exercises are of different lengths, level and type in order to serve different teaching and learning purposes, e.g. a long case study for students to read and prepare prior to seminars/tutorials as well as shorter cases and exercises which can be prepared in the session itself. The aim is to provide a good range of up-to-date, relevant material based upon actual HRM practice.

The book is divided into two parts; the first one, the 'Fundamentals of HRM', examines the core elements of HR practice (see Table 1.3 above). In this section there are chapters on selection and recruitment, performance appraisal, employee development, reward, industrial relations, line managers. The second half of the book, 'Contemporary Themes and Issues', addresses some key areas of rising importance in HRM practice. Here there are chapters on careers, downsizing, participation, ethics, work–life balance, emotion, knowledge management and diversity management. All these were topics covered in the first edition of the book.

To reflect the ever-changing nature of HRM, this third edition of the book has been revised in several key respects; in particular, we have added new chapters on topics that have grown in importance since the publication of the last edition. First, given the growing concerns with the quality of working life we have included a chapter on bullying. In response to the increasing importance of a global perspective on HRM we have added a chapter on comparative HRM.

Bibliography

Ackers, P. and Wilkinson, A. (eds) (2003) *Understanding Work and Employment: Industrial Relations In Transition,* Oxford: Oxford University Press.

Allen, M. and Wright, P. (2007) 'Strategic management and HR', in L.P. Boxall, I.J. Purcell and P. Wright (eds) *The Oxford Handbook of Human Resource Management,* Oxford: Oxford University Press.

Armstrong, M. (2004) *A Handbook of HRM,* London: Kogan Page.

Bach, S. (2008) 'Public sector HRM', in A. Wilkinson *et al.* (eds) *The Sage Handbook of Human Resource Management,* London: Sage.

Bacon, N. (2003) 'Human resource management and industrial relations', in P. Ackers and A. Wilkinson (eds) *Understanding Work and Employment: Industrial Relations In Transition,* Oxford: Oxford University Press.

Barney, J. (1991) 'Firm resources and sustained competitive advantage', *Journal of Management,* Vol.17, No.1, pp.99–120.

Barney, J. (1995) 'Looking inside for competitive advantage', *Academy of Management Executive,* Vol.9, No.4, pp.49–61.

Beardwell, I. (ed.) (1998) *Contemporary Industrial Relations,* Oxford: Open University Press.

Becker, B. and Gerhart, B. (1996) 'The impact of human resource management on organizational performance: progress and prospects', *Academy of Management Journal,* Vol.39, pp.779–801.

Beer, M. and Eisenstat, R. (1996) 'Developing an organisation capable of implementing strategy and learning', *Human Relations,* Vol.49, No.5, pp.297–619.

Beynon, H., Grimshaw, D., Rubery, J. and Ward, K. (2002) *Managing Employment Change, The New Realities of Work,* Oxford: Oxford University Press.

Boselie P., Dietz G. and Boon C. (2005) 'Commonalities and contradictions in HRM and performance research', *Human Resource Management Journal,* Vol.15, No.3, pp.67–94.

Boxall, P. (1992) 'Strategic human resource management: beginnings of a new theoretical sophistication?', *Human Resource Management Journal,* Vol.2, No.3, pp.60–79.

Boxall, P. and Purcell, J. (2000) 'Strategic Human Resource Management: Where have we come from and where should we be going?' *International Journal of Management Reviews,* Vol.2, No.2, pp.183–203.

*Boxall, P. and Purcell, J. (2003) *Strategy and Human Resource Management,* London: Palgrave.

Boxall, P. and Steenveld, M. (1999) 'Human resource strategy and competitive advantage: a longitudinal study of engineering consultancies', *Journal of Management Studies,* Vol.36, No.4, pp.443–63.

Boxall P., Purcell, J. and Wright, P. (eds) (2007) *The Oxford Handbook of Human Resource Management,* Oxford: Oxford University Press.

Brockbank, W. (1997) 'HR's future on the way to a presence', *Human Resource Management,* Vol.36, No.1, pp.65–9.

Brotherton, C. (2003) 'Industrial relations and psychology', in P. Ackers and A. Wilkinson (eds) *Understanding Work and Employment: Industrial Relations In Transition,* Oxford: Oxford University Press.

Caldwell, R. (2004) 'Rhetoric, facts and self-fulfilling prophecies: exploring practitioners' perceptions of progress in implementing HRM', *Industrial Relations Journal,* Vol.35, No.3, pp.196–215.

CIPD (2004) National Conference, Harrogate.

CIPD (2008) Annual report, London: Chartered Institute of Personnel and Development.

Clark, I. and Clark, T. (1990) 'Personnel management and the use of executive recruitment consultancies', *Human Resource Management Journal,* Vol.1, No.1, pp.46–62.

Collinson, M., Edwards, P., Rees, C. and Innes, L. (1997) *Involving Employees in Quality Management,* London: DTI report.

Cully, M., Woodland, S., O'Reilly, A. and Dix, G. (1999) *Britain at Work,* London: Routledge.

Delaney, J.T., Lewin, D. and Ichniowski, C. (1989) 'Human resource policies and practices in American firms', Washington, DC: US Government Printing Office.

Delery, J. and Doty, D. (1996) 'Modes of theorizing in strategic human resource management: tests of universalistic, contingency and configurational performance predictions', *Academy of Management Journal,* Vol.39, No.4, pp.802–35.

Dent, M. (1995) 'The new National Health Service: a case of postmodernism?', *Organization Studies,* Vol.16, No.5, pp.875–99.

Donovan (1968) 'The Royal Commission on trade unions and employers' associations, 1965–1968', Report, Cmnd. 3623.

Drucker, P. (1961) *The Practice of Management,* London: Mercury.

Dyer, L. and Reeves, T. (1995) 'Human resource strategies and firm performance: what do we know and where do we need to go?', *International Journal of Human Resource Management,* Vol.6, pp.656–70.

Eccles, R. and Nohira, N. (1992) *Beyond the Hype: Rediscovering the Essence of Management,* Boston, MA: Harvard Business School Press.

Eichinger, B. and Ulrich, D. (1995) 'Are you future agile?', *Human Resource Planning,* Vol.18, No.4, pp.30–41.

Exworthy, M. and Halford, S. (2002) *Professionals and the New Managerialism in the Public Sector,* Buckingham: Open University Press.

Ferris, G. Hochwarter, Buckley, M.R., Hamell-Cook, G. and Frink, D.D. (1999) 'Human Resource Management: Same New Directions', *Journal of Management,* Vol.25, No.3, pp.385–416.

Francis, H. and Keegan, A. (2006) 'The changing face of HRM: in search of balance', *Human Resource Management Journal,* Vol.16, No.3, pp.231–49.

Gennard, J. and Kelly, J. (1997) 'The unimportance of labels: the diffusion of the personnel/HRM function', *Industrial Relations Journal,* Vol.28, No.1, pp.27–42.

Giles, E. and Williams, R. (1991) 'Can the personnel department survive quality management?', *Personnel Management,* April, pp.28–33.

Glover, L. (2005) 'Listening to the shopfloor: broadening our conceptualization of the relationships that shape responses to quality management', Working Paper, De Montfort University.

Godard, J. (2004) 'A critical assessment of the high-performance paradigm', *British Journal of Industrial Relations,* Vol.42, No.2, pp.349–78.

Gospel, H. (2005) 'The management of labour and human resources', in G. Jones and J. Zeitlin (eds) *The Oxford Handbook of Business History,* Oxford: Oxford University Press.

Gratton, L., Hope Hailey, V., Stiles, P. and Truss, C. (1999) *Strategic Human Resource Management,* Oxford: Oxford University Press.

Green, F. (2005, forthcoming) 'Why is work effort becoming more intense?' *Industrial Relations.*

Greer, C.R., Youngblood, S.A. and Gray, D.A. (1999) 'Human resource management outsourcing: the make or buy decision', *Academy of Management Executive,* Vol.13, No.3, pp.85–96.

Grugulis, I. and Wilkinson, A. (2002) 'Managing culture at British Airways: hype, hope and reality', *Long-Range Planning,* Vol.35, pp.179–94.

Guest, D. (1987) 'Human resource management and industrial relations', *Journal of Management Studies,* Vol.24, No.5, pp.503–21.

Guest, D. (1998) 'Beyond HRM: commitment and the contract culture', in M. Marchington and P. Sparrow (eds) *Human Resource Management: The New Agenda,* London: Pitman.

*Guest, D. (1999) 'Human resource management: the workers' verdict', *Human Resource Management Journal,* Vol.9, No.3, pp.5–25.

Guest, D. (2000) 'Piece by piece', *People Management*, 20 July, pp.26–31.

Guest, D. (2007) 'Human resource management and the worker: towards a new psychological contract?', in P. Boxall, J. Purcell and P. Wright (eds) *Oxford Handbook of Human Resource Management*, Oxford: Oxford University Press.

Guest, D. and Conway, N. (1999) 'Peering into the black hole: the downside of the new employment relations in the UK', *British Journal of Industrial Relations*, Vol.37, No.3, pp.367–90.

Guest, D. and King, Z. (2001) 'Voices from the boardroom report: state of the profession survey', *Personnel Today*, pp.10–11.

Hendry, C. and Pettigrew, A. (1992) 'Patterns of strategic change in the development of human resource management', *British Journal of Management*, Vol.3, pp.137–56.

Hendry, C., Pettigrew, A. and Sparrow, P. (1988) 'Changing patterns of human resource management', *Personnel Management*, November, pp.37–41.

Herriot, P. and Pemberton, C. (1995) *New Deals: The Revolution in Management Careers*, London: Wiley.

Huselid, M. (1995) 'The impact of human resource management practices on turnover, productivity and corporate financial performance', *Academy of Management Journal*, Vol.38, No.3, pp.635–72.

Ichniowski, C., Kochan, T., Levine, D., Olsen, C. and Strauss, G. (1996) 'What works at work: overview and assessment', *Industrial Relations*, Vol.35, No.3, pp.299–333.

Kaufman, B. (2007) 'The development of HRM', in L.P. Boxall, L.J. Purcell and P. Wright (eds) *Oxford Handbook of Human Resource Management*, Oxford: Oxford University Press.

Keenoy, T. (1990) 'HRM: rhetoric, reality and contradiction', *International Journal of Human Resource Management*, Vol.1, No.3, pp.363–84.

Kersley, B., Alpin, C., Forth, J., Bryson, A., Bewley, H., Dix, G. and Oxenbridge, S. (2005) *Inside the Workplace: First Findings from the 2004 Workplace Employment Relations Survey*, London: Department of Trade and Industry.

Kochan, T., McKersie, R. and Cappelli, P. (1983) 'Strategic choice and industrial relations theory', *Industrial Relations*, Vol.23, No.1, pp.16–39.

Legge, K. (1995) *Human Resource Management: Rhetorics and Realities*, Basingstoke: Macmillan.

Lengnick-Hall, C.A. and Lengnick-Hall, M.L. (1988) 'Strategic human resources management: a review of the literature and a proposed typology', *Academy of Management Review*, Vol.13, No.3, pp. 454–70.

Lewin, D. (2003) 'Human resource management and business performance: lessons for the 21st century', in M. Effron, R. Gandossy and M. Goldsmith (eds), *Human Resources in the 21st Century*, New York: Wiley, pp.91–99, 454–70.

Lewin, D. (2007) 'HRM in the 21st century', in C. Wankel (ed.), *Handbook of 21st Century Management*, London: Sage.

Mabey, C., Clark, T. and Skinner, D. (eds) (1998) *The Experience of Human Resource Management*, Milton Keynes: Open University Press.

*Marchington, M. and Wilkinson, A. (2008) *Human Resource Management at Work* (4th edn), London: CIPD.

Marchington, M., Rubery, J., Grimshaw, D. and Willmott, H. (2004) *Fragmenting Work: Blurring Organizational Boundaries and Disordering Hierarchies*, Oxford: Oxford University Press.

McKinlay, A. and Starkey, K. (1992) 'Competitive strategies and organizational change', in G. Salaman (ed.) *Human Resource Strategies*, London: Sage.

Millar, M. (2004) 'HR must reduce bureaucracy to reduce business resilience', *Personnel Today*, 2 November 2004, p.2.

Miller, P. (1987) 'Strategic industrial relations and human resource management: distinction, definition and recognition', *Journal of Management Studies*, Vol.24, No.4, pp.347–61.

Monks, J. (1998) 'Trade unions, enterprise and the future', in P. Sparrow and M. Marchington (eds) *Human Resource Management: The New Agenda*, London: FT/Pitman.

Mueller, F. (1996) 'Human resources as strategic assets: an evolutionary resource based theory', *Journal of Management Studies*, Vol.33, No.6, pp.757–85.

*Noon, M. and Blyton, P. (2002) *The Realities of Work*, London: Palgrave.

Paauwe, J. and Boselie, P. (2007) 'HRM and societal embeddedness', in Boxall *et al.* (eds) *Handbook of Human Resource Management*, Oxford: Oxford University Press.

Pass, S. (2004) 'Looking inside the 'Black Box': employee opinions of HRM/HPWS and Organisational Performance', BUIRA Conference, Nottingham University, 1–3 July.

Patterson, M., West, M., Hawthorn, R. and Nickell, S. (1998) 'Impact of people management practices on business performance issues', *Institute of Personnel Management,* No.22, IPD.

Pfeffer, J. (1994) *Competitive Advantage Through People,* Boston, MA: Harvard Business School Press.

*Pfeffer, P. (1998) *The Human Equation,* Boston, MA: Harvard Business School Press.

Porter, M. (1985) *Competitive Advantage,* New York: Free Press.

Purcell, J. (1989) 'The impact of corporate strategy on human resource management', in J. Storey (ed.) *New Perspectives on Human Resource Management,* London: Routledge.

Purcell, J. (1999) 'Best practice and best fit: chimera or cul-de-sac?', *Human Resource Management Journal,* Vol.9, No.3, pp.26–41.

Purcell, J. (2001) 'The meaning of strategies in human resource management', in J. Storey (ed.) *Human Resource Management: A Critical Text* (2nd edn), London: Routledge.

Rucci, A.J. (1997) 'Should HR survive? A profession at the crossroads', *Human Resource Management,* Vol.36, No.1, pp.169–75.

Schuler, R.S. and Jackson, S.E. (1989) 'Determinants of human resource management priorities and implications for industrial relations', *Journal of Management,* Vol.15, No.1, pp.89–99.

Scott, A. (1994) *Willing Slaves?* Cambridge: Cambridge University Press.

Sheppeck, M.A. and Militello, J. (2000) 'Strategic HR configurations and organizational performance', *Human Resource Management,* Vol.39, No.1, pp.5–16.

Sisson, K. (1990) 'Introducing the Human Resource Management Journal', *Human Resource Management,* Vol.1, No.1, pp.1–11.

Smith, A. (2001) 'Perceptions of stress at work', *Human Resource Management,* Vol.11, No.4, pp.74–86.

Snape, E., Wilkinson, A. and Redman, T. (1993) 'Human resource management in building societies: making the transformation?', *Human Resource Management,* Vol.3, No.3, pp.43–60.

Sorge, A. and van Witteloostuijn, A. (2004) 'The (non)sense of organizational change: an essay about universal management hypes, sick consultancy metaphors, and healthy organization theories', *Organization Studies,* Vol.25, pp.1205–31.

Sparrow, P. and Hilltrop, J. (1994) *European Human Resource Management in Transition,* London: Prentice Hall.

Sparrow, P. and Marchington, M. (1998) *Human Resource Management: The New Agenda,* London: FT/Pitman.

Stewart, T. (1996) 'Taking on the last bureaucracy', *Fortune Magazine,* pp.105–8.

Storey, J. (1992) *Developments in the Management of Human Resources,* Oxford: Blackwell.

Storey, J. (ed.) (1995) *Human Resource Management: A Critical Text,* London: Routledge.

*Storey, J. (ed.) (2001) *Human Resource Management: A Critical Text* (2nd edn), London: Routledge.

Storey, J. (ed.) (2007) *Human Resource Management* (4th edn), London: Routedge.

Taylor, R. (2003) *Britons World of Work: Rights and Realities,* Swindon: ESRC.

Thompson, P. and O'Connel Davidson, J. (1995) 'The continuity of discontinuity: managerial rhetoric in turbulent times', *Personnel Review,* Vol.24, No.4, pp.17–33.

Torrington, D. (1993) 'How dangerous is human resource management?', *Employee Relations,* Vol.15, No.5, pp.40–53.

Torrington, D. (1998) 'Crisis and opportunity in HRM: the challenge for the personnel function', in P. Sparrow and M. Marchington (eds) *Human Resource Management: The New Agenda,* London: Prentice Hall.

Torrington, D., Hall, L. and Taylor, S. (2002) *Human Resource Management,* London: FT/Prentice Hall.

Truss, C. (2001) 'Complexities and controversies in linking HRM with organizational outcomes', *Journal of Management Studies,* Vol.38, No.8, pp.1121–49.

TUC (2004) *Workers are More Stressed than Ever,* London: Trades Union Congress.

TUC (2007) *Survey of Safety Representatives,* London: Trades Union Congress.

Tyson, S. (1987) 'The management of the personnel function', *Journal of Management Studies,* Vol.24, No.5, pp.523–32.

Tyson, S. (1995) *Human Resource Strategy: Towards a General Theory of Human Resource Management,* London: Pitman.

Ulrich, D. (1997) *Tomorrow's Human Resource Management,* New York: Wiley.

Ulrich, D. (1998) *Human Resource Champions,* Boston, MA: Harvard Business School Press.

Wall, T. D. and Wood, S. J. (2005) 'The romance of human resource management and business performance and the case for big science', *Human Relations,* Vol.58, No.4, pp.429–62.

Walsh, J. (2008) 'Work life balance', in A. Wilkinson, N. Bacon, S. Snell and T. Redman (eds) *The Sage Handbook of Human Resource Management,* London: Sage.

West, M., Borrill, C., Dawson, J., Scully, J., Carter, M., Anelay, S., Patterson, M. and Waring, J. (2002) 'The link between the management of employees and patient mortality in acute hospitals', *International Journal of Human Resource Management,* Vol.13, No.8, pp.1299–1311.

Whitfield, K. and Poole, M. (1997) 'Organizing employment for high performance', *Organization Studies,* Vol.18, No.5, pp.745–64.

Wilkinson, A. (2004) *Downsizing, Rightsizing or Dumbsizing? Human Resources, Quality and Sustainability,* Paper presented at the 9th World Congress for Total Quality Management, September, 2004, Abu Dhabi, UAE.

Wilkinson, A. (2007) 'Managing people', in B. Dale, T. Van Der Wiele and J. Van Iwaarden (eds) *Managing Quality* (5th edn), Oxford; Blackwell, pp.200–33.

Wilkinson, A. (2008a) 'Empowerment', in S. Clegg and J. Bailey (eds) *Encyclopaedia of Organizational Studies,* London: Sage, pp.441–42.

Wilkinson, A. (2008b) 'Industrial relations', in S. Clegg and J. Bailey (eds) *Encyclopaedia of Organizational Studies,* London: Sage, pp.652–53.

Wilkinson, A., Godfrey, G. and Marchington, M. (1997) 'Bouquets, brickbats and blinkers: total quality management and employee involvement', *Organization Studies,* Vol.18, No.5, pp.799–820.

Wilkinson, A., Bacon, N., Snell, S. and Redman, T. (eds) (2008) *The Sage Handbook of Human Resource Management,* London: Sage.

Wood, S. (1995) 'The four pillars of human resource management: are they connected?', *Human Resource Management,* Vol.5, No.5, pp.49–59.

Wood, S. (1999) 'Getting the measure of the transformed high performance organisation', *British Journal of Industrial Relations,* Vol.37, No.3, pp.391–417.

Wood, S., and de Menezes, L. (1998) 'High commitment management in the UK', *Human Relations,* Vol.51, pp.485–515.

Chapter 2

HUMAN RESOURCE MANAGEMENT AND ORGANISATIONAL PERFORMANCE:
IN SEARCH OF THE HR ADVANTAGE

Nicholas Kinnie and Juani Swart

Introduction

Research into the links between HR practices and organisational performance has become one of the main areas, some would say *the* main area of study, in the field of human resource management (Purcell and Kinnie 2007). The claims made, especially in the mid–late 1990s, for the impact of HR practices on business performance raised the profile of the issue among practitioners and policy makers. However, debate rages among academics over these claims and their theoretical, empirical and methodological underpinnings. While some authors regard the evidence as the Holy Grail they have been searching for, others question the basis of the research (Legge 2001). They say the research is too narrowly focused on business performance at the expense of other important measures such as employee well-being and corporate responsibility (Delaney and Godard 2001; Marchington and Grugulis 2000). Others warn of the risks of methodological weaknesses and confusion which cast doubt on the robustness of the relationship between HR and performance (Purcell 1999; Wright *et al.* 2005).

It is not difficult to see the reasons for the increased interest in the field. Senior managers were looking for ways to improve their performance by becoming more flexible and responsive in markets that became increasingly competitive because of globalisation and deregulation (Boxall and Purcell 2008; Becker and Gerhart 1996). The rise of the knowledge economy where firms rely almost completely on their human and intellectual capital for their competitive advantage elevated the importance of people management still further (Swart 2007). In this context managers of HR saw the opportunity to demonstrate their contribution to the business more convincingly than in the past (Wright *et al.* 2005). Some researchers in the field, it has been suggested, were motivated by the desire to demonstrate the policy relevance of their research (Legge 2001).

It is against this background that we aim in this chapter to:

- place the debate over HR and performance in the wider context of strategy and HRM;

- identify a suitable framework for analysing the HR and performance research;

- review the research in this field critically;

- examine some of the available data;

- provide case study examples.

Strategy and HRM

We first need to place the HR and performance debate in its wider context of the links between strategy and HRM. These debates have consumed many person hours and we are consequently able only to scratch the surface.[1] We will, however, briefly discuss the various perspectives on strategy.

The adoption of sets of HR practices is often thought to be strategic only if:

(i)   it contributes to organisational performance,[2] and in doing so

(ii) is aligned with the strategy of the organisation.

This leads us to question what strategy is and just what the variations in the alignment between the HR practices and the business strategy might be.

Boxall and Purcell (2008, p.34) follow Mintzberg (1994) and differentiate between the firm's strategic plan and its strategy. They ask whether an organisation, especially a small organisation, which does not have a strategic plan and strategic objectives, can be said to have a strategy. The existence of a strategy and the ability to strategise will, of course, differ from industry to industry. In some industries the market conditions change at a faster rate than others: some are characterised by novel and complex problems while others are more predictable.

We need first to understand the ways in which HR strategy might vary (Swart *et al.* 2004). The principal source of variation is the predictability of and knowledge about the environment. At one extreme, organisations will have a clear sense of how the environment may evolve. The environment in, for example, the public sector, and industries with large capital costs of configuration change like the energy industry, tends to be more stable or at least more predictable. At the other extreme firms do not know whether their environment will change rapidly nor what may trigger a change in the environment. For example, research and technology firms may not be able to predict what the next wave of scientific discovery may be. Firms respond to uncertainty in demand by creating a spread of responses at as low a cost as is practicable in order to capture the demand that eventually emerges (Powell and Wakeley 2003).

Each of these types of environment presents a different strategic paradigm and requirement for competence development (see Figure 2.1). Firstly, the left-hand position represents the classic perspective which views strategy as a plan or a set of strategic objectives (Ansoff 1965; Porter 1985). Success or failure, according to this school of thought, is determined internally through operational detail of the strategic plan (Whittington 2001). The more

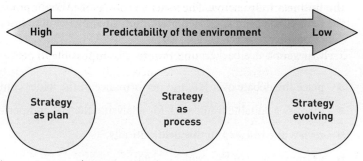

Figure 2.1 The strategy continuum

---

[1]Those looking for a more in-depth treatment are advised to consult Boxall and Purcell (2008).
[2]The link between HR and performance as it relates to strategy will not be discussed in this section as most of the chapter is dedicated to this exploration.

stable and predictable environment allows for environmental diagnosis, scenario-planning, gap analysis and forecasts with their relevant action plans. This approach to strategy has been criticised severely in recent years, mainly because of the dynamic nature of global markets which call for flexibility. This raises the further question as to whether it is possible, firstly, to write a strategic plan and, secondly, to implement this as planned (Boxall and Purcell 2008).

As we move along the continuum we arrive at a point which sees strategy as a process. According to this viewpoint the strategy process changes continually as a result of ongoing learning across the organisation and is therefore more adaptable throughout its enactment.

According to Pettigrew (1973), strategy as a process is influenced by individual and collective cognitions and the interplay of power and politics at every organisational level. This approach is essentially more fluid, with an emphasis on the enactment of strategy, as expressed through behaviours and cognitions. It is therefore more about *seeing* strategy than *planning* strategy.

This perspective can be illustrated by taking the example of a call centre whose customer relationship processes need to change considerably owing to technological development and labour market shifts. The call centre may not know exactly how this technological development could impact upon its processes but a strategy can be enacted through developing relationships with the originators of advanced technologies (in response to technological change and in preparation for customer demands) and as customers make their decisions.

Finally, the other extreme of the continuum represents an evolutionary approach to strategy (Foss 1994; Loasby 1991; Powell and Wakeley 2003). Here organisations operate in near-chaotic environments where change is typically too fast, too unpredictable and too implacable to anticipate and pre-empt and the advice is to concentrate on day-to-day viability while trying to keep options open (Whittington 2001, p.37). The strategic responses in these environments are characterised by a random generation of a spread of responses (since prediction is futile), together with a cost-sensitive trialling of these responses and a planned retention of knowledge gained by that trialling. If we recall the example of the research and technology organisation that develops several research innovations to an unexpected buyer demand, we can see that the organisation can 'keep its options open' through the design and initial development of several offerings. These are then exposed to developments in the market, both through professional networks and scientific partnerships and through market testing. Through the process of gauging responses to possible compounds, for example, the organisation can learn more about its environment and therefore develops an ability to enact future strategies and reinvests the knowledge gained in the development process.

Each of the points on the continuum in Figure 2.1 has implications for competence development. The key focus for the first position is on the development of core competence that will enable the enactment of the strategic plan. Competence development is, therefore, specific and relatively narrow. The focus on competence development is more broadly defined at the mid-point in the continuum where there are several options to a relatively familiar but changing environment. For example, the focus could be on customer service or technology development but given the uncertainty it is impossible to define exactly which core competence will be needed to compete successfully in the marketplace. Finally, the right-hand position calls for a development of a more generic meta-competence that is related to multiple-offering development, trial analysis and fast response once the source of change is known. The level of the competence development is therefore higher compared with the previous two cases and the focus is even wider.

This continuum takes a knowledge-based view to strategy and represents the strategic paradigms accordingly. Several other methods of representation are possible, including the strategic freedom perspective. Firms at each point along the continuum may experience various degrees of client pressure or influence upon their strategic choice. A large firm such as Toyota may not be in a position to plan for every eventuality but given its dominant position within its local network it has a greater degree of freedom of strategic choice

(Kinnie *et al.* 2005). Boxall and Purcell (2008, p.43) argue that it is important to steer between 'hyper-determinism' on the one hand and 'hyper-voluntarism' on the other. Firms therefore neither completely control their environment nor are they completely controlled by it. This is a general statement; we need to be aware of the varying degrees of freedom within and between industries that operate within each of the strategic paradigms. This has implications for the ways human resources are deployed and developed to achieve sustainable competitive advantage.

In this section we have considered the variety of forms that the links between strategy and HR might take. In particular, we have differentiated between three different links between strategy and HR by referring to a continuum based on the predictability of and knowledge about the environment. Having set the context through the consideration of strategy and HR we now turn our attention to how HR practices are linked to organisational performance.

HR and organisational performance: our approach and some background

Our aim is not simply to describe and evaluate all the available research in the field. This is a self-defeating task because the reader will quickly become lost in a mass of detail. Indeed, there are already a number of excellent detailed reviews to be found elsewhere (Becker and Gerhart 1996; Becker and Huselid 2006; Boselie *et al.* 2005; Boxall and Purcell 2008; Combs *et al.* 2006; Delery and Doty 1996; Huselid and Becker 2000; Lepak *et al.* 2006; Purcell 1999; Purcell and Kinnie 2007; Purcell *et al.* 2008; Wall and Wood 2005; Wright and Gardener 2004; Wright *et al.* 2005). One recent review of the research (Wall and Wood 2004) examined the 26 most cited studies published since 1994 and identified a number of characteristic features. Half were based in the industrial sector, most used a single respondent and were cross-sectional in design. Just over half the measures of performance were self-reported and were from the same source as the HRM measures.

We take a thematic approach to the research, referring to key studies as illustrations. More importantly, we use a much-needed theoretical framework based on the concept of human resource advantage (Boxall 1996, 1998; Boxall and Steeneveld 1999) to guide us through the maze of research findings. We use this framework to examine the research thematically in the following way. The next major section outlines the concept of HR advantage and explains how it will be used to structure our analysis of the impact of HR policy and practice.[3] This is followed by an examination of the research into the two forms of HR advantage referred to as human capital advantage and organisational process advantage. The chapter concludes by considering the theoretical, methodological and practical implications of our discussion. Before all of this we need to give some of the background to our discussion.

BACKGROUND TO THE RESEARCH

There has been a longstanding, almost intuitive view that the performance of an organisation is affected by the way its employees are managed. Indeed, this was virtually an unstated assumption behind much of the early research into scientific management, the Hawthorne studies and the total quality management movement. However, much of this early work lacked a strategic focus (Legge 1978; Golding 2004).

Research in the US in the early-to-mid-1980s looked in a more focused way at the possible links between HR and performance. The texts by Beer *et al.* (1985) and by Fombrun *et al.*

---

[3]Following Lepak *et al.* (2006, p.221) we define HR policies as expressing the broad HR aims in particular areas, e.g. the commitment to pay for performance, whereas HR practices are the specific organisational actions designed to achieve specific outcomes, e.g. profit sharing, individual appraisal-related pay.

(1984) were thought to be particularly influential and in some ways represented a major leap forward in the area. These studies were not, however, based on empirical research and there were no attempts at this stage to measure performance in any well-defined or systematic way (Truss 2001, p.1122).

It is only relatively recently that studies have explicitly focused on the performance issue and the data has been available and shown a positive relationship between the presence of key HR practices and organisational performance. Much of the recent interest can be traced back to the work of Huselid (1995) and Pfeffer (1994, 1998) in the US (which itself can be linked back to Peters and Waterman (1982)). The key work is that by Huselid (1995), who sought to measure the contribution of HR to performance in much more well-defined and precise ways than in the past. Drawing on a survey of 968 US firms and taking financial performance (although other outcome measures were also used, for example employee turnover and retention) as his dependent variable, he used sophisticated statistical techniques to consider the impact of high-performance work systems. Huselid found that 'the magnitude of the returns for investments in High Performance Work Systems is substantial'. Indeed, 'A one standard deviation increase in such practices is associated with a relative 7.05% decrease in (labour) turnover, and on a per employee basis, $27,044 more in sales and $18,641 and $3,814 more in market value and profits, respectively' (Huselid 1995, p.667). More recently, Huselid and Becker (2000) claimed that 'Based on four national surveys and observations in more than 2,000 firms, our judgement is that the effect of a one standard deviation change in the HR system is 10–20% of a firm's market value.'

Research by Patterson *et al.* (1997) in the UK came up with similar findings. Drawing on research in 67 UK manufacturing businesses studied over time they found that 18 per cent of the variation in productivity and 19 per cent of profitability could be attributed to people management practices. These were a better predictor of company performance than strategy, technology, and research and development.

Following the early research there have been over a hundred studies looking at the links between HR and performance and many of these have focused on the links between HR practices and performance. Boselie *et al.* (2005) report that there were 104 articles in the area in refereed journals between 1994 and 2003. Despite this extensive effort, the goal of establishing a clear link between HR practices and performance still seems some way off. As Purcell and Kinnie (2007, p.533) noted, 'numerous review papers . . . have found this field of research often wanting in terms of method, theory and the specification of HR practices to be used when establishing a relationship with performance outcomes'. Becker and Huselid (2006, p.921) put the same point in a slightly different way: 'Despite the remarkable progress the field of SHRM may be at a cross-roads.'

These studies have stimulated an intense debate surrounding the very nature, purpose and outputs of the research (Keenoy 1997; Legge 1995; Hesketh and Fleetwood 2006). However, before we explore the findings of this research in more detail we need to establish our framework for analysis.

Human resource advantage

Research in the field has often been criticised for an excessive emphasis on the quantitative analysis of data collected by the survey method. For example, when commenting on the early research Guest (1997, p.264) noted that 'While these studies represent encouraging signs of progress, statistical sophistication appears to have been emphasized at the expense of theoretical rigour. As a result the studies are non-additive, except in a very general way.' Wood (1999, p.408) in turn argued that 'The empirical work . . . has concentrated on assessing the link between practices and performance with increasing disregard for the mechanisms

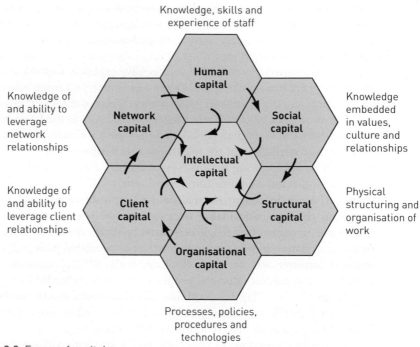

Figure 2.2 Forms of capital

Sources: Swart 2006; Kinnie *et al.* 2006

linking them'. Consequently Guest (1997, p.263) argued that 'if we are to improve our understanding of the impact of HRM on performance, we need a theory about HRM, a theory about performance and a theory about how they are linked'.

The work by Peter Boxall and his colleagues provides a way forward with their development of the concept of human resource advantage (HRA) (Boxall 1996, 1998; Boxall and Steeneveld 1999; Boxall and Purcell 2008). HRA is the series of policies, practices and processes that together contribute to the competitive advantage of the organisation. This advantage is comprised of a human capital advantage (HCA) and an organisational process advantage (OPA). There are various forms of capital which are critical to organisational performance (including human, social, structural, organisational, client and network capital – see Figure 2.2 for further details) and our discussion focuses on the generation of HCA which involves developing superior practices in key areas such as recruitment, selection, training and team building designed to ensure that the best people are employed and that these staff develop high levels of skill. However, HCA is unlikely to generate competitive advantage in the practices themselves because they are easily copied (Mueller 1996). It is the processes and routines required to put these practices into operation as intended that are more difficult to replicate and form the OPA (Boxall 1996, p.267). These processes, such as team-based learning and cross-functional cooperation, develop over time, are socially complex and causally ambiguous (Boxall and Purcell 2008, p.102).

Both HCA and OPA can generate competitive advantage, but they are most effective when they are combined. The form of HR advantage is likely to change as the firm grows through the establishment, mature and renewal contexts (Boxall 1998). Thus 'While knowledge of individual HR practices is not rare, the knowledge of how to create a positively reinforcing blend of HR philosophy, process, practice and investment *within* a particular context is likely to be very rare' (Boxall and Purcell 2003, p.86). This 'social architecture' is created and re-created at all levels in the firm and is therefore especially difficult to imitate (Mueller 1996, p.177).

For our purposes this creates a dual focus on the design and content of HR practices *and* the role of line managers and employees in putting these into action. We use this framework as a way of organising our discussion of the links between HR and performance. We look first at the research conducted into the influences shaping the HR practices that comprise the HCA. This can be broken down into two schools of thought typically referred to as 'best practice' and 'best fit'. Attention is then turned to studies of OPA looking at the role of employees and line managers.

Human capital advantage

Research into the impact of HR practices on performance can be divided into two groups. First, those who argue that a set of HR practices can be identified which can be applied in a wide variety of circumstances and will have a positive effect on business performance. The second view is that the effectiveness of HR practices depends on the external and internal context of the organisation. We review each of these using illustrations from the principal studies.

BEST PRACTICE

There is a long history of researching individual best practices, for example psychology-based research into psychometric testing (Boxall and Purcell 2008, pp.74–75). What is new is the concept of looking for a combination or 'bundle' of practices which need to be combined together (Lepak *et al.* 2006, p.218; MacDuffie 1995; Huselid 1995; Guest 1997). Making changes to individual practices will, it is argued, have a very limited effect whereas making changes together will have a more powerful effect. This suggests that there is a set of practices which can and should be adopted by firms and which will lead to improvements in performance. In practical terms not only must firms become aware of these practices, but they also need support from top-level managers to adopt them. Researchers have also highlighted the need to avoid what they referred to as 'deadly' combinations, for example the introduction of individual performance pay and teamworking (Delery 1998).

The terms for these bundles vary, indeed there is an array of acronyms used which seem designed to confuse the practitioner and the academic, including HR system, high-commitment management (HCM), high-performance work systems (HPWS) and high-involvement management (HIM).

These approaches seek to identify a distinctive set of successful HR practices that can be applied successfully to all organisations irrespective of their setting. Pfeffer (1994, 1998) developed a list of 16 best practices which were subsequently reduced to seven (1998). The seven practices are: employment security, selective hiring, self-managed teams/teamworking, high compensation contingent on organisational performance, extensive training, reduction of status differentials, and sharing information.

Huselid (1995) argued that there needs to be an integrated system of work practices to fit the particular needs of the organisation. This research involved collecting data relating to the number of practices the firm employs by means of a postal questionnaire completed by a single respondent representing the company as a whole. The resulting analysis produced impressive results linking the number of practices and various forms of performance – typically profit and market value.

More recent research by Guest *et al.* (2003), drawing on a survey of 366 UK firms, produced rather more mixed results. They found that increased use of HR practices was associated with lower labour turnover and higher profit per employee, but not with higher productivity. However, once profitability in earlier years is taken into account these associations ceased to be significant (Guest *et al.* 2003, p.306). Thus the association between HR practices and organisational performance is confirmed, but there is no evidence to show that the presence of HR practices causes a change in performance (Guest *et al.* 2003, p.307). Wright *et al.* (2005) also found that virtually all of their significant correlations disappeared when controlling for past performance. This type of research has a number of advantages because it focuses the debate on the role of HR practices but also raises various problems (Boxall and Purcell 2008, pp.78–82; Purcell 1999). Two kinds of problems have been identified: methodological and theoretical. Let us look at methodological problems first.

Methodological problems

Perhaps the easiest way of summarising the criticisms of this research is to pose a series of questions.

What is the direction of causation? It is possible that the direction of causation is in the opposite direction to that which is proposed since it may be only the successful firms that can afford these HCM practices (Guest *et al.* 2003, p.309). Indeed, Wright *et al.* (2005, p.432–33) argued for exercising 'extreme caution in inferring a direct causal impact on performance'. They suggest that dual causation provides a possible explanation for what they have observed: business units that perform well invest more in HR practices which pay off in terms of improved performance. There is also the possibility that respondents might believe that HR practices are good simply because the performance of their organisation is good (Gerhart 1999, p.42; Wright and Gardener 2000, p.8). Moreover, it is highly likely that there will be multiple causes of any improvement in performance and it is very difficult to unpick these satisfactorily.

What measures should be used? The measures of performance are typically narrowly focused on financial criteria, with very few studies examining the broader issue of employee attitudes and well-being. Similarly, there are issues over the extensiveness of HR practices: should they, for example, apply to all employees or only a selection? One study may examine whether the organisation has self-managed teams (i.e. yes or no), while another may look at the proportion of employees working in a self-managed team. Linked to this is the profound problem, discussed in more detail when we look at organisational process advantage, which has either been ignored or side-stepped by much of this research, that the practices that are being so carefully counted are not actually implemented in practice.

How should the data be collected, analysed and presented? Many studies rely on postal surveys where the main problem is mis-reporting by single respondents who have limited knowledge of the extent and use of the practices (Gerhart 1999). Much of the research makes use of highly sophisticated statistical techniques that produce results that are hard for the practitioner, as well as many students and academics, to understand.

Theoretical problems

As we have mentioned, there have been strong criticisms of the lack of theoretical development. This poses another set of questions which need to be addressed.

Best practice for whom? Is there room for an employee voice in this discussion or is the emphasis simply on the perspective of shareholders and managers? (Boxall and Purcell 2008, pp.73–74). Marchington and Grugulis (2000, pp.1105–6) consider the impact of these practices on employees and argue that these practices, such as teamwork or performance-related pay, 'which appear superficially attractive may not offer universal benefits and empowerment but actually lead to work intensification and more insidious forms of control; in other words quite different and more worrying interpretations from that portrayed in the "upbeat" literature – such as that by Pfeffer'. They are in short 'nice words and harsh realities'.

Ramsay *et al.* (2000) investigated the labour process explanation which argues that improvements in productivity are the result of the intensification of work, using the data from the Workplace Employee Relations Survey (Cully *et al.* 1999). However, they could not find support for either the labour process or the high-commitment management explanations.

More generally the absence of an independent employee voice is noted (Marchington and Grugulis 2000, p.1119), reflecting more generally a set of unitarist assumptions underpinning Pfeffer's work. Thus emphasis tends to be on the psychology-based techniques such as recruitment and selection, training, performance appraisal and pay rather than those based on pluralist assumptions, for example employee involvement practices and collective bargaining.

Which practices should be included? It is relatively easy to spot so-called 'bad' practices, for example the use of unstructured selection interviews or a poorly conducted performance appraisal. However, it is difficult to get agreement on what the good practices are, apart from the most obvious statements such as the need for careful planning. The lists of practices themselves vary (Boxall and Purcell 2008, p.78) and there is no agreement on what constitutes the best practices, such that 'studies of so-called high performance work systems vary significantly as to the practices included and sometimes even as to whether a practice is likely to be positively or negatively related to high performance' (Becker and Gerhart 1996, p.784). Guest and Hoque (1994), for example, list 23 practices, MacDuffie (1995) has 11 items and Pfeffer has seven. Marchington and Grugulis (2000, p.1114) note that employment security is included by Pfeffer but not by a number of other authors; similarly, the importance of employee voice varies: some include it but Pfeffer does it in a very limited way. Arthur (1994) gives low emphasis to variable pay whereas Huselid (1995) and MacDuffie emphasise this (Truss 2001, p.1124). Consequently, both Boxall and Purcell (2008) and Youndt *et al.* (1996, p.839) argue that there is a need for this kind of research to be more selective in the way findings are presented.

Do you need all of these practices and are they all equally important? The argument put forward by MacDuffie (1995), based on bundles of HR practices, suggests that these practices need to be combined and that just taking one or two is likely to be ineffective. Marchington and Grugulis (2000, pp.1112–15) argue that in practice we often find weak links between these practices or simply contradictory practices – one person's job security might be at the expense of another person's whether in the employing firm or a subcontractor.

Are all employees treated in the same way? Are these practices reserved for a minority of supposedly core employees or are they applied to all? (Marchington and Grugulis 2000, p.1117). This is not just an issue of differences between manual and staff employees but applies more widely in times of the decline of the internal labour market and the externalisation of the workforce through subcontracting and network relations. Early work on the 'flexible firm' suggested that employees would be treated differently based on how central they were to the core of the firm (Atkinson 1984). More recent work by Lepak and Snell (1999), discussed below, also addresses this issue.

What is the level and unit of analysis? This question is an important one. In some cases the research has been carried out at the level of the corporate head office (Huselid 1995) where the gap between HR practices, the employees they are intended for and performance is wide. Other research has collected data at the level of the business unit where the gap between the HR policy and performance data is narrowed (Wright *et al.* 2003). This issue is addressed to some extent by the sectoral studies discussed below.

If these practices are so effective, why aren't they used more widely? Evidence from the Workplace Employee Relations Survey (Cully *et al.* 1999) found that only 14 per cent of workplaces used HCM and in the US (Osterman 1994) only 35 per cent of firms used two or more HCM practices, a finding confirmed by Gittleman *et al.* (1998). Guest *et al.* (2000) found that only 1 per cent of their firms used three-quarters of 18 progressive practices and 20 per cent use less than a quarter. It is possible that just putting practices in on their own does not change very much, leading to a loss of enthusiasm because of the difficulty in identifying results.

More generally Guest *et al.* (2000) tell us that there were relatively few firms in their survey that had an HR strategy and a long tail of firms that did not. They found that while two-thirds of firms rely on people as their source of competitive advantage, only about 10 per cent gave people a priority above that of marketing and finance and in most companies people are not viewed by top managers as their most important asset.

How important is the context? Both national context, where customers, laws, cultures and styles vary (Boxall and Purcell 2008, p.78), and organisational sectoral contexts pose questions about the suitability of these practices, although multinational companies will attempt to standardise their practices across countries (Boxall and Purcell 2008, pp.79–80). There may well be circumstances where employers simply cannot afford these practices, most commonly in labour-intensive organisations, where arguably the difficulty of controlling costs is greatest (Marchington and Grugulis 2000, p.1117).

To sum up, we can see from these questions that although the best-practice view has gained a great deal of publicity because of the simplicity of the message, it has also attracted widespread criticism. Indeed, Purcell (1999) has characterised research in this area as leading into a *'cul-de-sac'* where no forward progress is possible. Many of the critics argue that what works in one organisational setting, for example a small knowledge-intensive firm, will be quite different from what is effective in another, for example a low-cost manufacturing company or an NHS Trust. This leads them to argue that in order to maximise performance managers must tailor their HR policies and practices to the contexts within which they are working – a view typically referred to as 'best fit'.

BEST FIT

This perspective is derived from the contingency view which argues that the effectiveness of HR practices depends on how closely they fit with the external and internal environment of the organisation. Business performance, it is argued, improves when HR practices mutually reinforce the choice of competitive strategy. This is the concept of vertical integration between the competitive strategy, the objectives of the firm, the HR practices and individual objectives (Fombrun *et al.* 1984; Wright *et al.* 1994) and it helps to explain lack of diffusion because the appropriate practices will depend on the context.

There are different views on the importance of particular contexts: some stress the stage in the life cycle whereas others draw attention to the 'outer context' of the competitive strategy or the 'inner context' of existing structures and strategy (Hendry and Pettigrew 1992).

Some authors (Kochan and Barocci 1985; Baird and Meshoulam 1988) argue that there needs to be a fit between the HR practices and the stage in the business life cycle. They suggest that the HR practices needed during the start-up phase are quite different from those needed during growth, maturity and decline. However, most organisations will have a series of products that are at different stages in their life cycles, producing the situation familiar to many managers whereby certain parts of their business are growing whereas others are shrinking, resulting in quite different pressures on HR practices.

However, perhaps the best-known examples of this perspective draw on analysis (Porter 1980) of the sources of competitive advantage (Miles and Snow 1978, 1984; Schuler and Jackson 1987), which argues that HR practices work best when they are adapted to the competitive strategy. Miles and Snow (1984) identify three types of strategic behaviour and link these to various HR practices: 'Defenders' will have narrow, relatively stable products and will emphasise internal, process-oriented training and internal pay equity; 'Prospectors' have changing product lines and rely more on innovation, leading to the use of external recruitment, results-oriented compensation and external pay equity; 'Analysers' have changing and stable product lines, leading them to use internal and external recruitment, pay equity measures and process-oriented performance appraisal.

Schuler and Jackson (1987) and Jackson and Schuler (1995) developed these approaches where they identified the different competitive strategies of organisations and the role behaviours which were needed with each of them. They drew attention to the different kinds of behaviours needed for innovation, quality enhancement and cost reduction and the types of HR practices needed to achieve these. For example, a strategy based on cost leadership will result in minimal levels of investment in human capital, with low standards for recruitment and poor levels of pay and training. In contrast, a strategy based on innovation calls for HR practices that encourage risk taking and cooperative behaviour. Youndt *et al.* (1996) and Delery and Doty (1996) provide some support for this perspective.

The 'best fit' approach is well illustrated in studies carried out in a single sector where most firms are operating within the same industrial context. For example, Arthur (1994) demonstrated how steel mini-mills firms pursuing cost leadership business strategies adopted cost minimisation approaches of the command-and-control type. Those seeking product and quality differentiation pursued HCM or HPWS approaches, with emphasis on training, employee problem solving, teamworking, higher pay, higher skills and attempts to create a work community. Batt and Moynihan (2004) found that HR practices emphasising investment in employees were more successful in the parts of the industry that required employees to exercise their discretion, when they examined call centres in the US telecommunications industry.

Thompson (2000) carried out two surveys of firms in the UK aerospace industry. In 1997 he found that establishments with higher levels of value added per employee tended to have higher penetration of innovative working practices among their non-management employees. These workplaces were more likely to engage in specialist production for niche markets and employed a richer mix of technical and professional employees. Later work in 1999 revealed 'compelling evidence that firms introducing a greater number of high performance work practices have much improved business performance' (Thompson 2000, p.10). Firms moving from less than five to more than six innovative practices made a 34 per cent gain in value added per employee.

Other research has highlighted the influence of the network of relationships within which firms, especially knowledge-intensive and professional service firms, are working (Swart and Kinnie 2003; Swart *et al.* 2007; Beaumont *et al.* 1996; Sinclair *et al.* 1996). Firms form relationships with clients, suppliers and collaborators who will seek to influence the HR practices pursued by the focal firm both directly and indirectly (see Box 2.1 and Figure 2.3). These external parties influence HR practices directly, for example through shaping recruitment and selection criteria or through requiring certain types of training to be conducted, or indirectly by setting performance targets that can be reached only by adopting, for example, team-based forms of work organisation (Kinnie and Parsons 2004).

Labour markets are also important because firms in certain industries and geographical areas find they have to compete much more intensively than others. Tight labour markets, for example where call centres are concentrated, will put pressure on particular HR practices such as recruitment and selection and reward (Kinnie *et al.* 2000).

Others argue that HR practices need to fit with and complement other important strategies and structures within the organisation. Organisational size will be important – larger firms will have complex internal structures, often with multiple layers, and more generally have just the resources needed to fund certain approaches, for example a formalised salary structure or recruitment scheme. The manufacturing strategy of the firm also needs to be taken into account (Purcell 1999; Boxall and Purcell 2008, pp.68–69; Baron and Kreps 1999).

Box 2.1: HRM in practice

Tocris Cookson

Tocris Cookson, with 60 employees, is a specialist chemical company with experience in the synthesis of a wide variety of compounds. They employ teams of skilled chemists (mainly at post-doctoral level) and operate from one site in the UK and one site in the USA. HR practices in Tocris Cookson can be understood only in the context of the network in which they operate (see Figure 2.3).

Tocris Cookson's key clients are life science researchers at universities or other research institutes. In order to build these client relationships and make the compounds, they need to maintain very strong ties with large pharmaceutical companies, patent lawyers and academics in the field. Pharmaceutical firms often have patents on some of the chemicals that need to be synthesised; however, these could lapse in an 8–10-year period. If a 'cool chemical is spotted' the patent rights need to be negotiated with the relevant firm. A senior manager in Tocris Cookson said, 'once our key to success was developing compounds, now it is building relationships'.

Relationships with universities also need to be maintained to:

i) update employees' skills in the pharmacological discipline;
ii) build client relationships, where the universities are often users of the compounds made;
iii) build an external recruitment pool by making top-performing research chemists aware of the business.

The process of building external relationships was regarded as 'an art' which could only be mastered over several years of experience: first as a doctoral chemist, then as a post-doctoral researcher and finally as a negotiator with major pharmaceutical firms.

Tocris Cookson recruits its employees during a post-doctoral placement at the company and this is often their first full-time employment. Managers regard this as a threat because the majority of their workforce is young, highly qualified and mobile (single). The threat is managed through the strong organisational culture, which employees describe as a family or home away from home.

Most formalised HR practices originated from an elaborate HR policy, which was written by the part-time HR manager. The drive towards more formalised HR systems coincided with the company objective of 'becoming more corporate'. Within the set of formalised practices, performance management was central to other HR practices both practically, given its links to reward and development, but also politically because it influenced the career development of this group of knowledge workers. Furthermore, the performance appraisal process was questioned by research chemists and there was a push to develop an in-house system because it is particularly difficult to appraise the outcome of research. This resulted in sets of HR practices evolving from formalised practices that may have originated outside the firm to sets of practices that grew from within the community of knowledge workers.

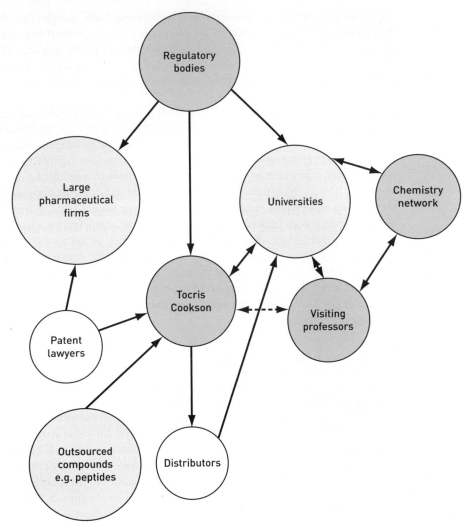

Figure 2.3 Tocris Cookson network

The best-fit approach has been subject to extensive review (see Boxall and Purcell 2008, pp. 64–73; Purcell 1999, p.32 for further details). Perhaps the most basic point of all is the assumption that firms have a competitive strategy with which HR practices can fit (Legge 1995; Ramsay *et al.* 2000). The second and related point is that it is possible to typify the firms in the way that has been suggested. Purcell (1999) suggests that this is unlikely for a variety of reasons. In practice, organisations may pursue a mix of competitive strategies, for example seeking both cost leadership and differentiation, leading to confusion over the most appropriate HR practices. Even if the firm does have a strategy, this view assumes that the one they have is the most appropriate for them. This may not be the case if firms do not have sufficient knowledge of their external environment or if they have misinterpreted the information that they have gathered.

Multiple contingencies

Perhaps the biggest problem is that most firms exist within complex external environments with multiple contingencies that cannot all be isolated or identified. There are particular problems with modelling the influences, with understanding what happens if the influences do not all pull in the same direction and with coping with change (Purcell 1999, p.34). This raises the issue of the dynamic fit between policy and context: if the external environment changes, should firms keep changing their practices to fit the market circumstances? There are strong arguments against this because HR practices are quite slow to change. Consequently, Purcell (1999) has argued that firms seeking a best fit are effectively chasing a 'chimera'.

In response to criticisms of the best-fit approach, Wright and Snell (1998) argue for the need to have both fit and flexibility (Boxall and Purcell 2008, p.73). This is not just the ability to move from one best fit to another, but to be able to adapt to the situation where the need to change is virtually continuous. 'Flexibility provides organisations with the ability to modify current practices in response to non-transient changes in the environment' (Wright and Snell 1998, p.757). In particular, there is a need to achieve fit between the HR system and the existing competitive strategy while at the same time achieving flexibility in a range of skills and behaviours needed to cope with changing competitive environments.

More broadly, there may be some characteristics of successful organisations that are impossible to model, usually referred to as idiosyncratic contingency or causal ambiguity (Purcell 1999, p.35). These are the patterns and routines of behaving or the cultural norms that have been built up slowly over a long period associated with success. It may simply not be possible to disentangle what exactly are the key factors in success when looking at a large complex organisation.

Treating employees differently

The need to respond to external pressures creates problems of treating employees with consistency of treatment, especially over time (Baron and Kreps 1999). In reality it is likely that a combination of practices will be needed depending on external circumstances: as products grow and decline there may need to be redundancies for some employees but also the need to retain good employees and to develop them (Boxall and Purcell 2008, p.65).

In response to some of these criticisms we have seen the development of the HR architecture model (Lepak and Snell 1999). This is based on the configurational view, which argues that it is unlikely that a company will use a single approach for all its employees. It suggests that the best-fit approach is too simple because there is a need to focus on combinations or patterns of practices which are needed – putting horizontal fit together with vertical fit (Delery and Doty 1996). Most organisations employ different groups of employees who will need to be treated differently and in effect there are different configurations of practices for different types of employees.

The Lepak and Snell model of HR architecture expresses these ideas in a more accessible form. They argue that 'To date most strategic HRM researchers have tended to take a holistic view of employment and human capital, focusing on the extent to which a set of practices is used across all employees of a firm as well as the consistency of these practices across firms. We believe that the most appropriate mode of investment in human capital will vary for different types of capital' (Lepak and Snell 1999, p.32). Their model distinguishes between employees on the basis of the value they create for the organisation (the extent to which they contribute towards the creation of competitive advantage) and the extent to which their knowledge and skills are specific to that organisation (uniqueness).

This approach represents a step forward but also raises various questions. In particular, there is the issue of consistency here: if an employer wishes to pursue an inclusive culture-based approach, why should they treat employees differently? If certain activities are externalised there is a danger that the core competences of the organisation will be lost. There is also a moral issue here – why should different groups be treated differently?

Recent work (Purcell et al. 2008) has examined this in a slightly different way, looking at the attitudinal outcomes such as organisational commitment and job satisfaction for different occupational groups (see Box 2.2 for further details).

Box 2.2: HRM in practice

Influences on the attitudes of different occupational groups

Much of the research assumes that the set of HR practices adopted will have the same effect on all employees who work for the organisation. We investigated this, drawing on an analysis of data drawn from the Workplace Employee Relations Survey, 2004 (Kersley 2006). We found[4] (Purcell *et al.* 2008) that a different practice mix is associated with high levels of organisation commitment for different occupations.

There are some practices (satisfaction with the work itself and with the level of managerial support) which seem to have a consistently positive influence on employee commitment across virtually all of the employee groups. However, there were other aspects of the work experience which were distinctively associated with particular work groups. Sales and customer service workers' commitment seemed to be closely tied to the flexibility of the job, whereas the role of line managers was unimportant. Pay satisfaction was important for skilled, personal service and elementary workers while teamwork was important only for the commitment of skilled and personal service employees. The role of line managers was important for all employees other than sales and customer service work. Variables for job stress, career opportunities, job involvement and training were not associated with employee commitment. Further details of the most important HR practices for each group are given below (the shaded areas indicate that there are negative correlations between the HR practice and employee commitment).

Lower skill employees: elementary

Satisfaction with work itself
Satisfaction with pay
Trust managers

Lower skill employees: operatives

Expect long-term employment
Satisfaction with achievement
Relationships with managers
Job security
Satisfaction with work itself
Trust managers

Zero hours
Job sharing
PBR
Selection by performance tests

Sales

Zero hours
Satisfaction with work itself
Able to reduce FT to PT hours
Job security guarantee

Skilled workers

Zero hours contracts
Satisfaction with achievement
Satisfaction with pay
Satisfaction with work itself
Teamworking
Job challenge
Trust managers

Able to work term time only
Five days training
Satisfaction with job security
Employee unease

Professionals

Ability to change work patterns
Select via performance tests
Satisfaction with work itself
Satisfaction with scope to use
  initiative
Trust managers

Ability to work same hours
Zero hours contracts

[4]We focused on the largest occupational group in each workplace.

In summary, we have considered the best-practice and best-fit approaches towards the generation of human resource advantage and examined the criticisms which have been made of these. It is possible, however, that these approaches can be reconciled. Boxall and Purcell (2008, pp.82–84) conclude that some general principles can be established, for example on selection interviewing, but that practices themselves are likely to be influenced by best-fit considerations at national and organisational levels. This combination of views remains, however, incomplete because it is still looking only at the formal practices and we now need to consider how these practices are actually used.

Organisational process advantage

The key theme running throughout our discussion has been that the acquisition of HR advantage depends on developing both a capital and a process advantage (Purcell 1999, p.36; Boxall and Purcell 2008, p.16). We need therefore to understand how HR practices are actually translated into operation before we can begin thoroughly to understand the links between HR and performance. It is important to look at the routines and processes, or, using another language, both the formal and informal practices which make up the day-to-day realities of organisational life.

Studying OPA is much more difficult than looking at practices because these processes are often tacit and intangible; they are immune to data collection by postal questionnaire and analysis by sophisticated statistical packages. In fact OPA is only seen most clearly when it is absent, when things go wrong: there is infighting between departments, poor knowledge sharing within and between project teams, or people do not work to their full potential.

The concept of OPA is derived from research carried out into the resource-based view of strategy.

RESOURCE-BASED VIEW

This draws attention to the intangible assets of the firm which make up its distinctive competencies and organisational routines (Purcell 1999, p.35). The resource-based view (RBV) has developed from business strategy literature that competitive advantage is based on what is difficult to imitate, not on what can be copied. There is a need to develop an exclusive form of fit. This is particularly important for knowledge-intensive firms that rely almost entirely on their human and intellectual capital for their success, and is effectively rebalancing an over-dependence on the Porter approach (Boxall and Purcell 2008, pp.101–3).

The RBV involves looking at the internal resources of the firm and considering the ways in which HR can maximise their contribution to development of competitive advantage. This focuses on how human resources can become scarce, organisation specific and difficult to imitate (Barney 1991; Barney and Wright 1998) and draws on the research into core competencies (Hamel and Prahalad 1994).

In particular, this view involves looking at how HR can develop the following (Barney and Wright 1998; Golding 2004, p.51):

- Value – how does the firm seek to distinguish itself from its competitors? What part does HR play in this?

- Rarity – is the firm doing something with its employees that its competitors are not?

- Inimitable – casual ambiguity means that the unique history of each firm makes it difficult to ascertain what causes the advantage and therefore makes it difficult to copy.

- Organisation – these internal resources need to be integrated into coherent systems so that the advantage is sustainable.

Research into the resource-based view tends to be associated with unpredictable environments and emphasises what is distinctive. However, we need to remember that firms also need to have the base-line characteristics right before developing distinctive characteristics, what Hamel and Prahalad (1994) and Boxall (1996) refer to as 'table stakes', the resources and skills needed simply to play the game. Once these have been established it is the differences between firms that are important. Truss (2001) notes that one of the problems with the RBV is its emphasis on the importance of synergy and fit between the various elements of the HR system and asks how compatible a systems-based approach is with flexibility (Becker and Gerhart 1996, p.789).

Becker and Huselid (2006, p.901) note, however, that 'the attention given to the independent influence of "implementation" in the strategy literature offers an opportunity to make the theoretical HR–performance link more concrete'. Indeed, they recall that Barney (2001, p.54) notes that 'the ability to implement strategies is by itself a resource that can be a source of competitive advantage'.

If we are to examine the implementation issues in the HR context we need to consider what has come to be known as the 'black box' research.

APPLICATION TO HR: EXAMINING THE 'BLACK BOX'

Becker and Gerhart (1996, p.793) noted the importance of examining the implementation of HR practices when they argued that 'future work on the strategic perspective must elaborate on the black box between a firm's HR systems and the firm's bottom line'. Moreover, 'more effort should be devolved to finding out what managers are thinking and why they make the decisions they do' (1996, p.794). This suggests that we need to understand how and why HR practices influence performance and to move away from basic input–output models which have policy inputs on the left-hand side of the model and outcomes on the right-hand side (Becker and Huselid 2006).

When we begin to look inside the 'black box' we find that there are differences between the espoused practices and the practices in use. Truss (2001) highlights the importance of the informal processes that exist alongside the formal practices, drawing on her research in Hewlett Packard. There were clear gaps between what the company claimed they were doing and what was actually experienced by employees: 'in areas such as appraisals and training and development the results obtained were not uniformly excellent; in fact some were highly contradictory' (Truss 2001, p.1143). Although the formal HP appraisal procedures rewarded employees' performance against targets related to the company's objectives, 'informally what counted was visibility and networking if people wanted to further their careers' (Truss 2001, p.1144). Despite espousing the value of training, less than half said they got the training they needed to do their job, fewer than half felt the appraisal system was working well and less than one-third felt their pay was fair. 'These are all examples of a strong disconnect between the "rhetoric" of human resource management as expressed by the human resource department, and the reality as experienced by employees' (Truss 2001, p.1143). This 'highlights the importance of the informal organization as mediator between policy and the individual' (Truss 2001, p.1144).

These findings were repeated in a study of 12 organisations where there was a clear gap between formal HR policy statements and actual practice in areas such as performance appraisals, training, involvement and communication (Purcell *et al.* 2003, 2008). For example, in organisations which claimed to have formal employee involvement schemes (such as team briefs) for all their employees, not all staff were aware of the existence of these initiatives and an even lower proportion of employees claimed to have been practically involved in such schemes (Hutchinson and Purcell 2003, p.36).

Research into formal and informal practices (Terry 1977; Brown 1972, 1973) has a long tradition in the industrial relations literature and sheds important light on contemporary concerns about the key processes involved. This makes a focus solely on formal practices inappropriate, and in particular we need to consider the role of the 'individual manager as agent, choosing to focus his or her attention in varying ways' (Truss 2001, p.1145). We consider this by looking at discretionary behaviour. However, we first need to examine the role of employees when engaging in discretionary behaviour.

Employee discretionary behaviour

The importance of employee discretionary behaviour has been highlighted by research in the US steel, clothing and medical equipment industries (Appelbaum *et al.* 2000). Drawing evidence from shop-floor employees and managers as well as a study of formal HR practices, Appelbaum and her colleagues found that the willingness of employees to engage in discretionary behaviour depended on the creation of opportunities to participate, skill development and motivation and incentives (Appelbaum *et al.* 2000, pp.118–20).

Their most important finding was that the positive effects of HPWS on plant performance were felt through increased discretionary effort by employees and an improved knowledge accumulation. These practices had a different effect on performance in different industries (Appelbaum *et al.* 2000, p.227). In steel, there was evidence that quality and employment security raised 'up time' by 8 per cent, incentives by 13 per cent, work organisation by 14 per cent and HPWS as a whole by 17 per cent (Appelbaum *et al.* 2000, p.108). In clothing, modular production involving self-directed teams reduced sewing time by 94 per cent and led to substantial cost savings. In medical equipment, the opportunity to participate is closely linked to value added per dollar and profits and quality (Appelbaum *et al.* 2000, p.108). The likelihood of employees engaging in this discretionary behaviour is also influenced by the role of line managers.

Role of line managers in bringing practices to life

Recent research has examined how the discretionary behaviour of managers, especially first line managers, contributes towards the development, or absence, of an organisational process advantage.

Over the past 15 years numerous studies have observed how line managers have played a more prominent role in the delivery of HR practices such as performance management, team leadership and communications as an increasing number of people management activities have been devolved to them (Hutchinson and Wood 1995; Renwick 2000; Larsen and Brewster 2003). The important role of line managers has been identified by both recent research (Marchington and Wilkinson 2002, pp.232–37) and earlier work on the 'forgotten supervisor' (Thurley and Wirdenius 1973; Child and Partridge 1982) and the role of the line manager in the emergence of informal practices (Brown 1972, 1973; Terry 1977; Armstrong and Goodman 1979).

Recent studies (Purcell *et al.* 2003, 2008) show that the way line managers implement and enact HR practices by 'bringing them to life' and show leadership strongly influences employees' attitudes. Employees' perceptions of line management behaviour (in terms of how they carry out their HR activities such as responding to suggestions from employees) was the most important factor in explaining variations in both job satisfaction and job discretion – or the choice people have over how they do their jobs. There is also evidence that a pattern can be traced between line manager activities, employee attitudes and the performance of comparable business units and changes over time. The Selfridges and Omega cases illustrate this well.

Bartel (2000) examined these issues in the banking industry in Canada and found that when controlling for environment and branch and managerial effects, the HR environment (as measured by the quality of feedback and communications) has a significant positive effect on loan sales. Although there were common HR practices, it was clear that there was discretion over how these were applied. One standard deviation increase in managerial effectiveness accounts for a 16–26 per cent increase in loan sales. Thus the discretion exercised by branch managers has a direct effect on performance through the education and motivation of branch staff.

These differences between 'espoused' and 'enacted' practices can be partly attributed to the line manager for a variety of reasons (Hutchinson and Purcell 2003; McGovern *et al.* 1997; Marchington 2001). Line managers may suffer from work overload partly because of organisational restructuring and the demise of the middle manager and simply lack the time to carry out all their duties. They may have inadequate training on how to operate the practices, lack commitment to them (Marchington 2001), be doubtful about the claimed benefits, or simply be ignorant of what is expected of them.

In an attempt to analyse this role Purcell *et al.* (2008) developed a model which places the discretionary behaviour exercised by line managers at the centre of the analysis, as shown in Box 2.3 and Figure 2.4. In particular, it sees the link between HR practices and performance as being the interaction between line manager behaviour and employee attitudes and behaviour. Line managers are important because of the key role they play in the generation of operational process advantage: most employees experience work through their contacts with their immediate team and their team leader.

The key role played by line managers opens up further lines of inquiry concerning how these line managers are themselves managed. Research (Hutchinson and Purcell 2003) suggests that the key factors influencing line managers' commitment and job satisfaction and their willingness to engage in discretionary behaviour are their relationships with their own line managers and the existence of career opportunities. In addition, work–life balance, the ability to discuss problems with their managers and job security are associated with organisational commitment, while involvement is linked with job satisfaction (Hutchinson and Purcell 2003, p.48; Hutchinson and Purcell 2007).

More broadly, this suggests that the values and culture of the organisation can be a form of organisational process advantage. There are positive links between this form of OPA and organisational commitment; for example, employees in firms which exhibit 'strong values' or

Figure 2.4 HR causal chain model
Source: Purcell *et al.* 2008

Box 2.3: HRM in practice

HR causal chain model

Many attempts to link HR policy and performance pay insufficient attention to the linking mechanisms. We draw on the work of MacDuffie (1995), Appelbaum *et al.* (2000) and Wright and Nishii (2004) to identify the key causal steps in the chain from intended HR practices to performance outcomes (Purcell *et al.* 2008).

The model has the following key features:

- *Intended HR practices* are those designed by senior management to be applied to most or all of the employees and concern employees' ability, motivation and opportunity to participate. These practices will be influenced by the articulated values of the organisation and found in the HR manual or the appropriate web pages. These also include the ways work is structured and organised since this has an impact on employee attitudes and behaviour.
- *Actual HR practices* are those which are actually applied, usually by line managers. There may often be a substantial difference between the espousal and the enactment of HR practices in an organisation (Hutchinson and Purcell 2003).
- *Experienced HR practices* require that attention is focused on how employees experience and then judge the HR practices that are applied to them. What they perceive may be different, or the same, as intended and may be judged through a lens of fairness and organisational justice.
- *Attitudinal outcomes* include attitudes employees hold towards their job and their employer and/or levels of morale or motivation. This especially includes employees' willingness to cooperate and their overall satisfaction with their job.
- *Behavioural outcomes* flow in the main from these attitudinal dimensions. This can be learning new methods of working, engaging in behaviour which is beyond that required, such as organisational citizenship behavior (OCB) (Coyle-Shapiro *et al.* 2004), or seen in levels of attendance and remaining in the job (or their opposites).
- *Performance outcomes* can be distal or proximal and can be restricted to short-term definitions of performance or can be expanded to include measures of effectiveness.

More precisely, the model draws attention to:

- the need to distinguish between intended HR and actual HR practices as experienced by employees;
- the key role played by line managers in the interpretation and implementation of HR practices;
- the link between experienced practices and employee attitudes and behaviours;
- the choice of performance measures that have meaning and significance for the companies and are close to the employee attitudinal data;
- the importance of organisational culture.

Box 2.4: HRM in practice

The Big Idea

In some companies it is not just the senior managers but also employees at all levels who identify strongly with the values and mission of the organisation. We came to call this 'the Big Idea' since it seemed there was something simple or easy to explain that captured the essence of the firm and clearly informed or enthused HR policy and practice. The essence of this is: 'A clear sense of mission underpinned by values and a culture expressing what the firm is and its relationship with its customers and employees'.

The Big Idea had a number of attributes:

- **Embedded** – it was embedded throughout the organisation, for example quality in Jaguar.
- **Connected** – it connected, and derived from the same root, the way customers were treated and employees managed, for example mutuality in Nationwide.
- **Enduring** – it was enduring, not a flash in the pan, not the product of a board discussion on an away day and had clear historical roots, for example a longstanding commitment to 'have fun and make money' in AIT.
- **Collective** – it was encapsulated in routines about the way work was done and how people behaved. In that sense it was collective, combining people in processes and routines in the sense of a taken-for-granted, everyday activity as seen in Nationwide.
- **Measured and managed** – it was measured and managed, often using broad measures of performance, as we found in Selfridges.

Source: Purcell *et al.* 2008

---

have a clear, well-established Big Idea have higher levels of commitment compared to employees in firms without these strong values (Purcell *et al.* 2003). Box 2.4 provides more details of this and again the Selfridges case illustrates this well. This supports the argument made by Barney (1986, p.656) some time ago that 'Firms with sustained superior . . . performances typically are characterised by a strong set of core managerial values that define the way they conduct business'.

Conclusions and implications

We have examined research into the links between HR and performance using the concept of HR advantage. This has highlighted the importance of gaining both a human capital and a process advantage. Our discussion has implications for method, theory and practice.

The methodological debates referred to here are likely to continue. The approach based on the sophisticated analysis of quantitative data collected by questionnaires is likely to remain popular, especially where it is supported by a wider research tradition and higher education infrastructure as in the US. However, the implication of this discussion is that this approach is unlikely to gain insights into the organisational processes that are clearly crucial to successful organisations. Indeed, Becker and Huselid (2006, p.915) argue that 'A clearer articulation of the "black box" between HR and firm performance is the most pressing theoretical and empirical challenge in the SHRM literature. This requires a new emphasis on integrating strategy implementation as the central mediating variable in the HR–performance relationship.' These critical processes and routines can only be effectively examined by means of the case study approach. However, the problems of generalisability of case study findings will remain. One possible way forward is the collection of a combination of quantitative and qualitative data perhaps within a restricted number of industries.

A whole series of theoretical issues are thrown up by our discussion. Perhaps the most basic issues of all revolve around questions such as: What do we mean by performance? Whose performance? How do we measure this? Delaney and Godard (2001) have argued that it is time for the research to move outside the narrow confines of financial performance. Not only should the narrow measures of organisational performance be broadened, but also concern should be given to wider measures such as employee well-being. This also points to the need to move away from the assumption that all employees are treated in the same way. Becker and Huselid (2006, p.908) argue that research needs to focus on the level of the business process because this is where strategic value is created, not at the level of the firm. This, in turn, means greater attention needs to be given to the differentiation of HR practices to support these business processes, which again takes us back to the importance of implementation since 'Designing an HR system with greater differentiation is not the problem. The challenge is motivating line managers to implement these systems' (Becker and Huselid 2006, p.919).

We also need to explore the concept of HR advantage in more detail, particularly the sources of organisational process advantage or disadvantage. We need to understand more clearly why gaps between espoused and operational policy emerge and what the consequences of this are for all parties. If line managers are critical to this, we need to know more about how they are managed and what factors influence their attitudes and behaviour. This raises the much broader issue of widening the focus of study away from human resource management to people management (Purcell and Kinnie 2007, p.543), from the tendency to study formal HR practices to a range of factors that impinge directly on the employee experience of work and which trigger discretionary behaviour. This would include the role of line managers in the operation of policy, the cultural context, and work organisation and job design.

The policy implications of this discussion are profound. The 'best fit–best practice' debate has largely been sidelined by the realisation that both fit and flexibility are needed. The most likely way of getting this is by employing staff who carry out the HR practices most closely to the way in which they were intended. More generally, the implication is that simply developing the appropriate practices is not in itself going to be enough because HR advantage also depends on how these practices are implemented. Consequently, looking for a link between HR practices and performance is a misguided activity because the main focus needs to be on the links between policy, practices, processes, implementation and performance.

This focus on process has potential benefits for HR specialists because these processes have to be carefully developed internally and cannot simply be copied from a textbook in the way that practices might be. Here the HR practitioner role becomes key because the development of what we might call 'best processes' can become a core competence which is embedded within the thinking and acting of the organisation, such that it cannot be imitated or outsourced.

Understanding performance in retailing: the case of Omega supermarkets[1,2]

Sue Hutchinson

Omega is a successful growth company and one of the largest supermarket chains in the UK, employing a large number of staff in stores across the country. Although the industry has seen very little growth in recent years Omega has successfully increased its market share through a policy of lowering prices (the company claims to have reduced prices by 7.5 per cent over the last four years) and improving customer service. It currently holds a dominant share of the UK market in its core business and is growing rapidly in related areas. The company plans to continue expanding in the UK, opening up new stores on brownfield sites in regeneration areas.

The organisation underwent considerable change in the mid-1990s in order to improve its competitive position, with a much greater emphasis on a customer-facing culture. As a senior human resources manager remarked, '1995 saw the evolution of a customer-focused business. With quality and price being very much the same across the sector, people and our service were seen as a differentiator.' One of the many changes introduced at this time was the balanced scorecard approach (Kaplan and Norton 1992) which helped define the business more strongly and bring about this culture change. The scorecard has four quadrants – people, finance, customers and operations – and each store's performance is measured against specific targets in each area. In the people quadrant, for example, targets include recruitment, development, retention, labour turnover, absence and staff morale (taken from the staff attitude survey). Although the four quadrants are not weighted, one retail director we interviewed considered the people quadrant to be the most important, as he explained 'if we can recruit, maintain and deliver fantastic people then operationally we can deliver'. The measures are updated each quarter and link to the corporate measures which underpin the organisation's strategic objectives. The introduction of this approach brought about a much greater focus on people and customer issues in the stores which historically had been driven by financial and operational results. Delayering also took place as part of the restructuring in the mid-1990s and within the stores there are currently four levels: store manager, senior managers (mostly operational managers), section managers and general assistants. Each store is run by a store manager whose job it is to provide coaching, guidance and support and to deliver the Omega 'standard'. As one store manager explained 'my role is to mobilise the team with a goal, to be energetic and to be able to motivate people'. There is a senior management team which includes operational managers responsible for departments and in an average-sized store (employing around 400 staff) this would comprise five or six managers which typically would include the store manager, personnel manager, customer services manager and operations managers. Each member of this team, including the personnel manager, takes a turn in managing the store for around 20 per cent of their working time so that they gain an understanding of the wider business issues. The personnel function within the stores (over two-thirds of stores have their own personnel manager) has undergone considerable change over the last five or six years, moving from a predominantly administrative and welfare role to a store-level senior management position. The role of the personnel manager includes taking responsibility for the payroll and controllable expenses and ensuring that the store maintains productivity

---

[1] Some details of the case have been change or omitted to preserve the anonymity of the organisation.
[2] Research for this case was undertaken as part of a project sponsored by the Chartered Institute of Personnel and Development.

levels. This means focusing on the people measures such as absence management, employee appraisal and development, resourcing and succession planning. One of the benefits of the balanced scorecard approach has therefore been to make the role of the personnel manager much clearer within the stores and enabled the function to measure themselves against specific goals.

A more recent change within Omega has been the drive for consistency across stores, and all policies, procedures and processes are centrally determined and their implementation closely monitored. Each store is governed by the company routines handbook which provides detailed information on how every task is to be performed – this is down to the minutest detail even including details on office layout, such as where pictures should go on the wall. On the HR side all policies and procedures are highly centralised and controlled – the wages budget for example is fixed for each store and there is no local flexibility on pay – something which was obviously a cause of great frustration in some of the stores where recruitment, retention and staff quality are on-going major problems. Although the stores cannot function without these routines it is the way in which the rules and routines are implemented that is considered a key ingredient to success. It is management, in particular store managers, who are responsible for how the policies and processes are implemented and their behaviour is therefore critical to a store's performance.

Section managers occupy first line manager position within the store. Spans of control are normally 12 general assistants to each section manager and in a large store there may be about 20 section managers covering different areas of the store. In addition to being responsible for the day-to-day running of their areas, section managers take responsibility for a range of people management tasks such as recruitment, training, performance appraisal, disciplinary and grievance issues, and pay enquires. The nature of the job is very demanding – these staff have to work long hours, perform a wide range of tasks and struggle to fill vacancies and absences on the shop floor. As one store manager explained:

Section managers have to work bloody hard . . . they are more task orientated than the senior team . . . ideally section managers should spend 70–80 per cent of their time managing, but they do not always do this because of the demands of the job.
Especially if they have gaps. It's one of the more pressurised roles.

This may partly explain why many stores face recruitment and retention difficulties with this position.

We focus on four stores in a single region. All are in market towns with similar socio-economic profiles, in other words demographic, labour market and income patterns in these towns are broadly similar. A total of 43 section managers were interviewed using a structured questionnaire, representing over two-thirds of the section manager population in those stores. Their views were sought on their job, the HR policies practised, the way their senior managers behaved and more general attitudes towards their work. Some of the results are summarised in Table 2.1.

We would expect to find low levels of variation in terms of exercise of management discretion at store level because Omega is a highly centralised organisation with clear routines and policies. However as Table 2.1 shows there are wide variations in satisfaction with certain HR policies, the controlling dimension of discretion and in the way these managers themselves are managed, as well as variations in more general attitudes such as job satisfaction, motivation and commitment. In particular it is clear that Store C is out of line with the others. For example section managers in Store C, in comparison to the other stores, consistently have a poorer perception of the way senior managers carry out their people management roles – or leadership. Only 18 per cent for example of section managers in Store C feel their managers (i.e. the senior managers) are good at responding to suggestions, compared to 82 per cent in Store B, 60 per cent in Store D and 27 per cent in Store A.

▶

Table 2.1 Employee satisfaction with aspects of HR policy and practice: Omega – four stores compared. Percentage of respondents who said 'very satisfied' or 'satisfied' (n = 43)

	Store A	Store B	Store C	Store D
(a) HR policies				
Training	46	82	36	90
Career opportunities	64	91	55	70
Pay	46	64	9	60
Appraisal	50	82	64	90
(b) Controlling				
Influence over how job is done (% a lot)	64	64	27	50
Job influence	82	82	36	100
Sharing knowledge (% good)	64	82	18	70
(c) Leadership % good				
Chance to comment on changes	53	72	18	30
Respond to suggestions	27	82	18	60
Deal with problems	73	82	55	70
Treating employees fairly	64	100	64	70
Provide coaching/guidance (% to a great extent)	46	55	27	40
Respect received from your boss	100	91	64	90
(d) Outcomes				
Job satisfaction	64	73	64	80
Motivation (% 'very' & 'fairly' motivated)	55	46	36	40
Commitment (% proud to tell people who I work for)	91	73	46	90

Table 2.2 shows some key operational performance measures for the stores. It is clear that again Store C was the poorest performer in a number of key areas. For example its expenses were 28 per cent higher than the average and its profit contribution was 34 per cent lower. It was particularly poor at managing wastage (shrinkage), which at the time was one of the key indicators used by Omega. In contrast, Store B had expenses which were 2.4 per cent lower than average and profits which were 21 per cent higher.

Table 2.2 Omega performance data, year 1 (2000/01). Percentage variation from regional average (20 stores)

	Store A	Store B	Store C	Store D
Availability	−0.1	0.6	−0.8	0.3
Waste/known loss	−5.5	4.7	−11.8	7.1
Shrinkage/unknown loss	5.4	63.5	−59.5	44.6
Operating expenses as % of sales	2.4	2.4	−28.2	−11.7
Waiting to be served	2.4	−6.8	−0.6	−3.3
Payroll costs as % of sales	−4.3	14.8	4.3	0.1
Profit contribution	−13.0	21.4	−33.7	−0.1
Turnover £m	42.6	71.1	48.2	54.8

NB. Data has been corrected to ensure that positive figures reflect better than average performance and negative figures show worse than average performance.

▶

Questions

1. How might the differences between the stores shown in Table 2.1 be explained?
2. How might the differences in performance between the stores (Table 2.2) be explained?
3. How does the case study help illustrate the concept of organisational process advantage (OPA) and the link with performance?

Human capital in the software industry: the case of MPC Data[3]

Juani Swart

This small software house is located on two sites in the southwest of England and originated 16 years ago. It was the brainchild of three software engineers who wanted to focus their commercial work on bespoke software development in embedded systems. A conscious decision was made at the outset by the owners to grow their business organically and to value quality of life. As the managing director put it: 'The quality of life is the most important thing for us. You have to remember our people are all we have. We don't have products, only people.'

The organisation has managed to maintain a flat structure (only three levels: five directors, senior software engineers and software engineers) through periods of growth. The market focus has also remained on bespoke software development and commercial efforts are directed toward the development of modules, subcomponents and hardware–software interfaces for multi-national clients.

A clear strategy is to steer away from the product route (a current trend in software development) because it is believed that this will have a devastating effect on their culture and staff retention. Their specific suite of software services means that it is difficult to recruit the right skills in the current labour market: this is intensified by universities taking a commercial approach, rather than technical specialist, in their education of software engineers.

This software house is cash rich with no funds owing to venture capitalists. According to the chairman it is due to their financial success that they can afford to be less traditional in their management approach. They are also successful at retaining both employees and clients: only four employees have resigned since the start of the business. Finally, the organisation occupies a dominant position within a niche market, with their main competitors being independent consultants.

Human capital

MPC employ 30 software engineers who specialise in systems software solutions. These employees are fluent in computing languages such as ANSI C and C++, Java, Visual Basic and Delphi (to name but a few). Most of these employees are recruited via their university

---

[3]Research for this case was carried out as part of a project sponsored by the Chartered Institute of Personnel and Development.

placements, thereby maintaining strong links with software education and influencing the quality of human capital upwards through the supply chain. Although most employees are software engineers, with only a couple of administrative staff, it would be incorrect to assume homogeneity. This is due to specific specialisms in software solutions. This causes software engineers to specialise in certain areas and almost to 'speak different languages', which then develops centres of expertise.

Organisational and organisational structure and clients

The particular substructures in the wider organisational structure that underpin the HR practices include:

(i) The mentoring structure, where each senior software engineer has two or three protégés whom they 'coach'. None of the protégés report to a mentor within the project structure (see (iii) below). In other words, no employee will be mentored by a senior software engineer who is working with them on a project. All mentors belong to a mentoring committee, which forms part of the second major organisational structure within which HR is practised.

(ii) The committee structure devolves what would be otherwise known as more traditional functions and all employees are members of at least two committees.

(iii) The third 'dynamic' structure, which facilitates HR practices, is the project structure. This structure is fluid, with either a software engineer, a senior software engineer or a director managing the project, and employees tend to circulate between projects over time.

This software house has a history of maintaining clients over long periods of time with contracts being renewed several times. Its key clients include: Hitachi Microsystems, Psion Dacom, Sony, Varian Oncology systems and Remote Metering Systems. Customer contact is not restricted to one level in the organisation and it is a common occurrence for student software engineers to have continuous contact with a client. However, one particular senior software engineer is responsible for new business development and uses the client knowledge base in the organisation to market new business.

The lengths of contracts vary with both short- and long-term projects running parallel: some contracts are shorter than two person-months while others can exceed ten person-years. Customers include both small and large multi-national organisations and span several markets including telecommunications, retail, instrumentation and consumer electronics.

Human capital advantage and organisational process advantage

Most HR practices are formalised[4] and the core HR roles are divided between several positions in the organisation. The business development director oversees recruitment and selection together with one other senior software engineer. He works closely with the chief technical officer (CTO) who oversees the performance management system, which is regarded central to other formal HR processes (skill enhancement and remuneration). Through involvement in the mentoring committee another senior software engineer suggested and implemented an induction programme, which has been running in this more formalised manner for the last three to four months. The responsibility for skill enhancement rests with mentors. The directors jointly determine pay levels and make

---

[4]The processes of formalisation takes place through the committee structure, where suggestions from directors, senior software engineers and software engineers are published on the intranet, discussed at a formal gathering, and approved by directors at their monthly meeting.

▶

decisions about increases based on the recommendations made by the mentors as the outcome of performance appraisal discussions.

Although HR practices are more formalised and the responsibility is split between directors and senior software engineers, the implementation of the HR processes is a lot more informal and the responsibility for these processes rest with mentors and project managers. Through the mentoring system the mentors, acting in a line management capacity, are responsible for the implementation of HR processes: focusing on personal and career development via the performance management system. Project managers take a leading developmental role in a technical skill enhancement capacity. A director could be reporting to a software engineer on a project and consequently be trained by a younger and more junior member of staff.

The HR architecture can therefore be presented as the relationship between HR practices (formalised with distributed responsibilities) and HR processes (informal and 'practised' by mentors and project managers). This is reflected in the presentation of the organisational structure (which reflects mentoring responsibility and sharing of cultural knowledge) alongside the project structure (which reflects technical development and houses software (skills) knowledge sharing).

Questions

1. To what extent would you say that MPC Data establish a human capital advantage?
2. Given that MPC Data is a knowledge-intensive organisation, what are the particular challenges that the organisation is faced with regarding the establishment of a human capital advantage?
3. Identify and describe the various ways in which an organisational process advantage has been created and established.
4. How do the HCA and the OPA work together to facilitate improved knowledge sharing?
5. How would the unique HCA and OPA of MPC Data be transferred to a larger organisation? What are the key lessons that larger organisations could learn from MPC Data in the establishment of HRA?

HRM and organisation turnaround at Selfridges[5]

Sue Hutchinson

Background

The Selfridges story is one where human resource management has played a vital role in delivering high performance, enabling the company to emerge in the late 1990s as an expanding and very successful, up-market retail department store. Formerly part of the Sears Group, Selfridges was widely described as the embodiment of 'Grace Brothers',[6] having acquired a rather old-fashioned, stuffy image in the 1980s and early 1990s and become,

---

[5]Research for this case was carried out as part of a project sponsored by the Chartered Institute of Personnel and Development.
[6]Grace Brothers was the retail department store portrayed in the 1970s television comedy *Are You Being Served?*.

▶

in the words of one senior manager, 'an organisation headed by senior managers with no logistical support, no idea of supply chain relationships, no use of technology and extremely hierarchical'. A process of renewal and growth began in the mid-1990s with the appointment of a visionary chief executive, Vittorio Radice (formally with Habitat) and a new senior management team. Almost three-quarters of senior managers left the organisation (then just a single-site store in Oxford Street, London), to be replaced by a younger, predominantly female team. In 1998 Selfridges de-merged from the Sears group and was launched as a public limited company investing £100 million in the Oxford Street site and opening a second store in Trafford Park, Manchester. Further stores subsequently opened in Manchester City centre (2002) and Birmingham (2003).

The vision of the company was 'to become the best and most exciting department store chain in Europe, by meeting the needs of customers in a unique and theatrical way whilst maximising operational efficiency' (mission statement, 1999). Staff, especially staff associates who serve customers, were seen to be central to creating and achieving this ambience and experience. As the commercial director explained: 'Selfridges see themselves at the upper end of the price market with customers prepared to pay a little bit more, so the service must be good – people will be critical to that.' This emphasis on employees was not new to the organisation and could be traced back to the founder of the store, Harry Gordon Selfridge, as this extract from a company document illustrates:

The aim of our Education Department is to develop to the utmost the human resource of the business. It aims at being a progressive force which seeks to promote happiness in work and, through happiness true efficiency. For the work of the department rests on the conviction that efficiency is the normal outcome of happiness, rather than an achievement accomplished through a system of instruction or mental gymnastics. (The Selfridges Education Department, 1920)

What is remarkable about this quote is not only its recognition of the importance of having a contented workforce, but its reference to 'human resources' – a term only popularised in the 1980s.

Selfridges re-invented itself as the 'House of Brands', and as part of the transformation process made major changes in almost every aspect of the business, including:

- A new approach to leadership and management style which was to be 'aspirational, friendly and accessible'.
- Managers would need to take more responsibility for people management (in the past even first-level disciplinary matters were sent to the personnel/HR department).
- Integrated IT systems linking suppliers to Selfridges and improved communication within the company.
- A new team of retail operations managers meeting weekly.
- A new approach to buying, with buyers taken off the department floor and no longer reporting to a senior manager in the department.
- Moving to seven-day-a-week trading with longer opening hours.
- New and more accurate performance measures especially in relation to profit per square foot, data on 'foot-fall' and key performance indicators (KPIs). The financial information and data were to be made available down to the lowest level so that economic literacy would improve.
- A different, more partnership-based relationship with concessionaires and their staff.

At the same time the company consciously set out to change the internal brand image of Selfridges among its staff, making it identical to, and consistent with the revitalised external image, introducing such values as 'brand champions', and 'brand experts'. The goal was to

▶

turn 'values into value' by acting out the values. These values were expressed in a more articulated form under four goals: 'Selfridges should be aspirational, friendly, accessible and bold.' These goals were, in turn, translated into statements so that all stakeholders (employees, customers, shareholders, suppliers and the community) could clearly understand what this meant for them. For example, the value 'everyone is friendly' was translated into the following

Employee values:	How does this make me want to work here?
Customer values:	How am I encouraged to shop?
Community values:	How does Selfridges reflect the spirit of the city?
Shareholder values:	Why should we invest in the store?
Supplier values:	What makes Selfridges an interesting proposition?

An example of how these questions are to be answered is provided in Table 2.3.

A number of HR initiatives were adopted to facilitate this change in culture. For example culture surveys were undertaken, employee focus groups organised and a new performance appraisal system was introduced. The old Hay job evaluation scheme was abandoned in favour of a broadbanding pay arrangement, replacing age and length of service with performance-based progression. A 'mystery shopper' programme was introduced to monitor staff effectiveness based on the acronym SHINE (Smile, Help, Inform, New product push, End the sale). The mystery shopper survey forms part of the monthly key performance indicators (KPIs) for each department, which also includes measures on stock control, labour turnover and absence. A new staff forum was created including staff representatives from the union USDAW, and National Vocational Qualifications (NVQs) were introduced for sales associates with financial rewards for advancement.

Selfridges, Trafford Park, Manchester

The Trafford Park, Manchester store was the first store to be opened outside London and became a test bed for the development of future stores. Located in the Trafford Centre, a shopping mall 3 miles outside Manchester, Selfridges was the anchor store for the site which houses around 280 stores. Visitors tend to come from a very wide geographic area (the site has good motorway connections), and the centre is perceived more as a leisure complex, providing restaurants and cinemas in addition to the shopping experience. The location however presents difficulties for staff as local transport is very poor, with all buses stopping at 8pm.

The store sells an extensive range of branded merchandise in fashion, cosmetics and homeware, in addition to providing specialist services such as hairdressing, a beauty salon, and a personal shopping department. In 1999 the workforce comprised 318 full- and part-time staff employed directly, and 250 full- and part-time staff employed by concessionaires. These staff are employed by concession owners who are responsible for their recruitment, pay, training and development, and discipline. They wear identical name badges to Selfridges' staff and mostly operate to Selfridges' policies and procedures. For example, if Selfridges are having a sale or promotion the concession staff will have an identical event, and they also promote and sell Selfridges account cards. The aim is to have these staff presenting an identical presence to the customer as Selfridges' staff. Concession staff are included in all Selfridges business and social activities and attend daily pre-opening store briefings.

The store opens 364 days a year, 7 days a week, from 10am until 9pm most days (which was subsequently extended to 10pm opening on some days). All staff work a range of shifts, with part-timers working as little as one day a week. Nearly 65 per cent of staff work on a part-time basis. Temporary workers, a high proportion of whom are students, are employed to cover peaks in the workload and absences, including holidays. This heavy reliance on

▶

Table 2.3 Selfridges: an example of the values matrix – everyone is friendly

Employee values	Customer values	Community values	Shareholder values	Supplier values
– how does this make me want to work here?	– how am I encouraged to shop?	– how does Selfridges reflect the spirit of the city?	– why should we invest in the store?	– what makes Selfridges an interesting proposition?
Selfridges is a very friendly place to work. I like my boss and my team.	People at Selfridges are always smiling and helpful – they seem to enjoy working there.	Selfridges promote an inclusive spirit.	Their annual reports are inviting and easy to read.	We help each other in the continuous improvement of our relationship.
I know my opinion and contribution is welcomed.	I like to buy and browse in Selfridges – I never feel under pressure but rarely come home empty handed.	It is a microcosm of all the different cultures and communities which make up the city.	Their financial information is transparent and their directors are open to any questions.	Their wide and diverse range of quality products adds value to my product.
I feel welcomed and this makes me welcome others.	Selfridges represents the good things about city living.	Through its managers and staff Selfridges gets involved in community projects.	I feel welcome when I attend shareholders' meetings.	My concession staff are treated well and made to feel welcome.

▶

concessionary staff, part-timers and to a lesser degree temporary staff undoubtedly presents strong challenges to the store in terms of managing people.

HR policies and procedures in Trafford Park

The HR department initially had a lot of autonomy from head office in terms of developing their own HR policies and procedures. Before the store opened to the public around 650 staff had to be recruited and trained off-site. Initially the need was to recruit staff who had deep product knowledge and were able to create a relationship with the customer. Preference was therefore given to those with retail experience and only a handful of staff transferred from the London store. Many managers, including team leaders, had previously worked for House of Fraser stores in Manchester and as a consequence were initially keen to adopt 'the House of Fraser way' in terms of policies and procedures. The store soon discovered that many of these people did not 'fit' with Selfridges' values and culture and the recruitment process was subsequently changed to focus on employee attitudes and behaviours, rather than experience. Concession staff were responsible for their own recruitment but had to obtain approval from the HR department in the store before they could appoint.

The store is committed to the training and development of all of its employees and in 1999 was awarded Investors in People (IiP) accreditation. The responsibility for training and development lies with line managers, with the HR department acting as a support function. Formal training is provided at the end of the week in the morning and also at the weekend. All new staff (full- and part-timers) undertake a two-day induction programme covering an overview of the company, its mission and values, security, health and safety and store familiarisation.

A great deal of emphasis is placed on communication and each day, for example, there is a 10-minute team talk prior to the store opening, which details daily targets, the previous day's performance, and important events for the day (a second team talk session was subsequently added later in the day to ensure coverage of some part-time staff). The mission statement (see earlier) is regularly referred to within the communication process and is on display in all staff areas and covered in the induction programme. Trade unions (USDAW is the main union) are involved in the consultation and communication process through the staff forum (although it is sometimes hard to get enough employee representatives to sit on the forum). Negotiations, however, do not take place over pay, which is decided by the employers. Pay rates are average for the area and sales associates are paid an annual salary based on an hourly rate – overtime is normally paid at time and a half of the hourly rate. Team leaders receive a bonus based on departmental targets (KPIs). Staff are not allowed to discuss pay and to do so is considered a disciplinary offence. There is also a generous staff discount of 35 per cent for all staff and a good pension scheme.

In 2000 a staff attitude survey was conducted in the store as part of a study looking at the link between people management and performance (Purcell *et al.* 2003). This showed very high levels of organisational commitment among sales associates (including concessionary staff) which compared very favourably with commitment levels in the other 11 organisations in the study. When compared with attitudes of retail trade staff nationally (taken from *WERS*)[7] the levels were even more impressive. For example:

- 97 per cent were proud to tell people who they worked for (*WERS* 56 per cent)
- 93 per cent were loyal to Selfridges (*WERS* 70 per cent)
- 72 per cent shared the values of the organisation (*WERS* 50 per cent).

There were no major differences between the views of concessionary staff and those of Selfridges' employees and 92 per cent felt the relationship between Selfridges' staff and concessionary staff to be good. These figures suggest that the emphasis on people

[7]*Workplace Employee Relations Survey 1998,* as detailed in Cully *et al.* 1999.

▶

management was working in terms of delivering positive employee attitudes. Further analysis of the survey findings showed a positive relationship between various HR practices and employee attitudinal outcomes (job satisfaction, commitment and motivation). For example, teamworking, career opportunities, performance appraisal, involvement and communication and line management behaviour showed positive correlations with job satisfaction and/or organisation commitment.

Team leaders

Despite these very positive findings, the store felt improvements could be made to certain aspects of HR policy and practice which had been identified as areas of possible weakness in the survey. This mainly concerned the delivery of people management by team leaders and the performance appraisal system. As a consequence the team leader role was redefined and team leaders were asked to re-apply for their positions through a new selection process which focused on behaviours as well as skill sets, which resulted in some losing their position. Improvements were also made to the performance appraisal process by linking it to succession planning and therefore working more on career opportunities. This ensured that team leaders took greater ownership of the process, and that appraisals actually got done properly. The second attitude survey (conducted in 2001) showed even more impressive results, with improved employee attitudes in terms of job satisfaction, commitment and job discretion, as shown in Table 2.4. These changes coincided with improved employee perceptions of team leaders' behaviour and better employee attitudes towards some HR policies (Table 2.5). As one sales associate remarked, 'we now have a manager that gets appraisals done . . . and we get praise now and little gifts, such as perfume'.

These were significant changes over a relatively short period of time and could be explained by changes to the team leader position and the appraisal scheme, since these were the only key changes that took place over this time period. Performance also improved in the store, with sales increasing by 23 per cent compared to the previous year, payroll costs down 5 per cent and 'contribution' – the key measure of sales against payroll costs – up 31.7 per cent.

Significantly, senior store managers themselves believed that these improvements (to performance and attitudes) were due to the changes made to the team leader role and continued to focus on this group of managers. In 2002 the role was again re-defined by issuing team leader role guides in order to give greater clarity to the role and more emphasis to the people management aspects. In terms of recruitment and selection, a task formally undertaken by the HR department, team leaders are now required to interview applicants, advise

Table 2.4 Employee attitudes (sales associates) in Selfridges

Employee outcomes	% of employees year 1 (2000) (n = 40)	% of employees year 2 (2001) (n = 40)
A lot of influence over the job	35	56
Satisfied with level of job influence	68	73
Satisfied with sense of achievement	68	83
Commitment: 'I feel proud to tell people who I work for' (% agree)	98	97
'I would recommend a friend or relative to work in Selfridges' (% agree)	83	90

▶

Table 2.5 Employee attitudes (sales associates) in Selfridges

Views on certain HR policies and practices	% of employees year 1 (2000) (n = 40)	% of employees year 2 (2001) (n = 40)
Managers are good at: – Keeping everyone up to date about proposed changes	58	61
– Responding to suggestions from employees	43	59
– Treating employees fairly	58	68
Satisfied with respect from immediate line manager	88	92
Line manager provides coaching and guidance to help improve your performance (% to a great extent or some extent)	58	78
Satisfied with performance appraisal	59	84
Satisfied with career opportunities	70	88

on the job evaluation and make the final decision to select. Team leaders also have a 'coaching and counselling' role. Coaching involves regularly observing sales associates, sometimes on a weekly basis, and providing instant feedback (rather than waiting for the formal development review). Counselling is concerned with monitoring absence, sickness, lateness and attitudes on a monthly bias, and conducting disciplinary meetings (team leaders can discipline up to the first level of written warning). In order to prepare them for this new role, all team leaders went through eight days of training in 2002, covering mainly aspects of people management such as discipline, recruitment, and selection, training, coaching and development.

In addition to these people management activities, team leaders have other responsibilities. These include:

- ensuring excellent customer services, including dealing with customer complaints;
- ensuring effective communication and team working – including communicating on a daily basis with team members, attending weekly management meetings and planning weekly rotas;
- ensuring excellent standards on the shop floor – for example ensuring that all staff wear badges and adhere to the dress code.

Team leaders are also responsible for key performance indicators which are incorporated into their performance reviews.

Selfridges' effort to improve the performance of team leaders also included addressing how the team leaders themselves were managed. Four areas in particular were focused on: involvement, coaching and guidance, career opportunities and management support. A team leader forum was set up (at their initiative) which meets twice a month to discuss, and try and resolve common issues and problems. Assistant sales managers (ASMs – those who manage the team leaders) have taken on the role of coaching and developing team leaders through both formal and informal means. On the formal side, for example, development reviews are conducted twice yearly which focus on monitoring team progress against performance indicators. In addition, weekly formal meetings are held with team leaders to assess their training needs. On a more informal basis the ASMs do weekly floor walks with the team leaders to assess sales and performance issues.

The whole process of re-defining the role of team leaders, particularly in terms of giving them more responsibility for people management activities, has been acclaimed a success by the store. As one senior manager rather bluntly explained, 'forcing the team leaders to be more disciplined, more planned and forcing them to be less reactive . . . partly because the HR team are no longer available on site to wipe their back sides!'

Questions

1. What are the main sources of human capital advantage (HCA) demonstrated in the case study?
2. Explain how the case study illustrates the concept of organisational process advantage (OPA).
3. How and why did the company try to influence team leaders' behaviour?
4. Explain how HCA and OPA were combined together to improve organisational performance.
5. What wider lessons do you draw from this case concerning the links between people management and performance, especially the importance of changes over time?

Bibliography

Ansoff, H.I. (1965) *Corporate Strategy*, Harmondsworth: Penguin.

Appelbaum, E., Bailey, T. and Berg, P. (2000) *Manufacturing Advantage: Why High-Performance Systems Pay Off*, Ithaca, NY: ILR Press.

Armstrong, P. and Goodman, J. (1979) 'Management and supervisory custom and practice', *Industrial Relations Journal*, Vol.10, No.3, pp.12–24.

Arthur, J. (1994) 'Effects of human resource systems on manufacturing performance and turnover', *Academy of Management Journal*, Vol.37, No.3, pp.670–87.

Atkinson, J. (1984) 'Manpower strategies for flexible organisations', *Personnel Management*, August, pp.28–31.

Baird, L. and Meshoulam, I. (1988). 'Managing two fits of strategic human resource management', *Academy of Management Review*, Vol.13, No.1, pp.116–28.

Barney, J. (1986) 'Organizational culture: Can it be a source of competitive advantage?', *Academy of Management Review*, Vol.11, No.3, pp.56–65.

Barney, J. (1991) 'Firm resources and sustained competitive advantage', *Journal of Management*, 2a Vol.17, No.1, pp.99–120.

Barney, J.B. (2001) 'Is the Resource-Based Theory a Useful Perspective for Strategic Management Research? Yes.' *Academy of Management Review* 26(1): 41–56.

Barney, J. and Wright, P. (1998) 'On becoming a strategic partner: the role of human resources in gaining competitive advantage', *Human Resource Management*, Vol.37, No.1, pp.31–46.

Baron, J. and Kreps, D. (1999) 'Consistent human resource practices', *California Management Review*, Vol.41, No.3, pp.29–53.

Bartel, A.P. (2000) 'Human resource management and performance in the service sector: the case of bank branches', *NBER Working Paper Series*, Cambridge: MA: National Bureau of Economic Research.

Batt, R. and Moynihan, L. (2004) 'The viability of alternative call centre models', in S. Deery and N. Kinnie (eds) *Call Centres and Human Resource Management*, Basingstoke: Palgrave.

Beaumont, P.B., Hunter, L.C. and Sinclair, D. (1996) 'Customer-supplier relations and the diffusion of employee relations change', *Employee Relations*, Vol.18, No.1, pp.9–19.

Becker, B. and Gerhart, B. (1996) 'The impact of human resource management on organizational performance: progress and practice', *Academy of Management Journal*, Vol.39, No.4, pp.779–801.

Becker, B. and Huselid, M. (2006) 'Strategic human resource management: where do we go from here?' *Journal of Management*, Vol.32, No.6, pp.898–925.

Beer, M., Spector, B., Lawrence, P. Quinn Mills, D. and Walton, R. (1985) *Human Resource Management: A General Manager's Perspective*, New York: Free Press.

Berg, P. (1999) 'The effects of high performance work practices on job satisfaction in the United States steel industry', *Relations Industrielles*, Vol.54, No.1, pp.111–34.

Berg, P., Appelbaum, E., Bailey, T. and Kalleberg, A. (1996) 'The performance effects of modular production in the apparel industry', *Industrial Relations*, Vol.35, No.3, pp.356–73.

Boselie, P., Paauwe, J. and Jansen, P. (2000) 'Human resource management and performance lessons from the Netherlands', *International Journal of Human Resource Management*, Vol.12, No.7, pp.1107–25.

Boselie, P., Dietz, G. and Boon, C. (2005) 'Commonalities and contradictions in research on human resource management and performance', *Human Resource Management Journal*, Vol.15, No.3, pp.67–94.

Boxall, P. (1992) 'Strategic human resource management: beginnings of a new theoretical sophistication?' *Human Resource Management Journal*, Vol.2, No.3, pp.60–79.

Boxall, P. (1994) 'Placing HR strategy at the heart of business success', *Personnel Management*, Vol.26, No.7, pp.32–35.

Boxall, P. (1995) 'Building the theory of comparative HRM', *Human Resource Management Journal*, Vol.5, No.5, pp.5–17.

Boxall, P. (1996) 'The strategic HRM debate and the resource-based view of the firm', *Human Resource Management Journal*, Vol.6, No.3, pp.59–75.

Boxall, P. (1998) 'Achieving competitive advantage through human resource strategy: towards a theory of industry dynamics', *Human Resource Management Review*, Vol.8, No.3, pp.265–88.

Boxall, P. (1999), 'Human resource strategy and industry-based competition: a conceptual framework and agenda for theoretical development', in P. Wright, L. Dyer, J. Boudreau and G. Milkovich (eds) *Research in Personnel and Human Resource Management (Supplement 4: Strategic Human Resources Management in the Twenty-First Century)*, Stamford, CT: JAI Press.

Boxall, P. and Purcell, J. (2000) 'Strategic human resource management: where have we come from and where should we be going?' *International Journal of Management Reviews*, Vol.2, No.2, pp.183–203.

Boxall, P. and Purcell, J. (2003) *Strategy and Human Resource Management*, Basingstoke: Palgrave Macmillan.

Boxall, P. and Purcell, J. (2008) *Strategy and Human Resource Management* (2nd edn), Basingstoke: Palgrave Macmillan.

Boxall, P. and Steeneveld, M. (1999) 'Human resource strategy and competitive advantage: a longitudinal study of engineering consultancies', *Journal of Management Studies*, Vol.36, No.4, pp.443–63.

Brown, W. (1972) 'A consideration of custom and practice', *British Journal of Industrial Relations*, Vol.10, No.1, pp.42–61.

Brown, W. (1973) *Piecework Bargaining*, Oxford: Heinemann.

Child, J. (1997) 'Strategic choice in the analysis of action, structure, organizations and environment: retrospect and prospect', *Organization Studies*, Vol.18, No.1, pp.43–76.

Child, J. and Partridge, B. (1982) *Lost Managers*, Cambridge: Cambridge University Press.

Combs, J., Yongmei, L., Hall, A. and Ketchen, D. (2006) 'How much do high performance work practices matter? A meta-analysis of their effects on organizational performance', *Personnel Psychology*, Vol.59, pp.501–28.

Cully, M., Woodland, S., O'Reilly, A. and Dix, G. (1999) *Britain at Work: As Depicted by the 1998 Workplace Employee Relations Survey*, London: Routledge.

Delaney, J.T. and Godard, J. (2001) 'An industrial relations perspective on the high performance paradigm', *Human Resource Management Review*, Vol.11, pp.395–429.

Delery, J. (1998) 'Issues of fit in strategic human resource management: implications for research', *Human Resource Management Review*, Vol.8, No.3, pp.289–309.

Delery, J. and Doty, H. (1996) 'Modes of theorising in strategic human resource management: tests of universalistic, contingency and configurational performance predictions', *Academy of Management Journal*, Vol.39, No.4, pp.802–35.

Dyer, L. and Reeves, T. (1995) 'Human resource strategies and firm performance: what do we know and where do we need to go?', *International Journal of Human Resource Management*, Vol.6, No.3, pp.656–70.

Dyer, L. and Shafer, R. (1999) 'Creating organizational agility: implications for strategic human resource management', in P. Wright, L. Dyer, J. Boudreau and G. Milkovich (eds) *Research in Personnel and Human Resource Management (Supplement 4: Strategic Human Resources Management in the Twenty-First Century)*, Stamford, CT: JAI Press.

Fombrun, C., Tichy, N. and Devanna, M. (eds) (1984) *Strategic Human Resource Management*, New York: Wiley.

Foss, N.J. (1994) 'Realism and evolutionary economics', *Journal of Social and Biological Systems*, Vol.17, No.1, pp.21–40.

Fox, A. (1974) *Beyond Contract: Work, Power and Trust Relations*, London: Faber.

Gerhart, B. (1999) 'Human resource management and firm performance: measurement issues and their effect on casual and policy inferences', in P. Wright, L. Dyer, J. Boudreau and G. Milkovich (eds) *Research in Personnel and Human Resource Management (Supplement 4: Strategic Human Resources Management in the Twenty-First Century)*, Stamford, CT: JAI Press.

Gittleman, M., Horrigan, M. and Joyce, M. (1998) '"Flexible" workplace practices: evidence from a nationally representative survey', *Industrial and Labor Relations Review*, Vol.52, No.1, pp.99–115.

Golding, N. (2004) 'Strategic human resource management', in I. Beardwell, L. Holden and T. Claydon (eds) *Human Resource Management. A Contemporary Approach* (4th edn), Harlow: Pearson, pp.32–74.

Goshall, S. and Napahiet, J. (1998) 'Social capital, intellectual capital and the organizational advantage', *Academy of Management Review*, Vol.23, No.2, pp.242–66.

Gratton, L., Hope-Hailey, V., Stiles, P. and Truss, C. (1999a) 'Linking individual performance to business strategy: the people process model', *Human Resource Management*, Vol.38, No.1, pp.17–31.

Gratton, L., Hope-Hailey, V., Stiles, P. and Truss, C. (1999b) *Strategic Human Resource Management: Corporate Rhetoric and Human Reality*, Oxford: Oxford University Press.

Guest, D. (1987) 'Human resource management and industrial relations', *Journal of Management Studies*, Vol.24, No.5, pp.503–21.

Guest, D. (1995) 'Human resource management, trade unions and industrial relations', in J. Storey (ed.) *Human Resource Management: A Critical Text*, London: Routledge.

Guest, D. (1997) 'Human resource management and performance: a review and research agenda', *International Journal of Human Resource Management*, Vol.8, No.3, pp.263–76.

Guest, D. (1999) 'Human resource management and performance: the workers' verdict', *Human Resource Management Journal*, Vol.9, No.3, pp.5–25.

Guest, D. and Hoque, K. (1994) 'The good, the bad and the ugly: employment relations in new non-union workplaces', *Human Resource Management Journal*, Vol.5, No.1, pp.1–14.

Guest, D. Michie, J., Sheehan, M. and Conway, N. (2000) *Effective People Management: Initial Findings of the Future of Work Study*, London: Chartered Institute of Personnel and Development.

Guest D., Michie, J., Conway, N. and Sheehan, M. (2003) 'Human resource management and corporate performance in the UK', *British Journal of Industrial Relations*, Vol.41, No.2, pp.291–314.

Hall, L. and Torrington, D. (1998) 'Letting go or holding on: the devolution of operational personnel activities', *Human Resource Management Journal*, Vol.8, No.1, pp.41–55.

Hamel, G. and Prahalad, C. (1994) *Competing for the Future*, Boston, MA: Harvard Business School Press.

Hendry, C. and Pettigrew, A. (1992) 'Strategic choice in the development of human resource management', *British Journal of Management*, Vol.3, No.1, pp.37–56.

Hesketh, A. and Fleetwood, S. (2006) 'Beyond measuring the human resources–organizational performance link: applying critical realist meta-theory', *Organization*, Vol.13, No.5, pp.677–700.

Huselid, M. (1995) 'The impact of human resource management practices on turnover, productivity and corporate financial performance', *Academy of Management Journal*, Vol.38, No.3, pp.635–72.

Huselid, M. and Becker, B.E. (2000) 'Comment on "Measurement error in research on human resources and firm performance: How much error is there and how does it influence effect size estimates?" by Gerhart, Wright, McMahan and Snell', *Personnel Psychology,* 53(4): 835–854.

Hutchinson, S. and Purcell, J. (2003) *Bringing Policies to Life,* London: Chartered Institute of Personnel and Development.

Hutchinson, S. and Purcell, J. (2007) *The Role of Line Managers in People Management,* London: Chartered Institute of Personnel and Development.

Hutchinson, S. and Wood, S. (1995) *Personnel and the Line: Developing the New Relationship: The UK experience,* London: Institute of Personnel and Development.

Hutchinson, S., Kinnie, N., Purcell, J., Rees, C., Scarbrough, H. and Terry, M. (1996) *The People Management Implications of Leaner Ways of Working,* Issues in People Management No.15, London: Institute of Personnel and Development.

Hutchinson, S., Kinnie, N., Purcell, J., Collinson, M., Scarbrough, H. and Terry, M. (1998) *Getting Fit, Staying Fit: Developing lean and responsive organisations,* London: Institute of Personnel and Development.

Ichniowski, C., Shaw, K. and Prennushi, G. (1995) 'The impact of human resource management practices on productivity', Working Paper 5333, Cambridge, MA: National Bureau of Economic Research.

Ichniowski, C., Kochan, T., Levine, D., Olson, C. and Strauss, G. (1996) 'What works at work: overview and assessment', *Industrial Relations,* Vol.35, No.3, pp.299–333.

Jackson, S. and Schuler, R. (1995). 'Understanding human resource management in the context of organizations and their environments', *Annual Review of Psychology,* Vol.46, pp.237–64.

Kaplan, R. and Norton, D. (1992) 'The balanced scorecard–measures that drive performance', *Harvard Business Review,* Vol.70, No.1, p.71.

Keenoy, T. (1997) 'Review article: HRMism and the languages of representation', *Journal of Management Studies,* 34(5): 825–841.

Kinnie, N. and Parsons, J. (2004) 'Managing client, employee and customer relations: constrained strategic choice in the management of human resources in a commercial call centre', in S. Deery and N. Kinnie (eds) *Call Centres and Human Resource Management,* Basingstoke: Palgrave, pp.102–26.

Kinnie, N., Purcell, J. and Hutchinson, S. (2000) 'Human resource management in telephone call centres', in K. Purcell (ed.) *Changing Boundaries,* Bristol: Bristol Academic Press.

Kinnie, N., Purcell, J., Hutchinson, S., Rayton, B. and Swart, J. (2005) 'Satisfaction with HR practices and commitment to the organisation: why one size does not fit all', *Human Resource Management Journal,* Vol.15, No.4, pp.9–29.

Kinnie, N., Swart, J., Lund, M. Morris, S., Snell, S. and Kang, S-K. (2006) *Managing People and Knowledge in Professional Service Firms,* London: Chartered Institute of Personnel and Development.

Kochan, T. and Barocci, T. (1985) *Human Resource Management and Industrial Relations,* New York: Basic Books.

Larsen, H.H. and Brewster, C. (2003) 'Line management responsibility for HRM: what is happening in Europe?' *Employee Relations,* Vol.25, No.3, pp.228–44.

Legge, K. (1978) *Power, Innovation, and Problem-solving in Personnel Management,* London: McGraw-Hill.

Legge, K. (1995) *Human Resource Management: Rhetorics and Realities,* Basingstoke: Macmillan.

Legge, K. (2001) 'Silver bullet or spent round? Assessing the meaning of the "high performance commitment management"/performance relationship', in J. Storey (ed.) *Human Resource Management A Critical Text* (2nd edn), London: Thompson Publishing.

Leonard, D. (1992) 'Core capabilities and core rigidities: a paradox in managing new product development', *Strategic Management Journal,* Vol.13, pp.111–25.

Leonard, D. (1998) *Wellsprings of Knowledge: Building and Sustaining the Sources of Innovation,* Boston, MA: Harvard Business School Press.

Lepak, D. and Snell, S. (1999) 'The strategic management of human capital: determinants and implications of different relationships', *Academy of Management Review,* Vol.24, No.1, pp.1–18.

Lepak, D.P., Liao, H., Chung, Y. and Harden, E.E. (2006) 'A conceptual review of human resource management systems in strategic human resource management research', *Personnel and Human Resource Management,* 25, pp.217–71.

Loasby, B.J. (1991) *Equilibrium and Evolution,* Manchester: University of Manchester Press.

Lowe, J., Delbridge, R. and Oliver, N. (1997) 'High-performance manufacturing: evidence from the automotive components industry', *Organization Studies,* Vol.18, No.5, pp.783–98.

MacDuffie, J.P. (1995) 'Human resource bundles and manufacturing performance: organizational logic and flexible production systems in the world auto industry', *Industrial and Labor Relations Review,* Vol.48, No.2, pp.197–221.

MacDuffie, J.P. and Pil, F.T. (1997) 'Changes in auto industry employment practices: an international overview', in T.A. Kochan, R.D. Lansbury and J.P. MacDuffie (eds) *After lean production: evolving employment practices in the world auto industry,* Ithaca, NY: ILR Press.

Marchington, M. (2001) 'Employee involvement at work', in J. Storey (ed.) *Human Resource Management. A Critical Text* (2nd edn), London: Thompson Publishing.

Marchington, M. and Grugulis, I. (2000) '"Best practice" human resource management: perfect opportunity or dangerous illusion?', *International Journal of Human Resource Management,* Vol.11, No.6, pp.1104–24.

Marchington, M. and Wilkinson, A. (2002) *People Management and Development,* London: Chartered Institute of Personnel and Development.

McGovern, P., Gratton, L., Hope-Hailey, V., Stiles, P. and Truss, C. (1997) 'Human resource management on the line?', *Human Resource Management Journal,* Vol.7, No.4, pp.12–29.

Miles, R. and Snow, C. (1978) *Organizational Strategy, Structure and Process,* New York: McGraw-Hill.

Miles, R. and Snow, C. (1984) 'Designing strategic human resources systems', *Organizational Dynamics,* Vol.13, No.1, Summer, pp.36–52.

Miles, R. and Snow, C. (1999) 'The new network firm: a spherical structure built on human investment philosophy', in R. Schuler and S. Jackson (eds) *Strategic Human Resource Management,* Oxford: Blackwell.

Miller, D. and Shamsie, J. (1992) 'The resource-based view of the firm in two environments: the Hollywood film studios from 1936 to 1965', *Academy of Management Journal,* Vol.39, No.3, pp.519–43.

Millward, N., Bryson, A. and Forth, J. (2000) *All Change at Work: British Employment Relations 1980–1998 as Portrayed by the Workplace Industrial Relations Survey Series,* London: Routledge.

Mintzberg, H. (1994) 'Rethinking strategic planning part 1: pitfalls and fallacies', *Long Range Planning,* Vol.27, No.3, pp.12–21.

Mueller, F. (1996) 'Human resources as strategic assets; an evolutionary resource-based theory', *Journal of Management Studies,* Vol.33, No.6, pp.757–85.

Osterman, P. (1987) 'Choice of employment systems in internal labor markets', *Industrial Relations,* Vol.26, No.1, pp.46–67.

Osterman, P. (1994) 'How common is workplace transformation and who adopts it?' *Industrial and Labor Relations Review,* Vol.47, No.2, pp.173–88.

Osterman, P. (2000) 'Work reorganization in an era of restructuring: trends in diffusion and effects on employee welfare', *Industrial and Labor Relations Review,* Vol.53, No.2, pp.179–96.

Patterson, M., West, M., Lawthom, R. and Nickell, S. (1997) 'Impact of people management practices on business performance', *Issues in People Management No.22,* London: Institute of Personnel and Development.

Peters, T. and Waterman, R.H. (1982) *In Search of Excellence: Lessons from America's Best-Run Companies,* New York: Harper & Row.

Pettigrew, A.M. (1973) *The Politics of Organizational Decision Making,* London: Tavistock.

Pfeffer, J. (1994) *Competitive Advantage Through People,* Boston, MA: Harvard Business School Press.

Pfeffer, J. (1998) *The Human Equation: Building Profits by Putting People First,* Boston, MA: Harvard Business School Press.

Pfeffer, J. and Salancik, G.R. (1978) *The External Control of Organizations: A Resource Dependence Perspective,* New York: Harper & Row.

Pil, F. K. and MacDuffie, J.P. (1996) 'The adoption of high involvement work practices', *Industrial Relations,* Vol.35, No.3, pp.423–55.

Porter, M. (1980) *Competitive Strategy,* New York: Free Press.

Porter, M. (1985) *Competitive Advantage: Creating and Sustaining Superior Performance,* New York: Free Press.

Powell, J.H. and Wakeley, T. (2003) 'Evolutionary concepts and business economics: towards a normative approach', *Journal of Business Research*, Vol.56, pp.153–61.

Prahalad, C. and Hamel, G. (1990) 'The core competence of the corporation', *Harvard Business Review*, Vol.68, No.3, May–June, pp.79–91.

Purcell, J. (1999) 'The search for "best practice" and "best fit": chimera or cul-de-sac?', *Human Resource Management Journal*, Vol.9, No.3, pp.26–41.

Purcell, J. (2004) 'The HRM–performance link: why, how and when does people management impact on organisational performance?', John Lovett Memorial Lecture, University of Limerick (available from the author).

Purcell, J. and Kinnie, N. (2007) 'Human resource management and business performance', in P. Boxall, J. Purcell, and P. Wright (eds) *The Oxford Handbook of Human Resource Management*, Oxford: Oxford University Press.

Purcell, J., Kinnie, N., Hutchinson, S. Rayton, B. and Swart, J. (2003) *Understanding the People and Performance Link: Unlocking the Black Box*, London: Chartered Institute of Personnel and Development.

Purcell, J., Kinnie, N., Swart, J., Rayton, B. and Hutchinson, S. (2008) *People Management and Performance*, Oxford: Routledge.

Ramsay, H., Scholarios, D. and Harley, B. (2000) 'Employees and high-performance work systems: testing inside the black box', *British Journal of Industrial Relations*, Vol.38, No.4, pp.501–31.

Renwick, D. (2000) 'HR–line work relations: a review, pilot case and research agenda', *Journal of European Industrial Training*, Vol.24, No.2–4, pp.241–53.

Richardson, R. and Thompson, M (1999) 'The impact of people management practices on business performance: a literature review', *Issues in People Management*, London: Institute of Personnel and Development.

Schuler, R. (1989) 'Strategic human resource management and industrial relations', *Human Relations*, Vol.42, No.2, pp.157–84.

Schuler, R. (1996) 'Market-focussed management: human resource management implications', *Journal of Market-Focussed Management*, Vol.1, pp.13–29.

Schuler, R. and Jackson, S. (1987) 'Linking competitive strategies and human resource management practices', *Academy of Management Executive*, Vol.1, No.3, pp.207–19.

Sinclair, D., Hunter, L. and Beaumont, P.B. (1996) 'Models of customer–supplier relations', *Journal of General Management*, Vol.22, No.2, pp.56–75.

Snell, S., Youndt, M. and Wright, P. (1996) 'Establishing a framework for research in strategic human resource management: merging resource theory and organizational learning', *Research in Personnel and Human Resources Management*, Vol.14, pp.61–90.

Snell, S., Lepak, D. and Youndt, M. (1999) 'Managing the architecture of intellectual capital: implications for human resource management', in P. Wright, L. Dyer, J. Boudreau and G. Milkovich (eds) *Research in Personnel and Human Resources Management: Strategic Human Resource Management in the Twenty-First Century*, Stamford, CT: JAI Press.

Swart, J. (2007) 'HRM and knowledge workers', in P. Boxall, J. Purcell, and P. Wright (eds) *The Oxford Handbook of Human Resource Management*, Oxford: Oxford University Press.

Swart, J. and Kinnie, N. (2001) 'Human resource advantage within a distributed knowledge system: a study of growing knowledge intensive firms', Paper presented at ESRC Seminar: 'The Changing Nature of Skills and Knowledge', Manchester School of Management, September 2001 (available from the authors).

Swart, J. and Kinnie, N. (2003) 'Knowledge intensive firms: the influence of the client on HR systems', *Human Resource Management Journal*, Vol.13, No.3, pp.37–55.

Swart, J. and Kinnie, N. (2004) *Managing the Careers of Knowledge Workers*, London: Chartered Institute of Personnel and Development.

Swart, J. Kinnie, N. and Purcell, J. (2003) *People and Performance in Knowledge Intensive Firms*, London, Chartered Institute of Personnel and Development.

Swart, J., Price, A., Mann, C. and Brown, S. (2004) *Human Resource Development: Strategy and Tactics*, London: Butterworth-Heinemann.

Swart, J. Kinnie, N. and Rabinowitz, J. (2007) *Managing Across Boundaries*, London: Chartered Institute of Personnel and Development.

Terry, M. (1977) 'The inevitable growth of informality', *British Journal of Industrial Relations*, Vol.15, No.1, pp.76–90.

Thompson, M. (2000) *Final Report: The Bottom Line Benefits of Strategic Human Resource Management, The UK Aerospace People Management Audit,* London: Society of British Aerospace Companies.

Thurley, K. and Wirdenius, H. (1973) *Approaches to Supervisory Development,* London: Institute of Personnel Management.

Truss, C. (2001) 'Complexities and controversies in linking HRM with organizational outcomes', *Journal of Management Studies,* Vol.38, No.8, pp.1121–49.

Ulrich, D. (1997) 'Measuring human resources: an overview of practice and a prescription for results', *Human Resource Management,* Vol.36, No.3, pp.303–20.

Ulrich, D. (1998) *Human Resource Champions,* Boston, MA: Harvard Business School Press.

Wall, T. and Wood, S. (2005), 'The romance of HRM and business performance, and the case for big science', *Human Relations,* Vol.58, No.4, pp.29–62.

Whittington, R. (2001) *What is Strategy – and Does it Matter?* (2nd edn), London: Thompson Learning.

Wood, S. (1996) 'High commitment management and payment systems', *Journal of Management Studies,* Vol.33, No.1, pp.53–77.

Wood, S. (1999) 'Human resource management and performance', *International Journal of Management Reviews,* Vol.1, No.4, pp.367–413.

Wood, S. and Albanese, P. (1995) 'Can we speak of high commitment management on the shop floor?', *Journal of Management Studies,* Vol.32, No.2, pp.215–47.

Wright, P. and Gardener, T.M. (2000) 'Theoretical and empirical challenges in studying the HR practice–firm performance relationship', Paper presented at the Strategic Human Resource Management Workshop, European Institute for Advanced Studies in Management, Insead, March (available from the Center for Advanced Human Resource Studies Working Paper Series Number 00-04, Cornell University).

Wright, P. and Gardener, T.M. (2004) 'The human resource – firm performance relationship: methodological and theoretical challenges', in D. Holman, T. Wall, C. Clegg, P. Sparrow and A. Howard (eds) *The new workplace: a guide to the human impact of modern work practices,* London: John Wiley.

Wright, P. and Snell, S. (1998) 'Toward a unifying framework for exploring fit and flexibility in strategic human resource management', *Academy of Management Review,* Vol.23, No.4, pp.756–72.

Wright, P., McMahan, G. and McWilliams, A. (1994). 'Human resources and sustained competitive advantage: a resource-based perspective', *International Journal of Human Resource Management,* Vol.5, No.2, pp.301–26.

Wright, P., McCormick, B., Sherman, W. and McMahan, G. (1999) 'The role of human resource practices in petrochemical refinery performance', *International Journal of Human Resource Management,* Vol.10, No.4, pp.551–71.

Wright, P.M., Gardener, T.M. and Moynihan, L.M. (2003) 'The impact of HR practices on the performance of business units', *Human Resource Management Journal,* Vol.13, No.3, pp.21–36.

Wright, P.M. Gardener, T.M., Moynihan, L.M. and Allen, M. (2005) 'The HR performance relationship: examining causal direction', *Personnel Psychology,* Vol.58, No.2, pp.409–46.

Youndt, M., Snell, S., Dean, J. and Lepak, D. (1996) 'Human resource management, manufacturing strategy, and firm performance', *Academy of Management Journal,* Vol.39, No.4, pp.836–66.

Chapter 3

RECRUITMENT

Anne McCormack and Dora Scholarios

Introduction

Recruitment is often neglected in the HRM literature. Most accounts combine the discussion of recruitment with selection, with greater emphasis on selection. However, the more effective organisations are at identifying and attracting a high quality pool of job applicants, the less important the selection stage of hiring becomes. According to some, recruitment is 'the most critical human resource function for organizational survival or success' (Taylor and Collins 2000, p.304).

Barber (1998) provided one of the first dedicated reviews of recruitment,[1] defining it as 'practices and activities carried out by the organization with the primary purpose of identifying and attracting potential employees' (p.5). Emphasis is usually on filling a position from outside a firm (rather than internal appointments or promotion). An important recent development is the greater attention devoted to how individuals become applicants – or the attraction element (Searle 2003). Sometimes referred to as an 'applicant perspective' (Billsberry 2007), this acknowledges a two-way relationship between organisations and applicants, where applicant decision making becomes an important factor shaping whether the recruitment process is successful or not. It is not just the efficiency of the organisation's procedures in identifying applicants which will ensure the desired outcome (a good match between the individual and the job) but also how potential applicants perceive and act on the opportunities offered. Thus, recruitment activities should 'enhance their [applicants'] interest in and attraction to the organization as an employer; and increase the probability that they will accept a job offer' (Saks 2005, p.48).

In this chapter, we use both an organisational and applicant perspective to understand recruitment. Our approach is represented in Figure 3.1. We begin with a summary of the context within which recruitment takes place (the external environment, organisational characteristics, and the nature of the job vacancy to be filled), focusing here on the environment within the UK, although the general conclusions are relevant for all organisations facing similar pressures. We show how each of these contextual drivers impacts recruitment activities, and emphasise the reasons why many organisations now pay more attention to the applicant perspective. This is the driving force behind many recent developments such as the growth in e-recruitment, the use of social networking sites, and 'employer branding'.

---

[1]For other reviews, see Breaugh and Starke (2000), Rynes (1991), Rynes and Cable (2003) and Taylor and Collins (2000).

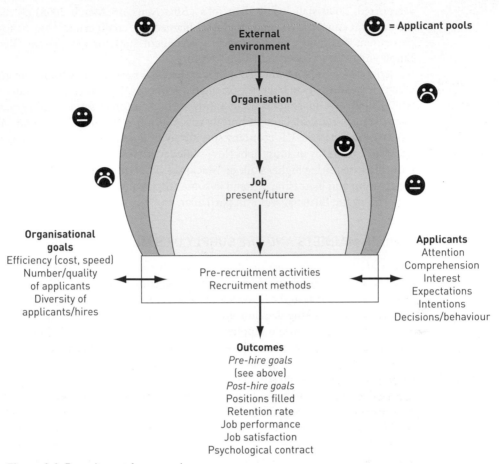

Figure 3.1 Recruitment framework

The external environment

At one time, it was thought that the aim of recruitment was simply to maximise the size of the applicant group which would then be reduced through a rigorous selection procedure for identifying the most qualified candidates. This assumed an abundant supply of qualified applicants and that those selected would accept the jobs offered. All recruiters had to do was advertise a job vacancy and appropriate candidates would apply and accept job offers. Although this approach may have sufficed for the job demands and labour force of the past, these assumptions are more tenuous in today's employment context. In this section, we consider how the organisation's external environment impacts recruitment.

THE ECONOMY

The wider economy exerts a positive or negative effect on hiring activity through job growth and contraction. In early 2008, many sectors of the economy were contracting and there was declining demand for some types of labour. The global 'credit crunch', fluctuating interest rates and the strength of the pound in relation to the dollar and euro were presenting challenges for many UK businesses. Falls in profits led to 'cautionary behaviour' when 'adding headcount', especially in the banking sector (*Personnel Today*, 8 April 2008) with one high-profile casualty resulting in the nationalisation of Northern Rock Building Society and a reported 2,000 staff losing their jobs (*BBC News*, 18 March 2008). A recent survey of recruitment consultancies and employers blamed the 'credit crunch' for the lowest growth in permanent positions and demand for permanent staff for over a year (Recruitment and Employment Federation and KPMG 2007).

Generally, in most advanced economies there has been a steady transition away from manufacturing industries to a service-orientated economy. This has meant greater job creation in white-collar, non-managerial occupations, such as customer services, and greater demand for managerial/professional and technical skills (Wilson *et al.* 2004). Goos and Manning (2007) recently described the UK economy specifically in this respect as polarised, with job creation occurring primarily in 'lousy' jobs (low-skilled work referred to as 'McJobs') as well as 'lovely' jobs (those requiring higher skills or 'Macjobs'). Thus, the current picture for the UK suggests job creation and increasing demand in some areas, but worrying contraction across the economy and in the financial sector in particular.

LABOUR MARKETS AND THE SUPPLY OF SKILLED JOB APPLICANTS

Economic conditions affect the degree to which employers find it difficult to fill job vacancies, i.e. whether the labour market provides appropriate people to fill existing posts at going wage rates. The crisis in the financial services sector is likely to create an oversupply of labour relative to the shrinking demand, and a 'looser' labour market. This will allow organisations easier access to appropriate supplies of skill and greater power to hold salaries constant and become more selective in their hiring processes. For job applicants, of course, there will be fewer job opportunities, greater competition for jobs, less bargaining power relative to employers and longer job search times.

In other sectors of the economy, where there is greater job creation, skill shortages still account for a large proportion of unfilled vacancies. As already noted, UK employers face tight labour markets at both ends of the job spectrum – in high-skilled, professional jobs, and in lower-end 'lousy' jobs which are generally poorly paid, physically demanding, have no upward mobility and high turnover. In 'tight' labour markets, firms compete for qualified staff or have difficulties finding staff at all, and have to become more creative in finding job applicants, for example through identifying non-traditional applicant groups or by offering additional incentives like pay and benefits.

Since 2004, UK employers have benefited from an increase in labour mobility from eastern Europe. From the eight EU accession states alone, 427,000 workers have successfully applied for work in the UK, over half (62 per cent) Polish. Many of these (young) migrants have taken employment in jobs which are difficult to fill, such as in agriculture and hospitality; 82 per cent are aged 18–34 and 56 per cent work in factories (Home Office figures between May 2004 and June 2006, quoted on BBC News Online, 2006). With respect to higher-end skills, the UK Health Service has had particular difficulties in attracting critical care nurses, midwives, dentists and pharmacists and has looked to skilled migrants to fill these gaps. It has also made greater use of incentives likely to attract both career and family-orientated health professionals, such as access to high-quality learning and development and flexible working practices (e.g. Department of Health 2007).

Skill supply is also affected by levels of educational attainment. The UK seems to be in a position where the skills which are being supplied do not always reflect those being demanded by employers, resulting in a skills deficit in important areas. More graduates are being produced than before – the graduation rate for the UK, the number of degrees awarded as a percentage of those of graduation age, is one of the highest in the OECD (Perryman 2003). Yet, employers are concerned about the quality of technical graduates and levels of numeracy (Barber *et al.* 2005), and report skills shortages in lower-level occupations, such as skilled technical or operative roles. This latter issue has been linked to an upgrading of the skills required to compete in a globalised economy. Research has shown that the supply of

Box 3.1: HRM in practice

Trends in qualifications used at work and skill supply (UK): 1986–2006

- The proportion of jobs not requiring qualifications has fallen from two-fifths to under a third.
- The proportion of jobs requiring degrees or their equivalent rose from about 16 per cent in 1986 to around 22 per cent in 2006.
- The use of generic skills has increased, including literacy, numeracy, technical know-how, problem solving, checking, planning, 'influencing' skills, and various forms of communication.
- A growing number of workers hold qualifications at a higher level than needed to do their job – 49 per cent of workers in 2006 compared to 35 per cent in 2001.
- There are mismatches between skills supply and skills required, especially in scientific, engineering and technical skills.

Source: Felstead *et al.* 2007

technical skills is not keeping pace with the expansion in jobs requiring the use of advanced technology in the production process (Haskel and Martin 2001).

Even though more jobs now require a degree or higher qualifications, recent evidence suggests that graduates' skills are being underutilised in many jobs and that skills shortages (i.e. unfilled vacancies due to inadequate qualifications) and recruitment difficulties persist. Box 3.1 summarises some of these issues, which emerged from a recent UK government Skills Survey (Felstead *et al.* 2007). Moreover, for those without the necessary skills for the Macjobs, most opportunities will most likely be in the low-security, poorly paid McJobs.

CHALLENGES OF DEMOGRAPHIC AND SOCIAL CHANGE

Immigration, an ageing population and more women seeking employment mean a far more diverse workforce. Some of these changes will address skill shortages (as with the recent European migrants) while others will exacerbate recruitment problems. One major concern facing employers is the size and composition of the UK labour force. This is projected to change dramatically, with a decline in 16–24-year-olds and a rapid increase in the number of people aged 50 or over, owing to longer life expectancy and the transition of the 'baby boom' generation to this age group (Madouros 2006). With a smaller labour force, organisations will increasingly turn to candidates from non-traditional 'talent pools', such as migrants, older workers, or women who are currently carers wishing to return to work.

This kind of targeted recruitment can be seen in some industries which continue to experience skill shortages. The youth-oriented ICT industry, for example, has been highlighted for the implicit age discrimination in its recruitment methods – the stereotypical attitudes of managers towards older workers or beliefs that older workers cannot keep pace with technological developments. Many have drawn attention to the reorientation of recruitment and selection methods as a way of encouraging a more age-diverse workforce which at the same time addresses skill shortages (see, for example, Healy and Schwarz-Woelzl 2007).

A second demographic shift is the changing priorities of job candidates and what attracts them to jobs and organisations. In one survey, the top attractions to a job listed by employees were holiday entitlement (43 per cent), location of work (47 per cent), flexible working and bonuses (39 per cent), and the company's workplace culture and environment (38 per cent) (YouGov 2006). Development opportunities came relatively low down the list of priorities (cited by 28 per cent). In another survey of 1,000 people aged between 25 and 35, 75 per cent admitted to looking for a new job because their life needs were not being taken into consideration (The Future Laboratory 2005). This indicates increasing overlap between life and work for many job seekers, who are considering what jobs can offer them in terms of their prospects for work–life balance. Similar evidence has been found in surveys of graduates during their first five years in the workplace (see Box 3.2), and employers seem to be taking

Box 3.2: HRM in practice

Attracting and retaining graduates

In a survey of two cohorts of graduates, both at their time of graduation and after six years in the workplace, the CIPD showed that new graduates rate 'happiness' as the most important aspect of a job. After a few years in the workplace, though, they become motivated by other aspects, such as additional benefits, work–life balance or the culture of the organisation (see a summary of these results below).

Other research shows that high levels of satisfaction can help in staff retention (CIPD 2006b). Given increasingly tight labour markets and competition for top talent, what do you think organisations should be doing to attract graduates? How might this impact their recruitment strategies? Rank the attributes in the table in terms of what kind of organisation you wish to work for when you graduate.

	2000 graduates (surveyed in 2006) %	2005 graduates %
Happiness	95	97
Career development	93	97
Challenging work	94	95
Training and development opportunities	90	94
Good relationship with manager	94	92
Company culture	89	90
Salary and bonus	88	86
Work–life balance	90	85
Supportive management structures	86	85
Job security	78	78
Company's overall reputation	68	72
Flexible working opportunities	68	65
Location of organisation	66	63
Company's ethical and environmental stance	59	63
Financial support for further study/qualification	52	61
Additional benefits	69	59
Coaching or mentoring	58	57

Source: CIPD 2006a

notice. In the 2007 Work–Life Balance Employer Survey, for instance, there was an increase since 2003 in the provision, and employee take-up, of flexible working arrangements like job sharing and compressed hours, while 42 per cent of employers cited recruitment as one of the positive benefits of offering such flexible working (Hayward *et al.* 2007).

Finally, changing social values are also evident in consumer preferences, which some have argued has created demand for higher-value, bespoke, quality goods and services (e.g. Leadbetter 2000). Expertise, personal attention, customer service and generic transferable skills, such as communication or service-orientation, therefore, have increased in importance.

EMPLOYMENT LEGISLATION

Employers face legal action and employment tribunals if their recruitment practices are not compliant with legislation. The basic principle of employment legislation is that all individuals should be considered according to their merits and provided with equality of opportunity. Discrimination in recruitment, selection or promotion is illegal, unless it can be 'objectively justified'. This applies both to direct discrimination on the basis of prohibited criteria (e.g. race), and indirect discrimination, where there is no intentional discrimination but the practice disproportionately impacts members of particular groups. For example, recruiting only from university campuses indirectly discriminates against ethnic minorities who may be underrepresented in higher education.

For many years, the UK seemed to lag behind the US and other parts of Europe with respect to specific legislation. Anti-discrimination laws relating to sex (1975) and race (1976) have been in existence for over 30 years. More recent legislation applies these principles also to disability (1995), sexual orientation, religion or belief (2003) and age (2006), while the Race Relations Amendment Act 2001 requires public authorities to monitor the race of all job applicants and employees eligible for promotion and training. (For more detail on legislation see Lewis and Sargeant 2007.)

This places the burden on employers to be aware of the composition of their workforce, whether this proportionately reflects the composition of the wider labour market, and whether their HR practices, including recruitment methods, treat groups differently. Underrepresentation can be addressed voluntarily by employers through setting targets for achieving a more diverse workforce or by using positive action – sometimes called positive discrimination or affirmative action – to recruit particular groups, for instance ethnic minorities or women. This is only acceptable, however, when its intention is to reverse past discrimination or lack of representation. For example, using our earlier example of ICT occupations, if an employer recognises underrepresentation of women and can attribute this to hiring procedures which mean women have fewer opportunities to apply for job vacancies (e.g. recruiting from engineering courses where women are already underrepresented), then a positive action recruitment campaign would identify alternative channels and aim to increase the number of applications from this group (e.g. recruit from Masters IT conversion courses).

Employers may decide to do this to avoid legal action or to manage the risk of costly tribunals. There is some evidence to suggest that employers do act on such legislation; Woodhams and Corby (2007), for example, showed an increase in the use of monitoring or positive action in recruitment (e.g. work introduction schemes) since the introduction of disability legislation in 1995 and 2003.

Increasingly, there are also arguments for a 'business case' (Cassell 2005), perhaps to gain access to a wider applicant pool or to project an image of a responsible employer. In fact, examples of positive action recruitment efforts are now prominently publicised on many organisations' websites; for example, Sikh recruitment by the British Army or female police officers in Scottish police forces.

Monitoring job applicants by ethnicity, gender, age and disability, when used to ensure representativeness and check that all groups have equal chances at all stages of recruitment, is considered good practice (ACAS 2006). However, equal opportunities policies and the practices to support them tend to be more common in public sector organisations, large workplaces, and those with HR specialists who seem to act as 'the guardians of equal opportunities' (Hoque and Noon 2004, p.497). McKay and Avery (2005) recommend caution in seeking numerical targets to satisfy diversity goals if workplace climates are not consistent with the principles of diversity. 'Otherwise firms will be apt to default on their implied recruitment promises, minority recruits will feel misled, and some form of backlash will be probable' (p.335). Hoque and Noon (2004), similarly, argued that policies introduced without the substantive practices to support them were nothing more than 'empty shell' policies, a situation which their evidence showed was more common in smaller private sector companies.

Other regulations affecting recruitment are less about avoiding discrimination and more about ensuring standards. These apply to the employment of particular groups, for instance ex-offenders, and specify procedures, like disclosure of previous convictions, to protect vulnerable people, e.g. children (see, for example, the Criminal Records Bureau). High-profile cases have revealed that if the applicant had been vetted at the recruitment stage, it might have been possible to prevent a tragedy occurring.

The discussion so far has focused on four aspects of the outer ring presented in Figure 3.1 – the external environment. We can summarise the effects of these pressures on recruitment as follows:

External environment	Impact on recruitment
Economy Labour market Social change Legislation	Skill needs and supply Composition of the applicant pool Recruitment strategy and practice • *degree of selectivity possible* • *use of incentives* • *monitoring and targeting applicants* • *need for efficiency/speed*

The organisation

Geographical location, industry sector and stage of growth or technological development all will impact skill shortages and the ability to access appropriate applicants. Employers in areas of high unemployment, for instance, usually experience looser labour markets, while those in larger urban conurbations will benefit from a more heterogeneous and skilled labour force. Some industry sectors have also been impacted more than others by globalisation, technological advances, changing business environments or legislation. Apart from the credit 'crisis' described earlier, the financial sector has already experienced intensified competition and restructuring of business operations throughout the 1990s which resulted in a growth in the use of temporary labour to staff more flexible and continuous customer service functions (Marshall and Richardson 1996). Although all organisations will be affected in some way by these external forces, some sectors, such as the public or health sector, have relatively more stable skill demands and supply. On the other hand, public sector organisations will be more likely to have systems in place, and be held accountable, for upholding employment legislation (Pearn 1993).

SIZE

The one feature which has perhaps the most significant impact on how an organisation manages recruitment is its size. Large organisations are more likely to recruit on a regular basis, use more recruiting sources, have dedicated HR staff for recruitment, adopt diversity policies and practices, and derive their recruitment strategy from wider organisational and HR priorities (Hoque and Noon 2004; Olian and Rynes 1984; Barber *et al.* 1999). Recruitment strategies in large organisations, therefore, tend to be more strategically driven and formalised. For example, diversity goals have had a significant impact on large-scale military or police force recruitment efforts, with more positive action to recruit ethnic minorities or women, and even the creation of a new role – the police community support officer – in an effort to increase the representativeness of public policing and respond to legislation on police reform (Johnston 2006). Large companies in the private sector are also more likely to adopt diversity policies and set recruitment targets. Here, though, this strategy may have more to do with cultivating the company image of being a responsible employer, as well as reducing the risk of potential tribunal cases (Purcell *et al.* 2002).

Most recruitment research has been directed at what happens in these large organisations; but small and medium-sized enterprises (SMEs) (those employing fewer than 250 employees) dominate most countries' economies. In the UK, SMEs account for approximately 99 per cent of establishments and more than half (59 per cent) of all UK employment (BERR 2008). Most recruitment activity, therefore, is likely to be informal rather than guided by a formal structure or specialist HR staff.

Generally, recruitment presents greater challenges for smaller companies. SMEs have, on aggregate, lower labour productivity and lower capital/labour ratios, which results in a more constrained pool of resources to expand the workforce or dedicate to recruitment. Unlike the larger organisations illustrated above, small companies are less likely to have the resources to meet demands for a more diverse workforce in keeping with demographic changes (Gallagher and O'Leary 2007). They are also less able to recruit from internal or national labour markets and are often thought to be disadvantaged by not having the promotional prospects offered by large firms to attract the best-qualified staff (Cable and Graham 2000; Vinten 1998). Research evidence confirms that smaller firms tend to rely on less formal methods of recruitment, such as word of mouth, and that this may in the long term create problems of high turnover (Carroll *et al.* 1999). This same research, however, also showed that informality and the use of trusted resources were seen as more cost effective in the short term.

Along the same lines, other research has shown that SMEs are better placed for utilising local labour markets and inter-firm networks – perhaps through these informal channels – and that this has some advantages in being able to adapt to recruitment problems. In a comparison of recruitment in small and large urban, suburban and rural hotels, Lockyer and Scholarios (2004) found that small hotels operated in a way that was more attuned to local labour market characteristics, and could therefore more easily identify and match potential employees with local customer expectations. Large hotels which were part of a chain operated a more bureaucratic approach, for example relying on advertisements in national newspapers or, as we explore further in the next section, the outsourcing of recruitment to agencies. In many cases, this meant they were less effective at utilising local networks to fill vacancies.

OUTSOURCING AND DEVOLUTION OF HRM

In larger organisations, the structure of HR functions and the responsibility for recruitment have shifted over the past few decades. This has occurred alongside important broader trends in HRM, including the devolution of traditional HR roles and functions to line managers

(Renwick 2006; Purcell and Hutchison 2007) and an upsurge in the number of companies claiming to implement Ulrich's HR partner model. The most recent version of the latter sees HR as a 'three-legged stool' consisting of business partners, shared administrative service centres, and centres of expertise (see also Ulrich and Beatty 2001).

According to the CIPD's most recent Recruitment, Retention and Turnover Survey (CIPD 2007a), the Ulrich model is the most common structure for the HR function among UK organisations, although less than 30 per cent of respondents said they had introduced the model in full, and an equal proportion had only partially introduced it. The recruitment function appears in various forms. For some it is carried out by HR partners or 'experts' as in the Ulrich model. Elsewhere, it is undertaken by a shared service centre which provides routine administration and sometimes more tailored additional HR services. Shared service centres can be resourced by in-house staff or they can be outsourced to specialist third-party outsourcing providers. Consequently, many companies have outsourced all or at least part of their HR functions, particularly those associated with recruitment. Some organisations have made the decision to outsource the recruitment function for particular grades of staff. In the 2007 CIPD survey, for example, 81 per cent of respondents used agencies for recruiting temporary workers.

This strategy, which is often referred to as 'recruitment process outsourcing' (RPO), is presented as a way of cutting costs, improving efficiency, for example by reducing the length of the recruitment process, and also attracting high-quality applicants. A vibrant business has emerged in RPO partnerships, particularly in the UK (*Personnel Today,* 10 July 2007). Many organisations work only with preferred supplier lists of agencies which re-tender periodically to retain their contracts. The agency then carries out the whole recruitment process on behalf of the organisation.

Such partnerships between organisations and outsourcers have developed to such a level of sophistication that some recent research has presented them as a template for a 'new model of recruitment' which would accommodate recruitment at all levels of an organisation (Gallagher and O'Leary 2007). This would combine more personalised, 'high value' approaches – high-cost strategies designed to attract candidates for high-skilled positions – with more standardised processes taking advantage of the efficiency gains offered by the use of new technologies. However, the CIPD survey also indicated that there had been a 10 per cent decrease in the use of agencies since the previous year, with 72 per cent of respondents attributing this to a wish to minimise costs and 53 per cent suggesting a preference for a direct-hire strategy. The latter reason may be an indicator of organisations wishing to build relationships directly with applicants at an early stage of the process, which lends support to the belief that both parties contribute to, and decide whether or not to continue to develop, the relationship. Thus, while RPO still is a popular strategy, there is some evidence that companies are bringing recruitment back in-house.

In organisations which retain the recruitment function, often this is centralised as part of a support function for line managers. If the responsibility for HR, including recruitment, has been devolved to line managers, HR may have a role in supporting the line manager in identifying their recruitment needs, suggesting appropriate strategies, advising them about legislation, assisting in drawing up staff requirements and recommending appropriate methods. In the case of agency partnerships, this becomes one of setting, agreeing and monitoring the standard of service provided by the agency, which thus removes the more routine tasks from HR. Arguably, these different roles and responsibilities enhance, or at the very least change, the role of HR practitioners, and demand a different set of skills from that required to carry out administrative tasks. Ulrich and Brockbank (2005) have claimed that HR professionals will need to be 'credible activists', 'culture and change stewards', 'talent managers/organisational designers', 'strategy architects' and 'operational executers'.

Taking each of these organisational characteristics into account, the importance of the second layer of the model in Figure 3.1 can be summarised as follows:

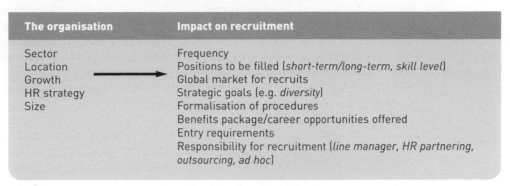

The organisation	Impact on recruitment
Sector Location Growth HR strategy Size	Frequency Positions to be filled (*short-term/long-term, skill level*) Global market for recruits Strategic goals (e.g. *diversity*) Formalisation of procedures Benefits package/career opportunities offered Entry requirements Responsibility for recruitment (*line manager, HR partnering, outsourcing, ad hoc*)

The job

We have already noted the changing nature of jobs and the effects this has on the skills demanded by employers. Recent research on the most valued qualities sought in job candidates shows that many companies are recruiting for 'attitude', and that this is consistent across jobs with different skill variety, autonomy and involvement (see Table 3.1). This further emphasises the increasing relevance of generic transferable, customer-orientated skills in all types of jobs.

Employers must also make a decision about whether the job should be allocated internally to existing employees or filled using externally resourced staff – either full-time, subcontracted, outsourced or temporary. This depends to a large extent on the expected employment relationship. Lepak and Snell (2002) describe a rational decision choice here with respect to the level of human capital required to perform the job. Jobs which require high skill and knowledge which is unique to the organisation (hence greater investment in training) are better managed as internal promotions or transfers, as these have implications for building a committed workforce. Jobs which do not require costly training and which can be performed at a lower skill level can be externalised with a view to a more short-term employment relationship.

This highlights the distinction between core and peripheral workers (Boxall and Purcell 2003). Those viewed as core to the success of a business are employed on a competitive salary and, in most cases, with a view to a long-term relationship. This longer-term investment is

Table 3.1   Main attributes that employers are looking for when recruiting, by job 'quality'

	Job quality			
	High %	Medium %	Low %	Total %
Specific/technical skills	25	16	13	19
Generic skills	15	19	20	17
Particular qualification or level of qualification	9	13	9	10
Particular type or number of years of work	7	7	1	5
Motivation and/or attitude	41	45	56	47
Others	1	0	1	1
Don't know	0	0	2	1
Total	88	31	71	

Source: Bates *et al.* 2008

reflected in the resources dedicated to recruitment. For high-value graduate positions, for example, large companies tend to have dedicated recruitment programmes managed by in-house staff. Those of less long-term value to the organisation are either outsourced entirely or employed in less secure, short-term contracts. In some industries, such as the IT sector, temporary agency staff are also used to fill skills gaps in specialist, 'cutting edge' areas, as well as in less skilled areas, such as helpdesk roles (Purcell *et al.* 2004). This allows the organisation to maximise workforce flexibility and operate more flexibly in unpredictable and competitive markets. (For further analysis of the human resource challenges of the use of temporary workers see Burgess and Connell 2006.)

Pre-recruitment activities

The previous section illustrates the diverse recruitment conditions which organisations face. It is hard to imagine a single, 'best practice' approach to actual recruitment which would be appropriate for all situations. However, there are some generalisations which can be made about how organisations should prepare for recruitment. Detailed accounts of these activities can be found in other texts (e.g. Lees and Cordery 2000; Marchington and Wilkinson 2005; Torrington *et al.* 2008). Here, we provide a brief review of two of the most fundamental pre-recruitment activities which are common across all situations – producing job descriptions and person specifications.

JOB DESCRIPTIONS

Filling a vacancy begins with a process called job analysis. This should be 'a purposeful, systematic process for collecting information on the important work-related aspects of a job' (Gatewood and Feild 1998, p.245), and should define what is required to perform the job successfully. Early approaches were based on producing a list of task-based and worker-based attributes (e.g. McCormick 1976), drawing from interviews/surveys with job incumbents or supervisors, observation, past job descriptions, or databases about occupational classifications (in the UK this is the Standard Occupational Classification). For example, a firefighter's job may involve 'applying water or chemical agents to extinguish flames' (a task-based attribute) and 'correctly identifying the nature of a fire and choosing the correct fire-suppressing or -retarding agent' (a worker-based attribute).

Various job analysis techniques have been proposed (e.g. position analysis questionnaire, functional job analysis, work profiling system) each using a slightly different approach to breaking down jobs into specific dimensions and ranking the importance of each to job success. Campion's (1988) multidimensional model of job analysis and design attempted to draw together many of these earlier approaches to provide the most comprehensive description possible of what a job entails. This proposed that jobs should be described using all of the following dimensions: tasks; worker characteristics (e.g. knowledge, skills, abilities, personality, motivation, perceptual-motor requirements); job context (e.g. tools/equipment needed, degree of social interaction); the reward structure (e.g. skill variety, autonomy); and demands (e.g. monitoring, problem-solving, intensity, speed).

There are at least two notable points about current thinking on describing jobs. The first is that the components of a job, whether the tasks or the worker characteristics, cannot be separated from the organisational setting in which it takes place; hence the position of the job at the centre of the concentric circles in Figure 3.1. The notion of skill, for example, may reflect specific product markets or organisational strategies. Grugulis (2007) distinguishes skill as residing in the individual, the job and the setting. Two call centre workers may each possess similar individual skills in interpersonal communication, but the setting means that one uses these skills in the context of a script to deal with customers, while the other may have more autonomy and scope to use their discretion. This has implications for job analysis methods, which some suggest should be refocused around the broader goals of work analysis rather than specific job tasks (Gatewood and Feild 1998). It also impacts decisions about matching the work context with the preferences of potential applicant groups, perhaps targeting temporary workers in the former example, and workers seeking long-term positions in the latter.

A second key point is that job descriptions should not be static or too narrow; they should take into account how jobs may change as a result of environmental drivers, like technological advances or competitive pressures, and consider the interconnections between specific jobs and other organisational roles (Sanchez 1994). As an example, organisational restructuring and delayering of middle-management levels has pushed many managerial responsibilities, like problem solving, on to non-managerial roles. 'Future-oriented' (or strategic) job analysis, which was described as a way of planning for future jobs (Schneider and Konz 1989), should intentionally include those involved in planning change in the organisation rather than rely on existing job incumbents as a source of information (see also Herriot and Anderson 1997).

PERSON SPECIFICATIONS AND COMPETENCY FRAMEWORKS

Person specifications, which are derived from the job description, detail the personal qualities that workers require to perform the job. The exact nature of person specifications has been influenced greatly by the competency profiling approach. This identifies the worker-based attributes (knowledge, skill, ability, personality etc.), or competencies, which are required to reach a required level of performance (or competence). The difference between this and traditional approaches is that the emphasis is on observable behaviours.

This approach emerged from the work of McClelland (1976) and Boyatzis (1982) who, focusing initially on managers, identified the behaviours which differentiated high- and poor-performing individuals and linked these to key underlying personal qualities. In the UK, there was an equally strong movement towards a functional competence approach based on minimum standards of observable performance outcomes rather than inferring underlying personal attributes. One such example was the Management Charter Initiative (1990), which consulted professional bodies for management development in order to identify a framework of competences required by managers at various levels. Today, this tradition continues in approaches which specify key performance indicators, or what behaviours the individual should achieve. Companies may purchase 'off the shelf' frameworks, which can then be amended to suit their needs, or develop their own competency frameworks in-house or with consultants (IDS 2008). This then might feed into the compilation of a competency dictionary which demonstrates each competency with positive and negative indicators (see Table 3.2 for an example related to the competency 'team-spirited' and Marchington and Wilkinson (2005) for further examples). As with 'future-oriented' job analysis, the competencies that organisations specify as the basis for recruitment and selection should be continually reviewed so that they can anticipate emerging and declining competency requirements (Robinson *et al.* 2005).

Competency frameworks are evident in large numbers of UK organisations. By 2007, 60 per cent of UK companies used a competency framework and of those who did not, almost all indicated an intention to introduce them (CIPD 2007a). Many companies identify 'core competencies' which are applied to all employees – for instance 'customer focus' and 'communication' – as well as specific competencies which may apply to different occupational groups. The most used competencies cited in the CIPD's 2007 Learning and Development Survey were teamworking, communication, customer service, communication skills, people management, team skills, customer service skills, results-orientation and problem solving. This provides further support that organisations are interested in recruiting for personal qualities as well as for specific skills and qualifications (see Table 3.1).

Table 3.2 Example competency statement and associated behaviours

Team-spirited

The way we pull together in an environment, which recognises and celebrates each other's strengths and contribution.

Positive behaviours	Negative behaviours
• Works effectively together to accomplish organisational goals • Builds positive working relationships with other teams and individuals • Shows consideration for the needs of the team; thinks about how colleagues will affect them • Happy to provide support to colleagues; doesn't wait to be asked	• Creates or tolerates an 'us and them' culture • Relies upon others to complete their work; doesn't take ownership • Doesn't build networks; sees themselves as self-sufficient • Avoids dealing with conflict between teams

Source: *IDS HR Studies 865,* March 2008, p.17

Returning again to Figure 3.1, we can now add further detail to how job requirements are likely to shape recruitment, as follows:

The job	Impact on recruitment
Current demands/skills Core/periphery Job/work analysis → Future job demands	Person specification Changes to competency profile 'Future orientation' of job analysis Effort in targeting applicant groups

Recruitment methods

As a result of the challenges discussed so far, organisations seem to be using more creative solutions, targeting diverse applicant groups and using internet channels to communicate to potential applicants alongside traditional methods, such as advertising, agencies and personal contacts. In 1989, the Institute of Personnel Management (IPM) reported that the majority of employers only advertised in regional or national press. Twenty years on, e-recruitment has become the method of choice for many organisations, although, as we saw with the rise of outsourced recruitment and the use of flexible labour, agency recruitment is also popular (see Table 3.3). In this section, we summarise the most popular methods, moving from those which provide advantages in terms of the efficiency of recruitment (e-recruitment, agencies) to those which are directed more at attracting the attention of candidates (referrals, word of mouth, networks). We conclude with a strategy borrowed from marketing which aims to solve recruitment difficulties by directly targeting applicant perceptions – employer branding.

INTERNET RECRUITMENT

Job information and recruitment channels are increasingly found on company websites, portals which host vacancies for similar types of posts (e.g. graduate jobs) or publicly funded

Table 3.3 Methods used to attract applicants, by industry sector (%)

	Total	Manuf. & production	Voluntary, community, not-for-profit	Private sector services	Public sector	2006 survey
Local newspaper advertisements	75	83	87	63	88	79
Own corporate website	75	65	69	76	87	75
Recruitment agencies	73	86	59	78	52	76
Specialist journals/ trade press	61	54	61	57	77	66
Employee referral scheme	47	49	22	66	11	47
Encouraging speculative applications/word of mouth	44	52	39	52	20	49
Jobcentre Plus	43	42	53	35	58	51
National newspaper advertisements	42	32	58	33	68	45
Links with schools/ colleges/universities	32	5	26	32	30	37
Apprentices/work placements/ secondments	33	36	28	29	37	36
Search consultants*	29	33	14	35	19	N/A
Commercial job boards	21	15	14	28	18	16
Physical posters/ billboards/vehicles	11	4	17	13	13	10
Radio or TV advertisements	6	5	6	6	9	7
Other	10	6	15	9	11	7

Source: CIPD 2007a

Base: 899

*included in the recruitment agencies figures for 2006

sites like the UK's Jobcentre Plus, which is one of the most popular sites used by the internet population to search for work (Hasluck *et al.* 2005). A recent trend is 'viral recruitment' where companies use social network sites like MySpace or Facebook to target 'Generation Y' applicants (school leavers, students and recent graduates); companies like Ernst and Young and BT already have such pages to help target their recruitment (Tenwick 2008).

As shown in Table 3.3, e-recruitment through corporate sites is used by 75 per cent of organisations, and more in the service sector, surpassing the popularity of most other traditional methods. The main reasons for this shift are related to issues of cost and speed. Rankin (2007) reported that more than 6 in 10 employers thought vacancies were filled more quickly than by other methods, more than 8 in 10 found it cheaper, 70 per cent found administration easier and slightly more (73 per cent) thought that they received more applications. Employers also cite the opportunity to offer jobs faster than other competitors who do not use internet sites. (See Case Study 3.1.)

For applicants, the internet allows easier access to job networks, enabling them to match their skills with the needs of employers (Cabinet Office 2004), and, in fact, for some may be the only job search medium. According to a survey of 400 graduate jobseekers by Reed Employment, 89 per cent looked at the web regularly for job opportunities while only 3 per cent consulted newspapers (*People Management*, 7 March 2008).

Internet recruitment, however, may not be fully compliant with disability discrimination legislation and there are concerns about accessibility for socially excluded groups, such as the unemployed or less IT-literate (Digital Europe 2003; Cabinet Office 2004). Research has shown that younger people, the better educated and those already in work are more likely to carry out job searches online (Kuhn and Skuterud 2000). As a result, equality legislation, generally, promotes also using traditional methods, such as application forms, and other ways of ensuring that all groups have equal access to job information.

AGENCIES AND HEADHUNTERS

Seventy-three per cent of employers report using agencies (Table 3.3). This compares with 62 per cent in the 1989 IPM survey cited above. The recruitment industry is reported to be worth £27 billion to the UK economy and is responsible for placing 1.2 million temporary workers each week and over 700,000 employees in permanent work each year (Recruitment and Employment Confederation 2008). Surveys of UK employers indicate that the main reason for using agency employment is to fill temporary vacancies in administrative positions or some professional posts, such as teachers or dentists (Welfare 2006). Although for employers this means a reduction in short-term labour costs, Forde and Slater (2006) argue that agency employment in many cases is also accompanied by low levels of commitment and greater job insecurity for employees.

A specific form of agency recruitment is carried out by executive search agencies or headhunters which identify candidates for senior management or executive roles. This involves cold-calling successful individuals with the intention of tempting them to apply for the post on offer, but can also involve the development of close relationships between the agency, the client and potential jobseekers (Finlay and Coverdill 2000). For such senior-level appointments, where discretion is required by both parties, headhunters are likely to remain the preferred route of recruitment over internet media.

TARGETING APPLICANT PERCEPTIONS: REFERRALS, NETWORKS, RECRUITERS AND INCENTIVES

Some methods are more directly focused on influencing the way that potential applicants perceive the job and their decision to apply. The 2007 CIPD survey of employers showed that such 'informal' methods are used by almost half of employers (Table 3.3). Employee referrals, for instance, have several apparent advantages. Candidates have already been vetted by an employee, are usually a better fit with the company and job, and have a better understanding of the business, often possessing some of the tacit knowledge which is accumulated through experience (*Personnel Today*, 29 May 2007; Yakubovich 2006). Employees feel that their reputation is at stake with a referral, which encourages them to refer only the highest-quality applicants. From the applicants' perspective, those referred receive valuable information about the job and organisation from their contacts. This 'realism' attracts people with more accurate expectations and better 'fit' to the job, allowing others to self-select out of the process at an early stage. Using referrals has also been shown to increase commitment to the company and reduce turnover (Breaugh and Mann 1984). The dangers of these informal methods, however, are that they can perpetuate existing social networks and working practices, hence acting as a barrier to change, as well as being open to challenge regarding their fairness.

One-third of employers reported building links with schools and universities to target students with specific skills that the organisation requires (Table 3.3). The traditional graduate 'milkround', in which companies visited almost all universities in the UK to promote their vacancies, has gradually been replaced with the forging of relationships with a limited number of universities, often offering internships and work placements to students, or other networking activities to target final year students. As well as affecting pre-hire concerns, such as enhancing the quality of applicants who ultimately apply for jobs, these methods are also thought to affect post-hire outcomes; for example, building a strong psychological contract, improving future employee satisfaction and commitment, and increasing retention rates (Anderson *et al.* 2001; Breaugh and Starke 2000).

There has also been considerable recent research on how the characteristics of initial contacts affect potential applicants' first impressions of the organisation, and their subsequent decisions to apply. One area often studied is the crisis facing military recruitment in many nations (because of changing social values, the unpopularity of recent conflicts such as Iraq, or the job prospects themselves). Focusing on the Belgian armed services, Schreurs *et al.* (2005) found that the perceived warmth and competence of career counsellors in recruitment outlets made potential recruits more likely to apply. However, they also were less likely to apply the more information they were given, suggesting that this process may also have imparted more realistic or too much (negative) information about the potential job. This finding is consistent with the large body of research on realistic recruitment information which shows that this leads to more accurate expectations and lower voluntary turnover after hiring (Phillips 1998).

Finally, financial incentives, such as increased pay or 'golden hellos', have been shown to increase the number of applications (Williams and Dreher 1992). The latter especially are evident in many areas of the current UK job market – cash lump sums or interest-free loans have been offered to new graduates in some areas of employment with hard-to-fill vacancies, such as engineering, teachers who indicate that they will accept a placement in any geographical area, or midwives in some health authorities. However, those recruited through financial inducements rather than through voluntary attraction based on value fit or a realistic expectation of the job – a process influenced more often by the informal processes discussed above – may be less likely to feel attachment to and remain with the organisation (Taylor and Schmidt 1983).

EMPLOYER BRANDING

Taking the applicant perspective further, there has been a surge of interest in the image of the employer (Saks 2005) and, in particular, 'branding' as a competitive attraction strategy; 69 per cent of respondents in a recent UK survey claimed to have an 'employer brand' (CIPD 2007a). The concept implies that organisations should think beyond just recruitment for specific job vacancies, and focus on communicating information about their image and the whole employment package to potential applicants. This has gained salience as the competition for skilled labour has intensified, as applicant decision making may be influenced by other job offers or informal information about a company; for example, negative comments on 'blogs' which may damage the employer 'brand' (*People Management,* 20 March 2008). One often-cited example is in graduate recruitment, where the primary reason given for difficulties filling vacancies was graduates' perceptions of the business sector (Association of Graduate Recruiters 2008).

Some writers are sceptical of the longevity of the concept of 'branding' as an explicit strategy, questioning whether it is no more than a passing fad (CIPD 2007b). It does seem, though, that various sources of information such as adverts, word of mouth, university sponsorship or publicity events can contribute to perceptions of 'the brand', particularly in conditions where organisations are competing to become the 'employer of choice'. High-profile surveys may influence applicant behaviour. Cable and Turban (2003) found that more applications were submitted to companies ranked high in US business publications, such as *Fortune,* while Lievens and Highhouse (2003) found that companies' symbolic attributes, such as what the company stands for, were more likely to influence applicant behaviour than objective (or instrumental) attributes, like pay or conditions. In the UK, one influential survey, the 2008 *Sunday Times* 'Best Companies to Work For', identified both instrumental and symbolic attributes when it asked existing employees to rate their companies on various dimensions, including leadership, personal growth, well-being/work–life balance, teamwork, 'giving something back', the way the company treated staff, and fair pay and benefits. The top-rated company of 2008 was Heat, a Belfast-based central heating installation company.

The need for an applicant perspective

The 'war for talent' and the search for more engaged and committed employees has meant that a purely selective approach to hiring based on matching job and person characteristics is often inadequate for finding the 'right' employees. As we examine further in the next chapter, staffing may be viewed as an interactive social process where the applicant has as much power about whether to engage in the application process as the organisation. This places greater importance on the perceptions of potential and actual applicants. In some situations companies will have to work harder to attract qualified applicants, maintain their interest in the company, and convince them that they should accept an offer of employment. As we saw in our analysis of the recruitment context, this has become acute in situations where there are skills shortages and an inadequate supply of quality labour, or for some organisations, such as SMEs.

Applicant 'attraction' to organisations implies getting applicants to view the organisation as a positive place to work. A considerable amount of research has been generated on just how applicant views are formed; for instance, how they are affected by recruiter behaviour, what draws their attention to corporate websites, how they process this information and how they use this to make decisions about the attractiveness of the organisation (e.g. Ehrhart and Ziegert 2005; Zottoli and Wanous 2000). This has provided information on the effectiveness of alternative recruitment sources, as well as investigating which sources provide the best employees in terms of post-hire outcomes like better job performance and lower turnover. We have reviewed some of this research in our consideration of each recruitment method above.

Conclusions

There is no 'best practice' recruitment approach, although methods which comply with equality legislation generally are a requirement. The model shown in Figure 3.1 demonstrates the factors which will impact recruitment outcomes, and hence the range of activities which organisations may adopt. The scarcity and criticality of the skills sought, decisions concerning the permanency of jobs, and the impact on particular applicant groups are just a few of the issues discussed in this chapter which will determine how employers choose to attract job applicants. For some organisations, recruitment is planned, integrated into wider HR strategies, and a key concern of senior managers who wish to attract and retain committed people. For others, it remains a low-priority task where ad hoc arrangements, increasingly through recruitment agencies, are made as the need arises. HR practitioners still have a role to play, but that role might range from one of simply sending out instructions in a service centre, to one of major strategic importance where specific expertise is required, as in the design and/or implementation of behavioural competency frameworks.

The 'applicant perspective' considers all recruitment methods as part of the developing relationship between applicants and organisations, which takes place in a changing external context. Recent interest in this approach has added considerably to earlier research which suggested that those hired through informal channels, such as referrals or realistic previews, would be different from those hired by formal methods, such as adverts or agencies. The former tended to be happier, more committed employees, with better fit to the needs of the organisation and less prone to turnover (see Barber 1998 for a review). More recent ways of looking at the effects on applicants have recognised that all recruitment channels, including traditional adverts, online systems and 'branding' efforts, send relevant messages to potential applicants which will affect their perceptions of the job/organisation and their intentions with respect to job search.

As well as trying to address objective recruitment goals, therefore, such as cost, the number of applications, diversity targets or time taken to fill a vacancy, organisations will also gain from using methods which communicate accurate information and attractive images of the job to applicants. These have been shown to influence interest in the application process and willingness to apply. Taking all these factors into account should mean a greater chance of successful recruitment, both in the short term with respect to recruitment goals and compliance with legislation, and in the longer term, with respect to the performance and attitudes of future employees.

CASE STUDY 3.1

Changing recruitment at Mercado supermarkets

Anne McCormack and Dora Scholarios

Mercado's HR strategy is: 'to provide improved capability to become the best retail HR function and make Mercado a great place to work'. New HR processes were introduced in 2007 which meant that many of the functions involved in recruitment and selection were centralised in the 'HR Shared Service Centre'. This was rolled out in Scotland, but is not yet operational throughout the whole of the UK.

Previously, there were issues with in-store recruitment processes because staff were dealing with a large number of CVs and application forms and this was time consuming and expensive. The number of applications at peak recruitment times, for example before Christmas, could be overwhelming, and this made them difficult to track on the old system. It was also recognised that the application screening process was not always robust, as department managers sometimes had to interview candidates who were not really suitable and this was not the best use of their time. Problems also existed in keeping up with the applicants' references. Eddie Pitt, the grocery manager in the Fenwick store, raised the subject regularly in the weekly meeting of department managers.

I am wasting so much of my time seeing people who just don't have what it takes to work here. I am not an HR manager and I've got bigger priorities than looking at application forms and preparing for interviews that turn out to be a waste of my time and theirs. Some of them have no common sense and no interest in working for the company. We need to get more colleagues who have a real desire to work with us and who are going to help our customers.

Now, applications are made online only and not on paper. This means that stores no longer accept or receive paper application forms and do not write advertisements to display in the store. Application forms are no longer scored manually. Offer letters and contracts are produced centrally.

For the company, this is an attempt to have a consistent recruitment brand and experience for applicants. It is hoped that 'prospect pools' for specialist and hard-to-recruit roles can be developed and thereby assist HR planning and induction training. The centralised system will also facilitate the production of management information, for example recruitment reports and statistics.

▶

The process begins with the store identifying the need to recruit; then it seeks authority to do this. The store then loads vacancy details onto the system, including interview slots and pay. Applicants browse the corporate website then apply for a specific vacancy and do a test. The vacancy automatically closes when a predetermined number of applicants have been successfully screened. The system then forwards the applicant to HR Shared Services, who arrange interviews directly with the applicants and then confirm the details. Eddie Pitt likes the new system so far, but it has taken a bit of time for him to learn how to put his vacancies on the website. 'I am more confident now that I have put three vacancies on. I had help and coaching from the store HR manager at first, but I did the last one by myself.'

From the store's perspective, it holds interviews at agreed times and returns notes to Shared Services, though the store ranks applicants and makes the decision. Eddie's colleague, the bakery manager, Jenny Jackson, was a bit unsure about setting aside interview times on a computer system. Her experience of her first interview arrangements has been positive.

I was a bit cynical about how it would work when you are dealing with people a couple of hundred miles away. I thought I would prefer to keep the old system. The applicants turned up for my interviews and seemed to know a bit about the job and the company. I had to plan my time to fit in the interview but it was worth it. It is hard to find qualified bakers, so if this is going to help get people more quickly, then it will be a good thing.

HR Shared Services makes a verbal offer, then sends out a contract and invitation to induction. It also sends for references when necessary. It means that department managers have to ensure that their department has the right skills and should plan ahead with vacancy requirements. They are also responsible for making sure that interviews take place at the planned time. An additional function for stores is that they can contact a 'prospect pool', or those applicants who have expressed a desire to work in specific skilled roles, like bakery, then advise them to apply online. They can also identify applicants with 'on hold' status who were successful but who were not offered a role. Stores can contact them and arrange a meeting to discuss a new vacancy. Jenny Jackson offered a job to a baker who was 'on hold' because he was second choice at the Paisley store.

This saved me so much time. I was able to get an offer made and start the new baker within a week. Peter was well impressed by how quickly we got him started – he decided to come to us and turn down another job that he has been waiting to hear from for three weeks.

A key objective is to improve the applicant's experience. The applicant browses the site for suitable opportunities. Those wishing to apply then create a user account. If there are no suitable vacancies, they can register interest in certain roles. In order to comply with the Disability Discrimination Act, applicants with special needs are referred directly from the website to Shared Services for assistance with their application.

Applicants normally apply online for vacancies and enter their details. They then complete a job-specific screening test online. If successful, they are contacted by Shared Services to arrange an interview, then attend interview.

The challenges of implementing this change to existing practice from the store's perspective have been about communicating the change to all relevant staff (including customer service staff, who can provide some information to applicants in store), training people who are directly involved in the process on the new system, and providing ongoing coaching support. Jean is a customer service adviser. In the past, she kept a supply of application forms at the desk, but now she has to refer all those who enquire to the company website.

At first, I felt that could not really help people asking about jobs, but the briefing I was at in the store explained the new system to me. I now understand what they have to do and I know where to get more help for them if they need it.

▶

This e-recruitment strategy is being monitored closely to determine its effectiveness from the point of view of the organisation. Measures are being taken of, for instance, the number of candidates registered, calls received, and average call handling time at the Shared Service Centre, offers made, percentage of references processed, and average time taken to fill a vacancy from advert to verbal offer.

While the experiences in one branch have been positive, the pilot study in another small store has highlighted some issues. There are only five user names and passwords allocated to staff and this means that not all managers can be authorised to use the system. Inevitably, there are problems of uploading vacancies, arranging interviews and making appointments.

It is too early to assess the impact on candidates, but there have been some success stories like Peter. Managers are still adapting to the new approach. Eddie Pitt is keeping an open mind, but his experience so far is that the system is 'letting me concentrate on managing the people I have already – and spending less time on interviewing people who don't want to be part of Mercado'.

Questions

1. What do you think were the main drivers for the company to develop its e-recruitment strategy?
2. Is e-recruitment appropriate for all types of vacancies in a retail store?
3. What are the advantages of this approach?
4. What are the disadvantages?
5. Which other methods would you suggest?
6. How would you design a research project to evaluate one aspect of the effectiveness of this example of e-recruitment from the point of view of the applicant?
7. To what extent has this new strategy 'improved capability to become the best retail HR function and make Mercado a great place to work'?

Outsourcing recruitment at Blueberry

Anne McCormack and Dora Scholarios

This case highlights two different issues. Firstly, it is an example of an outsourcing strategy adopted by a call centre, and secondly, it highlights some methods used to recruit for scarce skills. It is based on the authors' research with one of the largest global providers of human resources services (a Fortune Global 500 company) which provides career and staffing services for jobseekers and employers, and with a technical customer services call centre for a multinational IT company.

Blueberry is a subsidiary of a multinational IT company based in the US (Globalchip) which established its European help desk three years ago. Currently, it directly employs 40 staff whose contracts are permanent. New recruits need to be fluent in a European language other than English and have technical competence (computer skills, some product knowledge) and customer service skills. The recruitment of individuals with these relevant technical and language skills has been very difficult. Currently, the Customer Service Unit includes fluent speakers of Spanish, French, Italian, Finnish, Dutch, German and Greek. The majority are non-UK nationals.

▶

In the US, the parent company, Globalchip, operates a similar help desk for Asia. When the Asian help desk was established, the strategy adopted, after much discussion and deliberation, was to outsource the whole unit to an agency (Succuro) which recruits the staff, employs them and manages them with respect to personal development, discipline and performance management. There is a very tight budget for salaries. Blueberry managers are responsible for the overall operation of the unit.

The HR director of Blueberry's parent company asked the HR partner, Liz McDonald, who is responsible for liaising with the European help desk, to identify the steps which would need to be taken to put a similar outsourced help desk in place. She was also asked to collaborate with her US colleague to determine the difficulties that Succoro currently face in recruiting individuals with the required skills and competencies.

Her enquiries have shown that Globalchip has a three-year contact with Succuro, which is due for renewal soon. A 'service level agreement' was produced by the company, which clearly indicated what level of performance was expected of the agency, for instance time to fill vacancies, provision of statistical data about the levels of absence and performance of agents.

Succoro is finding it increasingly difficult to recruit suitable people within the budget constraints. However, it is an important contract which it wants to retain. The agency has been performing well and exceeding the service level agreement in some indicators. Succoro uses an online application form, and then screens applicants in a telephone interview. Globalchip managers are involved in the final selection decision.

Liz McDonald is a member of her local HR network, which is a group of HR practitioners who meet every three months to share their knowledge and experience in order to help with their continuing professional development. One of the other members, Jim Gray, works for an agency which runs a similar operation for a mobile phone company in a different area of the UK. Jim Gray offered to share his experience of recruiting those with languages and technical skills.

The main difficulty is trying to attract applicants to jobs which are paying a little below the average rate. Our agency cannot afford to use some of the more popular websites, because they are expensive. We need to use other ways of targeting people who might be willing to live and work in the UK – almost to sell the experience. We try to use networks, like websites for those who want to travel and work abroad, to advertise. We target social networking sites like Bebo, Facebook and Gumtree. We are having real difficulties getting speakers of, for example, Dutch and Finnish to come to work here in our UK site.

Jim added,

It takes about eight weeks to fill a vacancy, though for some of the more common languages there sometimes is a pool of applicants in our skills bank. We advertise on our website in the UK but have links to our agency posted in other national websites.

Liz is still investigating the implications of outsourcing for Blueberry.

Questions

1. How would outsourcing change the HR function?
2. What is a service level agreement?
3. Which methods would you use to attract applicants to their international call centre in the UK?
4. To what extent is this an example of 'viral' recruitment?
5. Companies target applicants who are predominantly young people under 30 years old who use social network sites. Is this potentially discriminatory?

Bibliography

ACAS (2006) *Recruitment and Induction, Advisory Booklet,* London: Advisory Conciliation and Arbitration Service.

Anderson, N., Born, M. and Cunningham-Snell, N. (2001) 'Recruitment and selection: applicant perspectives and outcomes' in N. Anderson, D. Ones, H.K. Sinangil and C. Viswesvaran (eds), *Handbook of Industrial, Work, and Organizational Psychology: Volume 1, Personnel Psychology,* London: Sage, pp.200–18.

Association of Graduate Recruiters (2008) *The AGR Graduate Recruitment Survey 2008: Winter Review,* available at www.agr.org.uk

Barber A. (1998) *Recruiting Employees: Individual and Organisational Perspectives,* London: Sage.

Barber, A.E., Wesson, M.J., Roberson, Q.M., and Taylor, M.S. (1999) 'A tale of two job markets: organizational size and its effects on hiring practices and job search behaviour', *Personnel Psychology,* Vol.52, pp.841–67.

Barber, L., Hill, D., Hirsh, W. and Tyers, C. (2005) *Fishing for Talent in a Wider Pool: Trends and Dilemmas in Corporate Graduate Recruitment,* IES Report 421, Institute for Employment Studies.

Bates, P., Johnson, C. and Gifford, J. (2008) *Recruitment and Training among Large National Employers,* Institute for Employment Studies and IFF Research on behalf of Learning and Skills Council.

BBC News Online (2006) 'Nearly 600,000 new EU migrants', updated 22 August 2006, available at http://news.bbc.co.uk.

BERR (2008) *BERR's Role in Raising Productivity: New Evidence,* BERR Economics Paper 1, London: Department of Business, Enterprise and Regulatory Reform.

Billsberry, J. (2007) *Experiencing Recruitment and Selection,* Chichester: John Wiley & Sons.

Boxall, P. and Purcell, J. (2003) *Strategy and Human Resource Management,* Basingstoke: Palgrave Macmillan.

Boyatzis, R.E. (1982) *The Competent Manager: A Model for Effective Performance,* New York: Wiley.

Burgess, J. and Connell, J. (2006) 'Temporary work and human resources management: issues, challenges and responses', *Personnel Review,* Vol.35, No.2, pp.129–40.

Breaugh, J. and Mann, R.B. (1984) 'Recruiting source effects: a test of two alternative explanations', *Journal of Occupational Psychology,* Vol.57, pp.261–67.

Breaugh, J. and Starke, M. (2000) 'Research on employee recruiting: so many studies, so many remaining questions', *Journal of Management,* Vol.26, pp.405–34.

Cabinet Office (2004) *Enabling a Digitally United Kingdom,* Report of the Digital Inclusion Panel, London: HMSO.

Cable, D.M. and Graham, M.E. (2000) 'The determinants of organizational reputation: a job search perspective', *Journal of Organizational Behavior,* Vol.21, pp.929–47.

Cable, D.M. and Turban, D.B. (2003) 'The value of organizational image in the recruitment context: a brand equity perspective', *Journal of Applied Social Psychology,* Vol.33, pp.2244–66.

Campion, M.A. (1988) 'Interdisciplinary approaches to job design: a constructive replication with extension', *Journal of Applied Psychology,* Vol.73, pp.467–81.

Carroll, M., Marchington, M., Earnshaw, J. and Taylor, S. (1999) 'Recruitment in small firms. Processes, methods and problems', *Employee Relations,* Vol.21, No.3, pp.236–50.

Cassell, C.M. (2005) 'Managing diversity', in T. Redman and A. Wilkinson (eds), *Contemporary Issues in Human Resource Management: Text and Cases* (2nd edn), Harlow: Pearson.

CIPD (2006a) *Graduates in the Workplace. Does a Degree Add Value?* London: Chartered Institute of Personnel and Development.

CIPD (2006b) *Working Life: Employee Attitudes and Engagement,* London: Chartered Institute of Personnel and Development.

CIPD (2007a) *Recruitment, Retention and Turnover Survey,* London: Chartered Institute of Personnel and Development.

CIPD (2007b) *Employer Branding. The Latest Fad or the Future of HR?* London: Chartered Institute of Personnel and Development.

Department of Health (2007) *Additionality Shortage Professions List,* available at www.dh.gov.uk

Digital Europe (2003) *European i2010 Initiative on e-Inclusion,* Brussels: European Commission.

Ehrhart, K.H. and Ziegert, J.C. (2005) 'Why are individuals attracted to organizations?' *Journal of Management,* Vol.31, pp.901–19.

Felstead, A., Gallie, D., Green, F. and Zhou, Y. (2007) *Skills at Work, 1996–2006,* Cardiff/Oxford: ESRC.

Finlay, W. and Coverdill, J. (2000) 'Risk, opportunism and structural holes: how headhunters manage clients and earn fees', *Work and Occupations,* Vol.27, No.3, pp.377–405.

Forde, C. and Slater, G. (2006) 'The nature and experience of agency working in Britain: what are the challenges for human resource management?' *Personnel Review,* Vol.35, No.2, pp.141–57.

Gallagher, N. and O'Leary, D. (2007) *Recruitment 2020. How Recruitment is Changing and Why it Matters,* London: Demos.

Gatewood, R.D. and Feild, H.S. (1998) *Human Resource Selection* (4th edn), Fort Worth, TX: Dryden Press.

Goos, M. and Manning, A. (2007) 'Lousy and lovely jobs: the rising polarization of work in Britain', *The Review of Economics and Statistics,* Vol.89, No.1, pp.118–33.

Grugulis, I. (2007) *Skills, Training and Human Resource Development: A Critical Text,* Basingstoke: Palgrave Macmillan.

Haskel, J. and Martin, C. (2001) 'Technology, wages, and skill shortages: evidence from UK micro data', *Oxford Economic Papers,* Vol.53, No.4, pp.642–58.

Hasluck, C., Mhonda, J., Winter, E., Durrant, C., Thompson, M., Dobbs, I. and Christou, G. (2005) *The Use and Development of Alternative Service Delivery Channels in Jobcentre Plus: a Review of Recent Evidence,* Research Report No.280, Department for Work and Pensions.

Hayward, B., Fong, B. and Thornton, A. (2007) *The Third Work–Life Balance Employer Survey: Executive Summary,* Employment Relations Research Series No.86, Department for Business, Enterprise and Regulatory Reform.

Healy, M. and Schwarz-Woelzl, M. (2007) *Recruitment Policies and Practices in the Context of Demographic Change. Critical Issues in the ICT Sector and Recommendations,* Report of MATURE Project, available at www.mature-project.eu

Herriot, P. and Anderson, N. (1997) 'Selecting for change: how will personnel and selection psychology survive?' in N.R. Anderson and P. Herriot (eds), *International Handbook of Selection and Assessment,* London: Wiley.

Hoque, K. and Noon, M. (2004) 'Equal Opportunities policy and practice in Britain: evaluating the "empty shell" hypothesis', *Work Employment and Society,* Vol.18, No.3, pp.481–506.

IDS (2008) *Competency Frameworks,* HR studies, 865, London: Income Data Services.

Johnston, L. (2006) 'Diversifying police recruitment? The deployment of police community support officers in London', *The Howard Journal of Criminal Justice,* Vol.45, No.4, pp.388–402.

Kuhn, P. and Skuterud, M. (2000) 'Job search methods: internet versus traditional', *Monthly Labor Review,* Vol.123, No.10, pp.3–11.

Leadbetter, C. (2000) *Living on Thin Air,* London: Penguin.

Lees, C.D. and Cordery, J.L. (2000) 'Job analysis and design', in N. Chmiel (ed.) *Introduction to Work and Organizational Psychology* (pp.45–68), Oxford: Blackwell.

Lepak, D.P. and Snell, S.A. (2002) 'Examining the human resource architecture: the relationships among human capital, employment, and human resource configurations', *Journal of Management,* Vol.28, pp.517–43.

Lewis, D. and Sargeant, M. (2007) *Essentials of Employment Law* (9th edn), London: Chartered Institute of Personnel and Development.

Lievens, F. and Highhouse, S. (2003) 'The relation of instrumental and symbolic attributes to a company's attractiveness as an employer', *Personnel Psychology,* Vol.56, pp.75–102.

Lockyer, C.J. and Scholarios, D. (2004) 'Selecting hotel staff: why best practice doesn't always work', *International Journal of Contemporary Hospitality Management,* Vol.16, No.2, pp.125–35.

Madouros, V. (2006) 'Projections of the UK labour force, 2006–2020', *Labour Market Trends,* January, Newport: Office for National Statistics.

Management Charter Initiative (1990) *Occupational Standards for Managers,* Department of Employment and NFMED.

Marchington, M. and Wilkinson, A. (2005) *Human Resource Management at Work: People Management and Development,* London: Chartered Institute of Personnel and Development.

Marshall, J.N. and Richardson, R. (1996) 'The impact of "telemediated services" on corporate structures: the example of "branchless" retail banking in Britain', *Environment and Planning A*, Vol.28, pp.1843–58.

McClelland, D.C. (1976) *A Guide to Job Competency Assessment*, Boston, MA: McBer and Company.

McCormick, E.J. (1976) 'Job and task analysis', in M.D. Dunnette (ed.), *Handbook of Industrial and Organizational Psychology*, Chicago, IL: Rand-McNally, pp.651–96.

McKay, P. and Avery, D. (2005) 'Warning! Diversity recruitment could backfire', *Journal of Management Enquiry*, Vol.14, No.4, pp.330–36.

Olian, J.D. and Rynes, S.L. (1984) 'Organizational staffing: integrating practice with strategy', *Industrial Relations*, Vol.23, No.2, pp.170–83.

Pearn, M. (1993) 'Fairness in selection and assessment: a European perspective' in H. Schuler, J. L. Farr and M. Smith (eds), *Personnel Selection and Assessment: Individual and Organizational Perspectives*, Hillsdale, NJ: Lawrence Erlbaum.

Perryman S. (2003) *The IES Annual Graduate Review: 2003 Update. Business as Usual? Trends in Student and Graduate Numbers*, Report 399, Institute for Employment Studies.

Phillips, J.M. (1998), 'Effects of realistic job previews on multiple organizational outcomes: a meta-analysis', *Academy of Management Journal*, Vol.41, pp.673–91.

Purcell, J., Purcell, K. and Tailby, S. (2004) 'Temporary work agencies: here today, gone tomorrow?', *British Journal of Industrial Relations*, Vol.42, No.4, pp.705–25.

Purcell, K., Rowley, G. and Morley, M. (2002), *Recruiting from a Wider Spectrum of Graduates*, May, London: Council for Industry and Higher Education.

Rankin, N. (2007) 'Online recruitment in 2007: The IRS report', *IRS Employment Review* No. 884, IRS.

Recruitment and Employment Federation and KPMG (2007) *Report on Jobs: October*, NTC Research on behalf of the Recruitment and Employment Confederation.

Recruitment and Employment Federation (2008) *About REC*, available at www.rec.uk.com/aboutrec, accessed December 2007.

Renwick, D. (2006) 'Line managers', in T. Redman and A. Wilkinson (eds) *Contemporary HRM* (2nd edn), London: Pearson Education, pp.209–28.

Robinson, M.A., Sparrow, P.R., Clegg, C. and Birdi, K. (2005) 'Forecasting future competency requirements: a three-phase methodology', *Personnel Review*, Vol.36, No.1, pp.65–90.

Rynes, S.L. (1991) 'Recruitment, job choice, and post-hire consequences' in M.D. Dunnette (ed.), *Handbook of Industrial and Organizational Psychology* (2nd edn), Palo Alto, CA: Consulting Psychologists Press, pp.399–444.

Rynes, S.L. and Cable, D. (2003) 'Recruitment research in the twenty-first century', in W.C. Borman, D.R. Ilgen and R.J. Klimoski (eds), *Handbook of Psychology: Volume 12: Industrial and Organizational Psychology*, Hoboken, NJ: Wiley, pp.55–76.

Saks, A.M. (2005) 'The impracticality of recruitment research', in A. Evers, N. Anderson, and O. Voskuijl (eds) *Handbook of Personnel Selection*, Oxford: Blackwell, pp.47–72.

Sanchez, J.I. (1994) 'From documentation to innovation: reshaping job analysis to meet emerging business needs', *Human Resource Management Review*, Vol.4, No.1, pp.51–74.

Schneider, B. and Konz, A. (1989) 'Strategic job analysis', *Human Resource Management*, Vol.28, pp.51–63.

Schreurs, B., Derous, E., De Witte, K., Proost, K., Andriessen, M. and Glabeke, K. (2005) 'Attracting potential applicants to the military: the effects of initial face-to-face contacts', *Human Performance*, Vol.18, No.2, pp.105–22.

Searle R. (2003) *Selection and Recruitment: A Critical Text*, London: Palgrave Macmillan.

Taylor, M.S. and Collins, C.J. (2000) 'Organizational recruitment: enhancing the intersection of theory and practice', in C.L. Cooper and E.A. Locke (eds), *Industrial and Organizational Psychology: Linking Theory and Practice*, Oxford: Blackwell, pp.304–34.

Taylor, M.S. and Schmidt, D.W. (1983) 'A process-oriented investigation of recruitment source effectiveness', *Personnel Psychology*, Vol.36, pp.343–54.

Tenwick, C. (2008) 'Generation Y requires a "viral" approach to recruitment', *HR Zone*, 27 March, available at www.hrzo.co.uk

The Future Laboratory (2005) *Freestylers and Work*, London: Standard Life Bank.

Torrington, D., Taylor, S. and Hall, L. (2008) *Human Resource Management* (7th edn), Harlow: Pearson Education.

Ulrich, D. and Beatty, D. (2001) 'From players to partners: extending the HR playing field', *Human Resource Management*, Vol.40, No.4, pp.293–307.

Ulrich, D. and Brockbank, W. (2005) 'Role call', *People Management*, 16 June, pp.24–8.

Vinten, G. (1998) 'Skills shortage and recruitment in the SME sector', *Career Development International*, Vol.3, No.6, pp.238–42.

Welfare, S. (2006) 'A two-way process: informing and consulting employees', *IRS Employment Review*, No.859, 17 November, pp.8–15.

Williams, M.L. and Dreher, G.F. (1992) 'Compensation system attributes and applicant pool characteristics', *Academy of Management Journal*, Vol.35, pp.571–95.

Wilson, R., Homenidou, K. and Dickerson, A. (2004) *Working Futures: National Report 2003–4*, Institute for Employment Research, University of Warwick.

Woodhams, C. and Corby, S. (2007) 'Then and now: disability legislation and employers' practices in the UK', *British Journal of Industrial Relations*, Vol.45, No.3, pp.556–80.

Yakubovich V. (2006) 'Passive recruitment in the Russian urban labor market', *Work and Occupations*, Vol.33, No.3, pp.307–34.

YouGov (2006) *Has Your Business Got the X Factor?* London: Croner.

Zottoli, M.A. and Wanous, J.P. (2000) 'Recruitment source research: current status and future directions', *Human Resource Management Review*, Vol.10, No.4, pp.353–82.

Chapter 4

SELECTION

Dora Scholarios

Introduction

'Best-practice' employee selection is usually associated with the 'psychometric' model. This recommends rigorously developed psychometric tests, performance-based or work simulation methods, and the use of multiple methods of assessment, all designed to accurately measure candidates' knowledge, skills, abilities, personality and attitudes.

This view has dominated literature on selection. Its popularity is no doubt due to its emphasis on objectivity, meritocracy and efficiency, which are all evident in the story of selection, and indeed the emergence of HRM, over the last century. Industrialisation and mass manpower planning during the early twentieth century required a systematic way of matching the attributes of individuals to the requirements of jobs, and early psychological research on understanding and scaling individual differences (for example, the work of Alfred Binet or Raymond Cattell in the field of education) provided tools for military and commercial organisations faced with this massive scale problem of person–job fit. These early assessment efforts became gradually refined to show how organisations of all types could gain from systematic selection methods. By the 1980s, it had become a core element of competitive strategy, and an essential part of an organisation's strategic capability for adapting to competition (Hamel and Prahalad 1989). Systematic selection is now regarded as one of the critical functions of HRM, essential for achieving key organisational outcomes (Storey 2007), and a core component of what has been called a high-commitment or high-performance management approach to HRM (Marchington and Wilkinson 2005; Pfeffer 1998).

This chapter begins with a review of the principles of the psychometric model and the range of assessment methods available to organisations that follow this model. The chapter then considers whether organisations have adopted these methods. This leads to a more sceptical account of sophisticated selection, and the possibility of alternative paradigms which move away from a techniques-driven approach. Three alternatives are covered: a 'best fit' approach; an 'interactive action-oriented' perspective (Newell 2006); and a discourse view, which describes selection as a contested, rather than rational, process, muddied by multiple possible interpretations and interests. We conclude by examining what these alternative paradigms imply for selection practice and for HRM.

A brief overview of psychometric quality

How do we identify people with knowledge, skill, ability and the personality to perform well at a set of tasks we call a job? Even more difficult, how do we do this before we have ever seen that person perform on the job? (Ployhart *et al.* 2006, p.10)

It is this latter task which gives the psychometric model its alias as the 'prediction' or 'predictivist' paradigm and takes up the majority of space in most textbooks on the subject of selection. Decisions whether to hire someone are usually based on their performance on a test assessing their suitability for the job – hence the prediction – but how do we make sure this test does what it is intended to do? Four standards are used to make this evaluation (more detail on each can be found in any textbook account of selection; e.g. Schmitt and Chan 1998; Searle 2003a).

1. The method of assessment must be *reliable*; i.e. accurate and free from contamination. Reliable methods have high physical fidelity with job performance itself, are standardised across applicants, have some degree of imposed structure, and show consistency across multiple assessors. Work samples or simulations, which measure performance on a structured task reflecting behaviours used in the job, are likely to have high reliability. Interviews are generally thought to have low reliability, although the use of panels, rather than individual decision makers, and structure and standardisation, like question-response scoring, have been shown to increase their reliability (McFarland *et al.* 2004).

2. Selection methods must also be *valid* – relevant for the work behaviours they are meant to predict. At minimum, to be valid, assessment must be designed around a systematic job analysis and person specification for the job, and be reliable. For example, introducing structure into interviews also enhances their validity (Schmidt and Zimmerman 2004). A valid method, though, should also show an association between scores on the assessment tool and desired job behaviours. This is often expressed as a correlation coefficient – known as a criterion-related validity coefficient – representing the relationship between scores on the predictor (or proposed selection method) and scores on a criterion (or proxy measure) of job performance. This correlation coefficient can range from 0 (chance prediction or no relationship) to 1.0 (perfect prediction). Table 4.1 summarises what values are considered to be low, moderate or high predictive validity coefficients for a range of selection methods.

3. *Subgroup predictive validity* should be the same for different applicant groups, such as men and women; i.e. the selection method should treat all groups the same. Members of one subgroup should not be selected disproportionately more or less often than members of another. The example of cognitive ability testing illustrates perfectly the trade-offs between predictive validity and different subgroup prediction. Psychometric tests which measure general cognitive ability (also known as general intelligence) provide the best predictors of future success in the workplace regardless of the specific job, with validity coefficients in the region of .60 (Schmidt and Hunter 1998). However, some minority groups, particularly blacks and Hispanics, tend to score lower as a group on such tests, even though the tests themselves are not inherently unfair. As a result of this differential predictive validity, the US federal government has encouraged the search for alternatives to cognitive ability testing for hiring purposes in order to minimise adverse impact against historically and socially disadvantaged groups.

4. The selection method should have high *utility* for the organisation. This usually takes into account cost and potential return on investment so that methods with high validity which are not expensive to develop or administer will have higher utility. This also is affected by the hiring context; for example, the number of applications received for a job opening and the proportion of these who will be hired (the selection ratio).

The 'what' and 'how' of selection

Each of these four psychometric standards is concerned with how we should design the assessment tools, or selection methods, for determining people's suitability for jobs. Also relevant is what underlying individual characteristics we wish to capture with these methods, as a range of methods (the 'how') could be used to tap into a single underlying construct (the 'what'). In this sense, application forms, interviews and psychometric tests could all be used to measure personality, but with varying degrees of psychometric rigour.

One useful framework distinguishes between cognitive, non-cognitive and performance-based individual differences. Cognitive characteristics reflect intellectual processes, academic achievements and knowledge; non-cognitive characteristics include personality traits, motivation, past experience and qualifications; and performance-based characteristics refer to more hands-on behavioural examples of job performance. Each of these constructs represents the 'what' to be measured; the selection technique used to do this represents the 'how'.

Table 4.1 brings together the psychometric standards and three types of individual differences to classify various selection methods. The table also indicates the general findings from research on user acceptability with respect to these methods, an issue to which we return later in the chapter. We discuss only some of these selection methods here. An important point to note from the discussion and Table 4.1 is that performance-based selection methods generally have higher reliability/validity, lower subgroup differences in predictive validity and higher user acceptability, all of which has resulted in their increasing popularity.

Table 4.1 The psychometric quality of alternative selection methods

	Psychometric quality			User acceptability
Selection method	Predictive validity	Subgroup differences (race/gender)	Utility	
Cognitive				
Ability/aptitude test	High	Large/small	High	Moderate
Achievement/job knowledge test	High	Moderate/small	High	Favourable
Non-cognitive				
Personality test	Low/moderate	Small/small	Moderate	Unfavourable
Biographical information	Moderate	Small/small	Moderate	Unfavourable
Experience	Moderate	Small/small	Low	Moderate
Performance-based				
Work sample	Moderate/high	Small-moderate/small	Moderate	Favourable
Interview – unstructured	Low	Small/small	Moderate	Low
Interview – structured	High	Small/small	Moderate	Moderate
Situational judgement test	Moderate	Moderate/small	High	Favourable

Source: Adapted from Ployhart *et al.* 2006 (Table 7.3) and Schmidt and Hunter 1998

Notes: Descriptors for criterion-related validity coefficients are based on the following accepted ranges: 0.10 = low; 0.20 = moderate; 0.30 and above = high

COGNITIVE ABILITY

Psychometric tests are standardised instruments designed to measure individual differences, most commonly cognitive ability or aptitude, achievement or personality. Although there is some blurring between cognitive ability and aptitude, measures of ability focus more on current levels of skill in specific areas, such as arithmetic or verbal ability, while aptitude refers to one's potential to learn or acquire skill, regardless of past experience, and is often associated with a broader measure of intelligence. Ability may underlie aptitude – high logical reasoning ability may be required for computer programming aptitude – which shows how aptitudes may be targeted at specific occupational areas (consider how an aptitude for making inferences from numerical data contributes to performance in financial services occupations). Tests of achievement include school examinations, typing tests or statutory professional examinations; e.g. for accountancy certification or where public safety may be at risk, as in the use of firefighting equipment or electrical safety.

During the 1980s, there was a flurry of influential research centred on tests of general cognitive ability (referred to as g), which include both ability and aptitude. Most test batteries measuring g consist of tests of numerical, verbal, reasoning and spatial ability, and emphasise future potential for learning or adapting to new situations. Research shows that tests of g provide the best way of predicting performance differences between job applicants in any type of job, with potentially high returns on investment (utility) for organisations. Using the statistical techniques of meta-analysis to aggregate across validity studies, g has been found to be a strong predictor of diverse measures of job success, including supervisory ratings, production quantity and quality, and training performance (e.g. Hunter and Hunter 1984). More recently, this has been shown to hold across different employment and cultural contexts. For example, Bertua *et al.* (2005) showed high validity for a range of UK jobs, and Salgado *et al.* (2003) did the same for 10 European Commission countries.

Current thinking on the structure of ability distinguishes between tests which measure fluid intelligence, representing general reasoning ability across situations, and crystallised intelligence, which represents a culturally specific view of intelligence which develops as a result of specific experiences (Carroll 1993). An example of how these tests are being used by graduate employers as a way of measuring fluid intelligence, and hence future potential, is described in Box 4.1. Today, over 70 specialised ability tests are available as aids to decision makers.

Box 4.1: HRM in practice

Psychometric testing in graduate jobs

The most recent survey of UK blue-chip graduate employers by the Association of Graduate Recruiters (2007) shows that psychometric testing is being used as a way of dealing with the oversupply of graduates qualifying with first or upper second class degrees; in the UK, this was thought to be 57 per cent in 2007. Although a 2:1 degree is still thought to be the 'gold standard' and used as a minimum requirement by 64 per cent of employers, university degrees of variable quality mean that qualifications alone are becoming less effective for initial screening. Blue-chip companies are increasingly using tests of numeracy, logical reasoning, literacy and verbal reasoning, which recruiters believe differentiate graduates with the highest potential.

That is not to say that g is now uncontroversially the psychometric test of choice in employment contexts. There are several areas of resistance. Firstly, performance on a test does not necessarily reflect intelligence or the test-taker's best possible performance, but may depend on whether the individual is interested in doing well, where they focus their attention and how much effort they expend. This leads to the distinction between typical and maximal performance. Rather than focusing on predicting someone's maximal behaviour, like most tests of cognitive ability, some argue that we should focus on finding out how a person typically performs a task in the actual job environment (Klehe and Anderson 2005). Later sections in this chapter consider the role of personality tests as one way of predicting typical behaviour.

A second development is in tests measuring different kinds of 'intelligence'. This includes dimensions of creative and emotional intelligence which cannot be captured by linguistically-based psychometric tests, but which some now argue affect many aspects of work performance (Weisinger 1998). Tacit knowledge, which represents practical knowledge of 'how' to do a job and is inferred from experience rather than academically acquired, has also received attention, especially in non-routine and unstructured jobs, such as management (Sternberg *et al.* 1995). Tacit knowledge also underlies the increasing use of situational judgement tests, which we consider later under performance-based methods.

Finally, as shown in Table 4.1, cognitive ability testing suffers from high subgroup differences in predictive validity; i.e. it has adverse impact on members of minority racial groups. Even though the reliability, validity and utility of cognitive ability testing have all been shown – that is, they are free from any bias – their use is a liability to employers who are concerned with maintaining a diverse workforce. Different applicant groups, for example Caucasian, Hispanic, Asian and African Americans, tend to score differently on these tests, which can lead to substantially different hiring rates, especially as organisations become more selective (i.e. hire fewer applicants or increase their cut scores on selection methods). In the US, federal law has battled with the issue of minority group preference in hiring and university entrance admissions and whether selection procedures should be race-neutral or race-conscious (see, for example, Kravitz 2008).

Internationally, the debate has tended to recommend careful design and validation of tests for particular groups (men/women, racial/cultural groups) to provide norm-referenced testing. If we remember the culturally specific element of intelligence (crystallised intelligence), though, we might question whether Western-designed tests are appropriate for other cultures' understanding of ability. Many multinational organisations face such issues when selecting staff who can work in any part of the world. There are interesting, unresolved dilemmas here with respect to culture-free and valid testing, as articulated by Searle (2003a, p.189). Should we aim for generic measures which tap into fluid (cultural-neutral) intelligence, or should we acknowledge the importance of cultural differences in what abilities are valued and develop different tests for different parts of the world? Another alternative may be that multinationals devise their own tests, which are valid for predicting performance in specific roles which transcend geographical boundaries.

PERSONALITY

Personality is a non-cognitive characteristic. With respect to the value of personality tests, there is continuing debate about fakeability, generally low predictive validity (Table 4.1), and even about the very existence of such a thing as personality (see, for example, Dilchert *et al.* 2006). Despite this, there has been a resurgence of interest focused especially on the Five Factor Model or the 'Big Five' dimensions. This claims that personality differences between people can be explained by five dimensions – extraversion, conscientiousness, agreeableness, neuroticism or emotional stability, and openness to experience (Costa and McCrae 1992). One of these in particular – conscientiousness – has emerged as a valid predictor of many aspects of work performance. This combines hard work, thoroughness, self-control and dependability, and is shown to have higher validity when used to predict pro-social aspects of work performance (also known as discretionary behaviour), such as altruism and (inversely) turnover or theft (Salgado 2002).

The most recent summaries conclude that personality tests are valid and useful when developers pay attention to possible moderators, such as social desirability effects or the specific task contexts which are being predicted (Viswesvaran *et al.* 2007). For instance, there are a number of studies showing that the dimensions of extraversion, agreeableness and neuroticism predict customer service behaviours but that in sales environments (closing a deal, for example), agreeableness may be a disadvantage (Liao and Chuang 2004).

Another application is in the use of personality tests to predict team performance. The aggregated score of team members on some of the Big Five personality dimensions, including the score of team leaders, is related to how well the team works together. Personality explains findings that homogeneous groups are more cohesive, while those which are heterogeneous are better at problem solving (Moynihan and Peterson 2004).

Ones *et al.* (2007) summarised the findings from accumulated validity studies and showed that the Big Five personality dimensions predict performance best for customer service, sales and managerial occupations. Although faking is a possibility, well-designed personality tests are most useful when used in combination with other information about the person and for specific work contexts. They also have lower adverse impact on women or racial minority groups than cognitive ability tests, which is one reason given for their increased use alongside other methods (Shackleton and Newell 1997).

Despite these developments, the debate about the role of personality testing in selection has continued, with prominent researchers arguing from both sides of the fence. The most recent exchange occurred over two 2007 issues of the prestigious journal *Personnel Psychology* (see Morgeson *et al.* 2007; Ones *et al.* 2007; Tett and Christiansen 2007).

Newer types of measures based on personality and other non-cognitive psychological constructs are also emerging. Two deserve mention here. First, emotional intelligence describes an individual's personal and social competence in managing their own and others' emotions, and is thought to be especially suited to predicting performance in roles requiring interpersonal interaction and leadership qualities (Zeidner *et al.* 2004). A second development is in the use of personality traits to form compound traits which are essentially custom-made personality measures based on combinations of traits designed to predict job-relevant behaviour in a specific context. These offer higher levels of predictive validity. Integrity, for example, which is often rated by employers as one of the most important employee characteristics, is made up of measures of hostility, impulsiveness, trust and dutifulness; these have been used to predict dishonest behaviour with high validity. Other compound scales have been designed for predicting customer service, stress tolerance, violence and managerial potential (see Ones *et al.* 2005).

BIOGRAPHICAL INFORMATION

Another non-cognitive characteristic is biographical information or biodata, where applicants describe retrospectively their past experience and work history. The assumption is that performance on past jobs predicts how someone will behave in future job situations, as it reflects underlying personal competencies such as attitudes or motivation. Application forms designed to collect biodata tend to be used by the majority of organisations as their initial screening device, and are now commonly found online (Hill and Barber 2005).

In general, biodata has moderate to high predictive validity for predicting tenure and performance (Reilly and Chao 1982). 'Hard', verifiable items, such as success in educational or occupational pursuits, tend to be more valid than 'soft' items related to values or aspirations, which are liable to faking (Lautenschlager 1994). Selectors must also avoid using information haphazardly without consideration of the important qualities to be judged for the job open-ing. The general principle behind making biodata job-relevant involves a process called 'cri-terion keying' – linking responses to each item with either high- and low-performing groups of employees and being able to specify what responses are the most desirable. Furnham (1997), for example, explains that items which showed an applicant's emphasis on financial responsibility, early family responsibility and stability were all good differentiators of good and bad insurance salesmen.

Instruments known as weighted application blanks or biographical information blanks make the weighting of important items more objective and may reduce adverse impact against protected groups (Chapman and Webster 2003). However, focusing on past accom-plishments is clearly suited only to those with experience, which excludes much of the youth applicant pool. This is one reason why many graduate recruitment schemes are designed with a view to focusing on personal competencies rather than experience. Similarly, many organ-isations use qualifications as a way of screening out a large number of applicants, for exam-ple by increasing the minimum level of qualifications required, from non-degree to degree. However, the requirement of a university degree may bear no relation to the knowledge, skills, abilities and personality characteristics actually required to do the job. For similar rea-sons, recent legislation addressing age and disability discrimination in the UK would place any items from which this information could be inferred (e.g. age) at risk of legal challenge; i.e. the selection method would adversely impact particular subgroups, such as older or dis-abled applicants. Practices such as only accepting candidates who are 'first jobbers' or those who have graduated within a restricted number of years, which can be inferred from biodata, would all be considered discriminatory.

PERFORMANCE-BASED METHODS

The third type of individual difference targeted by selection methods is performance itself. Performance-based tests and simulations focus on replicating a set of behaviours required on the job rather than an underlying psychological characteristic. The focus is on measuring present performance in order to predict future performance, although methods taking this approach can reflect varying degrees of complexity and physical fidelity to the actual tasks to be performed on the job, as shown in Table 4.1.

Work samples or job simulations are samples of the job, so represent 'high-fidelity' meth-ods which focus primarily on assessing current skills and performance of actual tasks – what a person can actually do rather than what they 'know'. Unsurprisingly, compared to cognitive and non-cognitive measures, these methods have higher validity and less adverse impact for non-traditional candidates (e.g. women, minority ethnic groups) (Schmitt and Mills 2001). Users, including managers and candidates, are generally more favourable towards perfor-mance-based methods. Selectors tend to pay more attention to observed behavioural infor-mation about a candidate than self-report data derived from personality or biodata, and candidates benefit from a realistic preview of the job itself. In a direct comparison of the psy-chometric qualities of a job simulation versus cognitive test for selecting insurance agents, Schmitt (2003) showed that while the simulation had lower validity (.36 versus .46 for the cognitive test), a higher proportion of capable minority individuals were selected using the simulation. Box 4.2 outlines the role simulation which was developed by Schmitt for these customer service agents.

Situational judgement tests have been called 'low-fidelity' simulations or 'white collar work samples' (Muchinsky 1986). These typically ask applicants to select from several possi-ble behavioural responses for a question about a work situation. This is essentially a test of judgement, which emerged originally as a measure of tacit knowledge or knowledge acquired through experience to complete everyday tasks. As there is no absolute correct answer, responses may vary depending on how the questions are designed, revealing some uncer-tainty about what is actually being measured. Ployhart and Erhart (2003) showed that asking

Box 4.2: HRM in practice

Increasing realism through performance-based methods

Job simulations

Schmitt (2003) describes a role-play simulation which replicates a typical day in the life of a service representative at an insurance company. Typical tasks were questions from customers about insurance rates and the various coverage options and products available to current or potential customers. A computer program first provided candidates with information about the company, how they should handle customer calls, and how to use several computerised databases to obtain information for customers. The candidates also had access to a policy-and-procedures manual and reference charts. Candidates had 30 minutes to review the material and to examine an abbreviated version of the customer database. The assessment began when two trained assessors made a series of 11 customer calls to the applicants. To respond appropriately to these calls, the applicants needed to draw together the information available to them, including the computerised databases, so that they could provide appropriate answers to the 'customer' queries. The assessors each used detailed scripts and took turns in playing the role of customer with the candidates. The assessor who was not role-playing listened to the conversation and took detailed notes.

Situational judgement tests

Lievens and Coetsier (2002) describe a video-based physician–patient situational judgement test for medical school admissions in Belgium. Scripts were written and verified by subject matter experts (professors) based on the identification of critical incidents, and videos were filmed with semi-professional actors, with the involvement of experienced physicians. In a follow-up study (Lievens *et al.* 2005), this test was shown to have validity for predicting medical school performance where interpersonal skill was important (e.g. situations involving patient interaction).

Situational interview

Maurer (2006) describes an engineering company's interview of technically qualified applicants for entry-level jobs. The aim of the interview was to assess their tendency to act in ways that 'fit' expected actions in critical job situations consistent with the values, goals and culture of the organisation and the work group. Incumbent project engineers created the following project management dilemma and rating criteria using a behaviourally anchored five-point scale:

> Suppose that you are in charge of a large-scale equipment installation project that must be completed on time to avoid significant penalties for exceeding the expected due date. The six-month-long project is now about 75 per cent completed and your PERT analysis indicates that, at best, it will be finished about two or three days ahead of schedule. However, an installation supervisor who works for you has just informed you that there may be a delay in material delivery that could add 7–10 working days to the project. What would you do to deal with this situation?

▶

1 = Poor. Ignore the situation since it is only a potential problem. Be prepared to deal with it when/if you hear that the delay is actually going to occur.

3 = Acceptable. Tell the supervisor that you expect him or her to deal with the problem. Remind the supervisor of the completion date and make it clear that you expect it to be met and that you want to be kept appraised of the situation.

5 = Excellent. Meet with the supervisor ASAP to determine the exact nature of the potential problem and formulate a plan for preventing or dealing with it. Set a follow-up procedure to make sure that the plan is being carried out.

The two points without specific anchors (i.e. the 2 and 4 points on the scale) would be used to evaluate answers that do not conform with all parts of the behavioural anchors. For instance, a response such as, 'Since it is not yet a problem, I would simply tell the supervisor to deal with it' would be a level 2 response since it contains parts of both the 1 and 3 anchors but does not comply with the full text of either.

people what they 'would do' in a certain situation tended to tap behavioural intentions, personality and past behaviour; asking what they 'should do' tapped job knowledge and cognitive ability. It may also be that 'would do' questions are more open to response distortion or faking – this remains an unresolved issue. Nevertheless, they have generally high validity, low subgroup differences, distinctiveness from other measures of past experience and job knowledge, and benefit from evolving delivery formats. New developments allowing multimedia, such as video-based clips, are better able to portray dilemmas or conflict encounters. As these become more powerful in representing the 'reality' of work, they may be able to increase fidelity for the assessment of judgement, prioritisation, decision making or diagnostic skills (Olson-Buchanan and Drasgow 2005) (see Box 4.2 for some examples).

Finally, structured interviews involve situational or behaviourally based assessments. The vast literature on the use of interviews for recruitment and selection highlights its various roles; e.g. as a way of selling the organisation to applicants or to prescreen applicants on minimum requirements. While the former involves a considerable amount of negotiation and subjective interaction – something we return to later in the chapter – the latter is based on simple, verifiable questions and is now frequently carried out by telephone. When interviews are used to assess more complex individual qualities, such as personality, knowledge, social skills or values which may or may not fit with the organisation, the need for reliable, valid techniques becomes much more apparent.

In short, structured interviews show high predictive validity (Table 4.1). Some examples of how structure can be introduced are by using a critical-incident-based job analysis for designing the questions, using multiple, trained interviewers and raters, minimising any use of prior information, such as applicant test scores, or limiting follow-up, prompting or elaboration.

With respect to our current interest in assessing performance, the use of questions based on hypothetical situations (situational interviews), past behaviour or experience (behavioural interviews) or direct job knowledge questions (either knowledge of facts or of procedures) provide the greatest potential in terms of psychometric quality (see Box 4.2 for an example). Like situational judgement tests, these do not directly measure an applicant's ability to do the job so they have lower fidelity to the job than work samples or simulations. Interview questions are usually tied to specific competencies which have been identified in the job analysis, however, and this emphasis on job relevance has been found to allow assessors to focus more on knowledge, skills, abilities and other qualities more directly linked to actual performance rather than relying on inferences about underlying characteristics. Structured interviews are not correlated with cognitive ability or personality tests, so it has been argued that companies can significantly enhance the validity of their selection methods by adding a structured interview to their hiring process (Huffcutt and Youngcourt 2007).

MIXED APPROACHES

The emphasis on behaviour is also visible in the competency movement. Competencies are transferable personal qualities, such as teamworking or business awareness, which draw from a range of skills, abilities, traits, job knowledge, experience and other qualities needed to perform a job effectively. Service-orientation for example, includes personality characteristics such as courtesy, consideration and tact (Hogan *et al.* 1984) but also behaviours displayed towards customers and colleagues during the service delivery process (Baydoun *et al.* 2001). The focus here is on behavioural outputs – individuals' achievements or what they should be able to do. In theory, therefore, different combinations of underlying psychological characteristics may achieve the same outputs (i.e. display competence in the job), which is why the focus is more on performance than the underlying cognitive or non-cognitive construct.

Of growing interest are 'future-oriented' behavioural competencies which go beyond immediate person–job fit. A typical example is in the selection of managers with leadership potential. Financial services firm HBOS uses a single behavioural competency framework based on 'leadership commitment' to guide selection across 18 different graduate schemes (e.g. HR, finance, IT, actuarial, corporate banking) and a range of methods, including online application forms, numerical and verbal reasoning tests, a telephone interview and teamwork and business scenario exercises (*People Management*, 4 October 2007).

Finally, an amalgam of many of these approaches is reflected in assessment centres which focus on a series of situational exercises designed to reveal various behaviourally based performance dimensions (Thornton and Mueller-Hanson 2004). As they use multiple methods, multiple assessors and systematic scoring procedures for integrating candidate data, they are thought to provide good validity for many occupations. They have high favourability both with managers and candidates because of their face validity (their appearance of measuring job-related factors), and the range of exercises ensures lower adverse impact against underrepresented groups. Some concern has been expressed about what assessment centres are actually measuring, despite the formalised systems and scoring. One critical account of graduate assessment centres describes a high degree of active, impression management by candidates, especially by those who are identified as 'stars' (the most employable candidates on paper), or the 'players' who were able to produce 'flashes of the appropriate behavioural competencies' (Brown and Hesketh, 2004, p.173). There was also inevitable subjectivity on the part of assessors whose evaluations of candidates might be based not on the objective test scores, but on performance in coffee breaks or even opinions formed when 'watching from afar'. From a more psychometric slant, careful attention to how assessors are trained and how they conduct their final evaluations, as well as to the design of the exercises themselves, is essential for improving reliability and maximising the potential validity of this approach (Lievens and Klimoski 2001). Given their high cost, though, they are likely to have utility only for the highest skilled, and more valuable, potential employees; for example, managers or professionals.

Summary of trends

From the review so far, we can detect several important trends in selection practice which build on the four indicators of psychometric quality.

- *More reliable and valid assessment tools.* This can be achieved, for example, by: conducting detailed job analyses, introducing structure and standardisation, training assessors, carrying out validation studies, and making more use of statistical aggregation and correction techniques, like meta-analysis, across validity studies to increase the precision of the prediction task (for a review see Sackett and Lievens 2008). Advances in these areas have resulted in increased confidence in the validity of many selection methods.

■ *Greater use of high validity/low adverse impact assessment tools.* As seen in Table 4.1, biodata, structured behavioural and situational interviewing, situational judgement tests, work samples and assessment centres have lower differential subgroup validity; i.e. they are less likely to adversely impact non-traditional applicant groups. Many selection processes use multiple methods in order to increase validity and lower adverse impact. For an example applied to call centre agents which combines biodata, psychometric cognitive or non-cognitive tests, and situational judgement tests see Konradt *et al.* (2003).

■ *Increasing importance of assessing non-cognitive qualities.* Across all types of jobs, interest has grown in a wider spectrum of behaviours, such as organisational citizenship or adaptability. The challenge has been to design valid tools to target these qualities. Some personality tests have been shown to be good predictors of this type of behaviour, and situational interviews can be designed to assess behaviours such as helping colleagues or volunteering (Latham and Skarlicki 1995).

■ *Increasing use of bespoke simulations.* These provide valid behavioural indicators of qualities relevant to a particular job or organisation, along with low adverse impact and high user acceptability. These organisationally specific approaches reflect a growing strategic orientation which links selection to wider competencies, not just job-specific skills, which are essential for ensuring competitive advantage and dealing with strategic pressures, such as restructuring. Searle (2003a) argues:

> the use of these tools reflects an increasing sophistication and confidence among human resource professionals, who see the adoption of more complex and rigorous assessment and development practices as demonstrating this professional group's pivotal place in helping to shape organizations for the future. (p.226)

■ *Online delivery of assessment.* This affects psychometric quality in various ways. Thirty per cent of UK organisations, and more among multinationals, report that they use online selection in some form (CIPD 2007), citing benefits like reaching a wider applicant pool, testing at a distance, and being able to confirm personality profiles usually gained through the 'gut-feel' of the interview (*People Management,* October 2007). Predictive validity and positive applicant reactions have been reported (Bartram 2000), especially for high-fidelity situational and behavioural assessments of performance, although questions remain about security, equality of access, and the quality of applicants (Anderson 2003).

What do organisations actually do?

Psychometric principles of good practice in the design and administration of tests are endorsed by professional psychological and HR associations in various countries. Whether employers pay heed to these recommendations, though, can be pieced together from various studies. Two of the most recent surveys of practice in the UK are summarised in Table 4.2. Consistent with past surveys across different countries (e.g. Ryan *et al.* 1999), the CIPD 2007 survey showed continuing reliance on interviews (generally a low-validity method), but over half of UK organisations (63 per cent) structured these around competency-based questions, which indicates a move towards questions based on systematic job analysis. The figures for psychometric tests of ability and personality show that three-quarters of companies use these in some way, and 18–29 per cent use them frequently. Leading

Table 4.2 Selection methods used by UK employers

CIPD Recruitment, Retention and Turnover Survey 2007[a]	Frequently use	Use in some way
Interviews (general/biographical/based on CV)	77	92
Structured interviews (panel)	58	88
Competency-based interviews	63	86
Tests for specific skills	29	80
General ability tests	26	72
Literacy and/or numeracy tests	25	70
Personality/aptitude tests	18	56
References	17	45
Assessment centres	16	47
Group exercise (e.g. role playing)	10	46
Online tests	9	30

Workplace Employment Relations Survey 2004[b]	Ever/routinely use performance/competency tests?	Use informal methods to fill vacancy
SME (private, <250 employees in UK)	40	79
Large enterprise (private, 250+ employees in UK)	50	76
Public sector	70	44
Managers/senior officials	39	68
Professionals	25	50
Associate professional/technical	19	50
Administrative/secretarial	41	40
Skilled trades	14	75
Caring, leisure, personal services	10	67
Sales/customer service	16	73
Process, plant, machine operatives	11	80
Routine unskilled	12	75

Note: 'Informal methods' include direct approaches to candidates, speculative applications, referrals and word of mouth.

[a] n=905 [b] Workplaces with more than 10 employees; n=2024 managers (see Kersley et al. 2006).

companies are more likely to use personality tests, for example 40 per cent of Fortune 100 companies, all of the top 100 in the UK (Rothstein and Goffin 2006) and those with more professional/managerial vacancies (Wolf and Jenkins 2006). Beagrie (2005) estimates that two-thirds of medium–large organisations use some type of psychometric test. Other studies show that 20 per cent of US companies use tests of cognitive ability, less than in the UK (Salgado and Anderson 2002), which is thought to be a sign of their low user acceptability and associated legal problems.

The WERS 2004 survey showed that performance-based and competency tests were used at some point by 70 per cent of public sector organisations compared to 50 per cent and 40 per cent of private sector large enterprises and SMEs, respectively. When asked if they were routinely used for particular occupations, these were most likely for managerial and administrative/secretarial positions. This may reflect the use of personal competency methods for management (e.g. application forms or interviews designed to assess leadership qualities or business awareness) and work samples/achievement tests for administrative/secretarial positions (e.g. for clerical tasks, or data manipulation). Wolf and Jenkins (2006) suggest that their use is more common in organisations which do more to ensure that recruitment and hiring practices are non-discriminatory and encourage diversity, a feature which is generally found in the public sector.

Also notable from Table 4.2 is the strong reliance on informal methods, such as responding to speculative applications and word of mouth. This was less likely in the public sector and for managerial/professional positions, but even here approximately half of all respondents admitted filling vacancies in this way. Informality was most likely in lower-skilled, elementary occupations.

Taking this evidence together, informal selection methods appear to dominate in most organisations, but there is some indication that larger organisations with a dedicated HR function, and especially those in the public sector, are more likely to adopt a psychometric approach, especially for managerial or skilled/technical positions.

Explaining practice

Selection is more than the application of assessment techniques. It is now accepted that selection can be thought of from at least three other perspectives which take into account the organisational and social hiring context (see also Iles 1999): (1) selection as 'best fit' for the organisation (as opposed to a normative, 'best practice' model); (2) selection as an interactive decision process involving multiple stakeholders; and (3) selection as discourse, where power and interests dominate what happens more than the validity and utility of assessment methods.

(1) SELECTION AS 'BEST FIT': THE ORGANISATION'S PERSPECTIVE

In the study of HRM generally, there is often an assumption of similar needs across sectors, organisations, occupations and even countries, which leads to 'best practice' guidelines, such as those of the psychometric model. These guidelines, however, are formulated almost completely in a vacuum. Valid methods are held always to have high utility, but this assumes a low selection ratio (i.e. a low number hired relative to the number of applicants), that the cost of poor selection is high (as it may be in a top management or skilled position), and that the top performers can always be selected (i.e. the 'best' actually accept the job offer). The reality of staffing is that these conditions are not always met.

Table 4.3 summarises a range of factors which shape selection practice. These are organised using Klehe's (2004) distinction between economic and social pressures as a way of illustrating the effects of the wider context of selection decisions and allow us to make predictions about when sophisticated (i.e. strategic/psychometric) approaches are likely to be adopted.

With respect to economic pressures, the higher the initial cost and development required, and the more dependent the organisation is on the approval of owners concerned with short-term financial impact, the less likely it will be to adopt sophisticated methods. Short-term resource considerations (e.g. the cost of more structured behavioural interviewing, training inexperienced assessors, relieving managers for multi-method assessment days, or evaluating procedures) often outweigh the longer-term potential returns. This is why competency-based methods are more common for managers (Table 4.2). Similarly, the fewer applicants the organisation has to choose from and the more dependent it is on filling the vacant post quickly, the less likely the organisation is to invest heavily in its selection procedure. This may be the position of many SMEs (as shown in Table 4.2), organisations located in suburban or rural areas, or sectors where there is high demand for key skills and skills shortages. The informality of unsolicited correspondence and face-to-face contact may be a more rational option for attracting suitable candidates where there is a small pool of qualified applicants or where the position must be filled quickly.

Social pressures are divided into two types in Table 4.3: legislative/institutional and stakeholder pressure. We consider the role of stakeholders in the next section. For now, it is

Table 4.3 Factors influencing selection practice and decisions

Economic pressures

Short-term financial impact
  Skills supply and labour market tightness
  Patterns of employment and turnover
  Organisation size
  Life cycle of the organisation
  Long-term versus short-term performance orientation
  Ownership (multinational, single owner, shareholder pressures)
  Presence of HR
  Experience/training of selectors
  Time resource constraints

Long-term financial impact
  High skill (managerial/professional) occupations/vacancies
  Career potential of position (internal labour markets, investment in training)
  Competition and rate of change
  Market segment/differentiation strategy
  Organisation values

Social pressures

Legislative/institutional
  Regulatory environment
  Visibility/accountability of organisation
  National culture
  Entry standards/statutory requirements

Other stakeholders
  Users
  Applicants
  Industry/profession
  Test developers

possible to identify the direct effects of employment legislation on hiring practice. Employers are increasingly required by law in many countries to pay attention to psychometric principles. Public sector organisations are especially affected. In an examination of 400 Canadian federal selection discrimination cases, Terpstra and Kethley (2002) showed that the government sector was more likely to have had litigation brought against it than any other sector. This kind of accountability and risk encourages the use of multiple methods, greater standardisation, and monitoring of selection procedures in order to ensure diversity (Jewson and Mason 1986; Pearn 1993) – a finding which is supported by the data in Table 4.2. US federal legislation also goes further in placing a burden on employers to justify the job-relatedness of all selection measures, and this is one of the reasons why psychometric testing is used more in some European countries (the UK, Spain and Portugal) than in the US (Salgado *et al.* 2003). UK employers, conversely to those in the US, perceive the rigour of a testing approach as a 'precautionary measure' which can protect them from legal challenge (Wolf and Jenkins 2006).

In other ways, though, the institutional context in Europe, Australia and Asia is more restrictive in terms of labour relations, with greater reliance on recruitment from educational systems or internal labour markets. Huo *et al.* (2002) speculated that a greater focus on individual candidate fit with cultural values in Australia was related to a recent tradition of joint consultation practice between employees and employers at the level of the enterprise.

In Box 4.3, we use this framework to illustrate the pressures faced in three different industry examples – hotels, construction companies and voluntary sector organisations. In these

Box 4.3: HRM in practice

Selection in three sectors

Economic pressures	Selection	Social pressures
Hotels		
Labour market (competition, shortages) *Short-term pressures to fill vacancies* (casualisation, high turnover) *Market segmentation* (chain, deluxe) *Resource pressures* (only chains have centralised HR/train selectors)	*Short-termist approach* Informal methods targeted at local transient labour market/unpredictability *Longer-term approach* Strategic alignment (high-quality localised approach, combines standardisation with informal networks) Emphasis on staff retention, permanent positions, person–culture fit	*Applicant perceptions* (low pay, poor prospects, antisocial hours, hard work, isolated locations)
Construction (manual and skilled/technical workers)		
Workflow (project-/network-based, local site decentralisation, flexibility due to design/supply variations) *Project ownership* (network of subcontractors and professionals, local focus) *Labour market* (skill shortages, limited training, competency-based skill certification, voluntary) *Resources* (working to contract, time, cost) *Change* (rapid technological change, changing markets, multiskilling)	Larger firms more formalised ('skills identity card', HR functions) Local variation even where formalised procedures existed (procedures called 'raindances') Strong emphasis on probationary days (work simulations) and site-manager local networks (time-served on other jobs) After technical ability, value honesty, conscientiousness, adaptability	*Applicant perceptions* (dangerous work, masculine culture, antisocial hours) *Industry* (Construction Industry Training Board common accreditation) *Customers* (pressures for improved quality, cost reduction) *Firm-specific demands* (work against industry standards) *Site-manager* (autonomous at local level) *Legislation* (Health and Safety)
Voluntary sector (front-line care and social services)		
Resources (insecure funding, 'full cost recovery' problematic, increased scope due to work transition from public services, increasing need to staff new business processes and functions) *Labour market* (competition with private/public sector, shortage of high skill/graduates) *High attrition/turnover* (unrealistic expectations)	Person–organisation fit essential Social process/attraction strategies (ensure value congruence, provide applicant power/choices, realistic job/organisation previews) Need for rebranding to attract wider applicant pool (flexible working, work–life balance, satisfaction, 'altruism payoff', underutilised graduates)	*Applicant perceptions* (uncompetitive salaries, insecurity, high emotional demands, women's work, need value-based high commitment, skills underused) *Public perception* (unprofessional, voluntary (unpaid), not a career, need for greater transparency)

Sources: Lockyer and Scholarios 2004, 2007; Nickson *et al.* 2008

situations, cost, time, and recruitment crises may be more salient than reliability and validity (Johns 1993; Muchinsky 2004). We return to these examples again in the next section.

(2) SELECTION AS AN INTERACTIVE DECISION PROCESS

Social pressures can also originate from other stakeholders in the hiring process. This includes the selectors (managers, HR) who implement the procedures, institutional bodies which set guidelines for entry into occupations or exert influence over assessment (e.g. professional associations), and applicants themselves. Searle (2003b) has argued that, with the growing use of online testing, test developers, whose interests are quite distinct from those of organisations and applicants, have become an increasingly powerful stakeholder because of the access they have to the results of testing processes. From this perspective, hiring is not just about the organisation choosing the right assessment tools for its needs, but involves an interactive process of information exchange and negotiation – a series of 'social episodes' (Herriot 1989) – between the organisation and its wider environment. This impacts two general areas.

How methods are perceived by stakeholders

In Table 4.1, we introduced the idea of user acceptability as a counterweight to the psychometric ideals of reliability and validity. This refers to whether the method is perceived as credible, and hence whether managers or practitioners will actually use it, as well as how it is perceived by the candidates who are exposed to it. Performance-based methods are more favourable as users can clearly see the relevance of the assessment for the job itself. This means these methods are more likely to be adopted and used appropriately than less transparent, psychometric tests.

The participation of users in the development of selection methods is also important. Millmore (2003), in his exploration of what makes recruitment and selection strategic, talks about the involvement of multiple stakeholders as equal partners in the process and the involvement of all levels of management and peers in the design of the process (e.g. defining person specifications, panel interviews). This should lead to greater consensus about the qualities being sought and hence more reliable assessment.

Applicants, too, should be considered equal partners. Schuler (1993) argued that applicants have the right to be treated with dignity, provided with information about what is expected of them and on their performance, and involved in the process by providing their consent and even their own input. Millmore suggested providing, at least, information packs and feedback on performance at all stages of the selection process. Candidates should also have their privacy respected, for example in questions asked in application forms or interviews, and the right to appeal against decisions which they think are unfair. This introduces the idea of perceptions of fair treatment, or what is sometimes called procedural justice (Cropanzano and Wright 2003). Some suggestions to improve fairness perceptions are to use a combination of methods, or modify how tests are administered. In general, research on applicant perceptions of fairness has shown that, consistently, across Europe, North America and Asia, the rankings for the most to least favourable methods are: (1) interviews, (2) CVs, (3) work sample tests, (4) biographical information, (5) written ability tests, (6) personal references, (7) personality tests, (8) honesty/integrity tests, (9) personal contacts and (10) graphology (Anderson and Witvliet 2008).

Going even further than this, some would argue that individuals entering a position should be able to influence the job demands rather than being fitted for the job requirements, thus making selection a truly two-way process. Work sample tests, for example, tend to imply that there is agreement about a single correct way to perform the job; however, candidates could be given freedom to demonstrate other ways of performing the job successfully rather

Box 4.4: HRM in practice

Has the power shifted to graduates?

A study by Reed Consulting (2007) found that 22 per cent of 2,500 graduates surveyed refused a job offer because they were unhappy with an organisation's recruitment process. Sixty-six per cent of job applicants did not receive a response – making potential talent feel disregarded and devalued – and this was especially the case in the financial services sector which receives high volumes of applications. Companies run the risk of losing qualified candidates to competitor organisations. The study also found that:

- more than one-third of UK graduates avoid products and services offered by a company that disappointed them in the recruitment process;
- 90 per cent of dissatisfied candidates tell family and friends about their bad experiences, with serious implications for damaging both the consumer and employer brand;
- failure to respond to a recruitment hotline phone call in 30 seconds results in 29 per cent of applicants hanging up.

Purcell *et al.* (2002) showed that, as a way of dealing with skill shortages, leading employers were doing more to attract non-traditional graduates. As well as identifying skills and competencies for specific jobs, they also

- encouraged underrepresented groups to apply;
- actively sold themselves as equal opportunities employers;
- established expectations at the recruitment stage (culture, career opportunities);
- offered work experience to allow graduates to make choices;
- responded to the diversity of the workforce with work–life balance flexibility.

than confined to the taken-for-granted views which are demanded by the psychometric approach (Searle 2003a, p.233).

The important point in all of these arguments is that applicant exposure to the assessment method influences important outcomes – whether qualified applicants maintain interest in the job for which they are applying, whether they decide to continue to the next stage of assessment, whether they accept the job if offered or even whether the method has 'negative psychological effects', such as lowering self-esteem (Anderson and Goltsi 2006, p.237). Box 4.4 illustrates how applicant perceptions have impacted graduate recruitment.

How applicants perceive the job or organisation

As we saw in Chapter 3 on recruitment, negative impressions may be caused by uninformative websites; disinterested recruiters; long, complicated application processes; or any message which communicates undesirable images of the employer brand (Van Hoye and Lievens 2005). The early stages of selection can be used to build identification with the organisation and encourage only those who see a match with the values of the organisation to remain in the application process. In an example from a police force in an American Midwest city, the interview stage provided a realistic preview of the job and prompted some candidates to withdraw from the process (Ployhart *et al.* 2002). Of most relevance to organisations is how potential applicants perceive 'fit' between their own goals and what is offered by the job, including issues such as pay, working conditions, organisational values and reputation, and career options.

This is important for several reasons. Firstly, if some applicant groups withdraw from the process more frequently than others, then potentially qualified candidates who are required to meet skill gaps are excluded. This seems to be the case for graduates who are not pursuing voluntary sector jobs vacancies because of the perceptions of what the jobs offer (see Box 4.3).

Secondly, this exclusion may adversely impact members of minority groups, such as women or blacks. These applicants withdrew disproportionately from the American police selection process indicated above. This also harms diversity staffing targets, an issue of some concern to police forces in many parts of the world who consider being representative of the community as essential to good policing.

Finally, in some employment situations, the balance of power lies with applicants rather than the organisation; for instance, Box 4.4 illustrates the competition to attract the brightest gradates. An example of this was shown in Box 4.3 where it was shown that the voluntary sector suffers recruitment difficulties because it competes with both the private and public sector for specialists and graduates. In another example, the hospitality industry is often portrayed as being in competition with higher-paying, 'cleaner', more flexible, temporary, part-time work offered by the likes of the call centre industry. Tackling negative perceptions of potential applicants and the use of informal methods of selection may be better practice in these situations. Of course, problems of inequality, bias and limits on diversity which are associated with informality still have to be recognised.

A further purpose of selection is to build relationships between the organisation and future employees. The interview has high social validity for both managers and candidates as it allows two-way communication and a richer environment for both to establish congruence or person–organisation 'fit'. Roe and van den Berg's (2003) survey suggested that European employers prefer interviews for this reason. In a similar vein, British Telecom replaced external assessors with their own managers in the final interviews at their graduate assessment centre in order to 'interface with the candidates themselves' (*The Guardian*, 19 January 2008).

One last consequence of paying attention to social processes in selection is their 'socialisation impact' (Anderson 2001). Methods which allow both parties to establish 'fit' will lead to employees who are more likely to be satisfied in their jobs, more committed to the goals of the organisation, and less likely to leave. A clear application of this is provided by the voluntary sector example in Box 4.4. Thus, as well as establishing hurdles, selection informs, attracts and increases the commitment of applicants to the job and organisation as the relationship progresses.

(3) SELECTION AS DISCOURSE

A more radical view is that selection is a process which cannot easily be reduced to the quality of assessment tools and rational decision making. The reference to discourse relates to the idea that there are many different ways of talking about (i.e. describing and understanding) selection. The choice of which discourse we focus on at a particular point in time will vary; for example, some may value meritocracy and hence use a discourse which focuses on developing neutral assessment techniques which are reliable and valid (a psychometric discourse), while others are more concerned with mutual respect, treating applicants in an ethical way and building relationships of trust (a social process or decision-interactive discourse). These two examples, in fact, are often used to describe the quite different dominant discourses which guide actual selection practice in North America versus Europe, respectively (de Wolff 1993). These selection discourses have become accepted by the culture as a result of societal values and guiding principles, established for example through legislation. Other discourses also may develop within organisations, clusters of organisations or professions as a result of other powerful forces. This may explain why 'blue-chip' multinational companies, which project themselves as global market leaders or 'good employers', often lead the way in adopting the most sophisticated, expensive and psychometrically sound selection systems, in order to be seen to comply with 'good practice' as presented by respected external bodies (e.g. those promoting equal opportunities legislation or human resource professionalism). This view goes as far as to argue that selection discourses, such as strict psychometric measurement, can be used as a way of making the management of people more explicitly controllable, e.g. to further particular interests (Townley 1989).

We use two examples here to illustrate this perspective and how it challenges the psychometric model (see also Iles 1999). The first questions whether job suitability can be objectively reduced to an agreed set of individual knowledge, skills, abilities and traits.

The 'good' firefighter In one of the author's research studies, the qualities of a firefighter were mused over by the Fire Service's personnel officer. They have to be able to put up with long periods of monotony and boredom but can suddenly be faced with emotional and harrowing situations. In many ways, the job is now so procedural that things rarely go wrong (e.g. virtual reality of many of the city's buildings means that firefighters no longer enter smoke-filled buildings without knowing where they are going). In fact, they have to be able to follow instructions without questioning orders in what can be a militaristic culture. At the same time, they are looking for general ability and the ability to think strategically. As well as basic physical ability and practical tests, assessors are looking for evidence of person–culture fit (prior knowledge of the service, commitment to a career and serving the community), all of which is assessed through self-report questions on an application form (e.g. why do you want to become a firefighter?) and interviews with senior officers. How can this complexity of demands be reduced to behaviours appropriate for every situation? Assessors often cannot agree on the suitability of candidates, and use other shortcuts, such as appearance, to justify their decisions, even though they all go through assessor training. 'State of the art' for firefighter selection recommends a combination of cognitive/mechanical and interpersonal/emotional skills tests (Blair and Hornick 2005), but this 'all rounder' view may just be the latest construction of the 'good' firefighter, which contrasts to earlier beliefs that firefighters should be the 'bravest and strongest' (shown through physical ability), 'smartest' (cognitive testing), or have the 'right' person profile (personality testing). Some may argue that this is just another discourse of what is 'acceptable', reflecting society, and the historical and cultural influences of those who draw up the person specifications and make final decisions. The effects of this are illustrated in a study of a similar profession, police work, which showed how good performance is constructed in terms of a 'masculine crime fighting' discourse (as opposed to an equally valid service discourse which privileges skills associated with femininity) and prevents potentially qualified women from applying. (Dick and Nadin 2006)

The second example raises the question whether formalisation and legislation can ever eliminate the inherent subjectivity of hiring decisions. This challenges the assumption of the rational assessor.

Graduate assessment centres Despite multiple assessors and careful exercise design, assessment centres have been portrayed as 'politically charged contexts', 'largely uncontrollable and permeated with problems of meaning', and a 'conspiracy of distortion' between assessors who rank subjectively while hiding behind a 'façade of systematic and scientific professionalism' (Knights and Raffo 1990, p.37). Brown and Hesketh's (2004) analysis of attempts to measure 'soft' competencies at graduate assessment centres showed that even after training on diversity issues, assessors were still inclined to resort to first impressions or compare people to the existing management in the company. In 'washing-up sessions' some opinions held more sway than others (e.g. a particularly negative view of how one candidate described what she gained from her gap year) and simplistic heuristics were used to organise the information from each exercise about the candidates. Candidates were labelled 'stars', 'geeks', 'razors' and 'safe bets'. Value was attached to 'appearance, accent and appropriate behaviour' (p.161), tending to favour the social capital possessed by Oxbridge candidates, while finding ways to match these to the 'objectively defined' behavioural indicators.

Conclusions and implications for HRM

There has been a recent frenzy of activity to develop the most valid assessment tool for predicting a diverse range of work behaviours, with 'best practice' showing a gradual shift towards holistic assessments encompassing a mix of measures of cognitive, non-cognitive and performance qualities. The move to performance-based methods, with their lower adverse impact against underrepresented groups, is particularly notable, as this seems to have accommodated the trend towards diversity as a strategic direction, whether among large private multinationals or the more publicly accountable government sectors.

Beyond this, though, different ways of understanding selection have also gained strength. These expand on the non-rational, unplanned, informal, social and power bases of selection, leading to an alternative language for evaluating the outcomes of any hiring process. Diverse contexts dictate alternative logics from that of prediction or formality, suggesting more of a 'best fit' approach than a normative one. For instance, the employee attributes required may shift alongside an organisation's strategic goals, and firms facing staffing problems will shape their selection strategies in ways which they consider will attract the 'right type' of employees or enhance employee retention. The 'best practice' model of selection offered by the psychometric model assumes that the number of applicants exceeds the positions available, and that the best applicants will always accept the jobs they are offered. This is clearly not the case.

Selection can also be judged in terms of the quality of the social exchange between organisations and other stakeholders. The treatment of applicants, their perceptions and attitudes, take on a more important role in ensuring they find the job and organisation attractive and whether person–organisation 'fit' is achieved. Also important is the way that selection techniques are used to further interests which often are only tenuously linked to the psychometric paradigm's aspirations of objectivity and fairness. Each of these perspectives – 'best fit', social process and discourse – highlights the deficiencies of the psychometric model for achieving a comprehensive understanding of all aspects of the selection problem (cf. Herriot 1993; Iles 1999).

Within HRM, selection has been viewed as a core function essential for achieving key organisational outcomes; high performance, low levels of absenteeism and turnover, and high employee well-being and commitment have all been linked with 'selective hiring' (Storey 2007). As argued in several HRM texts (Legge 2005), however, the reality of strategic integration and practice seldom has matched the rhetoric, and this seems equally as applicable to the adoption of 'best practice' selection. Based on 'best fit' perspectives, expensive testing and bespoke assessment may be reserved for higher-value core employees that organisations wish to retain or those at senior levels (Kwiatkowski 2003).

From the psychometric perspective, HR professionals (or those responsible for selection) should serve a monitoring function, ensuring that assessment methods are designed appropriately with a view to current legislation and practice developments and that relevant performance criteria (broad as well as job-specific) are used. Methods should be reappraised often and based on more frequent and focused validation programmes, although all this assumes that HR and HR issues are afforded an appropriate status and influence within the organisation. Social process perspectives may add to this the need to ensure that all stakeholders' views are accommodated in the design if not implementation of the assessment, and that selectors are encouraged to think of the applicant groups they wish to attract as potentially powerful decision makers with their own views about the attractiveness of the organisation and the job. The increased devolution of HR functions to line managers may also suggest the need for an additional level of support in managing the complexities of the process (Whittaker and Marchington 2003), although in many organisations, such as SMEs, this is rarely available. Nevertheless, these issues become particularly crucial if we acknowledge the discourse perspective's warnings of how persistent subjectivity, vested interests and less politically neutral forces are able to obstruct the ideal of creating meritocratic selection systems.

CASE STUDIES

Methods designed to reveal a service or sales orientation now form the basis of many hiring processes used in call centres. Baldry *et al.* (2007) described the following call centre selection processes.

CASE STUDY 4.1

Moneyflow

Dora Scholarios

One call centre in the financial services sector, Moneyflow, dedicated 3 hours 20 minutes to each candidate for the position of customer adviser. At the time of this example, there was a vibrant employment market in the area and this call centre was competing against 15 other companies for qualified staff. The demand for staff was high, as many of those recruited often left after the two days' training. Recruitment consultants were used to pre-select candidates for the company to interview. This recruitment agency was chosen because, in comparison to other agencies used, it seemed to understand the business and skill specifications required by the company and provide higher-quality candidates.

Stages of selection

1. A general register of candidates was developed (few active call centre workers were available, given the buoyant employment situation for call centre work in the area).
2. Ads were placed locally and nationally, including in universities. Local ads for part-time work were aimed at encouraging returners to work.
3. Candidates were asked to complete work history, details of present employment, and a financial planning questionnaire (to eliminate credit risks). The company designed and validated a self-assessment application form for the call centre adviser role based on work profiling and critical incident methods. This captured five customer-oriented competencies (customer focus, fact finding, relating to customers, convincing, oral communication) and two related to contextual performance (independent facilitation, job dedication) (see Bywater and Green 2005). It also acted as a realistic job preview to inform candidates of the sales component of the job and act as a self-selection tool.

▶

4. Skills testing: tests of visual accuracy; spelling; key depressions; arithmetic; and alphanumeric skill. All these were provided by the company to the agency.

5. Interview (20–30 minutes) based on CV/work history. Sales skills were explored further in the interview.

6. Telephone role play: 'You are a CA in a travel service . . .' Looking for questioning and listening skills as well as selling/additional sales.

7. Recruitment consultants sent a list of pre-selected candidates to the company to select for a 1 hour interview with two team leaders. Depending on need, the agencies often put all candidates forward for interview without pre-selection.

Questions

1. What underlying psychological characteristics are being assessed at each stage?

2. Based on the information provided in Table 4.1, what do you think the overall psychometric quality of such a procedure might be? Take into account what you know about the criterion of successful performance for call centre agents, the use of both recruitment agencies and team leaders to carry out the assessment, and the wider labour market context of the call centre.

3. Is user acceptability an important factor in this selection process?

CASE STUDY 4.2

Thejobshop

Dora Scholarios

Thejobshop is a growing city-based, multi-business outsourced call centre, which operates on behalf of 15 external clients. Outsourcing is attractive to organisations which do not have any call centre expertise and has the advantage of being able to set up a call centre in a very short period of time. Pay also tends to be lower in an outsourced call centre. The staffing numbers involved in a contract can range from approximately 200 to 3. There is some variation, though, in the extent to which client businesses retain autonomy over their operations. At the one extreme are 'co-sourcing' accounts, notably in the high-value operations, where the business retains greater controls over the service provided. These provide operators with distinct e-mail addresses and corporate slogans. At the other extreme are lower-value accounts where Thejobshop completely manages the operations on behalf of the client.

These differences are reflected in how selection is managed. Thejobshop tries to keep the clients out of the selection process as much as possible as they feel they know what they are looking for, although some, like the blue-chip IT company, are more hands-on and want to shape the type of person employed to match their culture. Carco (a luxury car sales business) wants 'tans and teeth' and 'young happy and shiny' people, even though most of their customer base is older and would prefer someone older to speak to. They make regular visits on site.

The operations manager said:

We perhaps show the client a half dozen who we feel are right and let them comment. We're looking for 'basic core competencies', although we try to tailor them for each set of interviews, for each individual client. We give clients the opportunity to give us details

▶

of the competencies they are looking for. For example, we asked drinks supplier DrinksNow to supply us with a list of the competencies they were looking for. They gave us a piece of A4 with a list of eight points, that's all. A new financial sector client has identified their target customer group as 95 per cent female and mostly over the age of 35. They want the customer service agents to reflect this. The match between client, product and agent tends to happen naturally.

Agencies are used to prescreen on keyboard skills (paste and copy, data entry) and basic numerical and literacy skills because of the need to find people quickly, 60 people within days. If Thejobshop is given a few weeks' notice they place their own adverts in the press and control the process. This is preferable as agencies often are less discriminating and just want 'bums on seats to get their cut'. They also tend to prefer people with previous call centre experience as they will be aware of the shift systems and nature of the work, so it won't be a shock.

Entcomm

Dora Scholarios

Entcomm, located in a small ex-industrial town near Glasgow, provides telecommunications and entertainment services for a large US multinational company. The call centre handles inquiries, billing, payments, new accounts and repairs maintenance. During a recent period of high-volume recruitment for 150 customer service adviser (CSA) posts it has found difficulties finding flexible staff. They advertise in local further education colleges and universities, and especially target training courses in IT for women returners and over-50s. This addresses the problem of employing young part-timers (high turnover) while achieving some flexibility in staffing to cover fluctuations in business. The vacancies are for 12–20 hours per week (4–6 hours per shift), in some cases finishing at 12.45am, and the starting pay is £6 per hour.

There is a friend and family recruitment scheme where the employee receives £300 for a full-time member of staff found acceptable. Referrals still have to pass the tests, though. The first filtering comes from a tele-screen interview which gives an initial indication of whether the prospective CSA has the required telephone manner and whether the shift preferences are compatible with the business needs. Keyboard skills are tested at this stage, followed by two role-play exercises. These will involve one difficult customer (who may shout and scream) and one technical issue from a customer.

This procedure is outsourced to an agency who receive £350 per CSA they supply for the next stages of selection. The final interview is competency-based and conducted by team leaders and HR. A lot of emphasis here is put on why the recruits find this an attractive job, e.g. entertainment sector, no cold calling. The interviews also include questions about coping with stressful situations building on the role-play simulation. Existing employees talk about how they cope with difficult situations, and some are better than others. Jenny, an agent in her early twenties, commented 'screaming customers I can cope with . . . one day though it was a really patronising customer and it just threw me completely . . . it was just the straw that broke the camel's back – I actually got up off the seat one day and I threw a booklet'.

Cathy, who is in her fifties, was more resilient. 'I can let a customer scream away and let them rattle on until they are finished and then say now I'll help you . . . it's just my experience I suppose.'

▶

Questions

1. Examine the economic and social pressure impacting selection in both Thejobshop and Entcomm. (Use the framework provided in Box 4.3.)

2. Explain the 'balance of power' in the selection process between employers, candidates and other stakeholders in each of the call centres.

3. Do these call centres operate a selection process which follows the psychometric process? Explain your answer.

4. What would the discourse perspective say about the definition of the competent call centre employee in the three call centres (Moneyflow, Thejobshop and Entcomm)? How does this affect the process and outcomes of selection?

Bibliography

Anderson, N. (2001) 'Towards a theory of socialization impact. Selection as pre-entry socialization', *International Journal of Selection and Assessment*, Vol.9, Nos.1/2, pp.84–91.

Anderson, N. (2003) 'Applicant and recruiter reactions to new technology in selection: a critical review and agenda for future research', *International Journal of Selection and Assessment*, Vol.11, pp.121–36.

Anderson, N. and Goltsi, V. (2006) 'Negative psychological effects of selection methods: construct formulation and an empirical investigation into an assessment center', *International Journal of Selection and Assessment*, Vol.14, No.3, pp.236–55.

Anderson, N. and Witvliet, C. (2008) 'Fairness reactions to personnel selection methods: an international comparison between the Netherlands, the United States, France, Spain, Portugal, and Singapore', *International Journal of Selection and Assessment*, Vol.16, No.1, pp.1–13.

Association of Graduate Recruiters (2007) *The AGR Graduate Recruitment Survey 2007: Summer Review*, available at www.agr.org.uk

Baldry, C., Bain, P., Taylor, P. and Hyman, J. (2007) *The Meaning of Work in the New Economy*, Basingstoke: Palgrave Macmillan.

Bartram, D. (2000) 'Internet recruitment and selection: kissing frogs to find princes', *International Journal of Selection and Assessment*, Vol.8, pp.261–74.

Baydoun, R., Rose, D. and Emperado, T. (2001) 'Measuring customer service orientation: an examination of the validity of the customer service profile', *Journal of Business and Psychology*, Vol.15, No.4, pp.605–20.

Beagrie, S. (2005) 'How to excel at psychometric assessments', *Personnel Today*, 25 March, p.25.

Bertua, C., Anderson, N. and Salgado, J. (2005) 'The predictive validity of cognitive ability tests: a UK meta-analysis', *Journal of Occupational and Organizational Psychology*, Vol.78, No.3, pp.387–409.

Blair, M.D. and Hornick, C.W. (2005) 'Fire selection in the new millennium', Paper presented at the 29th Annual Conference of the International Public Management Association Assessment Council, Orlando, FL.

Brown, P. and Hesketh, A. (2004) *The Mismanagement of Talent*, Oxford: Oxford University Press.

Bywater, J. and Green, V. (2005) 'Can scorable application forms predict task and contextual performance in call centre work?', *Selection and Development Review*, Vol.20, No.6.

Carroll, J.B. (1993) *Human Cognitive Abilities: A Survey of Factor-Analytic Studies*, Cambridge: University of Cambridge Press.

Chapman, D.S. and Webster, J. (2003) 'The use of technologies in the recruiting, screening, and selection processes for job candidates', *International Journal of Selection and Assessment*, Vol.11, Nos.2–3, pp.113–120.

CIPD (2007) *Recruitment, Retention and Turnover Survey*, London: Chartered Institute of Personnel and Development.

Costa, P.T., Jr. and McCrae, R.R. (1992) 'Normal personality assessment in clinical practice: the NEO Personality Inventory', *Psychological Assessment,* Vol.4, pp.5–13.

Cropanzano, R. and Wright, T.A. (2003) 'Procedural justice and organizational staffing: a tale of two paradigms', *Human Resource Management Review,* Vol.13, pp.7–39.

Dick, P. and Nadin, S. (2006) 'Reproducing gender inequalities? A critique of realist assumptions underpinning personnel selection research and practice', *Journal of Occupational and Organizational Psychology,* Vol.79, No.3, pp.481–98.

Dilchert, S., Ones, D. S., Viswesvaran, C. and Deller, J. (2006) 'Response distortion in personality measurement: born to deceive, yet capable of providing valid assessments?' *Psychology Science,* Vol.48, pp.209–25.

Furnham, A. (1997) *The Psychology of Behaviour of Work,* Hove: Psychology Press.

Hamel, G. and Prahalad, C.K. (1989) 'Strategic intent', *Harvard Business Review,* pp.63–74.

Herriot, P. (1989) 'Selection as a social process', in M. Smith and I.T. Robertson (eds) *Advances in Selection and Assessment,* Chichester: Wiley, pp.171–78.

Herriot, P. (1993) 'Commentary: a paradigm bursting at the seams', *Journal of Organizational Behavior,* Vol.14, pp.371–75.

Hill, D. and Barber, L. (2005) *Is graduate recruitment meeting business needs?* Web audit, Institute for Employment Studies.

Hogan, R.T., Hogan, J. and Busch, A. (1984) 'How to measure service orientation', *Journal of Applied Psychology,* Vol.69, No.1, pp.167–73.

Huffcutt, A.I. and Youngcourt, S.S. (2007) 'Employment interviews', in D. Whetzel and G. Wheaton (eds), *Applied Measurement: Industrial Psychology in Human Resources Management,* New Jersey: Lawrence Earlbaum, pp.181–200.

Hunter, J.E. and Hunter, R.F. (1984) 'Validity and utility of alternative predictors of job performance', *Psychological Bulletin,* Vol.96, pp.72–98.

Huo, Y.P., Huang, H.G. and Napier, N.K. (2002) 'Divergence or convergence. A cross-national comparison of personnel practices', *Human Resource Management Journal,* Vol.41, No.1, pp.31–44.

Iles, P. (1999) *Managing Staff Selection and Assessment,* Milton Keynes: Open University Press.

Jewson, N. and Mason, D. (1986) 'The theory and practice of equal opportunities policies: liberal and radical approaches', *Sociological Review,* Vol.34, No.2, pp.307–24.

Johns, G. (1993) 'Constraints on the adoption of psychology-based personnel practices: lessons from organizational innovation', *Personnel Psychology,* Vol.46, No.3, pp.569–92.

Kersley, B., Alpin, C., Forth, J., Bryson, A., Bewley, H., Dix, G. and Oxenbridge, S. (2006) *Inside the Workplace: Findings from the 2004 Workplace Employment Relations Survey,* London: Routledge.

Klehe, U. (2004) 'Choosing how to choose. Institutional pressures affecting the adoption of personnel selection procedures', *International Journal of Selection and Assessment,* Vol.12, No.4, pp.327–42.

Klehe, U.-C. and Anderson, N. (2005) 'The prediction of typical and maximum performance', in A. Evers, O. Smit-Voskuijl and N. Anderson (eds) *Handbook of Personnel Selection,* Oxford: Blackwell.

Knights, D. and Raffo, C. (1990). 'Milkround professionalism in personnel recruitment: myth or reality?' *Personnel Review,* Vol.19, No.1, pp.28–37.

Konradt, U., Hertel, G. and Joder, K. (2003) 'Web-based assessment of call center agents: development and validation of a computerized instrument', *International Journal of Selection and Assessment,* Vol.11, Nos.2–3, pp.184–93.

Kravitz D.A. (2008) 'The diversity-validity dilemma: beyond selection – the role of affirmative action', *Personnel Psychology,* Vol.61, pp.173–93.

Kwiatkowski, R. (2003) 'Devolving HR responsibility to the line: threat, opportunity or partnership?', *Journal of Managerial Psychology,* Vol.18, No.5, pp.245–61.

Latham, G.P. and Skarlicki, D.P. (1995) 'Criterion-related validity of the situational and patterned behavior description interviews with organizational citizenship behavior', *Human Performance,* Vol.8, pp.67–80.

Lautenschlager, G.J. (1994) 'Accuracy and faking of background data', in G.S. Stokes, M.D. Mumford and W.A. Owens (eds) *Biodata Handbook,* Palo Alto, CA: Consulting Psychologists Press, pp.391–419.

Legge, K. (2005) *Human Resource Management: Rhetorics and Realities*, Basingstoke: Palgrave Macmillan.

Liao, H. and Chuang, A. (2004) 'A multilevel investigation of factors influencing employee service performance and customer outcomes', *Academy of Management Journal*, Vol.47, pp.41–58.

Lievens, F. and Coetsier, P. (2002) 'Situational tests in student selection: an examination of predictive validity, adverse impact, and construct validity', *International Journal of Selection and Assessment*, Vol.10, No.4, pp.245–57.

Lievens, F. and Klimoski, R.J. (2001) 'Understanding the assessment centre process: where are we now?', *International Review of Industrial and Organizational Psychology*, Vol.16, pp.246–86.

Lievens, F., Buyse, T. and Sackett, P.R. (2005) 'The operational validity of a video-based situational judgment test for medical college admissions: illustrating the importance of matching predictor and criterion construct domains', *Journal of Applied Psychology*, Vol.90, No.3, pp.442–52.

Lockyer, C.J. and Scholarios, D.M. (2004) 'Selecting hotel staff: why best practice doesn't always work', *International Journal of Contemporary Hospitality Management*, Vol.16, No.2, pp.125–35.

Lockyer, C. and Scholarios, D. (2007) 'The "raindance" of selection in construction: rationality as ritual and the logic of informality', *Personnel Review*, Vol.36, No.4, pp.528–48.

Marchington, M. and Wilkinson, A. (2005) *Human Resource Management at Work: People Management and Development*, London: CIPD.

Maurer, S.D. (2006) 'Using situational interviews to assess engineering applicant fit to work group job and organizational requirements', *Engineering Management Journal*, 1 September.

McFarland, L.A., Ryan, A.M., Sacco, J.M. and Kriska, S.D. (2004) 'Examination of structured interview ratings across time: the effects of applicant race, rater race, and panel composition', *Journal of Management*, Vol.30, pp.435–52.

Millmore, M. (2003) 'Just how extensive is the practice of strategic recruitment and selection?' *The Irish Journal of Management*, Vol.24, No.1, p.87.

Morgeson, F.P., Campion, M.A., Dipboye, R.L., Hollenbeck, J.R., Murphy, K. and Schmitt, N. (2007) 'Reconsidering the use of personality tests in personnel selection contexts', *Personnel Psychology*, Vol.60, No.3, pp.683–729.

Moynihan, L.M. and Peterson, R.S. (2004) 'The role of personality in group processes', in B. Schneider and D.B. Smith (eds) *Personality and Organizations*, Mahwah, NJ: Erlbaum, pp.317–45.

Muchinsky, P.M. (1986) 'Personnel selection methods', in C. Cooper and I. Robertson (eds) *International Review of Industrial and Organizational Psychology*, New York: Wiley.

Muchinsky, P.M. (2004) 'When the psychometrics of test development meets organizational realities: a conceptual framework for organizational change, examples, and recommendations', *Personnel Psychology*, Vol.57, pp.175–209.

Newell, S. (2006) 'Selection and assessment', in T. Redman and A. Wilkinson (eds) *Contemporary HRM* (2nd edn), London: Pearson Education, pp.65–98.

Nickson, D., Warhurst, C., Hurrell, S. and Dutton, E. (2008) 'A job to believe in: recruitment in the Scottish voluntary sector', *Human Resource Management Journal*, Vol.18, No.1, pp.18–33.

Olson-Buchanan, J.B. and Drasgow, F. (2005) 'Multimedia situational judgment tests: the medium creates the message', in J.A. Weekly and R.E. Ployhart (eds) *Situational Judgment Tests: Theory, Measurement*, London: Routledge, pp.253–78.

Ones, D., Viswesvaran, C. and Dilchert, S. (2005) 'Personality at work: raising awareness and correcting misconceptions', *Human Performance*, Vol.18, pp.389–404.

Ones, D., Dilchert, S., Viswesvaran, C. and Judge, T.A. (2007) 'In support of personality assessment in organizational settings', *Personnel Psychology*, Vol.60, No.4, pp.995–1027.

Pearn, M. (1993) 'Fairness in selection and assessment: a European perspective', in H. Schuler, J.L. Farr and M. Smith (eds) *Personnel Selection and Assessment: Individual and Organizational Perspectives*, Hillsdale, NJ: Lawrence Erlbaum.

Pfeffer, J. (1998) *The Human Equation. Building Profits by Putting People First*, Boston, MA: Harvard Business School Press.

Ployhart, R.E. and Erhart, M.G. (2003) 'Be careful what you ask for: effects of response instructions and the construct validity and reliability of situational judgment tests', *International Journal of Selection and Assessment*, Vol.11, No.1, pp.1–16.

Ployhart, R.E., McFarland, L.A. and Ryan, A.M. (2002) 'Examining applicants' attributions for withdrawal from a selection procedure', *Journal of Applied Social Psychology*, Vol.32, No.11, pp.2228–52.

Ployhart, R.E., Schneider, B. and Schmitt, N. (2006) *Staffing Organizations. Contemporary Practice and Theory*, Mahwah, NJ: Lawrence Erlbaum.

Purcell, K., Rowley, G. and Morley, M. (2002) *Recruiting from a Wider Spectrum of Graduates*, May, London: Council for Industry and Higher Education.

Reed Consulting (2007) *Candidates as Customer: Changing Attitudes to Recruitment*. London: Reed Consulting.

Reilly, R.R. and Chao, G.T. (1982) 'Validity and fairness of some alternative employee selection procedures', *Personnel Psychology*, Vol.35, No.1, pp.1–62.

Roe, R. and van den Berg, P. (2003) 'Selection in Europe: context, developments and research agenda', *European Journal of Work and Organizational Psychology*, Vol.12, No.3, pp.257–87.

Rothstein, M.G. and Goffin, R.D. (2006) 'The use of personality measures in personnel selection: what does current research support?', *Human Resource Management Review*, Vol.16, No.2, pp.155–80.

Ryan, A.M., McFarland, L., Baron, H. and Page, R. (1999) 'An international look at selection practices: nation and culture as explanations for variability in practice', *Personnel Psychology*, Vol.52, pp.359–94.

Sackett, P.R. and Lievens, F. (2008) 'Personnel selection', *Annual Review of Psychology*, Vol.59, pp.419–50.

Salgado, J.F. (2002) 'The Big Five personality dimensions and counterproductive behaviors', *International Journal of Selection and Assessment*, Vol.10, Nos.1 & 2, pp.17–125.

Salgado, J.F. and Anderson, N.R. (2002) 'Cognitive and GMA testing in the European Community: issues and evidence', *Human Performance*, Vol.15, pp.75–96.

Salgado, J.F., Anderson, N., Moscoso, S., Bertua, C. and De Fruyt, F. (2003) 'International validity generalization of GMA and cognitive abilities: a European Community meta-analysis', *Personnel Psychology*, Vol.56, No.3, pp.573–605.

Schmidt, F.L. and Hunter, J.E. (1998) 'The validity and utility of selection methods in personnel psychology: practical and theoretical implications of 85 years of research findings', *Psychological Bulletin*, Vol.124, No.2, pp.262–74.

Schmidt, F. and Zimmerman, R.D. (2004) 'A counterintuitive hypothesis about employment interview validity and some supporting evidence', *Journal of Applied Psychology*, Vol.89, No.3, pp.553–61.

Schmitt, N. (2003) 'Employee selection: how simulations change the picture for minority groups', *Cornell Hospitality Quarterly*, Vol.44, pp.25–32.

Schmitt, N. and Chan, D. (1998) *Personnel Selection. A Theoretical Approach*, London: Sage.

Schmitt, N. and Mills, A. (2001) 'Traditional tests and job simulations: minority and majority performance and test validities', *Journal of Applied Psychology*, Vol.86, No.3, pp.451–58.

Schuler, H. (1993) 'Social validity of selection situations: a concept and some empirical results', in H. Schuler, J.L. Farr and M. Smith (eds), *Personnel Selection and Assessment: Individual and Organizational Perspectives*, Hillsdale: Lawrence Erlbaum Associates, pp.11–26.

Searle, R.H. (2003a) *Selection and Recruitment. A Critical Text*, Milton Keynes: The Open University.

Searle, R.H. (2003b) 'Organizational justice in e-recruiting: issues and controversies', *Surveillance and Society*, Vol.1, No.2, pp.227–31.

Shackleton, V. and Newell, S. (1997) 'International assessment and selection', in N. Anderson and P. Herriot (eds) *International Handbook of Selection and Assessmant*, London: John Wiley & Sons.

Sternberg, R.J., Wagner, R.K., Williams, W.M. and Horvarth, J.A. (1995) 'Testing common sense', *American Psychologist*, Vol.50, No.11, pp.912–27.

Storey, J. (2007) 'Human resource management today: an assessment', in J. Storey (ed.) *Human Resource Management: A Critical Text* (3rd edn), London: Routledge.

Terpstra, D.E. and Kethley, R.B. (2002) 'Organizations' relative degree of exposure to selection discrimination litigation', *Public Personnel Management*, Vol.31, No.3, pp.277.

Tett, R.P. and Christiansen, N.D. (2007) Personality tests at the crossroads: a response to Morgeson, Campion, Dipboye, Hollenbeck, Murphy, and Schmitt', *Personnel Psychology,* Vol.60, No.4, pp.967–93.

Thornton, G.C., III, and Mueller-Hanson, R.A. (2004) *Developing Organizational Simulations: A Guide for Practitioners and Students,* Mahwah, NJ: Lawrence Erlbaum.

Townley, B. (1989) 'Selection and appraisal: reconstituting "social relations"?', in J. Storey (ed.) *New Perspectives on Human Resource Management,* London: Routledge, pp.92–108.

Van Hoye, G. and Lievens, F. (2005) 'Recruitment-related information sources and organizational attractiveness: can something be done about negative publicity?', *International Journal of Selection and Assessment,* Vol.13, No.3, pp.179–87.

Viswesvaran, C., Deller, J. and Ones, D.S. (2007) 'Personality measures in personnel selection', *International Journal of Selection and Assessment,* Vol.15, No.3, pp.354–58.

Weisinger, H. (1998) *Emotional Intelligence at Work,* San Francisco: Jossey-Bass.

Whittaker, S. and Marchington, M. (2003) 'Devolving HR responsibility to the line: threat, opportunity or partnership?', *Employee Relations,* Vol.25, No.3, pp.245–61.

Wolf, A. and Jenkins, A. (2006) 'Explaining greater test use for selection: the role of HR professionals in a world of expanded regulation', *Human Resource Management Journal,* Vol.16, No.2, pp.193–213.

de Wolff, C.J. (1993) 'The prediction paradigm', in H. Schuler, J.L. Farr and M. Smith (eds) *Personnel Selection and Assessment: Individual and Organizational Perspectives,* Hillsdale, NJ: Lawrence Erlbaum.

Zeidner, M., Matthews, G. and Roberts, R.D. (2004) 'Emotional intelligence in the workplace: a critical review', *Applied Psychology: An International Review,* Vol.53, No.3, pp.371–99.

Chapter 5

TRAINING AND DEVELOPMENT

Irena Grugulis

Introduction

Training, development and skills are key aspects of economic life. At the levels of the firm and the national economy, training offers the hope of increased competitiveness through raising skill levels, productivity and 'value added'. For trade unions and professional associations, training enhances members' expertise, facilitating negotiations for pay and status. For individuals, given that life chances are still heavily influenced by the job a person does and the wages they earn, education and training can increase knowledge and opportunities, give access to more highly rewarded work and reduce the prospect of unemployment. Small wonder then that consensus exists in this area, that governments encourage training through regulation or exhortation, employers praise its importance in surveys. Yet despite this support, the levels and quality of vocational education and training in Britain are neither as high, nor as evenly distributed, as might be hoped. Excellent practice exists, but rarely 'trickles down' to less well-provided areas. This chapter, drawing on international practice, explores some of the advantages of developmental systems of vocational education and training (VET). It argues that, in common with other human resource practices, training should not be considered in isolation. Its effectiveness, or otherwise, hinges on the wider economic and organisational context as well as the way work is designed.

The case for training and development

The advantages of training and development are not illusory. Within organisations, it can equip workers to carry out tasks, monitor quality and manage complex products and services. Arthur's (1999) research into US steel mini-mills describes the way that switching between different types of steel or different shapes required close monitoring by melt-shop employees. The exact nature of changeover activities was difficult to predict and down-time was expensive so the quality and quantity of production relied heavily on the skills of operators and maintenance workers who had a considerable amount of discretion managing these shifts. Here, as elsewhere, quality products relied heavily on workers' expertise.

Training and development safeguards such productivity as well as supporting it, by preparing employees for future jobs and insulating firms from skills shortages. When jobs can be filled internally, firms are less dependent on the outside labour market and do not risk appropriate recruits not being available (or not being available at the price the organisation wishes to pay). Such security is welcome. Seven per cent of employers in England have skill-shortage vacancies and 16 per cent report internal skills gaps (in which not all employees are fully

> ## Box 5.1: HRM in practice
>
> ### Biscuits and skill: biscuit making in Britain and Germany
>
> *This is taken from a study of biscuit manufacture in ten British and eight German firms.*
>
> The type of biscuits produced varied greatly between the two countries, largely owing to national tastes and demand. In Britain, demand concentrated on relatively basic biscuits: either plain or with one simple coating of chocolate, cream or jam. In Germany, there was a much higher demand for decorated and multi-textured products (soft biscuits with jam filling in chocolate cases or layered variegated biscuits). Since this affected the type of biscuits that each firm produced, relative output figures were not easy to measure. On crude output figures, productivity per employee hour was 25 per cent higher in Britain than in Germany, largely because British firms produced large quantities of simple, low-quality biscuits. However, when these productivity figures were adjusted for quality, the British advantage disappeared, with German firms 40 per cent more productive per employee hour.
>
> In Germany 90 per cent of process workers were craft-trained bakers and could work in all of the main areas of operations (mixing, biscuit forming and oven control). This multi-skilling meant that three-person teams could be responsible for at least two oven lines at the same time. In German firms, employees were focused in areas that added value to the product. Maintenance staff were highly qualified and, in addition to undertaking regular maintenance, they worked with supervisors to customise equipment and increase productivity. In Britain, no process workers and few supervisors were vocationally qualified. As a result, each individual production line needed a three-person team to cover mixing and baking since workers were narrowly trained and tended to stick to their own jobs. Few firms had any regular system of machine maintenance since shift work meant that equipment was rarely scheduled to stop, but breakdowns were frequent and high staffing levels in areas such as wrapping were needed to sort out problems caused by equipment breakdown and malfunction. On the line, narrow training restricted the ability of shop-floor workers to anticipate problems (such as machine malfunctioning) and take appropriate action.
>
> Source: Mason *et al.*1996

proficient at the work that they do). The problems reported as a result of these gaps include difficulties with customer service, delays developing new products, increases in operating costs or problems introducing new working practices, difficulties with quality standards, the withdrawal of products or services and loss of business (LSC 2005, pp.13 and 14).

Within firms, training and development is a key element of human resource management, indeed Keep (1989) argues that it is the litmus test against which other aspects of management practice should be gauged. When firms compete on the basis of quality and adopt high-commitment work practices such as employee involvement, teamworking or merit-based pay, developing employees is the key element in performance. It can raise the capacity of the individuals and groups employed, enabling them to participate meaningfully in systems where their contribution is encouraged (Keep and Mayhew 1996). Arthur (1999) links the 'commitment'-oriented human resource practices in steel mini-mills to the strategic focus on quality and batch production, contrasting it with less developmental 'control' mechanisms in organisations where production was routine and where human resource practices focused on minimising labour costs.

Training also allows organisations to adapt to changes in the business environment – a point somewhat evangelically made in writings on the learning organisation (see, for example, Senge 1992). While this literature is problematic, focusing more on evangelical rhetoric, anecdote and prescription rather than considered evaluations of the ways that people learn in organisations, and while it is unlikely that a learning organisation either has or could have existed (Keep and Rainbird 2000), job design and organisational structure influence the way that people work and the amount they can learn. At the most basic level, as Hillage *et al.* (2002) reveal, organisations with skills shortages report difficulties introducing new products and working practices.

In addition to these substantive factors, training and development also serves an important and very positive symbolic function. Everything that a firm does sends messages (of one kind or another) to its employees (one of the key elements of the positive side of HRM). Organisations that spend money on raising skills are, quite literally, investing in their workers. Employees who participate in firm-sponsored training are more likely to see themselves as having better career prospects and say that they are intending to stay with their employer than those that do not (Heyes and Stuart 1996) – a finding that raises interesting questions on current discussions about 'employability' as a substitute for employment security.

However, while training and development can have an extremely positive impact on the quality of production, can insulate firms from skills shortages and is a pivotal element of most models of high-commitment human resource management, its links to productivity and profit are much harder to gauge. This is not to argue that such links do not exist, or that well-trained experienced workers do not outperform novices; rather, it is that the data that is collected is neither coherent nor robust enough for a convincing case to be made. At a national level Britain's lack of vocational preparation is consistently cited as one of the main reasons for its under-performance. Manufacturing productivity in the US is 81 per cent higher than in the UK, Germany is 59 per cent higher and Sweden 72 per cent (cited in Nolan and Slater 2003). However, VET here is one element of a much wider system and it is difficult to separate its impact from that of other factors, such as technology.

At the level of the firm, employers believe in the links between training, performance and profitability (Coopers and Lybrand 1985; DTZ Pieda Consulting 1999). And, according to some of the most recent estimates, firms spend around £33.3 billion on VET (LSC 2006, p.17). However, cross-firm comparisons are difficult to make since figures between (and occasionally within) firms are rarely consistent. Some organisations include costs of room hire and employees' salaries in their calculations, others give only the cost of training departments or external consultants and the costs of on-the-job training are almost impossible to collate. These inconsistencies, coupled with the fact that many organisations simply did not know how much they spent on training, were pointed out to employers by Coopers and Lybrand (1985). Most revealed that they would rather true figures were not collated since this would result in pressure to reduce training spend, a response which reveals the vulnerability of UK training, rather than its centrality.

To make this issue more confusing, organisations may use training as a means to escape from an economic downturn, increasing spending when profit levels are low; or symbolically, to motivate and reward. From the perspective of encouraging training and development, both of these approaches are welcome; but they do cause problems for academics attempting to establish links between an organisation's training activities and its performance. Then too, official measures of training success, such as increases in employment (a factor of key interest to governments), may not be welcomed by individual organisations whose managers are more concerned with the impact practice has on profitability and share-price (for a fuller discussion of these issues see Keep *et al.* 2002).

The benefits to organisations are matched by advantages that individuals can gain. According to human capital theory (Becker 1964), the more investment an individual makes in themselves the greater their lifetime returns, through increased earnings, fewer (and shorter) periods of unemployment and access to more interesting work. Training that leads to formal certification (qualifications) has the additional advantage of helping the labour market to function more efficiently. Qualifications are an uneasy proxy for skills, but they are simple to check and so, particularly in recruitment and selection, they tend to serve as a form of shorthand that enables individuals and employers to find one another.

Individuals can benefit at a collective level too, as members of a particular profession or craft. Indeed, many of the most respected forms of training (medical, engineering, apprenticeships) are designed to lead to full membership of an occupation. Professional bodies and trade unions then develop, market and defend the skills of their members, and are among the most active supporters of VET in Britain. Several professional bodies even have mandatory schemes to ensure that members' training is updated (Keep 1994; Rainbird 1994, 1990).

VOLUNTARIST AND REGULATED APPROACHES

While there is a consensus over the importance and value of training and development, this is not matched by agreement on how best to encourage good practice. At a national level the two principal approaches are voluntarist (market-based) and regulated (educational). Both the USA and Britain are broadly voluntarist. The principal assumption behind such systems is that organisations operate more effectively when unfettered by regulation. Market pressures (to remain competitive, produce quality goods and run efficiently) will ensure that, where training is appropriate, firms will invest in it and, in the absence of expensive and cumbersome official bureaucracy, investment can be accurately targeted to respond to market needs.

By contrast, in a regulated system, as in much of continental Europe, vocational education and training is supported by the state. Regulation may take a variety of forms. In France, employers are required to support training or pay a levy to the state, while in Germany there is a system of extensive and rigorous apprenticeships for young people entering the labour market, coupled with 'licences to practise' for particular occupations. The assumption behind this approach is that vocational education and training is a public good and it is in the long-term interests of all to have a highly skilled workforce. But left to themselves individual firms will prioritise profitability and may not invest in skills development or may fund only short-term and low-level training. Training and development is, after all, only one way of securing skilled workers and firms may choose to recruit workers trained elsewhere or de-skill production instead. By providing an appropriate infrastructure (or a system of levies, or by regulating practice) the state ensures robust skills development.

Both voluntarist and regulated approaches can be successful. Silicon Valley, California provides an excellent example of the way that skills can be developed in a market-based system. Silicon Valley is famously the site of a cluster of extremely high-tech computing firms. These are supported by the proximity of universities (University of California campuses in Berkeley, San Francisco, San Diego and Los Angeles and private institutions such as Stanford, USC and CalTech) that supply expert labour, share research and stimulate start-up companies. Stanford (whose graduates include William Hewlett and David Packard) even set up the first university science park to provide fledgling firms with support services. The infrastructure is conducive to growth, with good local transport, an international airport and a state-of-the-art telecommunications system, while the availability of venture capital, low levels of regulation and limited penalties on bankruptcy encourage start-ups. These small and often highly focused firms prosper through inter-dependency, forming partnerships with other organisations and participating in employer groups to pursue initiatives such as improving technical training in city colleges, which are to their mutual benefit.

Individuals also collaborate through professional associations, continuing education courses and alumni associations. In firms there is little formal training, but skills and expertise are developed through project work on cutting-edge technical challenges. Even labour mobility, a point of concern elsewhere, assists knowledge diffusion and increases personal and professional networks (Finegold 1999).

Such an unstructured 'ecosystem' is very successful at developing and supporting the most expert who work at the cutting edge of their profession. However, the USA as a whole is far less successful in training and development for the majority and it is here that a more regulated system triumphs. The highly regarded German apprenticeship system is one of the best-known routes to achieving vocational qualifications. Full apprenticeships last three years and trainees are taught technical skills in the classroom which are subsequently developed through participation in a series of problem-solving activities, graded in terms of difficulty. Care is taken to ensure that apprentices are exposed to a full range of different work situations, with central training centres supplementing workplace experience and providing additional workplace settings for trainees to learn in; an arrangement which gives smaller employers the capacity to offer high-level training. Technical training is supplemented with knowledge of work control and design (manufacturing qualifications involve familiarity with costs, design and planning, and administration and production) and, in addition to this, all apprentices are required to continue to participate in further education for the duration of their vocational studies (Streeck et al. 1987; Lane 1989; Marsden and Ryan 1995; though see also Culpepper 1999).

The German system is made possible by close, collaborative links between employers' associations, trade unions and regional governments cooperating on creating a system that works for the benefit of all. Taiwan is different; its economy is dominated by small and medium-sized enterprises (SMEs) that successfully resisted the introduction of a levy for vocational education and training in the 1970s. Yet, despite this it has managed to introduce extensive vocational skills development, increasing the amount of technical, vocational education and the numbers of scientists and engineers through the education system. Demand for education was for academic education (and this would have been cheaper to provide) but access to academic courses was officially restricted, more than half of school-children were channelled into technical training and, at university level, more courses were made available for scientists and engineers and new Institutes of Technology launched. Student numbers, textbooks and curricula were state-controlled and this meant that Taiwan succeeded in both the growing low-cost industrial products for export and also managed the transition from this to higher value-added production across many if not all sectors without significant reported skills shortages (Green et al. 1999).

Each system has its strengths and limitations. The 'high-skills eco-system' of Silicon Valley is highly responsive to developing new and expert skills, while regulation, as in Germany, does mean that skilled workers are widely available, with two-thirds of workers holding intermediate qualifications or above. By contrast, in unregulated systems some occupations neglect training even when this is to their detriment. After construction was de-regulated in the USA, training levels fell dramatically – as did investment in physical capital and productivity (Bosch 2003).

Perhaps the most notable feature of these examples is that they are systemic; success here goes beyond the simple provision of high-quality training (indeed, in the US example, formal training is one of the least significant elements of skills development). The high-skills eco-system of Silicon Valley is made possible by the fact that recruits are already extremely highly educated on entry (and many of them are IT experts). In Germany, the existence of employers' associations, trade unions and vocational colleges that are prepared to collaborate, and in Taiwan the government's readiness to both pay for skills development and take decisions that may be unpopular with individual students and their families, facilitate good intermediate skills training.

Box 5.2: HRM in practice

Expansive and restrictive approaches to training and development

Systemic approaches to training and development can also be observed *within* firms. One manufacturer of bathroom showers, described by Fuller and Unwin (2004), took an *expansive* approach to development. It had a long-established apprenticeship programme and many ex-apprentices had progressed to senior management. Apprentices were rotated around different departments to gain wider knowledge of the business and improve their skills. They also attended college on day release, working towards knowledge-based qualifications which would give them access to higher education, went on residential courses designed to foster teamworking and were involved with local charities through the company's apprenticeship association. Contrast this with the *restrictive* environment of a small steel-polishing company where apprentices had been reluctantly taken on only when managers were unable to recruit qualified staff. After less than a year, the two apprentices who had learned on the job had gained all the skills necessary for their work. There was no system of job rotation and formal training was limited to 10 half-day courses on steel industry awareness (the sum total of apprentices' outside involvement) and an NVQ.

Source: Fuller and Unwin 2004

This is an important point and a key element of the success of each of these approaches. It also has implications for attempts to identify and transplant 'best practice', which generally focus only on one narrow element of a successful system. Korea's attempts to replicate the German apprenticeship system are a case in point (Jeong 1995). This had government support and experienced German advisers were engaged, but little financial support was available, the firms employing the apprentices provided little training and used them as low-paid and low-skilled workers, few college tutors were sufficiently skilled to make up this deficit, and seniority, rather than skill, remained the key element in promotion. As a result, the initiative failed.

Training and development in the workplace

There are many reasons to support training and development and both voluntarist and regulated approaches can work, but the responsibility for developing workplace skills does not rest solely (or even primarily) with the state. Employers too should provide extensive high-quality training and development for staff, to enhance their competitive position and foster a reputation for being a 'good employer'. But even here there are problems. Excellent provision exists, but is rather unevenly distributed and not all training is developmental.

According to the Labour Force Survey, 15.9 per cent of workers in Britain received either on- or off-the-job training (Labour Force Survey 2008). But this experience of training (and particularly of the duration and content of training) varies greatly according to both occupation and sector. Employees in the public sector, younger workers, people who are new to the job and those working in professional or clerical occupations are far more likely to receive training than older workers in 'blue collar' jobs (Cully *et al.* 1999). While 14 per cent of managers and 25 per cent of professionals had received training, only 6.5 per cent of process, plant and machine operatives had done so. Overall, 29 per cent of training lasts for less than five days.

This is particularly significant when we step back from the data and recall what training is provided for. One of the main advantages of training and development was that it could enhance the skills base, equip workers with expertise and change the way that they worked. Given this, the overall statistics are of concern for, while training figures have risen since the 1980s, there is some evidence that this has been achieved by shorter training courses more evenly distributed. Clearly, duration is not a proxy for quality, but it is unlikely that fundamental changes to the skills base can be achieved in less than five days.

The content of training is also important. Workplace training can cover a multitude of activities. Graduate trainee accountants with major accountancy firms spend three years on a mixture of formal courses, guided work experience and personal study, leading to a prestigious professional qualification. By contrast, call centre workers can expect far more basic workplace training. In Callaghan and Thompson's (2002) study, one call centre worker, who had let his voice drop slightly during a conversation with a customer, was sent on a training course to teach him to keep intonation even and enthusiastic. Both of these activities count as training and both may increase organisational effectiveness, but the advantages they confer on workers are very different.

Reinforcing this, the two types of training most commonly funded by employers are health and safety and induction, a factor that may explain why temporary workers are more likely to receive training than their permanent colleagues (20 per cent as opposed to 15 per cent, DfES 2003, p.63). Heyes and Gray (2003), in their survey of SMEs after the introduction of the national minimum wage, found that training spend had risen, but that this was because employers were hiring younger (and cheaper) workers rather than up-skilling existing staff. Clearly it is important that workplaces are healthy and safe places to be and that new recruits receive adequate induction. However, it is highly unlikely that such forms of training will affect productivity, product quality or individual career development.

Training and development may also serve a social function, helping workers to form friendships and distracting them from alienating work. Two call centres investigated by Kinnie et al. (2000) used employee teams, games and spot prizes to motivate employees. These organisations also had three-week induction and technical training but their ongoing investment was in activities described by one supervisor as 'fun and surveillance'. An interesting modern variant on Adam Smith's (1993 [1776]) approval of publicly funded education for the working poor, who engaged only in simple, de-humanising and repetitive tasks, the better to support a 'decent and orderly' society (p.436).

PERSONAL QUALITIES AND GENERIC SKILLS

The type of training identified by Kinnie and his colleagues, the focus on games and the development of 'soft' or generic skills, is becoming more widespread. In part it reflects attempts to alleviate repetitive work, increase commitment or foster a particular organisational culture. But it also stems from the fact that workforce skills are increasingly being defined in attitudinal terms. The Department for Education and Employment's Skills Task Force included communication, problem solving, teamworking, an ability to improve personal learning and performance, motivation, judgement, leadership and initiative in its list of skills (DfEE 2000, p.24). The CBI's (1989) earlier suggestions included values and integrity and interpersonal skills; Whiteways Research (1995) extended this to cover self-awareness, self-promotion, political focus and coping with uncertainty. These are not isolated instances and some of the lists produced can be extremely long. Hirsch and Bevan (1988), drawing on lists of managerial skills, came up with 1,745 different items.

To a certain extent there is little here that is novel. Employers have always demanded appropriate qualities and attributes from their workers and this may be simply a modern variant of that. Moreover, the increasing numbers of service jobs demand very different qualities of those who carry them out compared to manufacturing work. In services, the process of being served is as much a part of the purchase as any product being sold and customers may conflate their delight at service levels with their appreciation of the product (Korczynski 2002). As a result, the way that employees look and feel and the impressions and emotions they provoke in others are important (see among others, Hochschild 1983; Leidner 1993). However, couching this in the language of skill causes a number of problems. Unlike formally accredited technical skills, it is not clear that soft skills are either transferable or give their holders power in the labour market. The communication skills needed to tell a customer which aisle the baked beans are in are very different from those needed to describe the rules of cricket or explain complex statistics. In each of these areas (just as for the exercise of judgement, leadership or problem solving), efficacy demands technical and local knowledge, a factor neglected by the compilers of generic lists. This is particularly worrying since there is some evidence that organisations attempting to train their staff in soft skills are neglecting the technical aspects of work (Grugulis and Vincent 2005).

Then too, soft skills may be reciprocal and relational rather than individual. In his study of the skills required by US employers, Lafer (2004) draws on research by Moss and Tilly (1996) in two warehouses in the same district of Los Angeles, both of which employed present and past gang members. While managers in one complained of high turnover, laziness and dishonesty, in the second, which paid several dollars per hour more, managers had few complaints and turnover was a modest 2 per cent. As Lafer (2004, p.117) argues: 'traits such as discipline, loyalty and punctuality are not "skills" that one either possesses or lacks; they are measures of commitment that one chooses to give or withhold based on the conditions of work offered'.

Focusing on motivation as an individual skill presupposes that people are unaffected by their conditions of work or the way that they are treated. Factors once considered the responsibility of management or personnel are individualised such that the emphasis on control systems, job design, pay rates or being a 'good employer' becomes the straightforward problem of hiring the most appropriately 'skilled' people (Keep 2001; Grugulis et al. 2004).

Nor is the exercise of soft skills particularly clear. Employers value them but often judge their presence or their absence through sexual and racial stereotypes. Women are favoured for call centres and reception desks (Collinson et al. 1990; Taylor and Tyler 2000; Hebson and Grugulis 2005). Asian women are not considered to be career-minded and men's marital status may be taken as a proxy for their reliability (Oliver and Turton 1982; Collinson et al. 1990). As Ainley (1994, p.80) argues, 'at rock bottom, the real personal and transferable "skills" required for preferential employment are those of whiteness, maleness and traditional middle-classness'. It is difficult to escape from the conclusion that in some environments focusing on soft skills can be used to legitimise prejudice and reinforce disadvantage.

This is a conundrum. At one level most jobs clearly require a mixture of both technical and soft skills and, given the existing lack of recognition for women's skills, rhetorical support for their importance should advantage them. At another, as Bolton (2004) argues, these skills – regardless of their complexity – seem to be the exception to the normal laws of supply and demand in the sense that, no matter how much employers require them, they are seldom highly rewarded when not accompanied by high levels of technical skill. The advantages that soft skills offer seem precariously dependent on their being noted, appreciated and rewarded by senior management (Grugulis and Vincent 2005). In isolation they provide workers with few of the labour market advantages of technical skills (Payne 1999, 2000; Keep 2001).

In part this is a systemic issue. A focus on soft skills (such as communication, loyalty or even punctuality) in low-level work confers few advantages on workers because it equips them only to perform low-level tasks, whereas an emphasis on teamworking, problem solving and responsibility for production integrated with technical skills in Thompson et al.'s (1995) cross-national comparisons of vehicle production provided employees with opportunities for progression. Similarly, in NUMMI's plant in Freemont, California, soft skills are

Box 5.3: HRM in practice

During the first week [of a US state-funded training programme] about a dozen women and two men sit around a conference table at the Dane county job centre. The instructor, who introduces herself as Kelly, shows flashcards. One flashcard says, *You'll never amount to anything.*

'Has anybody ever heard this in your life?' she asks.

No response.

'Good! Because it's not true!'

She holds up another flashcard: *You can do anything you set your mind to.*

'How about this one, how often do we hear this?'

No one says anything.

This is day three of the two-week . . . session. The topic: communication. From Kelly's point of view, things aren't going so well. 'People aren't talking a lot', she says.

Several participants are clearly trying though. Kelly holds up a flashcard that says *I'm so proud of you.* 'How do we feel when someone says this to us?' she asks.

'Good?', one participant offers.

'Yeah!', says Kelly. She hands out pieces of paper and asks everyone to write down the names of two people who have had a positive influence on their lives.

'It's the person who believes in you', she says.

She writes 'belives' in magic marker on a flip chart, then crosses it out and writes 'beleives'.

'Don't tell her,' the woman in front of me whispers.

'What?', Kelly asks, 'Don't tell me what?'

'You still spelled "believes" wrong', someone says.

Kelly stares at the flip chart.

'It's I before E except after C', another participant explains.

'That's OK', the woman in front of me says. 'That's a hard one.'

After a short break, Kelly lists some more rules for good communication. 'Here are two of the hardest things to say in the English language', she says, and writes 'Thank you' and 'I'm sorry' on the flip chart . . .

I interview some participants after class. 'I don't want to knock the programme or anything – maybe someone is getting their self-esteem raised', says one. . . . 'But . . . they've given me an ultimatum: you either go to this class or it's your check.'

Source: Conniff 1994, pp.18–21; quoted in Lafer 2004, p.121

combined with the development of technical skills and workers are given a great deal of discretion to address workplace problems (Rothenberg 2003). However, while integrating these generic qualities with challenging work may make them more 'skilful' and advantage those workers who possess or develop them, it does not overcome the tendency to read these virtues into gender, race, class, age or marital status.

THE DISADVANTAGES OF TRAINING AND DEVELOPMENT

The overall picture of training and development is not clear cut. Some courses, qualifications and on-the-job training are excellent at developing workforce skills which can then be integrated into the way work is designed and controlled. But developmental provision is set alongside narrow qualifications and training courses that serve only to entertain. At one level such behaviour is difficult to explain. If training and development is universally believed to have a positive impact, then why are so few firms training and why are the ones that do confining much of their activity to short courses, health and safety and induction? Equally, why do not individual employees respond to this by filling the gap themselves? Such lack of activity appears, at best, irrational.

There is, however, an explanation. Training and development does not occur in a vacuum, rather it is one aspect of an organisation's activities and exists to support the other activities. As Keep and Mayhew (1999) argue, training is a third-order issue, following on from decisions about competitiveness, product specification and job design. For organisations that choose to compete on the basis of quality, highly skilled workers are essential; for ones that compete on cost, they are an unjustifiable extravagance – and large sections of the British economy still compete on cost (Bach and Sisson 2000). The second reason, and this is related to the first, is that many jobs are designed to be tightly controlled, with employee discretion (and with it skill) taken away. One employer, interviewed by Dench *et al.* (1999), said that their ideal worker had two arms and two legs. When this is what jobs demand, it is difficult to see how training will help. Job design is not set in stone and it is perfectly possible to construct skilled work from the same jobs, the same market conditions and the same strategy. Boxall and Purcell (2003) provide an interesting example from two firms competing with one another in delivering bottled gas. British Oxygen decided to compete by using delivery drivers as key staff. Drivers were trained in customer relations, cab-based information systems and product knowledge, ensuring that customers were satisfied and encouraging them to trade up wherever possible. By contrast Air Products, a rival firm in the same industry facing the same pressures, decided to compete by outsourcing its haulage and distribution to an independent contractor. Their drivers were not expected to know anything about bottled gas beyond the standard health and safety guidelines. When large numbers of employers design jobs to be done without skill, pay low wages, and workers with little purchasing power buy products of low price and low quality, we have all the elements of what Finegold and Soskice describe as a 'low skills equilibrium' (1988).

This is an important point and worth exploring in a little more detail since job design can trap employees into vicious or virtuous circles. Jobs which allow employees discretion, encourage their input into work and allow them to make decisions in the workplace not only call on skills, they also enhance them, and such improvements are not confined to professional and managerial grade employees. In Rothenberg's (2003) study of Japanese-owned car plants based in both Japan and the USA, workers were actively involved in factory changes, from the rather passive consultation over whether fitting energy efficient light-bulbs would allow them sufficient light to work, to the very active involvement in problem solving, suggesting improvements and running with projects. This was more than simply a management device to secure commitment, it was an integral part of work, and worker expertise in where staff were purging paint guns or how drums of sealant were opened was as important to successful problem solving as more technical knowledge. Pye (1968) calls this the 'workmanship of risk' because it is the individual employees who are expected to make decisions (about, for example, work processes, product quality, service levels, intensity of work) and contrasts it with the 'workmanship of certainty' where all decisions are stripped from the front line and workers are simply required to follow instructions. Some types of call centre work illustrate this well. Here technological sophistication allows intense monitoring, so staff may be given scripts, calls are tightly timed, supervisors listen in and individual performance statistics are

Box 5.4: HRM in practice

McDonald's famously and relentlessly standardise every aspect of their product in order to eliminate the need for human input. The Operations and Training Manual (known to staff as 'the Bible') provides detailed prescriptions on every aspect of working life. Its 600 pages include full colour photographs illustrating the proper placement of ketchup, mustard and pickle on every type of burger, set out the six steps of counter service and even prescribe the arm motions that should be used in salting a batch of fries. Kitchen and counter technology reinforce these instructions as lights and buzzers tell workers when to turn burgers or take fries out of the fat, ketchup dispensers provide measured amounts of product in the requisite 'flower' pattern and lights on the till remove the need for serving staff to write out orders, as well as prompting them to offer additional items.

For more information on this see Leidner 1993; Ritzer 1998

publicly displayed (see, for example, Bain *et al.* 2002; Callaghan and Thompson 2002). Working in such tightly regulated environments is not only alienating for the individual employees, it is also de-skilling.

Then too, it is instructive to consider the areas of job creation; 77 per cent of UK jobs are now in the service sector (Labour Force Survey 2008). Service work includes many of the most highly skilled and knowledgeable workers, such as medics, teachers and IT professionals, but it also, and in far greater numbers, covers care workers, security staff and personal services, numbers of which are rising far faster. The sector as a whole is dominated by low-paid, part-time workers, few of whom are either highly skilled or allowed to exercise their skills in their work. This need not be the case. McGauran's (2000, 2001) research into retail work in France and Ireland shows how French employers expect their workers to be experts in the products sold and French customers request advice on products and product care when shopping. Gamble's (2006) research into British and Japanese-owned retailers in China reveals the importance of expertise there too. Not only were Chinese recruits 'frighteningly well educated', since the stores studied paid considerably more than local average wages and promotion was rapid, they were also exceptionally well informed about products and the regular and rigorous questioning to which customers subjected them ensured that they maintained this expertise.

However, it is not clear that this skilled variant of shop-work influences behaviour elsewhere. Rather, pressure for hyper-flexibility, described by Gadrey (2000, p.26) as 'tantamount to a personnel strategy based on zero competence', zero qualifications, zero training and zero career, means that retail work is dominated by poorly paid part-time workers and the flexibility demanded of them is availability for shift work at short notice. In Germany, this is threatening long-established traditions of training and qualifications as employers avoid training employees, since this would make them expensive to hire, and rely instead on large numbers of low-paid staff supported by small numbers of highly skilled 'anchor' workers (Kirsch *et al.* 2000).

At an individual level too there are good and sound reasons for not taking up vocational training. Human capital theory is neither as straightforward nor as axiomatic as some commentators argue. While some qualifications do indeed bring high returns, others do not and it is the low-level vocational qualifications that bring least reward. Then too, not all skills are equal and the status and labour market power of job holders influence the way their skills are perceived (Rubery and Wilkinson 1994). In practice this means that women's work, even when technically and objectively more complex than men's, tends to be under-valued (Phillips and Taylor 1986). Mechanistically assessing workers as a supply of skills neglects both this social construction and factors such as trust and motivation that are needed to put skills into practice at work (Brown 2001). Human capital theory also individualises the responsibility for acquiring and developing skills. Nor is it clear that highly skilled workers create their own demand. As the UK skills survey consistently demonstrates, more than a third of workers report that their skills are under-utilised in employment (Felstead *et al.* 2007).

Rethinking training and development

This chapter has deliberately extended the debate on training and development beyond the confines of formal courses and qualifications. These are important factors but, for students of HRM, they are only one aspect of a wider issue, the development of 'resourceful humans'. A knowledgeable workforce is the product, not of excellent training in isolation, but of a combination of a range of factors including training, job design, status, control systems and discretion. As Cockburn (1983) and Littler (1982) argue, skill reposes in the individual, in the job and in the social setting. In practice, this means that for development to be effective, individuals need enough discretion and challenge in their work to exercise their skills.

Given this, there are some reasons for optimism in Britain. Between 1986 and 2006 skills in work have risen against almost every indicator. Employers are demanding more (and more advanced) qualifications, training periods for jobs are rising and the amount of experience that employees need to do their work well is also rising (Felstead *et al.* 2007). However, while this trajectory is encouraging, it starts from a low base and most work still demands few skills, with 57 per cent of jobs requiring less than three months' training and 19 per cent less than one month's experience to do well (compared to 25 per cent which require more than two years' training, Felstead *et al.* 2007, pp.55 and 56). iMac jobs have not yet entirely replaced McJobs (Warhurst and Thompson 1998).

This skills survey also reveals two extremely worrying developments. The first emerged in the 1990s as more individuals gained qualifications and workplace demand failed to keep pace. The most recent results show that skilful people easily outnumber skilled jobs. In 2006 there were 1.1 million more graduates than graduate jobs, while at the other end of the spectrum jobs which required neither qualifications nor experience outnumbered unqualified people by nearly 5 million (Felstead *et al.* 2007, pp.59, 60).

This under-utilisation of skills is apparent in Rainbird and Munro's (2003) research. Drawing on an extensive study of low-paid workers, they found that rigid hierarchies, narrow job descriptions and cost constraints all acted as barriers that employees, who were often highly educated, skilled or anxious to progress, could not overcome. Nor was there any sign, despite the very significant differences that good managers could make, that this might

Box 5.5: HRM in practice

I've actually got the convenor saying to me, 'we've got to watch this multi-skill thing, because it's too interesting for them'.

Source: Managing director, GKN Hardy Spicer; cited in Hendry 1993, p.92

change. Indeed, the structural innovations observed, such as contracting out by the public sector, often reduced employees' areas of influence and took away aspects of their work that were interesting or skilful.

The second area for concern is the sharp decline in discretion employees can exercise, a trend that was particularly marked for professional workers. In 1986, 72 per cent of professionals reported that they had 'a great deal' of choice over the way that they worked. By 2001 this figure had fallen to 38 per cent (Rainbird and Munro 2003, p.71; see also Evetts 2002; Grugulis *et al.* 2003). Yet discretion is a prerequisite for skills to be put into practice.

Discussion and conclusions

It has frequently been argued that training is the 'litmus test' of human resource management (Keep 1989). The pivotal element of a system designed to harness the talents of those it employs (through well-designed jobs, teamworking, employee involvement and other human resource practices) is ensuring that employees are developed for their roles. However, the reverse also applies and human resource practices are the test of training. There is little point in training and developing employees if the jobs they are to undertake are tightly controlled with no trust or discretion given. Skill is an aspect of jobs as well as a part of individuals, and a highly skilled individual put in a job where they have little control, discretion or responsibility and which they have little power to change is likely to become frustrated. This means that, just as many excellent analyses of human resource management have queried the extent to which its ambitious rhetoric has been matched by its lived reality (see, among others, Legge 1995; Wilkinson and Willmott 1995), so training and development needs to be subjected to the same scrutiny. Good training and development has the capacity to significantly change lives. It can equip people for more interesting, better paid and more demanding work; help to mitigate the discrimination in the labour market experienced by women and members of minority groups; and provide an effective route out of poverty for people working in unskilled and low-paid jobs. However, just because some forms of training can do this does not mean that all can. Training and development is not straightforwardedly a 'good thing' – not all training is developmental and not all development is integrated into work. Before according our approval we really do need to examine what is involved in particular training systems, the effect it has on individuals and the way it is integrated into work. If this is not the case there is a danger that effort and resources will be put into systems which simply reinforce disadvantage and equip people only for minimum wage employment (Lafer 2004) or horizontal movement between a range of low-skilled jobs (Grimshaw *et al.* 2002).

Developing resourceful humans

Irena Grugulis

This chapter showed the way that training and development may be systemic and linked to product strategies, job design, the way that work is controlled and the level of discretion workers can use. For each of the jobs listed below set out:

(a) how people are trained to do the job;

(b) what (if any) continuing development they have on the job (remember that a challenging job provides opportunities for development, just as formal training does);

(c) how much discretion they can exercise;

▶

(d) what other human resource policies you would expect (on pay rates, involvement, career ladders, etc.);

(e) what would happen to these jobs if recruits received more developmental training or were more highly educated.

A secondary school teacher

A call centre worker

An anaesthetist

An accountant

A gardener

A shop assistant

A junior manager in a chain restaurant

A bank cashier

A factory worker

A cleaner

CASE STUDY 5.2

Soft skills and personal qualities

Irena Grugulis

In surveys of employers, the 'skills' that are most highly valued are often 'soft' skills or personal qualities and attributes such as customer handling, communication and problem solving (Hillage *et al.* 2002) or discipline, loyalty, punctuality and work ethic (Lafer 2004). For each of the jobs below consider:

(a) how important 'soft' skills are for doing the job;

(b) the advantages to the employer;

(c) the advantages to the employee;

(d) how complex these skills are;

(e) to what extent these are individual attributes and to what extent they are reactions to the way that people are treated;

(f) are all skills with the same name the same skill (are they interchangeable between jobs)?

A worker on a building site

A receptionist

A waiter/waitress

A chief executive

A university lecturer

A nurse

A computer programmer

A lawyer

A TV repairman/woman

A chef

Jobs, discretion and skill

Irena Grugulis, Steven Vincent and Gail Hebson

This case study explores two 'networks', an outsourced group of housing benefit caseworkers and production workers in a specialist chemicals company, and considers the effect that each network had on employee skills.

Total Customer Services (TCS) specialise in business operations outsourcing. With a turnover of over £200 million per year and more than 3,000 employees, TCS has one of the largest players in this emerging market and had a strategy of rapid expansion. It took over the management of the housing benefits office of a London borough as a loss-leader in order to break into an expanding area of outsourcing business. This housing benefits office had previously been underperforming and was identified as one of the worst in the boroughs in London. Here, claim processing was outsourced to improve the quality of service provided.

Scotchem was a pigment manufacturing plant. It was one of several UK-based chemical production facilities owned by Multichem, a large European multinational that specialises in developing and producing industrial chemicals. Pigments had been produced on the site for over 75 years and Scotchem is Multichem's centre of excellence in pigment manufacture. The company employs over 650 people on its unionised site and produces around 24,000 tonnes of pigment. A regular feature of this production process was that Scotchem collaborates with customers and suppliers in order to develop both processes and products for specific orders.

Both of these networks were organised, and gained their flexibility, in slightly different ways. In TCS claims processing was contracted out for seven years and initially contact between the council and TCS (with the exception of contract negotiation at senior level) took the form of council staff monitoring claims processed by TCS caseworkers. However, the original contract also set performance levels for TCS and these were not met. As a result, the council set a new series of targets and weekly meetings were held with senior TCS staff to discuss performance.

Scotchem's network was far more flexible, at least in terms of its relations with customers and suppliers. Since it produced chemicals in bulk and can both place and fill orders on a very large scale, many of its suppliers and customers were long-term, with 20- or 30-year relationships not uncommon. Formal contracts tended to be short-term, with quarterly negotiations used to set prices and agree approximate levels of consumption in order to manage work in progress. However, these agreements were part of very long-term relationships. As a result, a series of alliances and friendships have built up between various staff members, with informal contacts and tacit knowledge supplementing official agreements about cooperation.

Contracts, control and the decline of discretion

In theory, outsourcing only changes the responsibility for completing a task, not the task itself. In theory too, such a change may improve efficiency and effectiveness. The organisation that outsources may gain numerical flexibility, hiring staff only when needed, or secure access to expertise that it lacks internally. Yet these theories focus on organisational experience or expectations and assume that the way work is managed does not affect the way it is carried out. In practice, in TCS, outsourcing required a change in management structure which fundamentally altered the work processes. Such adjustments might have

▶

been predicted. There are, broadly, two distinct ways of controlling staff: 'status', in which employees are trusted to perform often ill-specified or 'extra-functional' activities (and through which they may gain certain rights), and 'contract', where tasks tend to be clearly specified and tightly controlled, completed at the order of employers (Streeck 1987). Most employment relationships tend to be a fluid mixture of both, influenced by organisational structures, individuals and contexts. According to the prescriptive literature, liberation from bureaucratic control should increase an individual's autonomy; in practice, in TCS, the reverse was the case. Here the process of contracting meant that tasks were more strictly defined and monitored and employees were able to exercise less discretion.

Housing benefit staff had previously been responsible for seeing an entire claim through from start to finish, ensuring that the documentation was complete and correct and often exercising their professional judgement to condone minor omissions. Since forms were complicated and demanded repeated pieces of evidence, these omissions were reasonably common. Under TCS, once the work was contracted out, processing was reorganised so that caseworkers 'specialised' in one part of the claims process or worked in the newly set-up call centre for extended periods of time (instead of part of a shift, as had been the case under the local authority). Housing benefit is a complex area and regulations are subject to change, so this specialisation not only made processing claims less pleasurable by taking away caseworkers' feelings of 'ownership' and making their work less interesting, it also meant that skills declined. Staff were no longer aware of changes that occurred outside their own narrow remit. Their power to make decisions was also lost. Caseworkers were required only to ensure that the paperwork was complete before passing the form back to the local authority, rather than approving it as it stood.

Under [the council] I had my own caseload, a set number of cases, surnames for a particular area, I go through all those cases from start to finish. If during the benefit period there was a change of circumstances it was my sole ability to do that case. I knew those cases. You could call the name and address and I could tell you what that entailed. We don't have that under [TCS]. What we have, it's even worse now . . . we come in and they give us this sheet and they say this is your work for the day. You don't really know the cases. Ten people could have touched that case since it came in before it gets to the person who finally pays the claim. So from the customer point of view it's not very helpful as they tend to receive letters from five or six different case workers – they say, who wrote to me? (TCS caseworker, female)

To a certain extent, this decline in discretion was an inevitable part of the contracting process. After all, tasks may be contracted out, but responsibility remains with the original organisation. This institutional separation of execution and authority has implications for work processes. While in-house staff might be controlled through trust, work undertaken by external bodies was regulated by 'contract'. Because local authorities must validate claims, council staff checked every detail of every form before authorising it. The in-house experts retained by the council found that the monitoring was as time consuming and tedious for them as it was for the ex-colleagues they monitored.

Changing skills, changing workers

This decline in employees' discretion was also matched by changes in personnel. In TCS the initial work group was of skilled staff who had transferred over from the local authority, but these were supplemented by agency staff (25 from a workforce of 110) whose levels of skill and experience varied. Further, TCS itself hired and trained new recruits but these were less well qualified than the existing caseworkers and the training that they were given was greatly shortened.

▶

Such increasingly active management was more a product of the subcontracting process than a reflection of changes in the skills base. The audit systems were imposed on all workers and even the most experienced and skilled staff, who had been accustomed to exercise discretion when working 'in-house', were subjected to higher levels of control as subcontractors. There was a reduction in the skills base that had existed prior to contracting out, but this reduction was a consequence, rather than a cause of, the increasing emphasis on audit. This reduction in skills was partly because the temporary nature of the agreements provided fewer incentives for organisations to develop and maintain employees' skills. TCS, which had a seven-year contract with the council, introduced a caseworker training programme, but they recruited less qualified people than the council had and their training programme then equipped workers with fewer technical skills since the redesigned work processes demanded fewer skills.

Scotchem and 'learning networks'

Scotchem's network was qualitatively different from TCS's outsourced work. Since it was one of the largest multinationals engaged in producing chemicals and pigments, several of its relationships with suppliers and customers were long-term. Specific contracts for services could be short, but they were repeated and inter-firm relationships could and did last 20 or 30 years. Many of these companies were competitors, but the size of their orders and the duration of the contacts meant that, here at least, market dependency resulted in the growth of trust. Officially contact took the form of contracts for particular services; unofficially it came close to a contract for service, allowing trust and status to develop.

In Scotchem, individual employees held permanent contracts and staff at all levels were expected to exercise responsibility and engage in 'extra-functional' activities. When a new plant was set up, one of the operatives commented that:

We've been left with quite a free role to prioritise ourselves, and sort our own team out, what we do and who does it, left to our own responsibility for that. . . . We know our responsibilities, we organise ourselves. I think the ownership has come from – because we understand the business and the needs of the business.

These expectations were extended to work with other firms. Orders for pigment would often involve developing products or improving delivery and, to achieve this, Scotchem employees at all levels were required to collaborate with customers and suppliers, a working arrangement which included shop-floor employees who would test new processes and equipment before developments were finalised. Two of the most recent results of such inter-organisational collaborations were a complex automated loading facility for part of the Scotchem site, and larger and tougher bags for the powdered chemicals. Extensive collaboration with one preferred supplier in producing bag specifications had maximised benefits for both parties by significantly reducing leakage which might foul the loading equipment.

Each of these collaborations was formally governed through contract, and the information that could be revealed to competitors was restricted. But the long-term relations between the firms and the friendships that often existed between employees meant that contracts were honoured more in breach than in observation. Exchanges generally went beyond permitted limits and several people commented that projects would not have succeeded were it not for both sides' generosity with information. Significantly too, contracts set out the aims of each collaboration and little attempt was made to specify or monitor detailed tasks.

▶

Questions

1. What were the main differences between the way work was organised at TCS and at Scotchem?

2. What implications did this have for skill?

3. What impact would improving or increasing training have had in these companies?

4. How important is discretion (a) in these two case studies, and (b) as part of skill?

5. Given the evidence here, what are the implications of a general increase in outsourcing work?

Source: Grugulis *et al.* 2003

Bibliography

Ainley, P. (1994) *Degrees of Difference*, London: Lawrence & Wishart.

Arthur, J.B. (1999) 'Explaining variation in human resource practices in US steel mini-mills', in P. Cappelli (ed.) *Employment Practices and Business Strategy*, Oxford and New York: Oxford University Press.

Bach, S. and Sisson, K. (2000) 'Personnel management in perspective', in S. Bach and K. Sisson (eds) *Personnel Management* (3rd edn), Oxford: Blackwell.

Bain, P., Watson, A., Mulvey, G., Taylor, P. and Gall, G. (2002) 'Taylorism, targets and the pursuit of quantity and quality by call centre management', *New Technology, Work and Employment* Vol.17, No.3, pp.170–85.

Becker, G.S. (1964) *Human Capital*, Chicago, IL: University of Chicago Press.

*Bolton, S.C. (2004) 'Conceptual confusions: emotion work as skilled work', in C. Warhurst, I. Grugulis and E. Keep (eds) *The Skills that Matter*, Basingstoke: Palgrave Macmillan.

Bosch, G. (2003) 'Skills and innovation – a German perspective', Paper presented at the Future of Work/SKOPE/Centre for Organisation and Innovation Conference on Skills, Innovation and Performance, Cumberland Lodge, Windsor Great Park, 31 March–1 April.

Boxall, P. and Purcell, J. (2003) *Strategy and Human Resource Management*, London: Palgrave.

Brown, P. (2001) 'Skill formation in the twenty-first century', in P. Brown, A. Green and H. Lauder (eds) *High Skills: Globalization, Competitiveness and Skill Formation*, Oxford: Oxford University Press.

*Callaghan, G. and Thompson, P. (2002) 'We recruit attitude: the selection and shaping of routine call centre labour', *Journal of Management Studies*, Vol.39, No.2, pp.233–54.

CBI (1989) *Towards a Skills Revolution – A Youth Charter*, London: Confederation of British Industry.

Cockburn, C. (1983) *Brothers: Male Dominance and Technological Change*, London: Pluto Press.

Collinson, D., Knights, D. and Collinson, M. (1990) *Managing to Discriminate*, London and New York: Routledge.

Conniff, R. (1994) 'Big, bad welfare: welfare reform politics and children', *The Progressive*, Vol.58, No.8, pp.18–21.

Coopers and Lybrand (1985) *A Challenge to Complacency*, London: Manpower Services Commission.

Cully, M., Woodland, S., O'Reilly, A. and Dix, G. (1999) *Britain at Work*, London: Routledge.

Culpepper, P.D. (1999) 'The future of the high-skill equilibrium in Germany', *Oxford Review of Economic Policy*, Vol.15, No.1, pp.43–59.

Dench, S., Perryman, S. and Giles, L. (1999) *Employers' Perceptions of Key skills*, IES Report 349, Sussex: Institute of Manpower Studies.

Department for Education and Employment (2000) *Skills for All: Research Report from the National Skills Task Force*, Suffolk: DfEE.

Department for Education and Skills (2004) 'First release: participation in education, training and employment by 16–18 year olds in England: 2002 and 2003', July.

Department for Education and Skills (2003) *Statistics of Education: Education and Training Statistics for the United Kingdom,* London: The Stationery Office.

DTZ Pieda Consulting (1999) *Evaluation of the IiP Small Firms Development Projects, Research Report RR135,* Nottingham: DfEE Publications.

Evetts, J. (2002) 'New directions in state and international professional occupations: discretionary decision making and acquired regulation', *Work, Employment and Society,* Vol.16, No.2, pp.341–53.

Felstead, A., Gallie, D., Green, F. and Zhou, Y. (2007) *Skills at Work 1986–2006,* Oxford and Cardiff: ESRC and SKOPE.

Finegold, D. (1999) 'Creating self-sustaining, high-skill ecosystems', *Oxford Review of Economic Policy,* Vol.15, No.1, pp.60–81.

Finegold, D. and Soskice, D. (1988) 'The failure of training in Britain: analysis and prescription', *Oxford Review of Economic Policy,* Vol.4, No.3, pp.21–43.

Fuller, A. and Unwin, L. (2004) 'Expansive learning environments: integrating organisational and personal developments', in H. Rainbird, A. Fuller and A. Munro (eds) *Workplace Learning in Context,* London and New York: Routledge.

Gadrey, J. (2000) 'Working time configurations: theory, methods and assumptions for an international comparison', in C. Baret, S. Lehndorff and L. Sparks (eds) *Flexible Working in Food Retailing: A Comparison Between France, Germany, the UK and Japan,* London and New York: Routledge.

Gamble, J. (2006) 'Multinational retailers in China: proliferating "McJobs" or developing skills?' *Journal of Management Studies,* Vol.43, No.7, pp.1463–90.

Green, F., Ashton, D., James, D. and Sung, J. (1999) 'The role of the state in skill formation: evidence from the republic of Korea, Singapore and Taiwan', *Oxford Review of Economic Policy,* Vol.15, No.1, pp.82–96.

Grimshaw, D., Beynon, H., Rubery, J. and Ward, K. (2002) 'The restructuring of career paths in large service sector organisations: "delayering", up-skilling and polarisation', *Sociological Review,* Vol.50, No.1, pp.89–116.

*Grugulis, I. (2007) *Skills, Training and Human Resource Development: A Critical Text,* Basingstoke: Palgrave Macmillan.

Grugulis, I. and Vincent, S. (2005) 'Changing boundaries, shaping skills: the "new" organisational form and employee skills', in M. Marchington, D. Grimshaw, J. Rubery and H. Willmott (eds) *Fragmenting Work: Blurring Organisational Boundaries and Disordering Hierarchies,* Oxford: Oxford University Press.

Grugulis, I., Vincent, S. and Hebson, G. (2003) 'The rise of the "network organisation" and the decline of discretion', *Human Resource Management Journal,* Vol.13, No.2, pp.45–59.

*Grugulis, I., Warhurst, C. and Keep, E. (2004) 'What's happening to skill?', in C. Warhurst, I. Grugulis and E. Keep (eds) *The Skills that Matter,* Basingstoke: Palgrave Macmillan.

Hebson, G. and Grugulis, I. (2005) 'Gender and new organisational forms', in M. Marchington, D. Grimshaw, J. Rubery and H. Willmott (eds) *Fragmenting Work: Blurring Organisational Boundaries and Disordering Hierarchies,* Oxford: Oxford University Press.

Hendry, C. (1993) 'Personnel leadership in technical and human resource change', in C. Clark (ed.) *Human Resource Management and Technical Change,* London: Sage.

*Heyes, J. and Gray, A. (2003) 'The implications of the national minimum wage for training in small firms', *Human Resource Management Journal,* Vol.13, No.2, pp.76–86.

Heyes, J. and Stuart, M. (1996) 'Does training matter? Employee experiences and attitudes', *Human Resource Management Journal,* Vol.6, No.3, pp.7–21.

Hillage, J., Regan, J., Dickson, J. and McLoughlin, K. (2002) *Employers Skill Survey 2002, Research Report,* Nottingham: DfES.

Hirsch, W. and Bevan, S. (1988) *What Makes a Manager?* Brighton: IMS.

Hochschild, A.R. (1983) *The Managed Heart,* Berkeley, CA: University of California Press.

Jeong, J. (1995) 'The failure of recent state vocational training policies in Korea from a comparative perspective', *British Journal of Industrial Relations,* Vol.33, No.3, pp.237–52.

Keep, E. (1989) 'Corporate training strategies: the vital component?', in J. Storey (ed.) *New Perspectives on Human Resource Management,* London: Routledge.

Keep, E. (1994) 'Vocational education and training for the young', in K. Sisson (ed.) *Personnel Management,* Oxford: Blackwell.

Keep, E. (2001) 'If it moves, it's a skill', Paper presented at an ESRC Seminar on *The Changing Nature of Skills and Knowledge*, Manchester, 3–4 September.

*Keep, E. (2005) 'Skills, training and the quest for the Holy Grail of influence and status', in S. Bach (ed.) *Managing Human Resources: Personnel Management in Transition* (4th edn), Oxford: Blackwell.

Keep, E. and Mayhew, K. (1996) 'Evaluating the assumptions that underlie training policy', in A. Booth and D.J. Snower (eds) *Acquiring Skills*, Cambridge: Cambridge University Press.

Keep, E. and Mayhew, K. (1999) 'The assessment: knowledge, skills and competitiveness', *Oxford Review of Economic Policy*, Vol.15, No.1, pp.1–15.

Keep, E. and Rainbird, H. (2000) 'Towards the learning organisation?' in S. Bach and K. Sisson (eds) *Personnel Management: A Comprehensive Guide to Theory and Practice*, Oxford: Blackwell.

Keep, E., Mayhew, K. and Corney, M. (2002) *Review of the Evidence on the Rate of Return to Employers of Investment in Training and Employer Training Measures*, SKOPE Research Paper No.34, Universities of Oxford and Warwick: SKOPE.

Kinnie, N., Hutchinson, S. and Purcell, J. (2000) 'Fun and surveillance: the paradox of high commitment management in call centres', *International Journal of Human Resource Management*, Vol.11, No.5, pp.967–85.

Kirsch, J., Klein, M., Lehndorff, S. and Voss-Dahm, D. (2000) 'The organisation of working time in large German food retail firms', in C. Baret, S. Lehndorff and L. Sparks (eds) *Flexible Working in Food Retailing: A Comparison Between France, Germany, the UK and Japan*, London and New York: Routledge.

Korczynski, M. (2002) *Human Resource Management in Service Work*, Basingstoke: Palgrave.

Labour Force Survey (2008) *Labour Force Survey Historical Quarterly Supplement*, Office for National Statistics, available at www.statistics.gov.uk/downloads/theme_labour/LFSHQS/LFS_HQS_CQ.pdf

*Lafer, G. (2004) 'What is skill?', in C. Warhurst, I. Grugulis and E. Keep (eds) *The Skills that Matter*, Basingstoke: Palgrave Macmillan.

Lane, C. (1989) *Management and Labour in Europe*, Aldershot: Edward Elgar.

Legge, K. (1995) *Human Resource Management: Rhetorics and Realities*, Basingstoke: Macmillan.

Leidner, R. (1993) *Fast Food, Fast Talk: Service Work and the Routinization of Everyday Life*, Berkeley and Los Angeles, CA: University of California Press.

Littler, C. (1982) *The Development of the Labour Process in Capitalist Societies*, London: Heinemann.

LSC (2006) *National Employers Skills Survey: Main Report*, June 2006, Coventry: Learning and Skills Council.

Machin, S. and Vignoles, A. (2001) 'The economic benefits of training to the individual, the firm and the economy: the key issues', London: Performance Innovation Unit.

Marsden, D. and Ryan, P. (1995) 'Work, labour markets and vocational preparation: Anglo-German comparisons of training in intermediate skills', in L. Bash and A. Green (eds) *Youth, Education and Work*, World Yearbook of Education, London: Kogan Page.

Mason, G., van Ark, B. and Wagner, K. (1996) 'Workforce skills, product quality and economic performance', in A. Booth and D.J. Snower (eds) *Acquiring Skills*, Cambridge: Cambridge University Press.

McGauran, A-M. (2000) 'Vive la différence: the gendering of occupational structures in a case study of Irish and French retailing', *Women's Studies International Forum*, Vol.23, No.5, pp.613–27.

McGauran, A-M. (2001) 'Masculine, feminine or neutral? In-company equal opportunities policies in Irish and French MNC retailing', *International Journal of Human Resource Management*, Vol.12, No.5, pp.754–71.

Moss, P. and Tilly, C. (1996) 'Soft skills and race: an investigation into black men's employment problems', *Work and Occupations*, Vol.23, No.3, pp.252–76.

Nolan, P. and Slater, G. (2003) 'The labour market: history, structure and prospects', in P. Edwards (ed.) *Industrial Relations: Theory and Practice* (2nd edn), Oxford: Blackwell.

Oliver, J.M. and Turton, J.R. (1982) 'Is there a shortage of skilled labour?', *British Journal of Industrial Relations*, Vol.20, No.2, pp.195–200.

Payne, J. (1999) *All Things to All People: Changing Perceptions of 'Skill' among Britain's Policymakers since the 1950s and their Implications,* SKOPE Research Paper No.1, Oxford and Warwick Universities: SKOPE.

Payne, J. (2000) 'The unbearable lightness of skill: the changing meaning of skill in UK policy discourses and some implications for education and training', *Journal of Education Policy,* Vol.15, No.3, pp.353–69.

Phillips, A. and Taylor, B. (1986) 'Sex and Skill', *Feminist Review,* Vol.6, pp.79–83.

Pye, D. (1968). *The Nature and Art of Workmanship.* Cambridge: Cambridge University Press.

Rainbird, H. (1990) *Training Matters: Union Perspectives on Industrial Restructuring and Training,* Oxford: Basil Blackwell.

Rainbird, H. (1994) 'Continuing training', in K. Sisson (ed.) *Personnel Management* (2nd edn), Oxford: Blackwell.

Rainbird, H. and Munro, A. (2003) 'Workplace learning and the employment relationship in the public sector', *Human Resource Management Journal,* Vol.13, No.2, pp.30–44.

Ritzer, G. (1998) *The McDonaldisation Thesis,* London: Sage.

Rothenberg, S. (2003) 'Knowledge content and worker participation in environmental management at NUMMI', *Journal of Management Studies,* Vol.40, No.7, pp.1783–1802.

Rubery, J. and Wilkinson, F. (1994) 'Introduction', in J. Rubery and F. Wilkinson (eds) *Employer Strategy and the Labour Market,* Oxford: Oxford University Press.

Senge, P. (1992) *The Fifth Discipline: The Art and Practice of the Learning Organisation,* London: Century Books.

Smith, A. (1993 [1776]) *Wealth of Nations,* Oxford: Oxford University Press.

Streeck, W. (1987) 'The uncertainties of management in the management of uncertainty: employers, labour relations and industrial adjustment in the 1980s', *Work, Employment and Society,* Vol.1, No.3, pp.281–308.

Streeck, W., Hilber, J., van Kevalaer, K., Maier, F. and Weber, H. (1987) *The Role of the Social Partners in Vocational Education and Training in the FRG,* Berlin: CEDEFOP.

Taylor, S. and Tyler, M. (2000) 'Emotional labour and sexual difference in the airline industry', *Work, Employment and Society,* Vol.14, No.1, pp.77–96.

Thompson, P., Wallace, T., Flecker, J. and Ahlstrand, R. (1995) 'It ain't what you do, it's the way that you do it: production organisation and skill utilisation in commercial vehicles', *Work, Employment and Society,* Vol.9, No.4, pp.719–42.

Warhurst, C. and Thompson, P. (1998) 'Hands, hearts and minds: changing work and workers at the end of the century', in P. Thompson and C. Warhurst (eds) *Workplaces of the Future,* London: Macmillan.

Whiteways Research (1995) *Skills for Graduates in the Twenty-first Century,* London: Association of Graduate Recruiters.

Wilkinson, A. and Willmott, H. (eds) (1995) *Making Quality Critical,* London: Routledge.

Chapter 6

REWARD MANAGEMENT

Mark W. Gilman

Introduction

Regardless of whether it is to do with the amount(s) paid or the method of payment, as a core element of the employment relationship the payment of employees has always been surrounded by controversy, especially when one considers employees' collective concern (Brown *et al.* 2003). Despite arguments telling us that equilibrium pay levels are determined by Adam Smith's 'invisible hand' (Smith 1986 [1776]), traditionally pay and payment systems have been examined against the objectives of recruitment, retention and motivation of employees (Kessler and Purcell 1996). This raises the notion that pay is not just the price of labour determined by the interaction of market forces but also that employers, managers and many other actors play an important role in pay determination. More recently, for example, reward systems are argued to have far-reaching aims and objectives. Nowhere is this starker than in debates concerning human resource management (HRM), where the role of employees is seen as crucial to the creation of an organisation's competitive advantage. As part of this, pay and reward are seen as an integral element of strategic HRM. Also, in today's global economy, multinational corporations (MNCs) face the added problems of managing pay and reward across different national systems, cultures, institutions, legislation and collective bargaining regimes, to say the least. As Dowling *et al.* (2008, p. 159) state, pay is

> increasingly seen as: a mechanism to develop and reinforce a global corporate culture, a primary source of corporate control, explicitly linking performance outcomes with associated costs, and the nexus of increasingly strident, sophisticated and public discourses on central issues of corporate governance in an international context.

It has been long known that variations in pay occur for a variety of reasons other than those stated by classical economic theories. In taking a prominent role in the search for incentives, employers, institutions, legislation, etc. determine the type and potency of variable pay. Therefore it is important to understand where variations in pay arise from and the nature of variable pay as an incentive to meeting various organisational objectives. This chapter will firstly examine why there are variations in pay by looking at pay-setting arrangements in practice, international comparisons and economic explanations for such variations. Secondly, it will examine more recent reward systems that aim to pay for performance, looking at what they are, the extent and growth, roles of the social partners and how strategic they are in relation to the organisation's overall strategy.

Why pay systems vary

Historically, there have always been different pay and reward systems operating, as employers and employees struggle over the most appropriate method to suit their requirements. However, pay and reward systems also seem to have 'mimetic' (Paauwe 2004) properties in that during certain periods, and in certain sectors, particular schemes have taken prominence over others. Having said this, there may be many considerations why an employer might want to vary their pay systems. First, employers may want to recognise an employee's ability or skill. If firms want to sort workers by ability, they will adopt pay systems that reward the most able and/or skilled. Second, they may want to consider the association between output and effort. If there is a clear relationship between effort and output it is easier to pay for performance. If not, they may choose a day rate. Third, they may want to consider monitoring costs. Paying for performance is more feasible if monitoring costs are low. Fourth, they may have to consider the risk preferences of workers, because 'risk averse' workers will be less willing to 'gamble' on pay related to performance than a guaranteed set amount of pay. Fifth, employers may have to consider whether trade unions or employers' associations are involved in deciding pay and what the effects of this may be. Sixth, fairness of the pay or system has to be taken into account. This is problematic because there are generally two notions of fairness involved: first, 'the rate for the job', in which it is only fair that employees doing the same job are paid the same rate of pay, and second, it is only fair that reward should reflect an employee's contribution or effort and hence their pay will vary accordingly. Finally, pay may be dependent on power. If labour is scarce, employees have more power and hence may be able to demand higher pay; if labour is plentiful, employers have more power and hence may be able to hold pay at lower rates.

Variations in pay can cause dispersion and compression. In reducing inequality of pay and bringing about fairness, institutions matter; particularly support for unions and collective bargaining. Institutions also reflect and influence the balance of power between labour (unions) and capital (employers). But it can be argued that there are costs and benefits to dispersion and compression. The cost of compression is that if top performers are underpaid, they may quit. One may create overpayment at the bottom and underpayment at the top. The benefits of compression are that greater cooperation may be generated with less emphasis on individual performance and more on quality consciousness. The costs of dispersion may be conflict, individualism, and worker dissatisfaction over perceived inequity. The benefits of dispersion may include the ability to use pay as a motivator and as a tool for attracting and retaining top performers: whatever the case, there may be spill-over effects for society and not just the organisation. In setting pay, a number of forces have to be understood. It is to these that we turn in the next section.

PAY SETTING IN PRACTICE

Time-based pay is a system under which employees of a similar grade receive the same pay expressed in hourly (waged) or salaried terms. Wages are distinguished by an hourly rate of pay, with a specified working week in terms of the normal expected hours. Under wage systems, earnings may consist of many elements, including a basic rate, shift or overtime payments, bonuses and allowances (Drucker 2000). Under time-based payment systems, employers' control over pace and performance is reliant on either direct supervision or the willingness of employees to engage with the task. Hourly-based pay often provides a baseline from which other wage systems are developed. In comparison, within time-based pay arrangements, salaries are calculated on an annual basis and are normally paid monthly.

Although traditionally blue-collar workers have been waged and white-collar workers salaried, there is no clear occupational classification which determines which categories of employees receive wages or salaries. The unpredictability of earnings has been a central feature of the experience of many waged earners, in contrast with the relative security and regularity of income for salaried workers. In fact the division between salaried and waged workers may have as much to do with mechanisms of control as pay systems.

The ultimate question always asked is: if you pay a worker by the hour, day, week or month, how can you make sure that the employee is going to work at full capacity? Take the hypothetical example of a garage that maintains and repairs cars. Taking out overheads, profit, etc., let's imagine that a mechanic can maintain a car per day at a value of £50. Their employer might thus agree to pay the mechanic £50 per day (a weekly wage of $5 \times 50 = £250$). But if there were problems, such as materials/parts not delivered on time, broken tools/machinery or other unforeseen problems, this might slow maintenance down to two cars every 2.5 days. The mechanic will still want paying £50 per day but the employer would only want to pay the mechanic £40 per day ($4 \times 50 = 200$ divided by 5 days = £40) to reflect the fact that only four cars are maintained per week. Here the employer will want to pay only for the direct output (effort) whereas the employee may say that they still exert effort in attending work and carrying out the job using different methods, even if they are not as productive as usual, etc.

Such situations are then interpreted as being one in which the employee will always want to work in a way which allows them to put in the minimum amount of effort for the highest amount of pay and the employer will want the maximum effort for the minimum amount of pay. Agency theory therefore assumes that it is difficult for the employer and employee to make a contract based on observed effort because monitoring is too difficult or expensive; the employee is averse to effort; the employee is also averse to risk; and by paying a worker for effort you will motivate them to work harder (Baron and Kreps 1999). The consequence of this is that employers might want to find a pay system that better relates performance to effort: incentive or variable pay. The problem of incentive pay then becomes how to relate effort, output and the price of labour in the correct proportions.

Setting the price of labour not only has to take account of perceived levels of knowledge and effort but has also to consider a number of interrelated factors to do with external and internal market factors, and in doing so a number of arrangements that act as intermediaries to the external and internal markets, such as job evaluation and collective bargaining.

External market

For classical economic theory, the level of wages is the competitive outcome of the forces of the supply and demand for labour. In competitive markets for labour, workers in similar occupations and with similar skills should ultimately receive the same wage. No individual employee or individual firm has the market power to sustain deviations and pay decisions are made by studying the 'going rate'. In reality, empirical observations do not match such a theory and there have been many attempts to explain why this is (see Box 6.2). Nevertheless, it is still the case that organisations cannot survive if they do not pay attention to competitive labour market rates. More recently, external labour market pressures have become apparent in a number of developments in pay practices (Kessler 2008). Firstly, organisations are placing a greater weight on making sure that wages compare with the external market when determining pay. Secondly, attention is increasingly being focused on how to cope with the uneven external market pressures, such as differing regional or occupational rates of pay. Thirdly, responses to these external market pressures have emerged as organisations have sought to modernise their internal grading structures.

Internal market

It has been long known that employers can sometimes deliberately seek to shelter employees from the effects of the external labour market. This can especially be the case in large organisations where internal relativities are more important than just external relativities. Therefore an organisation may make decisions concerning pay through a system of internal labour markets: that is, coherent wage and career structures internal to the firm (see Doeringer and Piore 1971). Kessler (2008) argues that the importance of internal equity emerged more recently in at least three different forms. The first relates to attempts to regulate pay at the extremes of the labour market. Organisations have therefore had to deal with the government's attempts to deal with inequalities at senior management/director level and low pay via the national minimum wage. Secondly, is the question of internal equality in light of the continuing question of gender differences in pay? Finally, linked to the issue of the pay process, organisations are increasingly attempting to give greater thought to the transparency underpinning pay determination.

Job evaluation

Internally developed pay systems can reward individuals who develop firm-specific human capital and the method most often utilised to maintain these internal constancies is job evaluation. In determining the value of its jobs, however, an organisation will have to consider both external and internal labour market equity (Kessler 2008). This it does by using job evaluation. Job evaluation is a systematic process for establishing the relative worth of jobs within an organisation. Pay is then usually allocated to jobs in line with a grading structure developed in conjunction with the system of job evaluation. Job evaluation is not an exact science but it can, at the least, bring a degree of objectivity to the decision-making process. There are a variety of schemes which fall under two main types (see Box 6.1): the first are 'analytical', where jobs are broken down into individual components, the second are 'non-analytical', where the job as a whole is assessed (Egan 2004). Analytical schemes are thought to be used by 86 per cent of companies while non-analytical are used by only 14 per cent (IRS 2007). In analytical schemes criteria are decided by the organisation and these factors are then used to evaluate jobs. The most commonly used are as follows (IRS 2007):

- knowledge and skills;
- responsibility;
- problem solving and decision making;
- people management;
- relationships and contacts.

Box 6.1: HRM in practice

Non-analytical job evaluation schemes

Ranking of whole jobs in order of 'size', complexity or business impact is the most straightforward method of job evaluation. The system works, as the title suggests, by listing jobs in their order of importance, comparing one criterion or multiple criteria. However, using only one aspect of the job is more likely to distort outcomes. Once all jobs have been listed, the job evaluators will need to make decisions about

▶

the number of grades they would like to use in their organisation and then lines are drawn through the rank order at agreed break points, e.g. at each point where there is perceived to be a step difference in the size of jobs.

Job categorisation – sometimes termed job classification. This is more of a top-down approach whereby the categories, classes or grades are determined in advance and roles are slotted or placed into the category in which they are perceived to fit best. The Federal US Fair Labor Standards Act (FLSA) is in effect a simple form of job categorisation inviting employers to classify jobs as exempt or non-exempt (for overtime pay).

Paired comparison is, in many respects, a more rigorous approach to job ranking. Paired comparisons force the employer to make a choice between two factors or two whole jobs and arrive at more objective decisions about the relative worth of a job.

Analytical job evaluation schemes

Points factor is by far the dominant form of job evaluation, the Hay job evaluation method being the leading proprietary brand of 'points factor' schemes. The points factor method is a highly analytical approach to job evaluation, breaking down jobs into a number of factors against which points are allocated. It highlights the importance of focusing on the job rather than the person. This is because the factors are intended to be impersonal objective lenses through which a job is deconstructed into its component parts, each part scored independently, and then the values are added together to give a total points value to the reassembled job.

Non-analytical job evaluation – the pros and cons

Pros	Cons
Straightforward to operate	No clear basis for grading or re-grading
No special 'technical' training is required to be a job evaluator	Quality of outcomes depends on evaluator's understanding of jobs
Relatively transparent and speedy	Not regarded as a scientific approach
More likely to result in 'felt fair' outcomes for those involved in process	Hard to justify outcomes to those who have not been involved in process

Analytical job evaluation – the pros and cons

Pros	Cons
Perceived to be a scientific method	Often regarded as too 'black-box'
Job evaluation panels are a means of involving trades unions in decisions	Panels are criticised for being time consuming, expensive and bureaucratic
Trained evaluators are more likely to deliver objectives' outcomes	Evaluators have to undertake quite extensive training
Judgements are more consistent and re-grading appeals are easier to handle	Despite the apparent objectivity of the process, subjectivity still plays a role

Source: Childs (2004)

In other schemes certain jobs may then be used as benchmarks to provide a basis of comparison for other jobs evaluated. Whichever scheme, a value is then created for the jobs and jobs are then placed within a grading structure which can contain either narrow bands to maintain jobs within small variations of pay, or broad bands that allow for larger variations. An important issue to note, though, is that internal and external equity can often be in conflict (Kessler 2008). An important method of dealing with such conflicting forces is the collective determination of pay.

The collective determination of pay bargaining

In most countries, to one extent or another, other than management prerogative, collective bargaining has been the most influential form of discussing and setting pay arrangements. It is a system of deciding pay through negotiation between employees (and their unions) and employers (and their associations). Sometimes even government can be involved, either as employers within the public sector or as interested parties in the health of the economy. The form of collective bargaining utilised can depend on union structure, bargaining structure, government, ideology and power. One has to take into account that while unions are democratic organisations and behave in ways that are solidaristic to employees' collective requirements, employers and their organisations are not. Yet, in reality the role of trade unions is seen as controversial and dependent on one's ideology and beliefs. For example, the process of collective bargaining can be viewed, on the one hand, as a 'distributive' relationship in which the parties acknowledge their mutual dependence and seek to coerce each other into an agreement on the distribution of a limited resource: a fixed-sum game, in which one party's gain is the other's loss. On the other hand, it can be seen as more 'integrative', more concerned with resolving problems facing them both and which may facilitate gain for both: a win–win outcome being possible, a variable-sum game (Walton and McKersie 1965).

The collective determination of pay and conditions became dominant throughout the twentieth century, particularly in the post-Second World War era, and peaking in the early 1980s. For example, in the UK during the 1950s and 1960s, in the main, there was a split between blue-collar (manual) wage earners and white-collar (office and professional) salaried employees. Pay was largely based on seniority even where schemes were related to performance, as with piecework and bonuses. Collective bargaining was widespread, with rates for the job determined through national or industry-wide agreements, often via multi-employer bargaining. In the UK, those not covered by collective bargaining were covered by the Fair Wages Resolution and Statutory Wage Councils. Towards the end of the period, problems of 'wage drift' began to occur, as employees sought to increase their rates of pay in line with the rising cost of living.

Consequently, during the 1960s and 1970s there were growing problems, with increasing inflation and unemployment. Increasingly different types of incomes policies were attempted by successive governments in a bid to reduce inflation and unemployment. In the late 1960s the Donovan Commission reported two systems of wage determination working side by side: formal bargaining by trade unions and employers' associations and informal bargaining being increasingly carried out between shop stewards and management at the organisational level (Hyman 2004). Both Labour, through the 1969 White Paper 'In place of strife', and Conservative governments (The Industrial Relations Act 1971) attempted to regulate the reform of industrial relations (Dickens and Hall 2003). The Donovan Report argued for the formalisation of industrial relations procedures at shop-floor level and the integration of shop stewards into the machinery of collective bargaining (Nolan and Slater 2003). The formalising of such systems was supposed to lead to greater productivity, but only if workers believed that they would also gain some benefit in the form of increased rewards (Hyman 2003). This period therefore experienced the reform of collective bargaining to the establishment level to allow for productivity agreements, the most famous of which was the agreement at the Fawley oil refinery (Flanders 1964). Productivity agreements were also used in times of incomes policies to allow employers to award higher than average increases in pay if they had achieved higher than average productivity increases.

The 1980s saw the end of government policy aimed towards maintaining prices and full employment within the economy. The Thatcher government of 1979 saw trade unions and collective bargaining practices as the main cause of rising inflation and unemployment. Trade unions were 'rigidities' in the market system, stopping wages from finding their market rate. To this end, many legal changes were made to curb the powers of the trade unions. There were key union defeats (e.g. National Union of Mineworkers) and a change in the balance of power between employers and employees. During this period, for this and a number of other reasons, collective bargaining coverage fell. The Fair Wages resolutions were revoked and replaced by compulsory competitive tendering, and statutory wage councils were abolished. There were also massive changes within the public sector as some industries were privatised and others were subjected to private sector practices (e.g. teachers, nurses, civil servants), regardless of whether they were suitable or not.

By the end of the 1990s collective bargaining coverage had fallen from 71 per cent in 1984 to 41 per cent in 1998. In the private sector, only 24 per cent of employees were covered by collective bargaining by 1998, signalling the widespread abandonment of collective bargaining and the introduction of what some have labelled 'procedural individualisation'. Management prerogative was now widespread within pay determination. Performance-related pay schemes were being increasingly introduced, along with broad banding to allow for wider variation. At the end of the period, after 18 years of Conservative governments, Tony Blair's 'New Labour' was elected, signalling the possibility that there might be changes to the way employment relations were viewed. For pay purposes, the most significant legal change during the period was the introduction of the UK's first legally binding national minimum wage (Gilman *et al.* 2002).

By 2004 the most common form of pay determination was unilateral pay setting by management, with 70 per cent of workplaces paying at least some of their employees in this way. On the other hand, only 27 per cent of workplaces set pay for at least some of their employees through collective bargaining with trade unions. Having said this, because most of this collective bargaining takes place in large organisations it is estimated that 40 per cent of employees still have their pay set through collective bargaining (Kersley *et al.* 2006). So overall, although it had slowed down, there has been a continual decline in collective bargaining since the 1980s. There has also been a trend away from mixed methods of pay determination to the use of single pay determination, with pay being set by management at workplace level: a growth from 32 per cent in 1998 to 43 per cent in 2004 within the private sector. Within the public sector there has also been an increase in the incidence of unilateral pay determination, from 21 per cent in 1998 to 28 per cent in 2004 (Kersley *et al.* 2006).

INTERNATIONAL COMPARISONS

Not only do reward practices and rates of pay vary within a particular country but they can also vary significantly depending on which country you live and work in. Changes to pay-setting arrangements have not been confined to the UK but are in fact an international phenomenon. Yet, despite the identification of some common trends, both in terms of the decentralisation of collective bargaining and the use of variable pay systems, consequences will differ significantly because employer practices, institutions, legislation, etc. can be very different to begin with. This is important for a number of reasons; in particular, because of the globalisation of the world economy. An increasingly global economy has huge significance for the pay and reward practices of multinational corporations (MNCs). In order to manage the pay and reward of the whole organisation they must understand the differing national and regional systems. For example, in the USA there have traditionally been very low levels of collective bargaining. Where bargaining does take place, it is mainly at workplace level, although once concluded the agreement can be very comprehensive. There has also been extensive use of variable pay supported by confidentiality clauses to stop employees discussing earnings with each other. By contrast, if we look at Germany, pay bargaining predominantly takes place at the industry level. More recently, there has been pressure on this system, with increasing options for more flexible workplace deals. In the German system non-union workers are also usually covered by collective agreements, although this practice is less widespread than it used to be. Employees still have some influence on the workplace through a dual system of representation, not only through collective bargaining but also through works councils and supervisory boards.

Another aspect to take into account is the wide variations found in the distribution of pay across countries. For example, there are wide differences between the CEOs and the average salary of production workers, as highlighted below:

	1997	2002
USA	325:1	600:1
UK	18:1	20:1
Japan	15:1	15:1
Germany	13:1	14:1
Sweden	11:1	11:1
France	12:1	12:1

Source: Kakabadse *et al.* 2006

Why do such differences come about, and what effects do they have on outcomes? Taking the example of the UK, there are wide variations within local labour markets and within occupations. Some have estimated that the 'range of indeterminacy' even within local labour markets and occupations is in the order of 20 per cent of average earnings (Blanchflower *et al.* 1990; Gilman *et al.* 2002). Internationally, what underlies the enormous difference in pay equality is shown to have a high correlation with trade union density, the degree of centralisation of collective bargaining, and to some extent whether a social democratic type of government is in power (Vernon 2006).

In developing an international compensation policy, a MNC will need to consider a number of objectives from its own and its employees' perspectives (Dowling *et al.* 2008). First, the MNC will want to consider whether the policy is consistent with its strategy, structure and needs. Second, it must recruit and retain staff in areas of greatest need. Third, it needs to facilitate the transfer of employees internationally. Fourth, the policy must be equitable and easily administered. From the employee's perspective it will want to consider, first, the employee's need for financial protection in terms of benefits and living costs in other countries. Second, the employee is likely to expect financial advancement from a foreign assignment. Finally, the employee will expect housing, education of children and other social issues to be covered. Taken together, the above thus raise the potential for many complexities and problems (Dowling *et al.* 2008).

The MNC will also have to consider the fact that, on the one hand, they have to be aware of the institutions, structures and actors in the different countries, while, on the other, through factors such as globalisation, the increasing use of information technology, European social legislation, etc., their practices in different countries are becoming more and more visible to other parties.

ECONOMIC EXPLANATIONS FOR VARIATION

For a long time economists did not have an explanation for these variations other than blaming them on rigidities and distortions to the market. But there have been growing attempts to establish theories that explain the day-to-day observations, which differ significantly from classical theory. Some of these are explained in Box 6.2. The first three of these remain within the orthodox framework of competitive equilibrium, while the latter three seek to explain why employers may choose wage rates higher or lower than those of their competitors (Brown *et al.* 2003).

Box 6.2: HRM in practice

Economic explanations for variation

Sorted by ability

Marshall (1920) argued that the differences in earnings reflect the different productive capacities among a group. Marshall's famous example was that farm labourers in the north of England, he said, were more adept at 'putting roots into a cart' than their brethren from the south, and the wages paid reflected this difference in physical efficiency in 'about the same proportion'. The outcome of this theory is that each establishment will employ only the best, the worst or the average worker for each job and will pay them accordingly. But this still leaves unexplained important elements of inter-firm wage differentials (Abowd *et al.* 1999).

Absence of perfect information

This explanation drops the neo-classical assumption that information is perfectly (and costlessly) available. Instead, employees incur (searching) costs in identifying the range of wages on offer within the labour market. These theories are essentially a specification of labour supply, rather than demand. They do not account for the empirical observation that wage offers are generally based on the job rather than on the individual and they 'fail to specify the behavioural and institutional processes which give rise to a particular structure of wage offers'.

Compensating differentials

Within this explanation, the wage or earnings do not accurately measure the net compensation for each job. Instead, it leaves out non-wage items such as fringe benefits and does not account for the variability in working conditions. The consequence is that firms offering undesirable jobs need to improve the working conditions or offer wages above the market rate. However, this forgets the practical fact that wages are very highly positively correlated with the advantages of employment.

Monopsony

This explanation examines why some firms can pay below the market rate without losing their employees to competitors. Two options are that a single employer is sole purchaser of a type of labour within the local labour market. Employees find it more costly to find work elsewhere, hence the employer is able to pay less than a

▶

competitor's rate. Secondly, even if employers cannot attract the right number of employees, they may operate with vacancies because this represents a lower-cost option than raising the wage.

Insider/outsider

This explains the importance of company-specific influences on pay in terms of the advantages enjoyed by workers already in employment (insiders) over those on the external labour markets (outsiders). In these models, workers can only be paid above market-clearing levels because the firm itself is operating in imperfectly competitive markets and hence able to earn profits above the norm. Employees are able to use their bargaining power, which comes from firm-specific skills. The wage level is thus indeterminate, depending largely on the bargaining power of the employer and employee. Some empirical evidence supports this, but it does not explain why employers should pay over the market rate unless coerced by trade unions.

Efficiency wages

This explanation posits a causal relationship between the level of wages and an individual worker's productivity. Firms will maximise profits by paying workers in excess of the market clearing rate. In return, this induces a more productive workforce. The increments in productivity will yield a higher profit. The increased productivity arises via reduced monitoring (or shirking) costs; decreased turnover; and sociological considerations (e.g. morale, loyalty, etc.). All have at their core the proposition, not accepted in orthodox neo-classical analysis, that individuals can vary their effort and, hence, their output.

Source: Adapted from Brown et al. 2003

The above therefore begins to raise the question that rather than the wage rate being market determined, there are in fact other factors involved, including employees and their representatives (trade unions), employers and their representatives (employers' associations), and government. Employers may want to vary the wage rate for a number of reasons, including prestige, competition, control, motivation, cost and change management. Yet they may also face constraints such as productive vs. allocative efficiency, discretion offered by product market conditions and discretion offered by production strategy, highlighting that pay is not an isolated device.

In fact, it was argued above that in balancing internal and external market factors management has been able to sustain variations in pay for a number of reasons. More recently, Kessler (2008) adds business strategy as one of the three fundamental principles on which pay systems and structures are founded (the others being external/internal equity as mentioned above). The major problem is that these three principles are often in competition and it is business strategy that organisations are likely to put the emphasis on, rather than equity.

Linking reward with business strategy is synonymous with the growth of HRM, especially its strategic versions, emphasising that reward is an integral part of the HRM cycle (Fombrum et al. 1984). Strategic HRM focuses on the overall direction of the organisation in pursuit of its stated goals and objectives. Increasing the core competencies of the firm, in particular human resources, is one of the key elements in the success of the firm. The idea that people management can be a source of sustained competitive advantage calls for the integration of both HRM and business strategy (Chen and Hsieh 2006).

Schuler and Jackson (1987) also talk about the fact that HRM, and the concentration on internal equity, would result in lower salaries that would allow employees to become stockholders and have the freedom to choose the mix of rewards which might make up their pay package (Paauwe 1994).

In linking reward with strategic HRM, two of the main keywords seen as integrally linked with variable pay in the 1980s/1990s were reward management and performance management. Both of these concepts are argued to be a move away from the static salary administration of the post-war period. Both do not necessarily have to include pay for performance as part of the process, yet for most it is seen as an essential reinforcement for the type of behaviours the organisation requires.

Reward management recognises that the motivation to improve must extend to all employees and not just high flyers. Secondly, they must be flexible and not tied to rigid salary structures and job evaluation schemes. There is both an implicit and explicit assumption that employees are the key to organisational success and that reward management is a means of helping to achieve the individual and organisational behaviour that a company needs if its business goals are to be met (Armstrong 1996).

Performance management is a form of reward management and akin to what Lawler (1990) calls the 'new pay'. It is 'about the agreement of objectives, knowledge, skill and competence requirements and work development plans' (Armstrong 1996, p.260). It mainly emphasises the importance of goal setting and feedback – reviewing performance in relation to agreed objectives. Fundamental is that it is not something handed down by employers, but all members of the organisation are regarded as partners. A CIPD (2005) survey highlighted that this approach is still strong, with over 80 per cent reporting that the primary objective of their reward systems was to support business goals. If the difference had to be summed up in one sentence, it would probably be that while both concepts utilise a connection to business goals, performance management is wedded to the use of the performance contract principle.

With business strategy, the personal element comes into play, with pay equating more directly to the person and their performance, skills, attitudes and behaviours and these being used for progression along the grades (Kessler 2008). Kessler argues that recently a range of external and internal labour market pressures have encouraged the review and restructuring of pay around 'total reward' packages. Such packages allow for employer choice around flexible packages of both intrinsic and extrinsic reward as well as aligning external and internal pressures, as will be outlined below.

Total reward

Recent developments have made it more important than ever for companies to make sure they have a strategic, holistic and integrated approach to reward (Chen and Hsieh 2006). In order to distinguish themselves from other organisations in the labour market it is necessary to offer more than just a good salary. It is argued that that a 'one size fits all' approach will not succeed. Instead, each organisation needs a tailor-made system to address its particular needs. 'Total reward' holds out the promise of recruiting and retaining better-quality staff, reduced waste from staff turnover, better business performance and enhanced employer reputation. There are many different models, but all include a balance between pay, benefits, work–life balance, individual growth and development, a positive workplace and future opportunities. Provision of total reward demonstrates that the organisation takes into consideration the needs of the employee and is prepared to be flexible in meeting those needs. The employee in return is supposed to feel that they have some control over the various options from a range of benefits (Thompson 2002). Therefore a strategic reward plan involving total reward can go beyond cash to include training, job redesign, flexible work, share options, etc. (Chen and Hsieh 2006).

Paying for performance: variable pay

Over the past three decades schemes relating pay to performance have generated a tremendous amount of interest but very little in the way of conclusive evidence concerning their effects on performance. The recent growth of variable pay experienced in the UK is also an international phenomenon (Arrowsmith *et al.* 2007). The defining feature of variable pay systems (VPS) is an explicit attempt to move away from time- or seniority-based pay to performance-related criteria. There are many different ways of paying for performance and there are also many different titles used for the various schemes: incentive pay, performance-related pay (PRP), variable pay, payment by results (PBR) are all labels commonly used. Although it is often the US that is seen as the leader in the promotion of variable pay, the UK is said to be among the leading European countries in the diffusion of VPS, with PBR long being a feature of the manufacturing sector (Arrowsmith *et al.* 2007; Drucker 2000).

DEFINITIONS OF VARIABLE PAY SYSTEMS

Definitions of variable pay are problematic, not least because more recently the term has become part of the rhetoric of 'new pay', a complete reward system prescribed for the modern strategically minded organisation (see Lawler 1990, 1995). In the UK sense, however, it is fair to say that the term is more often referred to under the umbrella of incentive pay. Incentive pay is described as a system of payment in which a proportion of earnings is related to either the level of worker effort (input) or the level of output (Gilman 2001).

Given the more 'all encompassing' rationale which will be outlined below, it is probably better to refer to such schemes as VPS. VPS can therefore include systems which have a direct relationship with output such as payment by results. It is, however, also used to cover schemes in which workers may be encouraged to perform well with only an indirect relationship with output (e.g. merit pay and performance-related pay). More recently, it is used to describe reward systems in which there is no necessary relationship at all with individual performance, but where workers are entitled to a share in the company's performance and profitability, such as profit-related pay and employee share ownership plans (i.e. financial participation (Gilman 2001)).

Casey *et al.* (1992) add a further dimension by distinguishing between those where the incentive is integrated into basic pay, such as PRP, and those where the incentive is clearly discernible from basic pay, such as bonuses, profit-related pay and share ownership schemes. More recently, however, some PRP schemes include a non-consolidated bonus that is not included into basic pay. Bonuses can therefore fall into one or all of the three categories, and can either be consolidated into a person's wage or salary, or unconsolidated and paid as 'one-off' payments (Gilman 2004).

Payment by results

This term is sometimes used in a strict sense to indicate a system in which there is a direct relationship between pay and output (e.g. piecework). At other times, the term may be taken to refer to any system in which an element of pay is related to employee performance, and thus could include such items as attendance bonus. Piecework is a payment system in which an agreed sum of money is paid in exchange for a specified unit of work. There are two basic types: money piecework, which attaches a price to each piece of work, and time piecework, in which a worker is given a fixed time to do a job but is paid the same amount if the job is finished early. The term 'piecework' is sometimes, incorrectly, used more generally as a synonym for payment by results. Systems of payment by results were the most common form of payment for manual workers in British manufacturing. Evidence now points to a shift away from strict output-based systems, especially for manual workers (Drucker 2000).

Performance-related pay

Sometimes referred to as 'merit pay', it is probably worth spending more time explaining this type of VPS as it has undergone more change and been more closely related to the logic of strategic HRM than any of the others. Also, the principles underlying its introduction have been used as a justification for other developments in VPS.

PRP is a method of payment where an individual employee receives an increase in pay based wholly or partly on the regular and systematic assessment of individual performance. The payment of salary increments, bonus and other incentives is determined by a process of systematic performance appraisal. The performance measures may concern inputs or outputs but generally focus on the achievement of specific individual objectives. There has been a growth of interest in such schemes and in some organisations they have been linked to the use of personal contracts. In the public sector, governments have used them to make a direct link between a person's contribution to the standards of service provided and their reward. Linking pay to individual performance is seen to contribute to the traditional objectives of pay systems (recruitment, retention, motivation) but also to play a role in organisational change, particularly instilling a more 'entrepreneurial' culture (see Marsden and Richardson 1994; Marsden and French 1998; Heery 1998; Gilman 2004). This objective appears to have influenced the development of such schemes in organisations following privatisation. A number of organisations have experienced difficulties in setting performance criteria, assessing performance objectively, and linking pay to performance, particularly where budget constraints limit the potential size of any reward. Individual performance-related pay systems have also been found to undermine teamworking. Some organisations have abandoned or modified their PRP systems but others are still moving towards this approach to pay.

The principle of PRP, or merit pay as it was known, has been well established since at least the late 1940s, in particular occupations and sectors, along with its counterpart, job evaluation. There was basically no change in the nature of these schemes until their new lease of popularity in the 1980s (Fowler 1988). Since then, five basic changes have been noted: there has been a move away from assessments based on personal qualities towards those assessed against working objectives (i.e. rewarding output rather than input); the schemes have been increasingly introduced into the public sector; there has been an extension of these schemes from their traditional area of managerial occupations downwards to all job categories in general; there has been a move away from a general two-part increase, which included a cost of living increase and a performance-related element, towards a single increase based solely on performance; and these pay systems, it is claimed, are linked more closely to the overall business objectives of the organisation.

Yet, it is still unclear exactly what PRP is and how it varies, if at all, from company to company and from sector to sector. Despite the simplicity of the title 'PRP', it is extremely difficult to say what it is in a simple sentence given its many guises. Useful characterisations are as follows:

> A means of translating and transmitting market based organisational goals into personalised performance criteria whilst at the same time preserving the integrity of a coherent grading structure. (Kessler and Purcell 1992)

> A means whereby 'an individual's increase in pay is determined solely or mainly through his/her appraisal or merit rating'. (Swabe 1991)

Storey and Sisson (1993) also differentiate between individual PRP, which is measured through output criteria, and merit pay, which is judged on behavioural traits. These descriptions, while embodying many of the sentiments involved with PRP, are mainly about different aspects of observed behaviours and are not applicable to all aspects and forms of PRP. While neither describes PRP adequately, owing to its complex nature, they provide an acceptable starting point.

PRP has obvious similarities with PBR schemes, but whereas PBR is measured by fixed output norms, PRP is measured by the attainment of previously set objectives or targets. Through these, effort within PRP is reconstituted to embrace not just levels of output, as is the case with PBR, but also the quality of that output, and the level of discretion and initiative exercised by the individual. In emphasising the individual, appraisal becomes a means of communicating both with and to the individuals involved, while reward systems based on contribution to the organisation's objectives for sustainable competitive advantage are highly favoured by employers. Another point is that whereas PBR is mechanistic, PRP involves an amount of subjective speculation of performance.

There are three ways of determining performance: via the individual, the group, or the establishment, although the latter two are relatively unusual since incentives are considered much stronger when applied to the individual level. Individual PRP can also be determined in various ways. They range from progression through set pay bands based on the attainment of certain criteria or performance targets/objectives (this is similar to progression based on seniority, which was commonplace in the public sector), to variable bonus payments that are utilised to target money to certain high-performing employees. Sometimes more than one type can run at the same time.

My preferred definition of PRP would be that it is characterised by the linking of an individual's increase in pay to an appraisal of their performance against the use of a set of predetermined criteria based on objectives, behaviours, competences, or some combination of the three. PRP is argued to have all the strengths and none of the weaknesses of other schemes. Individually based, it is a rewarder and a motivator, a supporter of organisational, cultural, skill and objectives based on change and performance – and capable of relating pay in the individual organisation to pay in the outside market (Gilman 2004).

Financial participation

This is a term applied to various forms of employee profit-sharing and share ownership schemes which give employees a financial stake in the company for which they work. Under the prompting of the Finance Acts of 1978, 1980 and 1984, employee shareholding schemes have grown in the UK in recent years. A recent survey showed that just over 20 per cent of public and private companies practised at least some form of employee share ownership, although not necessarily for all their employees. Extension of employee share ownership has been a much-publicised feature of the privatisation of some public sector corporations, such as British Telecom. They are subject to a number of limitations and restrictions under the Income Tax Act 2003 (Tew 2008). Although seen by some as a form of workers' participation and industrial democracy, in most cases the numbers of shares involved are small, providing workers with no real shareholder power, and in some cases may involve the allocation of non-voting shares only.

Employee share ownership plan (ESOP): An idea brought into the UK from the US, this provides a way for employees to obtain an equity stake in the company for which they work, which they would not otherwise be able to afford. A trust is established which purchases shares on behalf of employees, using money borrowed from a financial institution. The dividends on the preference shares are used to pay off the loan and the shares are then gradually released to the employees. They are still held in the trust but, if the scheme so allows, the employees can sell them. ESOPs have been used in connection with management and employee buy-outs of companies when new shares are acquired at the buy-out price.

Profit sharing scheme: This form of financial participation has a long history but has received renewed attention in the past decade because of legislative encouragement and tax advantages. Approved profit sharing (APS) schemes involve distribution of shares to employees free of charge. The shares are purchased by a trust established by the company and financed from company profits. The shares are allocated to individual employees and held by the trustees on their behalf for a minimum of two years. Since April 2003 such schemes have been largely replaced by employee share incentive plans (Tew 2008).

Another scheme with tax advantages is **SAYE (save as you earn)**, where an employee enters into a savings contract with the option to purchase shares at the end of the contract period at a price fixed previously. Both types of scheme must be open to all full-time employees who have been with the company for at least five years. In 1980, there were 184 APS and seven SAYE schemes in the UK. This had increased by June 1986 to 562 APS and 541 SAYE. There were also some 1,676 approved discretionary schemes (allowing companies to grant share options to selected employees, such as executives), and also non-approved schemes which do not enjoy the tax advantages.

Profit-related pay: This is an element in the total pay package which is related by some formula to the profitability of the company (or a unit thereof). Survey evidence indicates that some 20 per cent of private sector establishments had a cash-based profit sharing scheme in 1984 and 15 per cent paid value-added bonuses.

As with profit sharing, there were tax advantages for employees where the scheme was approved by the Inland Revenue. The intention of a profit-related pay scheme is that part of the employees' pay will move up or down according to the profits made by the company, thus making pay more responsive to company performance. As well as being seen as a way of improving individual performance and motivation through giving employees a direct interest in the success of the business, and as a means of fostering commitment to the company, profit-related pay is argued by its supporters to have employment implications in that labour costs will be automatically reduced when the company runs into difficulties (through the profit-related element), thus minimising the risk of layoff and redundancy. These claimed advantages of profit-related pay have yet to be substantiated by research findings.

Companies which have introduced financial participation generally express relatively long-term objectives, such as making employees feel they are part of the company, increasing employee commitment and making employees profit conscious. Conversely, arguments against financial participation are: the double risk it involves for employees in tying their jobs and savings to the success of the same organisation; the recruitment-inhibiting effects which may result from existing employees attempting to maximise their proportion of the profits; and the fear that employees, through their representatives rather than as shareholders, may demand a greater say than management is prepared to concede in the strategic decisions which can affect the company's profitability and consequently their pay.

THE ROLE OF TRADE UNIONS, EMPLOYERS' ASSOCIATIONS AND GOVERNMENT IN VARIABLE PAY

Trade unions do not like the idea of variable pay as they see it as a move away from collective to individual pay arrangements. A survey of trade union policy (Heery and Warhurst 1994) found that only 8 per cent of unions supported the idea of PRP, 69 per cent opposed it (although only 26 per cent of these were committed to resisting its introduction) and the rest had no policy or were pragmatic about it. Labour's determination to extend PRP into the public sector came despite union opposition to its proposals and a body of research evidence that casts doubt on its suitability and efficacy. According to research (Gunnigle *et al.* 1998), variable pay serves to increase the individualisation of the employment relationship and reduce the role of trade unions. Additionally, it poses a threat to fair treatment and procedural justice (Heery 2000). Despite the lack of support for such schemes, very few unions have organised industrial action against them. The dominant response has been to attempt to secure collective agreements which regulate its operation (Heery and Warhurst 1994), although this is not often possible with profit-related, share ownership and bonus schemes (Marginson *et al.* 2007).

The TUC stated that it supported wider share ownership and partnership. The government's All Employee Share Scheme was, however, criticised by the TUC as only being of benefit to employees of limited companies in the private sector. It excludes people in the public sector and those in the mutual sector (e.g. in building societies, co-ops, etc.). Rather than opposing such a scheme, the TUC argues that an equivalent scheme should be introduced for employees within mutual organisations so that there is no unfair advantage to share-issuing companies.

Employer organisations have continually promoted variable pay schemes as a means of providing individuals with the motivation to improve their performance. PRP schemes are seen as a far more efficient way of controlling the total wage bill while differentiating between employee performance. Because profit-related and employee share schemes usually attract certain tax benefits, they are seen as particularly cost-efficient forms of remuneration.

Governments have continuously promoted the idea of 'market forces' and 'individualisation' of the employment relationship, and have been determined to eliminate what they see as rigidities in the working of the labour market (Brown and Walsh 1991). Pay, according to government sources, ought to be linked only to what companies can afford (as in profit-related pay schemes which have been encouraged through direct tax concessions) as well as to an individual's performance as in PRP. Like its predecessors, the Labour government has embraced the concept of variable pay. For example, PRP is promoted for both private and public sector employees. The government's White Paper, 'Modernising government', set out changes reflecting their reward agenda of linking pay to individual performance. The introduction of PRP for teachers was particularly controversial (Payne 2000; Marsden 2007). In principle, paying for measurable performance has become increasingly blurred. It has led many public sector bodies to consider alternative PRP schemes that incorporate team-based rewards and a wider assessment of employees' overall contribution to the business. The Makinson Report (2000) noted, in particular, the damaging effects of perceived unfairness in the public sector organisations studied. It noted that although there was widespread acceptance of PRP in principle, there was also much disenchantment with it in practice. Marsden (2007) also noted much the same effect with the PRP scheme for teachers.

Governments have at various times explicitly encouraged profit/share schemes through the provision of tax incentives. Also, public consciousness of share ownership was increased dramatically by the privatisation of state enterprises such as water, gas and electricity. As mentioned above, the government introduced a new share ownership scheme in 2001, which it hoped would benefit a wider proportion of employees.

EXTENT AND GROWTH OF VARIABLE PAY

There are no overall detailed figures available in the UK or elsewhere to signify the true extent of variable pay, nor is there a commonly agreed definition of what it is. The 1990 Workplace Industrial Relations Survey (WIRS) and the 1998 and 2004 Workplace Employee Relations Survey (WERS), however, included data on incentive pay. Although overall comparisons can be made for some aspects, the structure of the questions differed within each survey, making meaningful comparisons difficult.

In the 1990 data, 63 per cent of workplaces had at least one type of incentive scheme. By 1998, the figure was 58 per cent. Despite this, the authors (Millward *et al.* 2000) argue that it would be safer to conclude that there was little overall change over the period. There were, however, changes in the way that incentive pay was used. In 1990, PBR schemes were more commonly used for manual rather than white-collar employees, whereas by 1998 the reverse was true. Also, there was a slight intimation that PRP was less commonly used than before, hinting that these types of schemes may have reached their peak. In 2004, 40 per cent of workplaces had incentive pay schemes: PBR was used in nearly one-quarter (23 per cent), merit pay in 9 per cent and both in 7 per cent. While the above does not give an accurate picture of the extent over time, the panel survey highlighted an increase from 20 per cent in 1998 to 32 per cent in 2004. Evidence also suggests that larger workplaces and those without recognised unions continued to make greater use of incentive pay (Kersley *et al.* 2006). Another survey (IRS 2006) reports that 21 per cent of organisations used PBR and 44 per cent used cash bonuses.

PRP, or merit pay as it is sometimes known, gained increasing popularity in the 1980s (Fowler 1988) but the precise extent of its coverage is not known because official data sources such as the New Earnings Survey only include PRP among the 'catch all' category of 'incentive pay' (Casey *et al.* 1992). However, those smaller-scale surveys which have been undertaken show that the proportion of companies which use PRP for at least some proportion of their employees varies between one-third (IRS 1991) and one-half (WIRS, 1992; IRS, 1991; Casey *et al.* 1992). One survey even found that two-thirds of respondents used PRP (IDS 1991). While the WERS 2004 survey found only a low presence of PRP for the largest occupational group, IRS (2006) found that it was the most commonly used form of reward strategy, with 55 per cent of organisations using it for at least some employees. Importantly, both surveys found that although this has been one of the most popular forms of pay system for the past decade, the use of such schemes seems to be on the decline.

In general, most studies find that there is a positive relationship between occupational hierarchy and PRP, profit-related pay and share ownership schemes, but that this narrowed somewhat over the period. The 2004 data highlights that incentive pay is most likely in sales and customer service and least likely in caring, leisure and personal services (Kersley *et al.* 2006).

Table 6.1 highlights the overall extent of financial participation. During the 1980s both profit-related and share ownership schemes became far more widespread owing to encouragement by consecutive Conservative governments via generous tax concessions. There was

Table 6.1 Financial participation 1980–98

	Cell percentages						
	Profit sharing			Employee share ownership			
	1984	1990	1998	1980	1984	1990	1998
All establishments	19	44	46	13	22	30	24
Broad sector							
Private manufacturing	16	33	50	8	14	25	22
Private services	21	50	46	17	27	34	25
Public sector – trading	1	4	17	–	–	–	–
Foreign owned	7	31	51	11	10	13	21
UK owned	21	45	47	14	24	33	25
Size of enterprise							
25–99 employees	12	29	29	3	2	4	3
100–999 employees	15	37	48	7	13	10	14
1,000–9,999 employees	18	50	59	19	33	53	38
10,000+	31	63	72	27	47	65	58

Source: Millward *et al.* 2000

only a slight growth of profit-related schemes during the 1990s, primarily in the manufacturing sector, among foreign-owned establishments and UK MNCs. The single most important characteristic of the extent of profit-related pay was the size of the workplace. At its peak in the mid-1990s, profit-related pay covered 4.1 million employees in 14,000 companies (IRS January 1999). Recent studies find that profit-related pay is prominent in financial services and electricity, gas and water but disagree on its extent (36 per cent, Kersley *et al.* 2006; 15 per cent, IRS 2006).

Share ownership schemes also grew throughout the 1980s but declined over the 1990s, particularly in the private service sector. The number of UK-owned companies using such schemes declined, while usage among foreign-owned companies increased. Four out of five workplaces with share schemes allowed all or most employees to participate. Take-up rates, however, were substantially smaller (Millward *et al.* 2000). According to data from the Inland Revenue (IRS May 2000), save-as-you-earn schemes are operated by 1,200 companies with 1.75 million participants; approved profit sharing is operated by 900 companies with 1.25 million participants; and company share option plans are operated by 3,700 companies with 400,000 participants. Recent figures (WERS 2004) highlight that 21 per cent of organisations (19 per cent, IRS 2006) had at least one share ownership scheme, the most common of which was SAYE (13 per cent). Overall, with both share ownership and profit-related pay there had been little change in the number of organisations using them since 1998.

There were differences in the overall utilisation of incentive schemes depending on sector: in the public sector, under half continued to use incentive pay; in the private sector, two-thirds continued to use incentive pay; and in the manufacturing sector, three-quarters continued to use incentive pay. In terms of the different types of variable pay, the WERS data highlighted that performance-related pay was concentrated within four main sectors:

- Distribution   25%
- Banking/finance   23%
- Manufacturing   21%
- Other services   17%

Table 6.2 provides a more detailed sector breakdown for financial participation schemes.

Table 6.2 Incidence of financial participation by sector

Industry	Profit-related pay % of workplaces	Share ownership % of workplaces
Manufacturing	50	22
Electricity, gas, water	81	80
Construction	29	9
Wholesale and retail	62	32
Hotels and restaurants	42	31
Transport and communication	61	30
Finance	80	56
Other business services	45	23
Education	8	0
Health	6	0
Other community services	28	28

Source: WERS Data

The criteria used in the award of variable pay

The following criteria were used as measures if pay was determined by individual performance/output (WERS data):

- Piece rates 7
- Other measure of output 45
- Assessment by supervisor 57
- Acquisition of skills/core competences 17

Casey *et al.* (1992) found that the criteria used for profit-related pay was split equally three ways: a third paid an amount at management's discretion; a third paid a fixed percentage of profit; and the final third used various other methods. With share schemes, employees are usually given an option to purchase shares, or awarded free or discounted shares dependent on individual, team or divisional performance (see IRS May 2000).

If payments are determined by individual or group PRP, the measures of performance used were as follows (WERS data):

- Individual performance/output 79%
- Group or team performance/output 47%
- Workplace based measures 33%
- Organisation based measures 39%

Similarly, the figures for profit-related pay are:

	1998	2004
Workplace	20%	48%
Division	10%	8%
Organisation	66%	40%
Other	4%	4%

The nature of VPS

Schemes are usually introduced, continued or abolished by employers. Schemes and the amounts awarded are sometimes the subject of negotiation with trade unions, but the employer tends to have most of the decision-making power. Although the use of PRP may have statistically peaked, such schemes continue to change in nature and prove just as controversial. Also, in the UK, profit-related schemes had their tax advantages phased out between 1996 and 2000, and have therefore declined in importance. Share schemes, however, continue to receive support from both the government and the unions. The WERS data suggests that more recently organisations are likely to use different types of variable pay in conjunction with each other rather than as alternatives (Millward *et al.* 2000).

Most VPS work in a way that means an individual is unlikely to receive an overall decrease in pay. The worst scenario is usually that no increase or bonus would be awarded, although in the case of share ownership schemes, depreciation is a possibility.

During the 1998/1999 pay round, all-merit rises added an average of 4.1 per cent to the annual pay bills of organisations making such awards. Where merit supplemented across-the-board increases this added an average of 2 per cent to the pay bill (IRS November 1999). An example of what this means in terms of individual increases can be found in the finance sector during the 2007 pay round (IRS 2007). The average merit award was 3.6 per cent within a range of 0–5 per cent. Profit sharing bonuses ranged between 5 and 9 per cent (IRS May 1999).

There is little or no information concerning the full extent of collective agreements over variable pay. If the extent of collective bargaining was taken as a general indication, by 1998 only 29 per cent of workplaces had their pay determined by collective bargaining. Sector differences were as follows:

- Private sector manufacturing   23%
- Private sector services   14%
- Public sector   63%

The greatest coverage of collective bargaining is in the public sector. Yet this sector is little affected by profit-related and share ownership schemes. The extent of collective bargaining over such schemes is therefore probably low.

With PRP, schemes are usually introduced, with unions then attempting to influence them in three main ways: to regulate the process of performance appraisal in a bid to ensure that management decision making involves rules and procedures; to reduce the financial risk to employees covered by such schemes; and to secure procedural rights to pursue appeals, have access to information concerning the running of the schemes and jointly review the schemes with management. Owing to the decentralised nature of industrial relations in the UK, bargaining usually occurs at the level of the organisation or in some cases the workplace. The increased importance of variable pay coincides with the decentralisation and decline in the extent of collective bargaining. Having said this, however, the emphasis on partnership in the workplace means that unions will look to play a role in variable pay wherever possible.

As noted previously, there are very few cases of industrial action over the use of variable pay schemes. One example was the case of Barclays Bank. The dispute began in August 1997 after the bank imposed a new PRP system without negotiating with the two main unions: Unifi and Bifu. The unions initiated three one-day strikes, a work to rule and an overtime ban. A fourth one-day strike was called off when the company agreed to talks with the unions. The dispute was settled in March 1998, with the company securing the introduction of PRP but the unions ending what would have amounted to an overall pay freeze for members (IRS March 1998).

A recent study (Arrowsmith *et al.* 2007) highlighted the use of collective bargaining over variable pay systems in the banking and machinery and equipment sectors of Austria, Norway, Spain and the UK. Comparing single employer bargaining (SEB) with multi-employers bargaining (MEB), it was found that variable pay in Spain and the UK were more employer driven than in Norway. In Austria, there was a difference between the savings banks (sector agreements) and the commercial banks (no agreements). In banking, multiple variable pay schemes were apparent in the majority of companies. Individual performance-related pay is subject to collective regulation in all four countries, but with the exception of Spain, account for only a small proportion of earnings. Rather it was bonuses and profit-related pay that yielded larger quantitative significance and was in all four countries subject to less collective regulation. In machinery and equipment variable pay was more employer driven in the UK than in Austria or Norway. Variable pay was rarely accompanied by collective bargaining in the UK whereas in Norway it was at the company level and in Austria at the sector level. Table 6.3 highlights examples of typical VPS within the banking sector of four European countries.

Table 6.3 Profile of VPS in four countries

	Type of VPS	Coverage	Criteria	Frequency	Quantitative significance (% of earnings)
UKC1	Merit pay	All employees	Individual appraisal around balanced scorecard (BSC) – matrix removed 2004	Incorporated into monthly salary	Varies. 2006 pay pot = 4% but 3% dedicated towards market and minima uplifts. Leaves 1% available to managers to distribute according to performance
	Bonus	Some 20 to 30 schemes covering all employees	Individual sales and BSC	Varies	5–6% for main retail workforce
	Share scheme	All employees	Free shares plus matching	Annually	3% salary (up to max. 3,000 shares)
	Flexible benefit package	All employees	Allowance to purchase benefits or take as cash	Annually	4%
NOC1	PRP – pay interview model	All, but varies who gets what	Competence, ability to cooperate, work performance (results), responsibilities, values	Pay interview annually. Incorporated into monthly salary on permanent basis	On average 1% annually (2005). Varies between individuals from no increase to substantial increases
	FP – profit-sharing scheme	All	No formal criteria, but based on company results. Discretionary decision by CEO/board	Payouts at retirement or if leaving the company	Approx. 3% of total wages allocated in 2005
	Ad-hoc bonus for commercial banking unit (one-time payments)	Employees in this unit	No criteria. Sum distributed to bank managers, who decide how to distribute	Was paid in 2005 (expected to be some arrangement for 2006 as well)	Limited information (2–3% average?)
	PBR – bonus, used by i.e. business market department plus international payments	All in units but only 125 of 7,000 employees	10 factors ranging from reducing loss to carrying out planned training. A total score set the total bonus pot	Annually	0.5=1.0% on average; 5–10% for those in receipt depending on wage level and size of bonus (varies between €2,400 and €3,600)
ESC1	Merit pay (1991)	Discretionary, pay revision for technical staff (75% of total)	Pay band systems and bonus reference (internal and external equity criteria), individual skills appraisal. Discretionary and consolidated, non-pensionable	Incorporated into monthly salary	n.d

▶

	Type of VPS	Coverage	Criteria	Frequency	Quantitative significance (% of earnings)
	Bonus (1991)	Individual bonus 8,149 employees; team 16,823	Management by results, reference bonus, individual score achievement, team performance appraisal and BSC. Discretionary, non-consolidated and non-pensionable	Annually	Individual: wage bill 8.2%, employee earnings 24,8%; Team: wage bill 5%; employee earnings 10.7%
	Extra bonus	High-performance staff (score 150+)	Reference bonus, results of each business unit division, discretionary, non-consolidated and non-pensionable	Annually	20–50% increase over ordinary bonus in employee earnings
	Commercial incentives	Those 10% branches in same classification with better results	Allowance to purchase benefits or take as cash, non-consolidated and non-pensionable	Annually	20% increase over ordinary bonus in employee earnings
ATS1	Performance pay (since 1993): savings from pay scheme reforms are redistributed as PP	100% all staff	Job evaluation factor and MBO with four criteria: job requirements, agreement on objectives, performance attitude, and executive functions.	Monthly	10% wage bill
	Voluntary balance bonus (since 1993)	100%	Company success	Annually	3.5% wage bill, max. half month's pay
	Incentive system market (since 2000)	68.8% (market employees)	40% is paid as team bonus and 60% as individual bonus; latter discretionary by supervisors	Annually	1.5% of the premiums; 12% wage bill.
	Incentive system back office (since 1990)	31% (administrative employees)	Extraordinary performance, discretionary proposal by supervisors (max. 50% of employees), subject to managing board confirming who/amount	Annually	2% wage bill

Source: Adapted from Arrowsmith *et al.* 2007

Pay for performance: how strategic is it?

BASED ON SIMPLISTIC VIEWS

Variable pay schemes have attracted increasing attention throughout the past decades. In particular, they have been seen to be linked with the concepts of human resource management (HRM), high-performance work systems (HPWS) and quality systems such as total quality management (TQM). Like these concepts, the research into VPS has produced indeterminate results. But this has not stopped them from being prescribed by academics and specialists alike as the reward systems to solve the problems of the past three decades.

As well as their traditional use as a means of aiding the recruitment, retention and motivation of staff, VPS are said to hold out the promise of a direct link between effort and reward, and to be a means of consolidating moves towards the creation of an internal labour market in line with other HRM/TQM techniques. Supporters even point to the fact that employees themselves have great difficulty in arguing against the logic of such schemes. It is also argued that such schemes are a fairer way of rewarding people as it is only 'fair' that reward should have a direct link with effort.

These views are simplistic for a number of reasons. First, and probably most important, the so-called 'positive' effects are rarely backed up by any systematic evidence. Second, specific company and/or sectoral factors are rarely taken into account, so that VPS are offered as a carte blanche recipe for all. Finally, the consequences for employees are largely ignored and/or seen as unproblematic 'teething' problems. It is assumed that the schemes will be beneficial to all employees and that they will understand and agree with the particular notions of fairness on which VPS are based, ignoring the possibility that perceptions of fairness can vary from employee to employee.

It is surprising that companies should place so much emphasis on particular pay systems without evidence as to whether they work or not, given that these schemes are rarely introduced independently and are usually argued to be part and parcel of other business goals and objectives to enhance competitiveness.

There have been various studies, mainly emanating from the US, which highlight the positive performance benefits of PRP (e.g. Lazear 2000). It is interesting to note that whereas these examples are used to promote the use of PRP they actually turn out to be piecework systems rather than PRP or merit pay. The relative merits and pitfalls of piecework were studied intensely in the UK throughout the post-war period (see Brown 1973) and do not need rehearsing here. The main point is that definition and terminology make it very difficult to have a serious discussion of the relative strengths and weaknesses of any VPS. To do so requires a deeper understanding of the different VPS on an international basis.

In the UK comprehensive studies within public sector organisations (Marsden and Richardson 1994; Marsden and French 1998; Heery 1998; Gilman 2004; Marsden 2004, 2007) tend to describe indeterminate results from PRP schemes in terms of performance but a widespread acceptance that such schemes lead to employee demotivation, thus leading some to argue that increased performance, where present, is more the result of work intensification than improved productivity. Marsden (2007) noted that the usual problems of line management bias in rating performance, poor-quality appraisal and goal setting, etc. can be improved by involving employees and their representatives in the design of and improvements to such schemes. Belfield and Marsden (2004, p.460) also argue that it 'is not so much the choice of pay system that drives organisational performance outcomes but the combination of pay system and monitoring environment'.

WHY SO POPULAR?

One reason for the popularity of VPS schemes, as mentioned above, is that they closely fit with government ideology throughout the past three decades. This factor certainly accounts for the increased use of PRP in the public sector.

A second reason is that PRP schemes are usually linked to notions of HRM/HPWS/TQM. Although the meaning and nature of these concepts remain elusive, they represent a strategic and coherent approach to an organisation's most important assets: its employees (Armstrong 1993). HRM and HPWS put emphasis on the development of the individual employee, while TQM emphasises the individual's responsibility to product quality and customer service. Thus individualised reward systems become an important part of the concepts of HRM/TQM. They are also symptomatic of broader shifts in management practices and the elaboration of strategy specific to the development of the individual organisation (Walsh 1992).

Finally, there have been increasing pressures on reward systems which have reinforced the trend towards PRP schemes (Vickerstaff 1992): both product market and labour market pressures have increased with the increasing competition of the past decades; new technology and new forms of work organisation have begun to challenge existing demarcation and pay structures; and reference points for market rates may have increasingly begun to internationalise.

THE EFFECTS OF VPS

The international study mentioned above found that different types of VPS had differing effects on the individualisation of the employment relationship. Whereas PRP schemes were more collective in nature, this was less the case for bonuses, share schemes and profit-related pay. Also, the strategic nature of VPS depended on factors such as the environment, structure and actors. For example, there was a bigger range of VPS in banking than in manufacturing, with a higher percentage of earnings related to performance. Different strategies were used in the two sectors. In banking, strategy was emergent, with intentions adapting over time to changing realities. In manufacturing, strategy was more deliberative, with a premium placed on reward systems that respond to customer requirements brought about by intense competition (Arrowsmith *et al.* 2007).

Discussion

It has been highlighted that reward is in fact an enormously complex issue which has to take account of three fundamental principles in determining systems and structures: internal equity, external equity and business strategy. In doing so it requires tools, such as job evaluation, and interacts with other interested parties, as in the collective determination of reward. Historically, there have been many changes introduced as the actors struggle with a combination of economic, political, social and technological pressures. These factors are intensified further when we include an examination of reward at international level.

Looking at the past 20 years, there is no doubt that variable pay has become much more important. In particular, VPS loom larger and have permeated further and further down the occupational ladder. There are also different types of VPS, with many organisations preferring to use them in combinations rather than any one individual type. It was also highlighted that in different sectors and countries schemes take on a variety of forms owing to factors such as competitive environment and institutional HRM arrangements. Simultaneously, collective bargaining over pay has declined significantly and coincided with a greater individualisation of the employment relationship. This is because incentives are argued to be most influential where they apply to the individual. Having said this, however, over the past few years the negative effects of such schemes as PRP are leading both government and companies to look at ways of incentivising employees.

There is very little evidence of any positive effects for performance or employees, especially in the case of PRP schemes. Most academic research shows that such schemes, on the whole, tend to have a demotivational rather than motivational effect. One of the main problems is the difficulty in balancing and maintaining salary structures while attempting to provide incentives. VPS do not seem to be meeting their traditional objectives, but other objectives have been found:

- to signal a change in organisational culture;

- to bring about a restructuring of the employment relationship;

- to allow selective reward without increase in the pay bill;

- to decentralise collective bargaining;

- to marginalise trade unions;

- to allow closer financial control;

- to balance the lack of promotional opportunities with selective reward for development.

Different schemes may even have different goals. Arrowsmith *et al.* (2007) found that bonus schemes were used as incentives, PRP was used for cost control and development (although these two are clearly in conflict) and profit-related pay to signal wider business goals and cultures. Some are now beginning to argue that PRP and other VPS are more about control, with employers wanting to re-establish more control over the effort bargain. Despite the above, there is no shortage of commentators willing to extol the virtues of variable pay schemes. Companies have consistently chosen an approach of altering schemes in an attempt to rectify problems, without any fundamental changes to the principles involved, with total reward presently being the flavour of the month.

So variable pay is presently confusing. While it is easy to discuss in broad terms, in reality the enormous variability and rhetoric surrounding such schemes has produced a state of uncertainty. More recently, companies are being advised to take a much more strategic approach to pay by utilising many different types of variable pay schemes in a way which 'fits' with the strategic intent of the company and its business plan. But as Arrowsmith and Sisson (1999) note, changes in pay arrangements reflect adjustments of management strategy in the light of intense competition, new production arrangements and key changes to the organisational context. All these factors are likely to be personal to each organisation and lead to 'personal' outcomes concerning variable pay, which fits with Kessler's (2008) argument that organisations are more likely to focus on business strategy than on internal or external equity.

Strategic success for reward systems relies on a whole range of factors (Marginson *et al.* 2007). The fact that integration of strategic HRM involves many practices (e.g. appraisal, training, corporate culture, etc.) combined with consideration of contingencies (technology, wider environment, etc.) means that it is difficult for any organisation to balance external and internal labour market factors while also offering the packages of VPS.

In offering systems under the label of 'total reward', organisations are clearly attempting to give themselves more flexibility to balance the three fundamental principles. The key question is what effects will this have on performance, with the answer likely to be that we are unlikely to find out until such schemes are examined based on solid empirical evidence rather than on rhetoric and mimetic adoption.

Total reward strategy at Kent County Council

Miral Metawie

About KCC

Kent County Council (KCC) is the largest council in the UK. The council governs the majority of the county of Kent in England and comprises 12 district councils and more than 300 town and parish councils. KCC employs a total of 45,500 employees, including schools, which accounts for almost two-thirds of KCC's workforce (30,500 employees). KCC is further divided into four main directorates. These are the Communities Directorate, which has the largest number of KCC's workforce with 4,277 employees; Children, Families and Education Directorate (4,179 employees); Adult Services Directorate (3,777 employees); Environment and Regeneration Directorate (902 employees); there is also the Chief Executive's Department (1,870 employees). KCC is one of the most successful local authorities. In three consecutive years the authority's comprehensive performance assessment has been rated 'excellent' and performance management framework as 'good' (4 out of 4). KCC encourages a strong performance management culture, where the aim is to provide value for money while lowering costs.

Pay structure at KCC: history of PRP

Like many parts of the public sector, KCC was faced with pressure by government to become more performance oriented and apply a reward system where pay is related to performance. As a result, KCC was one of the first local authorities to opt out of national pay arrangements. The traditional automatic incremental progression system was seen as being too remote to the performance culture KCC required in order to respond to the needs of the local environment. Consequently, KCC introduced 'Kent Pay Plus' in 1990, which was characterised by a move towards a performance-based system and the introduction of performance-related pay (PRP). The local pay determination was also aimed at placing greater emphasis on investing in employees' needs and development. The aim was to create a system where individuals were rewarded according to their individual performance and, hence, the introduction of differentiation between good and bad performers. As opposed to automatic increments, payment was made on three levels of assessment: these were level 3 which was one increment, level 2 which was two increments or a percentage of pay if at the top of the grade, and the top level which was placement on any pay point or a percentage of the pay if at the top of the grade. Levels 1 and 2 resulted in no pay progression.

According to a KCC reward project manager, however, the system was partially budget driven and was influenced by whether managers did or did not have enough money to reward those whom they thought deserved a level 2 or 1 assessment. Additionally, there was limited guidance as to how to measure performance, resulting in a lack of clear measurement against which employees were assessed and a lack of high-level moderation of the assessment results. For instance, managers who felt their team did well could award them a level 2 increment but might not have clear action plans or performance targets against which they could measure the assessment. Therefore, some decisions were fairly arbitrary. Consequently, the system was perceived to be unfair, costly and lacking consistency of application across the organisation. As a result, not all managers engaged with the system, which was finally abolished after 1996. According to employees who were employed by KCC during that period, PRP was also abolished because it created inequalities and failed to measure all aspects of the job, particularly for those in lower grades. It was also seen to lack the sophistication and consistency required of an appraisal system.

▶

Total reward strategy: a move to total contribution pay (TCP)

Since 1996, the local authority reverted to using the traditional automatic annual incre-ments where employees' progression was based on their length of service without linking to any formal performance review. The pay structure consisted of 12 grades for white collar employees, ranging from A to L. However, the persistent recognition of the need to improve service delivery and keep the council more responsive to Kent's changing environment and needs pushed KCC to revise its overall pay structure in 2000. The council argued that whereas the old system was unfair, inflexible and old-fashioned, the new reward strategy should be fair, simple, focused on delivery, promote dialogue in the workplace, motivate, develop staff full potential, and provide for two-way communication.

The result was the introduction of a new total reward strategy with a key element being the removal of automatic increments and the implementation of a pay progression system based on individual contributions – total contribution pay (TCP). The decision to introduce a 'contribution-based' system in KCC was taken at a political level in the organisation involv-ing the higher positions in the council (i.e. chief officer group – COG) as well as the cabinet members. Following the decision to introduce TCP, an ongoing process of consultation, design and development began in 2001 to formulate the new reward strategy. KCC devel-oped a partnership with the trade unions who were consulted over the new system and reward strategy, leading to a new agreement in 2003. Prior to the partnership, unions did not have a formal opportunity to state their opinion on pay.

The changes were accepted by a ballot of members of the union, with the council respond-ing to some of their concerns. Yet, there was a main philosophical difference between the union and the council about the individualistic nature of PRP and the union had concerns about the managerial capabilities of assessing individual performance. Overall, however, the KCC reward manager stated that less than one-third of KCC staff were union members.

Outside the union, employees who were consulted were mainly key managers at strategic levels. They were asked which aspects needed to improve. Consultation at the strategic level was mainly concerned with ensuring that TCP met the needs of the business. In addition, the COG examined the system in terms of its suitability to management. Overall, feedback was obtained from senior managers, elected members at cabinet level, trade unions, the reward strategy board, joint reward implementation team, and the operational HR teams.

Before the implementation of the new reward strategy KCC began to raise all staff awareness of the change, its nature and its benefits for individuals as well as the county as whole through what they called a comprehensive communication campaign. This campaign included circulating newsletters, carrying out road shows that were free to attend by all members of staff, sending out e-mails about TCP, as well as publishing information about the system on KCC's intranet site. Stated benefits for jobholders included:

- improved clarity about what is expected from staff;
- regular two-way discussion with managers on how well they are performing;
- ability to progress faster within their pay band;
- taking the whole job into account, not just objectives;
- performance development.

In addition to linking pay to contribution, another aim of the total reward strategy was to shorten the length of, and minimise the overlap between, job grades. This included changing the number of pay bands from 12 grades to 15. Figure 6.1 shows the KCC revised pay structure.

KCC also introduced a new approach to job evaluation using job families and profiles against which every member of staff was matched in order to fit the new grades. Following

▶

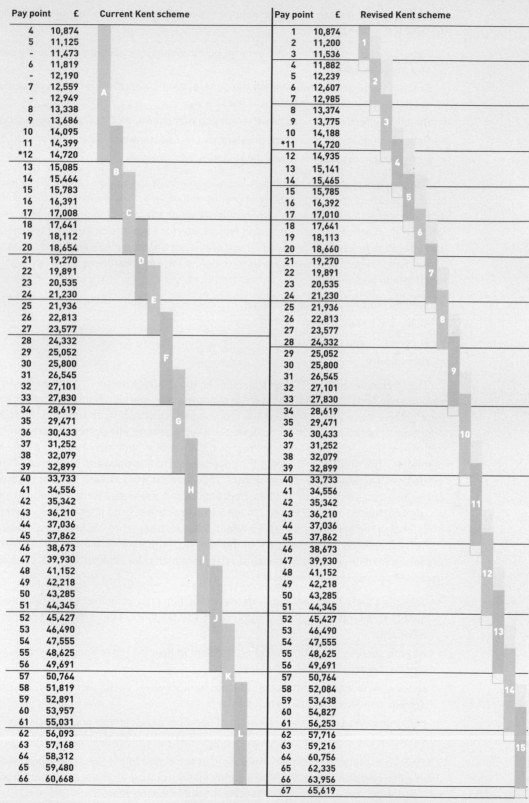

Pay point	£	Current Kent scheme		Pay point	£	Revised Kent scheme
4	10,874			1	10,874	
5	11,125			2	11,200	1
–	11,473			3	11,536	
6	11,819			4	11,882	
–	12,190			5	12,239	2
7	12,559	A		6	12,607	
–	12,949			7	12,985	
8	13,338			8	13,374	
9	13,686			9	13,775	3
10	14,095			10	14,188	
11	14,399			*11	14,720	
*12	14,720			12	14,935	
13	15,085	B		13	15,141	4
14	15,464			14	15,465	
15	15,783			15	15,785	5
16	16,391			16	16,392	
17	17,008	C		17	17,010	
18	17,641			18	17,641	6
19	18,112			19	18,113	
20	18,654			20	18,660	
21	19,270	D		21	19,270	
22	19,891			22	19,891	7
23	20,535			23	20,535	
24	21,230			24	21,230	
25	21,936	E		25	21,936	
26	22,813			26	22,813	8
27	23,577			27	23,577	
28	24,332			28	24,332	
29	25,052			29	25,052	
30	25,800	F		30	25,800	
31	26,545			31	26,545	9
32	27,101			32	27,101	
33	27,830			33	27,830	
34	28,619			34	28,619	
35	29,471	G		35	29,471	
36	30,433			36	30,433	10
37	31,252			37	31,252	
38	32,079			38	32,079	
39	32,899			39	32,899	
40	33,733			40	33,733	
41	34,556	H		41	34,556	
42	35,342			42	35,342	11
43	36,210			43	36,210	
44	37,036			44	37,036	
45	37,862			45	37,862	
46	38,673			46	38,673	
47	39,930	I		47	39,930	
48	41,152			48	41,152	12
49	42,218			49	42,218	
50	43,285			50	43,285	
51	44,345			51	44,345	
52	45,427	J		52	45,427	
53	46,490			53	46,490	13
54	47,555			54	47,555	
55	48,625			55	48,625	
56	49,691			56	49,691	
57	50,764	K		57	50,764	
58	51,819			58	52,084	
59	52,891			59	53,438	14
60	53,957			60	54,827	
61	55,031			61	56,253	
62	56,093	L		62	57,716	
63	57,168			63	59,216	15
64	58,312			64	60,756	
65	59,480			65	62,335	
66	60,668			66	63,956	
				67	65,619	

* = Top of current grade A becomes pay point 11

☐ = Transition range   ☐ = Advanced box

Figure 6.1 KCC pay structure

consultation with directorate representatives, five job families were identified as being able to cover the whole authority:

- Care (people) – roles which the general public would interact with in receiving services at a personal level.
- Community (places) – roles which the general public would interact with in receiving services at a business or technical level.
- Business effectiveness – administration and management of KCC as an organisation.
- Policy – medium- to long-term development of directorate services and/or KCC.
- Leadership – management and development of resources.

The purpose of developing job families was to enable individuals to see the bigger picture by being aware of the comparability of grades and roles across the organisation and to see a clear progression within their own 'family'. Additionally, a full job profile was written for each Kent scheme grade, including typical jobs for each directorate and typical skills and education levels to be attained. There are hence 15 job profiles equating to each of the 15 pay bands. Four key areas were used to define the key differences between a job placed in one grade and another:

- problem solving and accountability;
- skills and knowledge;
- supervision and management;
- competence.

The implementation of TCP was phased. Actual changes began in April 2005 and were complete by April 2007. Changes were brought in over a period of time to make it easier for employees who had to manage the process and for others to understand the changes. Adopting a phased approach also allowed KCC to 'fine tune' the system before the final implementation, following feedback received from senior staff after the first phase implementation. The first phase involved the coverage of 5,000 employees from grade D to grade L – all supervisory and senior staff. This phase started in April 2005 at the beginning of the new assessment year. In 2006, new grades and pay scales were introduced and pay progression based on contribution. In the same year the second phase was implemented by extending the system to all staff on Kent scheme grades 1 to 15, including schools.

TCP is based on the assessment of the individual's total contribution against their predetermined targets and personal development plans. An individual's total contribution is assessed against four key elements:

- objectives and accountabilities – delivery to action plan, effectiveness in job role, targets, quality standards, budgetary control, customer feedback, peer group/360 degree feedback;
- ways to success – meeting a higher standard in how the job is done, in accordance with agreed targets;
- wider contribution – contribution to team, project work, participation in KCC work activities not directly related to job role;
- personal development – achievement of personal development plan, application of development, attainment and use of required skills, qualifications attained.

Prior to the total contribution evaluation, at the beginning of the assessment year in April, employees and their managers jointly identify and agree the action plan targets as well as the personal development targets for the following year.

▶

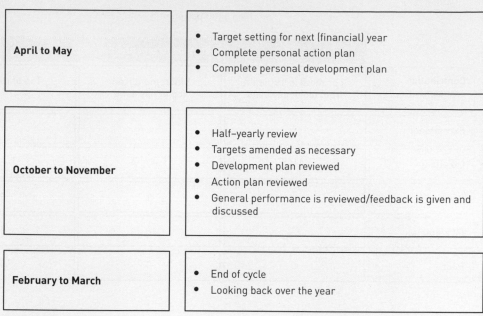

| April to May | • Target setting for next (financial) year
• Complete personal action plan
• Complete personal development plan |

| October to November | • Half-yearly review
• Targets amended as necessary
• Development plan reviewed
• Action plan reviewed
• General performance is reviewed/feedback is given and discussed |

| February to March | • End of cycle
• Looking back over the year |

Figure 6.2 The appraisal year

During the appraisal managers consider each assessment category within the context of total contribution; however, it is not necessarily the case that each individual will have every element shown for each assessment category. Figure 6.2 shows the suggested time for the appraisal year.

After the completion of the appraisal discussion, managers make the TCP recommendation, taking into account the four assessment categories of TCP.

Like the previous Kent scheme, TCP utilises the same overall pay budget, but distributes it differently to recognise individuals' contributions. For additional flexibility and to overcome problems with pay disparity, TCP enables progress on a scale of half-increments up to a maximum of two increments each year. In addition, individuals who are at the top of their grades can receive the equivalent of up to one additional pay point as a one-off award depending on their contribution assessment. TCP, hence, introduced five levels of performance rating using half-increments to provide shades of contribution. The ratings hence are as shown in Figure 6.3.

Not all elements in a category will apply to all people. Assessments, therefore, are expected to reflect individual differences. The appraisal form, containing the rating, is prepared by the manager and signed off by a 'grandparent' (a senior manager). The final rating decision is not shared with employees until all assessments have gone through a moderation process and been agreed by the chief officer group (see below) because any change in rating is likely to be demotivating. Managers provide summary evidence for the rating rewarded. A good rating can be the overall result of a combination of ratings for each category. However, an excellent rating should be the result of the combination of excellent ratings in all criteria, or with the combination of exceptional ratings. Similarly, an exceptional rating should be the result of the combination of exceptional performance ratings in all assessment categories.

There are also cash and non-cash awards. Cash awards can be also used throughout the year to reward specific actions or achievements. Managers should ensure that there is no double counting of an individual's contribution and should note any payments given earlier in the year. Managers can reward individuals for a good piece of work with up to £500.

▶

If on a full pay point:

Contribution assessment	Position in incremental pay band		
	2 or more increments from top of pay band	1 increment from top of pay band	Top of pay band
Exceptional	2	1 + A	A
Excellent	$1^1/_2$	$1 + ^1/_2$ A	$^1/_2$ A
Good	1	1	0
Incomplete	$^1/_2$	$^1/_2$	0
Poor	0	0	0

If on half pay point:

Contribution assessment	Position on incremental pay band		
	$2^1/_2$ or more increments from top of pay band	$1^1/_2$ increments from top of pay band	$^1/_2$ increment from top of pay band
Exceptional	2	$1^1/_2 + ^1/_2$ A	$^1/_2 + A$
Excellent	$1^1/_2$	$1^1/_2$	$^1/_2 + ^1/_2$ A
Good	1	1	$^1/_2$
Incomplete	$^1/_2$	$^1/_2$	0
Poor	0	0	0

Figure 6.3 Levels of performance ratings

Awards higher than £500 have to be signed off by a senior manager. Non-cash awards include buying a bunch of flowers, box of chocolates, etc.

After the manager's completion of their direct reports' assessments, the documents are sent to their grandparent for review. This process is repeated up the reporting line to the top of the directorate. At this point, results between directorates can also be compared, together with an equalities assessment. This is a moderation process that is used to assess the distribution of the manager's assessment and compliance against quality standards. Ultimately, directorates need to collate results to assess the distribution of the assessment

▶

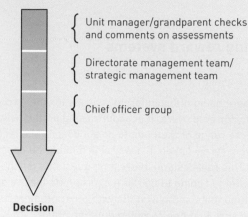

{ Unit manager/grandparent checks and comments on assessments

{ Directorate management team/ strategic management team

{ Chief officer group

Decision

Figure 6.4 The moderation process

scores on a wider basis and implications for budget expenditure. Figure 6.4 shows the stages of the moderation process.

Finally, TCP provides the opportunity for individuals who disagree with the outcomes of their assessment to appeal against the assessment result to their grandparent through the appeal process. Any disputes should be resolved at this level with the assistance of Personnel Business Support. It is hoped, however, that the appraisal process will be fair and objective, and decisions can be supported with evidence validating the final total contribution assessment rating.

TCP is one of the new elements of recognition that constitute what is called the total reward strategy, which includes the implementation of single status for former manual workers, a new approach to job evaluation using job families and profiles, and total contribution pay. The total reward package offers flexible benefits to all staff from buying and selling leave, health care, lifestyle screening, salary sacrificing, an employee discount and cashback benefits scheme (current offers include deals on finance, cars, gifts, days out, clothing, mobile phones, health and beauty, home and garden, holidays, entertainment, sport and fitness). All this is communicated to staff via an intranet site, www.KentRewards.com, telephone helpline and staff leaflet.

KCC has, for a long time, offered flexible working, employee benefits, cash awards and quality service awards (which is an amount of money to be spent on anything that improves the quality of the service, e.g. buying a new printer, changing furniture office, etc.). Though these benefits existed prior to the implementation of TCP, the total reward strategy aims at raising employees' awareness of these benefits. KCC expects the new reward strategy and the change in culture to enable employees to have greater ability to access their flexible benefits.

Questions

1. What are the advantages and disadvantages of the new pay arrangements?
2. Identify the key differences between the old PRP and the current total contribution pay.
3. What measures were taken by KCC to ensure that TCP will not meet the same fate as the old PRP system?
4. What other HRM practices and processes would you introduce to make sure TCP was successful?

Designing reward systems

Mark W. Gilman

Despite there being many different reasons for the introduction of pay for performance, essentially, for employers, it is about raising productivity. Yet companies use not only pay, but a diverse range of methods to do so, despite the fact that recent research argues that they are very rarely linked in a way which might be described as a 'productivity enhancing strategy'. This raises some interesting questions for the HR manager concerning which reward system is going to be more appropriate for the organisation and its employees, what are its components and how it fits with other elements of the productivity-increasing measures to ensure that one complements the other.

In this chapter we have highlighted not only the differing combinations of rewards available but also some of the differing internal and external pressures faced when deciding how to pay employees. Despite this, it is still common for employers to concentrate on performance-related pay schemes as their major form of reward. While a number of employers say that they have had a positive experience of tying pay to performance, there are a number of pitfalls, including encouraging different behaviours to those it was supposed to encourage. Below are a number of examples of recent schemes introduced by companies from a range of different sectors to meet a range of different priorities. The first, reintroducing an across-the-board increase, had a concern for overall pay equality; the second, despite being in the same industry, was moving in the opposite direction with a concentration on pay for performance; the third had to deal with employee market power; the fourth with a lack of flexibility; the fifth with consistency across European operations; and the final one not wanting to pay employees extra for what they should already be doing. In doing so companies were utilising similar schemes in different ways, attempting to balance internal and external factors and the requirements of the differing stakeholders.

Yorkshire Water implemented a new pay and performance management system in 1998. The scheme was considered ahead of its time and even credited with helping to turn the business round. It featured individual performance-related pay that offered employees the chance of consolidated merit awards, and formed the basis of a series of two-year pay deals.

However, unions representing the company's 2,200 skilled, technical and professional staff were unhappy with the individual performance element of the system. They were particularly concerned that an employee whose performance was poor in one year – leading to a zero pay increase – suffered not just in that year but for the remainder of their career and into retirement. Their calculations showed that a 40-year-old employee, who missed out on a pay rise in that one year while colleagues got a 3 per cent rise, would lose between £30,000 and £40,000 in pay and pension.

As a result of this and other concerns, Yorkshire Water and its recognised unions have now negotiated a new agreement which came into effect in 2005. It will include an inflation-linked increase for all employees until 2010, and non-consolidated individual merit bonuses. These non-consolidated bonuses are paid quarterly, and their value is known in advance. For 2005/2006, for example, each quarterly bonus is worth £250 to an 'over-achiever' and £150 to an 'achiever'. A system of consolidated bonuses is also available to those who consistently over-achieve, along with consolidated 'progression' increases. The move to the new scheme has been accepted by the unions, which say that their members are happier with the new approach.

Severn Trent Water operates 3,000 sites and employs around 5,000 staff. Frontline employees fall into two groups, including head office staff and contact centre employees

▶

and process and maintenance workers. Reward practices were considered out of date, with little provision for the desired flexibility or link to performance. Performance-related pay had been attempted for some of these groups in the past but had proved unsuccessful. The HR department had to devise an alternative model that provided clear performance-related progression for staff but at the same time retained a banded pay framework.

The company employed the Hay Group to provide consultancy services, enabling them to gain valuable insights into other reward practices and options, but decided that they wanted to create their own pay model. In its first two years up to 2004 the scheme involved an across-the-board pay increase, as it had done previously, and a performance-related increase. It was made clear that the basic pay increase would not be an entitlement and is not guaranteed – employees still have to meet the specified performance criteria.

From 2006 a new framework was negotiated linking pay to company profit targets and improvements in safety performance and attendance levels. A published formula shows how the amount of money available for the next year's pay increase can be enhanced by outperforming in all three areas.

In 2008 HR managers at **Yahoo Europe** were given the challenge of dampening down employee pay expectations. The company focused on rewarding only its best performers so that there were no expectations of linking pay to inflation or to what the employees themselves thought they were worth. The problem for the company was one in which global economic conditions are leading to recession but employees are well aware of their own value and hence perceive themselves to have a degree of market power to demand higher pay.

The company has introduced 'forced rankings', where managers have to identify who their best and worst performers are. The company commented that a significant proportion of employees would get zero in the 2008 pay round while performance would be rewarded more than normal. The company was hoping to get employees and managers to take accountability for their own performance and differentiate between strong and weak performance.

In 2002, insurance firm **DAS Legal Expenses** decided on an overhaul of their pay scheme after line managers complained that the scheme offered little flexibility. The new scheme is based on an appraisal system built around four core values – excellence, respect, improvement and cooperation – which, when broken down to individual targets, provides managers with both structure and a degree of flexibility.

The scheme operates by scoring employees on a quarterly basis from 0 to 14 for each aspect of their performance, and weighting the scores according to the perceived importance of each aspect to the department in which they work. Results are then compiled over the course of a full year ahead of the next pay review date. Although the merit element of pay rises can then be determined according to appraisal ratings, the system also includes room for collective bargaining with the Amicus trade union over the pay rise sum to be allocated to each grading.

The scheme is generally judged to be a success because it provides clarity to employees about company goals and their contribution to achieving them, and because it gives senior managers regular performance metrics that rapidly show up problems.

At business travel management consultancy **Carlson Wagonlit** merit pay is linked to a programme of performance reviews that take place at least once every year for each employee. A similar system operates for managers, who receive a bonus based on company and individual performance.

An intriguing aspect of the Carlson Wagonlit scheme is that the key competencies were developed by employees in the UK, rather than by consultants or the HR department, and have since been adopted for use throughout the company's European operations – although union resistance is likely to mean that these are not used to determine pay outside the UK.

▶

Sterilisation products manufacturer **Isotron** reviewed its reward systems after doubling its turnover and employee numbers in a takeover in 2006. Although it decided that performance-related pay was not right for it, the company does now have a performance-related bonus scheme. The company considered that rewarding managers with additional increases to their salary for jobs they were already paid to do was undesirable. Instead they wanted to reward for increased responsibilities only.

There had been a prior subjectively allocated performance bonus but the new bonus is decided via a performance review based on key values and reviewed by a senior manager. The company says that the scheme has involved a considerable culture shift in how pay and performance is viewed.

(Adapted from Personnel Today, 2008; IRS, 2004; Attwood, 2005)

Questions

1. Are the above companies utilising the appropriate reward system? Should they be using other rewards as part of their overall package? What would you advise for these companies?

2. Take an example of a company that you know and design a reward system, explaining the reasons for your design and ensuring that it incorporates the company's culture, strategy, employees, etc. Would you use the same system for all employees within the company?

Bibliography

Abowd, J., Kramarz, F. and Margolis, D. (1999) 'High wage workers and high wage firms', *Ecomometrica*, 67(2): 251–333.

Armstrong, M. (1993) *Managing Reward Systems*, Buckingham: Open University Press.

Armstrong, M. (1996) *Employee Reward*, London: Institute of Personnel and Development.

Arrowsmith, J. and Sisson, K. (1999) 'Pay and working time: towards organization-based systems', *British Journal of Industrial Relations*, Vol.37, pp.51–75.

Arrowsmith, J., Nicholaisen, H., Bechter, B. and Nonell, R. (2007) 'The management of variable pay in banking: forms and rationale in four European countries', 8th European Congress of the International Industrial Relations Association, September, Manchester UK.

Attwood, S. (2005) 'Performing flexible reward at Severn Trent Water', *IRS Employment review*, Issue 834.

Baron, J.N. and Kreps, D.M. (1999) *Strategic Human Resources: Frameworks for General Managers*, New York: Wiley & Sons.

Belfield, R. and Marsden D.W. (2003) 'Performance pay, monitoring environments, and establishment performance', *International Journal of Manpower*, Vol.24, No.4, pp.452–71.

Blanchflower, D., Oswald, A. and Garrett, M. (1990) 'Insider power in wage determination', *Economica*, Vol.57, pp.143–70.

Brown, W.E. (1973) *Piecework Bargaining*, London: Heinemann.

Brown, W., Marginson, P. and Walsh J. (2003) 'The management of pay as the influence of collective bargaining diminishes', in P.K. Edwards (ed.) *Industrial Relations: Theory and Practice*, Oxford: Blackwell.

Brown, W. and Walsh, J. (1991) 'Pay Determination in Britain in the 1980s – the Anatomy of Decentralization', *Oxford Review of Economic Policy*, Vol.7, Issue: 1, pp.44–59.

Casey, B., Lakey, J. and White, M. (1992) 'Payment systems: a look at current practice', Employment Department Research Series No 5.

Chen, H.-M. and Hsieh, Y.-H. (2006) 'Key trends of the total reward system in the 21st century', *Compensation and Benefits Review,* November/December, Sage.

Childs, M. (2004) 'Managing reward: job evaluation and grading. One stop guide', available at xperthr.co.uk

CIPD (2008) 'How to stand out from the crowd', summary of Thompson, P. (2002) *Total Reward: Executive Briefing,* London: Chartered Institute of Personnel and Development.

Dickens, L. and Hall, M. (2003) 'Labour law and industrial relations: a new settlement', in P.K. Edwards (ed.) *Industrial Relations: Theory and Practice,* Oxford: Blackwell.

Doeringer, P.B. and Piore, M.J. (1971) *Internal Labor Markets and Manpower Analysis.* Lexington, MA: D.C. Heath & Co.

Dowling, P.J., Festing, M. and Engle Allen, D. (2008) *International Human Resource Management,* (5th edn), London: Thompson Learning.

Drucker, J. (2000) 'Wage systems', in J. Drucker and G. White (eds) *Reward Management,* London: Routledge.

Edwards, P.K. (ed.) (2003) *Industrial Relation: Theory and Practice,* Oxford: Blackwell.

Egan, J. (2004) 'Putting job evaluation to work: tips from the front line', *IRS Employment Review,* Issue 792.

Flanders, A. (1964) *The Fawley Productivity Agreements,* London: Faber & Faber.

Fowler, A. (1988) 'New directions in performance pay', *Personnel Management,* November, Vol.20, No.11.

Fombrum, C., Tichy, N.M. and Devanna, M. (eds) (1984) *Strategic Human Resource Management,* New York: John Wiley.

Gilman, M. (2001) *Variable Pay: The Case of the UK,* Dublin, Ireland: European Industrial Relations Observatory.

Gilman, M. (2004) *The Characteristics of Performance Related Pay,* Canterbury Business School Working Papers, No. 59, March.

Gilman, M., Edwards, P., Ram, M. and Arrowsmith, J. (2002) 'Pay determination in small firms in the UK', *Industrial Relations Journal,* Vol.33, pp.52–67.

Gunnigle, P., Turner, T. and D'Art, D. (1998) 'Counterposing collectivism: performance related pay and industrial relations in greenfield sites', *British Journal of Industrial Relations,* Vol.36, pp.567–78.

Hay Group (2005) *Total Reward: Preliminary Report.*

Heery, E. (1998) 'A return to contract? Performance related pay in a public service,' *Work, Employment and Society,* Vol.12, No.1, pp.73–95.

Heery (2000) 'Trade unions and the Management of Reward', in J. Drucker and G. White (eds) *Reward Management.* London, Routledge.

Heery, E. and Warhurst, J. (1994) *Performance Related Pay and Trade Unions: Impact and Response,* Kingston University, Occasional Paper Series, August.

Hyman, R. (2003) 'The historical evolution of British industrial relations', in P.K. Edwards (ed.) *Industrial Relations: Theory and Practice,* Oxford: Blackwell.

IDS Focus (1991) 'Performance pay', December.

IRS (1991) 'Pay and benefits bulletin'. No. 587, September.

IRS (1998) 'Barclays settles pay dispute', *Pay and Benefits Bulletin,* 444, March.

IRS (1999) 'The end of the world is nigh: planning for the post-PRP age', *Pay and Benefits Bulletin,* 464, January.

IRS (1999) 'Pay report', *Pay and Benefits Bulletin,* 472, May.

IRS (1999) 'Pay prospects survey', *Pay and Benefits Bulletin,* 483, November.

IRS (2000) 'Assessing the value of share ownership', *Pay and Benefits Bulletin,* 496, May.

IRS (2004) 'Making merit work: One size doesn't fit all', *IRS Employment Review,* Issue 813.

IRS (2006) 'Pay prospects survey', *Pay and Benefits Bulletin,* 852, November.

IRS (2007) 'Job evaluation is thriving, survey finds', *Employment Review,* 667.

IRS (2007) 'Financial sector pay', *Employment Review,* 668, August.

Kakabadse, N.K., Kakabadse, A. and Kouzmin, A. (2005) 'Directors' remuneration: the need for a geo-political perspective', *Personnel Review,* Vol.33, No.5, pp.561–2.

Kersley, B., Alpin, C., Forth, J., Bryson, A., Bewley, H., Dix, G. and Oxenbridge, S. (2006) *Inside the Workplace: Findings from the 2004 Workplace Employment Relations Survey,* London: Routledge.

Kessler, I. (2008) 'Reward choices: strategy and equity', in J. Storey (ed.) *Human Resource Management: A Critical Text* (3rd edn), London: Thompson Learning.

Kessler, I. and Purcell J. (1992) 'Performance related pay objectives and application', *Human Resource Management Journal*, Vol.2, No.4.

Lawler, E. (1990) *Strategic Pay: Aligning Organizational Strategies and Pay Systems*, San Francisco: Jossey-Bass.

Lawler, E. (1995) 'The new pay: a strategic approach', *Compensation and Benefits Review*, July, pp.14–20.

Lazear, E.P. (2000) 'Performance pay and productivity', *American Economic Review*, Vol.90, pp.1346–61.

Makinson, J. (Chair) (2000) *Incentives for Change: Rewarding Performance in National Government Networks*, London: Public Services Productivity Panel, HM Treasury.

Marginson, P., Arrowsmith, J. and Gray, M. (2007) 'Undermining or reframing collective bargaining? Variable pay in two sectors compared', Pay and Reward Conference (PARC), Manchester.

Marsden, D.W. (2004) 'The role of performance related pay in renegotiating the "effort bargain": the case of the British public service', *Industrial and Labor Relations Review*, Vol.57, No.3, April, pp.350–70.

Marsden, D.W. (2007) 'Individual employee voice: renegotiation and performance management in public services', *International Journal of Human Resource Management*, Vol.18, No.7, July, pp.1263–78.

Marsden, D.W. and French, S. (1998) *What a Performance: Performance Related Pay in the Public Services Centre for Economic Performance, Special Report.* London: London School of Economics, available at www.cep.lse.ac.uk

Marsden, D.W. and Richardson, R. (1994) 'Performing for pay? The effects of "merit pay" on motivation in a public service', *British Journal of Industrial Relations*, Vol.32, No.2, June, pp.243–62.

Marshall, A. (1920) *Principles of economics: an introductory volume*, London: Macmillan.

Millward, N., Bryson, A. and Forth, J. (2000) *All Change at Work*, London: Routledge.

Millward, N., Stevens, M., Smart, D. and Hawes, W. (1992) *Workplace Industrial Relations in Transition*, Bath: Bookcraft Ltd.

Nolan, P. and Slater, G. (2003) 'The labour market: history, structure and prospects', in P.K. Edwards (ed.) *Industrial Relations: Theory and Practice*, Oxford: Blackwell.

Paauwe, J. (2004) *HRM and Performance: Achieving Long Term Viability*, New York: Oxford University Press.

Payne, J. (2000) 'School teachers' review body gives green light to performance-related pay,' EIRO online, UK0011100F.

Personnel Today (2008). *Yahoo Staff Face Performance Related Pay*, Feb. 12th.

Schuler, R.S. and Jackson, S.E. (1987) 'Linking competitive strategies with human resource management practices', *Academy of Management Executive*, Vol.1, pp.209–13.

Smith, A. (1986 [1776]) *The Wealth of Nations*, Books 1–3, London: Penguin.

Storey, J. and Sisson, K. (1993) *Managing Human Resources and Industrial Relations*, Milton Keynes: Open University Press.

Swabe, A.I.R. (1991) 'Performance related pay: a case study', *Employee Relations*, Vol.3, No.2.

Tew, P. (2008) *Employment Law*, Industrial Relations Services.

Thompson, P. (2002) *Total Reward*, Executive briefing, London: Chartered Institute of Personnel and Development.

Vernon, G. (2006) 'International pay and reward', in T. Edwards and C. Rees (eds) *International Human Resource Management: Globalisation, National Systems and Multinational Companies*, Harlow: Pearson.

Vickerstaff, S. (1992) 'Reward management', in S. Vickerstaff (ed.) *Human Resource Management in Europe: Text and Cases*, London: Chapman and Hall.

Walsh, J. (1992) 'Internalization v decentralization an analysis of recent developments in pay', Discussion Paper, Leeds University School of Business and Economic Studies.

Walton, R.E. and McKersie, R.B. (1965) *A Behavioural Theory of Labor Negotiations*, New York: McGraw Hill.

Workplace Employment Relations data set (2004).

Workplace Industrial Relations data set (1992).

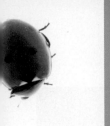

Chapter 7

PERFORMANCE APPRAISAL

Tom Redman

Introduction

The practice of performance appraisal has undergone many major changes over the past two decades. In the main, developments have been driven by large-scale organisational change (see Chapter 1) rather than theoretical advances in the study of performance appraisal. Particularly prominent here are the advent of downsizing, decentralisation and delayering, flexibilisation of the workforce, the move to teamworking, wave after wave of culture change programmes and new managerial initiatives such as total quality management (TQM), business process re-engineering (BPR), competency, knowledge management and, in particular in the UK, Investors in People. The Workplace Employee Relations Survey (WERS) data reports that organisations who are recognised as an Investor in People were significantly more likely to have a performance appraisal scheme in use (Cully *et al.* 1999; Kersley *et al.* 2006). Changes in payment systems have also fuelled the growth and development of performance appraisal. Developments in integrated reward systems, harmonisation and the increased use of merit- and performance-based pay have been strongly associated with the growth of performance appraisal.

Two main implications for performance appraisal practice arise from the new organisational context. First, it would be clearly inappropriate to expect those appraisal schemes operating 10 years or so ago to be effective in many organisations today (see Case Study 7.1 at the end of this chapter). Second, rather than new developments heralding the end of performance appraisal or diminishing its importance, they appear to have enhanced its contribution to helping achieve organisational objectives and have stimulated considerable experimentation and innovation in its practice. Performance appraisal, as we discuss below, has in fact become more widespread. It has grown to include previously untouched organisations and occupational groups. In particular, performance appraisal has moved down the organisational hierarchy to encompass manual, secretarial and administrative staff and from the private to the public sector. New forms of appraisal have also emerged. We thus now have competency-based appraisal systems, staff appraisal of managers, team-based appraisal, customer appraisals and '360°' systems. Old systems of performance appraisal have also been dusted down and have re-emerged in new forms (see Box 7.1).

This chapter's main aim is to critically review some of the key developments in the practice of performance appraisal. First, a brief history of performance appraisal is presented and current practice examined by considering how widespread it is, what it is used for, and its role as a managerial control tool within broader performance management systems. Second, we review some of the major innovations in the practice of performance appraisal. Third, some of the problems of performance appraisal in practice are considered; in particular, here we examine the compatibility of performance appraisal with TQM, continuous improvement and customer service initiatives. Finally, in light of the growing criticisms, we conclude by considering whether performance appraisal has a future in HRM practice.

Box 7.1: HRM in practice

Performance appraisal in hard times: ranking and yanking

A growing number of organisations are reported as having adopted a performance appraisal system in which best-to-worst ranking methods are used to identify poor performers. Such appraisal systems rank employees along a normal distribution curve in which the top 10 per cent typically receive an A grade or equivalent, the middle 80 per cent earn a B, and the bottom 10 per cent earn a C and dismissal if they do not improve. Such systems gained popularity in the 1990s, and about a third of companies now use them in the US, up from 13 per cent in 1997, according to *Time* magazine (Fonda 2003). The rationale for such performance systems is to punish the bottom as well as rewarding the top employees. The poor performers thus identified are first given help and a period of time to improve. If they fail to rise in the ranking, they must leave. The exit may be 'encouraged' with a redundancy package, but if the poor performer refuses to leave voluntarily, they face the possibility of termination without compensation. This strategy has become known as the 'rank and yank' system after the nickname given to the scheme by former Enron employees where it appears to have first emerged.

An example of the rank and yank appraisal is provided by Sun Microsystems. The company ranks its 43,000 employees into three groups. The top 20 per cent are rated as 'superior', the next 70 per cent as 'standard'. At the bottom is a 10 per cent band of 'under-performers'. The under-performers are told that they must improve and are provided with one-on-one coaches. The ultimate fate of these employees is clear from the CEO's view that these under-performers must be 'loved to death'. Informal variants of rank and yank appraisal systems seem to have emerged in some UK university departments in the run-up to the 2008 Research Assessment Exercise (RAE). The RAE ranks a department's research from sub-national to world-class levels (0 to 4*). In some mock assessment exercises university managers have ranked the research output and esteem of employees on this grading system, with 4* performers receiving 'retention packages' while those rated 1* and 0 rated have been made to feel, in the words of one dean, 'very unloved and uncomfortable'.

The advocates of rank and yank believe that forced rankings make managers and supervisors take the unpleasant but tough decisions that otherwise they would seek to avoid as being too fraught with conflict. Some organisations see the forced ranking approach as a way to create a continuously improving workforce. The view is that an annual culling system produces a 'hotbed of over-achievers' who increase the overall calibre of an organisation. However, despite its obvious Darwinian managerial appeal, there are many problems with the system. First, someone must always fall into the lower or under-performing category, even if everyone has performed at a very high level. It is also possible that those rated as 'poor performers' in highly productive departments may contribute more to the overall progress of the organisation than those rated as 'good performers' in other low-performing departments. Forced ranking thus does little for teamwork and can encourage high levels of in-fighting and dysfunctional internal competition as employees seek to protect their own position at the expense of their co-workers. The legality of such dismissals in many countries must be open to question and some ranking and yanking systems have been abandoned in the US following legal challenge. It must also be questioned whether the level of churn induced by such a system with an annual culling is good for the

▶

stable employee networks required to produce innovation and creativity, and whether it justifies the increased administrative costs associated with replacement recruitment and training. However, it is not clear that 'yanked' employees have been always replaced and some critics have suggested that the schemes are thinly disguised smoke screens for downsizing or to get rid of older workers who often populate the lower rankings. Thus the US has also seen forced ranking systems subject to a rising number of age discrimination lawsuits.

Development of performance appraisal

Informal systems of performance appraisal have been around as long as people have worked together; it is a universal human tendency to make evaluations of our colleagues at work. Formal performance appraisals have a shorter but still considerable history. Grint (1993) traces it back to a third-century Chinese practice. In the UK, Randell (1989) identifies its first use via the 'silent monitor' in Robert Owen's textile mills. Here a multi-coloured block of wood was hung over the employee's workspace with the front colour indicating the foreman's assessment of the previous day's conduct, from white for good through to black for bad. Owen also recorded a yearly assessment of employees in a 'book of character'.

Since these early developments, performance appraisal has become a staple element of HRM practice. Personnel managers themselves, however, have tended to be much keener on it than their line manager colleagues. Accompanying practitioner interest in performance appraisal has seen a mushrooming of academic research, notably by occupational psychologists. A key thrust of much of this research has been on improving performance appraisal's effectiveness and, in particular, its accuracy in assessing employee performance. We know rather less about a more strategic use of performance appraisal as an organisational change lever and managerial control tool. There is now a wealth of academic studies on performance appraisal. Computer literature searches on the topic show over 20 academic articles per month appearing with 'performance appraisal' in their titles. Despite the large and growing volume of research work on the subject, however, it is debatable how much influence such studies have had on the actual practice of performance appraisal. It seems that managers are peculiarly reluctant to heed the advice of researchers in this area of business practice and there is a persistant 'gap' between research and practice (Banks and Murphy 1985; Maroney and Buckley 1992).

This lack of impact of research on practice is not simply a question of general managerial indifference to the academic researcher, especially when compared to the wide influence of consultants and popular management 'gurus'. Rather, one explanation is that little of the research has considered the implications for practitioners who are faced with a plethora of organisational constraints not encountered in the research laboratory. More damning perhaps is the view that much of the research has had little to offer HR managers, except for the recommendation to train appraisers, as it has generally been unable to provide much improvement in terms of accuracy at least, over the simplest of supervisory ratings systems.

The practice of performance appraisal

HOW WIDESPREAD IS PERFORMANCE APPRAISAL?

Performance appraisal has become more widespread in Western countries. For example, surveys report performance appraisal in the US increasing from 89 per cent of organisations surveyed in the mid-1970s to 94 per cent by the mid-1980s (Locher and Teel 1988). In large and medium-sized US organisations performance appraisal systems are now virtually universally present. Similar surveys in the UK by the Chartered Institute of Personnel and Development report increasing coverage of formal performance appraisal arrangements (Long 1986; Armstrong and Baron 1998; IPD 1999; CIPD 2005). Performance appraisal is also now more common in many other non-Western countries such as China (Chow 1994), Hong Kong (Snape *et al.* 1998), Japan in the form of *Satei* (Endo 1994); Africa (Arthur *et al.* 1995) and India (Lawler *et al.* 1995). Performance appraisal appears to be one of the most commonly adopted HR practices in high-performance work systems (ILO 2002).

Appraisal is particularly prominent in some industrial sectors in the UK, such as financial services (IRS 1999), and it has grown rapidly in the public sector of late. It is now widespread in schools, hospitals, universities, local authorities, the civil service, etc. For example, some 80 per cent of local authorities surveyed either operated or were currently introducing performance appraisal (IRS 1995a). It has also grown from its main deployment in the middle of organisation hierarchies, particularly in middle management and professional occupations, to include a much broader group of manual and clerical employees (Kersley *et al.* 2006). Increasingly it seems, in line with harmonisation policies, all employees in an organisation are included in the performance appraisal system. An IRS survey found that 39 per cent of organisations' appraisal applied to every employee (IRS 1994) and a replication of the survey five years later found 75 per cent to do so (IRS 1999). The coverage of employees in the public sector, given the relative infancy of many schemes, is still rather more limited than the private sector. The IRS found only 17 per cent of public sector organisations surveyed included all employees in the scheme. However, these claims can be misleading. Employers who include the growing numbers of 'contingent' or 'peripheral' workers, such as part-time and contract staff, in performance appraisal schemes appear to be the exception rather than the rule.

HOW IS APPRAISAL CONDUCTED?

There is a wide range of methods used to conduct performance appraisals, from the simplest of ranking schemes through objective, standard and competency-based systems (see below) to complex behaviourally anchored rating schemes (see Snape *et al.* 1994). The nature of an organisation's appraisal scheme is largely a reflection of its managerial beliefs (Randell 1994), the amount of resources it has available to commit and the expertise it possesses. Thus smaller organisations with limited HR expertise tend to adopt simpler ranking and rating schemes while the more complex and resource-consuming systems, such as competency-based and 360° appraisal, are found mainly in larger organisations.

Most employers use only one type of appraisal scheme, often a 'hybrid form' of a number of methods, and a few companies even provide employees with a choice of methods in how they are appraised. The IRS surveys (IRS 1994, 1999) found many organisations with more than one system of performance appraisal operating. The main reason behind multiple systems was the wish to separate out reward and non-reward aspects of appraisal, different systems for different occupational groups (e.g. managerial and non-managerial employees) and separate systems for different parts of the organisation.

WHAT IS IT USED FOR?

Organisations use performance appraisal for a wide range of different purposes. Surveys commonly report the use of performance appraisal for clarifying and defining performance expectations, identifying training and development needs, providing career counselling, succession planning, improving individual, team and corporate performance, facilitating communications and involvement, allocating financial rewards, determining promotion, motivating and controlling employees, and achieving cultural change (Bowles and Coates 1993; IRS 1994, 1999; IDS 2007).

Recent trends suggest that the more judgemental and 'harder' forms of performance appraisal are on the increase and that 'softer' largely developmental approaches are declining (Gill 1977; Long 1986; Armstrong and Baron 1998; IPD 1999; CIPD 2005). Thus there has been a shift in performance appraisal away from using it for career planning and identifying future potential and increased use of it for improving current performance and allocating rewards. Here the arrival of flatter organisations has given rise to the need to uncouple, to some extent at least, performance appraisal and promotion, while competitive pressures have emphasised the need to incentivise improvements in short-term performance.

There are both advantages and disadvantages to such broad demands upon performance appraisal systems. A wide use helps to integrate various, often disparate, HRM areas into a coherent package of practices. For example, by providing a link between performance and rewards, and development needs and succession planning, more effective HRM outcomes are possible. However, it also gives rise to the common criticism that performance appraisal systems are simply too ambitious in that managers expect them to be able to accommodate a very wide a range of purposes. The breadth of use thus results in appraisal becoming a 'blunt instrument that tries to do too much' (Boudreaux 1994).

Further, many of the above purposes of appraisal are seen as being in conflict. Thus recording the past and influencing future performance is difficult to achieve in a single process. The danger is that appraisal, particularly given the trends identified above, concentrates on the past at the expense of the future performance, with a common analogy here being that this is rather like using the rearview mirror to drive future performance. Similarly, allocating rewards and identifying training needs are often seen as being incompatible objectives in a single appraisal scheme. The openness required for meaningfully assessing development needs is closed down by the need for the employee to 'explain away' performance problems in order to gain a merit rise. However, the danger of disconnecting reward allocation from appraisal is that appraisers and appraised would not treat the process as seriously because without it appraisal lacks bite and 'fires blank bullets' (Lawler 1994). Increasingly, as we now examine, performance appraisal is used as one element of a much broader performance management system.

PERFORMANCE MANAGEMENT

Performance management, like many HRM innovations, is a US import that has been a major driver in the increased use of performance appraisal by British organisations (IDS 2007). Performance management has been defined as 'systems and attitudes which help organizations to plan, delegate and assess the operation of their services' (LGMB 1994, p.6). Bevan and Thompson (1991) describe a 'textbook' performance management system thus:

■ a shared vision of the organisation's objectives communicated via a mission statement to all employees;

■ individual performance targets which are related to operating unit and wider organisational objectives;

■ regular formal review of progress towards targets;

■ a review process which identifies training and development needs and rewards outcomes;

■ an evaluation of the effectiveness of the whole process and its contribution to overall organisational performance to allow changes and improvements to be made.

A principal feature of performance management is thus that it connects the objectives of the organisation to a system of work targets for individual employees. In such models of performance management, objective setting and formal appraisal are placed at the heart of the approach. The development of performance management systems has had major implications for performance appraisal. A key trend has been away from 'stand-alone' performance appraisal systems and towards individual appraisal becoming part of an integrated performance management system.

There is a growing critique of performance management systems. First, they are seen as adding more pressure to a short-term view among British managers, which may well hamper organisational performance over the long term. Second, they are often proffered in a very prescriptive fashion, with many writers advocating a single best way for performance management, to the neglect of important variables such as degree of centralisation, unionisation, etc. This is in contrast to the actual practice of performance management in the UK, which is 'extremely diverse' (Fletcher and Williams 1992). The real danger is that performance management systems cannot be simply 'borrowed' from one organisation and applied in another, as many advocates appear to suggest. Third, it is supposed to be line-management 'driven' but case studies of its practices report the motivating forces in organisations as being chief executives and HR departments with often questionable ownership and commitment from line managers (Fletcher and Williams 1992). Fourth, there is a growing concern that performance management systems, because of their dedicated focus on improving the 'bottom line', have added unduly to the pressures and stresses of work-life for many employees. Many systems have been introduced with scant regard for employee welfare (see Box 7.1) and there is increasing concern that employees are now being performance managed to exhaustion (Brown and Benson 2003) and burnout (Gabris and Ihrke 2001). Lastly, and perhaps more damning, is the view that it is ineffective. The main driver of performance management is the improvement of overall organisational effectiveness. However, there is little support from various studies for the view that performance management actually improves performance. For example, Bevan and Thompson's (1991) survey of performance management in the UK found that there was no relationship between high-performing UK companies (defined as those demonstrating pre-tax profit growth over a five-year period) and the operation of a performance management system.

PERFORMANCE APPRAISAL AS MANAGERIAL CONTROL

With the decline of careers in the flat, delayered organisation, HRM techniques such as performance appraisal have become more important managerial tools in motivating and controlling the workforce. Appraisal is now seen by some commentators as being much more important in maintaining employee loyalty and commitment than in directly managing performance (Bowles and Coates 1993). Its use provides managers with a major opportunity to reinforce corporate values and attitudes and thus it appeals as an important strategic instrument in the control process. Thus we find an increasing use of appraisal systems for non-managerial employees that are based on social, attitudinal and trait attributes (Townley 1989). Employees are increasingly being appraised not only on 'objective' measures such as attendance, timekeeping, productivity and quality but also on more subjective aspects such as 'dependability', 'flexibility', 'initiative', 'loyalty', etc.

Recent analyses of performance appraisal, based upon the work of Foucault, have given particular emphasis to the power relations implicit in performance appraisal (Townley 1993, 1999; Coates 1994). For Townley, performance appraisal has the potential to act as the 'paper equivalent' of the panopticon with its 'anonymous and continuous surveillance' (1993, p.232). Thus recent developments in appraisal, which have both broadened the range of and increased the number of appraisers, via 360° appraisal, upward appraisal and the use of external customers, have increased the potential for managerial control and the utilisation of the panoptical powers of performance appraisal. In such systems the employee is now continually exposed to the appraisers 'constant yet elusive presence' (Fuller and Smith 1991, p.11). Every customer, peer, subordinate and colleague is now also a potential appraiser. Thus it is hardly surprising that employees have nicknamed peer reviews of performance 'screw your buddy' systems of appraisal.

Managers themselves are not immune from the disciplinary 'gaze' of performance appraisal (see below). Managerial attitudes, especially at middle-management levels, have often been identified as a barrier to the introduction of new ways of managing, such as introducing employee involvement and empowerment. Upward appraisal of managers by staff is increasingly being used to link managerial behaviour more closely with corporate values and mission statements by incorporating questions on these into appraisal instruments which are completed by the employee (Redman and Snape 1992). Thus at one and the same time organisations promote their required values to their employees and evaluate the commitment of their managers to these. Managers scoring badly in such appraisals are often 'culled' (see Redman and Mathews 1995). Thus, for example, at Semco, the much-discussed Brazilian company, managers are upwardly appraised every six months using a scale up to 100. The results are then posted on a noticeboard and those who consistently underperform are squeezed out or simply 'fade away'.

Recent developments in performance appraisal

As we noted in the introduction, there have been many innovations in performance appraisal practice. In this section we discuss some of the more influential of these.

UPWARD APPRAISAL

Upward appraisal is a relatively recent addition to performance appraisal practice in the UK. Although still far from common, the last decade or so has witnessed the introduction of upward appraisal in a range of UK companies. Upward appraisal is more common in the US and appears to have spread from US parent companies to their UK operations (e.g. at companies such as Federal Express, Standard Chartered Bank and AMEX) and from these to UK companies such as WHS Smith, The Body Shop and parts of the UK public sector (see Redman and Mathews 1995). Upward appraisal involves the employee rating their manager's performance via, in most cases, an anonymous questionnaire. The process is anonymous to overcome employees' worries about providing honest but unfavourable feedback on managerial performance. Anonymity limits the potential for managerial 'retribution' or what is termed the 'get even' factor of upward appraisal.

Advocates claim significant benefits for upward appraisal (Redman and Snape 1992; Bettenhausen and Fedor 1997), including improved managerial effectiveness and leadership through 'make-you-better feedback' and increased employee voice and empowerment. Equally, upward appraisal is seen as being more in tune with the delayered organisation where managerial spans of control are greater and working arrangements much more diverse. In such situations employees are in much greater contact with their manager than the manager's manager and thus traditional top-down boss appraisal is seen as being less effective. Upward appraisal, because of the use of multiple raters, is also seen as being more robust to legal challenge of performance judgements. Given the increasingly litigious culture in the UK and US, it is surprising that performance appraisal methods and the systems in which they are embedded are not attacked in the courts more often (Lee *et al.* 2004).

Managers have been reported as not being especially fond of upward appraisal systems. In part this may stem from the career-threatening use of upward appraisal schemes in some organisations. For example, one of BP Exploration's objectives in introducing upward appraisal was to return to individual contribution roles those managers 'clearly not cut out to manage people' (Thomas *et al.* 1992). Often it appears to the manager on the receiving end of upward appraisal that, according to Grint (1993), 'the honest opinions of subordinates look more like the barbs on a whale harpoon than gentle and constructive nudges'. Such a lack of managerial acceptance of upward appraisal, especially at middle and junior levels of management, may go some way to explaining its relatively low uptake in the UK after a flurry of activity in the early 1990s.

360° PERFORMANCE APPRAISAL

The so-called 360° appraisals appear to be taking root and becoming an established form of appraisal in the UK (see Box 7.2). Dugdill (1994) traces the origins of 360° appraisal to the US army in the 1970s. Here military researchers found that peers' opinions were more accurate indicators of a soldier's ability than were those of superiors.

The term 360° is used to describe the all-encompassing direction of feedback derived from a composite rating from peers, subordinates, supervisors and occasionally customers. It is again normally conducted via an anonymous survey, although some recent innovations include the use of audio and videotape to record feedback answers. Some organisations also use online computerised data-gathering systems. There is a wide variation in what is appraised in 360° feedback. Many companies use fully structured questionnaires based upon models of managerial competency. Others, such as Dupont's use of 360° appraisal in its individual career management programme, employ a much less structured approach. Here appraisers respond to open questions, which ask for descriptions of the appraiser's 'major value-adding areas for the year'; summaries of the manager's strengths; descriptions of key improvement needs; and a call for other general comments. Unstructured systems of appraisal have advantages in tapping into key aspects of managerial performance. However, the danger of using an unstructured approach is that the popular but incompetent manager may well fare better than one who is highly effective but not particularly pleasant. Mostly the appraisers remain anonymous but some systems, such as Dupont's, leave the option open to the appraiser whether or not to add their name to the appraisal form. However, unless a composite rating only is presented to the manager, and this tends to counter the value of having multiple perspectives in 360°, it is very difficult to provide the immediate supervisor with anonymity.

It seems that 360° appraisal is edging away from a management development tool and towards a broader organisational role (Toegal and Conger 2003). Increasingly, and controversially, it seems organisations are also experimenting with linking 360° and managerial remuneration. Given that 360° appraisal is now so popular for managers and professionals that some see it as replacing traditional performance appraisal systems, this trend to widening its remit raises some concerns. Toegal and Conger (2003) suggest that 360° appraisal is being 'overstretched' by including such broader administrative concerns and that these additions blunt its usage as a feedback tool. The solution, it seems, its to develop two distinct 360° appraisal tools, one for management development and one for performance feedback, a solution that, as we note above, could raise as many problems as it solves.

Rather a lot is claimed for 360° appraisal, and like many new initiatives we have seen a rash of articles announcing how it can 'change your life' (O'Reilly 1995) and deliver competitive advantage for the organisation (London and Beatty 1993). Because of its use of multiple raters with different perspectives, a sort of safety in numbers approach, it is often suggested that it provides more accurate and meaningful feedback. However, as Grint (1993) notes, this often simply replaces the subjectivity of a single appraiser with the subjectivity of multiple appraisers.

Undoubtedly, many organisations have gained some advantages from using it, particularly in management developmental terms. It has proved especially useful for providing feedback for senior managers who are often neglected at the top in appraisal terms. One key benefit of the broad group of appraisers used in 360° is that it can provide a more meaningful appraisal for employees with little contact with their workplace. In such situations traditional top-down appraisals are of little value. A strength of 360° is that management consultants proffering systems will tailor a basic questionnaire to meet the organisation's characteristics, such

Box 7.2: HRM in practice

360° appraisal at Northumbrian Water

Following the hot, dry summers and accompanying water shortages, adverse public relations and intense media interest, life has been particularly difficult for managers in the UK privatised water companies. One company, Northumbrian Water, has been helping its managers to cope with a range of management development practices, including 360° appraisal.

Northumbrian Water introduced a 360° feedback programme for its managers via a pilot group of 35 managers. A key reason behind the introduction was to provide data for the company's development centre for senior managers. The development centre was designed to enable managers to move to a position of managing their own career development. It was considered important that individual managers should have a view from their colleagues about their performance, potential and development needs in order to facilitate sound career decisions. The 360° appraisal instrument consists of a bank of questions asking respondents to comment on the effectiveness and performance of the appraised manager against three main categories: competence, style and role. Appraisers, for example, are asked to say how often they see the candidate behave in a particular fashion which is consistent with the behaviours listed for a senior manager. Space is also provided for open comments on the manager's performance and the company feels it is often these which prove the most enlightening.

The system is based upon a refined competency model originally developed in the early 1980s. The competency model was further developed following privatisation of the industry as the roles and styles of management appropriate to the company's new values were developed. For example, commercial awareness and customer care were not present in the original formulation. A study of HRM practices in the post-privatisation water industry considers Northumbria to have introduced the 'most dramatic changes' of all the companies (IRS 1992).

The feedback forms are distributed to 10–12 of the managers' colleagues in some form of distribution, such as two above, five sideways and four below, by the individual manager. Internal customers are often part of the process but the company has yet to incorporate external customers. The forms are returned directly to the company's consultants, who produce a summary data booklet, discuss the results with the manager, and help prepare them for the development centre.

The main benefit the company perceives it has obtained from 360° feedback is in providing individual managers with vital insights into some of their shortcomings, which would otherwise remain unaddressed. Although it has been somewhat of a shock for some, managers are considered to be much more self-aware about their leadership qualities and are felt to be working better with their staff. Also, 360° appraisal is seen as making a valuable contribution in encouraging managers to engage in continuous professional development and encouraging an approach where performance problems can be positively tackled through training and development. The main problems the company has found with its implementation are that in the early programmes there was some difficulty in convincing managers that such feedback was of value because their development and career planning was within their own remit rather than that of their of boss. A few individuals also had great difficulty in accepting the feedback and searched for reasons to rationalise their opposition.

Source: Interviews with managers

as culture, mission, business values and structure and management practices. It remains to be seen whether the benefits gained are outweighed by the considerable time, effort and costs involved. Indeed, it seems that some management consultants are 'gravy training' on the back of the current enthusiasm for 360°, with week-long feedback courses, facilitated by themselves, recommended to debrief managers.

Thus a number of questions remain unanswered about 360° appraisal, not least whether the data generated is accurate, valid and more importantly meaningful for the appraisee and whether the organisation stands to benefit from it. Ratings are only as good as the questions asked and often the interpretation of question wording is far from clear in many instruments. Such questions as 'Does the manager deal with problems in a flexible manner' are not uncommon in appraisal instruments. Items need to be clear, easy to understand and easy to rate given the raters' contact with the appraisee. One particular criticism of many 360° systems is that all raters are given the same instrument, despite the different nature of the contact with the appraisee. Some issues are clearly more visible to the rater from different vantage points and questionnaires should ideally be constructed accordingly. Items based on actual behaviours – key organisational competencies or critical incidents observed in the workplace indicative of superior performing managers – tend to be more effective. However, respondents will usually provide ratings on whatever questions are asked, whether or not they are in a position to do so.

There is also a certain tendency to produce overly bureaucratic systems. The danger here is that one common cause of failure generally in performance appraisal, that of requiring participants to fill in large quantities of paperwork, is being ignored. Making the feedback meaningful is also a challenge many users of 360° fail to rise to. To ensure meaningful feedback a process of self-appraisal, comparison against other managers' ratings and follow-up with facilitators and those who provided the ratings is the minimum required. Also there is an implicit expectation on the part of those providing the ratings that such feedback will lead to improvements and that managers will change their behaviour for the better. There is, however, yet little evidence that this actually occurs.

Lastly, many so-called 360° appraisal systems are actually far from an all-round view of managers; the external customer as a reviewer is often left out, but, as we discuss in the next section, customers are an increasingly heard voice in the assessment of employee performance. It seems 360° appraisal is also only a starting point, and as management consultants 'discover' new sources of raters we can look forward to such innovations as 450° and even 540° appraisal.

CUSTOMER APPRAISAL

TQM and customer care programmes are now very widespread in both the private and public sectors in the UK. One impact of these initiatives is that organisations are now increasingly setting employee performance standards based upon customer care indicators and appraising staff against these. A mix of 'hard' quantifiable standards such as 'delivery of a customer's first drink within two minutes' and soft qualitative standards such as 'a warm and friendly greeting', as used at one roadside restaurant chain, are now used in performance appraisal systems (IRS 1995b). The use of service guarantees, which involve the payment of compensatory moneys to customers if the organisations do not reach the standards, has also led to a greater use of customer data in performance appraisal ratings.

Customer service data for use in appraising employees is gathered by a variety of methods. First, there is the use of a range of customer surveys, such as via the completion of customer care cards, telephone surveys, interviews with customers and postal surveys. Organisations are now using such surveys more frequently and are increasingly sophisticated in how they gather customer views. Second, there is a range of surveillance techniques used by managers to sample the service encounter. Here the electronic work monitoring of factory workers is being extended into the services sector. For example, customer service managers at contact centres spend considerable time and effort reviewing staff performance by recording staff–customer conversations and giving immediate feedback, as well as using the data for the regular formal review process.

Third, and even more controversial, is the increasing use of the so-called 'mystery' or 'phantom' shopping. For some commentators, customer service can only be really effectively evaluated at the boundary between customer and organisation and this view has fuelled the growth of mystery shopping as a data-capturing process. Here staff employed by a specialist agency purport to be real shoppers and observe and record their experience of the service encounter. It is now commonly used in banks, pub companies, insurance companies, super-markets and parts of the public sector. Some local authorities evaluate the quality of tele-phone responses by employing consultants to randomly call the authority and assess the quality of the response (IRS 1995b).

Mystery shopping is argued to give a company a rich source of data that cannot be uncov-ered by other means, such as customer surveys. Such surveys, although useful for some pur-poses, are often conducted many months after the service encounter and thus exact service problems are difficult to recollect. Mystery shopping is also seen as being particularly useful in revealing staff performance that causes customers to leave without purchasing. In many service sector organisations a natural consequence of the use of mystery shoppers has been to utilise the data in the performance evaluations of staff (Fuller and Smith 1991). Although as yet relatively understudied, there are a number of concerns with mystery shopping, not least the psychometric quality of data collected in comparison to customer surveys. Few stud-ies have addressed this issue, but work by Kayande and Finn (1999) report that mystery shop-ping provides 'reasonably reliable ratings' of performance and that such data can be produced at considerably less cost than customer surveys. All this suggests that mystery shopping is very likely to grow in use in the future.

However, these data-gathering methods are, as one could well expect, not very popular with staff. Employees often question the ethics of introducing mystery shoppers and feel that it represents a distinct lack of managerial trust in them (Shing and Spence 2002). Thus employees describe shoppers in terms of 'spies' and 'snoopers' and react with hostility and 'shopper spotting' to their introduction. The introduction of mystery shopping for largely negative reasons of catching staff performing poorly only fuels such reactions. Cook (1993) advises that using them to reward staff for good performance rather than punish them for poor performance can help their acceptance. Staff who obtain good mystery shopping ratings should be rewarded and recognised, while those who obtain poor ones should use them as a source of identifying training needs.

In an increasing number of organisations internal service level agreements are also being established. The introduction of compulsory competitive tendering and subsequently 'best value' has given considerable impetus to such agreements in the public sector. Often in such agreements there is an internal customer-service 'guarantee' stating the level and nature of services the supplier will provide. It thus has been a natural progression of such a develop-ment for organisations, such as at Federal Express, to incorporate performance data from ser-vice level agreements into the appraisal process (e.g. Milliman *et al.* 1995). A key advantage claimed for using internal customers in this way is that joint goal setting helped provide both internal customer and provider with greater understanding of the roles that individuals and departments provide. It thus helps in breaking down internal barriers between departments.

TEAM-BASED APPRAISAL

Work is increasingly being restructured into highly interdependent work teams, yet, despite this, performance appraisal often remains stubbornly based on the individual. In some cases teams are increasingly being given responsibility for allocating work tasks, setting bonuses, selecting new staff, and even disciplining errant members. For such organisations it has thus been seen as entirely appropriate that performance appraisals should also be based upon and even conducted by the team themselves.

Two main variants of team appraisal can be identified. In some approaches the managers appraise the team as a whole. Targets are set, performance measured and assessments made, and rewards allocated as with traditional individual appraisals. The manager makes no attempt to differentiate one member from another in performance terms, in fact the creation of internal inequity with respect to rewarding performance is a deliberate aspect (Lawler 1994). Equal ratings and rewards ensue for all of the team regardless of performance. The team are then encouraged to resolve internally any performance problems or competence deficiencies in order to facilitate overall team performance and development. Team members themselves may then provide informal awards or recognition of superior performance. The other main variant is whereby individual appraisals of each team member are still made but not by management. Rather, in a form of peer appraisal, team members appraise each other, usually via the use of anonymous rating questionnaires.

COMPETENCY-BASED APPRAISAL

Interest in the concept of competency has been one of the major HR themes of recent times. Connock (1992) describes it as one of HRM's 'big ideas'. One consequence of this has been the attempt by some organisations to use the competency approach to develop an integrated human resource strategy. This has been particularly pronounced in HR practices targeted at managers but is also growing for non-managerial groups. A consequence of the development of organisational competency models has been that employers have increasingly extended their use from training and development, selection and reward into the area of appraisal. For example, the most widely reported innovation in performance appraisal systems during the 1990s has been the linking of appraisals to competency frameworks (IRS 1999).

The assessment of competencies in the appraisal process has a number of benefits. The evaluation of competencies identified as central to a good job performance provides a useful focus for analysing the progress an individual is making in the job rather than the static approach of many ability- or trait-rating schemes. Thus competency-based assessment is especially useful in directing employee attention to areas where there is scope for improvement. The use of competencies broadens appraisal by including 'how well is it done' measures in addition to the more traditional 'what is achieved' measures. It also helps concentrate the appraisal process on the key area of performance and effectiveness and provides a language for feedback on performance problems (Sparrow 1994, p.9). This latter benefit overcomes one of the problems of traditional objective-based appraisal systems in which the appraiser is often at a loss as to how to counsel an employee on what they should do differently if the appraisal objectives have not been achieved. However, these benefits must be counterbalanced against the development and running costs involved and the wider critical debate surrounding the 'competency movement' in general.

Problems of performance appraisal

Performance appraisals appear to be one human resource activity that everyone loves to hate. Carroll and Schneier's (1982) research found that performance appraisal ranks as the most disliked managerial activity. It is frequently suggested in the popular management literature that most managers would prefer having a dental appointment rather than conduct a performance appraisal. Many appraisees, it seems, would also prefer this! According to Grint (1993, p.64), 'rarely in the history of business can such a system have promised so much and delivered so little'.

Box 7.3: HRM in practice

Cronies and Doppelgangers in performance appraisal

The search for accurate performance appraisals is a seemingly illusory one, with many pitfalls and distorting effects strewn in the appraiser's path. Some of the main ones are:

Halo effects. This is where one positive criterion distorts the assessment of others. Similarly the *horns effect* is where a single negative aspect dominates the appraisal rating.

Doppelganger effect is where the rating reflects the similarity between appraiser and appraised.

Crony effect is the result of appraisal being distorted by the closeness of the relationship between appraiser and appraised.

Veblen effect is named after the economist Veblen, who gave all his students the grade C irrespective of the quality of their efforts. Thus all those appraised received middle-order ratings.

Impression effect is the problem of distinguishing actual performance from calculated 'impression management'. The impression management tactics of employees can result in supervisors liking them more and thus rating their job performance more highly. Employees often attempt to manage their reputations by substituting measures of process (effort, behaviour, etc.) for measures of outcome (results), particularly when the results are less than favourable.

The critics of performance appraisal argue that it is expensive; causes conflict between appraised and appraiser; has limited value and may even be dysfunctional in the improvement of employee performance; and, despite the rhetoric, its use contributes little to the strategic management of an organisation. It is also argued to be riddled with so many distorting 'effects' that its accuracy in providing an indicator of actual employee performance must also be called into question (see Box 7.3). Some appraisal systems, especially the more judgemental, those tied into merit pay systems and those with forced distributions, are argued to be especially problematic in these respects. Thus for many writers performance appraisal is 'doomed' (Halachmi 1993); a managerial practice 'whose time has gone' (Fletcher 1993; Bhote 1994) and whose end is imminently predicted (Roth and Ferguson 1994).

Why does performance appraisal not work? One reason is that despite their widely held belief to the contrary, most managers are not naturally good at conducting performance appraisals. According to Lawler (1994, p.17), it is an 'unnatural act' for managers, a result of which is that if they are not trained properly it is done rather poorly. Appraisal meetings are thus reported as being short-lived, ill-structured and often bruising encounters. Studies find that appraisers are ill-prepared, talk too much, and base much of the discussion on third-party complaints, with many of the judgements made on 'gut feelings'. It is then of little surprise when we find reports of how it takes the average employee six months to recover from it.

Being subject to 'political' manipulation also discredits appraisals. Managers, it seems, frequently play organisational games with performance ratings (Snape *et al.* 1994). Longenecker's (1989) research found that managers' appraisal ratings are often manipulated to suit various ends. Sometimes ratings were artificially deflated to show who was the boss; to prepare the ground for termination; to punish a difficult and rebellious employee; and even to 'scare' better performance out of the appraisee. One manager we interviewed described how he deflated the performance ratings of all new graduate trainees for their first few years of employment in order to 'knock some of the cleverness out of them' and show them that they 'did not know everything'. Equally, a poor performer may be given an excellent rating in order that they will be promoted up and out of the department and managers may inflate ratings in the hope that an exemplary set of appraisals reflects favourably on the manager responsible for such a high-performing team.

The move to more objective forms of performance appraisal, particularly encouraged by performance management models, and increasingly reported for managerial grades, is often argued to overcome some of the above 'subjective' problems. Legal challenges to personality- and trait-based performance appraisal schemes, particularly in North America and increasingly in the UK (Lee *et al.* 2004), have also encouraged the move away from personality- and trait-based systems. However, the so-called objective-based schemes are not without difficulties. First, measurement is often difficult and, according to Wright (1991), 'there are a number of jobs where the meaningful is not measurable and the measurable is not meaningful'. The tendency is also to simplify measurement by focusing on the short rather than the long term. Second, since objectives are set for individual employees or teams under such systems it can be especially challenging to achieve equitable ratings. Equally problematical is that the actions of the employee may account for little of the variability in the outcomes measured (a key criticism of the quality gurus) and thus the extent to which they are achievable is not within the employee's control. This has posed real problems with appraisals in industries such as financial services, where the economic climate and general business cycle arguably affect outcomes far more than individual effort. The potential here is thus for employee demotivation and disillusionment, especially when many such systems are now linked to reward structures.

Kessler and Purcell (1992) identify a range of further specific problems with objective-based systems. These include the difficulty in achieving a balance between maintenance and innovator objectives; in setting objectives that cover the whole job so that performance does not get skewed to part of it; and the lack of flexibility to redefine objectives as circumstances change during the appraisal cycle. The introduction of performance appraisal into the public sector has also given rise to many concerns. In particular, there are worries about its potential to undermine professional autonomy, with this concern being strongly expressed by clinicians in the NHS. A more general concern is that such a 'managerialist' intervention would undermine the public service values and public accountability of employees (Redman *et al.* 2000).

A range of more practical difficulties also results in problems with performance appraisal. Often the paperwork used to support the system can become excessive and give rise to a considerable bureaucratic burden for managers, particularly as spans of control grow. Some organisations have attempted to reduce this problem by designing paperless systems, requiring the employee to complete the bulk of the paperwork, or moving to a computer-based system. A real danger in many systems is that the paperwork dominates and the process is reduced to an annual 'cosy chat' and a ritual bureaucratic exercise devoid of meaning or importance for all concerned. Thus according to Barlow (1989, p.503), the performance appraisal of managers is little more than the 'routinized recording of trivialities'. Appraisers and appraised go through the motions, sign off the forms and send them to a central personnel department who simply file them away rather than utilising the data in a meaningful way (Snape *et al.* 1994). Given the lack of follow-up in many appraisal systems it is hardly surprising when they fall into disrepute and eventual decay.

Lastly, the growth of TQM and customer care programmes has triggered a considerable debate and a reassessment of the organisational value of appraisal. On the one hand there has been a high-profile barrage of criticism rejecting appraisal as being incompatible with TQM. In its strongest formulation it is suggested that managers face a stark choice between choosing either TQM or performance appraisal (Aldakhilallah and Parente 2002). On the other hand, some have suggested that appraisal may play a key role in developing, communicating and monitoring the achievement of quality standards (Fletcher 1993) and many organisations have been spurred by the introduction of TQM to revise their appraisal schemes in more customer-focused ways.

TQM has thus focused attention on some old as well as highlighting some new problems with performance appraisal. In relation to old problems some of the quality gurus, most notably Deming (1986), maintain that performance appraisal is inconsistent with quality improvement. He argues that variation in performance is attributable mainly to work systems rather than to variations in the performance of individual workers. Quality improvements are thus found mainly by changing processes rather than people, and the key is to develop cooperative teamwork. This, he claims, is difficult to do where the focus is on 'blaming' the individual, as in traditional appraisal, and where as a result there is a climate of fear and risk avoidance, and a concern for short-term, individual targets, all of which undermine the cooperative, creative, and committed behaviour necessary for continuous improvement.

Deming is careful to argue, in rejecting performance appraisal, not that all staff perform equally well but that appraisers are incapable of disaggregating system effects from individual staff effects. Thus what is needed for TQM is a shift away from the traditional focus on results and individual recognition, towards processes and group recognition. The TQM critics also raise some new problems with performance appraisal, in particular that it 'disempowers' employees by reducing variety and increasing homogenisation of the workforce, while for meaningful customer care we need the 'empowered' employee.

Conclusions

Performance appraisal is now more widespread that at any time in its history and the organisational resources consumed by its practice are enormous. At the same time its critics grow both in number and in the ferocity of their attacks. It is thus tempting to adopt a somewhat sceptical view of the value of performance appraisal. Following the rise of TQM and the prominence of its, mainly American, management gurus it has become rather fashionable of late to reject performance appraisal outright. Pathological descriptions of performance appraisal as a 'deadly disease' and an 'organisational virus' are increasingly common.

However, it would appear that the danger here is that such views are often based on little more than anecdote rather than solid empirical research. For example, one survey of employer reasons for introducing appraisal systems in the UK found that in over a third of cases it was developed to provide support for quality management initiative (IRS 1994). Our studies of managers' actual experience of being appraised finds many reporting its overall value to them and the organisation, with few suggesting it should be discarded altogether (e.g. Redman and Mathews 1995; Redman *et al.* 2000). Many of the criticisms are based upon a hard and uncompromising model of performance appraisal that is now less commonly found in practice, and the ineffective way that many organisations implement appraisal. The critics all too often have rather conveniently ignored many of the new developments we discuss above, which act to ameliorate some of these problems. Many of the problems of performance appraisal can be ironed out over time, as experience with its practice accumulates. Indeed, there is some evidence to suggest that employers who have utilised performance appraisal for longer report fewer problems (Bowles and Coates 1993).

Further, performance appraisal's detractors are usually silent on what should replace it. A common response is to suggest this is an unfair question in that it is the organisational equivalent of asking, 'What would you replace pneumonia with?'(e.g. see *People Management* 13 July 1995, p.15). The question of how to assesses individual performance, determine rewards and promotion, provide feedback, decide training and career needs and link business and individual goals without a performance appraisal system, however, cannot be so easily shrugged off.

Performance appraisal emerged in the first place to meet such needs and employees still need guidance in focusing their skills and efforts on important organisational goals and values. Hence we would suggest that performance appraisal will continue to have an important role in HRM practice. A good example here is that organisations often struggle to get managers committed to taking health and safety management as seriously as other aspects of their jobs. Tombs (1992) reports that 'safety leaders' in the chemical industry ensure that managers give safety management the attention it deserves by developing a 'safety culture', a key part of which is achieved by incorporating safety objectives into their performance appraisals. Thus the first objective of all ICI plant managers is always a safety one.

This is not to argue that the current practice of performance appraisal is unproblematic. Certainly some of the evidence also presented above would suggest that there are many concerns with its application. However, these are persistent but certainly not insurmountable or terminal problems, and it is argued strongly that organisations should think very carefully before abandoning it altogether. Rather, the evidence would seem to support the view that the key task facing most organisations in the millennium is the upgrading, renewal and reinvention of performance appraisal such that it is more compatible with new business environments.

CASE STUDY 7.1

Performance appraisal at North Trust

Tom Redman, Ed Snape and David Thompson

Organisation background[1]

This case study examines the practice of performance appraisal in an NHS Trust hospital. North Trust (NT) is a whole district Trust in the northeast of England serving a community of a quarter of a million people. It provides 32 major healthcare services, including the full range of in-patient, day case and out-patient services alongside a comprehensive primary care service including health visiting and district nursing services. It employs some 2,200 'whole time equivalent' (WTE) staff. The Trust has recently been relatively successful, meeting all its financial targets thus far. However, at the time of the study – the late 1990s–early 2000s – it was, similar to many other Trusts, experiencing increasing difficulties in meeting the demand for healthcare services within the constraints of its current resources.

The development of appraisal at NT

Appraisal at North Trust, a variant of the national Individual Performance Reviews (IPR) scheme, was first implemented for senior managers in 1988. Between 1988 and 1994 it was largely restricted to managerial and senior professional groups. In 1994 a review of IPR was conducted. An initial analysis found patchy coverage of IPR and a half-hearted commitment to it. Following the review a decision was taken to revise and re-launch the IPR scheme and 'roll it out' to a wider group of staff. There were two key influences underpinning this decision. First, a new chief executive with a much greater belief in the value of performance management was appointed. Second, a decision to pursue the Investors in People (IiP) award

---

[1]This case study draws on four main sources of data: interviews with managers and professionals, a fully structured postal questionnaire administered to a sample of 270 managers and professionals, the analysis of internal documents and procedures manuals and, finally, the observation of training workshops on appraisal and several senior management meetings reviewing appraisal practice at the organisation (see Redman *et al.* 2000).

▶

resulted in a decision to commit more time and effort to making IPR work. The next 18 months thus saw the revising of policy, the redesigning of supporting paperwork, and the committing of major training resources to IPR.

Final written agreement was secured in March 1995 and the new policy and procedure were 'signed off' by the chief executive in June 1995. The key aims of IPR at NT were articulated in the new policy document as ensuring all staff understand the Trust's goals and strategic direction; are clear about their objectives, how these fit with the work of others and the organisation as whole and are aware of the tasks they need to carry out; are given regular feedback and explicit assessment of performance; and are developed to improve their performance. The revised policy document made an explicit commitment to implement IPR for all employees.

The revised IPR policy at NT placed greater emphasis on measurability as a key aspect of the setting of individual objectives. The policy document outlines the principles underpinning individual objective setting as following the acronym 'SMART'. Here objectives should be specific, measurable, agreed/achievable, realistic and time-bound, with the form of measurement for each objective to be agreed at the time that they are set. According to the CEO, when he first arrived, this aspect was perceived as being very weak in practice:

Most people didn't know what an objective was if it sat up and bit them on the backside. Objectives here tended to be half-a-dozen or so generalised statements with no measurable outcome, no timescale, no agreement about how something is to be judged and whether it has been done or not, with the result that there is little accountability.

For the CEO the result of this was major problems in 'getting things done' at the Trust:

We don't have a performance culture here. This place was just great for talking about things. Only talking about things, not actually doing them.

Thus a key aim for the CEO was to 'toughen up' IPR. This was to be attained in part by an increased emphasis on the evaluation of the achievement of work objectives and to encourage detailed measures to be established for all new objectives. However, the CEO's view of the direction that IPR should go in did not seem to be shared by its 'owners': the personnel department. Here a softer, more developmental focus for IPR was envisioned:

What is important is the manager taking the time out to talk to the individual about how they are progressing. How they feel things are going. And talk about training and development. These things really help morale. Forget the form filling and objectives, and all the other bits. It is these things that really make the difference.

In the remainder of this case study we describe the practice of performance appraisal in North Trust.

The IPR process

Mechanics

IPR at NT is designed to cascade downwards through the organisation. The business plan is formulated by December/January each year and reviews conducted during February and March for senior managers. The majority of appraisals for other staff take place during April and May. A minority of managers, because of the large number of appraisals they conducted, in one case over 50, scheduled the appraisals over the full year, which in effect largely undermined the direct link with business planning for the majority of their staff. However, linkages with the business plan, especially for lower levels of staff, were also

▶

difficult to discern in the accounts of the IPR reviews conducted by those managers who did these in phase with the business planning process. Here managers' descriptions of how they appraised healthcare assistants, porters, domestics, catering staff, laundry workers and nurses rarely mentioned anything other than the loosest of connections with the business plan.

The IPR policy specifies a very much a 'top-down' process, noting that only occasionally might it be beneficial to involve another manager closely involved with the objectives being measured (such as a project manager). In practice no examples of this were found. A particular problem reported by the interviewees was that of continuity of appraisers between appraisal cycles. Owing to high levels of managerial turnover, caused by resigna- tions, promotions, transfers, secondments, etc. of both appraisees and appraisers, nearly a third of interviewees reported having different appraisers from one cycle to the next. This level of managerial change, because of the need for a close working relationship between manager and employee for appraisal to be effective (see below), was generally felt to limit IPR's potential. Interviewees described how continuity between appraiser and appraisee was important because reviews were generally perceived as improving as both parties got to know each other better and the discussion became more useful and open.

Coverage

There was an uneven application and use of IPR. Despite the avowed intention of the new policy to 'roll out' IPR uniformly over the trust, its use appeared to be distinctly patchy. The personnel department estimated that only around 25–30 per cent of staff received a perfor- mance review and that below management levels 'huge swathes' of staff were not involved. One of the tools to encourage its greater uptake was that senior managers were now being given personal objectives in their own appraisals to introduce IPR for all their staff. However, this strategy alone did not seem sufficient in gaining their commitment to making IPR process effective. As one manager explains:

Appraisal for lower level staff is a 5- minute wonder, get it out of the way. The supervisors say . . . 'I have got to go through this with you. You haven't been too bad a lad this year have you. See you next year.' We get the odd constructive thing coming out of it but the main thing is that the director will be happy that he can report we have now appraised all the staff in our department when he has his next IPR.

Such cynical attitudes were a source of irritation to the majority of managers who spent considerable time and effort on conducting IPRs in their departments. Here it was particu- larly resented that their managerial colleagues either did not conduct appraisals ('It's not fair that I have to do it if others don't'; 'Other staff feel they are missing out because they are not getting it') or gave mere lip service to them ('It brings the whole IPR process into disrepute and makes it much more difficult for me to get my staff to take it seriously').

Documentation

The standard Trust documentation was used for less than half of our interviewees' appraisals. The standard forms were felt to be too cumbersome and somewhat of an administrative chore, especially for use with employees at lower levels in the organisation. Thus those responsible for IPR often tailored the forms, usually reducing their length. A problem with some of the customised forms was that questionable performance categories, such as an appraisee's 'personality', featured prominently in these versions. In contrast, some professional groups found the forms rather too simplistic to capture the nature of their roles and again customised the standard forms to suit their needs. In a number of departments reviews were conducted without the aid of either customised or standard

▶

forms, and in one case an appraiser admitted that this was because he had never got round to actually reading them.

The IPR encounter

The heart of the IPR process, and the main source of participants' evaluation of it as either a success or failure, is the face-to-face meeting between appraiser and appraisee. Here for IPR is its 'moment of truth'. Table 7.1 shows that the majority of our appraisees reported interviews of at least 30 minutes, with 47 per cent having interviews of more than an hour. Judging from Table 7.2, appraisers were not usually dominating the interviews. The impression gained is that the majority of appraisees were having a sufficiently long and participative appraisal interview, an encouraging finding when we note that those who reported longer and more participative interviews also tended to report greater satisfaction with the appraisal process.

Table 7.3 sets out the extent to which various issues were discussed during the appraisal, as reported by our appraisees. The main emphasis appears to be on the achievement and planning of work objectives and on the planning of training and development. Not surprisingly, given the absence of performance-related pay for most staff, pay and benefits were only discussed in any detail during the appraisal interview. Overall, the approach seems to be one of performance management and development rather than of judgement and reward allocation.

A strong theme in the accounts of those who were positive about the overall IPR process was the notion that the interview represented 'quality time' between manager and managed. For some it was an 'employee's right' to have meaningful 'one-on-one time' with their manager and:

People value quality time to talk through with their immediate manager what they are doing, why they are doing it, and what they need to do in the future.

As we have seen, in these 'quality-time' appraisals, which were often between two to three hours' duration for managers, appraisees reported that a broad range of issues were discussed.

Table 7.1 How long did the appraisal interview last?

	%
Less than 30 minutes	11
Between 30 minutes and an hour	43
Between one and two hours	35
More than two hours	12

Table 7.2 During the appraisal interview approximately what proportion of the time did you and the appraiser talk?

	%
Mainly me (more than 75%)	13
Approximately 60% me	26
Approximately equal	48
Approximately 60% appraiser	12
Mainly the appraiser (more than 75%)	1

▶

Table 7.3   To what extent were the following issues covered in your appraisal?

	3 Thoroughly discussed	2 Briefly discussed	1 Not discussed at all
	%		
Your achievement of work objectives	63	32	5
Your future work objectives	65	31	4
Your personality or behaviour	17	42	42
Your skills or competencies	35	52	13
Your training and development needs	45	43	12
Your career aspirations and plans	30	43	27
Your pay or benefits	3	12	85
Your job difficulties	24	57	19
How you might improve your performance	16	40	44
How your supervisor might help you to improve your performance	15	45	40
Your personal or domestic circumstances	4	20	76

In contrast, the focus for lower-level grades was much more restricted and our in-depth interviews suggested that for such staff the time spent on the IPR interview varied between 10 and 45 minutes. Typical descriptions of the nature of appraisals for lower-grade staff were:

I discuss with them how they have worked this year. I say 'You've been a bit slack in these things. You are bloody good at that. You are one of my key workers for this. But your time-keeping wants pulling up a bit and your general attitude is not what should it be.'

To be honest there is very little to say to someone who feeds sheets into a machine five days a week. I have found it hard to think of positive things.

One manager reported the difficulty of getting lower-grade staff to relax during their appraisal because prior to IPR's introduction the only time such staff were called to her office was for a 'rugging'. Perhaps unsurprisingly, given such an approach, lower-grade staff were often reported as being 'indifferent' to and 'uninterested' in the IPR process.

It's the lower grades that feel 'Do I have to go through this again? I don't know why. I only want to do the job I'm doing and get my money at the end of the week.' These tend to be short interviews, most are less than 10 minutes.

Managers appeared to be coping with this lack of interest via a number of strategies. First, by renewing efforts in an attempt to encourage active staff participation and using developmental 'carrots'. Second, individual sceptics were labelled 'lost causes' and managers simply went through the motions in IPR and waited for such staff to leave. A more difficult problem was with 'clusters' of IPR-resistant employees. Here a coping strategy, often sold under the guise of self-development, appeared to be one of 'sharing the misery' more evenly with more junior managers and supervisors. The responsibility for conducting IPRs for 'difficult', 'obstructive' and 'awkward' staff was spread around the managerial team.
Generally, appraisees felt that their managers were good at giving performance feedback but fewer felt that they received regular feedback on their progress towards objectives

▶

Table 7.4 Perceived supervisor behaviour

	5 Strongly agree	4 Agree	3 Neither agree nor disagree	2 Disagree	1 Strongly disagree
			%		
POSITIVE ASPECTS					
My supervisor is good at giving me feedback on my performance	7	51	19	19	4
I receive regular informal feedback from my supervisor regarding my progress towards agreed targets and objectives	4	37	19	30	9
My supervisor takes my appraisals very seriously	21	50	15	12	2
My supervisor takes my career aspirations very seriously	5	50	24	17	3
I am confident that my supervisor is as objective as possible when conducting appraisals	10	60	20	8	1
NEGATIVE ASPECTS					
I have to keep on good terms with my supervisor in order to get a good appraisal rating	2	10	21	52	14
Supervisors use appraisals to reward their favourites	2	6	16	54	23
I am not entirely happy about challenging my supervisor's appraisal of my performance	3	18	17	52	11
I found it difficult during my performance appraisal to talk freely with my supervisor about what I wanted to discuss	4	14	9	52	21

(Table 7.4). The need for appraisal to be an ongoing, year-round exercise was emphasised in the IPR system (see below). It seems that at NT, significant minorities of appraisers were neglecting to do the expected follow-up. Judging from our interviews, constructive feedback was especially welcomed by the appraisees in providing direction ('You realise you are getting there'; 'Gives me some comfort I am getting there') and helping to boost confidence ('You know what you are doing is being done correctly'). Critical feedback was also valued but not often received by the interviewees, who in part blamed appraisal training here, which overly emphasised the 'positive' nature of IPR. Around a third of interviewees said they often 'watered down' their feedback in the reviews to ensure a positive IPR event and 'harmony' within their work-teams. Appraisees, especially female managers, emphasised the value of constructive criticism and 'meaningful' appraisals, with cosy chats being seen as a waste of their time.

Sound personal relationships between appraiser and appraised were emphasised by our interviewees as being a necessary but not sufficient condition for the appraisal to be effective. The large majority of appraisees felt that their managers were professional enough not to reward favourites, were confident that appraisers were objective, felt they could talk freely, were confident enough to challenge their appraisal, and that keeping on good terms

▶

with their manager was not a requirement in order to obtain a good appraisal (see Table 7.4). However, this still leaves a minority of appraisers whose appraisal behaviour was less positively rated by appraisees. Thus, some interviewees reported a poor relationship with their manager, describing IPR reviews in terms of conflict, verbal confrontation, point scoring, and 'edging about the real issues'. At its worst, this came down to appraisers using IPR to list what the appraisee had done wrong or badly over the year. A few appraisers, particularly those in clinical posts, described the problems of achieving an appropriate environment for conducting appraisal in a busy, emergency-led hospital:

When I had my IPR the phones were going, people were coming in and out of the office, the manager got called away. It spoke volumes to me about the value that was attached to IPR here.

Conducting IPRs on nights, at 2am, when people are not at their best, is hardly conducive to a quality process.

Mini-reviews

The formal annual reviews are supported by 'mini-reviews'. The policy document sees these as a 'crucial element' of IPR, providing constant review and monitoring such that the annual review itself becomes 'mainly a confirmation of agreements made during the year' or, as the title of the IPR training video suggests, appraisees should experience *No Surprises*. However, these appear to be rather sporadic in practice and, as we saw in Table 7.4, only 41 per cent of survey appraisees said that they received regular feedback from their supervisor on their progress towards their objectives.

A few departmental heads formally scheduled three-monthly reviews for all employees. The norm for the mini-reviews was a six-monthly, informal discussion, with a minority of interviewees receiving only the annual appraisal. Below management and professional levels, the impression gained was that mini-reviews were extremely rare or very ad hoc and rushed at best – 'corridor and canteen chats' – with managers struggling to find the time to conduct even the annual appraisal for some groups. However, the interviewees themselves often stressed the value of mini-reviews not only in providing a measure of progress and attainment but in a general updating of performance objectives. Several interviewees reported requesting, and receiving, additional mini-reviews. Here mini-reviews were especially useful to fine-tune, and often to replace, personal objectives that had been rendered obsolete by a rapidly changing organisational environment. Given the current level of change and 'churn' in the NHS, we suggest that it may now be appropriate to consider it a 'high-velocity' environment requiring fast, strategic decision making. In such circumstances static yearly objectives are clearly inappropriate. Interviewees reported how objectives set in April of one year were often irrelevant and obsolete by the following year. Mini-reviews allowed for individual objectives to be kept in line with changes in business strategy.

Objective setting

As we have seen, the increased emphasis on work objectives and measurability desired by the CEO is reflected in the issues covered in the appraisal process, with appraisees reporting that the achievement and planning of work objectives were the most thoroughly discussed issues in the appraisal process. Generally, appraisees found the emphasis on objectives a useful part of the IPR process. A picture that emerges from the survey findings is that objectives are generally clear, cover the most important parts of the job, and that appraisees are actively involved in the objective setting process (see Table 7.5). Interviewees reported being reassured they were on the 'right track', 'working along the right lines',

▶

Table 7.5 Objectives and feedback

	5 Strongly agree	4 Agree	3 Neither agree nor disagree	2 Disagree	1 Strongly disagree
			%		
The goals that I am to achieve are clear	8	61	13	15	2
The most important parts of my job are emphasised in my performance appraisal	3	58	24	13	2
The performance appraisal system helps me understand my personal weaknesses	5	48	19	26	3
My supervisor allows me to help choose the goals that I am to achieve	13	65	10	10	1
The performance appraisal system helps me to understand my job better	3	37	27	31	1
The performance appraisal system gives me a good idea of how I am doing in my job	6	55	23	14	2

'on-line', and 'knowing where they stood' ('You might think You are doing a good job but you need someone to tell you that and vice versa') in their jobs. For example:

Without IPR it would be so easy for you to drift and not do anything. It keeps you on your toes. It keeps you focused. You know exactly what you are aiming for. It makes you look at what you do and what the organisation's trying to achieve. If you didn't have appraisal it would be so easy just to not do anything. You'd just drift. It makes you think about where you are going and where you would like to be.

The setting of objectives provided direction in an increasingly complex and fast-moving organisational environment. The view of one manager was that by appraising her staff she:

Gives them something to hang on to. The job description is so vast and we are facing so many changes. The objectives give direction. It's a stepping stone for them. They give staff guidance and something to aim for, something constructive to aim for.

Interviewees reported how they often tended to 'push' and 'challenge' themselves to make 'progress', attain 'personal development' and 'growth' via the objective-setting process.

The general view was that in this respect the objectives they set for themselves were more challenging (and interesting) than those produced by their managers. For example:

Generally I can take them in my stride. There are one or two demanding ones but they are actually objectives I have brought forward myself. I probably tend to push myself harder than the organisation does.

I always put a new really challenging one in each time, like reducing sickness absence. I tend to challenge myself.

▶

However, for some interviewees their accumulated experience of objective setting had taught them not to challenge themselves 'too much' and restrict both the scope and the number of the objectives they set for themselves. Here we find managerial appraisees becoming sensitised to the objective-setting 'game'. For example:

What I've learnt, as time goes by, is you've got to be careful, right at the outset, how you set your objectives because you can be over optimistic, unrealistic. There's a danger of sitting down and thinking of all the things you'd love to do, or ideally should do, forgetting that you've got lots of constraints and you couldn't in a month of Sundays achieve it. So I think quite a few of us have learnt there is a skill in setting objectives which are reasonable and stand a chance of being achieved. I think that that bit is probably more important than anything else. There is nothing more demoralising than being measured against something which you yourself have declared as being in need of being done and finding that you couldn't possibly do it.

Some appraisees felt that objectives were 'imposed' on them but most accepted that this was 'just part of the job'. However, occasionally this caused some considerable irritation and anger, particularly in the clash with IPR's espoused developmental focus. One manager described 'ending up with nothing you really wanted to do' from his IPR and another described how when she pushed her appraiser to include a particular objective that she perceived as being a key issue for the department and which fitted well with her personal development needs, she was told 'either forget it or fit it into your own time'. The danger with imposing objectives on staff reluctant to accept them was that all that was achieved was lip service and half-hearted commitment, accompanied by subsequent 'fudge' in the appraisal review on the measures of achievement. For example:

I've got to do them [objectives]. I don't not do them but I don't give them the commitment they need if I don't feel it's right. And it never gets picked up at the next appraisal.

Measuring achievement

The use of data in measuring and evaluating individual performance was reported by interviewees as being very reactive on the part of appraisers. Here if the appraisee did not produce data there tended to be very little use of anything other than informed opinion in assessing whether objectives had actually been achieved. An effect of this lack of data use appears to be that although a majority appraisees felt that IPRs represented an accurate measure of their performance, a substantial number were unclear on the standards used to evaluate performance (see Table 7.6).

Some appraisees were prolific in their use of data in the IPR process. Interviewees who had also undertaken NVQ management programmes described a considerable use of reports and the production of memorandums to measure their achievement of objectives. Here, it seems that the NVQ requirement to produce a portfolio causes managers to start to document their work – at least until they attain the award. Our findings suggest this new-found enthusiasm for the memorandum and report generated by NVQs found a further outlet in the IPR process. Further, such documentation and the generally greater level of preparation on the part of the appraisee enabled them to control, to a considerable extent, the content and outcomes of the IPR process. For example:

I took lots of things along [to the IPR meeting]. One of my objectives was to set up team objectives on the ward. I copied examples of these objectives and took them along. I showed reports I had done on the empowerment of patients, and gave her copies of patients' meetings. I used information to show that I had done things. I used these things to prove to her that I had achieved them.

▶

Table 7.6 Measuring performance

	5 Strongly agree	4 Agree	3 Neither agree nor disagree	2 Disagree	1 Strongly disagree
			%		
My performance appraisal for this year represents a fair and accurate picture of my job performance	7	68	11	13	1
My supervisor and I agree on what equals good performance in my job	6	67	14	12	1
I know the standards used to evaluate my performance	2	40	26	29	4

In contrast, other managers usually reported a much less documented measuring process under IPR. The effective use of documentation by this group of managers and professionals thus raises the issue of 'impression management' in the performance measurement process. Impression management is a process by which people attempt to create and sustain desired perceptions of themselves in the eyes of others. In the employment context such others are colleagues, peers, internal customers, clients and especially bosses. The theory of impression management suggests that employees attempt to control, sometimes consciously and sometimes unconsciously, information on themselves which positively shapes others' perceptions of them. The performance-appraisal process is a particular important arena for the creation of favourable impressions at work. The effective use of performance documentation on the part of appraisees thus appears to be a very powerful tool in the production of an overall favourable impression of their managerial capability. A number of appraisers appeared to be very aware of staff's attempts at impression management via the IPR process. Such appraisers reported how they supplemented data from the IPR interview with views from an appraisee's peers and the 'grapevine'. Some declared that they were very wary of the accuracy of views offered by 'mouthy' and 'gobby' staff. For example:

A nurse who's an extrovert, who does a lot of mouthing off, may give the impression that they are doing a really wonderful job and the lass who is quiet could be doing an even better job. But because she's not there selling herself, telling you how wonderful she is, she often loses out here.

I am always wary of the gobby ones. Those who are always telling you how wonderful she is and how hard-worked she is.

It appears the key for managers in measuring individual performance under IPR was distinguishing between 'real' and 'created' performance achievements, the danger being that managers may actually measure an employee's ability to perform in the 'theatrical' rather 'task-oriented' sense.

Objectives and teamwork

The CEO was also keen to encourage wider sharing of objectives, particularly between managers. Here the IPR policy's emphasis on the confidential nature of the appraisal process and its individual nature was seen as discouraging the formal communication of

▶

personal objectives with others. The individualistic nature of IPR thus fitted rather uneasily with the considerable growth in teamwork across the trust. For example, according to one manager:

My boss knows how my objectives fit in with my colleagues, but I don't because I never see them.

The CEO was attempting to introduce change here by leading by example and then encouraging other managers to do the same. After setting objectives for his executive directors, all objectives for each manager, including his own, were circulated to the entire senior management team and also sent out to the clinical divisions. However, there generally did not seem to be much formal sharing of objectives among other managers and professionals. Many of our interviewees felt greater sharing of objectives would be valuable, not least in creating a better understanding of performance priorities within and between departments. On informal levels some staff were actively sharing objectives. One manager describes how she encourages this at team meetings with her managers and supervisors:

I'll say at meetings 'Have you looked at your IPR lately? Who's got that in their IPR? Somebody's got that in their IPR.'

Interviewees expressed how they found it easier to prepare their own objectives when their appraising manager provided copies of their own objectives in advance of the review process. Appraisees also reported that much of their work was now conducted in teams, and many felt that more team-based appraisals and the setting of team objectives would helpfully supplement the individualistic nature of IPR. For example:

I think IPR needs to achieve a better balance between individual performance and team performance. We need a much greater emphasis on team performance. Nowadays at NT we are all about teamwork. The IPR approach is too preoccupied with individual performance. It can become too narrow and it is often divisive.

A number also suggested that wider collaboration on the setting of objectives with other managers, project leaders, working parties, etc. would be beneficial in encompassing the full range of their activities.

IPR outputs

In this last section we report our findings on what the IPR process actually achieves. Here we structure our discussion under four main headings; management control; employee motivation; training and development; and rewards.

Management control

Clearly, as we discuss above, the setting and measuring of work objectives facilitates a direct form of managerial control over the labour process. Despite the rhetoric and policy of development, appraisers seemed to use IPR to exert their managerial authority. Occasionally, this was done in a very crude way. For example, a number of interviewees reported problems with managers waiting for the IPR to 'settle scores' for past conflicts. IPR was thus perceived as a vehicle by some appraisees for the line manager to 'tell me what I should be doing', and to 'tell me what I am not doing right in my job'. There is also evidence that IPR acts as a less manifest and more indirect form of managerial control. Here IPR appears to act as a vehicle to encourage 'self-discipline' and 'responsibility' among staff and thus to promote the reshaping of staff attitudes to fit new managerial values and

▶

beliefs in line with the changing form of work organisation. For example, even some of the sternest critics of IPR noted its subtle effects on them:

I achieve nothing from it. I suppose the main benefit is I actually discipline myself more with my time management. I think 'Oh, I have got to do so and so', and I chart out my work better so that I'll take all that in. I give myself deadlines for my work, saying 'I'll achieve that by March'.

The direction of control in the IPR process, however, is far from one way. Some managers described how their staff turned the IPR 'tables' on them:

The cooks use IPR to say 'This is why I cannot do my job. This is why I cannot achieve this objective.' And then they trot out a great list of problems with the job.

One manager described why he hated doing appraisals with lower-level staff because it reduced to 'a managerial witch-hunt and a general gripe and groan session about what I had or hadn't done over the year'. The manager became so fed up with being on the receiving end of this that he had written to all staff reminding them of the nature of the IPR process and asking for a more positive attitude and less moaning about perceived managerial inadequacies. However, the memorandum had only served to highlight his discomfort with the process and to increase the level of complaining behaviour from appraisees, such that he now admitted to merely 'going through the motions with IPR to get it over with as quickly as possible'.

Employee motivation

IPR, as we discuss above, was often perceived by appraisers and appraised as a good opportunity for managers and managed to talk meaningfully, and engage in 'quality time' together. Not only did IPR visibly and symbolically demonstrate to staff their value and importance to the organisation but the manager also personally cared about their well-being. In some of the accounts of appraisers there were classic human-relations descriptions of the IPR encounter going well beyond the boundaries of work relations. Here interviewees reported appraisals discussing broader personal and social issues and referred to this as 'getting to know your staff':

IPR helps people in knowing where their professional career and their lives are going.

It's your time that you devote to them. And some of them have aspirations that you wouldn't know about until you sit down and talk to them. You show that you are genuinely interested in them as people as well as nurses.

The language used to describe these encounters was often heavily redolent of the unitary ideology of human relations. Appraisees and appraisers stories were littered with references to 'progress', 'going forward together', 'participation', 'empowering the appraisee', 'boosting morale', 'becoming a proactive team', 'harnessing our collective energies' via IPR. Interviewees emphasised the importance of good communication, listening and being listened to particularly, as being a manager was often described as being a 'lonely job'. Thus some two-thirds of interviewees felt that they performed the duties of the post better and that IPR contributed positively to their personal motivation and job satisfaction:

If they scrapped it tomorrow, I don't think I would go home in tears but I would miss it. It helps me keep going, helps me keep motivated. It gives me some comfort, considering all the problems we have at the moment – I've got a service with a lot of problems – that I am achieving what I am supposed to do in my job.

▶

In contrast, other managers, again especially in relation to lower-level staff, were not convinced that IPR reviews delivered much other than a lot of 'hot air' and wasted time that could have been much more profitably employed doing other things. For example:

I have 49 staff. Appraisal takes at least 30–40 minutes each. That's a lot of man-hours to get nothing out of it other than hot air.

Senior management would like to think that if you appraise everybody it would instill in them some kind of belonging, some kind of corporate feeling. But for the rank and file they are just not interested.

Training and development

Despite the emphasis of IPR on training and development by the personnel department, as we can see from Table 7.3 the discussion of an appraisee's training needs takes second place to that on work objectives. Some 12 per cent of appraisees reported that training and development issues were not discussed at all. The majority of those interviewed emphasised training and development as an output of the IPR process. All interviewees claimed to have discussed their own 'personal development plan' (PDP) during the interview. However, this was often reported to be a relatively unfocused and vague discussion. Indeed, few interviewees, under persistent probing, could actually give details of what was in their PDP. The impression gained was that the PDP title signified a much more formalised, more detailed and rather grander training and development document in theory at least if not in practice. Many of the interviewees described a rather mechanical process whereby training and development was discussed as a distinct, almost stand-alone issue. The appraiser was often perceived as running through a checklist of items to be covered in the interview, of which training and development was one, rather than the identification of training needs emerging from a grounded discussion of appraisee performance. The large majority of interviewees felt that much of the training and development that was taking place would still have occurred without the use of IPR but possibly less systematically and at a slower pace.

Managers reported problems with the IPR process – especially coupled with the decision to pursue the IiP award – giving rise to appraisees producing training and development 'wish lists'. Here the key difficulty was finding the training resources to fund costly external courses in the face of increasingly tight training budgets. The demand for degree and diploma courses – particularly amongst nursing staff – fuelled in part by IPR, was causing managers problems in maintaining staff commitment to the appraisal process, given few employees could be supported in this way. Managers described a coping strategy here of encouraging employees to consider alternative, and less costly, development activities such as short secondments, work shadowing and job exchanges. Interviewees were also critical of the personnel department pushing the current training 'flavour of the month' via the IPR process. At the time of our study this was reported as being the managerial NVQ programme running in-house in conjunction with a local university.

Rewards

The PRP element of IPR was not particularly popular with either appraisers or appraisees. Whereas the general view of IPR was that a majority of both appraisees and interviewees considered it to be an overall positive experience, at least for managers and professionals, the views expressed in relation to performance-related pay were largely all negative. A strong view from those receiving PRP was that it was a lot of 'hassle' for little reward; more influenced by quotas than real performance; did little to motivate yet was often demotivating; unfair; arbitrary; inequitable; highly subjective; bias laden; ineffective and detrimental to professionalism; created dysfunctional interpersonal competition; and undermined the developmental focus of IPR. For some, IPR was 'sullied' by its linkage with PRP. At best appraisees felt PRP might possibly work with better and more stringent guidelines, where performance targets were clear and easily measurable rather than subject to an assessment based on ratings, and when they got on well with their line manager. However, PRP also ensured that appraisals were treated seriously. Many of these issues are very familiar 'moans and groans' from the growing PRP literature. A particular problem identified at NT was that performance was highly dependent on team effort and that work was increasingly being reorganised along teamwork lines yet PRP was individually based. The team–individual conflict in PRP may be at least partially resolved by including teamwork objectives in the appraisal process but as we discuss above this was rarely done at NT. Thus:

To achieve my objectives I have to rely on all my heads of departments. I have to rely on people outside our division to cooperate or to take things on board. It's a team effort yet I receive an individual reward that's largely determined on things beyond my control.

Equally, those who did not receive PRP were not keen to be subject to it. This seems to contradict the view that PRP is like an extramarital affair where those with no experience of such things think they are missing out on something terribly exciting and rewarding while those who were involved simply felt miserable. For example:

I don't need someone wielding a financial stick to tell me how to do my job or push myself.

PRP wouldn't affect me in the slightest. A few hundred pounds is neither here nor there for me.

Only one of the non-PRP managers was concerned that he was not receiving PRP. In essence this stemmed from his belief that it was unfair for some managers to receive PRP while others (such as himself) did not, rather than any great desire to be subject to it himself:

IPR was first introduced here for senior managers and was linked to their pay. Then they brought it down to other managers. This is not sour grapes, but when it got down to my level of management the pay was wiped out and just the appraisal was left.

Questions

1. Is IPR a failure at North Trust?
2. Should IPR be retained by the organisation? If you recommend retention, what changes would you advise? If you recommend it should be scrapped, what would you advise should replace it?
3. According to Wright (1991), a paradox of performance management systems is that the meaningful is rarely measurable and the measurable is rarely meaningful. What evidence is there to support such a criticism in North Trust?
4. A key for managers in measuring individual performance under systems of performance appraisal is distinguishing between 'real' and 'created' performance achievements. The danger is that managers may actually measure an employee's 'ability to perform in the theatrical rather than task oriented sense' (Randle and Rainnie 1997). What evidence is there that this is a problem at North Trust? How can the problems of 'impression management' be minimised?

▶

5. It has been suggested that the key challenge currently facing performance appraisal systems is their upgrading, renewal and re-invention such that they are more compatible with business environments. To what extent does IPR fit the business environment of the 'new, modern and dependable NHS' (Department of Health 1997)?

6. Some analysts have suggested that the NHS is moving from a bureaucratic mode of organisation to a network mode of organising. What are the implications of such a development for IPR practice?

Bibliography

Aldakhilallah, K. and Parente, D. (2002) 'Re-designing a square peg: total quality management performance appraisals', *Total Quality Management,* Vol.13, No.1, pp.39–51.

Armstrong, M. and Baron, A. (1998) *Performance Management,* London: IPD.

Arthur, W., Woehr, D.J., Akande, A. and Strong, M.H. (1995) 'Human resource management in West Africa: practices and perceptions', *International Journal of Human Resource Management,* Vol.6, No.2, pp.347–67.

Banks, C.G. and Murphy, K.R. (1985) 'Toward narrowing the research–practice gap in performance appraisal', *Personnel Psychology,* Vol.38, pp.335–45.

*Barlow, G. (1989) 'Deficiencies and the perpetuation of power: latent functions in management appraisal', *Journal of Management Studies,* Vol.26, No.5, pp.499–517.

Bettenhausen, K.L. and Fedor, D.B. (1997) 'Peer and upward appraisals: a comparsion of their benefits and problems', *Group and Organizational Management,* Vol.22, No.2, pp.236–63.

Bevan, S. and Thompson, M. (1991) 'Performance management at the crossroads', *Personnel Management,* November, pp.36–9.

Bhote, K.R. (1994) 'Boss performance appraisal: a metric whose time has gone', *Employment Relations Today,* Vol.21, No.1, pp.1–8.

Bowles, M.L. and Coates, G. (1993) 'Image and substance: the management of performance as rhetoric or reality', *Personnel Review,* Vol.22, No.2, pp.3–21.

Boudreaux, G. (1994) 'What TQM says about performance appraisal', *Compensation and Benefits Review,* Vol.26, No.3, pp.20–4.

*Brown, M. and Benson, J. (2003) 'Rated to exhaustion? Reactions to performance appraisal processes', *Industrial Relations Journal,* Vol.34, No.1, pp.67–81.

Carroll, S.J. and Schneier, C.E. (1982) *Performance Appraisal and Review Systems: The Identification, Measurement, and Development of Performance in Organizations,* Glenview, IL: Scott, Foresman and Company.

Chow, I. (1994) 'An opinion survey of performance appraisal practices in Hong Kong and the Peoples' Republic of China', *Asia Pacific Journal of Human Resources,* Vol.32, pp.62–79.

CIPD (2005) *Performance Management,* Survey report, London: Chartered Institute of Personnel and Development.

Coates, G. (1994) 'Performance appraisal as icon: Oscar-winning performance or dressing to impress?' *International Journal of Human Resource Management,* Vol.5, No.1, pp.165–91.

Connock, S. (1992) 'The importance of "big ideas" to HR managers', *Personnel Management,* Vol.21, No.11, pp.52–6.

Cook, S. (1993) *Customer Care,* London: Kogan Page.

CPCR (1995) *The Right Angle on 360-degree Feedback,* Newcastle: CPCR.

Cully, M., Woodland, S., O'Reilly, A. and Dix, G. (1999) *Britain at Work,* London: Routledge.

Deming, W.E. (1986) *Out of the Crisis: Quality, Productivity and Competitive Position,* Cambridge: Cambridge University Press.

Department of Health (1997) *The New NHS: Modern, Dependable,* London: The Stationery Office.

Dugdill, G. (1994) 'Wide angle view', *Personnel Today,* 27 September, pp.31–32.

Endo, K. (1994) '*Satei* (personal assessment) and interworker competition in Japanese firms', *Industrial Relations,* Vol.33, No.1, pp.70–82.

Fletcher, C. (1993) 'Appraisal: an idea whose time has gone?', *Personnel Management,* September, pp.34–38.

Fletcher, C. and Williams, R. (1992) 'The route to performance management', *Personnel Management,* 42–47.

Fonda, D. (2003) 'It's the B team's time to shine: under-appreciated corporate foot soldiers may be quick to bolt when the economy rebounds', *Time,* 15 September, pp.62–64.

Foucault, M. (1975) *Discipline and Punish: The Birth of the Prison,* New York: Vintage Books.

Fuller, L. and Smith, V. (1991) 'Consumers' reports: management by customers in a changing economy', *Work Employment and Society,* Vol.4, No.1, pp.1–16.

Gabris, G.T. and Ihrke, D.M. (2001) 'Does performance appraisal contribute to heightened levels of employee burnout?', *Public Personnel Management,* Vol.30, No.2, pp.157–72.

Gill, D. (1977) *Appraising Performance: Present Trends and the Next Decade,* London: IPD.

*Grint, K. (1993) 'What's wrong with performance appraisals? A critique and a suggestion', *Human Resource Management,* Vol.3, No.3, pp.61–77.

Halachmi, A. (1993) 'From performance appraisal to performance targeting', *Public Personnel Management,* Vol.22, No.2, pp.323–44.

IDS (2007) *Performance management,* HR Studies, London: Incomes Data Services.

ILO (2002) *Supporting Workplace Learning for High Performance Working,* Geneva: International Labour Organization.

IPD (1999) *Training and development in Britain 1999,* IPD Survey Report, London: Institute of Personnel and Development.

IRS (1992) 'Industrial relations developments in the water industry', *Employment Trends,* No.516, pp.6–15.

IRS (1994) 'Improving performance? A survey of appraisal arrangements', *Employment Trends,* No.556, pp.5–14.

IRS (1995a) 'Survey of employee relations in local government', *Employment Trends,* No.594, pp.6–13.

IRS (1995b) 'The customer is boss: matching employee performance to customer service needs', *Employment Trends,* No.585, pp.7–13.

IRS (1999) 'New ways to perform appraisal', *Employment Trends,* No.676, pp.7–16.

Kayande, U. and Finn, A. (1999), 'Unmasking the phantom: a psychometric assessment of mystery shopping', *Journal of Retailing,* Vol.75, No.2, pp.135–217.

Kersley, B., Alpin, C., Forth, J., Bryson, A., Bewley, H., Dix, G. and Oxenbridge, S. (2006) *Inside the Workplace: Findings from the 2004 Workplace Employment Relations Survey,* London: Routledge.

Kessler, I. and Purcell, J. (1992) 'Performance related pay: objectives and application', *Human Resource Management Journal,* Vol.2, No.3, pp.16–33.

Laabs, J. (1992) 'Measuring work in the electronic age', *Personnel Journal,* Vol.71, No.6, p.35.

Lawler, E.E. (1994) 'Performance management: the next generation', *Compensation and Benefits Review,* May–June, pp.16–28.

Lawler, J.J., Jain, H.C., Ratnam, C.S.V. and Atmiyanandana, V. (1995) 'Human resource management in developing economies: a comparison of India and Thailand', *International Journal of Human Resource Management,* Vol.6, No.2, pp.320–46.

Lee, J., Havighurst, L. and Rassel, G. (2004) 'Factors related to court references to performance appraisal fairness and validity', *Public Personnel Management,* Vol.33, No.1, pp.61–77.

LGMB (1994) *Performance Management and Performance-Related Pay. Local Government Practice,* London: Local Government Management Board.

Locher, A.H. and Teel, K.S. (1988) 'Appraisal trends', *Personnel Journal,* Vol.67, No.9, pp.139–43.

London, M. and Beatty, R.W. (1993) '360-degree feedback as a competitive advantage', *Human Resource Management,* Vol.32, Nos 2–3, pp. 353–72.

Long, P. (1986) *Performance Appraisal Revisited,* London: Institute of Personnel and Development.

*Longenecker, C. (1989) 'Truth or consequences: politics and performance appraisals', *Business Horizons,* November–December, pp.76–82.

Maroney, B.P. and Buckley, P.P.M. (1992) 'Does research in performance appraisal influence the practice of performance appraisal? Regretfully not', *Public Personnel Management,* Vol.21, No.2, pp.185–96.

Milliman, J.F., Zawacki, R.A., Schulz, B., Wiggins, S. and Norman, C. (1995) 'Customer service drives 360-degree goal setting', *Personnel Journal,* June, pp.136–41.

O'Reilly, B. (1995) '360-degree feedback can change your life', *Fortune Magazine,* 17 October, pp.55–58.

Personnel Management (1995) Vol.1, No.7, p.15.

Poon, J. (2004) 'Effects of performance appraisal politics on job-satisfaction and turnover intention', *Personnel Review,* Vol.33, No.3, pp.322–24.

*Randell, G. (1994) 'Employee appraisal', in K. Sisson (ed.) *Personnel Management: A Comprehensive Guide to Theory and Practice in Britain,* Oxford: Blackwell.

Randle, K. and Rainnie, A. (1997) 'Managing creativity, maintaining control: a study in pharmaceutical research', *Human Research Management Journal,* Vol.7, No.2, pp.32–46.

Redman, T. and Mathews, B.P. (1995) 'Do corporate turkeys vote for Christmas? Managers' attitudes towards upward appraisal', *Personnel Review,* Vol.24, No.7, pp.13–24.

Redman, T. and Snape, E. (1992) 'Upward and onward: can staff appraise their managers?', *Personnel Review,* Vol.21, No.7, pp.32–46.

*Redman, T., Snape, E., Thompson, D. and Ka-ching Yan, F. (2000) 'Performance appraisal in the National Health Service: a trust hospital study', *Human Resource Management Journal,* Vol.10, No.1, pp.1–16.

Roth, W. and Ferguson, D. (1994) 'The end of performance appraisals?', *Quality Digest,* Vol.14, No.9, pp.52–57.

Shing, M. and Spence, M. (2002) 'Investigating the limits of competitive intelligence gathering: is mystery shopping ethical', *Business Ethics: A European Review,* Vol.11, No.4, pp.343–44.

Snape, E., Redman., T. and Bamber, G. (1994) *Managing Managers,* Oxford: Blackwell.

*Snape, E., Thompson, D., Ka-ching Yan, F. and Redman, T. (1998) 'Performance appraisal and culture: practice and attitudes in Hong Kong and Great Britain', *International Journal of Human Resource Management,* Vol.9, No.5, pp.841–61.

Sparrow, P. (1994) 'Organizational competencies: creating a strategic behavioural framework for selection and assessment', in N. Anderson and P. Herriot (eds) *Assessment and Selection in Organizations,* Chichester: Wiley.

Thomas, A., Wells, M. and Willard, J. (1992) 'A novel approach to developing managers and their teams: BPX uses upward feedback', *Management Education and Development,* Vol.23, No.1, pp.30–32.

Toegel, G. and Conger, J. (2003) '360-degree feedback: time for reinvention', *Academy of Management Learning and Education,* Vol.2, No.3, pp.297–311.

Tombs, S. (1992) 'Managing safety: could do better . . .', *Occupational Safety and Health,* Vol.26, No.1, pp.9–12.

Townley, B. (1989) 'Selection and appraisal: reconstituting "social relations"', in J. Storey (ed.) *New Perspectives on Human Resource Management,* London: Routledge.

Townley, B. (1993) 'Performance appraisal and the emergence of management', *Journal of Management Studies,* Vol.30, No.2, pp.221–38.

Townley, B. (1994) *Reframing Human Resource Management,* London: Sage

Townley, B. (1999) 'Practical reason and performance appraisal', *Journal of Management Studies,* Vol.36, No.3, pp.287–306.

Tziner, A. (1999) 'The relationship between distal and proximal factors and the use of political considerations in performance appraisal', *Journal of Business and Psychology,* Vol.14, No.1, pp.217–31.

Wright, V. (1991) 'Performance related pay', in F. Neale (ed.) *The Handbook of Performance Management,* London: Institute of Personnel Management.

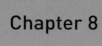

Chapter 8

INDUSTRIAL RELATIONS

Nicolas Bacon

Introduction

The purpose of this chapter is to outline some of the key contemporary developments in industrial relations issues and consider the implications. The term 'industrial relations' when broadly defined encompasses the study of all aspects of the employment relationship (see Heery *et al.* 2008, p.2); more narrowly defined, it has traditionally focused on those areas of the employment relationship in which managers deal with the representatives of employees rather than managing employees directly as individuals (Edwards 1995). The main parties to the employment relationship and the key actors are workers and workers' organisations (usually trade unions), employers and managers, and also the state. These actors create rules to regulate work, covering such issues as wages and working hours (termed 'substantive rules') and how to bargain, consult and resolve disputes over issues (termed 'procedural rules'). Whether substantive or procedural rules are set unilaterally by employers, the extent to which the state decides to intervene and regulate employment, and the role of workers and trade unions in the process of establishing rules, are among the central industrial relations issues explored in this chapter. Employers set rules to try to maximise efficiency, but other actors in the employment relationship may feel that employers often make choices that do not maximise efficiency, and that the decisions managers make may therefore damage organisational performance and threaten the terms and conditions of employees. In addition, workers and the state are also interested in the fairness of employment outcomes and seek to influence employer policies on a range of issues, such as what constitutes a fair day's work for a fair day's pay and the distribution of pay between different workers and between workers and managers, and to ensure equal opportunities for employees. As a result, industrial relations are often subject to joint regulation between employers and trade unions. Joint regulation of employer practices therefore requires employee participation in decision making and it is appropriate to start by considering how managers react to this challenge to their authority.

Management approaches to industrial relations

The suggestion that trade unions or the state should intervene, or intervene more, in regulating employment provokes a strong response in many employers and managers, many of whom prefer to make employment decisions unilaterally. Employers and managers responding in this way hold a set of assumptions about the right to manage (frequently termed the management prerogative) and the rights of workers, unions and the state to intervene in employment relations (Budd and Bhave 2008). These assumptions held by managers are the mixture of a complex blend of experiences, predispositions, learned behaviour and prejudice and are influenced and reinforced by incentives for managers either to act just in the interests of shareholders or to balance the interests of a broader range of stakeholders. The assumptions held by managers are termed 'frames of reference', (Fox 1966, p.1974) which describe managers' often deeply held assumptions towards a labour force and the rights of workers, trade unions or the state to influence management decisions. Three separate frames of reference can be identified: unitarism, pluralism and radical. A manager with one frame of reference will differ from a manager with an alternative frame of reference in terms of their beliefs about the nature of organisations, the role of conflict and the task of managing employees. Managers holding a unitarist frame of reference believe that the natural state of organisations is one of harmony and cooperation. All employees are thought to be in the same team, pulling together for the common goal of organisational success. The employee relations task of management is to prevent conflict arising from misunderstandings that result if they fail to adequately communicate organisational goals to employees. Any remaining conflicts are attributed to mischief created by troublemakers. A pluralist frame of reference recognises that organisations contain a variety of sectional groups who legitimately seek to express divergent interests. The resulting conflict is inevitable and the task of managers is to establish a system of structures and procedures in which conflict is institutionalised and a negotiated order is established. The radical critique of pluralism is not, strictly speaking, a frame of reference for understanding management views of the employment relationship. It draws upon Marxism and explains workplace conflict within a broader historical and social context and places a stress upon the unequal power struggle of opposing social classes.

There are no simple methods to assess whether most managers hold one frame of reference or another – indeed, they usually hold a complex set of ideas rather than falling neatly into a single and possibly oversimplistic frame of reference, and of course managers may hold different views in different countries. In Britain at least, most managers oppose sharing power with unions and prefer managerial unilateralism, express a preference for flexible labour markets and oppose government involvement in wage setting (Poole *et al.* 2005). As trade union power has declined, managers oppose state involvement in industrial relations issues, although this is not always the case, as managers in the past have supported state intervention to control the power of trade unions. Managers have, however, become less hostile to unions as union power has declined; for example, managers currently see less of a need for the state to intervene to restrict union power (Poole *et al.* 2005)

Answers to another question frequently posed to managers indicate that a majority of workplace managers do not have a single frame of reference. In the 2004 Workplace Employment Relations Survey (WERS04), most managers directly responsible for industrial relations issues in Britain (62 per cent) were 'neutral' about union membership, whereas 21 per cent were 'in favour', with 17 per cent 'not in favour' of union membership by employees in their workplace (Kersley *et al.* 2006, pp.112–13). However, when the same managers are asked more explicitly whether they prefer to manage employees directly or through unions then unitarist preferences emerge. For example, 79 per cent of all managers surveyed agreed with the statement 'we would rather consult directly with employees than with unions', increasing to 82 per cent of public sector managers and 88 per cent of managers in small workplaces with fewer than 50 employees (Kersley *et al.* 2006, p.50). Consequently, management approaches to industrial relations are often characterised as mixing and matching unitarist and pluralist beliefs (Edwards *et al.* 1998). Many managers hold such views because it reflects the reality of employees' need for representation to protect their interests from employers, or an acceptance that in some industries unions are powerful and employees will only regard rules as legitimate if employees and their representatives participate in management decisions. In some organisations, unitarist managers also actively seek to deter employees from joining trade unions, whereas pluralist managers in some cases in contrast encourage employees to join unions. Encouraging or deterring employees from joining unions appears to be important as employers' attitudes towards unions are significantly associated with union presence in the workplace (Kersley *et al.* 2006, p.114) and union membership across Europe (Schnabel and Wagner 2007) and no doubt outside Europe.

Frames of reference are also important because they underlie the broader management style adopted in organisations towards the workforce. The approach taken to industrial relations is often linked to broader work organisation and human resource management issues. It is common therefore to link managers' approach to industrial relations with a more general management style towards employees that also affects work organisation and human resource management practices (Fox 1974; Purcell and Sisson 1983; Purcell and Ahlstrand 1994; Storey and Bacon 1993; for a review see Bacon 2008). Later in this chapter we will describe the decline of joint regulation. An important question is whether employers have adopted a unitarist approach to industrial relations in order to facilitate high-performance work practices to improve organisational performance by developing employee commitment (Bacon 2003). Or, in contrast, do managers avoid unions in order to improve organisational performance by reducing employment costs and seeking to exercise greater control over employees? Before we look at this, however, employers cannot devise effective industrial relations approaches without carefully considering the views of their employees, and it is to employee views that we now turn.

Why employees join unions

A widespread criticism of management during the 1960s and 1970s, a point which still holds today, is that employees may not feel that everyone shares the same goals in their workplace and they may reject a unitarist perspective. In many, if not most, workplaces employees talk of 'us' and describe managers as 'them', believing that there are two sides with partially conflicting interests (Clegg 1979). Thus, many employees subscribe to a pluralist perspective and feel that workers and managers are on different sides with separate interests, rather than feeling that working for an organisation is like playing for a football team where all groups supporting a club are on the same side and pursuing a common goal (Ramsey 1975).

As many employees feel they have different interests from employers, they often join trade unions. Trade unions have approximately 320 million members worldwide, which amounts to between one-fifth and one-quarter of the global labour force (Visser 2003). Significant variation exists between countries. For instance, Russia, Ukraine and Belarus (58 per cent) and China (42 per cent) have high rates of union membership; around one-quarter (26 per cent) of European workers are union members; whereas a smaller proportion of workers in North America (13 per cent) and Asia (10 per cent) belong to unions. It is therefore important that employers understand why employees join trade unions.

Employees join unions for a wide range of reasons (Schnabel 2003, p.19). They may join a union because they feel dissatisfied with their work situation (termed the frustration-aggression thesis), joining a union may bring benefits such as higher wages that outweigh the costs of membership (a rational choice explanation), or employees may be encouraged to join by the traditions and opinions of their work group (an interactionist explanation). In a study across 18 EU countries, in addition to the strong effects of employers' attitudes in the workplace mentioned earlier to explain whether union members are present in the workplace, the probability of union membership is also affected by workplace characteristics, personal characteristics and an individual's attitudes (Schnabel and Wagner 2007). The types of workplace, the personal characteristics of the labour force and individual attitudes may of course vary between countries and alongside other factors help explain national differences in levels of union membership. State support for unions, the union role in social insurance schemes and of course national political history are also important to explain differences in national levels of union

Table 8.1 The reasons employees give for joining unions

Support if I had a problem at work	72%
Improved pay and conditions	36%
Because I believe in trade unions	16%
Free legal advice	15%
Most people at work are members	14%

Source: Waddington and Whitston 1997, p.521

membership. To illustrate in more detail, some of the factors identified in the study of 18 EU countries just mentioned were important in a survey of almost 11,000 union members in the UK (Waddington and Whitston 1997). In the UK survey employees revealed that they continued to join unions for collective protection and to improve their terms and conditions (Table 8.1). These findings are in line with studies suggesting that workers' perceptions of 'them' and 'us' are still strong, even though managers over the past 20 years have attempted to improve industrial relations through a wide range of initiatives described in other chapters in this book (see Coupland *et al.* 2005; D'Art and Turner 1999; Kelly and Kelly 1991).

The decline of joint regulation

The degree of joint regulation of industrial relations is not of course fixed but changes in response to global and national economic, social and political pressures. In a majority of countries union membership has fallen over the past 20 years, especially in Europe and North America. Increased market competition, for example, has reduced the willingness of employers to recognise and negotiate with trade unions in many, but not all, countries (Brown 2008). Table 8.2 shows the extent of decline in union density – the proportion of employees who are union members – in 20 OECD countries. In different European regions and in liberal market economies, union density has declined, although it has declined only marginally in northern Europe (Denmark, Finland, Norway and Sweden) and has declined most steeply in liberal market economies (Australia, Canada, Ireland, New Zealand, the UK and the US).

Declining union density is only one indication of joint regulation and it is also important to consider trends in collective bargaining coverage – the proportion of employees whose terms and conditions of employment are set by collective bargaining. Reflecting the comments made above about unionisation reflecting national economic and political differences, Table 8.3 shows that the most dramatic decline in collective bargaining coverage has occurred in liberal market economies (Australia, Canada, New Zealand, the UK and the US). Among central European countries collective bargaining coverage has remained stable (Austria and

Table 8.2 Average union density (%) and density change in 20 OECD countries, 1980–2000

Region	1980	1990	2000	Change 1980–2000
Northern Europe	71.5	71.5	71	−0.5
Mainland Europe	35	25	22	−12.8
Central Europe	42	36	32	−10.6
Liberal market economies	47	38	26	−20.7

Source: Hamann and Kelly 2008, p.138

Table 8.3 Average percentage of employees covered by collective bargaining in 20 OECD countries, 1980–2000

Region	1980	1990	2000	Change 1980–2000
Northern Europe	78	78	83	+5
Mainland Europe	73	78	83	+8
Central Europe	77	77	75	−2.5
Liberal market economies	55	47	36	−18.4

Source: Hamann and Kelly 2008, p.139

Belgium), declined (Germany and Switzerland) and increased in the Netherlands. In mainland Europe it has increased (France, Greece, Italy, Portugal and Spain), as it has in northern Europe.

Within each group of countries and within each country joint regulation has probably not declined at a uniform rate. However, in liberal market economies the steep decline of joint regulation appears to have affected all industrial sectors, if not evenly. If we consider a third indicator of joint regulation, union recognition, in the UK for example, the number of workplaces recognising unions declined between 1980 and 2004 in all sectors but the decline was modest in the public sector compared to the private sector (Table 8.4).

What are the main reasons for the decline in joint regulation? Focusing on liberal market economies, because this is where the decline is most evident, and using the UK as an example, the decline in union recognition in the UK since the 1980s is mainly due to the failure of unions to organise workers and gain recognition for collective bargaining in new firms and new workplaces (Machin 2000). Responding to heightened competitive pressures, managers have proved reluctant to recognise unions for fear of higher wages, and unions have found it difficult to recruit the growing numbers of female and service sector workers. As the number of large manufacturing plants and manual workers declined, the traditional habitat for the UK's system of industrial relations based on adversarial collective bargaining was disappearing (Millward *et al.* 1992). During the 1990s, these factors accounted for three-quarters of the decline in collective bargaining, although, in addition, managers in unionised workplaces were less likely to continue ongoing collective bargaining arrangements, with about one quarter of the decline in the 1990s explained by abandoning collective bargaining in ongoing workplaces (Charlwood 2007).

Trade union influence appears even lower than suggested by current levels of union recognition when we consider the scope and depth of joint consultation and bargaining. It is difficult to assess the extent to which managers rely upon collective agreements with trade

Table 8.4 Average percentage of workplaces with 25+ employees recognising unions, 1980–2004

	1980	1984	1990	1998	2004
Manufacturing	65	56	44	28	37
Private services	41	44	36	23	20
Public sector	94	99	87	87	88
All	64	66	53	42	39

Source: Blanchflower *et al.* 2007, p.288

unions in workplaces. Although formal collective agreements may include procedural arrangements for continued union influence in the workplace (Dunn and Wright 1994) managers have increasingly exercised their prerogative to make important changes unilaterally, particularly in working methods (Geary 1995). This suggests that although many employers retain agreements with unions, collective agreements have been hollowed out and in workplaces where union representatives are present only a modest level of joint regulation occurs. On average in British workplaces with recognised unions, for example, across seven different bargaining issues, employers report negotiating with union representatives in 10 per cent of workplaces, consult in 36 per cent, inform union representatives in 20 per cent, and neither negotiate, consult nor inform in 28 per cent of workplaces (Brown and Nash 2008). Managers in many workplaces appear to regard certain HR issues as off-limits to union representatives and do not even provide information on these issues to unions. As a consequence, trade union influence in many workplaces has 'withered on the vine', and where union representatives remain in place this resembles a unionised approach to industrial relations which in fact is little more than a 'hollow shell' (Hyman 1997).

Employers deny unions influence because they seek greater freedom to choose employment practices. From the mid-1980s, employers certainly appeared to exercise an increasing degree of strategic choice in redesigning employment practices as unions made significant concessions to employer demands. The strategic choice theory of industrial relations marked a paradigm shift from unions making demands and employers conceding to those demands, to managers, rather than unions, becoming the central industrial relations actor in liberal market economies such as the US, and making demands to which unions had to accede (Strauss 1984). At the core of strategic choice theory in industrial relations is the assumption that managers 'have discretion over their decisions; that is, where environmental constraints do not severely curtail the parties' choice of alternatives' (Kochan *et al.* 1984, p.21). However, declining union influence does not necessarily increase employer freedom of choice, for two reasons. First, the state has increasingly intervened to regulate employment practices to compensate for the decline of joint regulation between employers and unions (Piore and Safford 2006). To give one example, as unions are not able to easily organise workplaces with the lowest levels of pay, the British government introduced a national minimum wage and statutory recognition procedure for trade unions, both long-established features of US industrial relations. Second, intensive market forces have reduced employer discretion in employment practices in many instances. If all employers are, for example, forced to marginalise trade unions because they have to reduce employment costs then this is hardly a strategic choice but a market imperative (Lewin 1987: for a broader review see Bacon 2008). Whether employers have exercised significant levels of strategic choice in industrial relations or not, the implications of declining union influence are dramatic and tell us much about employer motives.

The implications of declining joint regulation

Trade unions have a range of beneficial effects, including forcing managers to improve human resource management practices (the 'shock effect' of unions requiring an improvement in management); increasing employee voice in the workplace to express the interests of employees, redistribution of outcomes and promoting equal opportunities (the 'sword of justice' effect); and increasing job satisfaction and reducing labour turnover. Union effects appear to have reduced remarkably in recent years; on some issues unions now appear to have no discernible effects and in other cases the effects only apply in specific circumstances (see Brown 2008, p.123). The long-term implications of the decline in joint regulation are potentially far-reaching.

According to the collective voice/institutional response model of unionism (Freeman and Medoff 1984), unions express employees' views and have an impact on managers greater than the views expressed by individual employees, which are frequently ignored by managers. With this collective voice unions seek to raise employee wages and bargain for a range of beneficial policies for members, such as greater training. As a result, unionised workers traditionally received higher wages compared to non-unionised workers (the union wage premium) and, as described earlier, employees act rationally in joining unions for higher wages that outweigh the costs of membership. At a time when unions are less powerful, employers correspondingly are less likely to recognise and work with unions in order to remove union pressure to provide improved terms and conditions. As a result, the union wage premium comparing the wages of unionised and non-unionised workers during a period of union weakness has reduced overtime (Blanchflower and Bryson 2003). Nevertheless, in 2005 the union wage premium in Britain was 10 per cent of gross hourly earnings (Bryson and Forth 2008). Trade unions also have a second important effect on wages by narrowing the pay distribution in attempting a fair redistribution of reward. It is therefore not surprising that declining unionisation results in increasing wage inequality (Charlwood 2007) and the salaries of executive directors and managers have risen exponentially as unions have been less able to increase members' wages.

Moving beyond wages, declining unionisation has also affected training provision and the ability of unions to raise training levels. Trade unions raise training levels in a variety of ways. Unions bargain directly for more training, increase wages so employers have to train employees in order for employees to contribute more and offset higher wages, and in expressing and seeking to resolve employee grievances, unions reduce employee turnover, thereby extending the period in which employers benefit from training investments. The positive union effect on training is also in decline. Whereas training was higher in unionised workplaces throughout the 1980s and 1990s in Britain, by 2004 unionised workplaces in the private sector no longer provided more training than non-unionised workplaces in the private sector, and the union training premium in the public sector was weak (Hoque and Bacon 2008). Even where unions have prioritised training (see the discussion of union learning representatives later in this chapter), and employers negotiated and bargained with union representatives over training, there is little evidence that employers respond to this pressure. In Britain at least, trade unions are currently not able to raise training levels above those provided in non-union workplaces in the private sector.

Trade unions also fulfil a 'sword of justice' role in promoting fairness and equality in the workplace and this may also have been harmed by the decline of joint regulation (Metcalf 2004). Unionised workplaces report more family-friendly policies and are more likely to have an equal opportunities policy (Noon and Hoque 2001; Walsh 2007). For example in Britain, whereas 63 per cent of non-union workplaces had an equal opportunities policy in 2004, 96 per cent of unionised workplaces had such a policy (Kersley *et al.* 2006, p.238). In the absence of union pressure and the willingness of employers to respond to this pressure, employers are less likely to adopt family-friendly and equal opportunities policies.

As the evidence reviewed so far suggests, unions are associated with many positive employment practices in the workplace, although employers are increasingly unresponsive to union pressure. There is also evidence that employers seek to offset the higher costs associated with unionisation by saving on employment costs elsewhere. For example, White (2005) reports that unionised compared to non-union workplaces not only report more high-performance work practices, fringe benefits and family-friendly practices, but unionised workplaces also report high levels of labour-cost-cutting policies such as reducing staffing levels, outsourcing and delayering management hierarchies. This suggests that where unions encourage managers to adopt expensive productivity-enhancing HR practices, employers look to reduce other employment costs by reducing staffing levels or employing staff on inferior terms and conditions through contractors.

Earlier in this chapter the declining influence of unions on employer policy was shown by the significant number of unionised workplaces in which managers did not negotiate, consult or inform union representatives on key employment issues. Recent evidence suggests that trade unions are no longer as effective in raising the concerns of their members because managers are increasingly less willing to listen to concerns expressed through union representatives and prefer to deal with individual employees. Trade unions rely on the logic of collective action – expressing the collective voice of employees has more influence than an employee acting alone. Managers appear increasingly unresponsive to union voice, with evidence that unions are no longer able to shock employers into better practices to raise productivity (Bryson *et al.* 2006). Trade unions find it increasingly difficult to resolve workplace grievances with unresponsive employers, and as a result find it increasingly difficult to increase the levels of satisfaction employees experience in their jobs. Guest and Conway (2004), for example, report that union members compared to non-union members report lower levels of job satisfaction, consistent with the suggestion that management unresponsiveness to union-expressed grievances and demands constrains union voice and increases the levels of dissatisfaction among union members. This is a worrying finding because job satisfaction is associated with turnover, and reduced turnover increases the incentive for employers to invest in commitment-enhancing human resource management practices, as the period over which they benefit from such investments is greater if fewer staff exit. Employer unresponsiveness to trade unions is gradually shutting off the productivity-enhancing impacts of trade unions.

Employers feel justified in avoiding unions or being unresponsive to pressure from recognised unions because unions may damage productivity by exercising monopoly power to defend restrictive work practices and raise wage costs above market rates. These issues have been extensively debated by labour economists without clear resolution one way or the other. Metcalf (2004), summarising the data on the productivity effects of unions, the impact of unions on financial performance and the probability of firm closure, notes that there is no difference in the productivity, financial performance or likelihood of closure of union and non-union workplaces. It certainly seems likely that at a time of union weakness, any union impact on productivity is minimal, whether the impact is positive or negative. The declining impact of unions has, however, affected their ability to encourage employers to adopt sophisticated human resource management practices, improve employee terms and conditions, and raise job satisfaction levels at work. The joint regulation of industrial relations has certainly declined but what does this mean for the increasing number of workers who find themselves in non-union workplaces, and how effectively are the interests of non-union workers represented?

Non-union workplaces

According to one estimate, the majority of UK workplaces had become non-union by 1995 (Cully and Woodland 1996). In the classic account by Fox (1974), to maintain a non-union status managers enforce management prerogative by coercive power to justify a unitarist ideology. Managers have often used a wide-ranging web of defences against unionisation that in their more extreme variants in the US include 'sweet stuff' to make management policies more acceptable to employees, 'fear stuff' to discourage union joining and 'evil stuff' to demonise unions (Roy 1980). Managers holding a unitarist frame of reference may adopt quite different approaches (Purcell and Ahlstrand 1994): a 'sophisticated human relations' approach requires investment in staff development and use of a wide range of human resource management policies to substitute for the services unions provide for members (a union substitution approach or 'sweet stuff'); a 'paternalist' approach seeks to build the loyalty and commitment of staff through consideration for employee welfare ('sweet stuff'); and a 'bleak house' strategy involves minimising labour costs and aggressively avoiding union recruitment ('fear stuff' and 'evil stuff').

Several key commentators in the late 1980s predicted a growth in the non-union 'sophisticated human relations' approach (Sisson 1989). A non-union environment appeared well suited to the demands of developing committed and flexible employees, as demonstrated by several large non-union US multinationals such as IBM, Hewlett Packard and Mars (Foulkes 1980; Kochan *et al.* 1986). For example, IBM had combined corporate success, a positive employee relations climate of low conflict, low labour turnover and long service, with good pay and conditions. In addition, the company provided procedures to fulfil many of the functions met by unions, including a complex array of alternative procedures (a no-redundancy policy, single status, equal opportunities policies, merit pay and performance assessments), a strong emphasis on internal communications and a grievance system. Most employees working at an IBM plant in the UK studied by Dickson *et al.* (1988) were positively attached to the individualistic ethos of the company and perceived little need for union protection. In the case of 'Comco', explored by Cressey *et al.* (1985), employees also identified strongly with the company and enjoyed 'greater benefits' and 'less disciplinary pressure'. Scott (1994) outlined a slightly different 'golden handcuffs' approach whereby employees in a chocolate works received good terms and conditions in return for accepting a high rate of effort and strict rules.

Despite this evidence, non-union companies with a sophisticated approach to managing employees appear to remain the exception. A study of high-tech companies in the southeast of England, where we might expect companies to reproduce the IBM non-union model, uncovered little evidence of sophisticated HRM, with companies either opportunistically avoiding unions or adopting the style of 'benevolent autocracies' (McLoughlin and Gourlay 1994). Furthermore, the assumed benefits of a 'sophisticated human relations' approach may be illusory. Blyton and Turnbull (2004) suggest that Marks & Spencer, so often held up as an exemplar non-union company, simultaneously pursued a 'union substitution' strategy in retail outlets while forcing suppliers into a cost minimisation approach. In another example, a steel plant that had introduced apparently exemplary human resource and work organisation practices subsequently derecognised trade unions, with employees reporting that managers insisted on attitudinal compliance, work intensification and the suppression of any counterbalancing trade union activity (Bacon 1999). It is also striking that among these cases, IBM lost its pre-eminence in its sector, Marks & Spencer now sources from Asian suppliers, leading to the closure of many UK suppliers, and the steel plant mentioned above closed.

Given the comments earlier in this chapter about the positive impact of unions on the adoption of high-commitment management practices (the 'shock effect' of unions), it is not surprising that sophisticated HRM practices are to be found alongside union recognition mainly in larger workplaces and those in the public sector rather than non-union private sector workplaces (Cully *et al.* 1999, p.111; Machin and Wood 2005; Sisson 1993, p.206). Furthermore, higher union density (the proportion of employees who are trade union members) is also associated with greater joint regulation and more high-commitment management (HCM) practices. There is also evidence that the combination of union recognition and high-commitment management practices has a powerful effect on workplace performance, with 'workplaces with a recognised union and a majority of the HCM practices . . . [performing] better than the average, and better than workplaces without recognition and a minority of these practices' (Cully *et al.* 1999, p.135). In private sector workplaces where managers withdrew from collective bargaining during the 1990s there was no compensating increase in high-commitment management practices, with lower productivity growth as a consequence (Charlwood 2007). It is not, however, clear that these positive associations will continue, given the evidence presented earlier in this chapter showing that union effects on employers continue to diminish in unionised workplaces. If unions cannot force employers to adopt more HCM practices than non-unionised companies then the differences between working in the union and non-union sectors will gradually disappear and this inevitably reduces the incentive for employees to join unions.

Non-union employee representation

As almost half of workplaces in Britain are effectively union-free, a 'representation gap' (Towers 1997) may have developed where managers operate without any independent employee voice. The representation gap is felt most keenly among the estimated 3 million workers who might join a union but a union does not exist in their workplace (Metcalfe 2004). In Britain, three-quarters of workplaces contain no employee representatives (either union or non-union employee representatives) and almost half of employees do not have an employee representative to speak up for them (Charlwood and Terry 2007, p.324). The absence of representation is important because dissatisfied workers who cannot effectively express their grievances may have little option but to leave the organisation (Hirschman 1971). In the absence of union recognition managers can provide employee voice through direct channels by communicating with workers in team briefings and problem solving, and there is evidence that managers are more responsive to these communications than in listening to unions (Bryson 2004). However, many organisations fail to provide either union or direct channels for employee voice.

Earlier it was mentioned that the state has increasingly intervened in industrial relations, partly to compensate for the decline in joint regulation through trade unions. The European Union Directive for informing and consulting employees, phased into the UK from 2005, provided rights for employees to be informed about the economic situation of their employer's business, employment prospects and substantial changes in work organisation or employment contracts (Hall 2006). This imposes obligations on all organisations, including those without unions, to consult with employee representatives. In Britain, an estimated 7 per cent of workplaces contain a non-union representative and 17 per cent of employees have access to a non-union representative (Charlwood and Terry 2007, p.324). Although workplace union representatives continue to have some effects on employer policies and employees' terms and conditions, the evidence to date reports that non-union forms of employee representation have no effects and are irrelevant (Charlwood and Terry 2007). There is little evidence to date that non-union employee representation, even backed by legislation, meets the basic requirement of representing employee interests to influence employer practices.

Partnership with unions

What of other developments in the unionised sector? In organisations where managers continue to recognise unions, an important innovation has been the signing of partnership agreements with trade unions. The election of 'New Labour' in the UK in 1997 produced a new public policy environment, with the Employment Relations Act 1999 and Fairness at Work programme introducing new rights for trade unions and individual employees (Dickens *et al.* 2005). As already mentioned, this legislative programme involved a statutory route for union recognition, an extension of rights for individual employees, a national minimum wage and closer engagement with the social policies of the European Union. A central aim of this legislative programme has been to 'replace the notion of conflict between employers and employees with the promotion of partnership in the longer term' (HMSO 1998) and reflects the increasing influence of a European approach in the UK.

Managers and unions have contested the meaning of 'partnership' and at times it appears an inherently ambiguous industrial relations aim with no agreed meaning (Undy 1999; Ackers and Payne 1998). As Undy (1999, p.318) has pointed out, 'What one party, or commentator, means by "partnership" is not necessarily shared by others'. As with so many terms in the area of employment relations, key pressure groups such as the Trades Union Congress (TUC), the Confederation of British Industries and the Institute of Directors (IoD) have sought to provide 'widely differing interpretations' of partnership (Undy 1999, p.318), defining the term for their own ends. The Institute of Personnel and Development, for example, explained that partnership 'has more to do with an approach to the relationship between employers and employees, individually and in groups, than it has to do with trade unions' (IPD 1997, p.8). Partnership can therefore be defined in both unitarist and pluralist terms. Rather unsurprisingly, the definition favoured by the TUC is pluralistic, with the stress placed on respecting union influence, whereas the IoD prefers a unitarist definition, whereby employees identify with the employer and trade unions are compliant to the wishes of management.

Despite these different views, the Involvement and Participation Association (IPA), an independent pressure group, developed an influential definition of partnership with leading companies and trade union leaders. This approach was endorsed by leading figures, including representatives from J. Sainsbury plc, the Boddington Group, the Post Office and the leaders of several trade unions (Involvement and Participation Association 1992). This definition requires managers to make several substantive and procedural commitments: declare security of employment as a key corporate objective; share the results of success with employees; and recognise the legitimacy of the employees' right to be informed, consulted and represented. In return, trade unions are required to: renounce rigid job demarcations and commit to flexible working; give sympathetic consideration to the continental model of representation of the whole workforce by means of election of representatives to new works councils; and recognise and then co-promote employee involvement methods.

The signing of partnership agreements is of potential importance in Britain (IRS 1997), and in contrast to critics who thought such agreement would not become widespread (Kelly 2004), employers and unions have signed significantly more partnership agreements than expected, with 248 partnership agreements signed between 1990 and 2007 (Bacon and Samuel 2007). These agreements at the end of 2007 covered almost 10 per cent of all employees and one-third of public sector employees in Britain. Furthermore, four-fifths of all agreements signed survived, suggesting that few employers and unions walked away from these agreements once signed in ongoing workplaces. However, the majority of partnership agreements have been signed in the public rather than the private sector, with private sector employers generally avoiding partnership agreements with trade unions. The growth of agreements in the public sector partly reflects union power in that sector compared to the private sector. In order to modernise public services, the New Labour government, and more importantly the devolved governments of Scotland and Wales, have sought strategic agreements to work closely with unions. These agreements may form the basis for a social democratic model of industrial relations in the public sector in forthcoming years.

Does the popularity of partnership agreements in Britain indicate that managers and unions have found a workable balance between disputed meanings of partnership and a range of other problems associated with partnership agreements? Careful study of the content of partnership agreements shows that few conform to the IPA definition of partnership, mainly because few contain substantive commitments by employers to provide job security for employees or to share the gains of productivity improvements with employees (Samuel and Bacon 2008). Partnership agreements in Britain are biased towards procedural rules over consultation and do not extend joint regulation or involve managers relinquishing control over unilateral determination of substantive terms and conditions. As employers relinquish so little in these agreements, more employers have signed partnership agreements than commonly appreciated.

Employers and unions signing partnership agreements have to deal with at least two critical issues. First, both sides have to commit fully to a single strategy of cooperative industrial relations throughout the organisation and avoid behaving in a short-term, contradictory or opportunistic manner. For example, at the Royal Mail several partnership initiatives have failed because not all managers in the company supported the partnership approach (Bacon and Storey 2000). For some other employers, partnership agreements form part of a longer-term strategy to marginalise trade unions (Claydon 1989; Gall and McKay 1994; Kelly 1996; Smith and Morton 1993).

Whereas one review of partnership agreements in six organisations reported that 'none gave serious consideration to ending recognition' (IDS 1998, p.4), a study of management attempts to restructure industrial relations in 10 organisations (Bacon and Storey 2000) revealed that de-recognition had been more seriously explored. According to Oxenbridge *et al.* (2003), employers working in partnership with unions to implement organisational change are sometimes simultaneously excluding unions from bargaining over issues such as pay.

A second important issue for the future of partnership agreements is whether they deliver greater returns for managers and trade unions. If returns are not forthcoming for either party then enthusiasm for the partnership approach may wane. Kelly (1996) has argued, for example, that unions have more to gain from militancy than cooperation with employers. Partnership is associated by Kelly with eroding the willingness and capacity of union members to resist employers, inhibiting the growth of workplace union organisation and generating apathy among union members; it involves union 'give' and management 'take', results in attempts to drive down terms and conditions of employment, and fails to genuinely represent member grievances. The extent to which Kelly is correct and unions will not benefit from partnership agreements is an interesting question. Kelly (2004) compared similar UK companies with and without partnership agreements and found that partnership firms shed jobs at a faster rate than non-partnership firms in industries marked by employment decline. In contrast, partnership firms in expanding sectors created jobs at a faster rate than non-partnership firms. Partnership appeared to have no impact on wage settlements or union density. In another study of 54 companies, Guest and Peccei (2001, p.207) discovered that the balance of advantage from partnership at work 'is skewed towards management', with improvements only in employment relations, quality and productivity. As few partnership agreements actually contain substantive clauses on job security or sharing gains with employees, gains for employees from partnership are particularly elusive (Samuel and Bacon 2008).

Union organising and new types of union representatives

As many employers have preferred not to recognise unions, or negotiate and consult with unions even where they are recognised, it is not surprising that workers and unions have sought to defend their interests. Unions have increasingly focused on organising workers and recruiting new members as an alternative to partnership (Heery 2002) and reversing falling membership levels and declining collective bargaining coverage. In training a new generation of union organisers to recruit members and organise workplaces (Fiorito and Jarley 2008), it is not surprising to see unions learning lessons from the US in how to organise when employers oppose unions (see Godard 2008). Union avoidance techniques used by employers in the US (Logan 2006) are also being learned by employers in other countries. A significant increase in new recognition deals has occurred in Britain, reflecting the work of union organisers and the backing provided by the statutory union recognition procedure of the Employment Relations Act 1999 (Gall 2004). To date, however, this has slowed rather than reversed the decline of union recognition in Britain, as described in Table 8.4.

Such has been the pace of trade union innovation that unions in Britain have also developed and recruited new types of workplace union representatives focused on single issues. These include union learning representatives (ULRs) and equality representatives, although there are others such as environment representatives. The emergence of new types of workplace union representatives constitutes an important and strategic initiative by unions to service existing members, recruit new members and represent members' interests on specific issues. A key aim in recruiting members into single-issue union posts is to increase membership activity in workplace unions and to work with employers on issues that employers have recently regarded as areas of management prerogative. The impact of these new representatives will have an important influence in the forthcoming years on whether unions are able to encourage employers to increase training provision and improve equal opportunities.

To assess the likely impact of these initiatives it is helpful to consider the case of ULRs as the most developed initiative, with 18,000 ULRs recruited by 2007 working to improve training provision for their members. The government provided important support to ULRs in the Employment Act 2002, which provided them with statutory rights to paid time off for five key tasks: analysing training needs; providing information and advice on training; arranging training; promoting the value of training; and consulting the employer over these activities. Have ULRs been able to increase training provision? Research to date has failed to identify a consistent relationship between ULRs and training, with ULR presence not associated with training among any employee group with the exception of male non-managers in the public sector (Hoque and Bacon 2008). The same research has, however, shown that ULRs may exercise a 'sword of justice' role. Employees who are traditionally less likely to report receiving training (for example, older workers, part-time workers, lower occupational groups, and workers with lower-level academic qualifications) are more likely to report training in workplaces with ULRs present. Whether ULRs are successful in raising training levels will depend on the extent to which employers value these new union representatives, employers are genuinely willing to consult and negotiate on these issues, and employers will provide paid time off from normal work duties for representatives to conduct these activities. A large proportion of ULRs in 2004, for example, did not spend any time on employee training in their role as a union representative and could therefore have little influence on levels of employer-provided training (Bacon and Hoque 2008a). Employer support is essential if these new types of representatives are to be effective, as the amount of time spent on the ULR role is strongly related to the number of hours the employer pays for the ULR to spend time on the role (Bacon and Hoque 2008b). ULRs are more likely to report that they are able to increase employee participation in training where the employer values their role, is willing to negotiate, consult or inform unions on training issues, and pay for ULRs to spend time on their role (Bacon and Hoque 2008b). Although other types of new union representatives are only just developing, it is anticipated that the degree of support from management for their role will affect whether unions are able to influence employer policies and develop workplace union representation through recruiting single-issue union representatives.

Conclusions

The aim of this chapter was to introduce the topic of industrial relations, outline some of the key contemporary developments in industrial relations and consider the implications. It covered management approaches to industrial relations, the reasons employees join unions, the decline of joint regulation and its implications, employer choice in industrial relations, non-union workplaces and employee representation in non-union workplaces, partnership with unions, union organising and new types of union representatives. Employers in liberal market economies and other countries are increasingly less inclined to support joint regulation of industrial relations. As a result, unions have found it increasingly difficult to represent effectively the interests of their existing and new members who continue to join trade unions. Employers avoid union recognition and influence in order to avoid the costs imposed by unions. The state has increasingly legislated on employment issues to protect employees from employer attempts to drive down terms and conditions and evade their responsibility for promoting equitable employment. The state is also the major sponsor of partnership agreements with unions as it attempts to reform public services with unions. Employers also have to deal with more sustained attempts by unions to challenge employers by organising workplaces against the wishes of employers. New types of union representatives focused on specific issues are potentially helpful allies for employers seeking to increase employee participation in training and increase the effectiveness of equal opportunities policies. These new representatives are only likely to be effective, however, if employers are willing to concede management prerogative over these issues.

CASE STUDY 8.1

Union–management partnership at NatBank

Stewart Johnstone

NatBank is a major UK bank with over 60,000 employees in the UK and over 100,000 employees worldwide. The partnership agreement at NatBank was born out of a very poor climate of industrial relations in the late 1990s, culminating in industrial action over pay in 1997. Union representatives and managers admitted that there was a need to end the hostile 'everybody out mentality' that prevailed within the bank whenever an issue arose, and that the 1990s situation of 'arm's-length adversarialism' was simply untenable. Improving employment relations was especially important as competition in the financial service sector was intense, and organisational performance had been disappointing. A formal partnership agreement was signed between NatBank and the recognised trade union in 2000, based upon an adaptation of six principles of partnership espoused by the Trades Union Congress:

The principles of partnership:

1. To secure and promote the long-term success of NatBank.

2. To promote the interests of employees, customers and shareholders.

3. To ensure that NatBank meets customer expectations by having people with the right skills in the right place at the right cost.

4. To facilitate the management of change.

5. To ensure employees are managed fairly and professionally.

6. To promote equality of treatment and opportunity for all, valuing diversity.

Partnership was described by senior managers as a modern and sensible approach to the management of industrial relations centred around a joint commitment to business success. In practice this was said to require greater dialogue and interaction with the trade union, and the ability to consider decisions from both an 'employee' as well as 'business' point of view. A senior manager contrasted this with a non-partnership approach, where the union may simply want what is best for the union/employees, while the business simply wants what is best for the business. For local managers, partnership concerned a more proactive problem-solving approach, and achieving a clear understanding of the rationale behind decisions. It was made clear by the management team, however, that the union representatives and officials need not necessarily agree with decisions. Rather, the focus was on early consultation regarding developments and the opportunity for representatives to provide feedback and input while decisions are still at 'the design stage'. When local representatives had strong feelings on an issue and no agreement could be reached locally, there was the option of escalating it to monthly national consultation for further detailed discussion. However, it was clear that under partnership the business retained the right to make the final decisions.

Similarly, for a senior union official, partnership concerned problem solving, mutual respect, transparency, and greater interaction between the union and the management team. However, he warned that the term 'partnership' for such an approach is perhaps inappropriate and potentially misleading. He suggested that the language of partnership often resulted in a debate regarding whether partnership suggests or requires an 'equal' relationship between unions and employers. He believed that such debates were actually

▶

unproductive, and that it is was better to view partnership in a more pragmatic way, as essentially an opportunity for unions to get 'inside the tent'. In turn, this was said to offer unions access to key business decision makers, the provision of better information, and a greater respect for each party's point of view. He suggested that senior management now had a clearer idea of the operation and purpose of trade unions, and equally full-time officials now had a greater appreciation of business issues and decision making. He contrasted partnership with an 'institutional conflict approach', without any real dialogue or regard for the other party's point of view. It was suggested that partnership provided a framework by clarifying the rights and responsibilities of the employer and the union, and setting out the 'rules of the game'.

Overall, several benefits were identified compared to the adversarial approach of the 1990s. A key benefit concerned the ability of the union to influence decision making. There was evidence to suggest that the union was involved across areas including pay and conditions, discipline and grievance, and organisational change. An example of this is the joint development of guidelines outlining various commitments regarding off-shoring practices. At the centre of this agreement were commitments to avoid compulsory redundancies and redeploy staff elsewhere in the business where possible, to provide early consultation, and to provide extensive support for employees who were ultimately displaced. With partnership it was suggested that the union now had a wider remit, especially in relation to organisational change issues, whereas prior to partnership much of the attention centred around pay and conditions. More generally, with partnership management were said to benefit from constructive feedback which assisted their decision making, meaning that pre-emptive changes could be made and leading to the greater legitimacy and acceptance of decisions. For the business, it was suggested that the partnership dialogue also encouraged a longer-term perspective than may otherwise have been the case. On the other hand, the union was said to benefit from the opportunity to have a say, often being consulted at a very early stage in the decision-making process. Though the partnership process was not viewed as one of joint decision making per se, union officials and representatives believed that there was evidence of the consultation process having an impact, and this was also recognised by employees.

Another benefit of partnership was said to be more local decision making and improved employment relations. The emphasis from the union had been on building a solid cadre of local representatives, and there was evidence to suggest that this had been successful. Representatives were active and knowledgeable, and appeared to be well respected by management and employees alike. Representatives described their role under partnership as one of questioning, challenging and persuading, as opposed to simply opposing management proposals. In this regard, a key issue was developing a strong basis on which to question proposals which took into account both business rationale as well as the impact on employees. There also appeared to have been an increase in union legitimacy. Prior to partnership, the union was said to have had few resources or facilities provided by the employer. Much of the work of a union representative was undertaken at home, and it was not unusual for vacancies for representative posts to be left unfilled. Since partnership, credible and active representative roles had been created, all union committee positions were filled, and previously weak trade union organisation was believed to have been revived. Representatives were now able to hold quarterly recruitment events, to distribute promotional materials, and to deliver a presentation at staff inductions for new staff. In addition, representatives were pleased with other arrangements in relation to the provision of sufficient time off for union duties, access to meeting rooms and use of office facilities.

In contrast to the frosty times of the 1990s, relationships between senior management and union officials, as well as between local management and union representatives, appeared to be very good. There was a belief that whereas prior to partnership relationships

▶

Charlwood, A. (2007) 'The de-collectivisation of pay setting in Britain 1990–98: incidence, determinants and impact', *Industrial Relations Journal*, Vol.38, No.1, pp.33–50.

Charlwood, A. and Terry, M. (2007) '21st-century models of employee representation: structure, processes and outcomes', *Industrial Relations Journal*, Vol.38, No.4, pp.320–37.

Claydon, T. (1989) 'Union de-recognition in Britain in the 1980s', *British Journal of Industrial Relations*, Vol.27, pp.214–23.

Clegg, H. (1979) *The System of Industrial Relations in Great Britain*, Oxford: Blackwell.

Coupland, C., Blyton, P. and Bacon, N. (2005) 'A longitudinal study of the influence of shop floor work teams on expressions of "us" and "them"', *Human Relations*, Vol.58, No.8, pp.1055–81.

Cressey, P., Eldridge, J. and MacInnes, J. (1985) *Just Managing: Authority and Democracy in Industry*, Milton Keynes: Open University Press.

Cully, M. and Woodland, S. (1996) 'Trade union membership and recognition: an analysis of data from the 1995 Labour Force Survey', *Labour Market Trends*, May, pp.215–25, London: HMSO.

Cully, M., Woodland, S., O'Reilly, A. and Dix, G. (1999) *Britain at Work*, London: Routledge.

D'Art, D. and Turner, T. (1999) 'An attitudinal revolution in Irish industrial relations: the end of "them and us"?', *British Journal of Industrial Relations*, Vol.37, No.1, pp.101–16.

Dickens, L., Hall, M. and Wood, S. (2005) *Review of Research into the Impact of Employment Relations Legislation*, Employment Relations Research Series, No.45, London: DTI.

Dickson, T., McLachlan, M.V., Prior, P. and Swales, K. (1988) 'Big Blue and the union: IBM, individualism and trade union strategy', *Work, Employment and Society*, Vol.2, pp.506–20.

Dunn, S. and Wright, M. (1994) 'Maintaining the "status quo": an analysis of the contents of British collective agreements 1979–1990', *British Journal of Industrial Relations*, Vol.32, pp.23–46.

Edwards, P. (1995) 'The employment relationship', in P. Edwards (ed.) *Industrial Relations*, Oxford: Blackwell, pp.3–26.

Edwards, P., Hall, M., Hyman, R., Marginson, P., Sisson, K., Waddington, J. and Winchester, D. (1998) 'Great Britain: from partial collectivism to neo-liberalism to where?', in A. Ferner and R. Hyman (eds) *Changing Industrial Relations in Europe*, Oxford: Blackwell, pp.1–54.

Fiorito, J. and Jarley, P. (2008) 'Trade union morphology', in P. Blyton, N. Bacon, J. Fiorito and E. Heery (eds) *The Sage Handbook of Industrial Relations*, London: Sage, pp.189–208.

Foulkes, F.K. (1980) *Personnel Policies in Large Non-union Companies*, Englewood Cliffs, NJ: Prentice Hall.

Fox, A. (1966) 'Industrial sociology and industrial relations', *Royal Commission Research Paper No.3*, London: HMSO.

Fox, A. (1974) *Beyond Contract: Work, Power and Trust Relations*, London: Faber and Faber.

Freeman, R.B. and Medoff, J.L. (1984). *What Do Unions Do?*, New York: Basic Books.

Gall, G. (2004) 'Trade union recognition in Britain, 1995–2002: turning a corner?', *Industrial Relations Journal*, Vol.35, No.3, pp.249–70.

Gall, G. and McKay, S. (1994) 'Trade union de-recognition in Britain 1988–94', *British Journal of Industrial Relations*, Vol.32, pp.433–48.

Geary, J. (1995) 'Work practices: the structure of work', in P. Edwards (ed.) *Industrial Relations*, Oxford: Blackwell, pp.368–96.

Godard, J. (2008) 'Union formation', in P. Blyton, N. Bacon, J. Fiorito and E. Heery (eds) *The Sage Handbook of Industrial Relations*, London: Sage, pp.377–405.

Guest, D. and Conway, N. (2004) 'Exploring the paradox of unionised worker dissatisfaction', *Industrial Relations Journal*, Vol.35, No.2, pp.102–21.

Guest, D.E., and Peccei, R. (2001) 'Partnership at work: mutuality and the balance of advantage', *British Journal of Industrial Relations*, Vol.39, No.2, pp.207–36.

Hall, M.J. (2006) 'A cool response to the ICE Regulations? Employer and trade union approaches to the new legal framework for information and consultation', *Industrial Relations Journal*, Vol.37, pp.456–72.

Hamann, K. and Kelly, J. (2008) 'Varieties of capitalism and industrial relations', in P. Blyton, N. Bacon, J. Fiorito and E. Heery (eds) *The Sage Handbook of Industrial Relations*, London: Sage, pp.129–48.

Heery, E. (2002) 'Partnership versus organising: alternative futures for British trade unionism', *Industrial Relations Journal*, Vol.33, No.1, pp.20–35.

Heery, E., Bacon, N., Blyton, P. and Fiorito, J. (2008) 'Introduction: the field of industrial relations', in P. Blyton, N. Bacon, J. Fiorito and E. Heery (eds) *The Sage Handbook of Industrial Relations*, London: Sage, pp.1–32.

Hirschman, A. (1971) *Exit, Voice and Loyalty,* Cambridge, MA: Harvard University Press.

HMSO (1998) *'Fairness at Work',* White Paper, London: HMSO.

Hoque, K. and Bacon, N. (2008) 'Trade unions, union learning representatives and employer-provided training in Britain', *British Journal of Industrial Relations,* December.

Hyman, R. (1997) 'The future of employee representation', *British Journal of Industrial Relations,* Vol.35, No.3, pp.309–36.

IDS (1998) 'Partnership agreements', *IDS Study,* 656, October.

Institute of Directors (1994) Evidence presented to the Employment Committee Enquiry, 'The future of trade unions', HMSO, HC 676-II.

Involvement and Participation Association (1992) *Towards Industrial Partnership: A New Approach to Management Union Relations,* London: IPA.

IPD (1997) *Employment Relations into the 21st Century,* London: Institute of Personnel and Development.

IRS (1997) 'Partnership at work: a survey', *Employment Trends,* 645, December, pp.3–24.

Kelly, J. (1996) 'Union militancy and social partnership', in P. Ackers, C. Smith and P. Smith (eds) *The New Workplace and Trade Unionism,* London: Routledge, pp.41–76.

Kelly, J. (2004) 'Social partnership agreements in Britain: Labour cooperation and compliance', *Industrial Relations,* Vol.43, No.1, pp.267–92.

Kelly, J. and C. Kelly (1991) 'Them and us: social psychology and the "new industrial relations"', *British Journal of Industrial Relations,* Vol.29, No.1, pp.25–48.

Kersley, B., Alpin, C., Forth, J., Bryson, A., Bewley, H., Dix, G. and Oxenbridge, S. (2006) *Inside the Workplace: Findings from the 2004 Workplace Employment Relations Survey,* London: Routledge.

Kochan, T.A., McKersie, R.B. and Cappelli, P. (1984) 'Strategic choice and industrial relations theory', *Industrial Relations,* Vol.23, No.1, pp.16–39.

Kochan, T., Katz, H. and McKersie, B. (1986). *The Transformation of American Industrial Relations,* New York: Basic Books.

Lewin, D. (1987) 'Industrial relations as a strategic variable', in M.M. Kleiner, R.N. Block, M. Roomkin and S.W. Salsburg (eds) *Human Resources and the Performance of the Firm,* Madison, WI: Industrial Relations Research Association, pp.1–41.

Logan, J. (2006) 'The union avoidance industry in the United States', *British Journal of Industrial Relations,* Vol.44, No.4, pp.651–75.

Machin, S. (2000) 'Union decline in Britain', *British Journal of Industrial Relations,* Vol.38, No.4, pp.631–45.

Machin, S. and Wood, S.J. (2005) 'Human resource management as a substitute for trade unions in British workplaces', *Industrial and Labor Relations Review,* Vol.58, No.1, pp.201–18.

McLoughlin, I. and Gourlay, S. (1994) *Enterprise Without Unions: Industrial Relations in the Non-Union Firm,* Milton Keynes: Open University Press.

Metcalfe, D. (2004) *British Unions: Resurgence or Perdition,* London: The Work Foundation.

Millward, N., Stevens, M., Smart, D., and Hawes, W.R. (1992) *Workplace Industrial Relations in Transition,* Aldershot: Dartmouth.

Noon, M. and Hoque, K. (2001) 'Ethnic minorities and equal treatment: the impact of gender, equal opportunities policies and trade unions', *National Institute Economic Review,* Vol.176, No.1, pp.105–16.

Oxenbridge, S., Brown, W., Deakin, S., and Pratten, C. (2003) 'Initial responses to the Statutory Recognition Provisions of the Employment Relations Act 1999', *British Journal of Industrial Relations,* Vol.41, No.2, pp.315–34.

Piore, M.J. and Safford, S. (2006) 'Changing regimes of workplace governance, shifting axes of social mobilisation, and the challenge to industrial relations theory', *Industrial Relations,* Vol.45, No.3, pp.299–325.

Poole, M., Mansfield, R., Gould-Williams, J. and Mendes, P. (2005) 'British Managers' attitudes and behaviour in industrial relations: a twenty-year study', *British Journal of Industrial Relations,* Vol.43, No.1, pp.117–34.

Purcell, J. and Ahlstrand, B. (1994) *Human Resource Management in the Multi-Divisional Company,* Oxford: Oxford University Press.

Purcell, J. and Sisson, K. (1983) 'Strategies and practice in the management of industrial relations', in G. Bain (ed.) *Industrial Relations in Britain,* Oxford: Blackwell.

Ramsey, H. (1975) 'Firms and football teams', *British Journal of Industrial Relations*, Vol.13, No.3, pp.396–400.

Roy, D. (1980) 'Fear stuff, sweet stuff and evil stuff: management's defences against unionization in the south', in T. Nichols (ed.) *Capital and Labour: A Marxist Primer*, Glasgow: Fontana, pp.395–415.

Samuel, P. and Bacon, N. (2008) 'Exploring the content of British partnership agreements signed between 1990 and 2007', Paper for BUIRA Conference, 25–27 June, University of West of England.

Schnabel, C. (2003) 'Determinants of trade union membership', in J.T. Addison and C. Schnabel (eds) *International Handbook of Trade Unions*, Cheltenham, Edward Elgar, pp.13–43.

Schnabel, C. and Wagner, J. (2007) 'Union density and determinants of union membership in 18 EU countries: evidence from micro data, 2002/03', *Industrial Relations Journal*, Vol.38, No.1, pp.5–32.

Scott, A. (1994) *Willing Slaves?* Cambridge: Cambridge University Press.

Sisson, K. (1989) 'Personnel management in transition?', in K. Sisson (ed.) *Personnel Management in Britain*, Oxford: Blackwell.

Sisson, K. (1993) 'In search of HRM', *British Journal of Industrial Relations*, Vol.31, No.2, pp.201–10.

Smith, P. and Morton, G. (1993) 'Union exclusion and decollectivization of industrial relations in contemporary Britain', *British Journal of Industrial Relations*, Vol.31, No.1, pp.97–114.

Strauss, G. (1984) 'Industrial relations: time of change', *Industrial Relations*, Vol.23, No.1: pp.1–15.

Towers, B. (1997) *The Representation Gap*, Oxford: Oxford University Press.

Undy, R. (1999) 'Annual review article: New Labour's "Industrial Relations Settlement": The third way?', *British Journal of Industrial Relations*, Vol.37, No.2, pp.315–36.

Visser, J. (2003) 'Unions and unionism around the world', in J.T. Addison and C. Schnabel (eds) *International Handbook of Trade Unions*, Cheltenham, Edward Elgar, pp.366–414.

Waddington, J. and Whitston, C. (1997) 'Why do people join unions in a period of membership decline?', *British Journal of Industrial Relations*, Vol.35, No.4, pp.515–46.

Walsh, J. (2007) 'Equality and diversity in British workplaces: the 2004 Workplace Employment Relations Survey', *Industrial Relations Journal*, Vol.38, No.4, pp.303–19.

White, M. (2005) 'Cooperative unionism and employee welfare', *Industrial Relations Journal*, Vol.36, No.5, pp.348–66.

Chapter 9

LINE MANAGERS

Douglas Renwick

Introduction

Involving line managers in human resource management (HRM) work appears to be such a common practice in work organisations today that it can perhaps be viewed as an obvious and core element of an HRM approach to the employment relationship. The logic of why line managers are used in HRM seems simple: they are closest to customers and employees, and occupy a key role in the people management aspects of the general management job (such as motivating, communicating, rewarding, disciplining and releasing people at work). Devolution in HRM to line managers also (supposedly) frees HR specialists to form HR policies and procedures, and to engage in the more complex and strategic parts of HR work, e.g. employment law (see Renwick 2006). But research in the field of involving line managers in HRM has revealed that a number of issues appear in doing so – questioning their involvement and their assumed usefulness in HRM per se. This chapter aims to unravel some of the developments, challenges and questions that surround the use of line managers in HRM, and contains cases to test the knowledge of students. This chapter proceeds by reviewing developments in the relevant international, European and British literature, and then raising some key issues that arise from them. Ideas for future research in this field are then detailed, which are followed by some conclusions.

DEFINITION

Some authors define line managers as those who engage in 'general management work – rather than being specialists in a particular functional area, like HRM, marketing or sales' (Legge 1995). But relevant studies also focus on different types of managers working at different levels in HRM. For example, some studies examine the role of middle managers (Currie and Procter 2001; Fenton-O'Creevy 1998, 2001), 'who are two levels below the CEO and one level above first-line supervisor' (Huy 2002, p.38), and who have direct responsibility over subordinates (Delmestri 2006, p.1523), while other studies focus on the role of frontline and/or first-line managers (FLMs) (Storey 1992; Marchington 2001; Purcell and Hutchinson 2007), supervisors (Lowe 1992), and production or first-line supervisors, i.e. shop-floor employees (Mason 2000, p.628). Additionally, differences exist in terms of what aspects of HRM such managers work on, and how they engage in HRM, as authors use different terms to denote this, such as 'involvement' (Gibb 2003; Marsh and Gillies 1983; Renwick 2006) or 'responsibility' (Larsen and Brewster 2003; Thornhill and Saunders 1998; Whittaker and Marchington 2003).

RATIONALE

One reason why line managers seem to be 'involved' in HRM is because HR work has been specifically 'devolved' to them – a trend of devolution in HRM (Brewster and Larsen 2000; Currie and Procter 2001; Guest and King 2001; Larsen and Brewster 2003; Renwick 2003, 2006; Storey 1992, 2001). However, involving line managers in HRM is not a totally new development. In the UK, for example, there has always been a recognition that line managers have had both accountability and responsibility for people management (Guest 1987; Legge 1995; Marsh and Gillies 1983; Poole and Jenkins 1997; Storey 1992). But it is the seemingly greater extent of their involvement in HRM via the use of HR devolution, and the attendant greater publicity and transparency associated with it, which mean it appears to make the headlines (in practitioner circles at least). In short, it is in vogue. Additionally, some studies argue that the increased role of non-specialist managers in HRM is a subject worthy of discussion itself (see Cully *et al.* 1999; Millward, Bryson and Forth 2000). So, while complexities that surround the definition, rationale and level of the devolution of HR work to line managers may appear to cloud our understanding of the role of involving line managers in HRM, some clear developments in the international, European and British literature on this topic are present. These are now outlined in turn.

Developments in the literature

THE INTERNATIONAL DIMENSION

Research on the different aspects of involving line managers in HRM has been seen in a number of countries across the globe, including specific national and comparative studies in the People's Republic of China (PRC), Hong Kong (HK), New Zealand (NZ), the United States (US), Canada and Ireland. These are now detailed. In the PRC, Mitsuhashi *et al.* (2000) examined the differences in perceptions of an expatriate (survey) sample of top HR and line executives on the importance and effectiveness of HR practices in 25 multinational Chinese firms, finding that line executives perceive HR performance effectiveness as 'significantly lower' than HR executives do in terms of strategic (non-administrative) HRM, i.e. communications, measurements and responsibilities (Mitsuhashi *et al.* (2000, p.197). They argue that the results from their study match those of other previous studies in Chinese HRM, i.e. that with the exception of compensation, line and HR perceptions of HR effectiveness do not alter significantly. They conclude that while their expatriate sample may be evaluating HRM on inappropriate (strategic HRM) criteria (as HRM in the PRC is in its infancy), some line managers there do not feel that HR are presently performing enough to become a strategic partner (Mitsuhashi *et al.* 2000, pp.209, 211–12).

In Hong Kong (HK), Wai-Kwong, Priem and Cycyota (2001, p.1325) studied the involvement of HR and line managers during strategy making and effects on performance, finding a positive and significant interaction between involving line managers in strategy and cost leadership being associated with higher levels of performance, and lower levels of line involvement and a cost leadership approach being related to much lower performance. They note that their own findings from line and HR managers in HK are consistent with those from Kanter (1983), i.e. that such middle managers encourage employee involvement programmes in the middle of production process redesign; create an environment where fears over change can be surfaced; and ensure that resistance and failure are reduced. They also see a comparison with later findings in the 1990s where changes to middle-management roles (such as increased speed, flexibility and empowerment over work roles) have seen line managers more willing in enacting strategy changes at the operational level where they have expertise. They conclude that more knowledge is needed on the contributions of HR and other middle managers to firm performance (Wai-Kwong *et al.* 2001, pp.1341–1342).

Dewe and O'Driscoll's (2002) survey on stress management involving 540 managers in New Zealand (NZ) revealed that such stress management interventions contain practices which offer scope for personal development and well-being, but that many stress interventions fall sort of achieving such goals. They argue that this is because such interventions offer partial solutions to the problem of stress, or do not appreciate the overarching issues of organisational context and structure within which such stress interventions occur, perhaps as there is little work attempting to understand what managers understand by stress itself, and the scope of responsibility their work organisations have for it (Dewe and O'Driscoll 2002, p.143). They note that managers may appear not to be interested in stress because of how they perceive it, i.e. it is seen as a 'high risk' issue which individuals should attend to, rather than being one that organisations need to manage. They found that only 33 per cent of managers thought that individual employees had some control over the factors that may bring stress on, but that individuals had a fair amount of responsibility (51 per cent) for managing any stress-related issues (Dewe and O'Driscoll 2002, pp.146, 153).

Dewe and O'Driscoll (2002, pp.157, 162–3) detail profiles for NZ managers on stress management. These include holding the organisation responsible for stress management, being older, having little control over stress factors, and being less likely to experience sources of pressure coming from work–life balance. They state that managers should move to think of stress as transactional between the individual and the environment (and not solely in either), because treating everyone as if they are all alike 'fails to capture the essential nature of the stress experience'. They conclude that a lot of stress management techniques fail as they are superficial, and because they are used in an ad hoc manner – due to a lack of managerial knowledge, and managerial attitudes and behaviour (Dewe and O'Driscoll 2002, pp.162–3).

In the United States, Huy's (2002) longitudinal (three-year) study of 104 middle managers in a large US firm (Servico) saw them displaying opposite emotion-management patterns to employees when radical change is taking place. Huy argues that some middle managers and union representatives at Servico maintain continuity in operations by practising a type of 'bounded emotionality' or 'emotional balancing', which attends to the psychological well-being of their subordinates and their families (regarding issues such as work and vacation scheduling, and exhaustion of young mothers caused by commuting). These managers recognise that private and work feelings are inseparable and need consciously attending to, when firms are consolidating workers on to one site and reducing workforce numbers. Although Huy details an instance of radical change at one firm which saw some managers being openly hostile to the personal concerns of staff, other managers deliberately broke company rules on 'emotional display', so as to maintain continuity of experience for subordinates (Huy 2002, pp.49–50). Huy concludes that the middle managers and union representatives that attend to the needs of their employees have a long tenure and know their subordinates well, which might partly explain their efforts to help them in a voluntary manner (Huy 2002, pp.61, 64).

Another study in the US by George and Zhou (2007) examined the ways in which supervisors can provide a supportive context towards employee creativity, via a survey of 161 (matched) supervisors and employees in an oil field services company. They found that such creativity was highest when contexts are supportive and when positive and negative moods are high, and that supervisors can provide a supportive context towards employee creativity by giving employees developmental feedback, in displays of interactional justice to them, and through being trustworthy in their dealings with them. They also noted that where such a supportive context exists, it is likely that both positive and negative moods contribute to creativity, as when positive moods are high and context is supportive, negative mood has a strong positive relation to creativity (George and Zhou 2007, pp.605, 610).

Other studies in the US include Mehra and Schenkel's (2007) survey on self-monitoring practices of 116 respondents in a high-tech firm, which revealed that when compared to 'low self-monitors' [rigids], 'high self-monitors' [chameleons] tend to experience greater role conflict because they are more likely to have 'boundary spanning positions' (i.e. are mediating between groups who have different values, beliefs and interests). They argue that these chameleons are caught in a 'cross-fire of competing expectations' and subject to high levels of role conflict from both intra and extra-organisational influences, and note that previous studies suggest that high self-monitors are likely to experience role conflict at work, leading to stress and negative consequences for their health (e.g. job burnout and low commitment) (Mehra and Schenkel 2007, pp.1, 2).

Comparative studies linking North American and European organisational contexts include McGuire *et al.*'s (2006) research into the relationship between the individual values of managers and HR decision making (i.e. concern for the individual) from a survey of 340 line managers in Canada and Ireland. They found a strong relationship between individual values and decision styles and that 'national or societal influences can affect the individual values of managers', namely that:

> Education was identified as a significant negative predictor of the importance of health and safety, indicating that the higher educated the person, the lower the perceived importance of health and safety issues . . . [And that] the nationality of respondents proved to be the strongest predictor of the importance of employment equity [5.4 per cent] . . . with Irish respondents placing a higher importance on matters of employment equity. Gender was identified as a significant negative predictor of employment equity, indicating that female respondents place a higher priority on employment equity than male respondents. (McGuire *et al.* 2006, p.263)

They argue that 'too much' of the HR discourse that is humanist oriented does not adequately treat the reality of corporate life, where senior managers may be as likely to lay off thousands of employees as they are to enquire about the 'affective states or personal feelings' of employees, and state that as line managers undertake many of the operational dimensions of HRM, it is in such decision situations that their individual values are likely to influence their decision choices. This means that 'potential for conflict exists' between organisational decision making and individual managerial values, which may be resolved through discussion and dialogue, and be ignored, denied and suppressed, or resolved by managers leaving the organisation (McGuire *et al.* 2006, p.255).

THE EUROPEAN CONTEXT

Within Europe, Larsen and Brewster's (2003) definitive Cranet study of 22 countries (and over 4,000 respondents) found that devolution to the line in HRM in the UK and Ireland was low compared to other European Union (EU) states (with most HR devolution in Denmark and Finland), and that while there are moves across the EU to hand line managers more responsibility for staff management, the extent of their autonomy in HRM tends to vary by subject. They argue that the most frequent pattern in HRM in the EU is one of shared responsibilities between HR and line managers (except on the matter of workforce expansion and/or reduction), and that many organisations are still very centralised in a lot of aspects of HRM. However, they also detail anecdotal evidence which could imply that both HR and line managers do not willingly accept devolution in HRM (see Renwick 2006 for details).

Andolsek and Stebe's (2005, p.311) study of changes of the HRM function in 20 European and five non-European countries found a shift of HRM tasks from HRM departments to managers, and that country (as an institutional environment) sets limits and encourages devolution in HRM, with HRM policy in institutional contexts second in importance. They argue that HR devolution has developed in all areas, but is lower in large organisations that have highly developed HRM teams (Andolsek and Stebe 2005, pp.326–27). They conclude that 'in the process of devolution, European organisations are gaining their autonomy through written HR policies', with such codified policies being the strongest factor that joins HRM practices in the EU in a common direction (Andolsek and Stebe 2005, pp.327–28).

Other European studies include Delmestri's (2006) survey of 418 Italian middle managers working for 72 local and international firms in Italy, which considered managerial identities as 'societal institutions'. He found that:

> The professional identity of the middle managers and their legitimacy, are based on either the capacity to personally solve technical problems (specifically German and Italian) or to demonstrate more managerial-like competencies (specifically British), whose identity is based on an idea of management as a mysterious mastery supported by the necessary personality traits and social skills. (Delmestri 2006, p.1521)

Delmestri found that job characteristics (hierarchical level and extent of contact with foreign colleagues) along with identification with both Italian and headquarters culture act as drivers towards an 'Italian profile', and that the adoption of the HR department into global integration (through HRM practices such as leadership, interfunctional careers, induction, diversity and appraisal), along with an identification with both a global and Anglo-Saxon culture, act as drivers towards an 'Anglo-Saxon profile' (Delmestri 2006, p.1531). He found some support for national culture and exposure to local and foreign influence helping to shape espoused managerial beliefs (as ideal types), and concludes that 'managers should try to detect opposite cultural streams which disconfirm stereotypical definitions' (Delmestri 2006, p.1537).

THE UK

The language writers used in the HR literature in Britain from the mid-to-late 1990s on the subject of involving line managers in HRM was of 'partnerships' being formed between HR and the line (Hutchinson and Wood 1995), cost/benefit analyses of devolution in HRM (Storey 2001; Sisson and Storey 2000), and that line managers should engage in boundary-spanning HR processes outside organisations, where 'they have freedom to experiment rather than being excluded from decision making' (Currie and Procter 2001, p.57).

In the UK, studies have (historically) seen that chief production managers wanted to pass personnel and industrial relations (IR) activity on to factory administrators as they did not consider it an efficient use of their time, and although they saw IR work as part of their workload, they preferred to rely on personnel/IR specialists for advice in it – even though they were not keen to be subject to their direction (Marsh 1971; Marsh and Gillies 1983, pp.32–38). More recently, the keenness of line managers to rely on the advice from specialist HR managers is particularly apparent in the area of Performance Management and Appraisal (PMA). For example, Harris (2001, pp.1182–90) notes managers disliking the 'bureaucracy' that surrounds PMA, which may lead them to engage in 'abdication management' in it, Redman's (2001) work saw line managers giving themselves good ratings in performance appraisal (even though they wish they could avoid it – but concluded that they do not tend to do it very well), and Guest and King (2001, p.26) found that managers tend not to do performance management properly, unless they get a stimulating 'kick' to do it.

In training and development, some line managers seem to take a 'learning by doing' approach to HRM, i.e. using experiential approaches (Brewster and Larsen 1992), while others argue that they do not need to train and develop themselves as managers in HRM, as 'most of this is common sense anyway' (quoted in Cunningham and Hyman 1995, p.18). But Gibb's (2003) analysis and review of the idea of 'managers as developers' found that line managers still need specialist HR advice in a knowledge management era, as there is a need to realign work, organisation and management together. We have also seen a call for greater comprehension of the role of line managers in terms of assessing and developing management and employee skills, which may contain a gender dimension, as Green and James (2003, p.63) found that in cases where the manager is male and the worker female, tendencies exist for bosses to underestimate the skill level of the worker, and also for workers to overestimate it when compared to other gender combinations.

In employee involvement (EI), Fenton-O'Creevy (1998, p.67) found 'middle management resistance' producing less positive outcomes in EI, and that senior managers may be blaming middle managers for the demise of failing EI schemes, whereas if middle managers resist such change they may see it as a 'pragmatic adaptation' (Fenton-O'Creevy 2001, pp.24, 38). Marchington (2001) revealed a series of 'unintended impacts' from involving non-specialist managers in EI, which include a lack of ability and commitment in it, deficiencies in time and training to do it, and an amount of doubt on why it needs to occur. Grievance and discipline cases also perhaps reveal a sense of line management expediency in HRM, as Rollinson *et al.* (1996) found HR managers being asked to 'sit in' in on such meetings to 'police' line management practices (and ensure that useful outcomes appeared), while IRS (2001) found line managers less involved than HR managers in terms of taking responsibility for disciplinary procedures. Regarding pay, line managers are being given more scope, with Currie and Procter (2001, pp.58–59, 63–66) finding them being given greater discretion in 'implementing' HR strategies and 'synthesising information', and others like Harris (2001, p.1184) noting a lack of line management enthusiasm towards performance-related pay schemes, a 'lack of ownership' of it as a process, and that they see HR in a negative light by trying to introduce such schemes, because doing so may overload the line management role.

Cunningham and James (2001) reveal a lack of willingness by line managers in terms of attending training to manage long-term sickness and disability cases, that such training was inadequate, and that specialist HR help was not present when such cases were being dealt with. Dunn and Wilkinson's (2002, p.245) study on absence management saw corresponding findings that some organisations had an 'ad-hoc' approach to it, with un-clarified responsibilities in it, which produced a 'muddling through' in some cases. The use of new technologies in HRM to provide HR services to line managers (like e-HR and HR call-centres) has limitations too, as line managers appear unwilling to take on additional HR work (seen at Marks & Spencer), and they have been perceived by line managers to increase their workloads (at British Nuclear Fuels) (Deeks 2000). Other empirical work on the devolution of specific HR tasks to line managers has seen difficulties arising. For example, Lynch (2003) found a department manager in retailing stating that employee development is difficult to complete as they do not have time to do it, and Whittaker and Marchington (2003) found that senior line managers still wanted specialist HR help because they found doing HR work difficult when other business pressures took priority. Additionally, other empirical work of the line management role in HRM from the viewpoint of middle managers has revealed both pros and cons present (see Renwick 2003).

More recently, Purcell and Hutchinson (2007, pp.5, 7) have identified three debates on the role of line managers in HRM that were 'interlocking' in the 1990s: the return of HRM to the line; clear evidence that front-line manager (FLM) roles in management and people management had been broadened; and studies on aspects of the FLM role in HRM (with distinctions between 'espoused and enacted HR practices'). Their own empirical survey of 608 employees in 12 'excellent' UK-based firms found employee commitment towards both their employer and their job being influenced by the quality of leadership behaviour and satisfaction with HR practices, which 'both have a strong effect on employee attitudes', and note that perceptions of leadership behaviour by employees 'are strongly negatively associated with tenure in the organisation, job and age', which suggest that employees with longer service and who are older have worse ratings for their managers. Their results show leadership behaviour and HR practices explaining 34.6 per cent of the variance in employee commitment (Purcell and Hutchinson 2007, pp.3, 9, 11).

SUMMARY

The review of the literature (above) has identified that the lack of capability and commitment by line managers to HRM identified by Brewster and Larsen (1992) still resonates today, as do the costs arising from it too – like a lack of consistency from line managers when dealing with matters such as employee relations (see Renwick 2006). The studies just mentioned (above) could perhaps be used to paint contrasting pictures of involving line managers in HRM, such as line enthusiasm, capacity and general positive attitude to doing it, or of their reluctance, scepticism and lack of skill in it, or of the factors that inhibit line managers from completing HRM duties well (e.g. lack of training and time to prepare; conflicting demands placed on them by other stakeholders; lack of visible help from HR managers; and the need to deliver business targets). Hence any issues that emerge from the use of line managers in HRM are arguably predictable and not due solely to line management intransigence in HRM, but partly a consequence of the organisational contexts within which they work. I now outline some general questions regarding involving line managers in HRM that emerge from the review of the literature just detailed.

General questions emerging

The literature reviewed (above) reveals that in addition to the issues of the capability, commitment and consistency of line managers and their practices in HRM that have been prevalent in the literature over the past decade (Larsen and Brewster 2003; Renwick 2006), line managers are under increasing pressure to focus on the 'hard stuff', the 'numbers' (Whittaker and Marchington 2003). This situation has left some line managers completing a wide range of both operational and HR tasks to a high level, when it is perhaps not clear that such non-specialist (line) managers can do all of them equally well and to a good standard. So questions occur as to which tasks line managers prioritise, and what effects their choices and skill levels in HRM have in terms of their role in linking into organisational performance and employee well-being, and any knock-on effects on their own careers too.

Some research studies are quite positive on the effects line managers have on organisational performance, and note the role of FLMs in making HR strategies 'come to life' from a fairly large British survey sample (e.g. Hutchinson and Purcell 2003; Purcell *et al.* 2003; Purcell and Hutchinson 2007). For example, Lazenby argues that at the British firm Nationwide:

> Our research has demonstrated that line manager behaviour has a significant impact on employee commitment, which has an impact on customer commitment, which has an impact on business performance. (Lazenby, quoted in Hutchinson and Purcell 2003, p.55)

But involving line managers in HRM is seen by some (again using a similar sample) to make for poorer organisational performance in general terms (Gibb 2001), and others like Gratton *et al.* (1999) have long argued for greater thinking in terms of the incentives line managers gain to develop people at work. Hence questions arise here on the exact role line managers play in contributing to organisational performance.

In terms of employee well-being, some research studies have found that line managers tend to 'marginalize, under-use, and under-develop part-timers' (Edwards and Robinson 2001), and that line incapability in HRM is a reason why some employees are leaving their jobs – as their 'poor boss' is the 'last straw' for them (Taylor 2002). So, questions arise here on the exact role line managers play in contributing to organisational performance, the extent to which they develop employee well-being, and whether line incapability in HRM accelerates employee exits from work organisations. Additionally, increasing employee rewards and career development are examples of the sorts of HR decisions that line managers take, but they seem to need more skill to make better choices when doing so (Tyson and Fell 1995; Marchington 1999). Hence auditing the skills of line managers in HRM may be one way of assessing the effects of their interventions in HRM. If such line skills appear low and are not improving over time, a different option could be to hand the more operational aspects of HR work back to HR managers.

The need to assess the skills line managers have in HRM is perhaps related to the career benefits available to line managers for developing such HR skills. Here, questions arise as to whether line managers feel that doing HR facilitates both job and career progression for them, or makes them so generalist that they then become easy to replace. Hence we may wish to assess whether doing HR work makes line managers more or less marketable, employable and powerful, overall, or not. That greater use of line managers in HRM does not always appear to enhance outcomes in terms of organisational performance, employee well-being and the career prospects of line managers themselves means that we may question models of HRM that include the involvement of line managers in HRM, like those associated with HR–line management partnerships such as the (US) one of Jackson and Schuler (2000). This is because such models look like ideal types when compared to some of the more negative results produced from involving line managers in HRM in countries like the UK. For example, it is seen in the UK that HR specialists sometimes do not give useful advice to line managers in HRM (Guest *et al.* 2001, p.67), and that line management incapability and lack of commitment/consistency in HRM can put a break on achieving such outcomes (Cunningham *et al.* 2004; Cunningham and James 2001; Harris 2001; Redman 2001). Indeed, questions arise as to whether line managers act in a professional and consistent way when completing HR duties (especially if they treat some employees less fairly than others), but research evidence on the latter so far is inconclusive (Budhwar 2000; Cunningham and Hyman 1999; Marchington 1999; Renwick 2003, 2006).

Some chief executives appear to be quite positive about increasing the involvement of line managers in HRM as they see it as 'good people management' (Guest and King 2001, p.25), meaning that whether line managers are keen on doing more HR work or not, their role in HRM may be with us for now (as their seniors exercise the strategic choice of using them in this way). A number of cases in the literature reinforce this view, as line management involvement in HRM has increased in some leading-edge firms (e.g. Hutchinson and Purcell 2003; Larsen and Brewster 2003; Purcell *et al.* 2003: Purcell and Hutchinson 2007). However, a question still arises as to whether involving line managers more in HRM is a positive development, and may well be contested terrain. This is because the contingencies of different work contexts seem to account for a lot of variance in such outcomes. For example, many of the studies (just mentioned) that are positive about involving line managers in HRM tend to come from 'excellent' firms where we might perhaps expect good outcomes to occur (as they invest resources to support and develop line managers in HRM). But in some other work organisations employees may be managed poorly by line managers as these organisations may not have the resources to fund such support and development, or an HR presence on site to 'police' line management practices in HRM – e.g. such as small to medium-sized enterprises (SMEs).

The data that does exist on assessing the usefulness of involving line managers in HRM (especially in the UK, but also now beginning to emerge from the PRC, NZ and US) arguably asks us to be cautious when doing so, as one finding from all of the research studies in the literature (above) is that there are fewer examples of the enhanced outcomes arising from involving line managers in HRM than studies that see many problems arising from doing so. For example, few quotes appear about 'my great boss', or how employees feel their line manager has motivated, developed and inspired them at work. Instead, several studies raise questions regarding the motivation, attitude, commitment, capability and consistency of line managers completing HR-related tasks. I now detail some challenges arising from involving line managers in HRM.

Challenges arising

One challenge for line managers in HRM lies in developing employees to help deliver organisational outcomes while attending to employee concerns regarding their well-being. But in delivering both organisational and employee needs/wishes, line managers may feel that they are the 'filling' in the HR sandwich (McConville and Holden 1999), or that they are stuck between a rock and a hard place. They seem to need to balance requests from their employer to make employees subject to the relevant performance criteria to help deliver the ever-increasing expectations of the stakeholders to whom they are accountable and responsible, and also need to develop people at work in a wider sense as resourceful humans (i.e. to ensure that employees are motivated and have job satisfaction). This is the (arguably classic) challenge of reconciling the soft and hard elements of HRM in practice (Legge 1995), or in Huy's (2002) terms, of line managers engaging in 'emotional balancing'.

While being involved in HR work may or may not help advance the careers of line managers, how line managers manage employees may perhaps affect employee careers (Walton 1999), as managers are asked which employees to recommend forward for development, rewards and promotions. So, while line managers may be the people that make HR strategies 'come to life' (Purcell *et al.* 2003; Purcell and Hutchinson 2007), they may also be the people that make employee careers flounder. Managing people well takes consideration and time, but it is unclear from the literature if line managers are being given the scope and opportunity to rise to the challenge of developing employees at work, as doing so requires such managers to make a mental leap away from using control and direct styles of management to embracing ones of tutoring, coaching and mentoring (Gibb 2003). Line managers may find making such an adjustment difficult, as they sometimes can be resistant to such change, and to the sort of mental reflexivity needed to embrace it too (Renwick 2003, p.275).

Producing useful outcomes in HRM from involving line managers in it also appears to rest on meeting another challenge – how to provide internal and/or external HR support to line managers undertaking HR duties, and give them good advice in HRM (Brewster and Larsen 2000). Marchington and Wilkinson (2002) (quoting Currie and Procter 2001) detail how HR managers can provide support to middle managers. Thus:

How HR managers can support middle managers

- HR strategies should be composed of broad themes that can then be contextualised by middle managers at an operational level.
- Middle managers should be encouraged to contribute towards an elaboration of these broad themes.
- Opportunities should be provided for middle managers to span boundaries within the organisation through membership of project groups.
- The HR function should be organised to allow HR professionals to work closely with middle managers at the point of delivery.
- The development of middle managers is directed towards their contribution to strategic change.

Source: Marchington and Wilkinson 2002, adapted from Currie and Procter 2001

But it is unclear if HR managers show the commitment, preparation and support to line managers in HRM (Brewster and Larsen 2000, p.208), and whether a 'simple, seamless transfer of responsibility' between HR and the line is achievable, owing to HR wanting to keep an operational role in HRM (Currie and Procter 2001, p.54).

If involving line managers in HRM is successful, then there may seem to be little need for work organisations to employ HR managers. Hence a challenge for HR managers is how to increase the involvement of line managers in HRM (to spread responsibility and accountability in HRM overall), without sowing the seeds of their own (HR) redundancy (i.e. the erosion of HR functions/departments, or an increase in HR outsourcing). Studies from the European and Chinese literature (above) could be seen to imply that HR also need to assess the challenge of how devolution in HRM helps the success of their work organisations (Andolsek and Stebe 2005), and to what extent such devolution supports a case for HR to become a strategic partner (Mitsuhashi *et al.* 2000). I now detail a research agenda for the involvement of line managers in HRM.

Future research[1]

While research studies on involving line managers in HRM do acknowledge some limitations in it, they also appear to be quite positive about it in general terms (e.g. Hutchinson and Purcell 2003; Huy 2002; Purcell *et al.* 2003; Purcell and Hutchinson 2007; Jackson and Schuler 2000). However, a fair (and higher) number of the other works reviewed (above) seem to suggest that the limitations associated with using line managers in HRM are more serious, as they appear to be both endemic and systemic. To move this research base forward we therefore need to know more on whether line managers are capable, committed and consistent in HRM or not, meaning that we need more studies to be completed to build clearer pictures, especially comparative and international ones, and those that give us insights into what is happening on these items in SMEs. Of particular importance is the need to seek the views of all the key actors in HRM: line managers, HR managers and employees – so we can triangulate their opinions to give us greater validity and reliability overall when drawing conclusions.

Additionally, we need to know more on how line managers cope with conflicting job demands, both operational and HRM (Lynch 2003), how they are recruited, inducted, trained, appraised and rewarded in the HR elements of their work, and what leadership roles senior line managers display in developing staff at work (Whittaker and Marchington 2003). Similarly, more research is needed on how line managers can develop different management styles of tutor, coach or mentor (Gibb 2003). Indeed, where the use of line managers in HRM in some studies is seen to be positive, we may want to ascertain more data on the capabilities and priorities of managers (Andolsek and Stebe 2005, p.327), and where it is negative, more data from employees on the role of their managers in motivating or inspiring employees to produce high performance (i.e. do line managers contribute to it, or do employees deliver high performance because they ignore their manager?). Moreover, we may also want to assess if employees are happy to be a means or channel to deliver increased organisational performance (hard HRM), or if they require career development for themselves also (soft HRM).

Technically, it may be useful for us to pursue Mehra and Schenkel's (2007) line of enquiry and see if FLMs gravitate to boundary-spanning positions within firms (and face heavy demands from other stakeholders), and if so, whether the demands from such groups produce role conflict for FLMs, and are leading FLMs to stress, job burnout and low commitment. It may be interesting to see if being an FLM is bad for the physical and psychological health of line management role occupants undertaking HR tasks, and if results on this question differ internationally. For example, we may be able to contrast findings here on what

---

[1]Further details on other research ideas for this field are detailed in Renwick (2003, 2006).

happens to role-holders in the US with those in the UK, and ask if we can state that FLMs undertaking HR work is good for the work organisations that employ them (as seen in some cases in the UK), but not good for the health of the managers in such positions (as seen in the US). It may be useful to chart what other patterns emerge on this issue internationally as well.

In the context of the work on issues such as stress management interventions (Dewe and O'Driscoll 2002), it may be useful to see how line managers view issues of stress when it applies not just to employees, but also to them as managers (perhaps as a result of taking on extra HR duties, and suffering from role conflict by completing them). By thinking through how line managers evaluate and re-evaluate their own managerial experiences in HRM, we may uncover whether they are reflective enough to explore the general tensions that they face between respecting employees and exploiting their human capital (McGuire *et al.* 2006, pp.254–55). We may also note the possibility of investigating the existence of centrifugal situational forces at work which may pressurise such managers to act in a spontaneous or automatic mode that buffers, mediates or rejects employee wishes and interests, i.e. those against the sort of 'emotional balancing' that Huy (2002) details. It may be useful here to understand (as per McGuire *et al.* 2006) the impact of various factors on such decision making by line managers, i.e. national culture, personality or institutional context, especially if managers do not engage in attending to employee needs in countries where such factors do not appear to support them to do so (e.g. Britain, where a lack of managerial training, of managerial commitment and general ad-hoc management practice are seen to dominate, and to be longstanding – see McGovern *et al.* 1997).

Lastly in this section, we may also wish to explore the role of factors like education, nationality and gender on how managers rate the importance of health and safety and employment equity (McGuire *et al.* 2006), as these may give new insight into how such managers view HRM issues in general terms. Of particular interest here may be new international patterns, and how the use of different (alternative) cultural streams can help managers break out of the stereotypical role definitions that surround them at work, especially those that relate to national culture (Delmestri 2006). In the case of Britain, for example, there may be some scope to see how imported practices can act as a lever to challenge any lack of managerial capability, commitment and consistency with respect to HRM that exists there. I now offer some conclusions forward.

Conclusions

Involving line managers in HRM requires them to manage in environments that are characterised by meeting the performance demands of a series of internal and external stakeholders, and managing in contexts of high levels of change and uncertainty. They have to reconcile the search for cost-control and higher creativity in HRM with demands of higher levels of responsibility for people and financial management, and to make choices on how they manage people at work. Coping with such expectations and demands places great pressure on line managers. But line managers need to practise HRM in a more consistent and professional way, as their expediency in it has long been understood. Hence we now face a series of questions. How do we want line managers to manage people at work? What roles should non-specialists and HR specialists take in HRM? And is involving line managers in HRM a positive development for all the stakeholders in HRM today? Answering these questions may help us understand if the greater involvement of line managers in HRM is a development that employers are pursuing to add value for all stakeholders in HRM, part of a cost-cutting exercise by them, a mixture of both, or something different altogether.

CASE STUDY 9.1

North Service Group (NSG)

William Hunter

NSG is a recently created work organisation, consisting of two operating companies – Cook and Dickens Services – which enjoy an equal partnership while retaining their separate identities and operating locations. They provide personal services to residents of local communities in the north of England. The services they provide are similar, but the communities they serve are very different, Cook operating mainly in a metropolitan borough, and Dickens in a rural district authority. Cook was formed nearly 30 years ago, and Dickens was formed in July 2006 when 17 staff transferred to it from local authority control. NSG is a non-asset-holding parent body, and a charitable association governed by the regulations of the Industrial and Provident Societies Act 1965. It qualifies as a society run for the benefit of the community, providing services for people other than its members. The NSG senior management team is primarily made up of the Cook senior management team. NSG was created to bring together the skills, resources and values of Cook and Dickens Services to create a strong body with a clear vision of what they want to achieve for their service users.

The organisational culture of NSG is, according to the chief executive and financial director, 'open'. Managers and staff are given their responsibilities and objectives, and then trusted to get on with their job. There is little or no 'checking up' or measuring of their performance. Owing to its reputation and quality service, Cook has maintained continuous employment for almost all staff. The future of NSG is thought to be secure, though individual projects can be vulnerable to changes in government policies and public spending reviews. NSG hopes that their growing size may help them survive, in addition to their good reputation. Cook has twice been awarded Charter Mark status and Investors in People recognition. HR policies and procedures tend to be designed by the directors of NSG, as there is no specialist professional HR presence on site. Cook makes use of a number of consultancies to assist with policy development in HRM as and when required, e.g. in health and safety, appraisal and recruitment. Occasionally line managers have been involved in developing such HR policies and procedures.

Questions

Considering all the relevant research literature (above) and the details of this case:

1. What priority do you think line managers at the British SME of NSG would give to their HR responsibilities (on a scale from HRM being 'very important' to HR issues 'sometimes are left in order to do operational tasks')?

2. Which HRM activities do you think line managers at NSG have most experience of, and why? (Choices here include induction, recruitment/selection, performance appraisal, training/development, coaching, grievance/discipline, communications, job evaluation, TQM, health/safety, motivation).

3. What areas of HRM do you think line managers at NSG will be strongest in, and which will they need to develop the most in? (Choices from list in 2 above).

4. What and who would you expect to guide line managers in taking decisions/actions in HRM at NSG, and how they learn to manage people?

5. To what extent do you think line managers at NSG will find formal written policies and procedures in HRM useful (on a scale of 1 = little use, to 5 = some use)?

6. Do you expect line management actions in employee relations and HRM at NSG to be consistent?

7. Do you think the context within which NSG operates (e.g. national culture, organisational size) will effect how line managers both view and undertake HR work?

Line managers and 'star' employees

Douglas Renwick

This case examines the issues surrounding how managers handle fluctuating employee performance in a high-performance work organisation – a football team. The actors are football player David Beckham and manager Fabio Capello at the English national team. The background to this case is the rise of Beckham as a football player at both Manchester United and Real Madrid, from his displays as a player on the right wing and his specialist ability as a free-kick expert. Capello was Beckham's manager at Madrid, dropping him from playing when Beckham announced his high-profile move to the (US) LA Galaxy (managed by Gullit). Then, with press speculation that Beckham had regained both form and fitness, Capello reinstated him in the Madrid team for their title challenge (and subsequent success).

The case in question involves Beckham's selection for the English national team in 2008, shortly after Capello (an alleged strict disciplinarian) took up the reins as the new England manager. Beckham has stated his desire to play for England and make himself available for selection for the next World Cup and European Championship campaigns. Capello was allegedly quoted in the English press as being at pains to state that while Beckham was a player 'who demands respect', he was not selecting him for the recent friendly (against Switzerland), reasoning that he was 'not match-fit'. Capello later reinstated him for the next friendly (against France). The non-selection of Beckham initially fuelled speculation as to whether he would play 100 caps for England (which he now has). But more importantly for the player, questions were being raised as to whether he would feature much, if at all, in the forthcoming World Cup and European qualifying games, owing to a lack of form, fitness and competitive edge – which some commentators view as arising from him playing in the US league.

Questions

1. Do you feel that Capello treated Beckham unfairly by excluding and then including him for England, or that Capello had good reason not to pick Beckham? Do you feel that the previous history between player and manager plays a part in the player not being selected?

2. Do you think that issues of management style and/or national culture enter the mix when thinking through how managers manage players, and how players feel about how they are managed? Do you see any similarities and/or differences on both items in relations between Beckham and his former and current managers, i.e. Ferguson (British), Capello (Italian) and Gullit (Dutch)?

3. What wider issues do you think this case raises in terms of performance management for managers and employees in general? Do you think that (as per stress management interventions) there is an onus on 'star' performers to look after their own form, fitness and competitive edge (or such like), or that it is the role of the manager to inspire them to perform, or something different?

Bibliography

*Andolsek, D.A. and Stebe, J. (2005) 'Devolution or (de)centralisation of HRM function in European organizations', *The International Journal of Human Resource Management*, Vol.16, No.3 (March), pp.311–29.

Brewster, C. and Larsen, H.H. (1992) 'Human resource management in Europe: evidence from ten countries', *The International Journal of Human Resource Management*, Vol.3, No.3 (December), pp.409–34.

Brewster, C. and Larsen, H.H. (eds) (2000) *Human Resource Management In Northern Europe: Trends, Dilemmas and Strategy*, Oxford: Blackwell.

Budhwar, P.S. (2000) 'Evaluating levels of strategic integration and devolvement of human resource management in the UK', *Personnel Review*, Vol.29, No.2, pp.141–61.

Cully, M., Woodland, S., O'Reilly, A. and Dix, G. (1999) *Britain At Work: As Depicted by the 1998 Workplace Employee Relations Survey*, London: Routledge.

Cunningham, I. and Hyman, J. (1995) 'Transforming the HRM vision into reality: the role of line managers and supervisors in implementing change', *Employee Relations*, Vol.17, No.8, pp.5–20.

Cunningham, I. and Hyman, J. (1999) 'Devolving human resource responsibilities to the line: beginning of the end or a new beginning for personnel?' *Personnel Review*, Vol.28, No.1/2, pp.9–27.

Cunningham, I. and James, P. (2001) 'Line managers as people managers: prioritising the needs of the long-term sick and those with disabilities', British Academy of Management Conference Paper, Cardiff University.

Cunningham, I., James, P. and Dibben, P. (2004) 'Bridging the gap between rhetoric and reality: line managers and the protection of job security for ill worker in the modern workplace', *British Journal of Management*, Vol.15, No.3, pp.273–90.

Currie, G. and Procter, S. (2001) 'Exploring the relationship between HR and middle managers', *Human Resource Management Journal*, Vol.11, No.1, pp.53–69.

Deeks, E. (2000) 'Self-service is hard work', *People Management*, 23 November, Vol.26, No.23, p.9.

Delmestri, G. (2006) 'Streams of inconsistent institutional influences: middle managers as carriers of multiple identities', *Human Relations*, Vol.59, No.11, pp.1515–41.

*Dewe, P. and O'Driscoll, M. (2002) 'Stress management interventions: what do managers actually do?', *Personnel Review*, Vol.31, No.2, pp.143–65.

Dunn, C. and Wilkinson, A. (2002) 'Wish you were here: managing absence', *Personnel Review*, Vol.31, No.2, pp.228–46.

Edwards, C.Y. and Robinson, O. (2001) '"Better" part-time jobs? A study of part-time working in nursing and the police', *Employee Relations*, Vol.23, No.5, pp.438–53.

Fenton-O'Creevy, M. (1998) 'Employee involvement and the middle manager: evidence from a survey of organizations', *Journal of Organizational Behaviour*, Vol.19, pp.67–84.

Fenton-O'Creevy, M. (2001) 'Employee involvement and the middle manager: saboteur or scapegoat?', *Human Resource Management Journal*, Vol.11, No.1, pp.24–40.

*George, J.M. and Zhou, J. (2007) 'Dual tuning in a supportive context: joint contributions of positive mood, negative mood, and supervisory behaviours to employee creativity', *Academy of Management Journal*, Vol.50, No.3, pp.605–22.

Gibb, S. (2001) 'The state of human resource management: evidence from employee's views of HRM systems and staff', *Employee Relations*, Vol.23, No.4, pp.318–36.

Gibb, S. (2003) 'Line manager involvement in learning and development: small beer or big deal?', *Employee Relations*, Vol.25, No.3, pp.281–93.

Gratton, L., Hope-Hailey, V., Stiles, P. and Truss, C. (1999) 'Linking individual performance to business strategy: the people process model', in R. Schuler and S. Jackson (eds) *Strategic Human Resource Management*, Oxford: Blackwell, pp.142–58.

Green, F. and James, D. (2003) 'Assessing skills and autonomy: the job holder versus the line manager', *Human Resource Management Journal*, Vol.13, No.1, pp.63–77.

Guest, D. (1987) 'Human resource management and industrial relations', *Journal of Management Studies*, Vol.24 (September), pp.503–22.

Guest, D. and King, Z. (2001) 'HR and the bottom line', *People Management*, 27 September, pp.29–34.

Guest, D., King, Z., Conway, N., Michie, J. and Sheehan-Quinn, M. (2001) *Voices from the Boardroom*, London: Chartered Institute of Personnel and Development.

*Harris, L. (2001) 'Rewarding employee performance: line manager's values, beliefs and perspectives', *The International Journal of Human Resource Management*, Vol.12, No.7.

Hutchinson, S. and Purcell, J. (2003) *Bringing Policies to Life: The Vital Role of Front-line Managers in People Management*, London: Chartered Institute of Personnel and Development.

Hutchinson, S. and Wood, S. (1995) *Personnel and the Line: Developing the New Relationship*, London: Institute of Personnel and Development.

*Huy, Q.N. (2002) 'Emotional balancing or organizational continuity and radical change: the contribution of middle managers', *Administrative Science Quarterly*, Vol.47, No.1 (March), pp.31–69.

IRS Employment Trends (2001) 'Managing discipline at work', No.727, May, pp.5–11.

Jackson, S.E. and Schuler, R.S. (2000) *Managing Human Resources: A Partnership Perspective*, London: International Thomson Publishing.

Kanter, R.M. (1983) *The Change Masters: Corporate Entrepreneurs At Work*, London: International Thomson Business Press.

Kelly, J. and Gennard, J. (2001) *The Effective Personnel Director: Power and Influence in the Boardroom*, London: Routledge.

Kelly, J. and Gennard, J. (2001) *Power and Influence in the Boardroom: The Role of the Personnel/HR Director*, London: Routledge.

*Larsen, H. and Brewster, C. (2003) 'Line management responsibility for HRM: what's happening in Europe?', *Employee Relations*, Vol.25, No.3, pp.228–44.

Legge, K. (1995) *Human Resource Management: Rhetorics and Realities*, Basingstoke: Macmillan.

Lowe, J. (1992) 'Locating the line: the front-line supervisor and human resource management', in P. Blyton and P. Turnbull (eds) *Reassessing Human Resource Management*, London: Sage, pp.148–68.

Lynch, S. (2003) 'Devolution and the management of human resources: evidence from the retail industry', Paper presented to the Professional Standards Conference, Chartered Institute of Personnel and Development, University of Keele.

Marchington, M. (1999) 'Professional qualification scheme: core personnel and development exam papers and examiners' reports May 1999', Institute of Personnel and Development, Paper given to the IPD Professional Standards Conference, University of Warwick, July, pp.1–12.

Marchington, M. (2001) 'Employee involvement at work', in J. Storey (ed.) *op. cit.*, London: Chartered Institute of Personnel and Development.

Marchington, M. and Wilkinson, A.J. (2002) *People Management and Development: Human Resource Management at Work* (2nd edn), London: Chartered Institute of Personnel and Development.

Marsh, A.I. (1971) 'The staffing of industrial relations management in the engineering industry', *Industrial Relations Journal*, Vol.22, No.2, pp.14–24.

Marsh, A.I. and Gillies, J.G. (1983) 'The involvement of line and staff managers in industrial relations', as quoted in K. Thurley and S. Wood (eds) *Industrial Relations and Management Strategy*, Cambridge: Cambridge University Press, pp.27–38.

Mason, G. (2000) 'Production supervisors in Britain, Germany and the United States: back from the dead again?', *Work, Employment and Society*, Vol.14, No.4, pp.625–45.

McConville, T. and Holden, L. (1999) 'The filling in the sandwich: HRM and middle managers in the health sector', *Personnel Review*, Vol.28, No.5–6, pp.406–24.

McGovern, P., Gratton, L., Hope-Hailey, V. and Truss, C. (1997) 'Human resource management on the line?' *Human Resource Management Journal*, Vol.7 No.4, pp.12–29.

*McGuire, D., Garavan, T.N., Saha, S.K. and O'Donnell, D. (2006) 'The impact of individual values on human resource decision-making by line managers', *International Journal of Manpower*, Vol.27, No.3, pp.251–73.

Mehra, A. and Schenkel, M.T. (2007) 'The price chameleons pay: self-monitoring, boundary spanning and role conflict in the workplace', *British Journal of Management* (online early), pp.1–7.

Millward, N., Bryson, A. and Forth, J. (2000) *All Change At Work? British Employment Relations 1980–1998, as Portrayed by the Workplace Industrial Relations Survey Series*, London: Routledge.

*Mitsuhashi, H., Park, H.J., Wright, P.M. and Chua, R. (2000) 'Line and HR executives' perceptions of HR effectiveness in the People's Republic of China', *The International Journal of Human Resource Management*, Vol.11, No.2, pp.197–216.

Poole, M. and Jenkins, G. (1997) 'Responsibilities for human resource management practices in the modern enterprise', *Personnel Review*, Vol.26, No.5, pp.333–56.

*Purcell, J. and Hutchinson, S. (2007) 'Front-line managers as agents in the HRM-performance causal chain: theory, analysis and evidence', *Human Resource Management Journal*, Vol.17, No.1, pp.3–20.

Purcell, J., Kinnie, N., Hutchinson, S., Rayton, B. and Swart, J. (2003) *Understanding the People and Performance Link: Unlocking the Black Box*, London: Chartered Institute of Personnel and Development.

Redman, T. (2001) 'Performance appraisal', in T. Redman and A. Wilkinson (eds) *Contemporary Human Resource Management*, Harlow: Pearson Education, pp.57–95.

*Renwick, D. (2003) 'Line manager involvement in HRM: an inside view', *Employee Relations*, Vol.25, No.3, pp.262–80.

*Renwick, D. (2006) 'Line managers: text and cases', in T. Redman and A. Wilkinson (eds) *Contemporary Human Resource Management* (2nd edn), London: Pearson Education, pp.209–28.

Rollinson, D., Hook, C., Foot, M., and Handley, J. (1996) 'Supervisor and manager styles in handling discipline and grievance: part two – approaches to handling discipline and grievance', *Personnel Review*, Vol.25, No.4, pp.38–55.

Sisson, K. and Storey, J. (2000) *The Realities of Human Resource Management*, Buckingham: Open University Press.

Storey, J. (1992) *Developments in the Management of Human Resources*, Oxford: Blackwell.

Storey, J. (2001) 'Human resource management today: an assessment', in J. Storey (ed.) *Human Resource Management: A Critical Text* (2nd edn), London: Thomson, pp.3–20.

Taylor, S. (2002) 'A poor boss can be the last straw', *Basingstoke Gazette*, 20 December, p.56.

Thornhill, A. and Saunders, M.N.K. (1998) 'What if line managers don't realize they're responsible for HR? Lessons from an organization experiencing rapid change', *Personnel Review*, Vol.27, No.6, pp.460–76.

Tyson, S. and Fell, A. (1995) *Evaluating the Personnel Function* (2nd edn), Cheltenham: Stanley Thomes.

Wai-Kwong, F.Y., Priem, R.L. and Cycyota, C.S. (2001) 'The performance effects of human resource managers' and other middle managers' involvement in strategy making under different business-level strategies: the case in Hong Kong', *The International Journal of Human Resource Management*, Vol.12. No.8, pp.1325–46.

Walton, J. (1999) *Strategic Human Resource Management*, Harlow: Pearson Education.

Whittaker, S. and Marchington, M. (2003) 'Devolving HR responsibility to the line: threat, opportunity or partnership?', *Employee Relations*, Vol.25, No.3, pp.245–61.

*Useful reading

Chapter 10

ORGANISATIONAL AND CORPORATE CULTURE

Alistair Cheyne and John Loan-Clarke

Introduction

In the study of organisations and their management, the concept of organisational culture (sometimes referred to as corporate culture) has become increasingly important, and the quantity of research in the area has increased dramatically since the early 1980s (Siehl and Martin 1990). This chapter outlines recent theory and research in organisational culture. In doing so it outlines definitions and categorisations of culture, discusses the assessment of culture and the related concept of organisational climate, investigates the links between culture and human resource management, and examines how organisations might attempt to manage culture.

The concept of culture

Culture as a concept derives from the fields of social anthropology and sociology. In general its description has been used to characterise an organisation or group of individuals within a social structure. Culture is, however, not a well-defined concept (Münch and Smelster 1992); it describes roles and interactions that derive from norms and values in the sociological tradition, or from beliefs and attitudes in the social psychological field (Wunthow and Witten 1988). In addition to these distinctions, there are at least two major approaches to the study of culture. The first views culture as an implicit feature of social life, and the second holds culture to be an explicit social construction (Wunthow and Witten 1988), in other words culture as the structure of a socio-political group or culture as a product of that group.

In the same vein, two models of culture have been proposed: that which defines culture in terms of behaviour and that which defines it in terms of meaning. The second of these models is supported by Trice and Beyer's (1984) assertion that culture is a system of publicly and collectively accepted meanings operating for a given group at a given time.

Such views of culture have been incorporated into organisational theory to give rise to the concepts of organisational culture (Brown 1998) and the similar corporate culture (Peters and Waterman 1982). The term 'organisational culture' tends to refer to a naturally occurring phenomenon that all organisations possess, whereas corporate culture is held to be more management driven, in an attempt to increase organisational effectiveness. Furthermore, it has been suggested (Shipley 1990) that culture is central to the understanding and control of, and resistance to, change in society, organisations and social groups. For organisations, Yu (2007) suggests that having an appropriate corporate culture is held as a vital element of many companies' successes, and failures.

Organisational culture

As noted earlier, the study of culture has been influential in the field of organisational studies for nearly 30 years (Denison 1996; Trompenaars and Hampden-Turner 1997). Its importance stems, in part, from the notion that it provides a dynamic and interactive model of organising (Jelinek *et al.* 1983; Smircich 1983) and as such can help explain how organisational environments might be characterised, assessed and ultimately controlled (Deal and Kennedy 1982; Schneider 1990). Furthermore, a number of authors have proposed that successful organisations have a strong or positive corporate culture (Deal and Kennedy 1982; Peters and Waterman 1982; Kilmann *et al.* 1985; Weick 1985; Yu 2007). The notion of culture can, therefore, imply a practical way of explaining how and why particular organisations enjoy differing levels of success (Trompenaars and Hampden-Turner 1997; Brown 1998). In the field of human resource management, organisational culture is increasingly held to be essential to success in organisations (see, for example, DeCenzo and Robbins 2002). The suggestion that organisational effectiveness is heavily influenced by a positive corporate culture has been particularly influential for practising managers. A key influence for the formation of this assumption was the 1982 book by Peters and Waterman, *In Search of Excellence*:

> Without exception, the dominance and coherence of culture proved to be an essential quality of the excellent companies. Moreover the stronger the culture and the more it was directed towards the marketplace, the less the need there was for policy manuals, organization charts or detailed procedures and rules. (p.75)

However, as more systematic, longitudinal research (for example, Kotter and Heskett 1992) has indicated, the causal link between culture and organisational effectiveness is not necessarily easy to identify. We will come back to the potential link between culture and performance later in this chapter, after we consider what culture is, and how we might assess it.

DEFINING ORGANISATIONAL CULTURE

A number of definitions of culture have been proposed and it is possible to discern some common themes among these. Moorhead and Griffin (1995) suggest that organisational culture is a set of values that help people in an organisation to understand which actions are considered acceptable and which are unacceptable to the organisation and its members. Similarly, Schein (1985) has defined organisational culture in terms of employees' shared values and perceptions of the organisation, beliefs about it, and common ways of solving problems within the organisation. Schein (1985) has also described organisational culture in terms of an ongoing process through which an organisation's behaviour patterns become transformed over time, installed in new recruits, and refined and adapted in response to both internal and external changes. Culture helps an organisation's members to interpret and accept their world, and so it is not so much a by-product of an organisation as an integral part of it, which influences individuals' behaviours and contributes to the effectiveness of the organisation.

Reviews of the concept of organisational culture (for example, Rousseau 1990; Furnham 1997) have detailed the abundance of definitions that have developed over the years. Examples of the range of definitions are detailed in Box 10.1.

While it is apparent that there have been a number of disagreements over the precise nature of organisational culture, these definitions do bear some resemblance to each other. Several salient points emerge upon comparing these definitions. Emphasis, in many cases, is on values, beliefs and expectations that are shared within the group and/or organisation, and which, in turn, can help the members make sense of their environment, and direct behaviour. Rousseau (1990) agrees that it is not really the definitions of organisational culture that vary widely but the approaches to data collection and operation (see, for example, p.250 below).

Box 10.1: HRM in practice

Definitions of culture

Kroeber and Kluckhohn (1952)	Culture consists of patterns of behaviour transmitted by symbols, embodied in artefacts, ideas and values.
Bowers and Seashore (1966)	The best way of doing things around here.
Becker and Geer (1970)	A set of common understandings.
Geertz (1973)	The fabric of meaning which allows the interpretation and guidance of action.
Van Maanen and Schein (1979)	Values, beliefs and expectations that members of organisations come to share.
Swartz and Jordon (1980)	Shared patterns of beliefs and expectations that produce norms shaping behaviour.
Ouchi (1981)	The set of symbols, ceremonies and myths that communicate the organisation's values and beliefs to its members.
Deal and Kennedy (1982)	A system of informal rules that spells out how people are to behave most of the time.
Louis (1983)	As having three aspects: (1) some content (2) specific to (3) a group.
Martin and Siehl (1983)	The glue that holds together an organisation through shared patterns of meaning, consisting of core values, forms and strategies to reinforce content.
Uttal (1983)	Shared values and beliefs that interact with an organisation's structures and control systems to produce behavioural norms.

Pettigrew (1990) offers one explanation of the problem in defining organisational culture. He suggests that it is, in part, due to the fact that culture is:

> not just a concept but the source of a family of concepts (Pettigrew 1979), and it is not just a family of concepts but also a frame of reference or root metaphor for organisational analysis. (p.414)

Pettigrew's explanation reflects two very different understandings of the concept of culture. Brown (1998) suggests that a clear distinction can be made between those who think that culture is a metaphor that helps us to understand organisations in terms of other entities (Morgan 1986), and those who see culture as an objective entity that distinguishes one organisation from another (Gold 1982). The view that culture is an objective entity can be subdivided, as pointed out by Rohner (1984), into something an organisation is (or its structure and meaning) or something an organisation has (for example, its behaviour), as embodied by most of the definitions summarised by Rousseau (1990) and detailed above.

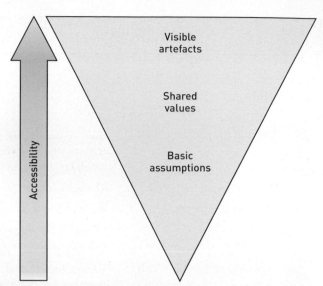

Figure 10.1 Schein's layers of organisational culture

LAYERS OF ORGANISATIONAL CULTURE

It may be that the use of culture as a concept can be seen to be too embracing, and some writers (Schein 1985; Morgan 1986; Rousseau 1990) describe culture as having a series of different layers. Schein (1985) suggests that there are three levels of culture: artefacts, values and basic assumptions. Figure 10.1 shows a representation of these layers of culture, organised from readily accessible, and, therefore, more easily studied, to difficult to access.

At the most accessible level are visible artefacts, or products of cultural activity. These might include patterns of behaviour (Cooke and Rousseau 1988), or the structures that reflect patterns of activity, observable to those outside the culture. Examples of these visible artefacts might include corporate logos and the physical layout of the organisation. The middle layer relates to values and priorities assigned to organisational outcomes. Such values might be reflected in group behavioural norms, or beliefs about what is acceptable and unacceptable behaviour within the organisation, similar to Moorhead and Griffin's (1995) definition of culture. This layer can be learned about through interaction with, and questioning of, group members. Patterns of unconscious assumptions (Schein 1984) are the deepest of the layers of culture, and these may not be directly known by the organisation's members and therefore require a period of intensive interaction to uncover. An appreciation of layers of culture could, therefore, be important when considering whether culture can be managed (see below).

This type of representation of cultural layers has been further embellished, to present a more complex picture. Hatch (1997) has adapted Schein's (1985) original layers model to incorporate organisational symbols and processes in a more dynamic model. Similarly, Hofstede *et al.* (1990) have divided the manifestations (or more accessible elements) of culture into values, at the deepest level, through rituals and heroes, to symbols at the shallowest.

Categorisations of culture

In addition to the various definitions of culture and descriptions of level, several researchers have developed a number of classifications of organisational culture, allowing organisations to be described as different types of objective entity. Indeed, Balthazard *et al.* (2006) suggest that much of the research on organisational culture has focused on describing types of cultures and producing dimensions of culture. These allow us to compare and evaluate different organisations in terms of their culture, and allow types of culture to be associated with successes and failures within those organisations. There are many such categorisations; here we will examine three of the better-known examples, those of Deal and Kennedy (1982), Harrison (1972) and Hofstede (1980, 1991).

DEAL AND KENNEDY'S FOUR CULTURES

One of the most popular classifications of corporate culture was proposed by Deal and Kennedy (1982). Their categorisation of culture was the result of visiting hundreds of organisations and is based on two organisational environmental factors: the degree of risk associated with business activities, and the speed of feedback to the organisation and individuals about the success of those business activities. Deal and Kennedy (1982) identified four distinct culture types:

- Tough-guy macho culture – an organisation of risk takers who receive immediate feedback; examples include police, management consultants, media.

- Work hard/play hard culture – a low-risk, quick-feedback culture which encourages people to maintain high levels of activity; examples include sales companies, computer companies.

- Bet your company culture – the high-risk, slow-feedback culture, where ideas are given time to develop; examples include large multinationals engaged in research and product development.

- Process culture – the classic bureaucracy where feedback is slow and risks are low, so individuals focus on the processes; examples might include local government and heavily regulated industries.

Deal and Kennedy (1982) recognise that organisations might not precisely fit into these four types, or indeed perhaps not fit at all, but they propose that this model is still a useful tool for managers beginning to identify an organisation's culture.

HARRISON'S TYPOLOGY

An early, relatively simple, yet extremely influential classification of organisational culture was suggested by Harrison (1972). This classification has been elaborated on by other scholars, including Handy (1978) and Williams *et al.* (1993), and, like the Deal and Kennedy model, includes descriptions of four main types of culture in organisations:

- Power culture – has a single source of power. Typically these types of organisation react quickly, but success often depends on those with the power at the centre and these organisations might be small, owner-managed businesses.

- Role culture – these types of organisations are more typically described as bureaucracies, with an emphasis on functions and specialities. These organisations are more likely to be successful in stable environments and could include public sector organisations.

- Task culture – the focus for these types of organisation is accomplishing goals; power is based on expertise and flexibility is important, for example management consultancies.

- Person culture – these types of organisation exist primarily to serve the needs of their members. Individuals are expected to influence each other through example and helpfulness, and have almost complete autonomy. This type of culture may be evident in those in professional practice, such as lawyers or doctors, or those involved in a collective organisation.

HOFSTEDE'S NATIONAL CULTURE DIMENSIONS

The consideration of organisational culture is complicated further when the effects of societal and national cultures upon individual organisations' cultures are considered. Hofstede (1980) studied these influences in relation to IBM, the American multinational company, operating in over 40 countries worldwide. Hofstede collected survey data concerning work-related values from international affiliates and found evidence of national cultural differences. Hofstede (1991) demonstrated that managers in different countries varied in the strength of their attitudes and values regarding various issues. Four dimensions were identified, including:

- power distance – the extent to which members are willing to accept an unequal distribution of power, wealth and privilege;

- uncertainty avoidance – the manner in which individuals have learned to cope with uncertainty;

- individualism – the degree to which individuals are required to act independently;

- masculinity – related to dominant values such as success and money.

A fifth dimension, 'confucian dynamism' – the degree to which long-termism or short-termism is the dominant orientation in life – was added after further sampling and analysis of the data.

The results of this work suggest, for example, that organisations in the UK will have low power distance, be individualist, masculine and able to cope with uncertainty. Hofstede's work is not only deemed to be important for the identification of specific cultural differences (Hatch 1997) but it has also shown that organisational culture is an entry point for societal influence on organisations. This notion has been developed further in the work of Fons Trompenaars (Trompenaars and Hampden-Turner 1977).

A number of similarities are apparent from these example classifications; for example, *tough guy, power* and *power distance* all seem to be tapping into similar types of culture, suggesting a degree of reliability in the observations of different research groups. However, while these typologies are a useful starting point in describing culture, as Deal and Kennedy (1982) acknowledge, we should remember that they represent ideal situations or models for us to compare actual organisations against, and no organisation will fit the types exactly. It is perhaps more useful for organisations to be able to describe the origin of their own cultures and the process by which they arise (Furnham 1997), and how they can enhance organisational effectiveness. A first step in achieving this might involve the detailed assessment of organisational culture.

It is clear from the literature examined above that there are certain inconsistencies in the way culture is defined. Many researchers agree that organisational culture involves beliefs and values, exists at a variety of different levels, and manifests itself in a wide range of artefacts, symbols and processes within any particular organisation. Culture helps an organisation's members to interpret meaning and understand their working environment. It is an integral part of an organisation and as such can influence individuals' behaviour and potentially contribute to the effectiveness or ineffectiveness of the organisation. Two examples of problems that can be encountered by individuals' interpretations of an organisation's culture and adherence to cultural norms are highlighted in Box 10.2.

A key issue for management is whether culture(s) will exist in the organisation irrespective of management action or whether management can proactively influence and change culture. These issues will be considered in more detail in the second half of the chapter; we now consider how an understanding of culture within an organisation can be acquired.

Problems of strong culture

The two instances which follow provide examples of the problems organisations and individuals can face when they feel bound by organisational culture to behave in a particular way.

Piper Alpha

An explosion and resulting fire destroyed the North Sea oil production platform the Piper Alpha on 6 July 1988, killing a total of 167 men. A leakage of natural gas condensate ignited, causing a massive explosion. The explosion ignited secondary oil fires and the released gas caused a second, larger explosion which engulfed the entire platform. The public enquiry (Cullen 1990) pointed out a number of managerial and organisational issues in the development of the disaster. One aspect of the disaster which might give an insight into the culture in the organisation was the delay in shutting down feeds from other neighbouring platforms. The fire might have burnt out sooner if it had not been fed new fuel from both the Tartan and the Claymore platforms. Both platforms could see that Piper Alpha was burning, but, it has been suggested, felt they did not have the authority to shut down production. There may be many explanations for these actions, but they could suggest that the parent organisation's culture might be characterised as a role or process culture where individuals adhered to a strong hierarchy.

Japan Airlines, Anchorage

On 13 January 1977, a Japan Airlines DC-8 crashed shortly after take-off from Anchorage International Airport, Alaska, killing three crew members and two cargo-handlers and destroying the aircraft. The flight was captained by a 53-year-old American pilot with 23,000 hours' flying experience; his Japanese co-pilot was 31 years old, with considerably less experience (1,600 hours). The investigation into the accident found that the captain was around three times over the legal limit for driving a car. The National Transportation Safety Board held that a contributing factor to this accident was the failure of other flight crew to prevent the captain undertaking the flight.

Anderson and colleagues (2003) suggest that, while it is difficult to gauge exactly what happened on the flight deck, the incident might have had something to do with the perception of command relationships. Given Hofstede's categorisations of national cultural dimensions, we might expect an American culture to be low on power distance and individualistic, while Japan has a culture that has high power distance and is collective. As Anderson *et al.* (2003) point out, the co-pilot would have been conscious of his role within the cockpit and the seniority of the captain, and so might have questioned the captain in a discreet way rather than the more assertive challenge that would have been needed in this situation.

Assessing organisational culture

Meyerson (1991) has noted that:

> culture was the code word for the subjective side of organisational life . . . its study represented an ontological rebellion against the dominant functionalist or 'scientific' paradigm. (p.256)

In other words, organisational culture research came about in part as a reaction to the existing approaches to the study of organisations, focusing on systems (Brown 1998). Despite this reaction, both quantitative and qualitative methods persist in the study of organisational culture (Rousseau 1990; Brown 1998). Moorhead and Griffin (1995) trace these differences back to the historical foundations, or antecedents, of current organisational culture and climate research. These include methodologies influenced by economics as well as those from psychology, sociology and anthropology.

As we might expect from an examination of definitions, approaches to assessment vary widely. Rousseau (1990) argues that debates over organisational research methods are the result of the resurgence of qualitative methodologies, originally based in anthropology and sociology, and the perceived shortcomings of quantitative approaches. Smircich (1983) proposes that standardised, quantitative measures cannot describe a culture, which is essentially a frame of reference. Similarly, Schein (1984) suggests that, since each organisation is unique, it is difficult for an outside researcher to form *a priori* questions or measures to tap into its culture. Furthermore, Schein (1984) asserts that the use of such quantitative methods is unethical in its use of aggregated data and not the participants' own words. Given the definitions of culture discussed earlier, it is important for quantitative organisational culture research to address these criticisms.

Quantitative approaches to the assessment of culture are, however, still popular. Many similar dimensions appear on several culture and climate assessment instruments, suggesting that values and behaviours can be expressed, and in turn assessed, in similar terms (Rousseau 1990). Furthermore, Xenikou and Furnham (1996) found significant correlations between four instruments and went on to suggest a six-factor model based on the work of Cooke and Lafferty (1989), Glaser (1983), Kilmann and Saxton (1983) and Sashkin and Fulmer (1985; cited in Rousseau 1990). The factors uncovered related to:

- openness to change;
- values of excellent organisations;
- bureaucratic culture;
- organisational artefacts;
- resistance to new ideas;
- workplace social relations.

Not surprisingly, these factors relate, almost exclusively to the more accessible layers of culture outlined in Figure 10.1, and bear more than a passing resemblance to some of the categorisations discussed above.

In addition to alternative research strategies and data collection methods, Pettigrew (1979, 1990) has identified several analytical issues, related to the complexity of the concept, that make the study of culture difficult. These include, among others, the fact that culture might exist at different levels (Schein 1985), is pervasive across the organisation, can include subcultures and is interconnected with the organisational system, subsystems and the external environment. These kinds of issues, together with varying data collection and research strategies, would seem to make a comprehensive study of organisational culture almost impossible.

Rousseau (1990) suggests that different approaches and strategies may suit the investigation of different levels and aspects of culture. Few empirical researchers claim to uncover everything about an organisation's culture in their investigations; they mainly focus on one or two of the elements discussed above, or the more accessible manifestations. In many cases attempts to assess the social psychological environment of an organisation have led researchers to focus on the similar concept of organisational climate. Indeed, much discussion of the concept and the study of organisational culture is related to that of organisational climate (Denison 1996).

ORGANISATIONAL CLIMATE

Climate has been held to be the individual descriptions of the social setting or context of which the person is part. James and Jones (1974) suggested that climate reflects employee perceptions of work and organisational practices. Investigations into organisational climate pre-date organisational cultural studies by at least a decade and some of the current interest in cultural perspectives of organisations is a result of the earlier research focus on climate (Brown 1998).

Moran and Volkwein (1992) propose that organisational climate is:

> a relatively enduring characteristic of an organization which distinguishes it from other organizations: and (a) embodies members' collective perceptions about their organization with respect to such dimensions as autonomy, trust, cohesiveness, support, recognition, innovation, and fairness; (b) is produced by member interaction; (c) serves as a basis for interpreting the situation; (d) reflects the prevalent norms, values and attitudes of the organization's culture; and (e) acts as a source of influence for shaping behavior. (p.20)

The above definition makes reference to organisational culture and highlights the similarities between the two concepts. Despite their distinct evolution, culture and climate are now often used as interchangeable terms (Denison 1996). However, distinctions can still be made between these concepts. Ashforth (1985) distinguishes between the shared assumptions of culture and the shared perceptions of climate and argues that culture informs climate by helping group members to define what is important. Reichers and Schneider (1990) suggest that culture and climate both deal with the ways by which members of an organisation make sense of their environment, and that both are learned through socialisation and interaction. However, culture exists at a higher level and relates to longer-term and overarching policies and goals, whereas climate has been more generally described as the way things are done on a day-to-day basis (Furnham 1997). Thus, measures of climate generally focus on individual or 'group' perceptions of the prevailing organisational structures, and culture measures generally focus on the patterns of values and beliefs that lead to the emergence of these structures (Cooke and Szumal 1983). A further distinction is offered by Hofstede *et al.* (1990), who see climate as describing shorter-term characteristics of the organisation which indicate how it treats its members. Culture, on the other hand, reflects longer-term characteristics which describe the types of people that the organisation employs.

Researchers in the field have proposed various connections between culture and climate, as described above. At the very least the two constructs are complementary (Schneider 1987), at most they provide different interpretations of the same phenomenon (Denison 1996). Schein (1985) proposes that climate can most accurately be understood as a manifestation of culture. In this way a 'positive' culture will be promoted and maintained by a 'positive' climate and vice versa. Culture and climate can be viewed as reciprocal processes in a cyclic relationship. Given developments in business activity facilitated by technology, particularly the use of internet-based business, Ogbonna and Harris (2006) have suggested that the culture concept will need rethinking. For example, employees will be interacting with customers, via technology, not face to face, and therefore understanding climate may become more important than understanding culture.

Denison (1996) offers a useful way of considering conceptual and research method differences between culture and climate, while recognising that the terms are often used interchangeably by many researchers. The definitional and assessment issues discussed above have proved particularly problematic when seeking to understand any relationships between culture and organisational performance.

Culture and organisational performance

Of particular interest to organisations and managers is the (assumed) link between organisational culture and organisational performance. Silverzweig and Allen (1976) were probably the first to claim such a link. Based on eight case studies of organisations seeking to change their culture in order to improve effectiveness, they identified that six of the organisations improved their performance. However, the real spur to popularity of the culture–performance link was Peters and Waterman's (1982) *In Search of Excellence*. Several researchers have sought to define and assess the link between culture and various organisational outcomes, often in the hope of identifying or nurturing the 'best' culture associated with those outcomes. Lee and Yu (2004) point out that much research on the link with performance has focused on a search for particular shared organisational traits or values that result in superior performance. One example of theoretical links being drawn between culture and outcome measures is given by the role for organisational culture and climate in productivity modelled by Kopelman and colleagues (1990). Their model is based on the influence of human resource management on productivity and individual satisfaction and motivation and illustrates how culture, management practices and climate can influence the outcome measure. Similarly, Bright and Cooper (1993) have proposed that quality management and organisational culture are closely aligned, with overall culture change being central to the development of quality management systems and essential to their functioning, although no empirical data is presented. Several attempts have also been made to link the assessment of organisational culture with financial performance (for example, Denison 1984; Gordon 1985; Gordon and DiTomaso 1992). Gordon and DiTomaso (1992) suggest that the appropriate culture for achieving results in the insurance organisations they examined may not be best described only as 'strong' in terms of consistency, but also as flexible. The organisational culture related to effectiveness may, therefore, best be conceived as a combination of several characteristics, which facilitate enhanced performance.

Petty and colleagues (1995) have endeavoured to link the assessment of organisational culture with broader performance measures. Their assessment of performance incorporated evaluations of operations, customer accounting, support services, marketing and employee health and safety into one overall performance measure. This study found evidence of associations between the measures of performance and organisational culture, with the strongest indication of the link being evident in the correlations between 'teamwork' and performance. They conclude that a culture that fosters cooperation may be the most effective in the organisations included in their study. Similarly, Lee and Yu (2004) studied the link between organisational culture and a number of performance outcomes in various Singaporean companies. They found some evidence to suggest that the cultural strength of organisations was related to performance, but only in some of the cases they studied. In recent work looking at public sector organisations, Garnett *et al.* (2008) suggest that communication has an indirect role by acting as moderator or mediator of organisational culture's influence on performance. Specifically, they state (p.266) that 'communication acts as a metamechanism for shaping and imparting culture in mission-oriented organizational cultures, thereby influencing performance. In particular, task orientation, feedback, and upward communication have positive effects on perceived organizational performance in mission-oriented organizations but potentially negative effects on performance in rule-oriented cultures.'

However, in a review of studies purporting to have examined the culture–performance link, Wilderom *et al.* (2000) are not convinced that meaningful conclusions can be drawn from the evidence available. They argue that different measures of culture are used in different studies and that the operationalisation of performance is inconsistent and lacks validity. Certainly subjective measures of performance, for example as made by the chief executive of an organisation, in comparison to key competitors (e.g. see Chan *et al.* 2004) seem to invite bias. This is particularly problematic in respect of the links between strong cultures supposedly leading to effective performance. Wilderom *et al.* (2000) suggest that assessment of the culture gap, the difference between employees' preferred organisational practices and their perceptions of actual practices, is a more fruitful line of research, because of the inconsistency in the way that culture is defined.

Organisational culture and human resource management

Having spent some time so far in this chapter outlining and debating conceptual issues relating to culture and climate in organisations, this section of the chapter will seek to explore the impact of the interest in culture on 'people management' practices. Consistent with the trends within the people management literature generally, this chapter will consider human resource management to be the most contemporary, if not the most commonly used, general approach to the management of people in the workplace. As a number of commentators within the UK have noted, human resource management and organisational culture seem to be highly intertwined concepts. So, for example, Storey (1995) and Legge (1995) have articulated the centrality of organisational culture to the development and practice of human resource management. Storey (1995, p.8) suggests that managing culture change coincides so much with the movement towards HRM that they 'become one and the same project'.

Fundamental assumptions which reflect managerial perspectives on organisational culture are also central to the beliefs and assumptions of human resource management. As Storey (1995, p.6), observes, management does not merely seek compliance with rules and the implementation of procedures and systems as a way of controlling employee behaviour, but seeks to develop high levels of employee commitment through the management of culture.

Mabey and Salaman (1995) comment that some have also welcomed the recognition that understanding culture changes the emphasis from focusing purely on formal/rational aspects of the organisation, for example organisational structure, rules, procedures and technical processes. However, like Sackmann (1991), they feel that 'managerialist' perspectives on culture are simplistic and ignore the complexities of the anthropological concept from which it is derived. For example, Deal and Kennedy (1982) seem to equate culture within organisations to culture in societies, and assume that the same processes will occur.

Some researchers consider that culture cannot be controlled by management within the organisation, whereas others tend to believe that it is at least possible. We shall return to this discussion later in the chapter. Nevertheless, there has been something of a convergence of approach to researching and understanding culture from those practitioners/consultants and academics who do believe that there is the potential to manage organisational culture. As Barley *et al.* (1988) have noted, both groups are interested in identifying how culture can be used as a mechanism to enhance performance.

There have been extreme concerns expressed by some academics regarding this new approach to the management of employees. Whereas previous rational approaches overtly used rules, regulations and procedures as a way of ensuring behavioural compliance from employees, many see culture management as equally controlling but in a covert way. The difference is that culture management techniques focus much less on rational rather than emotive approaches to employee management. Therefore, the winning of 'hearts and minds' and the legitimacy of seeking to manipulate employee emotions has been questioned by writers such as Casey (1995), Keenoy and Anthony (1992) and Willmott (1993), highlighting the ethical dimension.

Recognising that there are different perspectives in respect of the ethics and practicalities of manipulating culture within work organisations, we shall now assume that there is at least the potential for management to manipulate culture and explore how this might be done.

CULTURE MANAGEMENT AND HRM PRACTICES

It would seem logical that the human resources (HR) function ought to be centrally involved in attempting to influence organisational culture; however, this is not necessarily so in all organisations. A good example where it was the case is American Express. Fairbairn (2005) has outlined the role taken by HR in culture change. Particularly interesting in this account is the recognition that culture change was not necessarily problem centred and focused on overcoming current deficiencies. The espoused approach was developmentally focused, seeking, in large part, to build on aspects of the culture which were considered positive. The CEO (p.81) 'believed that any change must reflect the realities and expectations of stakeholder groups, including employees . . . '.

Employees, through focus groups, were asked to envision what the organisation should be like in five years' time, and propose how it should get there. By using a consultative process that was not management imposed, it was recognised that leaders might actually be resistant to change, particularly as the organisation was performing successfully. This approach is rather different to management-imposed culture change.

In contrast, Alvesson and Karreman (2007) suggest that even where extensive HR systems and practices exist, they may not work as effectively, or rationally, as they purport to do. They studied an international management consultancy firm and found, for example, that despite the existence of systematised performance rating systems, structured selection processes etc., promotion decisions could still be subjective, politicised and biased. However, inside the organisation the prevailing beliefs were that excellent HR practices existed and the culture was one of objectivity and career progression based on performance criteria.

Various facets of HR activity might be used either to reinforce the existing culture within an organisation or to support management-initiated culture change efforts. We shall now consider what these might be.

Recruitment and selection

Traditionally, organisations have sought to match individuals' abilities to job requirements, commonly known as person–job (P–J) fit. More recently, research has focused on the fit between the person and the organisation (P–O), particularly in respect of the organisation's culture. In this sense the individual's abilities/competencies are considered less important than their attitudes/values and the match of these with the organisation's culture. This is an interesting development and implies that it may be easier to change/enhance employees' abilities rather than their attitudes or values. Some recent research (Adkins and Caldwell 2004) explores whether the match of the individual with the subculture or group (P–G fit) of the organisation in which they are located may be more important to factors such as job satisfaction. They found that there were differences between groups (subcultures), even in an organisation seeking to maintain a strong overall organisational culture. This matching of the individual's values with the organisation's culture can be assessed, for potential employees, during the selection process. However, it is also important for individuals to assess whether the organisation's culture matches their own preferences. Examples of how the management of culture has been used to attract and retain employees are shown in Box 10.3. For multinational organisations a key staffing decision is the mix of parent country national (PCN) employees and home country national (HCN) employees. A number of factors, including

Box 10.3: HRM in practice

Managing culture to attract staff

Madame Tussauds, which runs waxworks in various countries, as well as other visitor attractions, relies on seasonal labour for up to half its staffing, during peak periods. The company emphasises that it is a fun place to work as one of its mechanisms for (re)attracting staff. It uses beer and pizza evenings, Halloween balls and other events for staff to reinforce the culture it wishes to project (Arkin 2004).

A recent study by Braddy *et al.* (2006) indicates that websites dedicated to recruitment can be useful in influencing potential applicants' perceptions of the organisation's culture. Perceptions of diversity (photos of staff from various ethnic backgrounds) and innovation (comments about how highly valued it was by the organisation, and the importance of risk taking) were the culture dimensions most effectively communicated. The importance of a rewards culture was also communicated through reference to organisational policies regarding bonuses and other incentives for performance. Website design could also influence perceptions of attention to detail (required of employees) and professionalism. Explicit statements about organisational values and employee testimonials regarding their work experience in the organisation were also influential.

Research (Arnold *et al.* 2003) regarding recruitment and retention problems in the UK National Health Service (NHS) has also highlighted the importance of realistic job previews (Wanous 1989). Arnold *et al.* (2003) identified that some potential employees were put off by what they saw as unrealistic advertising and promotion campaigns which portrayed NHS work as rather more positive and attractive than candidates perceived it to be, and underplayed difficulties. Therefore, key cultural values that participants wished to see associated with the NHS, such as honesty and integrity, appeared to be undermined by the recruitment campaigns which were simultaneously emphasising the high degree of expertise and professionalism expected of its staff.

A study by Van Vianen (2000) assessed new employees' perceptions of the organisational culture and whether this fitted with their personal preferences. Where new employees had a fit between their preference in respect of concern for people and this was shared with their supervisor, this was positively related to the newcomers' organisational commitment and (lack of) turnover intentions. However, general perceptions of the organisational culture had little influence on new employees' affective outcomes; thus it was less important that newcomers perceived the organisational culture in the same way as their supervisor/peers than that the culture fitted with the newcomers' preferences regarding value congruence.

Rather than seeking to ensure fit between applicants and the existing culture, Williams *et al.* (1993) identify the use of selection as a way of contributing to culture change. An electricity organisation increased the number of sales staff by 63 per cent over five years as part of a desired move from a technical to a sales culture. Iles and Mabey (cited in Stewart and McGoldrick 1996) have identified British Airways' use of Egyptian cabin crew and incorporation of Egyptian 'culture' on the London–Cairo route. As they point out, this was done to attract more customers, not simply to introduce international diversification into the workforce. The evaluation by Iles and Mabey did not indicate complete success in either respect.

cultural considerations, can influence the balance adopted. See Torbiörn (2005) for a useful discussion of this. Research shows, e.g. Harzing (2000), that north American multinationals tend to employ a greater proportion of HCNs, and Japanese multinationals tend to employ a greater proportion of PCNs, with European firms using more PCNs than American firms but fewer than Japanese organisations.

Employee induction

A key opportunity for the organisation to influence employee values is during the early stages of their employment. Marchington and Wilkinson (2005) suggest that there is little evidence in mainstream human resource publications to indicate that induction is used as a way of imparting the organisation's culture, and seeking to influence new employees in that respect. However, Harrison (2000, p.248) suggests that dialogic learning comprises a major component of induction programmes and 'should help [new starters] to understand and adapt to the vision of the organisation and its implicit values and norms'.

Dundon *et al.* (2001) have identified that an (unnamed) consultancy organisation employs a full-time culture manager, part of whose role is to ensure that new employees fit in with, and are committed to, the prevailing culture.

Trice and Beyer (1993) refer to different rites and identify induction and basic training as what they term a rite of passage, e.g. into the organisation. As they note, the manifest purpose of a rite of passage such as induction is to 'facilitate transition of persons into social roles and statuses that are new for them' (1993, p.111).

The extensive socialisation literature has referred to the impact of the socialisation process on organisational newcomers. For example, Ashforth (2001) identifies that formalised collective socialisation, for example in induction programmes, can help reduce the anxiety of role/organisational entry for newcomers. Even if organisations commit considerable time and effort to the formalised socialisation process at the point of organisational entry, individuals will still, over time, be influenced by informal events which affect the newcomer's perspectives (for example, Ricks 1997). Gundry and Rousseau (1994) have identified that new organisational entrants come to understand their organisation's culture by decoding 'critical incidents'.

Therefore, unless the formalised institutional socialisation represented by induction programmes is reinforced by the activities and contacts newcomers encounter in day-to-day organisational life, it may not necessarily achieve the desired effect (from the organisation's perspective).

Training and development

A traditional personnel management approach to training and development would tend to focus individuals on learning job-specific skills and knowledge rather than on personal development or broader career issues. However, Williams *et al.* (1993) indicate this may be a necessary first step as part of a culture change effort. For example, they suggest that it will not be possible to develop a customer-oriented culture if customer contact staff do not have the appropriate skills to interact effectively with customers.

Lee (1996) proposes that learning and development activities can focus on different components of the individual. Some focus purely on the acquisition of knowledge ('head'), some focus on the development of skills ('hands'), whereas some focus on affective aspects of the self and their relationships with others ('heart'). Some activities seek to integrate all these components.

Williams *et al.* (1993) suggest that training focused on employee behaviour is likely to be necessary in seeking to change employee values and attitudes. Indeed, Kunda (1992) argues that explicit attempts to change values can lead to employees feeling manipulated or brainwashed and therefore becoming very cynical. Ogbonna and Wilkinson (1988) indicate that even behaviourally focused change efforts can lead to what they called resigned behavioural compliance. Hopfl *et al.* (1992) have followed British Airways' long-term programme of culture management and highlight the need for consistency of message and practice from the organisation if employees are to consider the message credible. Perhaps more significantly, they stress the differing reactions from individuals subjected to the same culture change process. Thus management cannot assume that all employees will respond in the way that management would wish. Similarly, Scheeres and Rhodes (2006) have identified that in-house training programmes which are explicitly designed to inculcate managerially desired culture are unlikely to succeed where, as one training programme participant put it: 'what management would say . . . with the core values and one thing and another, is at odds with how it really is on a day to day basis' (p.232).

In this study, where employees' work experience was not consistent with espoused core corporate values, they were not allowed to debate such issues during the course. They were required to get the 'correct' answers to confirm their intellectual understanding of (but not lived experience of) management-articulated values.

Caligiuri *et al.* (2005) provide a useful discussion of a range of issues associated with training and development in a multicultural workforce. For example, delivery methods may need to be adjusted to reflect national cultural preferences. Americans may enjoy debating issues face to face in a training course but Chinese employees would be more reticent to express their opinions. The content of training could cover a range of issues, such as foreign language acquisition, understanding host country cultural norms and leading multinational teams.

In terms of corporate-level organisational learning and transfer across nations, Hong *et al.* (2006) have highlighted the importance of cultural considerations. In a study of Japanese subsidiary companies operating in south China, they noted that corporate values had to be taken into account as well as technical knowledge components. The use of parent company socialisation processes, as well as open plan factory and office designs, facilitated cross-border transfer of organisational learning systems.

Communication and integration activities

Communication is considered by many managers to be a central component of culture management (Williams *et al.* 1993). Manipulation of artefacts and symbols, Schein's (1985) top or surface level of culture, is the focus here. For example, Unisys used publications and audio cassette magazines as a way of reinforcing key cultural values such as customer orientation. Trice and Beyer (1993) identify two forms of rite which organisations may use to communicate culture. The rite of enhancement, for example the use of company newsletters, team briefings and employee of the month award schemes, can serve a number of purposes. It could be to spread good news about the organisation; equally, it could focus on individuals, and provide public recognition for their accomplishments. At the same time this recognition of individual achievement is designed to communicate to others what is expected of them and act as a stimulus for effort and motivation.

The rite of integration again uses non-work activities as a way of influencing employees' emotions. For example, organised social events, e.g. barbecues, visits to bowling alleys, etc., can be used to try to foster a sense of binding employees to the social system, i.e. the organisation. This may be particularly the case where the organisation seeks to foster a high degree of teamworking and team commitment. Williams *et al.* (1993) identify the way that Marley tried to break down formal divisions between functions within the organisation through the use of inter-functional social activities.

More recently, Crumpacker and Crumpacker (2007) have highlighted the importance of an increasingly diverse workforce in terms of the age range of employees. Because of increasing life-spans and the pressure this puts on pension systems, some older employees are having to work beyond what were traditional retirement ages, e.g. age 65. This means there could be four generations represented in an organisation's workforce, potentially spanning up to a 60-year age range. Proponents of a generational understanding of the workforce, such as Zemke *et al.* (2000), argue that different generations hold different values, attitudes and lifestyle preferences. These influence employee perspectives on issues such as ethics, work–life balance, authority and leadership, and technology. Therefore, the organisation needs to consider whether it is desirable and feasible to develop a uniform/integrated culture or whether diversity, based on generational perspectives, is more relevant.

Cross-cultural integration

We mentioned earlier in the chapter Hofstede's (1980, 1991) work regarding the influence of national culture. Continuing research suggests that national culture continues to override, in many instances, the desire of parent companies to impose their preferred organisational culture and associated HRM practices. Miah and Bird (2007) found that national culture in countries in South Asia (India, Pakistan and Bangladesh) was more influential in shaping HRM styles and practices in Japanese subsidiary and joint-venture activity in those countries. Auotocratic rather than participative approaches were preferred.

However, Dong and Glaister (2007) have studied Chinese parent firms involved in international strategic alliances (ISAs). Where corporate and national cultural differences are considered particularly important in their potential effects on ISA outcomes, proactive culture management is adopted, and reduces perceptions of cultural differences between ISA partners. Some caution needs to be attached to these findings as research participants only came from the Chinese organisations.

As Froese *et al.* (2008) discuss, there are various complex factors to consider when cross-national acquisitions occur. The type of strategy adopted by the acquiring organisation (e.g. assimilation, separation etc.), the cultural distance between the two organisations in respect of their existing organisational and national cultures, the expectations of the acquired organisation's employees in respect of degree of change, and the influence of contextual factors such as the prevailing economic conditions all need to be taken into account. Froese *et al.* (2008) found that Korean employees in firms acquired by Western organisations were more accepting of, and satisfied with, market-oriented reforms, because they expected them and saw the economic necessity of them in a Korean economy that was struggling. However, changes towards individualism which clashed with Confucian values were not well received.

Payment/rewards systems

Armstrong (1999) suggests that the organisation's remuneration policy is one part of its human resource strategy and the different components of that HR strategy need to be complementary and not contradict each other. While reward strategy impacts on various HR activities, for example recruiting, retaining and motivating staff, Armstrong emphasises that it can also be used as a way of communicating organisational values. Williams *et al.* (1993) stress that consistency is important if the organisation is not to send mixed messages to employees regarding management's preferred cultural values. For example, management may decide to reinforce the need for teamworking rather than individual 'stars'. However, if individually based performance-related pay, rather than team-based pay, is used, employee behaviour is likely to respond to the greatest potential for financial reward rather than consistency with management-espoused cultural values. Therefore, it is important for organisations to think through how the different components of HR strategy fit together and reinforce each other.

In multinational organisations the use of expatriate managers can be considerably more expensive than employing local managers. For example, Chen *et al.* (2002) have identified that employing expatriates in China can mean that they are paid up to 50 times more than local staff. However, Bonache and Fernandez (2005) note a number of reasons, including cultural ones, why the organisation may decide to incur these extra costs, for example if host country company-specific knowledge is required, possibly combined with the need to implement a global, rather than local, strategy (see also Chapter 11).

Redundancies

When an organisation is seeking to achieve culture change it may find that certain individuals or groups of staff are particularly resistant to the proposed new culture. Williams *et al.* (1993) have noted the use by various organisations of redundancy programmes as a way of reducing resistance to culture change efforts (see also Chapter 16). Similarly, after a merger, some individuals in the newly formed Unisys felt unable to be committed to the new organisation after long years of service with one of the merged organisations. In both instances, the importance of handling redundancy in a sensitive way is emphasised. More dramatically, Trice and Beyer (1993) talk about rites of degradation, the third example of which is the rite of removal. This is where an individual, for example the chief executive/managing director, or a group of people, e.g. the senior management team, are seen to be identified with failures within the organisation. Because of this it is considered appropriate to remove them from the organisation in order to move forward and introduce the required change. This is consistent with numerous models (see 'Leadership' section, below) where the role of leadership is considered crucial to cultural change. As Trice and Beyer (1993, p.115) note, the use of removal can 'can be dysfunctional if the person degraded did not contribute to the problems and if the degradation becomes a substitute for doing something more effective to deal with the problems'.

Performance management/appraisal

Stiles *et al.* (1997) undertook a study of performance management and its impact on perceptions of values. This study occurred in a distribution company, a telecommunications company and a bank, all of which had recently introduced values statements. While managers were aware of the corporate values being espoused by their organisations, they still saw that their short-term demands were primarily focused around financial targets and the need to achieve other organisational objectives. In addition, the setting of objectives was imposed from senior management without any negotiation. Perceptions were also influenced by the fact that organisational downsizing left managers in doubt whether even achievement of their objectives would be enough to facilitate career progression or, at worst, even job security.

We have already commented on the difficulty of identifying any relationship between culture and organisational-level performance. Recent research in the UK by Ogbonna and Harris (2000) suggests that cultures which are externally oriented incline towards risk taking and readiness to meet new challenges and tend to be more strongly associated with organisational performance (which was operationalised using a range of measures) than cultures that are predominantly internally focused. However, as with other studies this work was cross-sectional and correlational and therefore it is difficult to identify whether culture was actually a cause of performance.

Williams (2002) suggests that the performance management process might be seen as a way of developing, at least in part, a 'performance culture'. However, certain advocates of performance management, e.g. Armstrong (1994), tend to associate performance management with a set of values reflecting openness, trust, employee participation, etc. in the performance management process. In contrast, a performance culture may not place any emphasis on these things and simply focus on increasing employee productivity, etc.

For example, Fletcher and Williams (1992) identified that an organisation's performance culture placed particular emphasis on 'bottom line' results. Employees felt that fear was the driving force underpinning the performance culture rather than participation and openness.

In purely performance terms, many organisations may only be concerned with seeking to change employee behaviour rather than to change the deeper levels of cultural values and assumptions. Indeed Williams *et al.* (1993) recognised that behaviour change seems to be the central focus of many culture change programmes.

Leadership

In a useful analysis and evaluation of different models of culture change, Brown (1998) identifies the importance of leadership. The importance of leaders, particularly at the top of the organisation, as figureheads of, and role models for, preferred culture and values is seen as crucial. A new leader is often associated with a new approach to culture. We referred earlier to the compulsory removal of leaders as a signal to employees of a state of change. Leaders at different levels in the organisation have influence and control over various organisational rites (Trice and Beyer 1993). We have referred already to some of these rites. The rite of enhancement is a clear and generally public activity that enhances the status of an individual. Mechanisms that may be used here include employee of the month award schemes, articles in company newsletters and commendations at team briefings.

Schein (1992) stresses the roles that leaders at all organisational levels have to play, and that this will vary depending upon the organisation's stage of development and require different types of culture management at different stages. He also stresses that different strategic issues lead to a focus on different cultural dimensions.

Research conducted in China by Tsui *et al.* (2006) identifies interesting variations on leader behaviour and its interaction with organisational culture. Leaders described as 'performance builders' tended to be young, with management qualifications. Their focus was primarily on external adaptation of the organisation to its environment. They gave little attention to internal processes to develop/reinforce values, and their organisations had relatively weak cultures. In contrast, 'institution builders' focused strongly on internal processes/systems to reinforce values but were much less charismatic as leaders. They also relied on the support of other managers to reinforce culture. These organisations had stronger cultures, and used human resource systems, such as selection, reward and training, to reinforce and sustain culture.

Employee relations

While much of the HRM approach tends to downplay the role of trade unions and formal mechanisms for employee representation, Williams *et al.* (1993) indicate that some organisations considered formal trade union involvement and support as essential. For example, Toshiba introduced a single union agreement with the EETPU, and employee representation on the 'company advisory board' was designed to achieve greater employee understanding of, and commitment to, organisational goals and values. Organisations may also use other mechanisms to foster involvement from employees. Employee suggestion schemes, quality circles and/or project groups can all be used as a way of indicating to employees that they have a voice and their ideas are valuable. However, some authors have been critical of some of these mechanisms in the way that they have excluded formal employee representation and downgraded the role of trade unions. For example, Keenoy and Anthony (1992) have argued that HRM has often been used as a way of conducting anti-unionist policies. Indeed, they and others, for example Willmott (1993), see culture management as a way of increasing management control rather than empowering employees.

We have referred to a range of HRM practices that may be utilised as part of culture management efforts; however, as Williams *et al.* have indicated:

> It should not be assumed that culture can be changed simply by the introduction of, say, a new appraisal system, new reward practices or new methods of training. All of these are likely to have an effect on culture and each of these could be a crucial element of a culture change programme. In isolation though these personnel mechanisms are likely to be subordinated to the existing culture. (1993, p.28)

Is culture change feasible?

There is considerable scepticism regarding the feasibility of management proactively changing organisational culture, particularly at the deep fundamental levels. For example, Meek (1982) suggests that those who propose that culture change is feasible do not recognise that power differentials exist within organisations, that subcultures exist and that ultimately, in seeking to change culture, management is seeking to control employees. For example, within the healthcare sector Morgan and Ogbonna (2008) have identified that doctors and nurses (subcultures) may agree about certain core values of the National Health Service, but have different views about other issues. These are based on power, degree of expertise, desire for professional status and a range of other factors. Ogbonna (1992) suggests that the espoused aim of many culture change programmes, to enhance employee commitment, is not achieved. In many senses change is focused purely on employee behaviours and achieved through compliance rather than the commitment which is sought. Sackmann (1991) suggests that cultures are highly complex, dynamic systems with individual and group variability within them. Therefore, they are not really amenable to direct management. For some writers, attempts at culture management are ethically unacceptable. For example, Willmott (1993, p.517), argues that managers may like the idea of greater control over employees by using culture management to 'colonise the affective domain . . . promoting employee commitment to a monolithic structure of feeling and thought'. As he argues, the control has been transferred from managers to employees through high levels of self-monitoring and self-management. At one level employees are empowered to manage their own work, but in effect they have simply incorporated the organisation's desire for high standards of performance and behaviour and are only empowered to do what the organisation wants them to do. Thompson and McHugh (2002) reinforce this idea, suggesting that by managing the meanings and values of employees, management seeks to manipulate employees' internalised sources of control and commitment.

Despite the cynicism about both the ethics of attempting, as well as the feasibility of achieving, culture change, some writers have argued that culture change is feasible albeit with considerable difficulty. For example, Pettigrew (1990) has, on the basis of considerable research, proposed a number of factors for consideration in seeking to undertake culture change. He does note that this will be an arduous process and is more likely to affect surface levels of culture rather than core assumptions.

Harris and Ogbonna (1998) summarise the differing views on the feasibility of changing culture by suggesting three different perspectives: (a) culture can be managed, (b) culture cannot be managed, and (c) culture can be manipulated but only under certain conditions. They also stress that little research effort has been directed at understanding employee reactions to managerial culture change attempts. Therefore they conducted an empirical study in two contexts, one food and one clothing company in the British retail sector. They identified that employees could respond in a range of ways and that two key determinants seemed to be at play. One was willingness to change and the second was the existing strength of the particular subculture (for example, division of the organisation). Responses could range from active rejection through to active acceptance. Particularly interesting responses were reinvention and reinterpretation. Reinvention occurs where the attributes of the existing culture are recycled so that superficially, at least, they appear to be in line with the new culture being espoused by management. Reinterpretation occurs where employee values and behaviour are modified to some extent but in a way which is consistent with both the existing culture and the desired culture. While there appears to be some adoption of the espoused culture, this is filtered through the understanding of the existing culture and in that sense is not necessarily a predictable response. As we commented earlier, individuals can and do respond to culture change efforts in widely different ways. As Harris and Ogbonna (1998) note, there can be a range of responses between outright acceptance and rejection. This unpredictability of response makes culture change difficult to manage. Therefore Harris and Ogbonna suggest that attempts at culture change should not seek radical and transformational change but work on an incremental basis.

Conclusion

Based on the evidence reviewed in this chapter, what can we say about organisational culture? First, drawing on the vast number of definitions and classification systems, we can describe organisational culture as a phenomenon that involves beliefs, values and behaviours, exists at a variety of different levels, and manifests itself in a wide range of artefacts within any particular organisation. It is also apparent that culture is difficult to assess directly, given the varying data collection methods and the multi-level nature of the construct, but it is closely related to the concept of climate, which may be more easily assessed. Furthermore, culture might provide a useful description of organisational environments, which facilitate their comprehension, interpretation, acceptance and control, and might, but only might, help explain their success in terms of performance. Finally, if organisational culture is to be of use to managers and organisations, they must be able to adapt and change their culture when necessary.

It is clear from the research discussed in this chapter, however, that while culture change and the management of it by the organisation may appear feasible, there are practical problems associated with it. A number of such issues can be identified:

■   At what level is culture change occurring – is it at the artefacts level or at the level of fundamental assumptions?

■   Even if behaviour is changed, is this really culture change? If employee values and assumptions have not changed, does this really matter, if management is primarily interested in employees demonstrating appropriate behaviours?

■   Do organisations have unitary cultures, and, if so, is it feasible to change the culture of the whole organisation at once?

■   If it is accepted that organisations comprise subcultures, are strategies for culture change sophisticated enough to recognise the differential approaches required?

Martin (1992, 2002) has suggested that three differing perspectives can be adopted in seeking to understand culture and therefore interpret ways to approach culture change and its effectiveness. The integration perspective is most typical of management in that it assumes an organisation-wide consensus within the organisation and that consistency is feasible. The differentiation perspective assumes that there are likely to be subcultures within the organisation which will be inconsistent in their responses to culture change efforts. The fragmentation perspective assumes that there is such a multiplicity of views with little or no consensus that managing culture will be immensely complex. However, as Rodrigues (2006) points out, the same organisation may experience each of these perspectives at different points in time.

Understanding the culture of an organisation

John Loan-Clarke and Alistair Cheyne

Think about an organisation you know. This could be one you have worked in permanently (now or in the past), temporarily (e.g. vacation work) or during an industrial placement. Consider the following two questions about that organisation:

1. What do you consider the organisation's culture to be?

    Either use your own words to describe this or relate your understanding of the culture to one of the models we have covered in this chapter, e.g. Harrison, Deal and Kennedy, etc.

2. Does this culture apply equally across the whole of the organisation or just to a certain part(s) of it?

    You will initially need to think through these ideas on your own. Make some brief notes to help organise your thoughts. Having done this, exchange your ideas with others in a group.

Levels of culture

John Loan-Clarke and Alistair Cheyne

Various models of culture identify that it comprises a number of levels. For example, Schein's (1985) model comprises three. Choose one of these models and do the following:

Explain what each of the three levels means and what information would be needed to understand the culture at that level.

Culture and climate issues within a healthcare Trust

John Loan-Clarke and Alistair Cheyne

This case study organisation is an NHS community healthcare Trust (CHT) in England. It comprises two community hospitals and a number of health centres and clinics across a dispersed geographical region. Like all NHS Trusts in the UK over recent years, the organisation had been forced to react to a number of external pressures for change brought about by governmental reforms at a national level. The chief executive of the Trust, however, was proud to tell us that, despite the pressures and cuts in funding, no compulsory redundancies had been entailed and that he had fought hard behind the scenes to maintain funding and protect jobs. The Trust had recently achieved some of the best Patients Charter results in the region. This is an initiative introduced by the UK government which publicly announces the results of quantitative measures of Trust 'success' using criteria such as the length of time spent waiting for a consultation or operation and the numbers of patients

▶

seen. The Trust had also been awarded Investors in People status. This is another national initiative, which is granted to organisations which are able to demonstrate a high level of investment in their employees. Criteria used to judge the award include evidence of training and effective communication systems. In addition, two communications initiatives had recently been introduced by management: a monthly team briefing and a Trust newsletter. These were intended to help employees understand the broad implications of change for the Trust and, more specifically, to reassure staff about the relatively strong financial position of the Trust and the ongoing policy of no compulsory redundancies.

The Trust management team originally commissioned research to assess employees' reactions to these communication initiatives and to provide feedback to management regarding employees' overall perceptions of working for the Trust. A second major management consideration was the impending introduction of a computerised information system for healthcare professionals working in the community, for example district nurses. Management was keen to assess the impact of the introduction of this system on staff work practices and attitudes, and wished to establish a benchmark for doing this, in its desire to introduce what it termed an 'information-led culture'.

As Cavanagh (1996) has noted, the impact of UK NHS reforms has led to a need to investigate and possibly change the culture of UK healthcare organisations, and management at the CHT was keen to gather information from staff because of this.

Activity

Assume you have been commissioned by the management team at the CHT to assess reactions to the communication and information change initiatives. They are also interested in gathering data regarding employees' overall perceptions of working for the Trust.

Outline how you would go about conducting this assignment.

1. What sort of questions would you ask and why?
2. Who would you seek to gather information from and why?
3. What data collection and analysis methods would you use and why?
4. How and to whom would you report back your findings?

Managing culture at British Airways

Irena Grugulis and Adrian Wilkinson

The British Airways story

Even by the standards of modern management myths the British Airways transformation is impressive. At the end of the 1970s and the start of the 1980s BA was performing disastrously against almost every indicator. Its fleet was old, which meant journeys were uncomfortable and contributed significantly to the airline's record for unpunctuality; its productivity was considerably below that of its main overseas competitors; it was beset by industrial disputes; and it was recording substantial financial losses (£140 million or some £200 a minute in 1981). Staff discontent was more than matched by customer dissatisfaction and in 1980 a survey by the International Airline Passengers' Association put BA at the top of a list of airlines to be avoided at all costs. By the mid-1990s this picture was reversed. Not only had BA become the world's most profitable carrier, it was also voted the company that most

▶

graduates would like to work for and, in the year 2000, another survey declared it the second most admired company in Europe (Corke 1986; Warhurst 1995; Blyton and Turnbull 1998; *Financial Times* 9 July 1997; *Financial Times* 18 March 2000).

Much of the management literature attributes this turnaround to BA's own cultural change which remodelled staff attitudes and set customer care as the primary focus of activity. As Doyle (1999, p. 20) noted:

In the 80s BA had been transformed from a disastrous loss-making state enterprise – the British Rail of the sky – into the world's largest and most profitable international airline. It was a triumph for management, showing that Britain could produce world-class companies that could beat the best of the competition. Its success was the result of the process and strategy that management introduced. The process focused on creating a vision that would inspire the BA staff and gain their enthusiastic commitment.

It is certainly true that a great deal of effort and energy went into shaping BA's culture. At the heart of this was the 'Putting People First' (PPF) training programme launched by Colin Marshall, the company's new chief executive, in 1983. Originally intended for staff who had direct contact with customers it was, in fact, attended by all 40,000 employees by 1986 and it aimed to revolutionise their attitudes. In a direct challenge to the hierarchical and militaristic culture which existed in BA at the time, staff were instructed not to attend in uniform and, once on the course, put into cross-functional and cross-grade groups. Attendees were encouraged to take a more positive attitude to themselves, taught how to set personal goals and cope with stress, and instructed in confidence building and 'getting what they wanted out of life'. Lapel badges inscribed with the motto 'We're putting people first' provided a visible reminder of the course's message.

The approach was self-conciously 'indoctrinative' (Bate 1994, p.195). As Colin Marshall said

We . . . have to design our people and their service attitude just as we design an aircraft seat, an in-flight entertainment programme or an airport lounge *to meet the needs and preferences of our customers.* (cited in Barsoux and Manzoni 1997, p.14: emphasis added)

But the most impressive aspect of BA's cultural change was not so much the sophistication of the PPF programme itself, nor the commitment of executive time, but the extent to which other employment policies and practices were changed to fit the 'new' culture and the continued emphasis on these practices and programmes throughout the 1980s and 1990s. Three-quarters of the 100 Customer First teams, formed to propagate the message of PPF, survived into the 1990s. Not only were team briefings and teamworking introduced but these were developed and refined, with TQM, autonomous teamworking and multi-skilling introduced in many areas. Direct contact with all staff was considered so important that 'down route' briefings were developed to ensure that mobile and isolated staff were not neglected, and in 1996 BA became the first company to make daily TV broadcasts to its staff (Colling 1995).

The way cabin crew were rostered was also changed. 'Families' of staff were created to work the same shift patterns. These were intended to provide mutual support, make cabin crew feel happier about their work environments and, as a result, facilitate the production of emotional labour (Barsoux and Manzoni 1997). A new role of 'passenger group coordinator' was introduced and staff appointed based entirely on personal qualities. The importance of emotional processes was also reflected in the new appraisal and reward systems such that work was judged on the way in which it was performed as well as against harder targets (Georgiades and Macdonnell 1998; Höpfl 1993). Managerial bonuses could be as much as 20 per cent of salary and were calculated on a straight 50:50 split between exhibiting

▶

Table 10.1 The four-factor menu of practices used in British Airways in 1984–85

The menu of practices	
FACTOR I CLARITY AND HELPFULNESS Establishing clear, specific objectives for subordinates	*FACTOR II* PROMOTING ACHIEVEMENT Emphasising and demonstrating commitment to achieving goals
Helping subordinates to understand how their jobs contribute to the overall performance of the organisation	Giving subordinates feedback on how they are doing
Clearly defining standards of excellence required for job performance	Communicating your views to others honestly and directly about their performance
Providing help, training and guidance for subordinates	Recognising people more often than criticising them
Giving subordinates a clear-cut decision when they need one	Recognising subordinates for innovation and calculated risk taking
FACTOR III INFLUENCING THROUGH PERSONAL EXCELLENCE AND TEAMWORKING Knowing and being able to explain to others the mission of the organisation and how it relates their jobs	*FACTOR IV* CARE AND TRUST Behaving in a way that leads others to trust you
Communicating high personal standards informally through appearance and dedication	Building warm, friendly relationships
Noticing and showing appreciation for extra effort	Paying close attention to what people are saying
Sharing power in the interest of achieving overall organisation objectives	Responding non-defensively when others disagree with your views
Being willing to make tough decisions in implementing corporate strategy	Making sure that there is a frank and open exchange at work group meetings

Source: [Reproduced with permission.] From *Leadership for Competitive Advantage* by Georgiades N. and Macdonnell R., 1998, p.174. Copyright © John Wiley and Sons Ltd.

desired behaviours and achieving quantitative goals. 'Awards for Excellence' and an 'Employee Brainwaves' programme encouraged staff input. The personnel department was renamed 'human resources' with many decisions devolved to line managers and, in the first few years of the programme at least, a commitment was made to job security.

Closely following these developments, a 'Managing People First' programme targeted managerial employees and aimed to bring their behaviours into line with a list developed by two consultancy firms (see Table 10.1).

Other courses were developed to maintain the momentum created by 'Putting People First' and 'Managing People First'. These included 'Winning for Customers', 'A Day in the Life', 'To Be the Best', 'Leading in a Service Business' and 'Leadership 2000' and, while each was different, they all shared a focus on shaping staff emotions. The most dramatic form of this was probably the 'love bath' exercise in one of the early courses in which delegates took it in turns to sit in the centre of a circle while their colleagues complimented them (see Höpfl 1993). Nearly 20 years after the launch of PPF, BA managers attending a training course were still being told about understanding themselves and taking responsibility: 'understanding self is our starting point . . . That means that to make a change within the airline we need to start with you – what can *you* do differently'. In 1995, Bob Ayling, having newly taken over

▶

from Colin Marshall as chief executive, continued this active management of company cul-ture and said of his staff: 'I want them to feel inspired, I want them to feel optimistic, I want them to feel that this is a good place to be' ('Dangerous Company', BBC2 April 2000).

Such substantive change certainly seems to justify the plaudits heaped on it. But, as an account, it suffers from a number of flaws. Most significantly, as Anthony (1994) notes, together with other presentations of culture change it neglects structure. Yet the exis-tence of cultural factors does not negate more material ones and there were certainly structural reasons for BA's success. Colin Marshall's emphasis on putting people first and caring for one another had been preceded by a rule of fear. BA's first response to its prob-lems had been a massive series of redundancies, the largest in British history at the time, with staff numbers reduced by 40 per cent between 1981 and 1983 (albeit with generous severance).

More fundamentally, the company was well provided with slots in Britain's prestigious Heathrow airport and faced little competition on many of the routes that it served. European markets were still tightly regulated and market share often depended on negotiation skills rather than competitive success. In 1987, just before privatisation, BA controlled some 60 per cent of the UK domestic market and experienced competition on only 9 per cent of routes into and out of the UK (Monopolies and Mergers Commission 1987). Post privatisa-tion its position was actually strengthened when it gained a 75 per cent share of domestic routes (Colling 1995). Moreover, BA built up a series of alliances and mergers to consolidate this position.

While staff numbers were being drastically cut, the infrastructure was dramatically improved. The fact that new uniforms were provided is well covered in the human resource and marketing literature. Less commonly noted is that BA invested in control systems, terminal facilities and aircraft. Between 1980 and 1985 BA replaced over half its fleet (Colling 1995). Computer reservations were introduced, a series of hub and spoke routes through first Heathrow and then Gatwick networked flights, and selectively focused competitive pricing served to limit what little competition the airline faced (Blyton and Turnbull 1996). Nor was this the only strategy deployed against competitors. In 1993 BA used shared booking information to persuade Virgin customers to transfer to BA, informing them (incorrectly) that Virgin flights were no longer available. The subsequent court case fined BA £610,000 damages and £3 million costs. It raised questions about the extent of knowledge and involvement of Lord King, the chairman, Sir Colin Marshall, the chief executive, and Bob Ayling, the head of marketing, as well as criticising the impact of the BA culture itself.

Not only can much of the BA turnaround be attributed to structural factors, but also the extent of the company's cultural transformation itself is open to question. While cultural change interventions seek to influence the thoughts, values, attitudes and norms of others, employees are not cultural dupes. Cooperation may reflect ambition or pride in work as much as (or instead of) a belief in the organisation itself. Despite the claims of the prescrip-tive literature, the existence of 'culture management' does not ensure either that employees trust management, or that management trusts employees. So, in BA, 'new' management practices varied in the extent that they were introduced in departments and conflict between employees and management did not cease.

Nor was the much-vaunted job security quite as robust as it seemed. Alliances, mergers and franchising agreements with other airlines already supported what was, in effect, a 'tiered' system of terms and conditions, with employees based at Heathrow privileged over those in the regional airports. This emphasis on part-time, seasonal and subcontracted work was extended to most aspects of BA's operations. Its engine overhaul plant was sold off to GEC, data processing work was moved to Bombay, and job security for existing staff questioned (Colling 1995; Warhurst 1995; Blyton and Turnbull 1996). And all this at a time when BA was making record profits.

▶

In short, BA, while putting a great deal of effort into encouraging certain behaviours from staff, did not base its employment policies and practices around the new culture in the way that many accounts suggest. Their array of human resource management techniques was certainly impressive but not everyone benefited from them and those employed in partner, associate, merged or taken-over firms often experienced very different terms and conditions to the 'core' BA staff.

Staff reactions to 'culture change' included enthusiasm and acceptance but also doubt, concern, opposition and open cynicism. Such individual reactions were mirrored by the collective representations and the persistence of disputes even at the height of the 'cultural success'.

The 1997 dispute

By the end of the 1990s many of the structural factors that had provided the basis for the company's success were under threat. The emergence of low-cost carriers such as easyJet and Ryanair were undercutting BA's prices and, elsewhere, alliances between rivals Lufthansa and United Airlines ensured that cross-national traffic would be less likely to transfer to BA. The company's hold on Heathrow was also loosening under double pressure from Europe and the USA. In response, Ayling claimed that BA needed a second revolution. BA sought its own alliance with a different US carrier, American Airlines, as well as proposing £1 billion of cost savings from within the organisation, with the aim of doubling profits by the year 2000. Much of this was to come from staff savings, including 5,000 voluntary redundancies, with staff to be replaced by newly hired employees on lower pay (Blyton and Turnbull 1998). In addition, BA established links with a charter airline called Flying Colours, intending to continue its policy of outsourcing to other operators.

This policy of reducing labour costs was also extended to 'core' BA staff. In early 1997, BA attempted to change the structure of payments to cabin crew. It was proposed that the existing employees would be 'bought out' of their series of allowances (petrol, overnight stay, etc.) by receiving a higher basic wage. BA offered a three-year guarantee that no crew member would earn less under the new system but nothing beyond that, and it was clear to cabin crew staff that the measure was launched with the explicit aim of saving money. When these negotiations failed, one union, the TGWU, threatened strike action (Cabin Crew 89, a small breakaway union, had already accepted management's offer). Despite 14 years of espoused policy of caring for one another and putting people first, the tactics deployed by BA's management were described by two such different sources as the TUC and *The Economist* as bullying (*The Economist,* 27 July 1997; Taylor 1998). Members of the cabin crew were warned not to strike and BA managers were instructed to tell discontented staff that anyone taking industrial action would be summarily sacked, then sued for damages. Any who simply stayed away would face disciplinary action, be denied promotion and lose both pension rights and staff discounts on flights for three years. BA were also reported to be filming pickets.

The subsequent strike ballot had an 80 per cent turnout, with 73 per cent of employees voting in favour of strike action. The TGWU called a series of 72-hour strikes, with the first action scheduled for 9 July 1997. In response, temporary staff and an alternative workforce of 'volunteer managers' were given training to perform the key tasks of the ground handling staff and BA threatened to take legal action over claimed discrepancies in the ballot. On the eve of the first day of action airline cabin crew were telephoned at home and warned that 'they had a duty to cooperate with their employer'.

These managerial actions certainly influenced the impact of the strike. On the first scheduled day of action fewer than 300 workers declared themselves officially on strike but more than 2,000 called in sick. The company's threats and 'replacement workers' notwithstanding, more than 70 per cent of flights from Heathrow were cancelled. It seemed that

▶

BA's macho approach had ensured only that collective action took the form of collective illness.

Ironically this 'mass sickie' served to make things worse for BA. Not only did the pre-strike ballots (conducted to comply with legislation designed to discourage union activities) compound the effects of the strike by providing customers with advance notice of it; but also those employees who had called in sick tended to stay away longer than the official 72-hour strike. BA insisted that sick employees provide a doctor's note within 48 hours instead of the normal seven days but many employees still stayed off for the full two weeks that their sick notes allowed and, throughout this period, services were cancelled and passengers turned away. The strike was costly. Airline seats are a particularly perishable form of consumer good and aircraft scheduling is easily disrupted. When Bill Morris, the General Secretary of the TGWU, announced that he had written to Bob Ayling, suggesting that they resume negotiations, Ayling agreed before even receiving the letter.

The TGWU promised to save £42 million over three years. Catering was sold off but existing staff kept earnings and BA staff discounts, while sanctions against strikers were withdrawn and the TGWU increased its membership by 50 per cent to over 10,000. BA's management fared less well, despite Bob Ayling's claim that this agreement marked a 'new beginning and spirit of a cooperation'. The gulf between the managerial rhetoric on culture and official actions during the strike had a predictable effect on employee morale. One undercover employee publication, aptly named *Chaos,* advised on ways of maximising payments by delaying aircraft. These included throwing duvet feathers into the engine, superglueing down the toilet seat and poisoning the pilot: 'a particularly obnoxious captain can be made to suffer all the symptoms of violent food poisoning by emptying eye drops from the aircraft medical kit into his salad or drink'.

Moreover, the agreement itself fostered further dissent. By the end of 1997, 4,000 staff had left, but 4,500 more were recruited, including 2,000 in 1998. By the terms of the agreement, these new staff were employed on different contracts to existing employees. As a result, cabin crew working the same shifts on the same aircraft were (increasingly) on different payscales. The impact of this on both labour relations and BA's much-prized teamworking was problematic and problems were fuelled by suggestions that staff on new contracts were favoured by BA in promotion to purser (first-line manager).

Bob Ayling attempted to salvage the situation by placing more emphasis on managing the company's culture. Following Colin Marshall, he addressed staff training sessions and held question and answer forums with groups of employees. This time there were few positive reactions. The strike cost BA £125 million; morale never entirely recovered and profits suffered. Between 1998 and 1999 they fell by 61 per cent and in 2000 British Airways announced losses of £244 million on its main business. While gains from disposals succeeded in keeping the company out of the red, this was its worst performance (and first loss) since privatisation. The new logo Bob Ayling had launched (at great expense) during the 1997 dispute was unpopular and had to be withdrawn. These failures so coloured the public perception of the chief executive that even his attempts to refocus BA on to profitable routes and introduce a new seat for business class, long-haul passengers were not entirely welcomed. On 10 March 2000, Bob Ayling resigned as chief executive.

Source: Adapted from Grugulis and Wilkinson 2002

Questions

1. Explain employee reactions to culture change initiatives in this case.
2. What lessons can managers learn from this case about managing culture?

▶

Bibliography

*Adkins, B. and Caldwell, D. (2004) 'Firm or subgroup culture: where does fitting in matter most?', *Journal of Organizational Behavior,* Vol.25, No.8, pp.969–78.

Alvesson M. and Karreman D., (2007) 'Unraveling HRM: identity, ceremony, and control in a management consulting firm', *Organization Science,* Vol.18, No.4, pp.711–23.

Anderson, M., Embrey, D., Hodgkinson, C., Hunt, P., Kinchin, B, Morris, P. and Rose, M. (2003) 'The human factors implications for flight safety of recent developments in the airline indistry' *Flight Safety Digest,* Vol.22, No.3–4, pp.1–77.

Anthony, P.D. (1994) *Managing Culture,* Buckingham: Open University Press.

Arkin, A. (2004) 'Wax works', *People Management,* 25 November, pp.34–7.

Armstrong, M. (1994) *Performance Management,* London: Kogan Page.

Armstrong, M. (1999) *Employee Reward* (2nd edn), London: Chartered Institute of Personnel and Development.

Arnold, J., Loan-Clarke, J., Coombs, C., Park, J., Wilkinson, A. and Preston, D. (2003) *Looking Good? The Attractiveness of the NHS as an Employer to Potential Nursing and Allied Health Profession Staff,* Loughborough: Loughborough University.

Ashforth, B.E. (1985) 'Climate formation: issues and extensions', *Academy of Management Review,* Vol.4, pp.837–47.

Ashforth, B.E. (2001) *Role Transitions in Organizational Life,* Mahwah, NJ: Lawrence Erlbaum.

Balthazard, P.A., Cooke, R.A. and Potter, R.E. (2006) 'Dysfunctional culture, dysfunctional organization: capturing the behavioral norms that form organizational culture and drive performance', *Journal of Managerial Psychology,* Vol.21, No.8, pp.709–32.

Barley, S., Meyer, G. and Gash, D. (1988) 'Cultures of culture: academics, practitioners and the pragmatics of normative control', *Administrative Science Quarterly,* Vol.33, No.1, pp.24–60.

Barrett, S. and McMahon, L. (1990) 'Public management in uncertainty: a micro-political perspective of the health service in the United Kingdom', *Policy and Politics,* Vol.18, No.4, pp.257–68.

Barsoux, J.-L. and Manzoni, J.-F. (1997) *Becoming the World's Favourite Airline: British Airways 1980–1993,* Bedford: European Case Clearing House.

Bate, P. (1994) *Strategies for Cultural Change,* London: Butterworth Heinemann.

Becker, H.S. and Geer, B. (1970) 'Participant observation and interviewing: a comparison', in W. Filstead (ed.) *Qualitative Methodology,* Chicago, IL: Rand McNally, pp.133–42.

Blyton, P. and Turnbull, P. (1996) 'Confusing convergence: industrial relations in the European airline industry: a comment on Warhurst', *European Journal of Industrial Relations,* Vol.2, No.1, pp.7–20.

Blyton, P. and Turnbull, P. (1998) *The Dynamics of Employee Relations* (2nd edn), London: Macmillan.

Bonache J. and Fernandez Z. (2005), 'International compensation costs and benefits of international assignments', in H. Scullion and M. Linehan (eds) *International Human Resource Management,* Basingstoke: Palgrave.

Bowers, D. and Seashore, S. (1966) 'Predicting organizational effectiveness with a four-factor theory of leadership', *Administrative Science Quarterly,* Vol.11, pp.238–63.

Braddy, P.W., Meade, A.W., and Kroustalis, C.M. (2006) 'Organizational recruitment website effects on viewers' perceptions of organizational culture', *Journal of Business and Psychology,* Vol.20, No.4, pp.525–43.

Bright, K. and Cooper, C.L. (1993) 'Organizational culture and the management of quality,' *Journal of Management Psychology,* Vol.8, No.6, pp.21–27.

*Brown, A. (1998) *Organisational Culture* (2nd edn), London: Financial Times/Pitman.

Caligiuiri P., Lazarova M. and Tarique I. (2005) 'Training, learning and development in multinational organizations', in H. Scullion and M. Linehan (eds) *International Human Resource Management,* Basingstoke: Palgrave.

Casey, C. (1995) *Work, Self and Society: After Industrialization,* London: Routledge.

Cavanagh S.J. (1996) 'Mergers and acquisitions: some implications of cultural change', *Journal of Nursing Management,* Vol.4, pp.45–50.

Chan, L.L.M., Shaffer, M.A. and Snape, E. (2004) 'In search of sustained competitive advantage: the impact of organizational culture, competitive strategy and human resource management practices on firm performance', *International Journal of Human Resource Management*, Vol.15, No.1, pp.17–35.

Chen, C.C., Choi, J. and Chi, S.C. (2002) 'Making justice sense of local-expatriate compensation disparity: mitigation by local referents, ideological explanations, and interpersonal sensitivity in China–foreign joint ventures', *Academy of Management Journal*, Vol.45, No.4, pp.807–26.

Colling, T. (1995) 'Experiencing turbulence: competition, strategic choice and the management of human resources in British Airways', *Human Resource Management Journal*, Vol.5, No.5, pp.18–32.

Cooke, R.A. and Lafferty, J.C. (1989) *Organizational Culture Inventory*, Plymouth, MA: Human Synergistics.

Cooke, R.A. and Rousseau, D.M. (1988) 'Behavioural norms and expectations: a quantitative approach to the assessment of organizational culture,' *Group and Organization Studies*, Vol.13, pp.245–73.

Cooke, R.A. and Szumal, J.L. (1983) 'Measuring normative beliefs and shared behavioral expectations in organizations: the reliability and validity of the organizational culture inventory', *Psychological Reports*, Vol.72, pp.1299–1339.

Corke, A. (1986) *British Airways: The Path to Profitability*, London: Frances Pinter.

Crumpacker, M. and Crumpacker, J.M. (2007) 'Succession planning and generational stereotypes: should HR consider age-based values and attitudes a relevant factor or a passing fad?', *Public Personnel Management*, Vol.36, No.4, pp.349–69.

Cullen, Hon. Lord (1990) *The Public Inquiry into the Piper Alpha Disaster*, London: HMSO.

*Deal, T.E. and Kennedy, A.A. (1982) *Corporate Cultures: The Rites and Rituals of Organisational Life*, Reading, MA: Addison-Wesley.

DeCenzo, D.A. and Robbins, S.P. (2002) *Human Resource Management* (6th edn), New York: Wiley.

Denison, D.R. (1984) 'Bringing corporate culture to the bottom line', *Organizational Dynamics*, Vol.13, No.2, pp.4–22.

Denison, D.R. (1996) 'What is the difference between organizational culture and organizational climate? A native's point of view on a decade of paradigm wars', *Academy of Management Review*, Vol.21, pp.619–54.

Dong L. and Glaister K.W. (2007) 'The management of culture in Chinese international strategic alliances', *Asian Business and Management*, Vol.6, No.4, pp.377–407.

Doyle, P. (1999) 'From the top', *The Guardian*, 4 December.

Dundon, T., Grugulis, I. and Wilkinson, A. (2001) 'New management techniques in small and medium-sized enterprises', in T. Redman and A. Wilkinson (eds) *Contemporary Human Resource Management*, London: FT/Prentice Hall.

Fairbairn U. (2005) 'HR as a strategic partner: culture change as an American Express case study', *Human Resource Management*, Vol.44, No.1, pp.79–84.

Fletcher, C. and Williams, R. (1992) *Performance Appraisal and Career Development* (2nd edn), Cheltenham: Stanley Thornes.

Froese, F.J., Pak, Y.S. and Chong, L.C. (2008) 'Managing the human side of cross-border acquisitions in South Korea', *Journal of World Business*, Vol.43, No.1, pp.97–108.

Furnham, A. (1997) *The Psychology of Behaviour at Work*, Hove: Psychology Press.

Garnett, J.L., Marlowe, J. and Pandey, S.K. (2008) 'Penetrating the performance predicament: communication as a mediator or moderator of organizational culture's impact on public organizational performance', *Public Administration Review*, Vol.68, No.2, pp.266–81.

Geertz, C. (1973) *The Interpretation of Culture*, New York: Basic Books.

Georgiades, N. and Macdonell, R., (1998), *Leadership for Competitive Advantage*, London: Wiley.

Glaser, S.R. (1983) *The Corporate Culture Survey*, Bryn Mawr, PA: Organizational Design and Development.

Gold, K.A. (1982) 'Managing for success: a comparison of the private and public sectors', *Public Administration Review*, Vol.42, November–December, pp.568–75.

Gordon, G. (1985) 'The relationship of corporate culture to industry sector and corporate performance', in R.H. Kilman, M.J. Saxton and B. Serpa (eds) *Gaining Control of the Corporate Culture*, San Francisco, CA: Jossey-Bass.

Gordon, G. and DiTomaso, N. (1992) 'Predicting corporate performance from organizational culture', *Journal of Management Studies*, Vol.29, pp.783–98.

Grugulis, I. and Wilkinson, A. (2002) 'Managing culture at British Airways: hope, hype and reality', *Long-Range Planning*, Vol.35, No.2, pp.179–94.

Grugulis, I., Dundon, T. and Wilkinson, A. (2000) 'Cultural control and the "culture manager": employment practices in a consultancy', *Work, Employment and Society*, Vol.14, No.1, pp.97–116.

Gundry, L.K. and Rousseau, D.M. (1994) 'Critical incidents in communication culture to newcomers: the meaning is the message', *Human Relations*, Vol.47, pp.1063–88.

Handy, C.B. (1978) *The Gods of Management*, London: Penguin.

Harris, L.C. and Ogbonna, E. (1998) 'Employee responses to culture change efforts', *Human Resource Management Journal*, Vol.8, No.2, pp.78–92.

Harrison, R. (1972) 'Understanding your organization's character', *Harvard Business Review*, Vol.5, pp.119–28.

Harrison, R. (2000) *Employee Development* (2nd edn), London: Chartered Institute of Personnel and Development.

Hatch, M.J. (1997) *Organizational Theory*, Oxford: Oxford University Press.

Hofstede, G. (1980) *Culture's Consequences: International Differences in Work-related Values*, Beverly Hills, CA: Sage.

Hofstede, G. (1991) *Cultures and Organizations: The Software of the Mind*, Maidenhead: McGraw-Hill.

Hofstede, G., Neuijen, B., Daval Ohayv, D. and Sanders, G. (1990) 'Measuring organizational cultures: a qualitative and quantitative study across twenty cases', *Administrative Science Quarterly*, Vol.35, pp.286–316.

Hong, J.F.L., Easterby-Smith, M. and Snell, R.S. (2006) 'Transferring organizational learning systems to Japanese subsidiaries in China', *Journal of Management Studies*, Vol.43, No.5, pp.1027–58.

Höpfl, H. (1993) 'Culture and commitment: British Airways', in D. Gowler, K. Legge and C. Clegg (eds) *Case Studies in Organizational Behaviour and Human Resource Management*, London: PCP.

Höpfl, H., Smith, S. and Spencer, S. (1992) 'Values and valuations: corporate culture and job cuts', *Personnel Review*, Vol.21, No.1, pp.24–38.

James, L. and Jones, A. (1974) 'Organizational climate: a review of theory and research', *Psychological Bulletin*, Vol.18, pp.1096–1112.

Jelineck, M., Smircich, L. and Hirsch, P. (1983) 'Introduction: a code of many colors', *Administrative Science Quarterly*, Vol.28, pp.331–38.

Kilmann, R.H. and Saxton, M.J. (1983) *The Kilmann-Saxton Culture-Gap Survey*, Pittsburg, PA: Organisational Design Consultants.

Kilmann, R.H., Saxton, M.J. and Serpa, R. (1985) *Gaining Control of the Corporate Culture*, San Francisco, CA: Jossey-Bass.

Keenoy, T. and Anthony, P. (1992) 'Metaphor, meaning and morality', in P. Blyton and P. Turnbull (eds) *Reassessing Human Resource Management*, London: Sage.

Kopelman, R.E., Brief, A.P. and Guzzo, R.A. (1990) 'The role of climate in productivity', in B. Schneider (ed.) *Organizational Climate and Culture*, San Francisco, CA: Jossey-Bass.

Kotter, J.P. and Heskett, J.L. (1992) *Corporate Culture and Performance*, New York: Free Press.

Kroeber, A.I. and Kluckhohn, C. (1952) *Culture: A Critical Review of Concepts and Definitions*, New York: Vintage Books.

Kunda, G. (1992) *Engineering Culture: Control and Commitment in a High-Tech Firm*, Philadelphia, PA: Temple University Press.

Lawler, E. (1990) *Strategic Pay: Aligning Organisational Strategies and Pay Systems*, San Francisco, CA: Jossey-Bass.

Lee, M. (1996) 'Action learning as a cross-cultural tool', in J. Stewart and J. McGoldrick (eds) *Human Resource Development*, London: Pitman.

Lee, S.K.J. and Yu, K. (2004) 'Corporate culture and organizational performance', *Journal of Managerial Psychology*, Vol.19, No.4, pp.340–59.

Legge, K. (1995) *Human Resource Management: Rhetorics and Realities*, Basingstoke: Macmillan.

Louis, M.R. (1983) 'Organizations as culture-bearing milieux', in L.R. Pondy, P.J. Frost, G. Morgan and I.C. Dandridge (eds) *Organizational Symbolism*, Greenwich, CT: JAI Press.

Mabey, C. and Salaman, G. (1995) *Strategic Human Resource Management*, Oxford: Blackwell.

Marchington, M. and Wilkinson, A. (2005) *Human Resource Management at Work,* London: Chartered Institute of Personnel and Development.

Martin, J. (1992) *Cultures in Organizations,* New York: Oxford University Press.

Martin J. (2002) *Organizational Culture: Mapping the Terrain,* London: Sage.

Martin, J. and Siehl, C. (1983) 'Organizational culture and counterculture: an uneasy symbiosis', *Organizational Dynamics,* Vol.12, No.2, pp.52–64.

Meek, V.L. (1982) 'Organisational culture: origins and weaknesses', in J.G. Salaman (ed.) *Human Resource Strategies,* London: Sage.

Meyerson, D. (1991) 'Acknowledging and uncovering ambiguities', in P. Frost, L. Moore, M. Louis, C. Lundberg and J. Martin (eds) *Reframing Organizational Culture,* Beverly Hills, CA: Sage.

Miah, M.K. and Bird, A. (2007) 'The impact of culture on HRM styles and firm performance: evidence from Japanese parents, Japanese subsidiaries/joint ventures and South Asian local companies', *International Journal of Human Resource Management,* Vol.18, No.5, pp.908–23.

Monopolies and Mergers Commission (1987) 'British Airways plc and British Caledonian Group plc: a report on the Proposed Merger 247', London: HMSO.

Moorhead, G. and Griffin, R.W. (1995) *Organizational Behavior* (4th edn), Boston, MA: Houghton Mifflin.

Moran, E.T. and Volkwein, J.F. (1992) 'The cultural approach to the formation of organizational climate', *Human Relations,* Vol.45, pp.19–47.

Morgan, G. (1986) *Images of Organization,* Beverly Hills, CA: Sage.

Morgan, P.I. and Ogbonna, E. (2008) 'Subcultural dynamics in transformation: a multi-perspective study of healthcare professionals', *Human Relations,* Vol.61, No.1, pp.39–65.

Münch, R. and Smelster, N.J. (1992) *Theory of Culture,* Berkeley, CA: University of California Press.

*Ogbonna, E. (1992) 'Organisational culture and human resource management: dilemmas and contradictions', in P. Blyton and P. Turnbull (eds) *Reassessing Human Resource Management,* London: Sage.

Ogbonna, E. and Harris, L.C. (2000) 'Leadership style, organisational culture and performance: empirical evidence from UK companies', *International Journal of Human Resource Management,* Vol.11, No.4, pp.766–88.

Ogbonna, E. and Harris, L.C. (2006) 'Organisational culture in the age of the Internet: an exploratory study', *New Technology Work and Employment,* Vol.21, No.2, pp.162–75.

Ogbonna, E. and Wilkinson, B. (1988) 'Corporate strategy and corporate culture: the management of change in the UK supermarket industry', *Personnel Review,* Vol.18, No.6, pp.10–14.

Ouchi, W.G. (1981) *Theory Z: How American Business Can Meet the Japanese Challenge,* Reading, MA: Addison-Wesley.

Peters, T.J. and Waterman, R.H. (1982) *In Search of Excellence: Lessons from America's Best Run Companies,* New York: Harper & Row.

Pettigrew, A. (1979) 'On studying organizational cultures', *Administrative Science Quarterly,* Vol.24, pp.570–81.

Pettigrew, A. (1990) 'Is corporate culture manageable?', in D. Wilson and R. Rosenfield (eds) *Managing Organisations,* Maidenhead: McGraw-Hill.

Petty, M.M., Beadles, N.A., Lowery, C.M., Chapman, D.F. and Connell, D.W. (1995) 'Relationships between organizational culture and organizational performance', *Psychological Reports,* Vol.76, pp.483–92.

Reed, M. (1992) *The Sociology of Organization,* London: Harvester Wheatsheaf.

Reichers, A.E. and Schneider, B. (1990) 'Climate and culture: an evolution of constructs', in B. Schneider (ed.) *Organisational Climate and Culture,* San Francisco, CA: Jossey-Bass.

Ricks, T.E. (1997) *Making the Corps,* New York: Scribner.

Rodrigues S.B., (2006) 'The political dynamics of organizational culture in an institutionalized environment', *Organization Studies,* Vol.27, No.4, pp.537–57.

Rohner, R.P. (1984) 'Towards a conception of culture for cross-cultural psychology', *Journal of Cross-Cultural Psychology,* Vol.15, pp.111–38.

Rousseau, D.M. (1990) 'Assessing organizational culture: the case for multiple methods', in B. Schneider (ed.) *Organizational Climate and Culture,* San Francisco, CA: Jossey-Bass.

Sackmann, S. (1991) 'Managing organisational culture: dreams and possibilities', in J. Anderson (ed.) *Communication Yearbook,* Beverly Hills, CA: Sage.

Schein, E.H. (1984) 'Coming to a new awareness of organizational culture', *Sloan Management Review*, Vol.25, pp.3–16.

Schein, E.H. (1985), 'How culture forms, develops and changes', in R. H. Kilmann, M. J. Saxton, R. Serpa and Associates (eds) *Gaining Control of the Corporate Culture*, San Francisco, CA: Jossey-Bass.

*Schein, E.H. (1992) *Organizational Culture and Leadership: A Dynamic View* (2nd edn), San Francisco, CA: Jossey-Bass.

Scheeres, H. and Rhodes, C. (2006) 'Between cultures: values, training and identity in a manufacturing firm', *Journal of Organizational Change Management*, Vol.19, No.2, pp.223–36.

Schneider, B. (1987) 'The people make the place', *Personnel Psychology*, Vol.40, pp.437–53.

Schneider, B. (1990) *Organisational Climate and Culture*, San Francisco, CA: Jossey-Bass.

Shipley, P. (1990) 'The analysis of organisations as a conceptual tool for ergonomics practitioners', in J.R. Wilson and E.N. Corlett (eds) *Evaluation of Human Work*, London: Taylor & Francis.

Siehl, C. and Martin, J. (1990) 'Organizational culture: the key to financial performance?', in B. Schneider (ed.) *Organizational Climate and Culture*, San Francisco, CA: Jossey-Bass.

Silverzweig, S. and Allen, R.E. (1976) 'Changing the corporate culture', *Sloan Management Review*, Vol.17, No.3, pp.33–49.

Smircich, L. (1983) 'Concepts of culture and organizational analysis', *Administrative Science Quarterly*, Vol.28, pp.339–58.

Stewart, J. and McGoldrick, J. (1996) *Human Resource Development*, London: Pitman.

Stiles, P., Gratton, L., Truss, C., Hope-Hailey, V. and McGovern, P. (1997) 'Performance management and the psychological contract', *Human Resource Management Journal*, Vol.7, No.1, pp.57–66.

Storey, J. (1992) *Developments in the Management of Human Resources*, Oxford: Blackwell.

Storey, J. (1995) *Human Resource Management: A Critical Text*, London: Routledge.

Swartz, M. and Jordon, D. (1980) *Culture: An Anthropological Perspective*, New York: Wiley.

Taylor, R. (1998) 'Annual review article', *British Journal of Industrial Relations*, Vol.36, No.2 pp.293–311.

Thompson, P. and McHugh, D. (2002) *Work Organisations: A Critical Introduction* (3rd edn), Basingstoke: Palgrave.

Torbiorn I. (2005) 'Staffing policies and practices in European MNCs: strategic sophistication, culture-bound policies or ad hoc reactivity?', in H. Scullion and M. Linehan (eds) *International Human Resource Management*, Basingstoke: Palgrave.

Trice, H.M. and Beyer, J.M. (1984) 'Studying organizational cultures through rites and ceremonials', *Academy of Management Review*, Vol.9, pp.653–69.

Trice, H.M. and Beyer, J.M. (1993) *The Cultures of Work Organisations*, Englewood Cliffs, NJ: Prentice-Hall.

Trompenaars, F. and Hampden-Turner, C. (1997) *Riding the Waves of Culture: Understanding Cultural Diversity in Business*, London: Nicholas Brealey.

Tsui, A.S., Zhang, Z.X., Wang, H., Xin, K.R. and Wu, J.B. (2006) 'Unpacking the relationship between CEO leadership behavior and organizational culture', *Leadership Quarterly*, Vol.17, No.2, pp.113–37.

Uttal, B. (1983) 'The corporate culture vultures', *Fortune*, Vol.108, No.8, 17 October, pp.66–72.

Van Maanen, J. and Schein, E. (1979) 'Toward a theory of organizational socialization', *Research in Organizational Behavior*, Vol.11, pp.209–59.

Van Vianen, A.E.M (2000) 'Person-organization fit: the match between newcomers' and recruiters' preferences for organizational cultures', *Personnel Psychology*, Vol.53, No.1, pp.113–49.

Wanous, P. (1989) 'Installing a realistic job preview: ten tough choices', *Personnel Psychology*, Vol.42, pp.117–33.

Warhurst, R. (1995) 'Converging on HRM? Change and continuity in European airlines' industrial relations', *European Journal of Industrial Relations*, Vol.1, No.2, pp.259–74.

Weick, K. (1985) 'The significance of corporate culture', in P. Frost, L. Moore, M. Louis, C. Lundberg and J. Martin (eds) *Organizational Culture*, Beverly Hills, CA: Sage.

Wilderom, C.P.M, Glunk, U. and Maslowski, R. (2000) 'Organizational culture as a predictor of organizational performance', in N.M. Ashkanasy, C.P.M. Wilderom and M.F. Peterson (eds) *Handbook of Organizational Culture and Climate*, Thousand Oaks, CA: Sage.

Williams, A., Dobson, P. and Watters, M. (1993) *Changing Culture: New Organizational Approaches* (2nd edn), London: Institute of Personnel Management.

*Williams, R.S. (2002) *Managing Employee Performance: Design and Implementation in Organizations,* London: Thomson.

Willmott, H. (1993) 'Strength is ignorance, slavery is freedom: managing culture in modern organizations', *Journal of Management Studies,* Vol.30, No.4, pp.515–52.

Wunthow, R. and Witten, M. (1988) 'New directions in the study of culture', *Annual Review of Sociology,* Vol.14, pp.49–67.

Xenikou, A. and Furnham, A. (1996) 'A correlational and factor analytic study of four questionnaire measures of organizational culture', *Human Relations,* Vol.49, pp.349–71.

Yu, L. (2007) 'Corporate culture in the numbers', *MIT Sloan Management Review,* Spring, pp.4–6.

Zemke, R., Raines, C. and Filipczak, B. (2000) *Generations at Work: Managing the Clash of Veterans, Boomers, and Nexters in Your Workplace,* New York: American Management Association.

*Useful reading

Part II

CONTEMPORARY THEMES AND ISSUES

Chapter 11

INTERNATIONAL HRM

Geoffrey Wood, Leslie T. Szamosi and Alexandros Psychogios

Introduction

Simply stated, *international HRM* is the management of organisational personnel in an international environment (i.e. firms that operate across national boundaries). As such, it is distinct from *comparative HRM*, which merely compares how people are managed in different national contexts. Today, there are two central debates in international HRM. The first concerns the extent to which it is possible to retain a uniform set of organisational attitudes, norms and values – and HR policies and practices – across national boundaries, or whether these will be retrofitted within individual (or groups of) national locales. Or, will organisations inevitably mirror the paradigms and practices of the original country of origin? Secondly, there are a range of practical issues concerning the management of employees in different national contexts. These include the management of expatriates, and the role and relative importance assigned to nationals from the organisation's parent country vis-à-vis local personnel.

Thinking about international HRM: uniformity or diversity?

A key debate in international HR management is the extent to which firms should adapt their HR policies and practices to suit specific national contexts, whether they keep them in line with the dominant ways of doing business in their parent country, or whether a new transglobal model of HR management is emerging. Authors have begun suggesting that as globalisation increases, the genre of international human resource management spreads accordingly.

CONVERGENCE THEORIES

The neo-liberal perspective is premised on the belief that organisational and wider social outcomes reflect the choices of rational individuals seeking to maximise their personal gain. Throughout much of the 1990s, this perspective not only dominated the discipline of economics, but also influenced government policies in many Western countries. To neo-liberals, variations between national contexts represented variations in regulations (or 'market imperfections') on a continuum towards a desirable minimalism. There is an extensive body of literature in the neo-liberal tradition that suggests that modes of regulation and associated inter- and intra-firm practices are likely to converge towards the (largely free market) Anglo-American model. In other words, these perspectives assume that all economies – and associated institutional structures – will, over time, become more alike and, most likely, in line with

Box 11.1: HRM in practice

Factors leading to common HR strategies worldwide

Globalisation

Globalisation's effects are mainly related to homogeneity in values, habits, way of leaving and buying habits. Thus, this means that even in communities with a strong culture there is a trend of skipping core cultural values and citizens are becoming more 'Westernised'. For an HR department coming from the USA and operating, for example, in European countries, the differences in the way of living have prompted HR departments to adopt a common way of operating by setting up the same policies in hiring, evaluating and even motivating employees. There are many academics who stress that the time is not far away when even the last cultural obstacles will be abandoned and the 'global village' will have come into being. To summarise, where cultural differences in many countries are even smaller, HR departments do not need to be adapted and thus they are skipping any cultural aspects.

Cost-standardised and economy of scales

Continually establishing operations in many countries and markets is a costly endeavour for international companies. To avoid the cost of establishing a different tailored approach in order to respect cultural parameters, many companies are standardising policies and strategies in order to achieve economies of scale – one of which is the HR strategy. In such situations it is easier both to transfer and teach their strategies and thus avoid cultural adoption. This is a strategy that even more 'transatlantic' companies are following in their efforts to expand operations worldwide. Following this strategy, HR departments are adopting a holistic approach in the way they are treating employees.

Standardisation of a specific HR strategy globally

One of the greatest costs today, which for many companies constitutes an obstacle to expanding their operations, is labour costs. Even for big companies setting up from scratch, a new HR platform is a costly process. In order to avoid this process many companies are following a holistic approach for their HR departments only, while at the same time the other departments are following a more local approach.

The need to keep the same brand philosophy globally through implementing the same HR strategies worldwide

Another reason for companies to adopt global HR policies is the strong brand image that they have, and thus they are expanding their 'know-how' globally. This means that they have achieved significant levels of brand awareness such that employees are adapting to them and not the other way round. For example, Starbucks is following an HR strategy promoting the idea that 'everybody knows the way we operate, thus they know from the start which company they are joining and what they have to do'. This strategy, however, is efficient only in cases of very strong global brand images.

US models (Fukuyama 2000; cf. Friedman 1999). Freed from the restraints imposed by misguided attempts at regulation, an individual's desire for self-actualisation and recognition will unlock creativity and enterprise; firms will be able to operate without being hampered by unnecessary restrictions (Fukuyama 2000, p.320). Summarily, it is argued that the capacity to make use of similar organisational practices within different national locales is likely to optimise the firm's capacity; greater homogenisation is likely to infuse greater efficiency (Kostova and Roth 2002, p.215; cf. Zeira and Harari 1977, p.328). While the diffusion of HR practices across transnational firms may be uneven and disjointed, it will gradually make for similarities in different national contexts; firms will try to enforce their own view of the most efficient, effective and appropriate ways of accommodating HRM in other countries (Brewster *et al.* 2004).

CONVERGENCE: TOWARDS BEST PRACTICES?

Grounded in the above-mentioned rational choice tradition (in other words, neo-classical economics), convergence theories assume that firms pursue economic advantage through choices 'guided by unambiguous preferences and bounded rationality' (Gooderham *et al.* 1999, p.507). Hence, industries will adopt practices that promote the maximisation of economic goals; optimistic accounts suggest that this will result in a set of best practices diffusing across the parent economy and worldwide. The 'best practice' approach to strategic HRM holds that the adoption of an internally consistent set of high-performance work practices will result in superior outcomes (Huselid 2000, p.107). Conversely, it should be possible to identify optimal HR practices by analysing winning firms (ibid.). Further to this, these practices are often tacit and difficult or impossible to determine without being directly involved in the organisation.

'High-value-added' approaches base competitiveness on mutually rewarding employee–employee interdependence, with considerable delegation to employees (Pfeffer 1994; Ulrich 1997; Applebaum *et al.* 2000; Kochan and Ostermann 1994; cf. Whitley 1999). Such approaches are characterised by high levels of investment (of both time and money) in training and development and flat organisational structures, with broadly based employee participation, superior job security and innovative reward systems. In turn, these facilitate greater levels of participation, involvement and empowerment (Applebaum *et al.* 2000; cf. Webster and Wood 2005). Such interventions are likely to prove complementary: permanent employment reduces turnover, while investing in people and job redesign enhances organisational commitment, providing fertile ground for far-reaching involvement programmes (Lincoln and Kalleberg 1990). Again, leading multinational companies (MNCs) – sometimes referred to as transnational companies or TNCs – are likely to prove pioneers in the dissemination of best practices, given their greater resource bases and an ability to identify which specific sets of policies yield optimal results on a global basis.

Critics have questioned whether there may be a single set of optimal practices (Huselid 2000, p.107); indeed, lower-value-added approaches may prove highly profitable in specific industries and locales but their global applicability is tenuous at best. Moreover, individual interventions may elicit specific outcomes; a set of good practices may not necessarily result in an outcome that is coherent and mutually supportive.

CONVERGENCE: THE LOW ROAD

Alternatively, it can be argued that any pressures towards uniform practices are likely to be downwards; the range of pressures associated with globalisation – most notably, the intensification of competition, market break-up and the increased mobility of investor capital – have placed renewed pressures on firms to enhance their competitiveness through ongoing rounds of cost-cutting, primarily by workforce downsizing (Wright *et al.* 2005; Wood and Brewster 2002; Duysters and Hagedoorn 2001, p.348). Intense competition has placed particularly severe pressure on labour costs. Indeed, it has been argued that through the use of subcontractors, or simple relocation, MNCs have reverted to strategies centring profitability on steadily worsening employment conditions, including low standards of health and safety, extremely low pay, arbitrary management, a near-total lack of job security, and the discounting of skill (Greider 1997; Moody 1987). Inevitably, this involves a gradual shift of production to low-wage, low-cost, labour-repressive economies, forcing employees within core regions to gradually accede to worsening pay and working conditions in return for staving off threats to relocate. Given the pressures associated with globalisation, managers worldwide are gradually moving towards 'efficiency-enhancing' approaches; there is a general convergence in the direction of the lowest possible standards (O'Hagan 2002, p.40; Streeck 1995).

THE PERSISTENCE OF DIFFERENCE: INSTITUTIONAL ACCOUNTS

As noted earlier, rational choice theories depict organisational and social outcomes as the result of the combined choices of rational profit-maximising individuals. In contrast, institutionalist accounts see organisational and social behaviour as the product not only of individual actions, but of wider social structures and accumulated practices. In other words, institutional theories hold that pre-existing informal social conventions, as well as the regulations imposed by more formally constituted governmental structures, mould – and are remoulded by – human actions. Hence, what organisations do reflects not only the decisions of their members, but also formal and informal rules governing what can and should be done. In terms of the formal rules, Brewster (2002) argues that even greater restrictions are expected in the basic tenets of HRM practice (e.g. pensions, leave etc.), particularly in regions such as Europe.

More formally speaking, institutions can be defined as 'normative complexes relating to major aspects of our social activity' (Anderson and Parker 1964, p.136). Configurations of norms are established, formalised and regularised to ensure conformity in behaviour and allow for complex social transactions, while imparting greater predictability to social life. Within any given society, the major aspects of social structures influence daily life (ibid.); institutions may coincide with formal structures such as a national education and training system, or be rather less tangible sets of shared ways of 'doing things'. An example of the latter would be the common organisational practices shared by leading manufacturing exporters in Japan, centring on high security of tenure, mutual collegiality and commitment, and the sharing and dissemination of skills. Having said this, it has been more recently suggested that Japanese MNCs are having less direct influence on their subsidiaries (e.g. Miah and Bird 2007; Rose and Kumar 2007).

Accounts within the broad institutionalist tradition suggest that within specific national contexts, firm-level practices will gradually become homogenous or 'isomorphic' with the national context (Kostova and Roth 2002, p.215; cf. Brewster *et al.* 2001). Three forms of isomorphism may be identified: coercive (where the firm is forced to adopt specific practices, such as through force of law); mimetic (specific practices associated with success in individual firms are copied by others); or normative (behavior is tailored to fit what is considered suitable for the specific environment) (Haveman 1993, p.593; Kostova and Roth 2002, p.216; Brewster *et al.* 2004).

Recent institutional writings (cf. Whitley 1999; Gooderham *et al.* 1999; Brewster *et al.* 2004) have pointed to an emerging body of evidence that global economic pressures do not seem to have translated into uniform outcomes in terms of HR practices. In some national contexts, institutional strictures have been weak for many years, with national competitiveness being grounded on a purely cost-oriented basis, translating into HR policies centring on low wages, low security of tenure, and a lack of investment in training or development; good examples would include the Philippines and Nigeria. Others have been characterised by more active regulation, supported by coherent national industrial policies aimed at encouraging firms to adopt policies aimed at maximising productivity through strategic investments in people; examples would include South Korea and Mauritius. Institutional configurations are adaptable, and may evolve over time. For example, in apartheid South Africa, work organisation in large areas of the economy centred on racial Fordism – mass production coupled with a rigid racial division of labour, with Africans being confined to largely unskilled jobs and subject to the Pass Laws which made it difficult to switch employment or move between different areas of the country; the system, however, proved increasingly inefficient and uncompetitive in the face of mounting global competition; hence, even prior to the formal end of apartheid, more skilled occupations gradually opened up to Africans, and HR strategies became more focused and gradually diffused around issues such as cooperation and less around coercion.

TOWARDS TRANSNATIONAL INSTITUTIONAL MODELS?

As we have seen, theories of globalisation suggest that specific national practices are unlikely to prove durable given pressures towards transnational convergence. An alternative account would suggest that while specific institutional factors are likely to continue to mould and influence firm-level practices in different parts of the world, national institutions will increasingly give way to regional and transnational institutions. The most commonly cited example is that of the European Union. It is suggested that a broad social model is gradually diffusing, creating a region of highly competitive firms, based around high-value-added HR practices and policies (c.f. O'Hagan 2002, p.6). Examples include the European Works Council Directive, which compels firms with more than 1,000 employees operating in at least two EU states, with a workforce of 150 at least, to have a European works council (EWC). EWCs are, however, relatively weak, primarily consultative bodies which wield minimal influence and authority (Pulignano 2006).

Indeed, as writers such as Whitley (1999, p.133) have pointed out, the limited significance of pan-European agencies and European systems of economic organisation, despite 40 years of existence of the EEC and its successors, underscores the tenacity of national institutional arrangements and practices. Within the European context, MNCs are more likely to tailor their HR policies to national locale, or in line with prevailing international trends, than to one that is specifically in tune with emerging trans-EU norms and practices.

THEORIES OF ETHNOCENTRICITY

Growing up in a particular social context, individuals are socialised to believe that specific norms and values are the 'best' or the 'most proper'. Hence, as Anderson and Parker (1964, p.50) note, it is difficult for members of any specific society to be objective regarding 'new' ways of thinking and acting other than their own. A devotion to cultural norms reinforces in-group attitudes, strengthening customs and making change difficult (ibid.).

Consequently, originating within a specific national context, the core staff of an MNC is likely to have originated from a shared social context and be only mildly influenced by expatriates working within their locale. They may learn to adapt to the ways of doing business in other contexts, but shared socialisation – on both the individual and corporate levels – is likely to reinforce embedded beliefs that the ways of the parent country are the most appropriate, and should be disseminated to subsidiaries abroad. Hence, ethnocentric theories argue that MNCs will tend to mirror the dominant practices of their country of origin (cf. Zeira and Harari 1977, p.327). Based on comparative survey evidence, Mayrhofer and Brewster (1996) argue that, in practice, the vast majority of MNCs are ethnocentrically focused, despite potential inflexibility and lack of fit with local conditions (Janssens 2001). This runs contrary to other research (e.g. Andolšek and Štebe 2005), which suggests and foreshadows a much more intense decentralisation (at times referred to as devolution) of HRM functions within organisations at the local level.

THE PERSISTENCE OF DIFFERENCE: CULTURAL ACCOUNTS

In contrast to institutional accounts, cultural explanations believe that national differences cannot be ascribed to regulatory structures and norms, but rather to the content of the relevant social environment as a whole. Culture can be defined as the integrated, interdependent sum of socially produced and socially inherited patterns constructed around a corpus of socially created physical and biological materials (Anderson and Parker 1964, p.40). In other words, culture is not just about the effect of social structures, but also about localised patterns of human interactions that reproduce themselves and develop, over time, reflecting the effects of earlier interactions and the physical environment.

Cultural accounts would ascribe an even greater path dependence to nations – and firms located within them – than would the institutionalist tradition. Indeed, it is argued that assimilation of one culture by another is a relatively uncommon process. It is far more likely that, at best, representatives of different cultures can learn to collaborate (Sparrow and Hiltrop 2000, p.73). Hence, in MNCs, the 'corporate diplomat' who is experienced in the ways of diverse foreign climes has an invaluable role (Ferlie and Pettigrew 2000, p.204). Indeed, recent culturalist accounts have suggested that the world is irrevocably divided into rival cultures, leading to endemic clashes of belief systems (attitudes, values and morals) at macro and micro levels, clashes that may prove difficult to resolve (cf. Huntingdon 1996).

Within management studies, some of the most influential accounts on the effects of national cultures include Hofstede (1991), Fukuyama (1995) and Sako (1998). Cultural theories concede that specific cultures do not necessarily coincide with national boundaries – common distinctions are drawn between the Western and Chinese traditions, for example. However, what firms do in different national locales will gradually align with the dominant cultural context (Lao and Ngo 2001, p.95). This allows for prior knowledge to be harnessed most effectively, and for shared expectations, making for more efficient exchange relations. Specific national cultures mould behaviour and shape the perceptions managers have of the world (Sparrow and Hiltrop 2000, p.73). Not only does HRM impact national ways of doing things, but also local conditions and cultures mould the processes and problems of national models (ibid., p.73). For example, Wang and Zang (2005) found that China companies deemed to be more entrepreneurial were those that were collective based and globally oriented. This may suggest, perhaps, that there are positive impacts on people management practices when foreign companies locate in other markets.

Cultural explanations can be divided into two broad categories. So called *etic* approaches 'describe phenomena in constructs that apply across cultures' (Morris *et al.* 1999, p.782). In other words, there are certain 'universals' that can be applied to human behaviour. For example, in any context people may be more or less committed to their organisation; further to this, relative organisational commitment may be measured in objective terms. However, specific cultures may be associated with higher levels of organisational commitment, on account of specific attitudes, expectations and values. In applying the etic approach we must be wary of its limitations, including the proposition that implicit beliefs may be rooted in a deeper philosophical underpinning (Chang 2003).

More broadly speaking, different cultures have different characteristics that can be objectively identified and contrasted according to some external standard (ibid., pp.781–2). For example, Hofstede (1980) argues that different cultures vary according to certain objective dimensions, such as power-distance (the extent to which the least powerful accept their status), uncertainty avoidance (tolerance for risk), collectivism (group or individual orientation) and masculine/feminine dimensions (procedurality or intuition). Much criticism has been levelled at Hofstede's seminal work, including its lack of an underlying theory (Cray and Mallory 1998), sampling within a single multinational organisation (Smith 2002), and choosing a predominantly white, male, middle-management sample (Moulettes 2007).

A limitation of etic approaches is that the objective yardsticks against which cultures are measured are somewhat arbitrary, and may be ethnocentrically focused, perceived and interpreted. At worst, categorising nations according to predetermined standards may amount to little more than crude ethnic stereotyping, with some cultures inevitably being branded inferior, less desirable or less effective than others. Attempts to deploy etic approaches to understanding organisational failings in regions of the world characterised by poor economic performance, but where such performance can be directly traced to uneven natural resource endowments and a specific colonial legacy – an obvious example being Africa, are particularly problematic.

In contrast, *emic* approaches locate culture as an integral component of a broader social system (Parsons 1951; Giddens 1990). Within such systems, individual conceptualisations are defined by a specific historical-social trajectory; behaviourial patterns cannot be understood according to objective measures. Rather, it is necessary to attempt to see things from the 'insider's point of view', aiming to understand why specific actions make the most sense to those with particular sets of experiences. This would suggest that attempts to manage people across national contexts are likely to lead to persistent misconceptions, unless managers adopt more people-centred approaches that allow for open-ended employee involvement and constant feedback.

More recent work has suggested that emic and etic approaches are not necessarily mutually exclusive: aspects of behaviour may incorporate both emic and etic dimensions (Berry 1999, p.165; Helfrich 1999, pp.131–54). Again, all cultural approaches assume that culture is something of a given. In other words, it is not easy to transform cultures in such a manner as to enhance 'social capital', and hence, promote higher-skilled and higher-value-added production paradigms (Fukuyama 1995; Lane 1998; Wood and Brewster 2002).

COMMONALITIES BETWEEN INSTITUTIONAL AND CULTURAL APPROACHES

Both institutional and cultural approaches argue that MNCs have adapted their activities in line with local practices (Kostova and Roth 2002, p.215). As noted earlier, this process does reflect a particular *path dependence* – countries or regions tend to follow distinct trajectories, inter alia associated with specific sets of managerial and, specifically, HR practices, which are not easily altered and take time to adapt. MNCs entering a new country need to tailor/adapt their policies and practices to be more responsive to local expectations and realities, even if it means departing from long-established organisational practices.

It should also be noted that most cultural theories define culture as part and parcel of a wider social structure. In other words, although distinct from recent institutionalist writing, such cultural accounts are grounded in a shared recognition of the objective effects of formal and informal institutional frameworks. However, their interpretation is a relatively conservative one, in that structures are characterised as bodies that ensure continuity and order, rather than dynamic and ever-changing in response to internal and external pressures.

SIMILARITY AND DIFFERENCE: DUALITY PERSPECTIVES

Writing from within the institutionalist tradition, Whitley (1999, p.126) argues that MNCs are unlikely to change their existing practices unless foreign operations constitute a very large component of organisational activities, with these activities being concentrated in a national business system very different to – but more developed than – that of the country of origin. Moreover, the 'foreign business system' must be cohesive, with a high degree of institutional integration, while in the country of origin institutional agencies should not prevent significant changes (i.e. adapting to the local environment) (ibid., p.127). Again, the firm should be closely integrated across national boundaries to create synergies and, where possible, economies of scales. However, in such contexts, not only can multinational firms switch their dominant way of doing business, but they may also disseminate new practices back to their country of origin as well as to other operations throughout their sphere of influence.

Box 11.2: HRM in practice

International HR practices in McDonald's

Founded by Ray Kroc, McDonald's is one of the most valuable and well-known global brands that hold a leading global market share of the quick-service restaurant segment of informal eating. With more than 30,000 local restaurants serving nearly 50 million people in more than 119 countries each day, McDonald's as a market leader invests in its people. Its global people principles reflect its commitment to a supportive workplace environment. McDonald's provides growth and employment opportunities for large numbers of its employees. In their workplace, employees 'have the chance to learn what it takes to succeed'. McDonald's HR tactic gives employees the opportunity to move on to careers in different fields from the ones in which they began, carrying with them essential workplace skills and values. At McDonald's attention is paid to training courses at every level in the company. For example, in every branch of McDonald's around the world, crew members receive training and coaching in order to better understand the values of the company and to learn how they can provide outstanding customer service. It is also important for the employees to have the chance to get training via a computer-based training system and to learn more about the global market. However, a high staff turnover rate means that much of the training will perforce have to be aimed at the provision of the most basic skills to cope with food preparation, simple customer service and delivery in a highly standardised fashion.

Given the extent of barriers to the altering of corporate strategies and practices, it is likely that many firms will infuse elements of practices associated with the principal national contexts in which they operate. In other words, firms face conflicting pressures towards the homogenisation of practices around different national models, making for an uneven and dynamic integration process (Gooderham *et al.* 1998).

International HRM in practice

As Holden (2001, p.657) notes, there is some common ground between comparative and international HRM in that both are concerned with HRM issues in a global or regional context. However, international HRM exclusively concerns HRM in a transnational context; this would encompass the factors moulding the HR policies and strategies of MNCs, and the manner in which they are operationalised (ibid.).

STAFFING POLICIES

There are four approaches to staffing in MNCs, commonly referred to as ethnocentric, polycentric, geocentric and regional/regiocentric (cf. ibid.; Perlmutter 1969).

Ethnocentric approaches

This approach involves filling all key positions with parent country nationals – that is, those from the MNC's country of origin and/or where its headquarters are located. Posting existing staff from the parent country allows for similar cultural and practical expectations and may facilitate communication and coordination (Dowling *et al.* 2004, p.71). This is tempered, however, in terms of incomes or possibilities for upward mobility within the firm, between expatriates and locals in favour of the former, which is likely to prove bad for morale (ibid.) and may result in the firm losing touch with local realities. Furthermore, the wages of expatriates are likely to be higher than those of locals – as it is necessary to provide financial incentives to cover the inconvenience of location – and, hence, more costly for the firm. A good example of ethnocentric approaches to staffing would be US oil firms in a number of West African petrostates, such as Equatorial Guinea, which are characterised by both local skills shortfalls and a lack of an institutional environment that would encourage greater use of locals (Wood 2004).

Polycentric approaches

Polycentric approaches involve situations where locals fill the managerial positions in national subsidiaries, and parent country nationals those at headquarters. As Scullion (2001, p.298) notes, polycentric strategies minimise language barriers within any particular plant or locale, eliminate the adjustment problems experienced by recently relocated expatriates, allow for management continuity, are cheaper, and open up new career opportunities for locals, hence enhancing morale and organisational commitment. On the downside, this can hamper communication between subsidiaries and headquarters and it may be harder to exercise firm control over subsidiaries, while a lack of genuine cosmopolitanism within the firm may make it more difficult to compete in global markets. Moreover, it precludes the possibility of managers gaining broader experience by a series of postings into other areas where the firm has a presence (ibid.).

Regiocentric approaches

These are becoming increasingly important. They represent a form of functional rationalisation on a multi-country basis, dividing operations into several geographical regions, and allowing for freely transferring staff within each (Dowling *et al.* 1999, p.75). The advantage of this is that it allows for a level of sensitivity to regional conditions, while allowing an interaction between regional and parent country nationals at the regional headquarters level (ibid.). However, this policy can result in excessive federalism, and create an overall lack of synergy between different regions. While many motor firms have, in the past, used aspects of this policy, increasingly a trend in the industry is to rationalise design and production across continents, resulting in a need for closer liaison activities and more effective communication between regional entities.

Geocentric approaches

Here, the firms appoints staff on a worldwide basis, with the most suitable individuals, regardless of national origin, being appointed to key positions (Dowling *et al.* 1999, p.72). Problems include the high costs of relocating staff, the need to train staff to fit in with local conditions, and the fact that many developed countries have placed increased restrictions on the immigration and employment of individuals from the developing world (see ibid.); the latter problem has become particularly pronounced since the US embarked on its so-called 'war on terror'.

Towards a greater variety?

Recent research has suggested a tendency towards greater variety in MNC staffing strategies, reflecting a desire to tailor global strategies to local conditions and needs (Scullion 2001, p.300). More expatriates tend to be found in underperforming subsidiaries and in greenfield developments, and less so in local subsidiaries taken over by MNCs (ibid.). Finally, it seems that subsidiaries in Asian countries make a greater use of parent country nationals, although this could also be reflective of the nature of investments made (see ibid.).

MANAGING EXPATRIATES: RELOCATION AND LOCAL NEEDS

In practice, a central concern of the literature has been on managing expatriates (Bratton and Gold 2003, p.62). Expatriates can play a central role in transferring knowledge and information, developing the knowledge and skills base of staff and subsidiaries, and in ensuring that subsidiaries act in accordance with general group policies, strategies and procedures (Holden 2001, p.658). However, local managers may prove resistant to such processes, on account of blockages that the widespread use of expatriates may pose to their own upward mobility and/or persistent cultural differences. In short, the availability of expertise and the need for organisational solidarity have to be reconciled with local sensitivities and needs.

Relocating staff members abroad involves revisiting the original reward system (see p.289), provision of adequate training regarding local conditions, the organising of a removal company, the provision of short-term or long-term housing, and assistance regarding driving licences, banking, and the availability of social services in the new locale.

Box 11.3: HRM in practice

Female expatriates

According to Scully *et al.* (2002), the main difficulties experienced by female managers in the re-entry process are the following:

- failure to get credit from home-country management for their achievements internationally;
- not having a suitable position to return to;
- outgrowing their home organisations;
- problems of social readjustment for themselves and their families;
- missed promotional opportunities owing to home-country senior management overlooking them while abroad.

According to several researchers (Scully *et al.* 2002; Mayrhofer *et al.* 2004), many of the difficulties that female expatriates face are similar to those of their male counterparts; however, when the case is a managerial position, females experience uncertainty regarding re-entry because most of them are in pioneering roles. The female managers suggested that the re-entry stage should be built in as part of an overall career plan before the expatriate initially leaves their home organisation. This plan should be developed to identify the probable length of stay, projected responsibilities while abroad and subsequent job position upon repatriation (Scully *et al.* 2002). The executives suggested that two important factors influencing this were the clarity of the repatriation process and the repatriation training received prior to returning to their home countries. The managers expressed the view that clearer repatriation policies would have a positive impact on work adjustment. They also perceived that training for international managers and their families for the re-entry process, and for any likely problems related to repatriation, should reduce the uncertainty normally associated with re-entry (Scully *et al.* 2002; Scully *et al.* 2004; Mayrhofer *et al.* 2004).

Given the immediate costs of relocation, and the need to ensure that the individuals involved enjoy a standard of living abroad commensurate with what they had at home, which may involve either higher pay or assistance with housing or education, the use of expatriates is likely to be costly. On the one hand, the gradual diffusion of a global culture centring on consumerism has eroded great cultural divides between many regions and nations. Western society has become more individually oriented, with weaker extended family ties. On the other hand, the greater likelihood that spouses will have independent careers, and changing social expectations surrounding marriage or similar long-term relationships, have meant that fewer spouses are prepared to endure long separations or place careers on 'hold' until some future date. Again, the fact that fewer individuals are prepared to live relatively solitary lives abroad makes the process of relocation more difficult and the pool of qualified candidates more scarce. Indeed, one of the major causes of high failure rates – in other words, a situation where an individual fails to make a successful transition to a new locale and returns home – is family-related pressures.

Finally, there is the process of repatriating expatriates to their home country after they have completed their foreign assignments. Firstly, there is the preparation phase, including briefing the relevant employee as to their new job requirements, and practical issues to be considered in moving between nations (e.g. banking, housing arrangements, settling bills). Secondly, there is the actual physical relocation process, although this can be facilitated by the use of specialised firms offering comprehensive services. Thirdly, there is the transition phase, which may include assistance involving a broad range of issues such as the provision of bridging housing, finding appropriate schools, new banking and financial service arrangements, and the reissuing of driving licences (Dowling *et al.* 1999, p.206). Unfortunately, returning individuals may feel that their international experience is undervalued, and/or that their status, autonomy or career direction has been negatively impacted by their separation from the home country (Scullion 2001, p.305). This may account for the relatively high turnover among returning staff experienced by MNCs (ibid.).

Even more difficult is dealing with the inevitable reverse culture shock (Dowling *et al.* 2004, p.206). It is common for expatriates to idealise their home country when serving long assignments abroad, and equally common for them to be seriously disillusioned upon their return. In Britain, conservative newspapers such as the *Daily Mail* and *Daily Telegraph* promote a vision of a golden age somewhere in the imagined past, sharply contrasted to a

Box 11.4: HRM in practice

Expatriation in Europe

Expatriation in Europe is changing in some crucial ways. According to Scullion *et al.* (2001), some of the changes in Europe are common and close to other regions and others are unique. Taken together they are leading to new challenges for the management of expatriation and creating a new research agenda. 'There are significant changes in the international environment; in the international organizations; and in the expatriates themselves', claim Scullion *et al.* (2001). There have been changes in the location of expatriate assignments for European MNCs. The number of expatriates who go to Europe has been reduced because of substantial pressures from governments on MNCs to recruit and train local employees (Brewster *et al.* 2001; Opialy 2003).

decayed, disorganised and disobedient present, a vision that is particularly closely tailored to the sentiments felt by elderly expatriates who have spent a 'lifetime' abroad.

REWARD SYSTEMS

As Moorehead and Griffin (2004, p.212) note, when transferring a staff member to a different national locale they seek at least to match the relative compensation they previously enjoyed. Typically, this will involve an increasing salary when they are is transferred to a country where the cost of living is higher. More difficult is a transfer to a part of the world where the cost of living is substantially lower, but where there may be a lesser availability of suitable accommodation or social services, or where the physical or political climate is unpleasant. In the latter instances, firms commonly provide accommodation for expatriate staff, and, sometimes, a pay premium for overseas service. Unfortunately, both of these may increase the divide between expatriates and locals, and make the former less sensitive to the latter's culture and conditions of life (Wood 2004).

In developing an expatriate reward system, many firms divide pay according to three components – taxes, consumption and savings – and make sure that transferred employees enjoy equivalent coverage and benefits in each of these areas to what they would have enjoyed in the parent country, so that at the end of the assignment they are at least no further behind where they would have been had they stayed in their present position (Moorehead and Griffin 2004, p.212). In other words, they should have at least the same amount of money available for

Box 11.5: HRM in practice

Direct and incentive pay: contrasting Japan, US and the EU

In Japan, companies follow a direct payment system linked to age and skill, based on seniority. This system has been adopted by many Japanese companies in order to attract workers for lifetime employment and to reduce high turnover. On the other hand, EU countries have established strong trade unions that are supportive of employees and decisions on wages and skill-based payment are regulated by mutual agreement. Finally, the US differs from the EU and Japanese systems in terms of legislation and standards of payment. US trade unions have weakened over the past few decades, leaving employees less protected than ever before. A cost is that many US-based firms appear to battle to attain European or Japanese levels of productivity without imposing very long working hours and shorter leave periods, which, in turn, has had knock-on effects in terms of employee well-being. The US has also battled to retain competitiveness in incrementally innovative high-value-added manufacturing.

Incentive pay in the US, EU and Japan differs in terms of cultural issues. The US culture is more individualistic and practises salary compensation based on individual performance, mostly for white-collar workers. In contrast with the individual US appraisal, national systems that are more collectivistic, like Japan, choose to motivate their employees through group compensation. Also, in the Japanese culture employee rewards are based on age and experience. Although until the 1980s collectivism was more integrated in the European compensation system, more recently there have been pressures in many EU countries to move towards individualism.

savings (as they will probably wish to retire to their country of origin), adequate compensation in those cases where they would be prejudiced by a different tax regime, and sufficient pay to enjoy similar standards of housing, transport, food and social provision as the home country. Understandably, such provision does not come cheaply, even when an employee is transferred to a country where the cost of living seems very much lower (see ibid.).

PLANNING AND MANAGING INDIGENOUS CAREERS

As can be seen, MNCs face conflicting pressures towards greater use of parent country nationals and localisation; inevitably, this will involve certain trade-offs (Brewster *et al.* 2005). In many situations it can be extremely difficult to secure the commitment of talented local staff if they perceive that more senior positions are dominated by expatriates, closing off their own prospects for upward mobility. Moreover, there is growing pressure on organisations to ensure that they represent the wider community in ethnic and gender terms (Tummala 1999, p.495). Moreover, many governments in the developing world place formal (legislative) or informal pressures on firms to develop and implement coherent affirmative action policies aimed at redressing the historical disadvantages suffered by women and/or specific ethnic groups, through targeted employment structures and development and/or promotional policies (Serote *et al.* 2001, p.166).

HUMAN RESOURCE DEVELOPMENT IN A TRANSNATIONAL CONTEXT

As Elger and Smith (2001, pp.449–50) note, MNCs have the potential to be major carriers of innovations in managerial practices across the global economy, allowing for distinct competitive advantages associated with one part of the world to be diffused to another. However, while there is some evidence of specific sets of innovative practices spreading across very different national contexts, such practices will often require modification or adaptation to fit in with differing cultural or institutional realities.

In practice, human resource development (HRD) in a transnational context involves three distinct processes. Firstly, there is the process of disseminating and institutionalising existing knowledge and best practices within the firm to subsidiaries operating in different national contexts. While new technologies – and the practical skills needed to make use of them – are relatively portable, innovations in organisational processes may be harder to transplant (Elger and Smith 2001, p.450). In other words, it is relatively easy to train people how to make the best use of 'hard' technological innovations, such as the use of new machinery to make innovative new products, such as flat panel TVs. However, it is rather harder to infuse new forms of socially organising work, or implement new managerial strategies that challenge pre-existing local cultures (attitudes, norms and values). The latter requires a detailed understanding of the implications of differing cultural and institutional contexts, and the manner in which changes in organisational practice may be adjusted to meet the needs and expectations of a different society and sold to affected employees. There is also the possibility for 'upfusing' existing knowledge from subsidiaries or 'junior' partners. For example, in its alliance with Nissan, Renault was able not only to impart its design expertise, allowing Nissan to make use of the running gear from some of its highly successful model lines, but gained access to Nissan's specific knowledge regarding key aspects of work organisation.

Secondly, given the need to fully develop the capacity of talented local employees and to meet possible equity targets, MNCs need to have coherent training policies and interventions for indigenous staff. Given possible shortfalls in local training, and the need to continuously develop and upgrade the skills of those earmarked for upward mobility, there has been a growing emphasis on internal development, or the use of programmes that have been commissioned by an outside body specifically to suit organisational needs (Favennec-Hery 1996, pp.665–74).

Thirdly, there is the issue of training expatriates to work within a different country. The type of training is impacted by the type of job, country of assignment, time available and mode of delivery; such training may include language training, field experiences, and area studies programmes that include briefings on the relevant national context and cultural and/or sensitivity training (Dowling *et al.* 1999, p.157).

Conclusion

At a policy level, it is important to understand the extent to which the policies of MNCs are moulded and impacted by specific national contexts. It has been variously suggested that MNCs mould their policies in the different locations in which they operate according to the specific cultural and/or institutional setting, that they inevitably mimic the policies that predominate in their parent countries, or that they are gradually converging towards a common international model of HRM. However, there is a growing body of critical research that suggests that there remains considerable variety in the HR policies followed by MNCs, reflecting a combination of pressures towards localisation, internationalisation and ethnocentricity.

At a practical level, people management in MNCs poses specific problems and challenges. These include the management of both expatriate and local staff careers, the development of skills and knowledge bases both within and across specific national settings, and the design of functional reward systems for an international environment as opposed to within a particular national context. Again, while it is possible to implement specific policies and procedures across an entire enterprise, the nature and implementation of specific HR practices are likely to be shaped by the socio-economic contexts in which the firm operates. Clearly, there is insufficient evidence to conclude that there is an emerging international model of HRM. However, there is evidence that the most successful MNCs are those with a consistent track record of investing in people, and capable of reconciling the pressures of operating in a global market with those posed by specific national settings.

CASE STUDY 11.1

International HRM: the practice of oil and gas companies in West Africa

Geoffrey Wood

The West African microstate of Equatorial Guinea is one of the fastest-growing economies on the African continent, owing to the discovery and exploitation of substantial offshore oil and gas reserves in the past few decades. A former Spanish colony, the country has, since independence, been ruled by a single family, the Nguemas; as such, its political development has been very much closer to the former Latin American family dictatorships, such as the Samosas in Nicaragua and the Batistas in Cuba, than other countries on the African continent. During the colonial era, the country developed a significant plantation economy, centring on the export of cocoa and, to a lesser extent, bananas. However, the founding president, Macias Nguema, systematically destroyed this sector through his expulsion of the Nigerian contract labourers and his wholesale personal expropriation, and subsequent

▶

poor management, of the plantations. Macias's excesses led to the death or exile of at least one-third of the population. Finally, he turned to murdering members of his own family, leading to his being overthrown, and subsequently executed, by his nephew and security chief, Obiang Nguema Mbasogo. Initially, Obiang pledged to end the excesses of the Macias years. A multi-party constitution was later introduced. However, Obiang has won all subsequent elections with at least 98 per cent of the vote, thanks to systematic intimidation and fraud. The opposition is weak and divided, while Obiang is regularly ranked as one of the most brutal despots in the world. By the late 1980s, many aid agencies had left the country, owing to the voraciousness of the ruling elite and death threats or attacks on both foreigners and locals who questioned the status quo. Finally, the US withdrew its ambassador after he had received death threats by members of the ruling elite. Owing to the termination of significant foreign aid and the failure to rebuild the plantation economy, there is considerable evidence that the ruling elite turned to crime as a means of revenue generation, including trafficking in drugs, women and children, and allowed the country to serve as a base for arms smuggling and pirate fishing and as a dumping ground for nuclear and chemical waste. President Obiang currently has very poor health, which has variously been ascribed to a cardiac or prostate condition.

The discovery of sizeable oil reserves ended the country's isolation. The ruling family has been courted by both major oil companies and foreign governments and, under the Bush administration, full diplomatic relations were restored with the US. The oil industry is dominated by major US oil companies such as ExxonMobil and oil logistics companies such as Schlumberger. Recently, it transpired that oil companies were paying royalty payments directly into an account at Riggs Bank, New York, controlled by members of the ruling family. The oil reserves are all offshore, mostly in ultra-deep water (typically 7,500 feet below sea level, and a similar distance into the seabed); commercial exploitation has only been possible owing to very recent technological advances. Consequently, the development of the oil industry has been on highly capital-intensive lines, with skilled and managerial jobs being almost exclusively filled by expatriates; there are currently few opportunities for local employment, other than in a relatively small number of menial support tasks. There is no tertiary educational institution in the country, while the school system is in very poor condition; most of the population are functionally illiterate. When recruiting local labour, oil companies make use of labour bureaux controlled by members of the ruling family; wages are paid direct to the bureaux, who are responsible for disciplining labour. There is little evidence of significant firm-based internal training programmes aimed at upgrading the skills of local employees.

In contrast, in Angola, another West African petrostate with an exclusively offshore oil industry and persistent governance and transparency problems, locals have managed to gain access to a wide range of skilled and managerial positions. While in part this has resulted from a decision by the Angolan government to encourage and support a limited number of Angolans to gain engineering training abroad, it has also reflected decisions by a number of major foreign investors to make significant use of local staff, on account of their better understanding of local conditions, and to promote sustainability.

All oil companies investing in Equatorial Guinea centre their staffing policies around the use of parent country nationals. Expatriate oil workers are housed in closed and largely self-sufficient compounds, with almost all supplies being imported from abroad. However, while in many respects the compounds accurately reproduce suburban America, the persistence of a particularly severe strain of malaria has deterred foreign recruitment, leading to proposals to spray large proportions of the country with DDT. Recently, direct commercial flights have been introduced to Houston, Texas, in order to facilitate the

▶

exchange of staff and leave breaks. The offshore nature of the industry makes much of the development 'invisible' to locals, despite the glow flaring from the offshore fields in the night sky. There is currently no refinery, and oil is simply exported on an unrefined basis. Meanwhile, in a goodwill gesture, ExxonMobil recently donated large numbers of mosquito nets to the Ministry of Health; it is commonly held that most were then resold in a neighbouring country by members of the ruling family.

The rich pickings from the oil industry have led to bitter feuds over the division of spoils within the ruling family. In March 2004, a bizarre coup attempt mounted by a grouping of foreign mercenaries, ostensibly to replace the family with an exiled opposition leader, Severo Moto, seems really to have been aimed at securing the succession for the president's brother Armengol, rather than his appointed heir, the notoriously unstable Teodorin, best known for his pretensions as a Hollywood rap artist and producer. It has since transpired that both the US and British governments had prior knowledge of the attempt, as did senior management of at least one major US oil company.

There is little doubt that the present policies and practices of major oil companies investing in Equatorial Guinea raise a range of ethical and practical HR questions.

Source: Wood 2004

Questions

1. What alternative HR policies could oil companies investing in Equatorial Guinea adopt?
2. What are the practical, training, development and resourcing implications of a shift to the alternative policies identified in question 1?
3. What benefits could the oil companies gain from a move away from the near-exclusive use of parent company nationals in skilled and managerial posts?
4. Why do you think the oil companies investing in Equatorial Guinea chose the HR policies identified in the case?

CASE STUDY 11.2

MNCs and suppliers

Geoffrey Wood

Autocom Ltd is a supplier for a Japanese automobile manufacturing plant based in the UK. Autocom itself is situated at a greenfield industrial site in Bedfordshire, to which it relocated from a brownfield industrial site in the mid-1980s.

Historically speaking, the firm had relied on a very stable workforce of long-serving workers. They were unionised, with a long tradition of militancy. In part, the relocation was driven by a desire to break with the past, and to develop new HR policies. Management sought to 'regain their prerogative', above all on the right to upsize and downsize the workforce without risking a dispute with the union. In addition, since the relocation, management has frequently stated its commitment to develop greater task flexibility, although in practice this has amounted to little more than a limited job rotation among the workforce.

▶

In order to 'make a fresh start', the firm has had a policy of employing younger workers since its relocation, as these are 'less likely to have the wrong ideas'. Training is done on an informal 'on the job' basis. Although the workforce is, on average, a relatively productive one, the firm has been dogged by a high staff turnover. The firm is beset by high levels of absenteeism, especially on Fridays. In the end, both these problems have driven the limited job rotation that takes place, rather than particular innovations in work organisation.

This has made it particularly difficult to meet orders for the principal customer, which operates on a strict just-in-time system, and requires supplies to be competitively priced. As a result, Autocom has recently considered reviewing its staffing policy.

Moreover, it seems that workers derive little satisfaction from the work. Indeed, their sole interest in the job seems to be in terms of the pay received. The HR manager has often overheard workers voicing sentiments such as: 'Well, it's just another job'; 'I don't want to do this for the rest of my life, but it pays the rent'; 'The firm is OK, but the work is fairly boring'.

There is currently no union operating at the firm, although two unions have recently approached management with a view to organising the workforce.

Questions

1. Do you think the HR policies followed by Autocom are a product of its relationship with a MNC?
2. What are the possible effects an MNC could have on a supplier's HRM policies and why? In other words, what determines the HR policies of multinationals, and how could this 'rub off' on suppliers?

CASE STUDY 11.3

Staffing in multinational organisations: reflective exercises

Geoffrey Wood, Leslie T. Szamosi and Alexandros Psychogios

Exercise a

Think of any multinational organisation you know well.

1. Identify what approach you think it employs in staffing its national subsidiaries (e.g. convergence models, ethnocentric, emic, etic, etc.).
2. Why do you think this approach has been adopted?
3. Could organisational effectiveness be enhanced by the adoption of an alternative approach? (You may want to benchmark your chosen organisation against others in the particular industry.)

▶

Exercise b

Critically analyse and discuss whether an international organisation should implement similar human resource management practices across the world or adapt them to suit local conditions. Discuss these with particular reference to various aspects of HRM in a single country context. You may choose to critically evaluate HRM practice(s) of a particular organisation(s) in relation to one country location or give various examples to illustrate your argument.

Exercise c

1. Study two to three MNCs, focusing on investigating their approach to staffing in international assignments. Then, classify each of the MNCs according to their policies in:

    - strategy;

    - staffing mix;

    - performance evaluation criteria;

    - career development;

    - purpose of socialisation processes;

    - information and resource flows.

2. To what extent can you argue that the above issues influence their approaches to staffing?

Bibliography

Anderson, W. and Parker, F. (1964) *Society: Its Organization and Operation,* Princeton, NJ: Van Nostrand.

Andolšek, D. M. and Štebe, J. (2005) 'Devolution or (de)centralization of HRM function in European organizations', Vol.16, No.3, pp.311–29.

Applebaum, E., Bailey, T., Berg, P. and Kalleberg, A. (2000) *Manufacturing Advantage: Why High Performance Work Systems Pay Off,* Ithaca, NY: Cornell University Press.

Berry, J .W. (1999) 'emics and etics: a symbiotic conception', *Culture and Psychology,* Vol.5, No.2, pp.165–72.

Bratton, J. and Gold, J. (2003) *Human Resource Management: Theory and Practice,* London: Palgrave.

Brewster, C. (1995) 'Towards a "European" model of human resource management', *Journal of International Business Studies,* Vol.26, No.1, pp.1–21.

Brewster, C. (2002) 'Transfer of HRM practices around the world', Second International Conference on Human Resource Management in Europe, University of Athens.

Brewster, C., Sparrow, P. and Harris, H. (2001) *Globalization and HR,* London: Chartered Institute of Personnel and Development.

Brewster, C., Brookes, M. and Wood, G. (2004) 'Convergence, isomorphism or duality?: recent survey evidence on the HRM policies of MNCs', unpublished Working Paper, Henley Management College/Middlesex University, London.

Brewster, C., Sparrow, P. and Harris, H. (2005) 'Towards a new model of globalizing HRM', Vol.16, No.6, pp.949–70.

Chang, W-W. (2003) 'Considering the limitations of etic approaches to cross-cultural study', *Human Resource Development Quarterly*, Vol.14, No.4, pp.483–85.

Cray, D. and Mallory, G. R. (1998) *Making Sense of Cultural Change*, London: International Thompson Business Press.

Dowling, P., Welch, D. and Schuler, R. (1999) *International Human Resource Management*, Cincinnati: South West Publishing.

Duysters, G. and Hagedoorn, J. (2001) 'Do company strategies and structures converge in global markets? Evidence from the computer industry', *Journal of International Business Studies*, Vol.32, No.2, pp.347–56.

Elger, T. and Smith, C. (2001) 'The global dissemination of production models and the recasting of work relations in developing societies', in J. K. Coetzee, J. Graaff, F. Hendricks and G. Wood (eds) *Development: Theory Policy and Practice*, Oxford: Oxford University Press.

Favennec-Hery, F. (1996) 'Work and training: a blurring on the edges', *International Labour Review*, Vol.135, No.6, pp.665–74.

Ferlie, E. and Pettigrew, A. (2000) 'Managing through networks', in C. Mabey, G. Salaman and J. Storey (eds) *Strategic Human Resource Management*, London: Sage.

Friedman, T. (1999) *The Lexus and the Olive Tree*, New York: Farrar and Strauss.

Fukuyama, F. (1995) *Trust: Social Virtues and the Creation of Prosperity*, New York: Free Press.

Fukuyama, F. (2000) 'One journey, one destination', in R. Burns and H. Rayment-Pickard (eds) *Philosophies of History*, Oxford: Blackwell.

Giddens, A. (1990) *The Consequences of Modernity*, Cambridge: Polity.

Gooderham, P., Nordhaug, O. and Ringdal, K. (1998) 'When in Rome, do as the Romans?: HRM practices of US subsidiaries in Europe', *Management International Review*, Vol.38, No.2, pp.47–64.

Gooderham, P, Nordhaug, O. and Ringdal, K. (1999) 'Institutional and rational determinants of organizational practices: human resource management in European firms', *Administrative Science Quarterly*, Vol.44, pp.507–31.

Greider, W. (1997) *One World, Ready or Not*, Harmondsworth: Penguin.

Haveman, H. (1993) 'Follow the leader: mimetic isomorphism and the entry into new markets', *Administrative Science Quarterly*, Vol.38, pp.593–627.

Helfrich, H. (1999) 'Beyond the dilemma of cross-cultural psychology: resolving the tension between emic and etic approaches', *Culture and Psychology*, Vol.5, No.2, pp.131–54.

Hofstede, G. (1980) *Culture's Consequences: International Differences in Work-Related Values*, Beverly Hills: Sage.

Hofstede, G. (1991) *Cultures and Organizations*, London: McGraw-Hill.

Holden, L. (2001) 'International human resource management', in I. Beardwell and L. Holden (eds), *Human Resource Management: A Contemporary Approach*, London: FT/Prentice Hall.

Huntington, S. (1996) *The Clash of Civilizations and the Remaking of the World Order*, New York: Touchstone.

Huselid, M. (2000) 'The impact of human resource management practices on turnover, productivity, and corporate financial performance', in C. Mabey, G. Salaman and J. Storey (eds) *Strategic Human Resource Management*, London: Sage.

Janssens, M. (2001) 'Developing a culturally synergistic approach to international human resource management', *Journal of World Business*, Vol.36, No.4, pp.429–50.

Kochan, T. and Osterman, P. (1994) *The Mutual Gains Enterprise*, Boston, MA: Harvard Business School.

Kostova, T. and Roth, K. (2002) 'Adoption of an organizational practice by subsidiaries of multinational corporations', *Academy of Management Journal*, Vol.45, No.1, pp.215–33.

Lane, C. (1998) 'Theories and issues in the study of trust', in C. Lane and R. Bachmann (eds) *Trust Within and Between Organizations*, Oxford: Oxford University Press.

Lao, C. and Ngo, H. (2001) 'Organizational development and firm performance: a comparison of multinational and local firms', *Journal of International Business Studies*, Vol.32, No.1, pp.95–114.

Lincoln, J. and Kalleberg, A. (1990) *Culture, Control and Commitment: A Study of Work Organization in the United States and Japan*, Cambridge: Cambridge University Press.

Mayrhofer, W. and Brewster, C. (1996) 'In praise of ethnocentricity: expatriate policies in European multinationals', *International Executive*, Vol.38, No.6, pp.749–78.

Miah, M. K. and Bird, A. (2007) 'The impact of culture on HRM styles and firm performance: evidence from Japanese parents, Japanese subsidaries/joint ventures and South Asian local companies', *International Journal of Human Resource Management*, Vol.18, No.5, pp.908–23.

Moody, K. (1987) *Workers in a Lean World: Unions in the International Economy*, London: Verso.

Moorehead, G. and Griffin, R. (2004) *Organizational Behaviour: Managing People and Organizations*, Boston, MA: Houghton Mifflin.

Morris, M., Leung, K., Ames, D. and Lickel, B. (1999) 'A view from the inside and the outside: integrating emic and etic insights about culture and judgment', *Academy of Management Review*, Vol.24, No.4, pp.781–96.

Moulettes, A. (2007) 'The absence of women's voices in Hofstede's cultural consequences: a postcolonial reading', *Women in Management Review*, Vol.22, No.6, pp.443–55.

O'Hagan, E. (2002) *Employee Relations in the Periphery of Europe: The Unfolding of the European Social Model*, London: Palgrave.

Parsons, T. (1951) *The Social System*, Glencoe: Free Press.

Perlmutter, H. (1969) 'The tortuous evolution of the multi-national company', *Columbia Journal of World Business*, Vol.4, pp.9–18.

Pfeffer, J. (1994) *Competitive Advantage Through People*, Cambridge, MA: Harvard University Press.

Pulignano, V. (2006). 'The diffusion of employment practices of US-based multinationals in Europe. A case study comparison of British and Italian-based subsidiaries between two sectors', *British Journal of Industrial Relations*, Vol.44, No.3, pp.497–518.

Rose, R. C. and Kumar, N. (2007) 'The transfer of Japanese-style HRM to subsidiaries abroad', *Cross Cultural Management: An International Journal*, Vol.14, No.3, pp.240–53.

Sako, M. (1998) 'Does trust improve business performance?', in C. Lane and R. Bachmann (eds) *Trust Within and Between Organizations*, Oxford: Oxford University Press.

Scullion, H. (2001) 'International human resource management', in J. Storey (ed.) *Human Resource Management: A Critical Text*, London: Thomson Learning.

Serote, P., Mager, A. and Budlender, D. (2001) 'Gender and development', in J. K. Coetzee, J. Graaff, F. Hendricks and G. Wood (eds) *Development: Theory Policy and Practice*, Oxford: Oxford University Press.

Smith, P. B. (2002) 'Women in management: reflections and projections', *Women in Management Review*, Vol.22, No.1, pp.6–18.

Sparrow, P. and Hiltrop, J-M. (2000) 'Redefining the field of European human resource management', in C. Mabey, G. Salaman and J. Storey (eds) *Strategic Human Resource Management*, London: Sage.

Streeck, W. (1995) 'Neo-voluntarism: a new European social policy regime', *European Law Journal*, Vol.1, No.1, pp.31–59.

Tummala, K. (1999) 'Policy of preference: lessons from India, the United States and South Africa', *Public Administration Review*, Vol.59, No.6, pp.495–508.

Ulrich, D. (1997) *Human Resource Champions*, Cambridge, MA: Harvard University Business School Press.

Wang, Z. and Zang, Z. (2005) 'Strategic human resources, innovation and entrepreneurial fit', *International Journal of Manpower*, Vol.26, No.6, pp.544–59.

Warner, M. (2005) 'Whither international human resource management?', *International Journal of Human Resource Management*, Vol.13, pp.870–74.

Webster, E. and Wood, G. (2005) 'Human resource management practice and institutional constraints', *Employee Relations*, Vol.27, No.4.

Whitley, R. (1999) *Divergent Capitalisms: The Social Structuring and Change of Business Systems*, Oxford: Oxford University Press.

Wood, G. (2001) 'Globalization and human resource development', in J. K. Coetzee, J. Graaff, F. Hendricks and G. Wood (eds) *Development: Theory Policy and Practice*, Oxford: Oxford University Press.

Wood, G. (2004) 'Business and politics in a criminal state: the case of Equatorial Guinea', *African Affairs*, Vol.103, No.413, pp.547–67.

Wood, G. and Brewster, C. (2002) 'Decline and renewal in the British labour movement', *Society in Transition*, Vol.33, No.2, pp.241–58.

Wright, P. M., Snell, S. A. and Dyer, L. (2005) 'New models of strategic HRM in a global context', *International Journal of Human Resource Management*, Vol.16, No.6, 875–81.

Zeira, Y. and Harari, E. (1977) 'Genuine multinational staffing policy: expectations and realities', *Academy of Management Journal*, Vol.20, No.2, pp.327–33.

Chapter 12

COMPARATIVE HUMAN RESOURCE MANAGEMENT

Geoffrey Wood and David Collings

Introduction

This chapter is about ways of comparing human resource management[1] (HRM) from context to context. This raises a number of questions. Firstly, in a world that is supposedly 'globalising', does this mean that HRM is likely to become more similar over time, regardless of context? Secondly, what makes HRM different in different places? Thirdly, what are the key differences likely to be found in HRM in different places? Fourthly, what ways have researchers used to study and understand such differences?

Let us start with the first question. A longstanding debate in the management literature concerns the extent to which management practices are converging or diverging across nation states. This is not a terribly new question, of course: even in the nineteenth century, scholars such as Durkheim and Marx sought to understand the nature of modernisation of societies and workplace practices, and the extent to which they were becoming more alike. Over the past two decades, the debate about globalisation – the extent to which the opening of markets, more mobile investors and the apparent homogenisation of global consumer taste has made the planet more unified – has rekindled all this. A key underlying consideration in this debate is the extent to which globalisation is facilitating the convergence of national economies and the HR and other management practices that encompass this, and the homogenisation of the modus operandi of multinational corporations (MNCs) operating in the global economy (Ferner 2000).

Indeed, a good starting point in looking at the globalisation and HRM debate is in the latter area: surely firms that operate on a global basis are the pioneers of a common HRM practice? The issue of multinational HR practices is examined in Chapter 11. However, for the purposes of this chapter, it is worth noting that that multinational corporations, one of the principle agents responsible for foreign direct investment (Hirst and Thompson 1999), are the key drivers in the internationalisation process (Ferner and Hyman 1998). Thus these corporations can be perceived as significant in transferring practices from their country of origin with them when they establish operations in foreign countries (Ferner 1997).

---

[1]HRM has been defined in a number of ways ranging from 'a distinctive approach to employment management' (Storey 1992, p.5) with particular characteristics in regard to employee management to 'anything and everything associated with the management of employment relationships in the firm' (Boxall and Purcell 2000, p.184) (see also Chapter 1 of this text). In this chapter we adopt the latter definition and thus define HRM quite broadly and also incorporate issues external to the firm, such as the nature of the labour market, issues relating to trade unions and the like, which may have an impact on HRM policy and practice within the walls of the organisation.

Looking specifically at human resource management, there is broad consensus that dominant modern conceptions of the field are heavily influenced by US thinking (Brewster 2007; Guest 1990). Thus, there is a degree of expectation that these US models enjoy a hegemonic position in global business contexts and that all HRM practice will converge on this US model. Writers such as Kidger (1991) and DiMaggio and Powell (1983) argue that US multinationals, business schools and consultants will contribute to global convergence on US conceptualisations of HRM, reflected in HRM practice across the world (see Brewster 2007 for a recent review). In illuminating the convergence/divergence polemic in the context of cross-national management practice, we can point to a number of significant studies. For instance, Gunnigle *et al.*'s (2002) study found a clear variation between HRM practice in firms of different national origin (see also Gooderham *et al.* 1999). In a similar vein, Harzing and Sorge (2003) found that while internationalisation strategy was more closely related to industry and size than other variables, the country of origin of firms was significant in explaining differences in control mechanisms utilised by firms. Thus there was continued divergence in control mechanisms utilised in firms of different national origin and they argue that, on balance, divergence remains in place. Geppert and his colleagues also pointed to differences in the change management strategies pursued by organisations of different nationalities (Geppert *et al.* 2003). Thus, on balance, the literature suggests that management practices continue to be characterised by divergence across national borders (Brewster *et al.* 2004; Harzing and Sorge 2003), and indeed Hirst and Thompson (1999, p.95) go as far as to suggest that 'in many ways . . . [national business] systems are being reinforced and strengthened by the internationalization of business' (see also Hall and Soskice 2001, pp.56–60; Whitley 1999).

The debate is, however, a complex one and there are a number of theories advanced which posit a universalist (convergence) or continued divergence of business systems and management practices. These theories merit some discussion and the key debates are outlined below. Our discussion is framed in the arena of comparative human resource management, which is defined as 'about understanding and explaining what differences exist between countries in the way that human resources are managed' (Brewster 2006, p.68). Thus, comparative HRM stands in contrast to international HRM, which Scullion (1995, p.325) defines as 'the HRM issues and problems arising from the internationalization of business, and the HRM strategies, policies and practices which firms pursue in response to the internationalization of business': comparative HRM is about comparing what firms do in different national contexts, irrespective of whether they are multinational or not. While Boxall (1995, p.5), writing in the mid-1990s, described comparative HR as a poorly theorised, emerging field, there is little doubt that we have witnessed significant theoretical and empirical development in the field in the past decade, and these developments inform our chapter.

There are two principal strands of literature on comparative HRM. The first draws on a range of different theoretical traditions to make assumptions as to the direction of national economies, supported by a mixture of case study evidence and macroeconomic data – in short, top-down approaches. This area of study concerns itself primarily with what makes HR different from case to case, and what the general differences encountered are likely to be: in other words, the second and third questions with which we opened our chapter. In contrast, bottom-up approaches seek to shed more light on national commonalities and variations in human resource management through pragmatic empirical work. The primary focus of the latter school of thought is, hence, on cataloguing HRM practices, rather than trying to explain them in terms of a broader theoretical template. Again, it is about what distinguishes HR practices in particular national contexts. However, its bottom-up focus means that such studies often provide richer detail on precisely how HR is practised in specific contexts – often enriched with case study evidence – although this may be at the expense of ease of comparative analysis. Finally, such studies draw on a range of different methods – be that surveys (economy, region, industry or firm wide) or more qualitative methods. This diversity makes for richness in detail, but, of course, makes direct comparisons between contexts more difficult!

Convergence or divergence in HRM systems

UNIVERSALISTS: THE CONVERGENCE DEBATE

The key underlying philosophy of the universalists is the general applicability of a common system of social and economic organisation (Rubery and Grimshaw 2003). In other words, they assume that a specific general model is of universal worth. Inspired by Francis Fukuyama's (2000) suggestion that the ending of the Cold War saw the 'end of history', such perspectives assume that all national economies will move towards the neo-liberal ideal, which would be mirrored by similar shifts in firm-level practices (see also Friedman 1999). Allowing space for individual self-actualisation and fair recognition in line with market incentives will unlock creativity and enterprise; firms will be able to operate without being reigned in by distortions (Fukuyama 2000, p.320). While universalists do acknowledge that there may be variations between different countries, these are underscored by 'objective' economic or technological differences between societies or institutional barriers to the implementation of 'best practice' as opposed to fundamental differences in what constitutes 'the best way' (ibid.). At an organisation level, convergence 'implies a relative degree of disembeddedness of practices and structures, overriding more regionally or nationally specific institutions or behavioural predispositions' (Harzing and Sorge, 2003, p.188). Within the universalist school a number of distinct variations emerge. The most influential strand of this thinking is the so-called new-institutionalists (cf. Harbison and Myers 1959; Kerr *et al.* 1960; DiMaggio and Powell 1983) and we focus on this as an example in this chapter.

New-institutionalism

New-institutionalism was popularised by the writings of Harbison and Myers (1959), Kerr *et al.* (1960) and DiMaggio and Powell (1983) among others, drawing on the works of Douglass North (1990). Underlying this broad tradition is a view of institutions as a provider of incentives to rational actors: institutions may help people make the right decisions, or deter them from making the wrong ones. Institutionalisation has been defined as the 'process by which social processes, obligations, or actualities come to take on a rulelike status in social thought and action' (Meyer and Rowan 1977, p.341). Organisations have a tendency to copy what is done elsewhere in an attempt to gain legitimacy or the support of external agencies within a society (Strauss and Hanson 1997). While functional or technical criteria may be key determinants of adoptions of innovations at an early stage, the importance of these determinants become weaker over time (Tolbert and Zucker 1996). In a similar vein, Meyer and Rowan (1977) argue that organisations may not conform to a set of institutionalised practices simply because they are taken for granted or 'constitute reality' but because they are rewarded for doing so through increased legitimacy, resources or survival capabilities. In other words, there are some external incentives which inform the organisation's decision to adopt the practices.

Organisations sharing the same environment are likely to demonstrate isomorphism (in other words, experience pressures to do similar things) as they are believed to become structurally similar as they respond to like pressures (Gooderham *et al.* 1999). Broadly speaking, differences between economies are regarded as deviations from established 'best practice' and are expected to dissolve as nation states catch up with those countries higher up the technological or organisational ladder. The bulk of work in this genre makes the assumption that the US model of weak unions and a heavily deregulated labour market is the optimal model to be followed: all societies will inevitably move towards this model, if institutional distortions are removed. A central feature of the US model is strong rights for property owners, and weak ones for other parties: this is seen as a central prerequisite for the efficient operation of markets.

The implications for labour are quite profound and, as Thelen (2001, p.75) postulates, the convergence of human resource management and industrial relations systems is regarded by this school as:

> A seemingly inexorable, inevitable slide toward deregulation, as high unemployment and increased capital mobility allow employers to dispense with strategies based on accommodating labour and instead shop for the best (i.e. least restrictive, least expensive labour regime). The result is a convergence theory that sees changes in the 'strong labour' countries as moving them in the direction of the weak labour countries.

In practice, attempts to apply such theories to the management of people has two key characteristics. The first is its prescriptive nature: it aims to highlight best practices, aimed at what things should be – and perhaps, inevitably will be – rather than taking account of divergences from this model that are likely to manifest themselves even within the US context (Brewster 2007). Secondly, it makes some very definite assumptions as to what best practice HRM is likely to be like (Brewster 2007). In practice, this will translate into the type of HRM where the employer has a relatively free hand to set the terms and conditions of the employment contract and work organisation without the 'interferance of extraneous parties such as trade unions' (ibid.). This may translate either into a type of 'soft HRM', where the firm emphasises communication and consultation – but little in the way of genuine co-determination by way of collective bargaining and works councils – or into 'hard HRM', where the firm tightly monitors employee performance, tailoring pay to individual effort and outcomes, and where employees can be readily hired and fired according to day-to-day organisational needs. Such approaches, of course, ignore the fact that individual forms of communication tend to be primarily top-down – junior employees will be reluctant to express unpopular opinions or be seen as bearers of bad news, if this opens them to retaliation by their superiors. Again, weak job security may allow the firm to rapidly adjust its workforce size according to organisational needs and the relative demand for its goods or services, but it also weakens the commitment of employees to the organisation. And, such approaches discount the knowledge and wisdom that employees may have accumulated over a time period of working for the organisation; the worth of this may be extremely difficult to cost accurately, and it will be lost forever, should such employees be dispensed with arbitrarily.

Finally, while the heyday of such studies was the 1990s and early 2000s, when the US was doing rather better than many of the advanced societies of Western Europe, the tables have now turned: to many, the US model appears to be one of speculation, insecure living standards and labour repression, rather than that of a new and better future. It was argued that the US model encouraged firms to create new jobs: this ignored the fact that in the US, unemployment is a lot worse than might initially seem apparent based on national statistics. These statistics obscure the fact that 6 million US workers hold highly insecure 'contingent' jobs, 15 million work in part-time or reduced jobs without benefits, 3 million unemployed are not counted as such because they fail to qualify for benefits, 1.5 million are in the armed forces, and a further 2 million are in prison (Harcourt and Wood 2007). What about in firm HR practices? Things are, again, a lot less efficient than might first seem apparent. While acknowledging that there is a good degree of heterogeneity in the nature of US industry, with some firms displaying paternalistic attitudes underscored by supportive welfare capitalist traditions (Jacoby 1997), there is also a more dominant tradition in the US context which is less favourable to employees. Nonetheless, US firms invest relatively large amounts in training, partially to compensate for an extremely poor vocational training system, and also because of the recurring need to provide basic induction training to new staff in the case of firms that have high staff turnover rates (cf. Harcourt and Wood 2007). Again, high levels of productivity in the US reflect long working hours and fewer holidays: continental Western European workers appear capable of producing similar amounts in significantly shorter periods of time, and thus are able to enjoy more leisure time and have better work–life balances, which, again, is likely to make them more useful when they are at work.

At a theoretical level, new-institutionalism has been criticised from a number of perspectives since its emergence (cf. Sorge and Warner 1986; Sorge and Streeck 1988). For example, Sorge and his colleagues pointed to the fact that in the context of the UK and Germany, factories of similar size, producing similar products with similar technology, could demonstrate dissimilar forms of organisation: there was no evidence that a US or US-like model was necessarily the best, or that it was driving out other models. They also pointed to the persistence of both corporate and free market models as responses to economic and technological change in different countries (see also Turner 2006).

DIVERGENCE: THE ENDURANCE OF NATIONAL SYSTEMS

A key principle underlying most theories of divergence is that, contrary to management rhetoric which is obsessed with efficiency, organisational life is heavily influenced by factors which have very little to do with organisational goals and which may indeed thwart these very goals. The wider societal collectives in which organisations are embedded are quite significant in influencing management practices in organisations (Sorge 2004). The key schools which are generally associated with these arguments are broadly classified as culturists (cf. Hofstede 1980, 2001; Trompenaars 1993) and institutionalists (cf. Whitley 1999; Hall and Soskice 2001). We now look in turn at these schools.

The culturalists

Although there have been a number of studies which have attempted to classify different nationalities on the basis of cultural dimensions (cf. Schneider and Barsoux 2003 for a synthesis of the literature), we focus on the work of Geert Hofstede, as the underlying premise of all of the studies is broadly similar and Hofstede's work is generally considered the seminal study in the field. Hofstede (2001, p.9) defines culture thus: 'the collective programming of the mind that distinguishes the members of one group or category of people from another'.

Key to this definition, he argues, is the fact that social systems exist only because human behaviour is not random, but rather to a certain extent predictable. In developing his theory Hofstede identifies three levels of human mental programming, the individual, collective and universal (2001, pp.2–3). While the universal level of mental programming is, as the name suggests, shared by almost all of humankind, 'a kind-of biological operating system', and the individual is unique to each individual, it is the collective level that is key to understanding national cultures. Most of our mental programming is learned at this collective level; this is illustrated by the fact that we share traits with people who have gone through the same learning processes but with different genetic makeup. This level of culture is shared by people belonging to a certain group. Examples of collective cultural similarities include language and deference shown to elders, among other traits. Key to our discussion is Hofstede's (2001, p.11) thesis that although societal norms reflective of the collective level of human programming originate in a variety of ecological factors, they have resulted in 'the development and pattern maintenance of institutions in society with particular structures and ways of functioning'. Examples of these institutions include the education system, political systems, legislation and the family. Hofstede continues that although the institutions may change over time, the underlying societal norms prevail, reflecting the persistent influence of

Box 12.1: HRM in practice

Hofstede's dimensions of cultural difference

1. **Power distance,** which is related to the different solutions to the basic problem of human inequality.
2. **Uncertainty avoidance,** which is related to the level of stress in a society in the face of an unknown future.
3. **Individualism versus collectivism,** which is related to the integration of individuals into primary groups.
4. **Masculinity versus femininity,** which is related to the division of emotional roles between men and women.
5. **Long-term versus short-term orientation,** which is related to the choice of focus for people's efforts: the future or the present.

Source: Hofstede, 2001, p.29

the majority value system. Any new institutions which emerge over time are smoothed by these underlying norms until their structures and functioning eventually adapt to the norms.

Hofstede differentiated between national cultures on five different criteria. These criteria are outlined in Box 12.1 Hofstede's study was based on a sample of some 116,000 IBM employees in 72 countries who completed pen-and-paper questionnaires between 1967 and 1973. In a later stage data from 10 more countries and three multicultural regions were added (see Hofstede 2001, chapter 2 for further detail on the methodology of the study).

The key underlying premise of the culturist approach is that cross-national differences in industrial relations systems and in organisations and the management of human resources are rooted in strong values and beliefs of the people in a given country. Practices are sustained because people find it unappealing, unethical or even repulsive to do otherwise (Sorge 2004). For example, individuals in countries which are classified as high on the collectivist dimension are more likely to be ideologically committed to the trade union movement; conversely, where individualist preferences prevail, individuals are likely to be less ideologically committed to the trade union cause.

Although quite influential, the culturalist approach has never been universally accepted and indeed the approach and specifically Hofstede's work have been subject to a number of criticisms. Most notable is the argument that although the approach is useful in explaining differences between nationalities, it fails to account for heterogeneity within the citizens of a given country. Rather it represents a central tendency within a nation (Evans *et al.* 2002). Although the culturalists point to the link between the evolution of a country's business system or institutional structures and the characteristics of a national culture, they generally fail to explore the relationship between the cultural values and the structural and institutional characteristics of national economic systems (Ferner *et al.* 2001). The results of Hofstede's study have also been specifically criticised. Tayeb (1996) points to the limitation that the study is based on an attitude-survey questionnaire which she argues is the least appropriate way of measuring culture. His choice of dimensions of cultural difference (see Hofstede's Box 12.1) has also been criticised (McSweeney 2002). A further significant criticism is the fact that the research is limited to a single organisation (IBM) and thus the sample may not be representative (McSweeney 2002).

At a theoretical level, the perspective has been condemned as overly functionalist – i.e. that national systems work, and that they work as a coherent whole (Bacharach 1989). It assumes both that the culture corresponds with national boundaries and that national cultures are immutable. This raises the awkward questions as to whether some cultures are more conducive to doing business than others, and whether some nations are condemned to a particular path on account of their cultural heritage. Of course, this cannot explain why nations can reinvent themselves. Prior to the Second World War, Austria was a poverty-stricken and unstable backwater, characterised by authoritarian and conflictual employment relations. Today, Austria is a highly prosperous country: Austrian employment relations are held up as a model of cooperation between managers and workers. More recently, both New Zealand and Ireland have enjoyed strong economic recoveries linked to legal reforms that have promoted cooperation and mutual dependence, rather than conflict and 'winner takes all' relations, at the workplace.

Recent years have witnessed the development of a less quantitative and more historical perspective on the divergence of modern industrial societies, the institutionalist perspective, and we now consider the key arguments of this school.

Institutionalist perspectives

Rational-hierarchical approaches. The persistence of national diversity challenged new-institutional accounts of convergence. From within the economics and finance literature, new approaches – which again saw institutions as providers of incentives and constraints on rational actors – now sought to explain the persistence of national diversity. Such accounts focused on the relative strength of property (and hence, owner) rights, looking at the effects of law, constitutions and politics (Djankov *et al.* 2003, p.596). Roe (2003) argues that specific political contexts are likely to encourage co-determination between managers and employees in the workplace: in turn, this will make for poor managerial accountability to owners as the system will both divide supervisory boards and encourage collusion between workers and managers at the expense of owners. For example, many managers seek personal aggrandisement through running a disproportionately large organisation, which, in turn, encourages the inefficient use of labour: in turn, the workforce colludes in the myth of needed bigness.

In their work on the effects of judicial systems and corporate governance, La Porta and colleagues (2000) suggest that a country's legal tradition will determine investor rights. In common law countries, investor rights vis-à-vis other stakeholders are likely to be stronger, at the expense of other stakeholder interests; the converse is true in civil law countries (La Porta *et al.* 2000). La Porta *et al.* further argue that national legal systems mould the regulation of labour (Botero *et al.* 2004, p.1379). In civil law countries, employee rights are more clearly delineated, while governments are more likely to directly regulate labour markets (ibid., p.1340). Hence, industrial relations will affect the manner in which a corporation is governed in the same manner as investor rights will (Botero *et al.* 2004, pp.1379–80). When worker rights are strong, those of owners will be relatively weak, resulting in the 'bottom line' not receiving the same degree of priority as it would in a common law setting.

Pagano and Volpin (2005) propose a further variation on such accounts, and focus on the effects of electoral systems: proportional representation electoral systems are likely to promote coalition building, again constraining the rights of shareholders at the expense of other interest groupings; such systems also are likely to encourage neo-corporatist arrangements, promoting co-determinism at workplace level, again at the expense of owner rights. Both these schools of thought follow a long tradition of 'property rights' approaches to understanding management: shareholders have ultimate authority and it is necessary for managers to follow their wishes, with owners' rights taking precedence over the interests of all other groups in the firm (Rollinson and Dundon 2007, p.73).

What this literature has in common is that it sees employee and owner rights as a zero-sum game. If employees have rights, it must be to the detriment of owners and vice versa. Hence, in contexts where owner rights are stronger, one is more likely to encounter hard

HRM policies geared to the bottom line: performance-based pay, close monitoring of output, effective performance appraisals and insecure job tenure. In contrast, where employee rights are stronger, one is more likely to find strong unions, collective bargaining, high job security and, indeed, structures such as works councils that give employees a say in the organisation of work.

Varieties of capitalism approaches. This broad body of literature rejects the rational actor model: individuals make decisions not always on the basis of information, but also owing to commitments and relations with other actors. Hence, the varieties of capitalism literature locate the firm within a centre of relations with stakeholders: owners, employees, community and community associations, and government. The theoretical origins of this tradition are diverse, drawing on both functionalist and radical theories. Within the North American industrial relations literature, abiding influences have been Dunlop and Bendix's essentially functionalist accounts (see Bendix 1956): national industrial relations practices constitute a coherent and incrementally developing system. Firms within a business system tend to adopt similar HR practices in the interests of familiarity, and because they are closely fitted to wider economic, social and cultural realities. Some of the criticisms levelled at cultural accounts can also be focused on this literature.

Within Europe, there are many different accounts, including Whitley (1999) and Amable (2003). However, probably the most influential account has been that of Hall and Soskice (2001): the 'varieties of capitalism' approach; this builds on earlier work by Dore (2000) and Lincoln and Kalleberg (1990) that pointed to the key distinctions both in firm-level HR practices and wider governance between Anglo-American liberal market economies (LMEs) and collaborative market economies (CMEs). Examples of the former would include the US and the UK, and of the latter, Germany, the Low Countries, Scandinavia and Japan. Hall and Soskice seek out national-level differences in the nature of capitalism and attempt to develop terms that classify these more generally than has previously been the case. They conceptualise political economies as terrains populated by political actors, each with a rational self-interest to advance their own interests. While acknowledging a multiplicity of actors, such as individuals, governments, trade unions, suppliers and others, firms are regarded as the critical actors in any capitalist economy. Firms are viewed relationally, in that the relationships which they develop with key internal and external actors are inextricably linked to the firms' ability to develop core competencies or dynamic capabilities, for developing, producing and distributing goods or services profitably.

The most significant characteristic of firms operating in LMEs in this regard is management's unilateral right to manage. This is reflected in the principle of 'employment-at-will' which dominates the American industrial relations landscape. This places little obligation of firms to provide employees with a guarantee of employment and thus employees can be hired and fired 'at will' on the basis of business needs. This results in highly fluid labour markets characterised by the ease of release or hire of labour and the investment by employees in general, transferable skills as opposed to company-specific ones. This can be linked to the nature of corporate governance and the fact that the interests of shareholders are emphasised above those of any other stakeholder in the business relationship (Almond et al. 2003).

Closely linked to the individuals' investment in general, transferable skills is the nature of the training and education system in LMEs. Vocational training is generally provided by institutions offering formal education emphasising general skills rather than company-specific apprenticeships, as companies are unwilling to invest in specific training as there is no guarantee that employees will remain with the firm. The imperative of employees gaining general training is further emphasised by the fluid nature of labour markets, where general, transferable skills determine employment potential. This high investment in general training lowers the cost of company-specific training; however, as firms generally focus on providing employees with in-house training it is not as expensive as traditional apprenticeship-type programmes. Rather the focus is on further developing general, marketable skills (Hall and Soskice 2001).

Conversely, in coordinated market economies industrial relations systems are characterised by strong industrial relations institutions. These institutions have evolved in response to companies' dependence on highly skilled employees with substantial work autonomy, who could potentially hold their employers to ransom by moving to other firms, while employees may be exploited if they share information with management. In the German system, many of these problems were addressed through the development of industry-level bargaining between employer organisations and trade unions. As Jacobi *et al.* (1998, pp.190–91) argue, while unions and employer organisations are in legal and formal terms independent, in reality they are mutually dependant, and should be considered 'reliable partners within a network of stable cooperation'. These provisions arguably protect employees against arbitrary management decision making, including changes to working conditions and layoffs, thus encouraging employees to invest in company-specific skills and extra effort.

Hall and Soskice link these differences to different national strengths. The pluralist HRM policies found in CMEs is likely to be conducive to high-quality, incrementally innovative production (exemplifiers of the latter including Toyota, Volkswagen, Siemens, etc.). In contrast, the managerially dominant types of HRM found in LMEs are likely to be associated with either low-value-added service sector activity or high-technology innovation. This is likely to result in a number of key distinctions in terms of skills needs and HR practices. Incremental innovation requires good industry-specific skills, high security of tenure (in order to encourage the development of firm-specific human capital) and cooperation and knowledge sharing through advanced forms of participation that genuinely empower employees (such as found through centralised collective bargaining and works councils) (Thelen 2001). In contrast, hi-tech industry requires generic tertiary skills (e.g. university education), a mobile workforce and more individually oriented reward and incentives systems (Thelen 2001). The low-value-added sweatshop paradigm requires little investment in people, with pay being tied to output or held at the lowest acceptable level. The fact that clusters of HR practices continue to be found within particular regions and nations points to the importance of understanding national context.

Hence, Locke, Kochan and Piore (1995, p.143) point to the significance of the historical development of the employment relations system within a nation state, noting:

> although a particular approach to employment relations has emerged in all the advanced industrial nations . . . [in their study] . . . the particular from [of the employment relations approach] it has taken and its extent vary considerably within countries, between firms, industries and regions, and between countries with different historical traditions and institutional arrangements.

This argument is articulated by a number of other authors based on empirical study. Sorge and Streeck (1988) have argued that there has been an explosive divergence in industrial relations, rather than an implosive convergence towards one central best practice. Morley *et al.*'s (1996, p.652) study pointed to elements of convergence and divergence in European industrial relations, but concluded that overall, any coherent move towards convergence was 'a long way off'. Indeed, Hall and Soskice's argument that variance between the types of capitalism alluded to above will reinforce differences in national institutional frameworks seems to have significant merit based on the empirical evidence. This is a view shared by Geppert *et al.* (2003) whose case-based data suggest that the more globalised the organisational strategy pursued by a firm, the more it perpetuates and reinforces cross-national specifics. Thus they posit 'from this perspective one could argue that globalisation ultimately reinforces the importance of different national contexts' (2003, p.833).

Box 12.2: HRM in practice

What makes for common practices within countries?

What encourages firms to do similar things in particular countries? And, why are some countries better at certain types of economic activity than others? There are many explanations for this. From the classic economics literature, the concept of 'economic man', that society is made up of profit-maximising competing individuals, has developed the argument that institutions provide incentives for people to make certain kinds of decisions. For example, if property rights are strong, firms will be particularly likely to pursue profits, particularly in the short term. From sociology and socio-economics come alternative explanations that see institutions as webs of relationships. Social life is not just about competition for resources, but also about relationships between individuals, and between individuals and associations. Such relationships are likely to make for a great degree of continuity and more effective exchange relations (as people know what to expect of others they interact with). Finally, drawing on both sociology and psychology, cultural accounts argue that national cultures (and sets of national cultures) are likely to result in individuals in particular societies behaving in particular ways. All these perspectives suggest a degree of path dependence (i.e. people and companies in societies are likely to carry on doing much the same type of thing over extended periods of time) and uniformity (certain sets of decisions and actions are likely to be particularly common in specific contexts). More recent critical work has suggested that societies undergo periods of crisis and rupture, leading to fundamental institutional changes which, in turn, will provide for a new period of stability and growth. This would explain, for example, why Ireland has transformed itself from a poor – and poorly performing – economy to one of Europe's most successful. Again, it has been argued that there is likely to be considerable diversity within individual societies, with not one but several paradigms – or ways of doing things – coexisting. Particular types of institutions may work well with more than one set of practices. This would explain why in the US the high-value-added production paradigms of Silicon Valley coexist with the cost-cutting approaches characterised by McDonald's and Wal-Mart.

Empirical ways of understanding diversity

The preceding discussion has illustrated that we can see that diversity in HR practice may be understood from a range of different theoretical starting points. At an empirical level, there is a rich body of literature aimed at understanding variations in HR practices at a country level. While sometimes employing some of the above theories as a starting point, this literature is primarily concerned with documenting key HR practices within specific national contexts. Sometimes these have been consolidated into books about HRM in specific regions or continents, an example being Routledge's *Global HRM* series of edited books on HRM in specific regions, such as Europe (Holt Larsen and Mayrhofer 2006), Africa (Kamoche *et al.* 2003), Asia Pacific (Budhwar 2004) and the Middle East (Budhwar and Mellahi 2006), and the Wood and Brewster (2007) volume on industrial relations in Africa. These books have been distinguished by high-quality contributions by often locally based country experts, with the editorial team drawing out common themes and trends. A further recent innovation has been Morley *et al.*'s (2006) and Ackers and Wilkinson's (2003) contributions which take a regional perspective on the comparison of industrial relations systems.

Similar country-study-type articles have been published in a range of academic journals, most notably *International Journal of Human Resource Management* and *Employee Relations*. These articles tend to focus on defining features of HRM from either a functional areas or relationship approach. Articles in the first genre seek to document and explain national or regional practices in recruitment and planning, motivation and reward, industrial relations and/or human resource development. In contrast, articles following the second approach tend to focus on issues such as the degree of employer–employee interdependence and the extent of delegation to employees (Whitley 1999). The former would include job security and the extent to which employers will invest in their people and how employees are inclined to accumulate organisation-specific skills. Meanwhile, the latter would include the degree of participation and involvement. In practice, the comparative lessons of individual national experiences are often only briefly alluded to, or presented in a highly attenuated form, it being left up the reader to decide what the experience of a particular nation or region reveals about the practice of HRM more generally.

A variation of such approaches are subnational studies and supranational studies. As Boyer and Hollingsworth (1997) note, institutions are nested at supra-, national and sub-national levels. In other words, although national setting heavily impacts on HR policies, institutions – be they rules (formal laws and informal conventions), training structures, development incentives and/or physical infrastructural provisions and support – may also vary within states, or may be shared between countries. For example, European Union directives governing labour standards have encouraged moves towards common continent-wide HR practices in many areas, an example being the treatment of elderly workers. This has led some commentators to suggest that a European-wide social model is emerging, associated with cooperative HR policies; other, more pessimistic writers have argued that Europeanisation has been associated with the introduction of more hardline management-oriented 'Anglo-Saxon' practices that have seriously damaged more cooperative continental European forms of HRM (O'Hagan 2002; see also Morley *et al.* 2006, section two, for a discussion on these issues).

Within countries, regional development initiatives (and local training realities and historical legacies) have led to some regions pursuing distinct trajectories. An example of this would be the Grenoble hi-tech cluster in France: such regional concentrations of industry have encouraged firms to tailor their HR policies accordingly, given specific sectoral needs and local skills realities. People management here centres on the efficient use of a relatively young incoming (from other parts of France, and abroad) workforce, with high levels of tertiary education, and the support of a number of excellent public research centres (Anniello 2004, p.314). In a 2004 edited collection by Colin Crouch *et al.* (2004), it was found that local production systems could be encountered in many countries across Europe, each bringing with them associated sets of HR policies and practices, in many respects different from national norms.

Conclusion

This chapter has aimed to introduce some of the major debates within the field of comparative HRM. A growing body of theoretical enquiry and empirical evidence points to the fact that individual nations and regions remain distinct in many areas. This would appear to vindicate the varieties of capitalism and other similar institutional approaches. At the same time, in studying comparative HRM, we need to be aware that, even if countries and regions may not be becoming more alike, they are all subject to change. In other words, we are studying a moving target in many respects. This would reflect the role of supranational institutions such as the EU, technological changes, changes in laws and innovations in policy and firm-level practices and in some instances the impact of innovations introduced by foreign multinational companies operating in the host country (Gennard 1974; Gunnigle 1995; Ferner and Quintanilla 2002). Hence, the new Irish HRM model, for example, is rather different from that encountered 20 years ago (see Gunnigle 1995; Collings *et al.* 2008). This makes the empirically oriented studies that formed the focus of the second part of this chapter of particular importance: keeping abreast of innovations in practice is an essential part of being an excellent HR manager and, indeed, an excellent student in HRM.

CASE STUDY 12.1

HRM in Mozambique

Geoffrey Wood and David Collings

After almost 500 years of a particularly exploitative form of colonial rule, a failed socialist experiment and a bloody civil war, Mozambique underwent radical economic adjustment in the late 1980s and 1990s in line with the then prevailing neo-liberal orthodoxy. While the latter had severely adverse consequences for large areas of an already fragile manufacturing sector, it also led to an – albeit limited – increase in foreign investment and a partial revitalisation of the transport and tourism industries.

A nationwide survey of HR practices in Mozambique revealed little evidence of innovation or of leading-edge practices. While most firms had a specialised people management function, the techniques employed remained personal, informal, but also top-down. At the same time, HRM techniques cannot be considered to be uniformally 'bleak house' or 'low road'; the 'low road' hypothesis is thus falsified. Rather, HRM practices seem to have much in common with those noted in other African countries; this would include a reliance on personal networks for recruitment, the use of informal training structures, and poor pay and working conditions being mitigated by a willingness by management to make informal concessions to workers in the event of personal difficulties. In contrast to the 'low road' model, Mozambican managers do not make use of rigid sets of rules, little communication, fixed bare minimum wages and an unwillingness to depart from fixed procedures (cf. Taylor and Bain 2003). The dominant 'informal' managerial style is founded on autocratic partriarchalism, underpinned by personal ties. On the one hand, external shocks to the Mozambican economy have resulted in large-scale job shedding that must have done much to erode any sense of mutual commitment. On the other hand, managers retain close personal contact with the workforce – inter alia, through general meetings – and remain willing to adjust terms and conditions of service in response to individual need. The survey would thus provide further evidence to support Harrison (2000) and Pitcher's (2002) arguments that the Mozambican context is one characterised by long-term continuities, despite seemingly radical socio-political changes.

At the same time, the survey revealed evidence of a range of 'best practice' techniques among a small minority of firms. While there is little doubt that the latter are likely to be best equipped to escape reverting to a low-wage, low-skill, low-value-added trajectory, it remains uncertain whether such a path is viable in a context of institutional weakness and cut-throat competition from abroad.

In summary, the survey revealed that relatively few firms make use of a full and complementary range of high-performance work practices. However, most firms have not reverted

▶

to the 'low road'/'bleak house' model that has become a feature of people management in specific sectors within the advanced societies. Indeed, many firms rely on traditional patri-archal-authoritarianism, and are reluctant to concede their workers even basic benefits such as paid vacations and sick leave. On the other hand, many are willing to grant leave at short notice and/or advances on wages, in the event of individual workers experiencing per-sonal difficulties. Contact is maintained with the workforce through irregular meetings, both scheduled and ad hoc, while most firms made use of informal on-the-job training. The dominant Mozambican paradigm of people management shares these common features with that found in many other tropical African countries; such practices represent the product of adverse external environments, periodic systemic shocks and colonial and/or precolonial traditions.

However, in Mozambique, the ability of this highly personal/patriarchal managerial paradigm to engender any sense of mutual commitment is likely to have been eroded by episodic rounds of redundancies, while firms are unlikely to invest systematically in their people through formal training programmes or systematic career planning given a highly competitive environment. Less principled rivals may not only gain a short-term cost advan-tage, but are able to poach staff from those firms that provide effective training and devel-opment. The diffusion of higher-value-added production paradigms is only likely in a more supportive institutional context which encourages firms to buy into mutually advantageous sets of rules governing fair play (cf. Marsden 1999) and which limits the rewards accruing to bad practice. While the more efficient enforcement of legislation may encourage the broader diffusion of 'high road' practices, their sustainability is, at least in part, contingent on the diffusion and reconstitution of supportive conventions (Dore 2000); regrettably, this makes it extremely difficult to depart from the dominant existing paradigm.

Source: Webster and Wood 2005

Questions

1. What are the key features of HRM in Mozambique?
2. Why has HRM in Mozambique been characterised by many continuities, do you think?

Ireland and the multinationals

Geoffrey Wood and David Collings

Ireland is one of the most globalised countries in the world, owing to the significance of foreign-owned MNCs which have established subsidiaries there. The scale of foreign direct investment (FDI) there is driven by a consistent public policy agenda, pursued by successive governments, of providing incentives to attract MNCs to invest in Ireland. This policy has proved very successful and recent research confirms that there are some 470[2]

---

[2]This figure only includes all wholly or majority foreign-owned organisations operating in Ireland, with 500 or more employees worldwide and 100 or more employed in their Irish operations.

▶

foreign-owned MNCs in Ireland (McDonnell *et al.* 2007), employing over 140,000 people. American-owned multinationals are particularly significant players there, with 226 US-owned subsidiaries. These include large high-profile firms such as IBM, Microsoft, Dell, Google, Pfizer, Wyeth and the like. These firms are estimated to employ over 7 per cent of the private sector non-agricultural labour force and also contribute significantly through indirect employment through suppliers and the like and make a very substantial contribution to taxation revenues in Ireland.

Given the disproportionate significance of FDI and American FDI in particular in Ireland, combined with the expectation that HRM policies and practices are likely to converge on the US model, Ireland represents a very interesting context to study the convergence of HRM through looking at subsidiary practice in subsidiary operations. Further, if we do expect to witness convergence of HRM practice, Ireland would represent an interesting test case. The expected convergence would be even more likely to emerge in US MNCs owing to the fact that they tend to be quite ethnocentric in managing the foreign operations and display a preference for centrally developed, standardised policies in their foreign operations.

There is a broad consensus that MNCs have been an important source of innovation in management practices in Ireland, particularly in the application of new HRM/industrial relations approaches and in expanding the role of the specialist HR function. For example, MNCs have been associated with innovation in areas such as the diffusion of so-called 'high commitment' work systems and performance-related pay innovations which appear to have transferred to a degree at least in indigenous firms. Further, US MNCs have been particularly strong in their resistance to recognising trade unions, a trend which stands in contrast to Irish traditions, which were generally supportive of trade unions' role in the workplace. Recent research reveals that over time, as the country's reliance on the FDI sector has increased, MNCs have found it easier to establish and operate subsidiaries on a non-union basis.

However, we do still see evidence of divergence between US MNCs and indigenous firms, suggesting that divergence remains important in the Irish context. For example, based on Gunnigle *et al.*'s (2002) study, we see that American subsidiaries in Ireland put substantially more emphasis on performance appraisal and reward than did Irish organisations. Significantly, US MNCs displayed a degree of adoption of HR practice to account to local standards. This study also unearthed differences between US firms and subsidiaries of other nationalities, providing further evidence of sustained divergence. More recently, Collings *et al.* (2008) argued for elements of an essentially hybrid system with regard to industrial relations in US MNCs, reflecting some particularly 'American' practices in these firms, again suggesting divergence with indigenous firms.

Thus, despite the relative power of US MNCs in the Irish context and the reliance of the Irish economy on the FDI sector, there is little evidence of complete convergence between US MNCs, other foreign MNCs and indigenous firms in the Irish context.

Questions

1. Consider the reasons why differences remain between foreign MNCs and indigenous firms in the Irish context.
2. What challenges may a heavy reliance on FDI have on a host government in terms of balancing the needs of powerful firms and employees in the host economy?

Bibliography

Ackers, P. and Wilkinson, A. (2003) *Understanding Work and Employment: Industrial Relations in Transition,* Oxford: Oxford University Press.

Almond, P., Edwards, T. and Clarke, I. (2003) 'Multinationals and changing national business systems in Europe: towards the shareholder value model?', *Industrial Relations Journal,* Vol.34, pp.430–45.

Amable, B. (2003) *The Diversity of Modern Capitalism,* Oxford: Oxford University Press.

Anniello, V. (2004) 'Grenoble Valley', in C. Crouch, P. Le Galès, C. Trigilia and H. Voelzkow (eds) *Changing Governance of Local Economies,* Oxford: Oxford University Press.

Bacharach, S. (1989) 'Organizational theories: some criteria for evaluation', *Academy of Management Review,* Vol.14, No.4, pp.496–515.

Bendix, R. (1956) *Work and Authority in Industry,* New York: John Wiley.

Botero, J., Djankov, S., La Porta, R., Lopez-de-Silanes, S. and Shleifer, A. (2004) 'The regulation of labor', *Quarterly Journal of Economics,* Vol.119, pp.1339–82.

Boxall, P. (1995) 'Building the theory of comparative HRM', *Human Resource Management Journal,* Vol.5, No.5, pp.5–17.

Boxall, P. and Purcell, J. (2000) 'Strategic human resource management: where have we come from and where should we be going?', *International Journal of Management Reviews,* Vol.2, No.2, pp.183–203.

Boyer, R. and Hollingsworth, J.R. (1997) 'From national embeddedness to spatial and institutional nestedness', in J.R. Hollingsworth and R. Boyer (eds) *Contemporary Capitalism: The Embeddedness of Institutions,* Cambridge: Cambridge University Press.

Brewster, C. (2006) 'Comparing HRM policies and practices across geographical borders', in G.K. Stahl and I. Björkman (eds) *Handbook of Research in International Human Resource Management,* Cheltenham: Edward Elgar.

Brewster, C. (2007) 'Comparative HRM: European views and perspectives', *International Journal of Human Resource Management,* Vol.18, No.5, pp.769–87.

Brewster, C., Mayrhofer, W. and Morley, M. (eds) (2004) *Human Resource Management: Evidence of Convergence?* Oxford: Elsevier Butterworth Heinemann.

Budhwar, P. (2004) *Managing Human Resources in Asia Pacific,* London: Routledge.

Budhwar, P. and Mellahi, K. (eds) (2006) *Human Resource Management in the Middle East,* London: Routledge.

Collings, D.G., Gunnigle, P. and Morley, M.J. (2008) 'Boston or Berlin: American MNCs and the shifting contours of industrial relations in Ireland', *International Journal of Human Resource Management.*

Crouch, C., Le Galès, P., Trigilia, C. and Voelzkow, H. (eds) (2004) *Changing Governance of Local Economies,* Oxford: Oxford University Press.

DiMaggio, P.J. and Powell, W.W. (1983) 'The iron cage revisited: institutional isomorphism and collective rationality in organizational fields', *American Sociological Review,* Vol.48, pp.147–60.

Dore, R. (2000) *Stock Market Capitalism: Welfare Capitalism,* Cambridge: Cambridge University Press.

Djankov, S., Glaeser, E., La Porta, R., Lopez-de-Silnes, F. and Shleifer, A. (2003) 'The new comparative economics', *Journal of Comparative Economics,* Vol.31, pp.595–619.

Evans, P., Pucik, V. and Barsoux, J.L. (2002): *The Global Challenge: Frameworks for International Human Resource Management,* New York: McGraw Hill/Irwin.

Ferner, A. (1997) 'Country of origin effects and human resource management in multinational companies', *Human Resource Management Journal,* Vol.7, No.1, pp.19–36.

Ferner, A. (2000) 'The embeddedness of US multinational companies in the US business system: implications for HR/IR', Occasional Paper 61, Leicester, DeMontfort University.

Ferner, A. and Hyman, R. (1998) 'Introduction', in A. Ferner and R. Hyman (eds) *Changing Industrial Relations in Europe* (2nd edn), Oxford: Blackwell.

Ferner, A. and Quintanilla, J. (2002) 'Between globalisation and capitalist variety: multinationals and the international diffusion of employment relations', *European Journal of Industrial Relations,* Vol.8, pp.243–50.

Ferner, A., Quintanilla, J. and Varul, M.Z. (2001) 'Country of origin effects, host country effects, and the management of HR in multinationals: German companies in Britain and Spain', *Journal of World Business,* Vol.36, pp.107–27.

Friedman, T. (1999) *The Lexus and the Olive Tree,* New York: Farrar and Strauss.

Fukuyama, F. (2000) 'One journey, one destination', in R. Burns and H. Rayment-Pickard (eds) *Philosophies of History,* Oxford: Blackwell.

Gennard, J. (1974) 'The impact of forigen-owned subsidiaries on host country labour relations: the case of the United Kingdom', in A.W. Weber (ed.) *Bargaining Without Boundaries,* Chicago IL: University of Chicago Press.

Geppert, M., Matten, D. and Williams, K. (2003) 'Change management in MNCs: how global convergence intertwines with national diversity', *Human Relations,* Vol.56, pp.807–38.

Gooderham, P.N., Nordhaug, O. and Ringdal, K. (1999) 'Institutional and rational determinants of organizational practices: human resource management in European firms', *Administrative Science Quarterly,* Vol.44, pp.507–31.

Guest, D.E. (1990) 'Human resource management and the American dream', *Journal of Management Studies,* Vol.27, pp.977–87.

Gunnigle, P. (1995) 'Collectivism and the management of industrial relations in greenfield sites', *Human Resource Management Journal,* Vol.5, No.3, pp.24–40.

Gunnigle, P., Murphy, K.M., Cleveland, J., Heraty, N. and Morley, M. (2002) 'Localisation in human resource management: comparing American and European multinational corporations', *Advances in International Management,* Vol.14, pp.259–84.

Hall, P. and Soskice, D. (2001) 'An introduction to the varieties of capitalism', in P. Hall and D. Soskice (eds), *Varieties of Capitalism: The Institutional Basis of Competitive Advantage,* Oxford: Oxford University Press.

Harbison, F.H. and Myers, C. (eds) (1959) *Management in the Industrial World: An International Analysis,* New York: McGraw Hill.

Harcourt, M. and Wood, G. (2007) 'The importance of employment protection for skill development in coordinated market economies', *European Journal of Industrial Relations,* Vol.13, No.2, pp.141–59.

Harrison, G. (2000) *The Politics of Democratization in Rural Mozambique,* New York: The Edward Mellon Press.

Harzing, A.W. and Sorge, A. (2003) 'The relative impact of country of origin and universal contingencies on internationalization strategies and corporate control in multinational enterprises: worldwide and European perspectives', *Organizational Studies,* Vol.24, pp.187–214.

Hirst, P. and Thompson, G. (1999) *Globalisation in Question* (2nd edn), Cambridge: Polity.

Hofstede, G. (1980) *Cultures Consequence,* Thousand Oaks, CA: Sage.

Hofstede, G. (2001) *Cultures Consequences: Comparing Values, Behaviors, Institutions and Organizations across Nations* (2nd edn), Thousand Oaks, CA: Sage.

Holt Larsen, H. and Mayrhofer, W. (eds) (2006) *Managing Human Resources in Europe: A Thematic Approach,* London: Routledge.

Jacobi, O., Keller, B. and Müller-Jentsch, W. (1998) 'Germany: facing new challenges', in A. Ferner and R. Hyman (eds) *Changing Industrial Relations in Europe,* Oxford: Blackwell.

Jacoby, S.M. (1997) *Modern Manors: Welfare Capitalism Since the New Deal,* Princeton, NJ: Princetown University Press.

Kamoche, K., Debrah, Y., Horwitz, F. and Nkombo Muuka, G. (eds) (2003) *Managing Human Resources in Africa,* London: Routledge.

Kerr, C., Dunlop, J.T., Harbison, F.H. and Myers, C.A. (1960) *Industrialism and Industrial Man: The Problems of Labour and Management in Economic Growth,* London: Penguin.

Kidger, P.J. (1991) 'The emergence of international human resource management', *International Journal of Human Resource Management,* Vol.2, No.2, pp.149–63.

La Porta, R., Lopez-de-Silanes, F., Shleifer, A. and Vishny, R. (1997) 'Legal determinants of finance', *Journal of Finance,* Vol.52, pp.1131–50.

La Porta, R., Lopez-de-Silanes, F., Shleifer, A. and Vishny, R. (1998) 'Law and finance', *Journal of Political Economy,* Vol.106, pp.1113–55.

La Porta, R., Lopez-de-Silanes, F., Shleifer, A. and Vishny, R. (2000) 'Investor protection and corporate governance', *Journal of Financial Economics*, Vol.58, pp.3–27.

Lincoln, J. and Kalleberg, A. (1990) *Culture, Control and Commitment: A Study of Work Organization in the United States and Japan*. Cambridge: Cambridge University Press.

Locke, R., Kochan, T. and Piore, M. (1995) 'Reconceptualizing comparative industrial relations: lessons from international research', *International Labour Review*, Vol.134, pp.139–61.

Marsden, D. (1999) *A Theory of Employment Systems*, Oxford: Oxford University Press.

McDonnell, A., Lavelle, J., Gunnigle, P. and Collings, D.G. (2007) 'Management research on multinational corporations: a methodological critique', *Economic and Social Review*, Vol.38, No.2, pp.235–58.

McSweeney, B. (2002) 'Hofstede's model of national culture differences and their consequences: a triumph of faith – a failure of analysis', *Human Relations*, Vol.55, pp.5–34.

Meyer, J.W. and Rowan, B. (1977) 'Institutional organizations: formal structure as myth and ceremony', *American Journal of Sociology*, Vol.83, pp.340–63.

Morley, M., Brewster, C., Gunnigle, P. and Mayerhofer, W. (1996) 'Evaluating change in European industrial relations: research evidence on trends at organisational level', *International Journal of Human Resource Management*, Vol.7, pp.640–56.

Morley, M.J., Gunnigle, P. and Collings, D.G. (eds) (2006) *Global Industrial Relations*, London: Routledge.

North, D.C. (1990) *Institutions, Institutional Change and Economic Performance*, Cambridge: Cambridge University Press.

O'Hagan, E. (2002) *Employee Relations in the Periphery of Europe: The Unfolding of the European Social Model*, London: Palgrave.

Pagano, M. and Volpin, P. (2005) 'The political economy of corporate governance', *American Economic Review*, Vol.95, pp.1005–30.

Pitcher, A. (2002) *Transforming Mozambique: The Politics of Privatization*, Cambridge University Press, Cambridge.

Poole, M. (1986) *Industrial Relations: Origins and Patterns of National Diversity*, London: Routledge.

Roe, M. (2003) *Political Determinants of Corporate Governance*, Oxford: Oxford University Press.

Rollinson, D. and Dundon, T. (2007) *Understanding Employment Relations*, London: McGraw Hill.

Rubery, J. and Grimshaw, D. (2003) *The Organization of Employment: An International Perspective*, Basingstoke: Palgrave.

Schneider, S.C. and Barsoux, J.L. (2003) *Managing Across Cultures* (2nd edn), Harlow: Prentice Hall.

Scullion, H. (1995) 'International human resource management', in J. Storey (ed.) *Human Resource Management: A Critical Text*, London, Thompson.

Sorge, A. (2004) 'Cross-national differences in human resources and organisation', in A.W. Harzing and J. van Ruyssevekdt (eds) *International Human Resource Management* (2nd edn), London: Sage.

Sorge, A. and Streeck, W. (1988) 'Industrial relations and technological change: the case for an extended perspective', in R. Hyman and W. Streeck (eds) *New Technology and Industrial Relations*, Oxford: Blackwell.

Sorge, A. and Warner, M. (1986) *Comparative Factory Organization*, Aldershot: Gower.

Storey, J. (1992) *Developments in the Management of Human Resources*, Oxford: Blackwell.

Strauss, G. and Hanson, M. (1997) 'Review article: American anti-management theories of organization: a critique of paradigm proliferation', *Human Relations*, Vol.50, pp.1426–29.

Tayeb, M. (1996) 'Hofstede', in M. Warner (ed.) *International Encyclopaedia of Business and Management*, London: Thompson Press.

Taylor, P. and Bain, P. (2003) 'Call centre organising in adversity: from Excell to Vertex', in G. Gall (ed.) *Fighting for Fairness at Work: Campaigns for Union Recognition*, London: Routledge.

Thelen, K. (2001) 'Varieties of labor politics in the developed democracies', in P. Hall and D. Soskice (eds) *Varieties of Capitalism: The Institutional Basis of Competitive Advantage*, Oxford: Oxford University Press.

Tolbert, P.S. and Zucker, L.G. (1996) 'The institutionalisation of institutional theory', in S. Clegg, C. Hardy and W.R. Nord (eds) *Handbook of Organization Studies*, London: Sage.

Trompenaars, F. (1993) *Riding the Waves of Culture* (2nd edn), London: Nicholas Brealey.

Turner, T. (2006) 'Industrial relations systems, economic efficiency and social equity in the 1990s', *Review of Social Economy*, Vol.64, No.1, pp.93–118.

Webster, E. and Wood, G. (2005) 'Human resource management practice and institutional constraints', *Employee Relations*, Vol.27, No.4, pp.369–85.

Whitley, R. (1999) *Divergent Capitalisms: The Social Structuring and Change of Business Systems*, Oxford: Oxford University Press.

Wood, G. and Brewster, C. (eds) (2007) *Industrial Relations in Africa*, London: Palgrave.

Chapter 13

UNDERSTANDING AND MANAGING CAREERS IN CHANGING CONTEXTS

Laurie Cohen and Amal El-Sawad

When the Editor of *Everywoman's World* asked me to write 'The Story of My Career,' I smiled with a little touch of incredulous amusement. My career? Had I a career? Was not – should not – a 'career' be something splendid, wonderful, spectacular at the very least, something varied and exciting? Could my long, uphill struggle, through many quiet, uneventful years, be termed a 'career'? It had never occurred to me to call it so; and, on first thought, it did not seem to me that there was much to be said about that same long, monotonous struggle. But it appeared to be a whim of the aforesaid editor that I should say what little there was to be said . . . So I shall cheerfully tell my tame story. If it does nothing else, it may serve to encourage some other toiler who is struggling along in the weary pathway I once followed to success. (Lucy Maud Montgomery, 1917, Canadian author, whose first book, *Anne of Green Gables,* was published in 1908)

When my children grow up I don't want them to have a job, I want them to have a career. (Prime Minister Tony Blair on a visit to the Sheffield Job Centre, *Sheffield Star*, 5 February 1998, p.1. Cited in Mallon 1998, p.48)

Introduction

This chapter is about career: how we can understand the concept of career, and how we might go about managing our own careers and other people's. Academics have examined career in a whole range of ways: from psychological and sociological perspectives, as objective realities or subjective constructions, from individual and organisational points of view. Similarly, in everyday language career has a number of different meanings and is used in a variety of contexts: the career of the footballer, the bureaucrat, the politician or the patient; career education, career breaks, career mentoring. If we were to analyse what career means in each of these cases, we would come up with a rich, diverse and probably ambiguous picture. In spite of this diversity, though, what many of these examples have in common is a relationship between an individual and an organisation. The nature of this relationship is a fundamental issue within HRM.

This chapter has five sections. The first focuses on the concept of career, considering a number of academic and popular definitions and usages, while the second examines changing work contexts and raises questions about the implications of these changes for people's thinking about career, and for career management. The mainstream careers literature has been widely criticised for its failure to account for the different ways in which people from diverse groups construct their careers. In light of such critique, the third section focuses on careers and diversity. The next section explores the way in which academic thinking about career has developed, considering traditional psychological and sociological approaches, as well as interdisciplinary and interpretive perspectives. Finally, the chapter examines organisational interventions in career management, considering these in the context of current debates about changing careers.

An 'elastic' concept: diverse understandings of career

The term 'career' conjures up an array of images. We might use it to refer to a lifetime of service in a bureaucracy, or to a professional career like law or medicine. In contrast, we could talk about the more temporary career of a professional sports person. In years gone by, 'career girl' was used to differentiate a woman in paid employment from housewives and mothers. We could refer to the career of a drug addict or of a patient. We could also consider a career in crime, as 42-year-old Razor Smith (2004) has done in the published account of his life to date entitled *A Few Kind Words and a Loaded Gun: The Autobiography of a Career Criminal*. In contrast, we might also talk about the career of an academic subject, for example the career of organisational analysis. In short, it is a term we use every day, unproblematically, in a whole variety of situations and contexts. But what do we actually mean by career? Is it just another way of talking about paid employment? Could any job be described as a career, or is the term exclusive to a particular type of position? And what role, if any, does one's life outside work play in the definition of career? An academic analysis of career and its management clearly requires some consideration of these questions.

A traditional view of career is illustrated in Wilensky's (1961) classic definition:

> Let us define career in structural terms. A career is a succession of related jobs arranged in a hierarchy of prestige, through which persons move in an ordered (more or less predictable) sequence. (p.523)

Implicit within this definition is the idea of career as paid work. The reference to 'hierarchy of prestige' suggests a bureaucratic context. Notably, Wilensky describes career as a structural phenomenon, that is, it seems to have its own existence independent of the individual. This view implies that careers are real things, prescriptions, available for people to take part in, in a particular, set way. This conflation of the concept of career with bureaucracy (with implicit notions of hierarchy and steady advancement), persisted through the mid to late twentieth century. Indeed, paths and ladders are familiar metaphors in talk about careers. While the path suggests career as a journey towards an ultimate destination, implicit in the ladder image is the notion of career as hierarchical and, again, oriented to a goal. Other popular metaphors for describing careers include tracks and arrows (and of course, the more cynical rat race).

In contrast are those definitions of career which extend beyond the domain of paid employment, to the sequence of an individual's life experiences more generally. Interestingly, although this more inclusive notion of career is becoming increasingly popular, its origins date back to the 1930s, when Chicago sociologist Hughes (1937) explained:

> A career consists, objectively, of a series of statuses and clearly defined offices . . . subjectively, a career is the moving perspective in which the person sees his [*sic*] life as a whole and interprets the meaning of his various attributes, actions, and the things that happen to him. (p.413)

While acknowledging the structural, objective dimension of career, Hughes' definition also highlights the notion of the career as situated within the individual, thus emphasising its subjective dimension. Thus it is not the case that a person simply acts out a prescribed career pattern; instead, they construct their career in dynamic negotiation with their social, economic and cultural context. Hughes' work stimulated research into career in a whole variety of social situations: from funeral directors to tubercular patients and marijuana users. Goffman (1961)

Box 13.1: HRM in practice

A challenge to bureaucratic notions of career

Traditionally the term 'career' has been reserved for those who expect to enjoy rises laid out within a respectable profession. The term is coming to be used, however, in a broadened sense to refer to any social strand of any person's course through life . . . Such a career is not a thing that can be brilliant or disappointing; it can no more be success than a failure. One value of the concept is its two-sidedness. One side is linked to the internal matters held dearly and closely, such as image of self and felt identity; the other side concerns official position, jural position and style of life and is part of a publicly accessible institutional complex. The concept of career, then, allows one to move back and forth between the personal and the public, between the self and its significant society. (Goffman, 1961, p.127)

- How does this compare to other definitions introduced thus far?
- Would you say that Goffman places more value on certain kinds of careers?
- How might a researcher go about studying the 'two sides' of career?

further developed Hughes' notion of career, subverting conventional definitions which equated career with occupational advancement. More recent definitions, particularly those put forward by academics writing in the fields of HRM and career guidance, tend to reflect this broader, more inclusive approach: 'the individual's development in learning and work throughout life' (Collin and Watts 1996, p.393).

Interestingly, Savickas (2002) has argued that this subjective element is not simply a way of looking at a career, but that it is fundamental to the career concept. In his words: 'the essential point is that career denotes a reflection on the course of one's vocational behaviour; it is not vocational behaviour' (p.384).

Finally, different subject disciplines lead to and often explain variations in definitions of career. For example, economists may define career as 'the vehicle through which human capital is accrued through a lifetime of education and experience' whereas those from the discipline of politics might understand career as 'the sequence of endeavours to maximise self-interest, through successive attempts to gain power, status and influence' (Adamson *et al.* 1998, p.253).

However, notwithstanding the 'elasticity' (Collin and Young 2000) of the career concept and its diverse constitution within particular national-cultural, organisational and occupational contexts and from different disciplinary perspectives, we agree with Savickas (2002) who suggests that central to all of these are notions of development and movement through time.

Changing contexts of work and career

There is a growing consensus that careers are changing, from traditional, hierarchical, linear and organisationally bound models to more fluid arrangements, based on the accumulation of skills and knowledge and the integration of personal and professional life. It is notable that, in spite of the very different ways in which individuals' careers develop, much of career theory remains staunchly bureaucratic in its orientation, emphasising (albeit implicitly) linearity, hierarchy and the division of work and home life.

Kanter (1989), in a challenge to this traditional perspective, offers a very different model for understanding career development and change. Her starting point is that as bureaucratic forms of organising are beginning to wane, so too are bureaucratic careers. Kanter identifies three career forms: bureaucratic, professional and entrepreneurial. To Kanter, a bureaucratic career is characterised by: 'the logic of advancement. [It] involves a sequence of positions in a formally defined hierarchy of other positions' (1989, p.509). The bureaucratic career has been the basis of much HRM thinking about career management.

Kanter defines professional careers as: 'craft or skill, with monopolisation of socially valued knowledge the key determinant of occupational status, and "reputation" the key resource for the individual' (pp.510–11). She argues that a professional's relationship with their organisation is more complex than that of a bureaucrat. For Kanter, the entrepreneurial career is: 'one in which growth occurs through the creation of new value or new organisational capacity . . . the key resource in an entrepreneurial career is the capacity to create valued outputs' (1989, pp.515–16). There is a significant body of research which investigates the relationship between professional work and management (Raelin 1985; Cohen *et al.* 2002), although a relative paucity of work on entrepreneurship in the careers literature.

Kanter takes a broad, macro-view and does not examine in detail the processes through which these career forms are constructed. Furthermore, although she identifies three principal forms, there could of course be more. Nevertheless, Kanter's model provides a very valuable starting point for examining career in the early twenty-first century, and her suggestion that we need to know more about these forms and the ways in which they are enacted in organisational contexts is a significant issue for HRM.

There is an emerging consensus that we are experiencing an irreversible change in the organisation of our working lives and the structures and cultures of our working environments. This raises important questions about the ways in which these changes are impacting on our perceptions and experiences of career.

What might be some implications of these changes for career development and management?

Arnold (1997a) cites a number of key changes which he sees as particularly relevant to individuals' understandings of career and career management, including macro-level changes in demography and the labour market, as well as at the level of the organisation. The composition of the UK workforce is changing in important ways – it is ageing, and becoming increasingly diverse, with growth in the numbers of women working, students in employment, and foreign workers. The employment rate for women of working age has risen from 51 per cent in 1971 to 66 per cent in 1995 and 70 per cent in 2005. For men the rate rose from 76 per cent in 1995 to 79 per cent in 2005. The proportion of self-employed people has remained steady throughout 2005 at just under 13 per cent. Service sector employment grew

Box 13.2: HRM in practice

'Flexible capitalism' – what does it mean for career?

Today the phrase 'flexible capitalism' describes a system which is more than a permutation on an old theme. The emphasis is on flexibility. Rigid forms of bureaucracy are under attack, as are the evils of blind routine. Workers are asked to behave nimbly, to be open to change at short notice, to take risks continually, to become ever less dependent on regulations and formal procedures. This emphasis on flexibility is changing the very meaning of work. (Sennett 1998, p.9)

from 61 per cent in 1978 to 82 per cent in 2005 while employment in manufacturing fell from 28 per cent to 12 per cent. The percentage of teleworkers doubled between spring 1997 and spring 2005, from 4 per cent to 8 per cent of the total workforce (National Statistics, *Labour Market Review,* March 2006).

Gender splits in sectoral patterns of employment have persisted over the past decade. Women are more likely to work in services and men are more likely to work in manufacturing and production. Women are four times more likely than men to work in personal service occupations such as hairdressing and childminding and over twice as likely to work in sales or customer service. They are also likely to be paid less than their male counterparts, despite equal pay legislation. In 2005 females earned on average 87 per cent as much as males, compared with 85.5 per cent in 2004 (National Statistics, *Labour Market Review,* March 2006). According to the Labour Force Survey 2001, nearly one in five people of working age have a long-term disability – 3.7 million men and 3.4 million women. Of these, just 3.4 million were in employment in autumn 2001. The employment rate for those without a disability is 81 per cent compared to 48 per cent for those with a disability, and 36 per cent for those with a disability and from an ethnic minority.

Legislation to protect against sex and race discrimination has been in place for some 30 years and yet women and ethnic minorities remain disadvantaged in the labour market. Both men and women from ethnic minorities experience higher levels of unemployment than whites. Interestingly though, self-employment varies significantly by ethnic group. Numbers of those in self-employment rose from around 2.2 million in the late 1970s to around 3.8 million in the late 1980s, with little change since. As of December 2003 the figure remains at around 3.8 million. Except for those of black African and black Caribbean origin with a self-employment rate of 7 per cent, rates among all other ethnic groups are higher than the rate for whites. One wonders if self-employment offers minority groups an escape route from workplace discrimination and the subsequent disadvantage this creates.

As the labour force becomes more diverse, the structures of opportunity afforded to people are changing significantly. With more people involved in paid work, and changing structures of employment opportunities, it follows that individuals' and organisations' expectations of career and career development are also undergoing some transformation.

CHANGE AND CONTINUITY IN CAREER FORM

There is an emerging consensus that individuals can no longer expect a job for life. Whether this kind of arrangement was ever available to the majority of workers is a moot point. However, a recognition of increasingly short-term employment arrangements has consequences for both individuals and organisations. It has been suggested that in today's world of movement, diversity, flexibility and short-term relationships, organisations need to rethink their approaches to human resource development and career development. The causes and extent of change in today's world of work are still a subject of vigorous debate. Nevertheless, in contrast to the (mythical?) job for life, careers today are characterised by uncertainty and frequent change – of organisation, role, colleagues and required skills. It is a world of movement.

Scholars have argued that not only are bureaucratic careers seen as less and less likely, but they are also less and less appealing. In the literature on emerging careers, organisations are frequently depicted as 'stultifying individuals' initiative and creativity and promoting an unhealthy dependence on organisations for the conduct of one's working life' (Cohen and Mallon 1999). People are encouraged to weaken their links with organisations, and to develop relationships based on short-term contracts and financial arrangements. Scholars have argued for more embracing notions of career and have developed metaphors of boundaryless and protean careers (Mirvis and Hall 1996; Arthur and Rousseau 1996) to capture this changing landscape. While different in significant ways which we will discuss briefly below, both see careers as typically cyclical rather than linear, characterised by ongoing learning and development and involving movement and change.

Although the notions of boundaryless and protean careers have sometimes been used synonymously, as a way of describing new kinds of careers and especially careers which do not conform to bureaucratic norms (Briscoe and Hall 2006), in a number of recent articles scholars have sought to highlight their differences. Regarding the boundaryless career, introducing the concept for the first time Arthur and Rousseau (1996) identified what they saw as its six key components:

1. Careers that transcend the boundaries of different employers.

2. Careers that draw validity and marketability from outside the present employing organisation.

3. Careers that are sustained and supported by external networks.

4. Careers that challenge traditional assumptions about career advancement and movement up through an organisational hierarchy.

5. Careers in which individuals reject opportunities for advancement for personal or family reasons.

6. Careers that are based on an actor's interpretation, who may see their career as boundaryless regardless of contextual constraints.

Central here is the idea of careers becoming less dependent on a single employing organisation, and more in the hands of individuals to develop as they see fit.

Whereas the boundaryless career is seen as involving both physical and psychological dimensions, the protean career is conceptualised more in terms of the latter – about individuals constructing their own careers, guided by their personal value systems and subjective notions of success. Coined by Hall in 1976, the metaphor has been developed (Briscoe and Hall 2006; Briscoe *et al.* 2006) to describe careers in which 'the individual, not the organization, is in charge, the core values are freedom and growth, and the main success criteria are subjective (psychological) vs. objective (position, salary)' (Hall 2004, p.4).

While boundaryless and protean career metaphors are widely celebrated, voices have been raised about their potentially negative implications for both individuals and organisations. And questions are raised about the concepts themselves – both analytically and as a way of capturing people's understandings of their career enactment (Arnold and Cohen 2008). Regarding the latter, as Cohen and Mallon argued in their study of women who left jobs in organisations to pursue portfolio careers: 'the stories we heard were less about breaking free than about *reconstructing* the boundaries . . . It appeared that participants were attempting to establish new employment contexts which in some ways approximated those that they had only recently left' (Cohen and Mallon 1999, p.346). At the level of values, we are concerned about the strong sense of individualism embedded within these ideas. In placing such emphasis on the individual career actor, we would suggest that both boundaryless and protean metaphors downplay the important role that institutions play in people's career lives. We do not believe that people have unfettered opportunities to pursue their careers in whatever way they choose. Rather, economic, political, cultural, occupational and organisational factors all contribute to the structuring of what is available.

Notwithstanding our reservations about these metaphors and the values and assumptions on which they are based, they have become a part of the current career lexicon – both in academic and popular discourse. To that extent, they clearly have resonance for people seeking to construct meaningful careers in our rapidly changing, early twenty-first-century context.

Gender and ethnicity in career debates

A persistent criticism of mainstream career theory is its exclusivity – its central concern with those most privileged in traditional career terms (Sullivan 1999): white, middle-class and usually male-dominated occupational groups. Through such a focus, career theory has effectively constructed women, as well as people from minority ethnic groups, blue-collar workers, the disabled, the poor, the uneducated, as 'the other', as deviations from a dominant pattern (Marshall 1989; Thomas and Alderfer 1989). In what follows we consider how (if at all) career scholars have sought to redress this imbalance, in relation to gender and ethnicity.

DIVERSE CAREERS: WOMEN'S CAREERS AND MEN'S THEORIES

Turning first to gender, career theorists, mindful of the exclusion of women from the mainstream career canon, have sought to develop understandings which more adequately reflect women's lives. Taking career development as an example, apart from a few early studies which suggested that the process of career development is essentially the same for women and men (Fitzgerald and Crites 1980), there is now a general consensus that women's lives are fundamentally different from men's, and that they construct their careers in different ways. Feminist psychologists take issue with theories of adult development based on male experiences (Gilligan 1982), while feminist sociologists emphasise the significance of gender in an individual's experience of life's choices and chances (Evetts 2000).

In recent years research on gender and careers has focused on a whole array of issues, including constructions of career success (Sturges 1999; Höpfl and Hornby Atkinson 2000); family roles and responsibilities (Hakim 2006; Hite and McDonald 2003); women's careers in management (Wajcman 1996; Crompton 2005; White *et al.* 2003) and women's experience of career transition (Mallon and Cohen 2001); work and leisure careers (McQuarrie and Jackson 2002); and women's involvement in 'non-traditional' and new careers (Whittock 2000; Belt 2002). These studies offer illuminating insights into the day-to-day issues which women confront as part and parcel of their unfolding careers.

To understand the ways in which career theory has or has not engaged with women, back in 1989 Marshall identified three overlapping phases of feminist thought. She describes the first as a consciousness-raising period, whereby the absence of women from career theory was noted and calls for more inclusive approaches were made. The second is identified as a reform period whose central purpose was to facilitate women's access to the career world, hitherto dominated by men. Arguably, much career theory remains in that phase (Brett and Stroh 1994; Hakim 2000). Finally Marshall discusses the emergence of a radical voice, which elucidates women's subordination through patriarchal social structures and cultural meaning systems. The intent of this phase is not so much to fit women into existing structures, but to assert women's perspectives, and in so doing, to challenge the status quo. The aim is emancipation and social transformation (Tomlinson 2006; Crompton *et al.* 2005; Gambles *et al.* 2006).

On one hand, it could be argued that the new and emerging definitions of career discussed above are particularly appropriate to women's career experiences, in so far as they blur out paid work as a distinguishing feature of career, celebrating instead a greater variety of career forms and lifestyle choices. Through the mobilisation of such discourses, women could be seen as deriving a sense of social legitimacy for their 'non-linear' career choices, and need not see themselves as falling off a career path.

On the other hand, though, current research evidence suggests that these new meanings do not simply eclipse the old in such neat ways (Pringle and Mallon 2003). Rather, so embedded are traditional notions of career development and success that they continue to resonate, even when they appear to no longer 'fit' the lives and experiences of many people. Similarly, within these new career discourses, important questions about power relations and inequality (questions central to researchers working in Marshall's third phase) are sometimes lost from view in the wide-open definitions of what now constitutes a career.

ETHNICITY AND CAREERS

While career scholars seem to have woken up to the androcentricity which has characterised much career theorising, and are beginning to tune in to the experiences of women, there remains a persistent (if not intentional) blind spot when it comes to the ethnocentric nature of much existing career theory (Fearfull and Kamenou 2006). There is a dearth of work which explores the career experiences of individuals from ethnic minority groups. It is telling, for example, that in edited books within the mainstream careers literature – notably Peiperl *et al.* (2000), Collin and Young (2000) and Peiperl *et al.* (2002) – not a single chapter is devoted to exploring the experiences of ethnic minorities (though all three books do devote one chapter to the experiences of women). It is difficult to fathom why such neglect, noted by Thomas and Alderfer in (1989), persists. They recall two interest groups set up by the Academy of Management in the 1970s – one on women in management which evolved into a division, the other on minorities and management which disbanded within five years. Thomas and Alderfer (1989) offer a number of possible explanations for why so many people seem so uninterested in race-related issues: the underrepresentation of ethnic minorities in the academic community; a belief that race only becomes a pertinent issue worthy of attention when overt acts of discrimination occur; and the difficulties of researching a sensitive and potentially 'controversial' issue 'fraught with tension' (p.153).

Ethnic minorities, who make up 8 per cent of the UK population, some 4.6 million people or 1 in 12 of the population, are without doubt disadvantaged in the workplace. There is much diversity of experience though, and some ethnic groups, notably those of Indian origin, fare better than others (Cabinet Office Strategy Unit 2003). However, according to figures published by the Office for National Statistics (2006), the percentage of the working-age population in employment is far higher for whites than for most other ethnic groups. Among men, those from Bangladeshi, black African, black Caribbean and mixed ethnic groups have the highest unemployment rates (between 13 and 14 per cent), around three times the rates for white British or Irish men. The unemployment rates for Pakistani and Chinese men are around twice the rates for white British or Irish men. Chinese men have the highest male economic inactivity rate, at 37 per cent, more than twice the rate for white British men, though it is important to note that the vast majority of economically inactive Chinese men are students. In 2004, Bangladeshi and Pakistani women had the highest working-age economic inactivity rates in Britain (75 per cent and 69 per cent respectively), up to three times the rates for white British, white Irish and black Caribbean women. The majority were looking after their family or home.

Such disadvantage is not merely a feature of the UK labour market. For example, Lamba (2003) examined the employment experiences of refugees living in Canada and found that many were held back by structural barriers and experienced downward occupational mobility. In 2003 the UK government set itself the goal of ensuring that, within 10 years, ethnic minority groups living in Britain will 'no longer face disproportionate barriers to accessing and realizing opportunities for achievement in the labour market'. Measures to track progress towards this goal include 'increased employment rates and earnings' and 'improvements in the career profiles of ethnic minorities' (Cabinet Office Strategy Unit 2003). The available practical evidence suggests that the government has much work still to do for UK police officers.

In research terms, what is needed to begin to plug the gap in our understanding of the relationship between ethnicity and careers? Pringle and Mallon (2003) point to the paucity of research conducted in non-Western industrialised cultures. There is thus a need for research which is carried out in different national and cultural contexts where ethnic groups

Box 13.3: HRM in practice

Institutional racism and career implications

Once in employment, individuals from ethnic minorities face considerable hurdles in their attempt to pursue career. This is perhaps best documented in the UK police service. Bland *et al.* (1999) studied the career progression of ethnic minority police officers in order to assess whether and in what ways the careers of ethnic minority and white officers differed. Though the career aspirations of all groups were found to be similar, ethnic minority officers were significantly disadvantaged. For example, although they applied at roughly the same time, ethnic minority officers took on average 12 months longer than their white colleagues to secure promotion to sergeant. For promotion to inspector, black officers took on average 23 months longer and Asian officers 16 months longer than their white colleagues, despite Asian officers being more likely to have 'A' levels and graduate qualifications than their white colleagues.

Following the inquiry into the death of Stephen Lawrence and the subsequent publication of the MacPherson Report in 1999, police forces across the country were directed to take action to tackle the 'institutional racism' inherent in their policies and procedures. After five years there was little sign of improvement. An investigation by the Commission for Racial Equality found that police forces were failing to implement race equality regulations; and 90 per cent of police race equality schemes did not meet the minimum legal requirements. Just one of the 15 police force schemes investigated was seen to be fully compliant with the Race Relations Act.

who are a minority group in one context are studied in contexts where they represent the majority. We also need studies which focus specifically on the career experiences of all minority groups, not just ethnic minorities. Without such studies career theories will become increasingly detached from the experiences of these groups and the millions of people which they represent.

Career lenses and approaches

Traditional studies of career tended to approach career from the perspective of a single academic discipline: typically sociology or psychology: 'While psychologists say "people make careers", sociologists claim "careers make people" and the careers literature shows a dearth of cross referencing between these two frames of reference' (Derr and Laurent 1989, p.454). Although these approaches have been criticised for being partial and fragmented, given their prominence within career theory, they are a really useful and important starting point.

Sociological approaches see the career as something which is organisationally based, planned, progressive and enacted by rational individuals (Inkson 1995). This literature typically explores careers in terms of particular occupational paths, focusing on issues such as turnover patterns, organisational demographics and internal labour markets. Such perspectives are based on the concept of the career as objective, external to the individual.

'Individuals are portrayed as if they join the organisation practically as lumps of clay, ready to be shaped by all those around them' (Bell and Staw 1989, p.232). This view emphasises social structures over individuals' ability to act and affect change. It sees the career as something with its own prescribed existence, as something real and external to the individual.

In contrast, early psychological work on career focused on the individual, and on the notion of the career as situated within the individual. This literature is concerned with issues such as personality traits and their implications for occupational choice, and the importance of person–environment 'fit' for occupational stability (Super 1957; Holland 1973). Psychological approaches were influenced by trends in developmental psychology. Consistent with psychologists' interest in adult change and development (Hall 1976; Levinson 1978), career development theorists study the ways in which careers develop over the span of an individual's adult life. Here the work of Super (1957) has been particularly influential. His five-stage model (reworked in 1985): from 'growth' to 'decline', though criticised for its exclusivity and its apparent lack of flexibility, has been the basis of much thinking and theorising about career development over the past 40 years. (This revised model is illustrated in Table 13.1.)

Such models continue to influence academic and popular thinking about career, and indeed available computer packages which help people to make career decisions are typically based on psychological models of person–occupation fit and career development. Nevertheless, questions have been raised about the adequacy of psychological models of understanding. Scholars have criticised personality traits approaches for being too static and determining, and for their failure to account for social processes and contexts (Nicholson and West 1989; Potter and Wetherell 1987). As regards life-stage models, academics have taken issue with the male orientation of much of this research. In addition, they have been criticised for their over-emphasis on age, and their lack of attention to social and organisational change.

Table 13.1 Typology of adult career concerns derived from Super *et al.* 1985 framework

Exploration phase

Clarification	Development of one's ideas about suitable and meaningful employment
Selection	Move from general ideas to specific choices
Enactment	Execution of plan for entering chosen occupation

Establishment phase

Becoming secure	Settling into occupation and adoption of a lifestyle consistent with its imperatives
Cementing	Process of gaining security in occupation
Advancement	Progression: in terms of position/earnings/responsibility

Maintenance

Retention	Holding of position in context of internal and external pressure and change
Keeping up to date	Proactively keeping abreast of developments in field
Creativity	Finding innovating ways of performing roles

Disengagement

Slowing down	Easing off of workload and pace
Ideas for retirement	Financial and lifestyle planning
Retirement	Establishing alternatives to work

MORE DYNAMIC, LESS STATIC APPROACHES?

Seeking to understand what gives a career its continuity, Schein (1978, 1993, 1996), Driver (1982) and Derr (1986) all attempt to look at careers as they unfold and develop through time: for Schein it is the anchor, for Driver enduring shapes and patterns, and Derr's work focuses on 'career logics'. Schein used the anchor image to describe what he saw as those fundamental ideas around which individuals construct their careers. Through his research into American male Masters students, he identified eight such anchors: technical/functional competence, general management competence, autonomy/independence, security/stability, entrepreneurial creativity, service/dedication, pure challenge, and lifestyle (Schein 1996). In contrast to the anchor's solidity, Driver's 'concept' model is about shapes and patterns: transitory, steady-state, linear and spiral, while Derr's five 'career logics': getting ahead, getting secure, getting free, getting high and getting balanced, are based on the idea of career development as an essentially rational process.

It could be argued that these approaches are now somewhat dated, reminiscent of an employment context which offered more choice and opportunity than many experience today. Nevertheless, we find them interesting in their attempt to integrate the individual and the organisation, and their radical departure from the idea of career as hierarchical. Instead, they acknowledge the diverse ways in which individuals construct their careers, and recognise the significance of non-work aspects of life in the experience of career.

As discussed in the section on definitions, Hughes and the Chicago sociologists were interested in the ways in which people make sense of their careers. While these interpretive approaches were to some extent eclipsed by more mainstream sociological and psychological research, they have nevertheless persisted, providing an illuminating – and often missing – perspective. Examples of interpretive work include Cohen and Mallon's research into individuals' transition from organisational employment to self-employment (Cohen and Mallon 1999), Fournier's (1998) on careers and the discourse of enterprise, Collin and Watts' (1996) study into career guidance and El-Sawad's (2002) research into career sensemaking of graduate employees in a blue-chip multinational, against a backdrop of large-scale change.

Recently attention has turned to using constructivist and social constructionist approaches in careers research (Young and Collin 2004). Fundamental to both perspectives is the idea of social reality as subjectively constructed. However, while the former derives from development and cognitive psychology and sees social experience as subjectively constructed by individuals through cognitive processes, the latter is more interdisciplinary, with roots in sociology, literary studies and cultural anthropology, focusing on the construction of reality as a fundamentally social process (Bruner 1990; Burr 1995; Gergen 2001).

In a special issue of the *Journal of Vocational Behaviour* dedicated to the use of constructivist and social constructionist perspectives in career theory (Young and Collin 2004), the editors argue that both offer challenges and opportunities to the career field. In particular, the articles highlight how these perspectives move beyond static, individualised analyses, providing understandings which take account of the processes through which careers are developed, the dynamic contexts in which individuals enact and make sense of their careers, and illuminating, in particular, patterns of dominance and subordination played out within these contexts. Furthermore, it is argued that the narrative and discursive approaches characteristic of constructionism provide access into the 'unique interaction of self and social experience' (2004, p.381) which career represents, but which is difficult to tap through positivistic, survey-based methodologies.

From this perspective, scholars have recently begun to think about careers as stories (Sugarman 2005). Indeed, if we consider some popular definitions of career, like Collin and Watts' 'individual's development in learning and work throughout life' (1996, p.393) we get a protagonist; a sense of sequence and causality; the merging past and present; individuals embedded in social contexts; and of how, through the telling, patterns emerge with beginnings, middles and ends. Elements of career of course, but they are also elements of narratives. As Inkson suggests:

> When we talk about our careers, we tell stories about ourselves. For example, every time we leave a job, get a new job, or experience a career crisis, there is a story to tell, an account of what happened. Such incidents are, as it were, chapters in a book, and each book is the story of a life, and it is not finished until the person dies. Any career is essentially a story. (2007, p.277)

Of course, Inkson is speaking metaphorically, but the aptness of the comparison is such that we sometimes think that careers and stories are one and the same. Researchers (and we would include ourselves here) have found that considering careers from a narrative perspective can be useful in a number of ways. First, attending to sequence can help us to better understand the temporal element of a person's career – that is, how they see it as unfolding through time, incorporating aspects of both change and continuity. Second, it can illuminate contradictions, inconsistencies and ambiguities that are sometimes smoothed over through other approaches. Third, stories can help us to understand people's relationships with their social worlds. Although thus far we have focused on the individual as author of their own career story, we are not suggesting that this happens in a social vacuum. On the contrary, we see it as fundamentally social, framed by cultural norms. As Savickas argues, 'Individuals mentally structure the story of their own work life using the social structure provided by society's grand narrative of careers. The narrative frames people's stories of work and its consequences as they think about and take stock of their work lives' (Savickas 2005, p.49, cited in Inkson 2007). These 'grand narratives' thus work as the backdrops against which our own career stories are set.

HOLISTIC PERSPECTIVES: NEW METAPHORS FOR THINKING ABOUT CAREER

In contrast to scholars who see career as either external or internal, residing within the organisation or within the individual, are those who seek to explore career more holistically, as an ongoing process central to which is the relationship between the individual and the organisation. To this end, metaphor analysis has been argued to offer a powerful tool in the study of careers (e.g. Gunz 1989; Mignot 2000, 2004; Inkson 2002, 2004; El-Sawad 2005).

The language we use to describe careers is often metaphorical: successful careers are described in terms of climbing to the top, reaching targets and being at the pinnacle, while unsuccessful careers are attributed to losing one's sense of direction, getting lost or hitting glass ceilings. It has been suggested that metaphors 'are used to make sense of the situations we find ourselves in' (Grant and Oswick 1996, p.1); they are 'a way of thinking and a way of seeing' (Morgan 1986, p.12). These familiar metaphors which we use to talk about career are no accident. Rather, underpinning them are fundamental assumptions about what a career is and is not, about career success and failure. These assumptions are typically based on notions of career as external to the individual, organisationally based and prescribed, linear and hierarchical.

Within the careers literature the dominant metaphors which scholars have used to talk about careers fall into four broad groups: spatial, journey, competition and horticultural metaphors (El-Sawad 2005). Spatial career metaphors draw attention to entrenched notions of vertical mobility, with frequent reference to hierarchies, pyramids, career ladders, high-flyers and so on (Gunz 1989; Barley 1989). Journey metaphors frame careers as, for example, travel along paths. Competition metaphors represent careers as uphill struggles or rat races on fast tracks. Gunz (1989) notes the use of horticultural metaphors in the careers literature, conjuring both positive career images of growing, flowering and blossoming, as well as negative ones such as being pruned and cut back. But what of the metaphors employed by those having rather than studying careers? What do these tell us about the ways in which people make sense of their careers and the contexts in which they are played out?

In a study of the careers of graduates employed in a large blue-chip organisation, El-Sawad (2005) analysed the metaphors contained in their career accounts. Like career scholars, graduates drew on 'established' metaphors to describe their careers. In addition, they drew on other essentially disciplinary metaphors not reflected in the careers literature – imprisonment, military, school-like surveillance, 'Wild West' and nautical metaphors. Through imprisonment metaphors, graduates likened their careers within the organisation to serving a life sentence. Military metaphors included references to political battles, fighting, tending wounds and the need to wear body armour for protection. Through 'school-like surveillance' metaphors graduates presented themselves as children and their managers as the parental figures who could reward good behaviour with the opportunity to get involved in more responsible and interesting 'grown-up' work. Such metaphors highlight the graduates' understanding of the power held by managers to determine their career fates. The imagery conjured up by 'Wild West'-type metaphors was of good and bad guys (rather than children). Through nautical metaphors, graduates described feelings of anxiety and insecurity created by the pursuit of career progression. They spoke of their experiences of floundering and even drowning and of their desire to bail out. Taken together, these metaphors present a rich and textured reading of career, uncovering disciplinary dimensions of career and career contexts which, except for a handful of notable exceptions (Grey 1994; Savage 1998; Fournier 1998), are currently under-explored in the mainstream careers literature. Indeed, issues of power have been largely neglected in studies of career to date (Collin and Young 2000). There is clearly a need for more research in this area.

The latest contribution to the career metaphors literature comes from Inkson's (2007) book in which he views career through a series of metaphorical lenses and devotes separate chapters to each. He considers career variously as inheritances, as cycles, as action, as fit, as journeys, as roles, as relationships, as resources and as stories. Each metaphor helps illuminate particular aspects of, and dimensions to, career and offers a way of organising existing career theories.

Managing careers: implications for HR practice

Assumptions about how we might define career are embedded within organisational approaches to career management and development. Some scholars have argued that traditional approaches to career management, based on notions of lifelong employment and hierarchical development, have become obsolete. However, others maintain that employees continue to attach real importance to managed career development initiatives, and certainly available evidence supports this (CIPD 2003). Many organisations do make an attempt to intervene in individuals' career development. Arnold (1997a) identifies a number of such interventions, illustrated in Table 13.2.

Baruch (2002) presents a list of career management practices in order of the level of implementation which an earlier survey (Baruch and Peiperl 2000) found. These are: advertising internal job openings; formal education as part of career development; performance appraisal as a basis for career planning; career counselling by direct manager; career counselling by HRM department; lateral moves; retirement preparation programmes; succession planning; mentoring; common career paths; dual ladders; booklets on career issues; written personal career planning; assessment centres; 360° appraisals; career workshops; induction; special programmes, e.g., for high flyers; creating psychological contracts; and secondments. Greenhaus *et al.* (2000) also offer a summary of typical career management practices: anticipatory socialisation via, for example, apprenticeships; realistic recruitment;

Table 13.2 Career management interventions in organisations

Internal vacancy notification. Details about jobs available within the organisation prior to external advertising. Should include necessary experience and qualifications, and a job description.

Career paths. Information about the sequence of jobs that people can do, or competencies they can acquire within the organisation, with details of how high the path goes, potential lateral moves, required qualifications/skills/experience.

Career workbooks. Exercises designed to guide individuals in analysing their own strengths and weaknesses, identifying opportunities and assessing action necessary to achieve goals.

Career planning workshops. Deal with similar issues as workbooks, but in a more 'managed' way, offering opportunities for discussion and feedback. Sometimes include psychometric testing.

Computer-assisted career management. Packages which help employees to assess their skills, interests and values, and translate these into employment options. Sometimes these are organisationally specific.

Opportunities for training and development. Information, financial support and sometimes delivery of courses. Could be within or outside the organisation. Designed to enable employees to update, or to acquire new skills and knowledge. Often used in preparation for seeking promotion.

Personal development plans. Statements of how an individual's skills and knowledge might develop, given a particular employment context and timescale. Often arise from performance appraisal or development centre assessment.

Career action centres. Resources (paper, video and electronic) available to employees on a drop-in basis. Sometimes also offer counselling.

Development centres. Employees are assessed on the basis of their performance in a number of different exercises and tests. Focus on identifying an individual's strengths and weaknesses for the purpose of development.

Mentoring programmes. Attaching employees to more senior colleagues who act as advisers, advocates, counsellors.

Job assignment/rotation. Careful use of work tasks can help a person to stay employable. Organisation will benefit from staff adaptability, flexibility.

Outplacement. Purpose is to support people who are leaving organisation, to help them clarify future plans. May include a variety of the above interventions.

Source: Adapted from Arnold 1997a. Reprinted by permission from Arnold, J., *Managing Careers into the Twenty-first Century*, copyright © Sage Publications Ltd, 1997

employee orientation; individual learning and development; on-the-job experiences; performance feedback and coaching; mentoring and supportive alliances; dual promotion ladders; dealing with career plateau; late career activities; redeployment and outplacement programmes; pre-retirement programmes.

The CIPD (2004) suggests that effective career management should adhere to a number of principles: consistency and coherency within organisations in messages about what career and career management is; proactivity; collaboration between employer and employee; and dynamism, requiring both 'flexibility and compromise over time as changing organizational and individual circumstances mean that each party wants and expects different things from the employment relationship' (p.8). In practice, organisations struggle to uphold these principles, as the CIPD's (2003) survey of the career management practices of 700 UK-based employers helps to illustrate (See Box 13.4).

Arnold (1997a) concludes that career management interventions are most likely to have most impact in situations where, first, there is openness and trust. Although one could argue that these are becoming increasingly rare in these days of flexibility and changing psychological contracts, Macauley and Harding (1996) maintain that it is precisely in this context that

Box 13.4: HRM in practice

Findings from the CIPD survey of career management practices

The CIPD's (2003) survey on the career management practices of 700 UK-based employers provides an indication of how career management in UK organisations is played out in practice. This makes for interesting reading. The survey found the following:

- 48 per cent of organisations surveyed have a formal written career management strategy.
- The majority claim to follow a 'partnership' approach to career management – individuals managing their own careers but with the support and guidance of their employer.
- 95 per cent of organisations hold the view that individuals will be expected to take responsibility for managing their own careers, though 90 per cent think individuals should be offered support by their employer for this to work effectively.
- There is firm commitment from senior managers to career management in only 34 per cent of organisations.
- 56 per cent believe that line managers do not take career management seriously.
- Practices considered most effective are: an open internal job market, development or assessment centres, online vacancy boards, development programmes and graduate entry schemes.
- Practices considered to be least effective are: succession planning, career information/advice from staff in a learning centre or career unit, and informal support from managers.
- Most respondents feel that certain groups need special attention to ensure non-discriminatory treatment. However, current practice does not reflect this. Less than a third of organisations offer additional career support or assistance to 'atypical' employee groups, e.g. part-time or older workers.
- Career progression paths are still based on a traditional, inflexible, male-oriented model.
- The main factors felt to influence career progression positively are gaining extra qualifications, undertaking work-related training, taking on extra work responsibilities and working in a number of business locations/areas.
- The factors felt to influence career progression negatively are taking a long period of sickness, needing time for family responsibilities, working flexible or reduced hours and taking a career break.

such qualities are needed most. Second, Arnold suggests that the goals of career management processes must be explicit, and that this will be most easily achieved if there is a limited number of compatible interventions. Furthermore, it is important that interventions stay in existence long enough to become established. Third, the way in which these processes are managed and delivered is crucial. On a theoretical level, Arnold (1997b) suggests that given current changes in career patterns and expectations, providers of careers guidance need to be more aware of process, rather than focusing exclusively on outcomes. Not only do Arnold's propositions relate to individual career management, but they likewise have implications for those involved in managing the careers of others.

On a more practical level, managers should themselves be appraised on how well they carry out career interventions, and top management should be seen as actively supportive of such initiatives (Mayo 1991). Here it is vital that career management programmes are seen as integrated in the organisation's daily practices, and consistent with its more general strategic orientation. Finally, it is essential that career management interventions are not perceived as only available to a select few: rather, organisations should be seen to take an interest in the careers of all their employees, including minority groups.

It is interesting to consider HR interventions in career management in light of current debates on changing careers. As noted earlier, traditional approaches to career management were based on the notion of the career as lifelong, existing within and defined by the organisation, and sought to establish the right 'fit' between the person and the position. In this case the role of the HRM practitioner 'became one of defining position requirements, identifying and selecting individuals capable of meeting those position requirements and assisting organizational members to progress through a sequence of positions within the organization' (Templar and Cawsey 1999, p.72). However, the emerging discourse on new careers sees the career as situated within the individual, focusing on individual choice, self-development and 'employability' (see also Ball and Jordan 1997). From this perspective, career management is contract-oriented, concerned with defining core competencies and identifying the 'core' workforce, and is short-term in focus. Templar and Cawsey describe these, respectively, as 'position centred' and 'portfolio centred' career development procedures. Whereas the former sees HR practitioners as having a central role to play in the employees' long-term training and development, within a portfolio perspective individuals are responsible for their own training and career growth. In this case, HR managers must ensure that individuals have the requisite skills needed to fulfil the terms of a specific contract.

Given these two perspectives, we can then ask where the interventions outlined in Table 13.2 can be situated. Although certain interventions (such as career planning workshops and job assignment/rotation) are often associated with an individual's long-term relationship with the organisation, this does not have to be the case (Ball and Jordan 1997). Taking opportunities for training and development as an example, such programmes could be offered by the organisation to help individuals prepare for promotion. However, in other cases individuals might opt into particular training courses as a way of updating their knowledge and skills – thus enhancing their personal portfolio. Thus, it is not the intervention per se which is significant, but the way in which it is understood and used.

Conclusion

This chapter began with two quotes about career. Together these quotes raise some fascinating questions about what careers are, the relationship between personal and work-life, about where careers are located and the extent to which (and by whom) they can be managed. While not aiming to provide definitive answers, this chapter has explored these questions, considering, in particular, emerging debates on changing careers and the implications of these debates for HR practice.

The chapter began by discussing the changing contexts in which careers are enacted. While the precise nature and extent of change is still an open question, there is a growing consensus that careers are increasingly characterised by uncertainty and instability. One way of engaging with these debates is by considering how career thinking has developed – examining traditional definitions and the extent to which these are being reproduced/challenged or transformed in current employment contexts. While some might argue that conventional definitions are outdated, metaphors of ladders, arrows and getting to the top continue to send powerful messages about career success and failure. In addition to these traditional conceptualisations, broader, more inclusive definitions were introduced, emphasising both subjective and objective dimensions of career, and the integration of professional and personal life.

The chapter then briefly discussed the theoretical frameworks on which these definitions are based, with particular reference to the experiences of women and ethnic minorities. Not only were conventional definitions found to be wanting in their failure to account adequately for the diverse patterns of different individuals' working lives, but also within these approaches there is often an implicit assumption that careers take place in large organisations and are based on bureaucratic notions of success. Alternatives to this traditional model were introduced. The final section of the chapter focused on organisational intervention in career management.

CASE STUDY 13.1

Making sense of careers

Laurie Cohen and Amal El-Sawad

Understanding careers

1. Working in a group, make a list of 20–30 jobs – make your list as wide-ranging as possible.
2. Which of these jobs would you consider to be 'careers'? Which would not be careers? Why?
3. Construct a definition of career that justifies your categorisation. How does this definition compare to those introduced in the chapter?
4. Apply this definition to your own experiences. Which aspects of your life would it include? Which aspects would be excluded from this definition? Based on this definition, would you say that your experiences constitute a career?

Reflecting on career experiences

1. Make a 'time-line' of your career to date. Choose an appropriate shape, and include significant events, decisions, people and transitions. Should aspects of personal life be included? What about voluntary or community activities, education, training? Who have been the key stakeholders in your career development?
2. Consider this time-line in terms of the theoretical approaches introduced in this chapter.
   - Do you see your career as objective or subjective? Who 'owns' your career?
   - To what extent do sociological/psychological approaches shed light on your career experiences?
   - Explore the relevance of career anchors, shapes or logics. What are the relative merits/weaknesses of these approaches in relation to your own experience of career?
   - Consider the issue of career diversity in terms of your experience of career. To what extent do feminist calls for 're-visioning' the career concept have resonance for you?
   - How does your career compare to traditional, bureaucratic conceptualisations?
   - Consider Kanter's model in light of your career time-line. Would you say that your career could be described in terms of one of her career forms? Could more than one of these forms apply? Simultaneously or at different times? How might you account for movement between these career forms?
3. Describe any career interventions you have experienced (in terms of your own career, or in terms of managing the careers of others). Critically examine the apparent strengths/weaknesses of this intervention, for the individual and the organisation. ▶

4. Using your accumulated understanding of careers, develop a metaphor that describes your career and reflects key concepts introduced in the chapter.

5. Based on your experience and observations, to what extent and in what ways do you think careers are changing? What are the implications of these changes for individuals and organisations?

A journey into the unknown

Bradley Saunders

Steve is 36, single, and originally from Newcastle. After university, he joined a major retailer as a trainee area manager in Leeds in a job which he described as 'an emotional roller coaster – total stress for a minimum of six days a week'. After only a few years, he felt disheartened by the 'sink or swim, dog-eat-dog mentality' and asked for a six-week vacation. 'Such a request was unheard of and friends warned me not to rock the boat, but I was at the end of my tether. Fortunately, my request was granted, but without pay.'

Steve decided to use his frequent-flyer miles to get as far away as he possibly could. After a short stay in Singapore, he took a boat to Sumatra in Indonesia. The boat developed engine problems and drifted for a few days and Steve found himself bonding with the other passengers, none of whom spoke much English.

On arrival, a family took him in and he was touched by their hospitality. One day he was passing by a building when he heard English being spoken so he walked in to what was an English class for young children. By the end of the day, Steve had accepted a post as English teacher there for a salary of 25 dollars a month and board and lodging. He returned to Newcastle to sell everything and set off, but then decided to look for similar work overseas but with a better salary. 'I knew I wanted a fresh start but I'd got used to a certain level of income and realised I couldn't live on fresh air.'

Steve decided he could make good money teaching English in Japan. Shortly after starting work there, he became convinced that teaching was definitely what he wanted to do as a career. 'Looking back, I'm so glad I quit the rat race when I did. Teaching English allows me to travel, to see other cultures, to feel them first hand and do something far more valuable than retail management, valuable in terms of contribution to the world.'

Over the next few years, Steve gradually realised that his lack of qualifications was holding him back from getting better jobs, 'so I enrolled on a one-year Master's degree back home'. He thoroughly enjoyed his year studying but was left with quite a substantial student loan to repay. Rather than return to Japan, he decided to go to the Middle East as he had heard that the salaries there were much higher. He found a job teaching male students in a college in Riyadh. He enjoyed the teaching but was not too happy with the administration of the institution. 'They smothered the creativity out of you. They didn't care about how well you taught, just about how thoroughly you completed all the paperwork.'

Steve was quickly able to get back on a good financial footing. After two years, despite being offered the chance to renew his contract, he returned to the UK and spent a year teaching freelance there. 'After being micro-managed for so long in Saudi, I wanted to make my own decisions. I wanted a bit of freedom. I had an enjoyable, if precarious, time but I got fed up with spending most of my time and effort on finding new business, rather than on

▶

becoming a better teacher. I missed the lifestyle in the Middle East and one day I just decided to apply for a teaching post at a university in Dubai.'

Steve soon settled into his new job. 'First and foremost, as a teacher, what makes you look forward to a day at school is the students' attitude. My students here are terrific. They're hard-working and respectful. Not angels, you understand, but they do want to learn.' He also found that the cosmopolitan nature of the population meant that he could meet a wide variety of people. 'Did you know that here at the university, we employ 32 nationalities? I've got friends and colleagues from all over the world here. It's great!' However, he disliked being on short-term renewable contracts. He explained that he worried at times about the prospect of not being given a contract renewal every three years. 'I'm fairly confident my current contract will be renewed next year but I'd really like a bit more security. Then again, I suppose if I did lose this job for whatever reason, I could always find work elsewhere and be happy.'

Steve found Dubai an interesting place to be. 'Even though it's a big city, with all that entails, it's easy to grab a few minutes of peace and quiet. I love going into the desert at weekends. It's near to a number of places I've always wanted to visit – last year I saw the pyramids, a lifelong dream! And yet I can find anything I want here, from the latest blockbuster to Newcastle United live on the TV. And English is widely spoken, so there's no pressure to learn a new language.'

Steve often thinks about the unusual way in which he 'stumbled into teaching as a career'. Looking back, he wonders why he ever went into retail management when 'all my life my main desire was to help people who needed helping'. He attributes this decision partly to a desire to 'make my parents proud of me', adding that he was the first member of his family to go to university.

'It's strange,' Steve explained, 'that even though I didn't originally plan on leaving the UK for an extended period, a decade later I've spent only two years back in the UK apart from the odd visit. Unless my parents suffered a major health setback, I have no plans to return there to live and work in the foreseeable future.' One reason is the realisation that he would find it hard financially if he were to return to the UK and work there as an English teacher. 'I wouldn't want to do any other kind of work – especially not retail management! As a teacher I would either really struggle to make ends meet or work myself silly freelancing. But money isn't the reason I want to stay here. The real reason why I have no desire to return to the UK is that I learn so much more living overseas. When I'm in the UK I feel like I'm missing something.'

Steve sometimes thinks about looking for a teaching job in another country, such as Turkey, but is aware that the money he would earn there is far less than in the Middle East. Therefore, he wishes to stay for the next few years since he is making very good money there and is even able to start thinking about planning for his retirement. 'I really don't know how long I'll be able to stay here or where I'll be in 10 years' time. But, truly, I feel very fortunate in that I've had the freedom to do what I want to do when I want to do it. I know now that I'm doing what I want to do, what I need to do, and I hope in my old age that will give me satisfaction.'

Questions

Having read Steve's account, consider the following questions.

1. Would you say that Steve's career could be described as a 'boundaryless career'?
2. In what ways, if any, does Steve seem to reconstruct career boundaries, rather than break free of them?

▶

3. In your view, could Steve's career be described as external, having an objective existence, or internal, subjectively constructed by Steve himself?

4. Is Steve's story more about change or continuity?

5. What metaphors does Steve employ to describe his career? In what ways do his career metaphors help us to understand how he makes sense of career?

6. To what extent can Schein's career anchors be applied to this story?

7. Examine Steve's story in light of Kanter's bureaucratic, professional and entrepreneurial career forms. Does Kanter's model work? To what extent do you think it can accommodate the transitions he described? Is there a fourth (or even a fifth) career form which you feel would enhance Kanter's framework?

CASE STUDY 13.3

An organisational career at Compucan

Amal El-Sawad and Laurie Cohen

Alison is 28 years old, is married with no children and no plans for any. She has worked for Compucan for the last six years. After graduating from university Alison struggled for some months to find a job. Having applied for a number of management training schemes without success, she decided to apply for programming roles in order to try to get her foot in the door of a company and was delighted when Compucan finally offered her a position as a computer programmer. Though she did not enjoy programming work (she felt she was no good at it), she hoped that eventually she would be able to move into a management role. The turning point for her came after two years when she worked on a programming project which enhanced her visibility by bringing her into contact with senior managers in the company. Soon after the project ended, she was promoted to the position of team leader, responsible for managing a small team of programmers. Following this she was appointed to a first-line manager position with responsibility for a whole department. Recently she has secured another promotion to a second-line manager role. Alison now has several managers reporting to her and assumes overall responsibility for a number of different departments. While she describes her first role as a programmer as 'just a job', she is clear that what she has now is a career. She explains:

I've been here six years and in the six years I've done five jobs. Each job has been a step up the career ladder. I know where I'm going next. I can see the natural steps, the sort of stepping-stones to get more responsibility. That's what I believe a career is. I think I'm very fortunate because I happen to have got on a very nice path and was recognised early and have been given lots of opportunities.

Beyond attributions to luck, Alison is hard-pressed to explain her meteoric rise at Compucan. She is surprised at how well she has done and struggles explain her success:

I was offered the team leadership job after two years and that came as a surprise to me. I really wasn't expecting it then. I seem to have just fallen into things, you know? I didn't plan to become a first-line manager but it, sort of, just happened. I certainly didn't plan to get this job as a second-line manager. I was just offered it.

▶

Alison suspects that her promotions may be connected to the visibility she secured within the organisation early on. She wonders whether the senior managers she met at this time have, behind the scenes, acted as her career sponsors:

I think if you've been recognised then I think you continue to be recognised. I think the senior management look after you quite heavily and worry about what you're doing, that kind of thing.

Now in a senior managerial role herself, Alison describes how she now keeps a lookout for younger employees whom she feels to be 'rising stars'. She instructs the managers who report to her to scout for stars on her behalf so that she can collate a list of high-potential employees. A committee of senior managers meets regularly at Compucan and the lists which managers have drawn up are discussed. A small number of employees considered to have the highest potential are singled out for special attention and are placed on the 'high-flyers database'. Their progress is monitored closely and they are often given extra projects to work on, over and above their daily roles, to help increase their visibility within the organisation. As Alison puts it: 'We grow our people by giving them opportunities.'

While many employees, in particular graduate recruits, aspire to be placed on the high-flyers database, only some of those that are on the database are actually informed of the fact. Ambitious employees therefore do not know whether they are being 'watched' because their name is on the database or 'watched' because someone somewhere deems them to have the potential to be placed on the database. The net effect is to make them feel as though they are under constant surveillance. To be seen to ease off work is to jeopardise one's chances of being identified as a high-potential employee. This in turn ensures that the maximum effort goes into their work.

When it comes to promotion decisions, there are no set criteria written down. Indeed, like Alison, Compucan employees are not really sure what qualities and abilities are required to achieve promotion, which makes it difficult for them to know how best to attract the attention of selectors. Alison is particularly drawn to enthusiastic employees. She explains:

I think the thing that I notice with people and what I appreciate in people and would encourage is enthusiasm because I think if somebody is enthusiastic then you can teach them anything and you can get them to do anything.

Despite acknowledging the role that senior managers have played in her own promotion, and the role that she plays in identifying and grooming the next generation of 'stars', Alison is frustrated by the views held by some employees that what matters at Compucan is 'not what you know but who you know' and that promotion decisions are political ones. Alison protests:

I don't think [career progression] is political. To be promoted in Compucan you need to do your job, plus you take on extra responsibilities round it. The people who call it political are the people who just do their job and who are only willing to do their job. They're only willing to do the nine to five and that is their choice. You know, it's 'no pain no gain'.

Alison works very long hours and 12-hour days are the norm. For her, employees who have chosen to devote time and effort to commitments outside of work – for example to family life – should not expect to achieve the kind of career progression available to those prepared to 'devote all' to Compucan. Alison is attempting to communicate this message to the employees for whom she is responsible. She is currently mentoring two junior staff,

▶

*El-Sawad, A. (2005) 'Becoming a "lifer"? Unlocking career through metaphor', *Journal of Occupational and Organizational Psychology*, Vol.78, pp.23–41.

Evetts, J. (2000) 'Analysing change in women's careers: culture, structure and action dimensions', *Gender, Work and Organization*, Vol.7, No.1, pp.57–67.

Fearfull, A. and Kamenou, N. (2006) 'How do you account for it? A critical exploration of career opportunities for and experiences of ethnic minority women', *Critical Perspective on Accounting*, Vol.17, pp.883–901.

Fitzgerald, L.F. and Crites, J.O. (1980) 'Toward a career psychology of women: what do we know? What do we need to know?', *Journal of Counselling Psychology*, Vol.27, pp.44–62.

Fournier, V. (1998) 'Stories of development and exploitation: militant voices in an enterprise culture', *Organization*, Vol.5, No.1, pp.55–80.

Gambles, R, Lewis, S. and Rapaport, R. (2006) *The Myth of Work–Life Balance: The Challenge of our Time for Men, Women and Societies,* Chichester: Wiley

Gergen, K. (2001) *Social Construction in Context,* Thousand Oaks, CA: Sage.

Gilligan, C. (1982) *In a Different Voice. Psychological Theory and Women's Development,* Cambridge, MA: Harvard University Press.

Goffman, I. (1961) *Asylums,* New York: Anchor.

Grant, D. and Oswick, C. (eds) (1996) *Metaphor and Organization,* London: Sage.

Greenhaus, J.H., Callanan, G.A. and Godshalk, V.M. (2000) *Career Management,* Orlando, FL: Harcourt.

Grey, C. (1994) 'Career as a project of the self and labour process discipline', *Sociology*, Vol.28, No.2, pp.479–97.

Gunz, H.P. (1989) *Careers and Corporate Cultures: Managerial Mobility in Large Corporations,* Oxford: Blackwell.

*Hakim, C. (2000) *Work–Lifestyle Choices in the Twenty-First Century,* Oxford: Oxford University Press.

Hakim, C. (2006) 'Women, careers and life preferences', *British Journal of Guidance and Counselling*, Vol.34, No.3, pp.279–94.

Hall, D.T. (1976) *Careers in Organizations,* Pacific Palisades, CA: Goodyear.

Hall, D.T. (2004) 'The protean career: a quarter century journey', *Journal of Vocational Behavior*, Vol.65, pp.1–13.

Hite, L. and McDonald, K. (2003) 'Career aspirations of non-managerial women: adjustment and adaptation', *Journal of Career Development*, Vol.29, No.4, pp.221–35.

Holland, J.L. (1973) *Making Vocational Choices,* Englewood Cliffs, NJ: Prentice-Hall.

Höpfl, H. and Hornby Atkinson, P. (2000) 'The future of women's career', in A. Collin and R. Young (eds) *The Future of Career,* Cambridge: Cambridge University Press.

Hughes, E.C. (1937) 'Institutional office and the person', *American Journal of Sociology*, Vol.43, pp.404–13.

Inkson, K. (1995) 'Effects of changing economic conditions on managerial job changes and careers', *British Journal of Management*, Vol.6, pp.183–94.

Inkson, K. (2002) 'Thinking creatively about careers: the use of metaphor', in M. Peiperl, M. Arthur and N. Anand (eds) *Career Creativity: Explorations in the Remaking of Work,* Oxford: Oxford University Press.

Inkson, K. (2004) 'Images of career: nine key metaphors', *Journal of Vocational Behavior*, Vol.65, pp.96–111.

Inkson, K. (2007) *Understanding Careers: The Metaphors of Working Lives,* London: Sage.

Kanter, R.M. (1989) 'Careers and the wealth of nations: a macro-perspective on the structure and implications of career forms', in M.B. Arthur, D.T. Hall and B.S. Lawrence (eds) *Handbook of Career Theory,* Cambridge: Cambridge University Press.

Lamba, N.K. (2003) 'The employment experiences of Canadian refugees: measuring the impact of human and social capital on quality of employment', *Canadian Review of Sociology and Anthropology*, Vol.40, No.1, pp.45–64.

Levinson, D. (1978) *The Seasons of a Man's Life,* New York: Knopf.

Macauley, S. and Harding, N. (1996) 'Drawing up a new careers contract', *People Management*, 4 April, pp.34–5.

Mallon, M. (1998) 'From managerial career to portfolio career: making sense of the transition', unpublished PhD thesis, Sheffield Hallam University.

Mallon, M. and Cohen, L. (2001) 'Time for a change? Women's accounts of the move from organizational careers to self-employment', *British Journal of Management*, Vol.12, No.3, pp.217–30.

Marshall, J. (1989) 'Re-visioning career concepts: a feminist invitation', in M.B Arthur, D.T. Hall and B.S. Lawrence (eds) *Handbook of Career Theory*, New York: Cambridge University Press.

Mayo, A. (1991) *Managing Careers in Organisations*, London: Institute of Personnel Management.

McQuarrie, F.A.E. and Jackson, E.L. (2002) 'Transitions in leisure careers and their parallels in work careers: the effect of constraints on choice and action', *Journal of Career Development*, Vol.29, No.1, pp.37–53.

Mignot, P. (2000) 'Metaphor: a paradigm for practice-based research into career', *British Journal of Guidance and Counselling*, Vol.28, No.4, pp.365–380.

Mignot, P. (2004) 'Metaphor and "career"', *Journal of Vocational Behaviour*, Vol.64, No.3, pp.455–69.

Mirvis, P.H. and Hall, D.T. (1996) 'Psychological success and the boundaryless career', *Journal of Organisational Behaviour*, Vol.15, pp.365–80.

Montgomery, L.M. (1917) 'The Alpine Path: the story of my career', originally published in instalments of *Everywoman's World*, available at http://digital.library.upenn.edu/women/montgomery/alpine/alpine.html, accessed 22 April 2008.

Morgan, G. (1986) *Images of Organization*, London: Sage.

Nicholson, N. and West, M. (1989) 'Transitions, work histories and careers', in M.B. Arthur, D.T. Hall and B.S. Lawrence (eds) *Handbook of Career Theory*, New York: Cambridge University Press.

Office for National Statistics (2003) *Labour Market Trends*, February, London: ONS.

Office for National Statistics (2003) *Labour Market Trends*, October, London: ONS.

Office for National Statistics (2006a) *Annual Population Survey January 2004 to December 2004*, London: ONS.

Office for National Statistics (2006b) *Labour Market Review*, March, London: ONS.

Peiperl, M., Arthur, M., Goffee, R. and Morris, T. (2000) *Career Frontiers*, Oxford: Oxford University Press.

Peiperl, M., Arthur, M. and Anand, N. (eds) (2002) *Career Creativity: Explorations in the Remaking of Work*, Oxford: Oxford University Press.

Potter, J. and Wetherell, M. (1987) *Discourse and Social Psychology*, London: Sage.

*Pringle, J.K. and Mallon, M. (2003) 'Challenges for the boundaryless career odyssey', *International Journal of Human Resource Management*, Vol.14, No.5, pp.839–53.

Raelin, J. (1985) *The Clash of Cultures: Managers and Professionals*, Boston, MA: Harvard Business School Press.

Savage, M. (1998) 'Discipline, surveillance and the "career": employment on the Great Western Railway 1833–1914', in A. McKinlay and K. Starkey (eds) *Foucault, Management and Organization Theory*, London: Sage.

Savickas, M. (2002) 'Reinvigorating the study of careers', *Journal of Vocational Behavior*, Vol.60, pp.381–85.

Savickas, M. (2005) 'The theory and practice of career construction', in S.D. Brown and R.W. Lent (eds) *Career Development and Counselling: Putting Theory and Research to Work*, Hoboken, NJ: Wiley, pp.42–70.

Schein, E.H. (1978) *Career Dynamics*, Reading, MA: Addison-Wesley.

Schein, E.H. (1993) *Career Anchors: Discovering your Real Values*, London: Pfeffer.

Schein, E.H. (1996) 'Career anchors revisited: implications for career development in the 21st century', *Academy of Management Executive*, Vol.10, pp.80–8.

Sennett, R. (1998) *The Corrosion of Character: The Personal Consequences of Work in the New Capitalism*, New York: W.W. Norton & Co.

Smith, R. (2004) *A Few Kind Words and a Loaded Gun: The Autobiography of a Career Criminal*, London: Viking.

Sturges, J. (1999) 'What it means to succeed: personal conceptions of career success held by male and female managers at different ages', *British Journal of Management*, Vol.10, pp.239–52.

Sullivan, S. (1999) 'The changing nature of careers: a review and research agenda', *Journal of Management*, Vol.25, No.3, pp.457–84.

Sugarman, L. (2005) *Life-Span Development. Frameworks, Accounts and Strategies* (2nd edn), Hove: Psychology Press.

Super, D.E. (1957) *The Psychology of Careers,* New York: Harper & Row.

Super, D.E., Thompson, A.S. and Lindeman, R.H. (1985) *The Adult Careers Concern Inventory,* Palo Alto, CA: Consulting Psychologists Press.

Templar, A.J. and Cawsey, T.F. (1999) 'Rethinking career development in an era of portfolio careers', *Career Development International,* Vol.4, No.2, pp.70–76.

Thomas, D.A. and Alderfer, C.P. (1989) 'The influence of race on career dynamics: theory and research on minority career experiences', in M. Arthur, B.S. Lawrence and D.T. Hall (eds) *Handbook of Career Theory,* Cambridge: Cambridge University Press.

Tomlinson, J. (2006) 'Women's work-life balance trajectories in the UK: reformulating choice and constraint in transitions through part-time work', *British Journal of Guidance and Counselling,* Vol.34, No.3, pp.365–82.

Wacjman, J. (1996) 'Desperately seeking differences: is management style gendered? *British Journal of Industrial Relations,* Vol.34, pp.333–49.

White, M., Hill, S., McGovern, P., Mills, C. and Smeaton, D. (2003) 'High performance management practices, working hours and work-life balance', *British Journal of Industrial Relations,* Vol.41, No.2, pp.175–95.

Whittock, M. (2000) *Feminising the Masculine: Women in Non-traditional Employment,* Aldershot: Ashgate.

Wilensky, H. (1961) 'Work, careers and social integration', *International Social Science Journal,* Vol.12, No.4, pp.543–74.

Young, R. and Collin, A. (2004) 'Constructivism and social constructionism in the career field', *Journal of Vocational Behaviour,* Vol.64, No.3, pp.373–88.

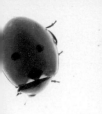

Chapter 14

MANAGING DIVERSITY

Catherine Cassell

Introduction

Within the management and organisation literature there has been an increased interest in managing diversity as a way of addressing equal opportunity issues. A broad term that encompasses a number of concepts, managing diversity refers to the systematic and planned commitment on the part of organisations to recruit and retain employees from diverse demographic backgrounds (Thomas 1992). Building on the notion that all differences between groups and individuals within an organisation should be recognised and valued, managing diversity presents a business case for equal opportunities. Noon and Ogbonna (2001, p.1) suggest that the concept of equal opportunities is increasingly being replaced with the notion of management of diversity: 'It has been a gradual drift, emanating from writers and organizations in the USA, traveling across the U.K. and seeping into mainland Europe.' A key issue here is that in linking equal opportunities initiatives directly with business strategy, the concept of managing diversity is inextricably linked with strategic HRM.

The aim of this chapter is to outline the principles behind the managing diversity approach and examine some of the key issues and tensions around diversity debates. The chapter begins by outlining the context in which managing diversity has arisen. The principles of managing diversity strategies are then discussed, together with some of the techniques and tools that managers can use to this end. The challenges facing the creation of global diversity programmes are then considered. The chapter concludes by examining some of the key issues and debates within this field. These include a consideration of the evidence for the effectiveness of managing diversity initiatives, and a critique of the business case within which managing diversity initiatives are located.

The managing diversity context

The management of diversity first emerged within the business literature towards the end of the 1980s. Therefore, in the history of personnel and HRM more generally, it is a relatively new concept. It is important to consider why the concept emerged when it did, and the currency that it currently has among HR academics and practitioners. By way of context, the triggers that led to a focus of attention towards diversity management are now considered. Two particular factors are important here: changing demographic trends and the emergence of the business case for the progression of equal opportunities.

DEMOGRAPHIC TRENDS

The development of managing diversity strategies is clearly located within the context of shifting demographic trends. The composition of the international workforce is changing dramatically. Prasad and Mills (1997, p.4) pointed out the impact that these shifts initially had in North America:

> Few trends have received as much publicity or gained as much attention in management circles as the recent interest in managing diversity. It can be argued that much of this interest can be traced back to Johnston and Packard's (1987) influential report, *Workforce 2000*, which alerted organizations to the dramatic demographic changes that were in the process of transforming the North American workforce.... Confronted with the prospect of these major imminent changes, management practitioners, business educators, and organizational consultants quickly began preparing to meet the challenges of a new and diverse workforce in a number of ways.

Kandola (1995, p.138), one of the pioneers of managing diversity initiatives in the UK and Europe, highlighted at the time that similar demographic changes to those that were occurring in North America were anticipated throughout Europe. Specifically, it was anticipated that there would be increasing numbers of women and ethnic minorities entering the labour market, and the overall age of the working population would increase. The argument was that such demographic trends had created the necessity to expand the labour pool to include those groups traditionally disadvantaged in the employment market. Roberson and Kulik (2007, p.24) highlight how when these trends were first identified they were 'heralded as an opportunity for organizations to become more creative, to reach previously untapped markets, and in general to achieve and maintain a competitive advantage'. The key aim of diversity management, therefore, was for companies to turn such demographic trends to their own advantage and make the most of the talents of the new diverse workforce that were now available to them. Recent European statistics have highlighted that the issue of demographic trends is one that is here to stay. Egan and Bendick (2003) highlight the dramatic changes predicted in the EU workforce for the next 30 years. Apart from the increased migration of those workers from newly recognised EU states, the workforce is expected to become on average older; be more dominated by women; to have more workers working part-time; and also to shrink considerably.

THE BUSINESS CASE FOR EQUAL OPPORTUNITIES

The development of managing diversity perspectives came at a time when there was considerable disillusionment among activists, practitioners and employers about the effectiveness and achievements of equal opportunities (EO) policies, particularly in the UK (e.g. Wilson 1995). Concerns were also expressed that such policies were unattractive to employers. For example, Ross and Schneider (1992, p.36) suggested that employers had resisted EO legislation precisely because it has been imposed upon them:

> So long as equal opportunities was equated simply with complying with legislation, then it's always going to be about group parity, and getting the numbers 'right'. This was a recipe for inertia over the last fifteen years, this is pretty much what we experienced.

Rather, they argued that EO needed to be seen as business driven in order to be attractive to employers, clearly a different case from the traditional case of fairness, justice and group parity. In a similar vein Davidson and Fielden (2003) suggest that one of the criticisms of the equal opportunities approach is that it is seen as a negative attempt to address issues of inequality because the focus is on punitive measures for those employers who do not comply with legislation. Diversity policies, on the other hand, are likely to be seen as more positive with regard to their recognition and celebration of the characteristics of diverse groups. The debate about equal opportunities versus managing diversity is, however, not that clear-cut. For example, Liff and Dickens (1999) argue that a comparison between the two approaches can lead to an over-emphasis of the creation of a false dichotomy between them. Indeed, other authors such as Kaler (2001, p.58) suggest that 'what is unclear is whether they are two entirely separate approaches to employee management or whether diversity is offering a new and potentially more successful way of achieving the moral objectives of equal opportunity'. What is apparent, however, is that the managing diversity approach is based upon a business case for equal opportunities.

The business case focuses on the business benefits that employers accrue through making the most of the skills and potential of all employees. The argument is that the loss or lack of recognition of these skills and potential, usually as a result of everyday discriminatory practices, is very costly. Consequently the business case is fundamentally linked to the principles of strategic HRM where the human resource and its full utilisation is seen to give a company the competitive edge (Storey 1995). Additionally it is crucial that equal opportunities initiatives are seen to tie in with the overall strategic direction of a company. A business case sees achieving equality as essential to achieving organisational goals. Again, in the same way that HRM is linked into the general strategy of a firm, so equal opportunities pervades every aspect of business policy, rather than being an add-on.

In 1995 the Equal Opportunities Commission launched a campaign to highlight the business case for equal opportunities. The aim was to demonstrate that, in economic terms, equality made good business sense. A leaflet produced at the time outlines the 'Benefits of Equality' and 'Costs of Inequality'. The benefits of equality include:

- best use of human resources;

- flexible workforce to aid restructuring;

- workforce representative of the local community;

- improved corporate image with potential employees and customers;

- attracting ethical investors;

- managers can integrate equality into corporate objectives;

- new business ideas from a diverse workforce.

The costs of inequality include:

- inefficiency in use of human resources (high staff turnover, low productivity and restricted pool of talent);

- inflexible workforce, limiting organisational change;

- poor corporate image with prospective employees and customers;

- management time spent on grievances;

- losing an industrial tribunal case.

These costs and benefits were linked into the demographic trends outlined earlier. The business case blossomed as a rationale for the effective management of diversity within the workplace and became an important underpinning argument for furthering equality at work. For example, most recently the CIPD (2007) has outlined three major benefits associated with the business case for equal opportunities and managing diversity. These relate to people issues such as drawing on a wider range of labour who will be more creative, innovative and happier in their work environment; market competitiveness where a diverse workforce can, for example, open up new market opportunities; and corporate reputation, where diversity and inclusion are linked into the wider issues of corporate social responsibility.

To summarise, it is worth examining the differences between the diversity model based on the business case and traditional models of equal opportunity. Kandola and Fullerton (1994) propose that whereas EO is externally initiated, legally driven and focuses on numbers and problems, diversity is internally initiated, business-needs driven and focuses on qualitative and opportunity outcomes. EO approaches tend to assume assimilation and are reactive, whereas diversity approaches assume pluralism and are proactive. Finally, EO approaches focus on a particular set of differences, usually race, gender and disability, whereas diversity approaches focus on all differences. Therefore diversity approaches based on a business case represent a different way of looking at equal opportunities.

General principles

Underlying diversity management is the notion of difference and the effective management of difference. Valuing difference is seen as an important concept because it is specifically linked to an organisation's culture and values. A key element is to move towards 'cultures of inclusion' (Thornberg 1994), recognising that various organisational practices lead to certain groups feeling left out or unwelcome.

Exponents of the management of diversity perspective (Thomas 1990; Cox 1992; Jackson 1992; Kandola and Fullerton 1994; Montes and Shaw 2003) argue that all differences must be valued, including those of white males. Kandola and Fullerton (1994, p.8) provide a useful working definition of managing diversity:

> The basic concept of managing diversity accepts that the workforce consists of a diverse population of people. The diversity consists of visible and non-visible differences which will include factors such as sex, age, background, race disability, personality and work style. It is founded on the premiss that harnessing these differences will create a productive environment in which everybody feels valued, where their talents are being fully utilized and in which organizational goals are met.

The concept of managing diversity has become very popular, particularly in North America. The language surrounding diversity initiatives focuses on the notion of celebrating differences, as Prasad and Mills (1997, p.4) suggest:

> Diversity is celebrated with the help of evocative metaphors such as the melting pot, the patchwork quilt, the multicolored or cultural mosaic, and the rainbow. All of these metaphors evoke enormously affirmative connotations of diversity, associating it with images of cultural hybridity, harmonious coexistence, and colorful heterogeneity.

A consideration of some organisational policies about diversity highlight some of the differences that need to be managed. A typical policy will include differences such as gender, race, disability, spent criminal convictions, sexual orientation, religion and beliefs, socio-economic background, and age, and potentially others such as personality differences and working styles. For example, the general manager of Global Diversity and Inclusion at Microsoft states that:

> Microsoft needs the insight, creativity and diverse perspectives that a range of employees can bring to the table. This means not only having a workforce balanced by race, ethnic origin, gender, sexual orientation, and gender identity and expression, but also having a workforce that embraces differences in approaches, insights, abilities and experiences. (Microsoft 2008)

Kandola and Fullerton (1994) suggest that managing diversity must pervade the entire organisation, if it is to be successful. They propose a MOSAIC vision, which summarises the key characteristics of the diversity-oriented organisation. MOSAIC is used here as an acronym for **M**ission and values, **O**bjective and fair processes, **S**killed workforce: aware and fair, **A**ctive flexibility, **I**ndividual focus, and **C**ulture that empowers. Therefore the HR professional should, in theory, have a key role in the implementation of such initiatives. Jackson (1992, p.27) suggests that making the most of workforce diversity is a key challenge for HR professionals. She suggests that it is those professionals who are 'best able to educate business leaders about the strategic importance of working through diversity to mobilize them to take immediate actions'. She also suggests that HR professionals have a wide range of tools available to them for changing the attitudes and behaviours of their organisation's employees. Such tools include recruitment and selection systems, performance evaluation and appraisal, compensation and reward, and training and development. Celebrating diversity could, therefore, be reinforced through the use of these tools. This approach sees diversity as a strategic imperative and therefore clearly linked into HRM. The focus of diversity initiatives is that of ensuring that all individuals within an organisation can maximise their potential, regardless of any groups they may belong to. It is an all-embracing concept where the focus is cultural change and learning, rather than promoting fairness and avoiding discrimination. Crucially, managing diversity is seen as a key element of overall business policy, linked into an organisation's strategy, rather than a personnel or HR policy. Given that, the emphasis is clearly on the business benefits that the successful management of diversity can accrue for a company.

Implementing diversity initiatives

A whole range of initiatives can be subsumed under the heading of diversity initiatives. Arnold (1997, p. 179) lists some of the interventions that characterise diversity initiatives. They include:

■ multicultural workshops designed to improve understanding and communication between cultural groups;

■ multicultural 'core groups' which meet regularly to confront stereotypes and personal biases;

■ support groups, mentoring, and relationships and networks for women and cultural minorities;

■ advisory councils reporting to top management;

■ rewarding managers on the basis of their record of developing members of targeted groups;

■ fast-track development programmes and special training opportunities for targeted groups.

Detailed examples of the use of different types of these interventions can be found in relation to DEC (Walker and Hanson 1992); National Transportation Systems (Ellis and Sonnenfeld 1994); American Express (Woolfe Morrison and Mardenfeld Herlihy 1992); Pepsi-Cola (Fulkerson and Schuler 1992); International Distillers and Vintners (Kandola and Fullerton 1994); the construction industry (Gale *et al.* 2003); BBC Scotland (Maxwell 2003); and Royal Mail (Foster 2004). A key element in most of these interventions is some form of diversity training. This usually focuses on the importance of the successful management of diversity for achieving business benefits, and highlighting how stereotypes of different groups may hinder their opportunities in the workplace.

It is apparent that specific interventions will not work without a consideration of the environment within which they are being introduced. Other aspects of organisational processes are also important. For example, Gilbert and Ivancevich (2000) identify five factors related to the success of diversity initiatives. These are the initiation and support of the chief executive; human resource initiatives; organisational communication; corporate philosophy; and measures of success. Wholesale organisational support needs to be available, as evidence suggests that individual one-off initiatives are not enough to make a noticeable difference. The processes by which the interventions are planned is also important, as these are part of change strategies. Friday and Friday (2003), for example, provide a framework for using a 'planned change–corporate diversity strategy' based on Lewin's (1951) unfreezing model, arguing that any strategy needs to be carefully planned.

In a similar vein, Thornberg (1994) outlines three phases which represent a company's evolution towards a more diverse heterogeneous culture. The first is to bring in more women and minorities, the second to emphasise working on problems of individual and group behaviour associated with race and gender, that is, to begin to understand how people are different and why; and the third a focus on company culture which involves evaluating all of the organisation's policies and procedures. Therefore diversity interventions are characterised as comprehensive and inclusive.

Although most case studies of diversity initiatives are North-American-based, there is some European-based research. Rather than assessing the success of comprehensive diversity initiatives, a couple of studies have looked at comparisons between firms that have elements of a diversity policy and those that do not. Shapiro (2000) describes research designed to explore the link between organisational approaches to employee involvement and managing diversity. Using eight case studies from five European countries, she argues that employee diversity can be seen as the missing link that can encourage the success of innovations such as TQM and employee involvement. Indeed, Shapiro suggests that unless organisations take explicit consideration of the differences that exist between employees then they will have difficulty in meeting their key corporate improvement objectives. Research conducted in Britain (Hicks-Clarke and Iles 1999) has also demonstrated that positive employment attitudes (e.g. job satisfaction and employee commitment) are related to a company having a positive climate for diversity (as indicated by perceptions of policy support; organisation justice; support for diversity; and recognition of the need for diversity).

Other research has recently investigated the extent to which diversity initiatives are now being implemented in Europe. Süß and Kleiner (2007) outline how, in contrast to the USA, the starting point for managing diversity in Germany has been a focus on gender differences. They conducted a survey of 160 companies listed on the German stock exchange and found that 39. 4 per cent had implemented diversity management; 18.2 per cent had heard of the concept; but 42. 4 per cent knew nothing about it. The authors conclude that in the German context 'the concept is far from being a widespread and naturally employed management concept'.

Organisations may also be using diversity policies to meet different strategic aims and objectives. Maxwell *et al.* (2003) examined the use of diversity policies in UK public service and hotel organisations and found that the public sector areas they examined seemed to be actively considering the intrinsic value of managing diversity, such as treating the workforce fairly, whereas the hotel cases seemed more concerned with external organisational benefits. Foster and Harris (2005) reviewed the use of diversity management in the UK retail industry. Within that industry there are some well-publicised examples of companies claiming considerable business benefits from diversity policies. For example, ASDA in a press release highlighted the benefits of removing an age restriction to the employment of their workforce:

We have always been really proud of the fact that we have such a diverse workforce with colleagues as young as 16, whilst others are in their 80s. We're in no doubt that this benefits everyone, especially our customers. We've understood for many years now that an older workforce offers maturity, commitment and knowledge which our customers value. Over the years we've found that some of our best colleagues are also some of our oldest, with loads of experience to share with younger colleagues – they make a massive difference to our stores. (ASDA 2006)

Foster and Harris's (2005, p.14) research focused on how line managers were interpreting the concept of diversity management in practice. They found that line managers in different companies were interpreting the concept in diverse ways. They also highlight an interesting tension that the line managers were experiencing:

> Growing numbers of organizations have corporate diversity statements that acknowledge the importance of employing a diverse workforce and valuing individual difference. Yet the reported line management practice revealed that a standardized approach to dealing with employee differences was widely regarded as more sustainable and workable within the framework of the UK's present anti-discrimination legislation than more 'customised' approaches designed to accommodate individual diversity in the employment relationship.

A further finding from Foster and Harris's research is that few line managers had experienced diversity training. This may also be characteristic of other UK industries. For example, the annual CIPD Training and Development Survey in 2004 highlighted that of the different types of training asked about in the survey, diversity training was seen as the least important, with 46 per cent seeing it as 'somewhat important' and 22 per cent as 'not important' or 'not offered'.

It would seem, then, that there is increased evidence of the use of diversity initiatives in parts of the UK and Europe. A complicating issue, however, is the impact of increased globalisation. Individual companies may develop their own approach to diversity, but these approaches may be inappropriate within the different locations where a company is based. Global diversity management has therefore increasingly become the key challenge in this area.

Global diversity management

With the increased globalisation of the workforce, managing diversity across international borders has become an important issue. Sippola and Smale (2007) suggest that we know very little about how multinational firms are responding to the increasingly globalised nature of their workforce and operations. The extent to which diversity policies focusing on managing difference translate neatly across borders has been questioned. Nishii and Özbilgin (2007, p.1883) suggest that 'American' labels regarding difference are 'simply ridiculous' outside the US context. They give the example of Canada where an important difference in the workplace, regardless of ethnicity or gender, is whether one is primarily English or French speaking. Other challenges about whether a US or Western model of diversity is appropriate have been posed with regard to India (Wilson 2003), Australia (Strachan *et al.* 2004) and New Zealand (Jones *et al.* 2000). Egan and Bendick (2003) also highlight that the US has different priorities about diversity owing to the different legal, political and cultural environments. This raises the issue of whether global diversity initiatives should focus upon multi-domestic approaches which are individual to each cultural location of the company, or focus on attempting to achieve a global strategy with a similar approach in all locations.

Nishii and Özbilgin (2007, p.1886) suggest that global diversity initiatives based on the 'exportation of US based diversity programmes abroad have failed due to their lack of attention to local cultural and demographic differences'. They outline a conceptual framework that examines the leadership and cultural foundations and the organisational outcomes of global diversity management. The framework also includes four important components that need to be in place for successful global diversity management. Firstly, global units need to be included in the decision-making processes of the company. This is in line with the strategies for inclusion that underlie diversity initiatives. Secondly, human resource management policies need to be designed flexibly in order to take account of local context. Thirdly, although there need to be locally defined goals for addressing particular forms of discrimination that take into account power differences between groups within a cultural context, the overall goals of the global diversity initiative need to be unified across global units. This prevents fragmentation of the overall company approach (Nishii and Özbilgin, 2007, p.1888).

There is some evidence that multinational companies are adopting the kind of approach recommended. Egan and Bendick (2003, p.723) examined how US multinationals were seeking to implement global diversity initiatives in European locations. They conducted a survey of 30 large US MNCs from a range of industries and services. They concluded that although diversity management is likely to become important in human resource management practices of US MNCs located in Europe, there is no one best approach. Rather 'for each company, the soundest approach is likely to be that which matches the degree of centralization that the firm applies to other important aspects of corporate operations'. They also draw attention to the issue that the business case may be different in different European contexts. A further point is that it may be difficult for diversity staff to cover both local and international work. Clearly there is the need more generally for the development of staff with expertise in international diversity management.

In summary, it would seem that the issues encountered with regard to global diversity management are similar to the debates about integration or national differentiation that characterise the nature of global HRM more generally (Sippola and Smale 2007). Time will tell the extent to which global diversity initiatives manage to achieve their objectives.

Do diversity initiatives deliver?

A key question about managing diversity initiatives is to what extent do they actually work? The search for empirical evidence to validate the success of managing diversity programmes can be a fairly frustrating exercise. One of the problems is that many of the case studies of diversity programmes that are reported in the literature do not contain any evaluative element. Indeed, sometimes these case study reports focus more on promoting a particular company approach with evangelical zeal, rather than assessing and evaluating the success of a given programme. An additional source of concern is that most of the studies that do look at diversity interventions are American based. This in itself is not a problem, but, as highlighted earlier, there is the issue of how transferable the context is. Jones *et al.* (2000) point out the paradox that as managing diversity develops as a worldwide vocabulary for examining or celebrating difference, US cultural dominance may be reinforced by a US model of difference being applied globally.

As was suggested earlier, the impact of diversity on the business bottom line is difficult to assess. There are a couple of studies that consider the financial benefits of diversity programmes. One such analysis is provided by Wright *et al.* (1995). Using data from 1986 to 1992, they examined the impact that announcements of US Department of Labor awards for exemplary affirmative action had upon the stock returns of winning corporations, together with the effects that announcements of damage awards from the settlement of discrimination lawsuits had on the stock returns of guilty corporations. Their results indicated that announcements of quality affirmative action programmes were associated with an increase in stock prices, and conversely, announcements of discrimination settlements were associated with significant negative stock price changes. The authors conclude from this study that:

> the prevalent organizational ethnic and gender bias (Hitt and Barr 1989) should be eradicated not only because such bias is not ethical or moral, but also because it does not make economic sense. As the climate of competition becomes more intense, no enterprise can afford the senseless practice of discrimination. In fact, America's cultural diversity may provide a competitive advantage for unbiased US corporations over both domestic rivals that discriminate and European and Japanese companies in the world marketplace. (p.284)

A number of authors have drawn attention to some of the problems that emerge in seeking to evaluate diversity initiatives in organisations. Ellis and Sonnenfeld (1994) review three pioneering diversity programmes in US companies. They conclude that although it makes sense that the benefits of such programmes may translate into higher productivity and lower turnover, few organisations actually measure the transfer of the educational interventions into actual changes in human resource practices such as recruiting, management development and promotion. Their article highlights some of the emerging pitfalls with corporate diversity programmes. They suggest that the programmes:

> are positive in tone, yet often lack systematic firm-wide integration into other human resource policies and do not tap the passionate disagreement that often rages beneath a platitudinous facade. (Ellis and Sonnenfeld, 1994, p.80)

One of the problems they highlight is the lack of time actually spent on training in some diversity initiatives:

> These programes seem to be based on the premise that contact with members of different ethnic groups – if only for a few hours – or propaganda announcing the benefits of diversity, will clear up any misperceptions or ill will that some employees feel towards certain ethnic groups. Evidence often shows the contrary; simply pointing out differences among various groups, if not handled sensitively, can increase hostility and misunderstanding. (Ellis and Sonnenfeld, 1994, p.83)

Of significance here is the danger that diversity training may actually reinforce old stereotypes, or create new tensions. Ellis and Sonnenfeld point out that when evaluating a 'Valuing Diversity' seminar they found that a minority of respondents disliked it. In particular, white males complained that they were 'vilified' in the training materials, which depicted bias and miscommunication in their interactions with women and minorities. The authors suggest that leaders need to monitor continuously the messages that are being put across through diversity initiatives. They also conclude that studies of the effects of managing diversity programmes are rarely conducted. So although an individual may be asked to evaluate the training they have received through an evaluation questionnaire, the impact is rarely measured at the level of the firm, for example through the business benefits accrued.

Other evidence that diversity programmes are not being evaluated comes from the work of Kochan *et al.* (2003, p.8). They argue that there are few studies that look directly at the impact of diversity policies on objective measures of organisational performance. They attempted to conduct research with over 20 large and well-known Fortune 500 companies who had expressed an interest in being involved in diversity research. However, the research team encountered difficulties in following through the research in these firms. As the authors outline:

> After often considerable discussion of the data, confidentiality, and time commitments, all but four companies declined to participate. In some cases, the diversity advocates and professionals in the company lacked sufficient influence to convince line managers to spend the time required to collect the necessary data. In other cases, these professionals were reluctant to examine the effects of their organization's policies, with a view that they had sufficient top management support for their current initiatives and did not need to demonstrate a business case to maintain this support.

As the authors suggest, one of the first interesting lessons from their research was that as well as managers not knowing the impact of diversity strategies on objective performance measures, few of them were interested in discovering this information. Within the four cases that were conducted the authors concluded that there was 'simply no evidence to support the simple assertion that diversity is inevitably either good or bad for business' (Kochan *et al.* 2003, p.17). Perhaps this was one of the reasons why the managers were unhappy about keeping data about the impact of their policies in this area.

CRITIQUING DIVERSITY INITIATIVES

A number of other critiques have emerged about the managing diversity approach. Cassell and Biswas (2000) suggest that much of the literature that exists on the subject is largely atheoretical. Prasad and Mills (1997, p.5) outline the 'distant cheerleading' approach taken by some management academics and suggest that some of the potential difficulties of diversity initiatives are rarely challenged:

> Metaphorically speaking, the melting pot may well have become a cauldron (Nash, 1989), the quilt may have been torn, cracks may have begun to appear in the mosaic, and the rainbow may have become twisted out of shape. Yet, much of the management literature on workplace diversity (with few exceptions) tends to ignore or gloss over these dilemmas while continuing to stress the potency of workshops and training to accomplish the goals of workplace diversity.

Other authors suggest that structural change in itself may not be enough. Kossek, Markel and McHugh (2003), for example, propose that HR strategies that focus on structural change without focusing also on developing supportive group norms and an appropriate climate may be inadequate strategies for change in this area.

Arnold (1997) points out that there is a significant difference between learning to like diversity and learning to manage it. He suggests that much social psychological research has shown us that the former is difficult enough and that most of us tend to equate difference from ourselves as being worse or wrong. He proposes that even when we learn to appreciate difference, it does not mean that we necessarily know how to manage it. McEnrue (1993) has argued that the successful management of diversity at the interpersonal level requires the acceptance of the relativity of one's own knowledge and perceptions together with a tolerance for ambiguity and the ability to demonstrate empathy and respect while being willing to change one's own beliefs. This could, of course, be a list of skills required to be a good manager, rather than those explicitly linked with managing diversity.

A final important issue to consider is the extent to which the business case on which managing diversity is based holds any weight in relation to equal opportunities. Prasad and Mills (1997) suggest that the economic showcasing of diversity is both credible and persuasive to the public. However, the underlying economic assumptions of that case are drawn from human capital theories where people are treated explicitly as economic resources, with their skills, qualifications and characteristics having potential value for the firms that employ them. If we take women as a group, for example, it could be argued that opportunities for women employees in the labour force are enhanced when the perceived economic climate necessitates it. Studies of the employment of women during wartime have documented this (e.g. Alpern 1994; Farley 1994). In evaluating the business case, the key question must be what happens when demographic trends alter and skill shortages disappear? In other words, one can envisage a time when there is no business case for employing or promoting women and their diverse skills.

The problem with an economic case is that it is only persuasive within a given economic climate. Consequently, its impact in facilitating long-term change must be seriously questioned. A further issue is put forward by Richards (2001, p.29) who highlights how the difficulties with employer-driven equal opportunities agendas are that the priorities they usually support are those seen as important by the employer. These tend to address the more visible aspects of equal opportunities such as the number of women in senior positions, for example. In this context 'they are unlikely, therefore, to offer measures dealing with "stone floor" inequalities'. A further concern is that the links between valuing diverse skills and business success can be problematic. For example, Adkins (1995) in her analysis of gender relations in the tourist industry outlines how women workers were recruited to a variety of jobs at a theme park on the basis of their physical appearance. The reasons given for using such selection criteria were 'because of the customers'. Consequently women deemed as sexually attractive were employed in order to please the clients, 'sexual servicing' as Adkins calls it. Similarly, Biswas and Cassell (1996) outline a case study of a hotel where the work was clearly divided on gender lines. It was argued that it was crucial that receptionists were physically attractive; as they were the first point of contact for the customer, they would have an impact on whether that customer used the hotel again. In this context, then, it was argued that accentuating the sexuality of women employees through styles of dress etc. made business sense. There was a business case for women doing typically female jobs and men doing specifically male jobs, because the customers liked it.

Such examples render the perceived clear link between equal opportunities and business benefits problematic. Dickens (1994b, p.13), for example, suggests that some organisations will benefit from the absence of equal opportunities in that discriminatory practices can contribute to the bottom line. As she puts it: 'Organizations can, and do, obtain cost benefits from the non-recognition (but utilization) of women's skills, the undervaluing of women's labour, and from the exploitation of women as a cheap, numerically flexible (easily disposed of) workforce.' Indeed, a business benefits argument could, in this context, be used to legitimise a gendered status quo.

A final point is that the business case may not apply equally to all diverse groups. Woodhams and Danieli (2000) suggest that there is very little written within the diversity literature about the business case for employing disabled people. They suggest that the rationality underlying the diversity approach falters in relation to the employment of disabled people in a number of ways. As a considerably heterogeneous group who are not segregated within the labour market, a managing diversity approach based on the identification of group-based characteristics has little to offer. This leads us to the view that some diverse groups maybe more suitable to the business case than others, or indeed whether there is actually a business case for equal opportunities at all. Dickens (1994b, p.5) is suspicious about this. She suggests:

> In practice in the UK, there is not a business case for EO, but rather a number of business arguments which have greater or lesser attraction for particular employers in particular circumstances. The business-case arguments, although valid, are contingent on, and made within, variable decision-making contexts. Receptiveness to them, therefore, is likely to be uneven and they will not guarantee action on the part of all employers, at all times.

This discussion highlights the complicated nature of the processes through which issues of power, fairness and equality are reformulated into issues of competitive advantage. The potential for fundamental change within such an approach becomes questionable.

Conclusions

To conclude, four key issues emerge from this analysis of the managing diversity literature. The first is the extent to which there is evidence that organisations that manage diversity are more successful than organisations that do not. As suggested earlier, there is clearly the need for more research in this area. Ideally, research needs to focus on longitudinal assessment of diversity programmes, using a range of criteria from impact on economic performance to the attitudes of those groups that the interventions have been designed to address. Only then can the claims made for the success of managing diversity be properly evaluated.

Secondly, there is the question of the extent to which a movement that originated in North America translates easily into the distinctive HR contexts that exist in other parts of the world. It would seem that the business case for managing diversity is more partial in other economic contexts. A further issue in this context is the problematic nature of universalistic notions of managing diversity. In practice, the term does not have a unitary meaning; it means different things to different people, and can mean different things in different cultures or organisations. As stated earlier, increasingly there are challenges from other cultures about whether the Western model is appropriate. This is particularly important in relation to the development of global diversity initiatives and questions about the international application of locally derived diversity policies.

My predecessor went on maternity leave: why didn't she come back? Women just become frustrated.

The vast majority of Educate employees in the UK are white. This creates issues with regard to selling multicultural texts in that region. In the past couple of years Educate UK has tried to recruit a number of ethnic minority publishers and sales people. Dan Walker's view is that they will serve to keep the company on top of the growing multicultural educational market, therefore employing a more diverse workforce would make business sense. Indeed, a number of clients purchasing multicultural texts have commented on the lack of ethnic diversity among Educate UK staff. This is particularly apparent in the schools market where sales staff meet regularly with multicultural education coordinators in schools. Despite actively trying to recruit ethnic minority staff, there has not been much success in both recruiting and retaining ethnic minority employees. Where ethnic minority workers have been employed, they have rarely stayed at Educate UK long, commonly complaining about the lack of access to 'real' opportunities. One particular salesman expressed his feelings of tokenism in the following way:

I'm sick of being the only black face around the place, the guy who goes out just to get orders from the black customers. There doesn't seem to be any other role for me here apart from that. This is not what I expected when I came to work with a big multinational that wins awards for its diversity policies.

Dan Walker is concerned that some of the smaller, newer publishing firms are making inroads into the UK multicultural market, and are enticing away those customers who were previously loyal to the company. He wonders whether Educate UK actually has a problem with its image as an employer of the white, well-spoken, middle classes. He is also concerned that some of the older members of the workforce who have been around for a long time are reinforcing this traditional image of the firm by their very presence. In such a competitive market, where sales is a primary driver, Dan is concerned that the parent company is starting to ask questions about the image that the UK wing currently has and how it fits into the overall global profile. Although he knows that he has problems in this area, he is concerned that some of David Nolan's ideas about how to promote diversity may not go down too well in Educate UK. In particular, the legislative context of the UK is different from the US where those who are different are more 'loud and proud'. His view is that a more specific diversity strategy is required for the UK division of Educate. Therefore David Nolan is demanding immediate changes. His view is that the implementation of a global diversity strategy will not only deal with the problems in the UK subsidiary, but also be useful in the expansion into the new Chinese and European markets. He thinks it is important that employees of Educate throughout the world toe the line with the progressive diversity policies currently at work in the USA.

Questions

1. What advice would you give to David Nolan about developing a global diversity strategy to cover Educate worldwide? What are some of the difficulties he may face in his attempts to implement a global diversity strategy?
2. What advice would you give to Dan Walker about how he can deal with the diversity issues currently faced in the UK division of Educate? What type of diversity interventions can be introduced locally that will both satisfy the staff that progress is being made and also satisfy David Nolan that the UK is coming into line with US diversity practices?

Hinchcliffe Cards

Catherine Cassell

Hinchcliffe Cards was started by William Hinchcliffe in 1874. Hinchcliffe had an artistic talent which he used for drawing individual greetings cards for his family and friends. As demand for the products he made increased, members of William's family joined him in creating the more intricately decorated cards. As the products of the firm grew in popularity, Hinchcliffe cards began to expand, investing in its first printing press in the early 1900s. The business continued to grow and moved into the mass production of greetings cards for the family market. William, who by then was managing director of the firm, was keen that some element of the origins of the company remained, and despite the focus on mass production, a small sideline in the design and production of handmade cards remained.

After William Hinchcliffe died in 1934 the firm remained in the family and is now managed by chief executive James Hinchcliffe, who is William's great-grandson. The company headquarters, warehouse and packaging plant are housed in the same Lancashire town in England where William originally started the business in his own home. Indeed, the firm prides itself on being a family firm and having a paternalistic culture. James Hinchcliffe is often to heard to say 'Now, what would great-grandfather do in this situation?', when discussing any key strategic or problem issues. Despite the paternalistic culture, James is keen that the company moves with the times. Having recently completed an MBA at a local business school, he is keen to hear about new ideas and new methods of working that he can introduce into the company.

The company employs about 250 people. Seventy per cent of the workforce are women, who work mainly on the production line, and 10 per cent are from ethnic minority backgrounds. All the managers and senior management team, except the human resource manager (a white woman), are white males. Turnover in the company is generally low, though James Hinchcliffe suspects that there is a growing unease among the workforce about a number of issues.

The cards produced by the company feed into two main markets. First, there is the mass production of greetings cards. In particular, the firm recently won a couple of key contracts to produce Christmas cards for two of the larger chain stores which are internationally located. These contracts meant a considerable expansion of business, which has caused some problems in terms of work scheduling as production needs to be far higher in the spring months to meet the Christmas demand. In particular, some of the more sophisticated machines that are used occasionally, for foiling for example, are in 100 per cent use at this particular time. Putting coloured or silver foil on a card is an expensive process and the two men who work that machine are highly skilled. Currently there is a shortage of such skills within the printing industry. To deal with the increase in output required at this time of year, the firm has tended to employ around 20 casual workers for the spring period when these cards are produced. There is evidence, however, that the permanent production workers display animosity towards the temporary workers. As one suggested:

They're just here to make a quick buck, they don't seem bothered about the quality of what they do, their mistakes affect all of our bonuses.

The production workers have also recently been complaining about some other issues to do with their opportunities in the workplace. Some of the female workers have been asking

▶

Questions

1. What are the diversity issues currently faced by Hinchcliffe Cards?
2. Imagine that you are the consultant who has been approached by James Hinchcliffe to advise the company about how it can address each of the diversity issues you have outlined in question 1 above. What advice would you give?
3. How do you think the advice you have provided in answer to question 2 will be received by:
   a. the homeworkers;
   b. the male factory workers;
   c. the female factory workers;
   d. the senior management team?
4. Bearing in mind your answers to the above three questions, what advice would you give the company about how it can develop its international strategy?

CASE STUDY 14.3

Diversity training exercise

Catherine Cassell

You are an HR manager working in a busy training department in a local government office. The department has a well-established managing diversity policy. Within that policy it is explicit that discrimination against certain groups within the workforce based upon any differences will not be tolerated. Your training department provides regular courses for line managers about areas such as recruitment, selection, assessment and appraisal. As part of these courses there is a focus on the country's employment legislation. These parts of the courses focus on providing advice to managers about how to avoid inadvertently discriminating against staff as part of their general employment processes.

Recently it has been suggested that there may be a need for specific diversity training in your organisation. Your manager has asked you to put together a one-day training event about managing diversity that is aimed at middle managers. She has also asked that you make some suggestions about how the impact of the diversity training can be evaluated.

The task

1. Provide an overview of the schedule for the day's training session.
2. What is the aim of each of the sessions you have scheduled?
3. What kind of material will be included in each of the sessions?
4. What difficulties do you anticipate with the training you have suggested?
5. How will the impact of the training be evaluated?

Bibliography

Adkins, L. (1995) *Gendered Work: Sexuality, Family and the Labour Market,* Buckingham: Open University Press.

Alpern, S. (1994) 'In the beginning: a history of women in management', in E.A. Fagenson (ed.) *Women in Management: Trends, Issues and Challenges in Managerial Diversity,* Newbury Park, CA: Sage Publications.

Arnold, J. (1997) *Managing Careers into the 21st Century*, London: Paul Chapman Publishing.

ASDA (2006) 'DWP recognizes ASDA's continued good practice on age diversity', available at www.asda-press.co.uk/pressrclase/65, accessed 21 January 2008.

Biswas, R. and Cassell, C.M. (1996) 'The sexual division of labour in the hotel industry: implications for strategic HRM', *Personnel Review*, Vol.25, No.5, pp.51–66.

Cassell, C.M. and Biswas, R. (2000) 'Managing diversity in the new millennium', *Personnel Review*, Vol.29, No.3, pp.268–74.

CIPD (2004) *Annual Training and Development Survey*, London: Chartered Institute of Personnel and Development.

Cox, T., Jr (1992) 'The multi-cultural organization', *Academy of Management Executive*, Vol.5, No.2, pp.34–47.

Davidson, M.J. and Fielden, S.L. (2003) *Individual Diversity and Psychology in Organizations*, Chichester: John Wiley and Sons.

Dickens, L. (1994a) 'What HRM means for gender equality', *Human Resource Management Journal*, Vol.8, No.1, pp.23–40.

Dickens, L. (1994b) 'The business case for women's equality. Is the carrot better than the stick'? *Employee Relations*, Vol.16, No.8, pp.5–18.

Egan, M.L. and Bendick, M. (2003) 'Workforce diversity initiatives of US multinational corporations in Europe', *Thunderbird International Business Review*, Vol.45, No.6, pp.701–27.

Ellis, C. and Sonnenfeld, J.A. (1994) 'Diverse approaches to managing diversity', *Human Resource Management*, Vol.33, No.1, pp.79–109.

Equal Opportunities Commission (1995) *The Economics of Equal Opportunities*, Manchester: EOC.

Farley, J. (1994) 'Commentary', in E.A. Fagenson (ed.) *Women in Management: Trends, Issues and Challenges in Managerial Diversity*, Newbury Park: Sage.

Foster, C. (2004) 'Royal Mail: delivering dignity at work', *Equal Opportunities Review*, No.132, August, pp.8–15.

Foster, C. and Harris, C. (2005) 'Easy to say, difficult to do: diversity management in retail', *Human Resource Management Journal*, Vol.15, No.3, pp.4–17.

Friday, E. and Friday, S. (2003) 'Managing diversity using a strategic planned change approach', *Journal of Management Development*, Vol.22, No.10, pp.863–80.

Fulkerson, J.R. and Schuler, R.S. (1992) 'Managing worldwide diversity at Pepsi-Cola International', in S.E. Jackson (ed.) and associates *Diversity in the Workplace: Human Resource Initiatives*, New York: Guilford Press.

Gale, A.W., Davidson, M.J., Somerville, P., Sodhi, D., Steele, A. and Jones, S.R. (2003) 'Managing racial equality and diversity in the UK construction industry', in M.J. Davidson and S.L. Fielden (eds) *Individual Diversity and Psychology in Organizations*, Chichester: John Wiley and Sons.

Gilbert, J.A. and Ivancevich, J.M. (2000) 'Valuing diversity: a tale of two organizations', *Academy of Management Executive*, Vol.14, No.1, pp.93–107.

Hicks-Clarke, D. and Iles, P. (1999) 'The effects of positive climate for diversity on organizational and career perceptions and attitudes', Proceedings of the 1999 British Academy of Management Conference, Manchester, 1–3 September, Vol.1.

Hitt, M.A. and Barr, S.H. (1989) 'Managerial selection decision models: examination of configural cue processing', *Journal of Applied Psychology*, Vol.59, pp.705–11.

Jackson, S.E. (ed.) and associates (1992) *Diversity in the Workplace: Human Resource Initiatives*, New York: Guilford Press.

Johnston, W.B. and Packard, A.H. (1987) *Workforce 2000: Work and Workers for the 21st Century*, Indianapolis: Hudson.

Jones, D. (2004) 'Screwing diversity out of the workers? Reading diversity', *Journal of Organizational Change Management*, Vol.17, No.3, pp.281–91.

Jones, D., Pringle, J. and Shepherd, D. (2000) '"Managing diversity" meets Aotearoa New Zealand', *Personnel Review*, Vol.29, No.3, pp.364–80.

Joplin, J.R.W. and Daus, C.S. (1997) 'Challenges of leading a diverse workforce', *Academy of Management Executive*, Vol.11, No.3, pp.32–47.

Kaler, J. (2001) 'Diversity, equality, morality', in M. Noon and E. Ogbonna (eds) *Equality, Diversity and Disadvantage in Employment*, Houndmills: Palgrave.

Kandola, R. (1995) 'Managing diversity: new broom or old hat?', in C.L. Cooper and I.T. Robertson (eds) *International Review of Industrial and Organizational Psychology*, Vol.10, Chichester: John Wiley and Sons.

Kandola, R. and Fullerton, J. (1994) *Managing the Mosaic: Diversity in Action*, London: Institute of Personnel and Development.

Kochan, T., Bezrukova, K., Ely, R., Jackson, S., Aparna, J., Jehn, K., Leonard, J., Levine, D. and Thomas, P. (2003) 'The effects of diversity on business performance: report of the diversity research network', *Human Resource Management*, Vol.42, No.1, pp.3–21.

Lewin, K. (1951) *Field Theory in Social Science*, New York: Harper and Row.

Maxwell, G. (2003) 'Minority report: taking the initiative in managing diversity at BBC Scotland', *Employee Relations*, Vol.26, No.2, pp.182–202.

Maxwell, G., McDougall, M., Blair, S. and Masson, M. (2003) 'Equality at work in the UK public-service and hotel organizations: inclining towards managing diversity?' *Human Resource Development International*, Vol.6, No.2, pp.243–58.

McEnrue, M.P. (1993) 'Managing diversity: Los Angeles before and after the riots', *Organizational Dynamics*, Vol.21, No.3, pp.18–29.

Microsoft (2008) 'Message from Claudette Wilding, General Manager, global diversity and inclusion', available at www.microsoft.com/about/diversity/fromoffice.mspx, accessed 21 January 2008.

Montes, T. and Shaw, G. (2003) 'The future of workplace diversity in the new millennium', in M.J. Davidson and S.L. Fielden (eds) *Individual Diversity and Psychology in Organizations*, Chichester: John Wiley and Sons.

Nash, M. (1989) *The Cauldron of Ethnicity in the Modern World*, Chicago: University of Chicago Press.

Nishii, L.H. and Özbilgin, M.F. (2007) 'Global diversity management: towards a conceptual framwork', *International Journal of Human Resource Management*, Vol.18, No.11, pp.1883–94.

Noon, M. and Ogbonna, E. (2001) *Equality, Diversity and Disadvantage in Employment*, Houndmills: Palgrave.

Prasad, P. and Mills, A.J. (1997) 'From showcase to shadow, understanding the dilemmas of managing workplace diversity', in P. Prasad, A.J. Mills, M. Elmes and A. Prasad (eds) *Managing the Organizational Melting Pot: Dilemmas of Workplace Diversity*, Thousand Oaks: Sage.

Prasad, P., Mills, A.J., Elmes, M. and Prasad, A. (1997) *Managing the Organizational Melting Pot: Dilemmas of Workplace Diversity*, Thousand Oaks: Sage.

Richards, W. (2001) 'Evaluating equal opportunities initiatives: the case for a transformative agenda', in M. Noon and E. Ogbonna (eds) *Equality, Diversity and Disadvantage in Employment*, Houndmills: Palgrave.

Roberson, L. and Kulik, C.T. (2007) 'Stereotype threat at work', *Academy of Management Perspectives*, Vol.21, No.2, pp.24–40.

Ross, R. and Schneider, R. (1992) *From Equality to Diversity: A Business Case for Equal Opportunities*, London: Pitman.

Shapiro, G. (2000) 'Employee involvement: opening the diversity Pandora's box?', *Personnel Review*, Vol.29, No.3, pp.304–23.

Sippola, A. and Smale, A. (2007) 'The global integration of diversity management: a longitudinal case study', *International Journal of Human Resource Management*, Vol.18, No.11, pp.1895–1916.

Strachan, G., Burgess, J. and Sullivan, A. (2004) 'Affirmative action or managing diversity: what is the future of equal opportunities policies in organizations'?, *Women in Management Review*, Vol.19, No.4, pp.196–204.

Storey, J. (1995) *Human Resource Management: A Critical Text*, London: Routledge.

Süβ, S. and Kleiner, M. (2007) 'Diversity management in Germany: dissemination and design of the concept', *International Journal of Human Resource Management*, Vol.18, No.11, pp.1934–53.

Thomas, R.R., Jr. (1990) 'From affirmative action to affirming diversity', *Harvard Business Review*, Vol.68, No.2, pp.107–17.

Thomas, R.R. (1992) 'Managing diversity: a conceptual framework', in S.E. Jackson (ed.) and associates *Diversity in the Workplace: Human Resource Initiatives*, New York: Guilford Press.

Thornberg, L. (1994) 'Journey towards a more inclusive culture', *HRMagazine*, February.

Totta, J.M. and Burke, R.J. (1995) 'Integrating diversity and equality into the fabric of the organization', *Women in Management Review*, Vol.10, No.7, pp.32–39.

Wahl, A. and Holgersson, C. (2003) 'Male managers' reactions to gender diversity activities in organizations', in M.J. Davidson and S.L. Fielden (eds) *Individual Diversity and Psychology in Organizations*, Chichester: John Wiley and Sons.

Walker, B.A. and Hanson, W.C. (1992) 'Valuing differences at Digital Equipment Corporation', in S.E. Jackson (ed.) and associates *Diversity in the Workplace: Human Resource Initiatives*, New York: Guilford Press.

Wilson, F.M. (1995) *Organizational Behaviour and Gender*, London: McGraw-Hill.

Wilson, E.M. (2003) 'Managing diversity: caste and gender issues in India', in M.J. Davidson and S.L. Fielden (eds) *Individual Diversity and Psychology in Organizations*, Chichester: John Wiley and Sons.

Woodhams, C. and Danieli, A. (2000) 'Disability and diversity: a difference too far'?, *Personnel Review*, Vol.29, No.3, pp.402–17.

Woolfe Morrison, E. and Mardenfeld Herlihy, J. (1992) 'Becoming the best place to work: managing diversity at American Express travel related services', in S.E. Jackson (ed.) and associates *Diversity in the Workplace: Human Resource Initiatives*, New York: Guilford Press.

Wright, P., Ferris, S.P., Hiller, J.S. and Kroll, M. (1995) 'Competitiveness through management of diversity: effects on stock price valuation', *Academy of Management Journal*, Vol.38, No.1, pp.272–87.

Chapter 15

WORK–LIFE BALANCE

Keith Townsend and Paula McDonald

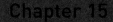

Introduction

We live and work in interesting times. By all accounts, people in the industrialised world are richer, have more opportunities for employment, leisure and travel, and have more possessions or 'stuff' to enjoy – mobile phones, computers, internet, big screen televisions and so on. However, many of us struggle to enjoy all these opportunities and possessions. Many people are working longer hours, feeling more pressured in their jobs and at home and are struggling to maintain a healthy balance in their lives. As a result, work and non-work aspects of life seem to be on a collision course and the casualties are mounting.

The way individuals balance or integrate their work and non-work lives is an area of interest that has received increasing scrutiny over the past two decades. Research has developed in response to, or at least in parallel with, the progressively higher profile of work–life balance (WLB) issues and concerns in the media, in the rhetoric of political and business leaders, and in organisational policy and human resource priorities. These factors, in turn, have arisen from significant demographic and technological shifts in industrialised societies. These shifts include an increased proportion of women (particularly mothers) in the paid workforce, greater numbers of dual-earner couples and single parents, demand for workplace flexibility and public support for childcare and eldercare, and the rapid expansion of information technology allowing work portability (Greenhaus and Powell 2003; Noor 2002; Pitt-Catsouphes and Christensen 2004; Sullivan and Lewis 2001).

This chapter explores a range of work–life issues, practices, debates and critiques. It begins with a definition of terms and a brief historical overview of how work–life concepts have become part of everyday language and organisational strategy, particularly in managing employees – a key factor in organisational success. The chapter then examines the way organisational policies and practices operate to facilitate or constrain work–life boundaries. A number of concerns are canvassed, including the importance of who initiates flexible working arrangements, what factors influence the take-up of available policies and the gendered nature of such use. The legal framework supporting work–life boundaries in the EU and elsewhere is then discussed, followed by the role of unions in driving WLB arrangements. Finally, the chapter looks at the way the boundaries of work and non-work life are managed. At the end of the chapter, two case studies help to illustrate the complexities of WLB in the modern workplace.

Is it work–life balance or something else?

For very many decades there has been an interest in the interface between paid work and other domains. Until the 1990s, the term 'work–family' was commonly used, with an implicit focus on how employees, and mothers in particular, integrated paid work and family responsibilities.

For example, the ILO (International Labour Organisation) Convention 156 on 'Workers with Family Responsibilities' makes no mention of 'work–life' terminology in 1981. In the past decade or so, this has given way to a broader and more gender-neutral focus on 'work–life' (Lewis *et al.* 2007). The term 'work–life' is suggestive of issues that extend beyond immediate family and therefore reflects the concerns of workers with and without dependent children, sick or elderly parents or others requiring care (Lambert and Haley-Lock 2004). Furthermore, while work–family balance encompasses work and home (Clark 2000; Lyness and Kropf 2005; McFarland 2004), work–life (balance, integration, conflict, fit) tends to be broader in scope, encompassing domains such as home, financial security, friends, community, profession and leisure, under the umbrella of 'life' (Crooker *et al.* 2002; Gurvis and Patterson 2005; Warren 2004).

In a similar way to developments in terminology such as work–family and work–life, terms which reflect the way employees fulfil their commitments to paid work and other domains have evolved and changed. To date, two constructs have dominated WLB research. The first is 'balance', which has been defined as harmony or equilibrium between work and life domains (Clarke *et al.* 2004; Comer and Stites-Doe 2006). The second is 'conflict' or 'interference', which means negative or unbalanced outcomes of combining paid work and non-work activities. Work–family conflict consists of two separate, though related, concepts: work conflict or interference with family, and family conflict or interference with work (Greenhaus and Powell 2006). However, other perspectives have also recently emerged, including work–life articulation (Crompton *et al.* 2007), harmonisation of paid work and personal life (Gambles *et al.* 2006) and work–life integration (Kossek and Lambert 2006).

Other ways to look at work–life integration or balance are also potentially important. These include 'work–family enrichment', which is defined as the extent to which experiences in one role improve the quality of life in the other role (Greenhaus and Powell 2006). Work–life enrichment tries to refocus conflict and tension towards some of the positive outcomes of work–life participation. The term 'work–life culture' has also recently emerged as an area of interest. It is defined as 'the shared assumptions, beliefs, and values regarding the extent to which an organization supports and values the integration of employees' work and family lives' (Thompson *et al.* 1999). Work–life culture has been used in previous research to explain different phenomena, such as how organisations develop work–life policies, rates of uptake of flexible work arrangements (including fathers' uptake) and the success or otherwise of work–life programmes (Haas and Hwang 1995; Sherer and Coakley 1999; Wise and Bond 2003). In short, academics and practitioners are constantly reconsidering all the conditions that have traditionally been taken for granted to better understand what people want and need in order to balance or integrate their work and non-work lives.

Why WLB is important to employers

Organisational policies, which are often introduced by employers as a means to assist employees in their work–life integration, can be broadly discussed under three categories. These are:

- specialised leave policies (e.g. parental leave, career break schemes);

- dependent care benefits (e.g. subsidised childcare, childcare referral);

- flexible working practices (e.g. part-time work, flexible hours arrangements).

For many organisations, the development and implementation of work–life balance policies are an important component of their HR strategies. Known as the 'business case approach', such strategies rest on the assumption that work–life balance policies are 'good for business'(Baird *et al.* 2002). Benefits to organisations include reduced absenteeism and turnover and higher organisational performance and productivity (Allen 2001; Konrad and Mangel 2000; Perry-Smith and Blum 2000). However, the business case approach, which is voluntary, may not benefit all employees. For example, industries with low rates of unionisation may not implement such policies, and benefits may only be delivered under certain economic conditions, such as when the labour market is tight and employees are difficult to recruit and retain (Doherty 2004). As the section on legislation later in the chapter explains, the voluntary approach to the implementation of work–life policies and practices has increasingly been supplemented with statutory employment rights.

Of the three types of policies, flexible working practices have received by far the greatest attention in previous research. Flexible working practices are those that either enable WLB (i.e. 'employee-friendly' policies which are usually sought by employees) or those which constrain it (i.e. 'employee-unfriendly' policies are those which are usually sought by employers). Examples of employee-friendly policies which enable work–life integration include flexitime, term-time working and nine-day fortnights, while examples of employee-unfriendly policies which constrain work–life integration include annualised hours, night shifts or split shifts (Fleetwood 2007). Policies in either category may also be 'neutral' in that they are 'friendly' to both parties or benefit employees without incurring additional costs to employers. However, it has been argued that any introduction of WLB policies has to be compatible with superordinate business needs, which ensures profit is realised (IDS 2000, cited in Warhurst *et al.* 2008).

INITIATION OF FLEXIBLE WORKING

An example of the importance of how flexible working practices are initiated is part-time work. Like many forms of non-standard working arrangements, there are winners and losers. Many full-time students, for example, embrace the opportunity to have flexible working hours. However, casual, part-time work has long been recognised as being associated with a shortfall in rights and benefits in comparison with permanent work, such as a lack of tenure, no career path and low present and uncertain future income (Harley and Whitehouse 2001; Junor 1998; Pocock *et al.* 2004). Some casual employees do, however, seek longer-term and more permanent working-time arrangements. It has been argued that flexibility is essential in the modern workplace to ensure a competitive business environment and to be productive. Equally, though, employment insecurity can be costly for society.

Permanent part-time employment has been offered as a solution to the conflict of full-time work hours and the demands of caring, while maintaining at least some of the benefits of standard employment. However, the quality of permanent part-time jobs seems to depend at least partly on whether they are employee- or employer-initiated. That is, so-called work–family measures such as reduced hours employment can be introduced for reasons other than family-friendliness and subsequently constrain rather than enhance the ability to integrate work and care commitments (Pocock *et al.* 2004; Whitehouse and Zetlin 1999). An example of employer-driven flexibility that constrains WLB is adjusting employees' start and finishing times without giving them any control over when they begin and end a shift. Another example is averaging the number of hours an employee works over a year while requiring them to work longer hours during peak times, without overtime payments or penalty rates. These forms of flexibility may be especially a problem for parents, who may be locked into paying for a fixed amount of childcare each week, regardless of how much they use or need.

Thus, permanent part-time employment offers tenure and may provide a career path if it is employee-initiated, but employer-initiated part-time work is often available only at entry-level grades and offers few prospects of career advancement or income security normally associated with standard employment (Junor 1998). Furthermore, even where permanent part-time workers enjoy protected conditions, other more entrenched disadvantages may arise which makes their employment different to their full-time counterparts. For example, part-time employees often experience reduced responsibilities and lesser access to high status roles and projects, along with a lack of access to promotion opportunities (McDonald *et al.* 2008). Part-time employees may also be expected to complete a full-time workload in their part-time hours and therefore have increased work intensity. These problems are inconsistent with many of the principles of WLB as well as organisational policies which support the integration of paid work and outside work responsibilities.

UNDERUTILISATION OF FLEXIBLE WORKING POLICIES – A JOB FOR THE HR TEAM!

Another issue for HRM professionals is that even if diverse and generous policies are documented and available in an organisation, this does not mean that they will be widely utilised by employees. A number of factors are thought to influence this problem, including the supportiveness of managers and colleagues, working-time expectations and perceived career consequences (Jahn *et al.* 2003; McDonald *et al.* 2007; Soonhee 2001).

The level of support provided by direct line managers for adopting flexible work practices is especially critical. Where supervisors enthusiastically support the integration of paid work and non-work responsibilities, employees will be more likely to take up available work–life programmes (Bardoel 2003). Conversely, managers may send negative signals indicating that the use of flexible benefits is inconvenient to the 'usual' flow of work and threatens productivity for the organisation as a whole (Rapoport and Bailyn 1996). Furthermore, it is argued that the long-term success of flexible work arrangements relies on the use of such arrangements at all levels of the workforce, including management (Kossek *et al.* 1999). Some UK evidence suggests, though, that much smaller numbers of employees, compared to managers, believe that flexible working arrangements such as part-time work, change in shift patterns and home-working are available to them (Kersley *et al.* 2006).

The willingness to utilise WLB policies is related to values shared between managers and employees (Blair-Loy and Wharton 2002). That is, employees are more likely to use flexible work policies if they work with powerful supervisors and colleagues who can buffer them from perceived negative effects on their careers. Career implications in WLB policy utilisation are also central to research, which has found that flexible workers are perceived to have decreased organisational commitment, which subsequently affects the allocation of organisational rewards, including advancement opportunities and salary increases. The availability of genuine work–family provisions also has a class bias, with managers and professionals having greater access to these benefits than low-wage employees, even among those who are employed in the same organisation (Holcomb 2000). For example, professionals are estimated to be around 14 per cent more likely to have flexibility in their working hours than salespersons or personal service workers (Gray and Tudball 2002).

FLEXIBLE WORK FOR BOTH SEXES?

Over the past four decades, women have made substantial gains in labour market participation and employment-related achievements. Despite these gains, there is empirical evidence that women continue to be restricted and disadvantaged in the workplace and do not participate equally with men because they perform the unique reproductive function of bearing children (Acker 1998; Moyle 2002). Since the 1990s, understandings of work–family, with the implicit focus on the labour force participation of mothers, has given way to a

Box 15.1: HRM in practice

Two women: different opportunities for WLB

Pocock (2008) illustrates the extremes of class bias through comparing the experience of two women – Gail Kelly and Rosa*. Gail Kelly is often promoted within Australia as an icon for success in both career and family aspects of life. The mother of four children (including triplets), Gail Kelly is the CEO of one of Australia's largest banks, reportedly earning $6 million (AU$) a year in fixed salary and incentive bonuses. Rosa is a sole parent of five dependent children and works part-time as a room attendant at a luxury hotel. Rosa earns less than $15 an hour and is entitled to government allowances (rent subsidy and tax benefits). Her income does not allow residence close to her workplace, hence, a long daily commute. Gail Kelly can earn each week more than four times Rosa's annual wage. Thus, the work–life balance of the wealthy and even middle classes relies heavily on the support provided by a low-paid workforce, to clean, cook, provide childcare and other ostensibly 'less important' duties.

*Rosa was interviewed as part of a research project investigating low pay in Australia by The Brotherhood of St Laurence, the Liquor Hospitality and Miscellaneous Workers Union and the Centre for Work + Life at the University of South Australia.

gender-neutral focus on work–life (Lewis *et al.* 2007). This is despite the fact that women remain the predominant users of flexible work arrangements. This practice has proven to be very resistant to change and one which may have far-reaching consequences. For example, the predominance of women using flexible work arrangements entrenches women's place as carers (Strachan and Burgess 1998), illustrating and reinforcing the strongly gendered way in which employment and care-giving is combined in Western societies. In other words, the continuation of gender inequality has been attributed to working arrangements in neo-traditional families whereby the woman continues to perform most unpaid work in the household and holds a subordinate and/or part-time position in the labour market (Moen and Yu 2000). Liff and Cameron (1997) also note that the predominance of women using flexible work arrangements may lead to women being seen as deficient and needing help.

In contrast, men do not take up available flexible work arrangements in nearly the same numbers as women. There are three main reasons for this: the organisation of the workplace, including doubts about the legitimacy of men's claims to family responsibilities; the business environment, including competitive pressures to maintain market share and increase earnings; and the domestic organisation in employees' own homes, including the centrality of the father's rather than the mother's career (Bittman *et al.* 2004). Bittman *et al.* (2004) showed that despite a commitment to the ideal of shared parenting, most of the male employees in their study tended to give work priority over family. European evidence also suggests that despite offering longer periods of parental leave, the use of this leave by male employees remains low (International Labour Review 1997). The low response to paid paternity leave indicates that the ideas of policy makers do not match the reality of equal parenthood (Haas and Hwang 1995). It also illustrates the relative difficulty in changing social practices through policy channels alone.

Box 15.2: HRM in practice

Job-sharing – does WLB lead to more work?

PublicSchools is a church-based educational system, receiving funding from three key sources: government funding, church funding, and via a user-pays school fee system. In total, this organisation operates almost 150 separate educational centres. The employees within this organisation can be divided into three key groups: administrative/support staff; management staff (including school principals); and teachers.

The majority of teachers within this organisation are employed on a full-time continuing basis. Both the organisation and the union have taken the approach that full-time continuing positions are in the best interests of all parties. However, this approach has led to difficulties for the organisation. For example, by employing people on a full-time continuing basis, there has been limited flexibility for the organisation to react to changes in the population of particular school communities and staffing levels that are required. A rather strict employment policy was in place and full-time continuing positions were rarely offered and certainly never in abundance. Hence, the core level of teaching staff stayed rather lean, while the organisation began to offer a growing periphery of fixed-term contracts.

Within this regime, should a woman choose to have a family and spend more than the legislated 12-month (unpaid) maternity leave out of the workforce, she would lose her continuing position and often find it difficult to return to the system. Hence, many women were forced to sacrifice either their career or the care for their family to maintain an ongoing position within the organisation. As a result, a system of job-sharing was introduced.

While this policy is open to all teachers, there are two obvious groups of people who are taking advantage of job-sharing. They are women who have or are starting to have a young family, and women who are considering retirement and choose to reduce their hours slowly rather than remove themselves from the workforce completely. The organisation is maintaining a pool of wisdom and skill that might be otherwise lost. In many cases, more experienced staff are teamed with those less experienced in a mentoring relationship.

While a comparatively costly approach to employment, this organisation recognises that simple bottom-line costs are not the only indicator of success. As a community-based organisation, PublicSchools views the work–life balance of its staff and the stability of the school community as essential aspects of its successful enterprise. Related to this, the additional professional development and increased staff retention and morale indicates that there are many ways in which the organisation benefits that are not apparent on financial breakdowns.

Employees who are engaged in a job-sharing position point to two significant outcomes. Firstly, the significant improvement in their ability to manage their work and non-work lives. And secondly, the realisation that to perform a job-share teaching position effectively and successfully, they need to do 'more than their share' of work. That is to say, a 50 per cent job-share load (and hence 50 per cent pay) means something closer to a 60 per cent teaching workload. Despite this anomaly, all participants enjoy what it is providing them professionally, socially and privately.

When the government gets involved

In addition to voluntary organisational policies and practices which support employees' work–life integration, a number of legislative reforms have been implemented to varying degrees and with varying success in different countries. These provisions have developed in response to a recognition of the potentially negative impacts on families with caring responsibilities, compared to those without such responsibilities. This section provides two examples of such legislation: 'right to request' regulation and paid parental leave. Right to request legislation offers a workplace process for making and considering employee requests to change working-time arrangements, and for employers to seriously or reasonably consider the request (Charlesworth and Campbell 2008). Paid parental leave and the right to return to the same job arguably encourage fathers' involvement in the care of young children and allows working women to maintain their links with the labour market following family formation.

RIGHT TO REQUEST LEGISLATION

A number of European countries provide workers the right to a part-time schedule and all have enacted legislation to implement a European Union directive to prohibit discrimination against part-time workers (Kornbluh 2005). In the UK, the right to request flexible working was introduced in 2003 for parents of young and disabled children, with the scope extended to carers of certain adults in 2007 (Department for Business Enterprise and Regulatory Reform [BERR] 2008). The right enables eligible employees to request a flexible working pattern and places a duty on employers to consider their requests seriously, refusing the application only where there is 'a clear business ground for doing so' (BERR 2008). In Germany, this right applies more inclusively, being available to all workers, regardless of parental status. In the Netherlands, employees have a right to change their working hours via their employment contract and this can only be refused on the basis of 'serious business interests' (Kornbluh 2005). In contrast, US employers have no obligation to allow parent employees to work part-time or flexible schedules, even if the cost to the employer would be inconsequential (Kornbluh 2005).

Until very recently in Australia, the availability of part-time work for a carer up to a child's second birthday, while documented in legislation and related to established precedents in a few examples of case law (Moyle 2002), was dependent on the agreement of the employer. In August 2005, an Australian Industrial Relations Commission (AIRC) test case decision, similar to the 2003 changes to the Employment Rights Act in the UK (Fraser 2004), granted award workers an additional 52 weeks' unpaid parental leave (104 weeks in total) and the right to request part-time work until their child reached school age.

PAID PARENTAL LEAVE

There are several international standards relevant to paid maternity leave and family-friendly provisions at work. These include the 1979 United Nations Convention on the Elimination of Discrimination Against Women (CEDAW); ILO Convention 183 (C183), Maternity Protection 2000 (with associated Recommendations); and ILO Convention 156, Workers with Family Responsibilities, 1981 (C156 and Recommendations) (Pocock 2007). These standards reflect the international view that at least 14 weeks' paid maternity leave is essential to the promotion of equal opportunity and treatment for women workers, and to substantive equality of opportunity and treatment between men and women with family responsibilities.

UK maternity rights have existed since 1975 but it was only after the adoption of the Social Chapter at Maastricht in 1992 that a broader set of provisions began to appear. Along with working-time regulations, statutory entitlements to parental leave and time off work for family emergencies were introduced by the Maternity and Parental Leave Regulations 1999 and the ERA 1999 (Dickens and Hall 2003). The 2003 Employment Act in the UK provided enhanced support for new parents in the form of extended paid maternity leave for 26 weeks, regardless of how long the woman has worked for her employer. These extensions of paid maternity leave were viewed as being central to goals of a flexible labour market and a society where being a good employee and a good parent were not in conflict (Department of Trade and Industry 2005; James 2007). Paid paternity leave was also provided for fathers to take time off from work around the time of the birth of their child.

It is worth noting that not all countries have such statutory entitlements as those in the EU. More traditional European societies such as Poland operate under a 'male as breadwinner' model and provide few formal supports for work–life integration. Even among some OECD countries, notably the US and Australia, there is no formal entitlement to paid maternity leave (though there are unpaid provisions for eligible employees). The absence of a paid maternity leave scheme arguably threatens mothers' attachment to employment, contributes to inequities between women in different sectors, has negative effects on fertility rates and undermines women's dual roles as producers and reproducers (Baird 2004; Jaumotte 2004; Pocock 2007).

As the previous sections have outlined, there are variations in the strength of right to request legislation, the conditions under which employers can deny such requests, and paid parental leave provisions, in different countries. Organisations also vary markedly in the types of flexible work arrangements offered and the degree to which they actively support work–life integration. When we also consider the normative social and cultural roles of certain demographic groups such as women, fathers, youth or older people, it is clear that employees are subject to very different rights frameworks and have differential access to WLB entitlements, depending on who they are, where they live and how and where they are employed.

WHEN THE GOVERNMENT IS NOT ENOUGH: BRINGING HR BACK IN

Despite the provisions that exist in work–life and anti-discrimination legislation, and voluntary business programmes which support work–life integration, employees with caring responsibilities all too often face significant difficulties in achieving career development opportunities and effectively juggling their responsibilities in and out of the workplace. The large number of reports each year of pregnancy and family responsibilities discrimination is testament to these problems. For example, despite much of the work–life balance rhetoric, pregnant employees and those with dependent children are often perceived as an inconvenience and potentially a threat to the profitability and functioning of the business (Chester and Kleiner 2001; McDonald 2008). These perceptions may be underpinned by assumptions about the incompatibility of being an effective caregiver as well as a committed worker (Hays 1996; Walzer 1997). They may also be influenced by presumed return to work decisions and assumptions that part-time workers demonstrate less commitment to their jobs (Chester and Kleiner 2001). Hence, the organisation of work around the unencumbered 'ideal worker' needs to be comprehensively challenged to address the combined effects of skilled labour shortages and ageing populations, which many industrialised countries are facing (Baird 2004; Charlesworth 2005). In short, work–life balance policies and their successful implementation are considered a key tenet of high-performance workplaces (HPW) (Marchington and Wilkinson 2008).

There is a strong potential role for HR managers in addressing unsupportive work cultures which constrain WLB. Importantly, the first responsibility is to acknowledge that negative attitudes and assumptions about employees with caring responsibilities are likely to exist in at least some areas of the organisation. The implementation of training and development modules for managers which cover information about employee entitlements, practical strategies in managing a flexible workforce and an opportunity to challenge assumptions may help counter these attitudes.

Ensuring high levels of awareness of organisational flexible work policies is also important. This could be achieved through incorporating relevant information into induction programmes, ensuring that all employees have access to web-based or paper-based policy information and providing regular communications to employees about changes to organisational or legislative provisions. HR managers may also have a role in monitoring long working hours and/or requirements or expectations that employees respond to unreasonable work demands during unpaid hours.

In order to address equity issues associated with transitions from full-time to part-time work, HR managers should monitor career progression rates across their organisations, comparing part-time to full-time staff and men to women. At an individual employee level, human resource specialists have a role in ensuring that necessary reductions in job content (associated with reduced hours) are commensurate with reductions in the visibility and status of the remaining tasks undertaken. Human resource managers could also allow, or even encourage, part-time employees to internally contest situations where job quality or opportunities for advancement have been halted. It is possible, however, that these measures may elicit strong protests from full-time workers for undermining their current advantage and from managers for infringing on their decision-making prerogatives (Gaze 2005).

Unions and WLB

Working time has long been an area of contest for unions and management (Blyton, 2008). More than 150 years ago, workers celebrated the success of an eight-hour working day, campaigning under the slogan 'Eight Hours Labour, Eight Hours Recreation, Eight Hours Rest'. Employees had successfully negotiated one of the earliest officially sanctioned 40-hour working weeks (Love 2006). In 1965 a US Senate subcommittee predicted a 22-hour working week by 1985 and a 14-hour working week by 2000. However, these predictions did not eventuate as expected. While in the UK working hours appear to have declined marginally in the past decades, in Australia and the US employees are working longer hours now than they have for 30 years.

As a result, working time continues to be on the agenda of unions. The TUC has a range of campaigns aiming to redress the imbalance in working-time expectations and practices, for example the 'Work Your Proper Work Hours Day' as a means of highlighting the significant number of unpaid hours of overtime worked. Working-time and holiday arrangements are the second and third most frequently negotiated issues in UK workplaces (pay is number one) (Kersley *et al.* 2006, p.194). In several European countries, growing decentralisation has been accompanied by national agreements on the number of hours people can work each week. For example, following the statutory 35-hour week in France, there has been a significant increase in union and management bargaining over temporal flexibility, often with agreement to average and limit 'annual hours' (Alis 2003). The Australian Council of Trade Unions (ACTU) initiated a 'Reasonable Hours Test Case' in 2005 to force working time on to the mainstream agenda.

The percentage of women in the paid labour force has increased over the past 30 years in OECD countries. As such, trade unions have reacted through organising around broader issues such as family-friendly employment policies. In the UK unions have actively supported regulatory developments to reflect the changing gendered patterns of the workplace, suggesting that there is an important business case for employers. The logic suggests that if there are more women working, then greater WLB rights provide employers with an economic benefit related to retaining skilled workers, recruitment and training. In Australia, the ACTU initiated the Work and Family test case in 2004, aiming to improve rights for workers with caring responsibilities. Furthermore, the ACTU has led the campaign in Australia for paid parental leave.

Finding the boundaries

There is a recent stream of literature that critiques the WLB research for failing to adequately capture empirically key aspects of work and life (Warhurst *et al.* 2008). One of the reasons for this is that much of the existing research assumes that 'work' and 'life' are two distinctly different spheres of a person's existence. In contrast, there is a great deal of post-war industrial sociology literature that captures the entwined nature of people's work and non-work lives (cf. Mayo 1946; Roy 1973; Cunnison 1966; Salaman 1974). This literature, which appears to be long forgotten by recent WLB debates, reveals the way that the overlap or penetration of the work and non-work spheres can be beneficial to workers.

However, we must acknowledge that some people, and indeed, people in particular occupations, appear to have much less success in managing the boundaries between what is work and what is non-working life. For example, the manufacturing workers of Roy or Cunnison's studies could not take their work home or to the beach – rather, it was the social structures of the workplace that permeated their non-workplace time and vice versa. The professionals and managers of the modern era on the other hand, who engage in 'mental' labour, can find themselves in work-mode for every waking, and many sleeping, moments!

Just as there is a significant class dimension to WLB, as discussed earlier in this chapter, there is also an occupational dimension. It is hard to imagine how people employed in some areas of the media can manage a boundary between their work and non-work life. High-profile television personalities, actors and sporting celebrities are constantly in the sights of the paparazzi. There have been recent media frenzies about the manner in which some people employed in these areas are engaging in recreational use of drugs and alcohol. Khoshoba (2008), for example, investigated the manner in which the boundaries between an athlete's work and non-work life were blurred, particularly in relation to recreational performance-enhancing drug use. On Monday morning, very few employees need to be concerned about how they spent their time over the weekend. Employees who are constantly in the public arena, however, do have that concern.

There is an increasing literature examining the role of information technologies and WLB (Hislop 2008). However, while the use of mobile technologies has enabled a great deal of spatial and temporal flexibility which is valued by some, many professionals and managers lament the 'flexibility' that enables them to be contacted anywhere and at any time, and which subsequently leads them to feel that they are constantly working. One-third of managers have reported allowing work-related mobile phone calls to interrupt sexual activity – clearly indicating a problem with determining the boundaries between work and non-work activities (Townsend and Batchelor 2008). Much of this recent literature calls, not for a greater division between work and life, but for a greater understanding of the relationship between work and life and the overlapping boundaries between the two.

Conclusions

Regardless of the label placed on the area of research or practice, there are many important dimensions to the interface between people's work and the non-work aspects of their lives. For some it is a clear distinction. For others it is a blur between what is work and what is pleasure, when time is work time and when it is social. The changing nature of labour markets (increased numbers of women and working parents), developing information and communication technologies, and notions of a 24-hour consumer culture all impact on the work–life boundaries. Clearly, there is a role for a range of actors – the government, employers, HR professionals, unions and, indeed, the individual in deciding what boundaries are appropriate, how they should be established and how much control employees should have over deciding when work ends and life begins. Work–life balance must be addressed by all these actors in order to develop a range of alternatives available in a modern, developed democratic country.

CASE STUDY 15.1

Flexibility denied

Keith Townsend and Paula McDonald

State Department is a large, Australian government agency. Government employment in Australia has historically been seen as having high job security but low job challenge, although this has changed in the past 10 years with a greater emphasis on efficiency and productivity, in line with new public management principles. State Department has a broad and varied array of work–life integration policies documented and available to its employees. These include specialised leave policies (e.g. paid parental leave, career-break schemes); dependent care benefits (e.g. childcare and elder care referral services); and flexible working practices options (e.g. part-time work, job-share, telecommuting, flexible start and finish times). However, despite the availability of these measures to support and improve employees' work–life integration, a recent employee survey indicates a number of problems.

First, many manual workers and those employed outside the major metropolitan area were not aware of the range of policies available. Second, many employees across most areas of the organisation indicated in the survey that they felt unable to use the policies that were available. The reasons given for this were varied. They included unsupportive immediate line managers, fears that working in a flexible manner (particularly telecommuting and reduced hours arrangements) would lessen their ability to advance in their careers, and high workloads which prevented them using accrued time and taking leave. Third, the number of employees using the more 'substantial' forms of flexible work (part-time, job-share, telecommuting) was very low – around 5 per cent of the overall workforce and almost exclusively women. Given the predominance of male employees (80 per cent), the overall number of workers who were not full-time and present in the workplace at least five days per week was very small indeed.

The HR manager is concerned with these findings, not least because the organisation and indeed the construction industry itself is facing severe skill shortages and finds it difficult to attract appropriate staff, particularly in the manual trades and professional areas such as surveying, architecture and engineering. The organisation has also attempted to position itself in the industry as an 'employer of choice', offering a range of flexible work options that are not necessarily available in private sector organisations. Thus, the organisation's flexible work policies have been designed as an intentional recruitment and retention strategy as well as being consistent with its statutory obligations as a public sector employer. Clearly, the organisation needs to address the problem of underutilisation to address the work–life integration needs of its employees and to ensure future competitiveness in the industry.

Questions

1. Employees can have requests for flexible work arrangements denied by their line managers at State Department, particularly if the employees are not women returning from maternity leave (in which case they would be legally entitled to part-time work).

   • What reasons might a manager give for denying such requests?

   • How should an employee go about requesting flexible work arrangements? What issues would they need to think through and what factors might influence the success or otherwise of the request?

   • What might be the likely impacts on the individual and the work team of denying a request for flexibility?

▶

2. Many managers and co-workers want and expect employees to be consistently physically present in the workplace during 'normal' working time to attend meetings, respond to requests and to ensure they are being productive. Unfortunately, these expectations are sometimes at odds with employees' needs for fulfilling caring responsibilities or with their preferences to work at another location away from the workplace. How might the use of information and communication technologies help address these perceptions?

3. What would be some of the likely impacts of having diverse and generous policies available at the human resource level, but not available in practice?

4. What 'cultural' factors in State Department might be influencing the low take-up of flexible work arrangements?

5. HR policy in relation to all State Department policies which support work–life integration are framed in gender-neutral terms. The organisation has also actively promoted flexible work arrangements and leave policies as being available to both men and women. Although men and women both use flexible start and finish times, part-time work and job-sharing is used almost exclusively by women. Discuss this trend.

6. In a recent survey at State Department some work–life integration problems were identified. The HR manager is responsible for designing strategies and policies to address these problems. What strategies, programmes or tasks could be implemented and how should they be prioritised?

CASE STUDY 15.2

Longer days, better balance?

Keith Townsend and Paula McDonald

TunnelCorp has been commissioned to build a major piece of infrastructure – a road and tunnel designed for buses to reduce congestion in the city. There is nothing particularly unusual about TunnelCorp – it is a standard organisation operating within a male-dominated industry where long hours – often six-day working weeks – is the acceptable norm. However, this management team sought to reduce the number of working hours as a means of improving the employees' work–life balance.

The construction industry is an important one in any country, simply because buildings, roads, tunnels, bridges and the like cannot be imported. Certainly, aspects of the production process can be performed off-shore; however, the actual construction must occur on-site. As such, there are many different 'types' of workers present at each construction site. Typically, there will be unskilled labourers, truck and machinery drivers, tradespeople (plumbers, electricians, etc.), supervisors, engineers, surveyors, managers, administrative staff and designers, to name just a few. This is where WLB gets interesting and indeed, very complicated for managers of construction sites.

Quite often WLB can be seen as an issue affecting men and women differently. The TunnelCorp workforce can be divided into two groups; however, not on gender lines. The first of the two groups at TunnelCorp are those who are paid a yearly salary, for example supervisors, administrative staff, managers, engineers, etc. The second group are those employees who are paid an hourly wage, consisting of tradespeople and labourers. Salaried staff will take home the same pay every week regardless of whether they work 40 hours or 70 hours. In contrast, waged staff are paid overtime payments – in some cases, waged employees can earn up to 60 per cent of their base pay through paid overtime. This differing payment system, regardless of the two types of employees working the same long hours, is problematic for managers.

▶

Charlesworth, S. (1997) 'Enterprise bargaining and women workers: the seven perils of flexibility', *Labour and Industry*, Vol.8, No.2, pp.101–15.

Charlesworth, S. (2005) 'Managing work and family in the "shadow" of anti-discrimination law', *Law in Context*, Vol.23, No.1, pp.88–126.

Charlesworth, S. and Campbell, I. (2008). 'Right to request regulation: a panacea for work/family imbalance?' Proceedings of the 22nd Conference of the Association of Industrial Relations Academics of Australia and New Zealand, Melbourne, Australia, 6–8 February.

Chester, N. and Kleiner, B. (2001) 'Pregnancy in the workplace', *International Journal of Sociology and Social Policy*, Vol.21, No.8–10, pp.137–48.

CIPD (2007) *Factsheet on Managing Diversity*. Available at http://www.cipd.co.uk/subjects/dvsequl/general/divover.htm?IsSrchRes=1 Last accessed 3rd July 2008.

Clark, S.C. (2000) 'Work/family border theory: a new theory of work/family balance', *Human Relations*, Vol.53, No.6, p.747.

Clarke, M.C., Koch, L.C., and Hill, E.J. (2004) 'The work–family interface: differentiating balance and fit', *Family and Consumer Sciences Research Journal*, Vol.33, No.2, pp.121–40.

Comer, D.R. and Stites-Doe, S. (2006) 'Antecedents and consequences of faculty women's academic-parental role balancing', *Journal of Family and Economic Issues*, Vol.27, No.3, pp.495–512.

Crompton, R., Lewis, S. and Lyonette, C. (eds.) (2007) *Women, Men, Work and Family in Europe*, Basingstoke: Palgrave.

Crooker, K.J., Smith, F.L. and Tabak, F. (2002) 'Creating work–life balance: a model of pluralism across life domains', *Human Resource Development Review*, Vol.1, No.4, pp.387–419.

Cunnison, S. (1966) *Wages and Work Allocation: A Study of Social Relations in a Garment Workshop*, London: Tavistock Publications.

Department for Business Enterprise and Regulatory Reform (BERR) (2008) 'Flexible working: the right to request and the duty to consider', available at www.berr.gov.uk/employment/employment-legislation/employment-guidance/page35663.html

Department of Trade and Industry (2005) 'Work and families: choice and flexibility: a consultation document', London: HMSO.

Dickens, L. and Hall, M. (2003) 'Labour law and industrial relations: a new settlement', in P. Edwards (ed.) *Industrial Relations: Theory and practice* (2nd edn), Oxford: Blackwell.

Doherty, L. (2004) 'Work–life balance initiatives: implications for women', *Employee Relations*, Vol.26, No.4, pp.433–53.

Fleetwood, S. (2007) 'Why work–life balance now?', *The International Journal of Human Resource Management*, Vol.18, No.3, pp.387–400.

Fraser, M. (2004) 'New rights for old. Flexi-working and sex discrimination', *Employee Relations*, Vol.26, No.2, pp.167–81.

Gambles, R., Lewis, S. and Rapoport, R. (2006) *The Myth of WLB: The Challenge of Our Time for Men, Women and Societies*. Chichester: Wiley.

Gaze, B. (2005) 'Quality part-time work: can law provide a framework?' *Labour and Industry*, Vol.15, No.3, pp.89–111.

Gray, M. and Tudball, J. (2002) *Family Friendly Work-Practices: Differences Within and Between Workplaces, Research Report No. 7*, Melbourne, Australia: Australian Institute of Family Studies.

Greenhaus, J.H. and Powell, G.N. (2003) 'When work and family collide: deciding between competing role demands', *Organizational Behavior and Human Decision Processes*, Vol.90, No.2, pp.291–303.

Greenhaus, J.H. and Powell, G.N. (2006) 'When work and family are allies: a theory of work-family enrichment', *The Academy of Management Review*, Vol.31, No.1, pp.72–92.

Gurvis, J. and Patterson, G. (2005) 'Balancing act: finding equilibrium between work and life', *Leadership in Action*, Vol.24, No.6, pp.4–9.

Haas, L. and Hwang, P. (1995) 'Company culture and men's usage of family leave benefits in Sweden', *Family Relations*, Vol.44, No.1, pp.28–36.

Harley, B. and Whitehouse, G. (2001) 'Women in part-time work: a comparative study of Australia and the United Kingdom', *Labour and Industry*, Vol.12, No.2, pp.33–59.

Hays, S. (1996) *The Cultural Contradictions of Motherhood*, New Haven CT: Yale University Press.

Hislop, D. (ed.), (2008) *Mobile Work/Technology: Changing Patterns of Spatial Mobility and Mobile Technology Use in Work*, London: Routledge.

Holcomb, B. (2000) 'Friendly for whose family?', *Ms.*, April/May, pp.40–5.

IDS Studies (2000) *Work–life Balance*, No.698, November.

International Labour Review (1997) 'Perspectives: parental leave', *International Labour Review*, Vol.136, No.1, pp.109–28.

Jahn, E., Thompson, C. and Kopelman, R. (2003) 'Rationale and construct validity evidence for a measure of perceived organizational family support (POFS): because purported practices may not reflect reality', *Community, Work and Family*, Vol.6, No.2, pp.123–40.

James, C. (2007) 'Law's response to pregnancy/workplace conflicts: a feminist critique', *Feminist Legal Studies*, Vol.15, pp.167–88.

Jaumotte, F. (2004) *Female Labour Force Participation: Past Trends and Main Determinants in OECD Countries*, Geneva: OECD Economics Department, p.10.

Junor, A. (1998) 'Permanent part-time work: new family-friendly standard or high intensity cheap skills?', *Labour and Industry*, Vol.8, No.3, pp.77–95.

Kersley, B., Alpen, C., Forth, J., Bryson, A., Bewley, H., Dix, G. and Oxenbridge, S. (2006) *Inside the Workplace*, London: Routledge.

Khoshoba, T. (2008) 'Recreational use or performance enhancing? Doping regulation and professional sport', in C. Warhurst, D. Eikhof, and A. Haunschild (eds) *Work Less, Live More? Critical Analysis of the Work–Life Boundary*, London: Palgrave Macmillan, pp.210–23.

Konrad, A. and Mangel, R. (2000) 'The impact of work–life programs on firm productivity', *Strategic Management Journal*, Vol.21, pp.1225–37.

Kornbluh, K. (2005) *Win-Win Flexibility. Work and Family Policy Proposal*, Washington, DC: New American Foundation.

Kossek, E. and Lambert, S. (eds) (2006) *Work and Life Integration: Organizational, Cultural and Individual Perspectives*, Mahwah, NJ: Lawrence Erlbaum.

Kossek, E.E., Barber, A.E. and Winters, D. (1999) 'Using flexible schedules in the managerial world: the power of peers', *Human Resource Management*, Vol.38, No.1, pp.33–46.

Kossek, E.E., Markel K.S. and Mc Hugh P.P. (2003) 'Increasing diversity as an HRM change strategy', Journal of Organizational Change Management, Vol.16, No.3, pp.328–52.

Lambert, S.J. and Haley-Lock, A. (2004) 'The organisational stratification of opportunities for work–life balance: addressing issues of equality and social justice in the workplace', *Community, Work and Family*, Vol.7, No.2, pp.179–95.

Lewis, S., Gambles, R. and Rapoport, R. (2007) 'The constraints of a "work–life balance" approach: an international perspective', *International Journal of Human Resource Management*, Vol.18, No.3, pp.360–73.

Liff, S. and Cameron, I. (1997) 'Changing equality cultures to move beyond "women's problems"', *Gender, Work and Organisation*, Vol.4, No.1, pp.35–46.

Liff, S. and Dickens, L. (1999) 'Ethics and equality: reconciling false dilemmas', In J. Marshall and D. Winstanley (eds.) *Ethical Issues in Contemporary Human Resource Management*, London: Macmillan.

Love, P. (2006) 'Melbourne celebrates the 150th anniversary of its eight hour day', *Labour History*, Vol.91.

Lyness, K.S. and Kropf, M.B. (2005) 'The relationships of national gender equality and organisational support with work-family balance: a study of European managers', *Human Relations*, Vol.58, No.1, pp.33–60.

Marchington, M. and Wilkinson, A. (2008) *HRM at Work*, London: Chartered Institute of Personal and Development.

Mayo, E. (1949) *The Social Problems of an Industrial Civilisation*. London: Routledge & Kegan Paul.

McDonald, P. (2008) 'Family responsibilities discrimination in Queensland workplaces: where business and caring collide', *Journal of Industrial Relations*, Vol.50, No.1, pp.45–67.

McDonald, P., Pini, B. and Bradley, L. (2007) 'Freedom and fallout in local government: how work–life culture impacts employees using flexible work practices', *The International Journal of Human Resource Management*, Vol.18, No.4, pp.602–22.

McDonald, P., Bradley, L. and Brown, K. (2008) '"Full-time is a given here": part-time versus full-time job quality', *British Journal of Management*, Vol.19.

McFarland, L.A. (2004) 'Work–family balance', *The Industrial-Organizational Psychologist*, Vol.41, No.4, pp.47–53.

Ministerial Task Force on Work and Family (2002) 'Review of work and family in Queensland', (Issues Paper), Queensland Government Department of Industrial Relations, Brisbane, Australia.

Moen, P. and Yu, Y. (2000) 'Effective work/life strategies', *Social Problems*, August, pp.291–326.

Morgan, H. and Milliken, F.J. (1992) 'Keys to action: understanding differences in organisations' responsiveness to work and family issues', *Human Resource Management*, Vol.31, pp.227–48.

Moyle, S. (2002) 'Pregnancy in the workplace: employer obligations to pregnant employees', speech delivered at the NSW Young Lawyers, Discrimination Seminar Series NSW Leagues Club, Sydney, 22 October.

Noor, N.M. (2002) 'The moderating effect of spouse support on the relationship between work variables and women's work-family conflict', *Psychologia: An International Journal of Psychology in the Orient*, Vol.45, No.1, pp.12–23.

Perry-Smith, J. and Blum, T. (2000) 'Work–family human resource bundles and perceived organisational performance', *Academy of Management Journal*, Vol.43, pp.1107–17.

Pitt-Catsouphes, M. and Christensen, K. (2004) 'Unmasking the taken for granted', *Community, Work and Family*, Vol.7, No.2, pp.123–42.

Pocock, B. (2007) 'A time to act: paid maternity leave for all south Australian women', Submission to the Selection Committee on Balancing Work and Life Responsibilities, Adelaide, Australia: Centre for Work and Life.

Pocock, B., Buchanan, J. and Campbell, I. (2004) 'Meeting the challenge of casual work in Australia: evidence, past treatment and future policy', *Australian Bulletin of Labour*, Vol.30, No.1, pp.16–33.

Pocock, B., Skinner, N. and Williams, P. (2007) 'Governing work–life intersections in Australia over the life course: policy and prospects', Paper presented to the Social Policy Research Conference University of New South Wales, 11–13 July 2007.

Rapoport, R. and Bailyn, L. (1996) *Relinking Life and Work: Toward a Better Future*, New York: The Ford Foundation.

Roy, D. (1973) 'Banana time: job satisfaction and informal interaction', in G. Salaman and K. Thompson (eds) *People and Organisations*, London: Longman, pp.205–22.

Salaman, G. (1974) *Occupation and Community*, Cambridge: Cambridge University Press.

Sherer, P.D. and Coakley, L.A. (1999) 'Questioning and developing your part-time employee practices', *Workforce*, October, pp.4–8.

Soonhee, K. (2001) 'Perceived impacts of family leave policy: Do organisational factors matter?', *Public Personnel Management*, Vol.30, No.2, pp.221–39.

Strachan, G. and Burgess, J. (1998) 'The "family friendly" workplace: origins, meaning and application at Australian workplaces', *International Journal of Manpower*, Vol.19, No.4, pp.250–65.

Sullivan, C. and Lewis, S. (2001) 'Home-based telework, gender, and the synchronization of work and family: perspectives of teleworkers and their co-residents', *Gender, Work and Organization*, Vol.8, No.2, pp.123–45.

Thompson, C.A., Beauvais, L.L. and Lyness, K.S. (1999) 'When work–family benefits are not enough: the influence of work–family culture on benefit utilisation, organisational attachment, and work–family conflict', *Journal of Vocational Behavior*, Vol.54, No.3, pp.392–415.

Townsend, K. and Batchelor, L. (2008) 'Freedom and flexibility with a ball and chain', in D. Hislop (ed.) *Mobile Work/Technology: Changing Patterns of Spatial Mobility and Mobile Technology Use in Work*, London: Routledge.

Walzer, S. (1997) 'Contextualizing the employment decisions of new mothers', *Qualitative Sociology*, Vol.20, No.2, pp.211–26.

Warhurst, C., Eikhof, D. and Haunschild, A. (eds) (2008) *Work Less, Live More? Critical Analysis of the Work–Life Boundary*, London: Palgrave Macmillan.

Warren, T. (2004) 'Working part-time: achieving a successful "work–life" balance?', *British Journal of Sociology*, Vol.55, No.1, pp.99–122.

Whitehouse, G. and Zetlin, D. (1999) 'Family friendly policies: distribution and implementation in Australian workplaces', *Economic and Labour Relations Review*, Vol.10, No.2, pp.221–39.

Wise, S. and Bond, S. (2003) 'Work–life policy: does it do exactly what it says on the tin?', *Women in Management Review*, Vol.18, No.1/2, pp.20–31.

Chapter 16

DOWNSIZING

Tom Redman and Adrian Wilkinson

It was the best time (for stockholders), it was the worst of times (for employees). The corporation was restructuring. (DiFonzo and Bordia 1998, p.137)

Introduction

In this chapter we first introduce the subject of organisational downsizing by discussing its extent and potential for causing problems when mismanaged. The breadth and depth of organisational restructuring seen in the industrialised economies has been significant in recent years. Second, we review the methods by which downsizing occurs and consider a range of alternatives to its use. Third, we examine the processes involved and focus in particular on consultation, redundancy selection and support for both those made redundant and the survivors of downsizing. Lastly, we conclude by asking whether the costs of downsizing are worth it and whether downsizing translates simply into 'increased stress and decreased job security' (De Meuse *et al.* 1997, p.168).

Downsizing: the reality of HRM?

Downsizing is the 'conscious use of permanent personnel reductions in an attempt to improve efficiency and/or effectiveness' (Budros 1999, p.70). Since the 1980s, downsizing has gained strategic legitimacy (Cameron *et al.* 1991; Boone 2000; McKinley *et al.* 2000). Indeed, recent research on downsizing in the US (Baumol *et al.* 2003, see also the American Management Association annual surveys since 1990), UK (Sahdev *et al.* 1999; Chorely 2002; Mason 2002; Rogers 2002), and Japan (Mroczkowski and Hanaoka 1997; Ahmakjian and Robinson 2001) suggests that downsizing is being regarded by management as one of the preferred routes to turning around declining organisations, cutting cost and improving organisational performance (Mellahi and Wilkinson 2004).

Downsizing and restructuring are often used interchangeably but organisations can restructure without shrinking in size and vice versa (Budros 1999). In the UK downsizing has been seen as an all too easy solution to management problems.

The lack of labour market protection, the weakness of unions and the intense pressure on private and public sector companies alike to improve their profitability and efficiency have meant that the fashionable doctrine of downsizing has spread like a contagion. (Hutton 1997, p.40)

The above comment from Hutton reflects that organisational downsizing is thus now firmly established as a central aspect of HRM practice in the UK. Equally, Guthrie and Datta

(2008, p.108) observe that millions of American workers have been laid off or downsized over the years, a trend that shows no sign of abating. However, after a perusal of the growing numbers of textbooks on HRM a reader could be forgiven for thinking that HRM practice is largely associated with a positively virtuous image in the organisation. Righteous HRM managers recruit, train, devise strategies, manage rewards and careers, involve employees, improve labour relations, solve problems, etc. for the mutual benefit of the organisation and workforce (see, for example, Torrington *et al.* 2005). Most management books take an upbeat tone, with little reference to the more unpalatable aspects of downsizing and redundancy. Revitalising change is seen as an entirely positive process to do with 'rooting out inertia', promoting efficiency and fostering innovation. Change is to be achieved not incrementally but by 'big leaps' (Hamel 2000). Downsizing is more apparent in the Dilbert books (Adams 1996), the Doonesbury cartoons (Anfuso 1996) and Michael Moore's journalism (Moore 1997). When managers do discuss downsizing it tends to be couched in very euphemistic terms (see Box 16.1). However, an examination of managerial practice over the past decade or so also finds a darker side to HRM in organisational downsizing. Worrall *et al.* (2000) note over 200,000 notified redundancies in the UK each year and Cascio (2008) estimates 900,000 as the typical number in the US. This, however, does pale in comparison with the 25 million laid off from state-owned firms in China between 1998 and 2001.

Box 16.1: HRM in practice

The sanitisation of dismissal: sacking goes out of fashion

Redundancy and dismissal are one area of HRM practice that particularly suffers from euphemistic jargon. Some of the terms HRM managers use include:

building down	downsizing	re-engineering
career re-appraisal	exiting	releasing
compressing	headcount reduction	resizing
decruiting	involuntary quit	re-structuring
de-hiring	lay-off	retrenchment
dejobbing	letting-go	rightsizing
de-layering	non-retaining	severance
demassing	outplacing	slimming
de-selection	payroll adjustment	streamlining
disemploying	rationalising	termination
downscoping	rebalancing	wastage

The motor industry seems especially afflicted in this respect, perhaps as a result of the large scale of workforce reductions. For example, General Motors described one plant closure as a 'volume-related production schedule adjustment', Chrysler had a 'a career alternative enhancement program', while Nissan introduced a 'separation program'. Two motor industry personnel managers interviewed about the effects of lean production methods talked of 'increasing the velocity of organisational exit' and 'liberating from our organisation' those who could not accommodate the new system. One also talked of getting rid of the PUREs (previously unrecognized recruitment errors). In contrast, the language of the shop floor is much more direct and includes being sacked, canned, given your cards, axed and being sent down the road.

Despite its importance and growing prominence, this aspect of HRM rarely merits treatment in the texts. In those few texts that recognise its existence the focus is usually on a discussion of how to avoid the legal pitfalls when reducing the workforce or a simple attempt to quantify its use. Much rarer is any discussion that examines the nature, significance and aftermath of making people redundant. This neglect is a serious and somewhat puzzling one. As Chadwick *et al.* (2004) note, successful performance following downsizing requires HR practices that continue to promote discretionary efforts of employees, retain valuable human capital and reconstruct valuable organisation structures.

One possible explanation for the neglect of this issue lies in the view that workforce reduction is considered to be an isolated and unpleasant element of HRM practice and one that is best hurriedly carried out and quickly forgotten: the so-called 'Mafia model' of downsizing (Stebbins 1989). The statistics for redundancy and dismissal in Britain would, however, suggest that unpleasant though it may be, workforce reduction is not an isolated event, rather it is a central aspect of HRM practice in recent years. Particularly worrying here is the numbers of organisations downsizing who are actually making healthy profits. As Cascio (2002) points out, these are not sick companies trying to save themselves but healthy companies attempting to boost earnings. Organisational size is no longer a measure of corporate success. Western managers, it seems, have a bent for sacking employees. Jack Welch, for example, was known as 'neutron Jack' for his actions in getting rid of employees and leaving only the buildings intact (Welch 2001; Haigh 2004). Chainsaw Al Dunlap managed to terminate 11,000 staff in two months, representing around 35 per cent of the workforce. Shareholder value was the banner under which these cuts were made (Lazonick 2005, p.594).

One trigger for increasing interest and attention for downsizing, above and beyond its greater extent and scale than in the past, is that as Sennett (1997, p.18) notes: 'Downsizings and reengineerings impose on middle-class people sudden disasters which were in an earlier capitalism much more confined to the working classes.' Effectively managing workforce reduction is thus of increasing importance in HRM practice, not least because of its greater scale and frequency but also because of the potentially serious negative effects of its mismanagement (Thornhill and Saunders 1998; Wilkinson 2004). The mismanagement of workforce reduction can clearly cause major damage to both the organisation's employment and general business reputations. Damage to the former can seriously affect an organisation's selection attractiveness with potential future employees by producing an uncaring, hire-and-fire image and affect the employer brand (Dewettinck and Buyens 2002). Similarly, bad publicity over retrenchment can cause customers to worry that the firm may go out of business or give rise to problems in the continuity or quality of supplies and services.

There have also been increasing recent concerns about the organisational effectiveness of the post-downsized 'anorexic organisation'. The benefits, which organisations claim to be seeking from downsizing, centre on savings in labour costs, speedier decision making, better communication, reduced product development time, enhanced involvement of employees and greater responsiveness to customers (De Meuse *et al.* 1997, p.168). However, some writers draw attention to the 'obsessive' pursuit of downsizing to the point of self-starvation marked by excessive cost cutting, organ failure and an extreme pathological fear of becoming inefficient. Hence 'trimming' and 'tightening belts' are the order of the day (Tyler and Wilkinson 2007, 2003).

Research suggests that downsizing can have a negative effect on 'corporate memory' (Burke 1997), employees' morale (Brockner *et al.* 1987), destroys social networks (Priti 2000), increases labour turnover (Trevor and Nyberg 2008), and causes a loss of knowledge (Littler and Innes 2003). As a result, downsizing could 'seriously handicap and damage the learning capacity of organisations' (Fisher and White 2000, p.249). Further, given that downsizing is often associated with cutting costs, downsizing firms may provide less training for their employees, recruit less externally, and reduce the research and development budget (Mellahi and Wilkinson 2008). Consequently, downsizing could 'hollow out' the firm's skills capacity (Littler and Innes 2003, p.93). It is interesting to note that the problems BA experienced in the summer of 2004 with angry travellers, people sleeping rough at airports, etc. was said by the unions to be the result of 13,000 redundant posts since 2001, leaving staff shortages in key areas (Inman 2004).

Paradoxically, restructuring has also been seen as a sign of corporate virility and stock market prices have boomed in the context of such plans. Barclays Bank shares soared after its announcement to axe 6,000 staff (Garfield 1999) and, in the political arena, the Labour and Conservative parties have been attempting to outdo each other in announcing the number of civil service jobs they could reduce (BBC News, 12 July 2004), with the Labour government announcing the axing of 104,000 civil servants' jobs and being accused by the Conservative party of failing to 'slim down its fat government'. As Haigh observes (2004, p.141), 'it remains the case that the quickest way for a CEO to obtain an ovation is to propose eliminating a layer of managers, as though dusting a mantelpiece or scraping off a coating of rust'. In the light of such reports it is interesting to note that in a 2002 CIPD survey on redundancy, 37 per cent of HR professionals felt that organisations were too ready to make people redundant to meet short-term changes in demand.

Industrial conflict and workforce resistance (e.g. via strikes, sit-ins, work-ins, etc.) is also a potential problem that arises in periods of retrenchment. However, given the unparalleled levels of workforce reductions, the relatively low level of disputes overall is perhaps more surprising. It may reflect not only reduced trade union and worker power but also that redundancy is now so commonplace and woven into the fabric of industrial life that it is seen as an inevitable consequence of work in hyper-competitive times (Turnbull and Wass 2004). The form of union resistance to redundancy has thus changed to one of attempting to secure the best deal possible for members via job security agreements which incorporate consultation mechanisms, severance payments and supportive measures, alongside a general lobbying and campaigning role, with industrial action a very rarely used last resort.

The potentially negative impact of downsizing is not restricted to those who leave but also has a major effect on the remaining employees. Such employees are by their very nature now much more important to the employer but are often overlooked in downsizing situations. The impact of downsizing on the remaining employees is such that commentators now talk of 'the survivor syndrome' (Brockner 1992). This is the term given to the collection of behaviours such as 'decreased motivation, morale and loyalty to the organisation, and increased stress levels and skepticism' that are exhibited by those who are still in employment following restructuring (Doherty and Horstead 1995). Studies also report how the health of surviving employees deteriorates after downsizing (Kivimaki *et al.* 2000).

Cascio (2008) suggests that there are only two sets of circumstances where downsizing may be warranted. The first is when companies find themselves saddled with non-performing assets or consistently unprofitable subsidiaries. Here he says they should consider selling them to buyers who can make better use of those assets, and employees associated with those assets or subsidiaries often go with them to the new buyers. The second case is when jobs rely on technology that is no longer commercially viable; for example, in the newspaper industry when after computer-based typesetting, compositors were no longer required.

Methods of downsizing

There are a number of ways that organisations can reduce the size of the workforce. In this section we first examine the ones employers use the most: natural wastage, compulsory and voluntary redundancy and early retirement. Second, we consider a range of alternatives to dismissing workers, in particular redeployment and wage reduction.

NATURAL ATTRITION/WASTAGE

Natural wastage is often proffered as the most positive and humane method of workforce reduction. It is seen as giving individuals a free choice in whether to leave or stay and thus reduces the potential for conflict and employees' feelings of powerlessness. Evidence suggests that it is not the exact equivalent of normal labour turnover. It appears that in a redundancy situation both the rate and nature of labour turnover change. Early research reported that labour turnover increases in retrenchment situations (Wedderburn 1965; Bulmer 1971), but this may reflect more on the nature of the labour market, with alternative jobs easier to obtain during this period. This form of workforce reduction poses problems for management in that it is unplanned and uncontrollable. Some evidence also suggests that it depresses workforce morale more than the short, sharp, shock approach of redundancy. Natural wastage is also a form of job loss that is much more difficult for employees and unions to resist because of its incremental nature.

VOLUNTARY REDUNDANCY

This method is increasingly most employers' preferred method of downsizing. Some common concerns are that it is expensive, because employees with long service find it attractive, that the best workers leave because there is demand for their skills, while poorer workers stay because they are less marketable. There is little evidence to make a judgement here but Hardy's (1987) research suggests the reverse actually occurs in practice. Marginal performers are more likely to take up voluntary redundancy packages because of either disillusionment with the job or the fear of dismissal without any financial cushion at a later date. Savery *et al.* (1998) report that high absenteeism and low commitment are associated largely with those who have expressed an interest in voluntary redundancy. The main advantages are that at least employees are given a choice and this de-stigmatises, to some extent, the loss of the job. Although voluntary redundancy is much preferred to compulsory forms, it is sometimes seen by unions as 'selling jobs'.

There is, however, considerable evidence that voluntary redundancy is often far from a willing choice on the part of employees, with many reports of managers 'leaning' on targeted employees, leading to the question of did they jump or were they pushed? Research on teacher lay-offs, for example, found a wide range of informal and very threatening tactics used by managers to 'encourage' particular teachers to volunteer. In one case this included a manager threatening to disclose to an employee's spouse his extramarital affairs if the teacher did not 'volunteer' for redundancy (Sinclair *et al.* 1995).

COMPULSORY REDUNDANCY

Compulsory redundancy – where no choice is presented to the departing employee – is normally a 'last resort' strategy for employers and is usually seen as the least acceptable face of downsizing. However, as it is based on managerial decision making, it gives employers the opportunity to design and implement criteria based on business needs. Compulsory redundancy is also more common where downsizings are large-scale or involve complete plant closures. According to WERS data, compulsory redundancy is also much more common in the private sector than in the public sector (Kersley *et al.* 2006; Cully *et al.* 1999). However, it has also been suggested that compulsory redundancy is rising in usage in the public sector as the potential for voluntary redundancy and early retirement has been exhausted and more generally because of doubts about the latter's effectiveness.

RETIREMENT

Early retirement is usually utilised alongside other methods of workforce reduction, although it may often be sufficient to generate the required cuts of itself. It is often seen less as a method of redundancy and more as a way of avoiding it. The mechanics differ from other methods in one key respect; employees opting for early retirement are less likely to seek to re-enter the workforce. The increasing use of early retirement can be detected in surveys which measure the declining economic activity rates of older employees.

Ill-health is one cause for the increase in early retirement, but other developments at both company and national level also lie behind the increase. There has been a major increase in level of ill-health retirements in recent years. A commonly voiced argument is that this is a consequence of intensification of work and associated increases in stress levels which result in more long-term sickness.

At national level there has been a desire by governments in the US and Europe as well as other industrialised countries to increase work opportunities for younger workers. At company level the expansion of occupational pension schemes and the inclusion of standard arrangements for redundancy retirement have facilitated the use of early retirement as a method of workforce reduction (McGoldrick and Cooper 1989). The use of enhanced early retirement benefits makes it more palatable. It would also appear that many managers, usually with little supporting evidence, associate increasing age with declining levels of productivity and poorer-quality performance. Ageism in managerial circles, it seems, is rife, and some companies even had formal 'first in first out' redundancy policies until the advent of legislation on age discrimination throughout the EU. The view that older workers have critical experience and expertise with 'seasoning', an asset not a liability, is not widely shared (Clabaugh 1997). The main exception here appears to be senior managers themselves. The increasing age profile of directors has caused some to question whether there should be a 'sell-by' date for such a group (Weyer 1994).

There are a number of advantages of early retirement ('downsizing with dignity' – Barbee 1986); in particular, it is seen as carrying less stigma than other forms of redundancy; 'retired' is a much more socially acceptable 'r' word than 'redundant'. However, there are also a number of drawbacks. The decline of last in first out (LIFO) redundancy selection criteria, which protected older workers by virtue of seniority, has left them disproportionately vulnerable to enforced early retirement under employers' labour-shedding policies. People are now living longer and retiring earlier and thus need sound financial provision if demeaning financial dependency is to be avoided. The adequacy of early retirement benefits is under increasing question. It is now clear that the past trends in early retirement will not continue, not least because of uncertainty over the capacity of pension funds to sustain the costs. EU-wide legislation on age discrimination and a changing policy on mandatory retirement look set to radically alter early retirement trends.

Alternatives to redundancy

Employers are often encouraged to consider alternatives to redundancies, and to view compulsory redundancy, especially, only as a last resort. There is a wide range of possible alternatives to redundancy. These include redeployment, freezing recruitment, disengaging contractors and other flexible workers, reducing overtime, secondments, career breaks, and introducing more flexible working patterns such as job-sharing and part-time work.

However, despite such calls there is little evidence for any widespread development of redundancy alternatives in Britain. For some commentators an explanation lies in the ease with which British employers can dismiss their workers without having to consider alternatives. Turnbull and Wass (1997) argue that deregulation has made redundancy, or what the European Union term 'collective dismissal', easier than other forms of workforce reduction. A consequence of a more protracted dismissal process is that it seems other countries have a much greater emphasis on avoiding redundancy. Japan and Scandinavian countries have the most developed forms of employment protection, with graded steps for cost reduction. In the case of Japan, this includes redeployment, relocation, retraining, transfer and even suspending dividends and cutting the salaries of senior managers. As Turnbull and Wass (1997) point out, this is the exact reverse of the British picture, where dividends and the bonus payments of senior managers are boosted by making workers redundant in the pursuit of short-term profit improvements.

Cascio (2008) points out that there is a very limited research that examines the relative financial effects of these alternatives on firms, and the effects on individual employees, partly because there are few examples. He attributes this to the mental models that senior managers have about human resources. From his work he identifies two groups. One group of firms saw employees as *costs to be cut*. The other, much smaller, group of firms saw employees as *assets to be developed*. From here we can see a major difference in the approaches they took to restructure their organisations.

- **Employees as costs to be cut** – the downsizers. They constantly ask themselves, what is the minimum number of employees we need to run this company? What is the irreducible core number of employees the business requires?

- **Employees as assets to be developed** – the responsible restructurers. They constantly ask themselves, how can we change the way we do business, so that we can use the people we currently have more effectively?

As Cascio puts it, the downsizers see employees as commodities – like paper clips or light bulbs – interchangeable and substitutable, one for another. This is a 'plug-in' mentality: plug them in when you need them, pull the plug when you no longer need them. In contrast, responsible restructurers see employees as sources of innovation and renewal. They see in employees the potential to grow their businesses. A key issue is how HR can influence these mental maps and hence influence practice.

Some of these main alternatives to redundancy are now briefly discussed.

WAGE REDUCTIONS

Wage cuts as an alternative to job cuts tend to be sparingly used, although there have been a number of prominent examples, as a method of cost reduction in the UK and elsewhere, such as Hong Kong. A particular use has been in the introduction of US concession-style bargaining arrangements wherein employees forgo a wage increase for some form of job security agreement. In the UK Thomas Cook in 2001 cut jobs by 1,500 and asked staff to take pay cuts of 10 per cent as business collapsed in the wake of terrorist attacks in the US. Senior executives cut their own pay by 15 per cent and all those earning more than £10,000 had salaries cut by 3–10 per cent (McCallister 2001).

The phenomenon that wages are 'sticky' downwards and labour markets respond to falls in demand by employment adjustments is well established in economic theory. What Sullivan and Hogge term 'wage fix/employment flex' was found to operate widely, with managers faced by a recession seeking to control labour costs (via redundancies), improve productivity and maintain employment reputation and workers' morale (Sullivan and Hogge 1987). The mechanisms that best achieved this were adjustments to employment rather wage levels. Neither management nor unions sought to negotiate on maintaining employment as an alternative to real wages as this would damage the 'implicit contract' between workers and managers. An alternative might be reducing hours, as VW did in the early 1990s as part of a large cultural change which involved removing layers of management, introducing teamwork and raising skill levels (Pfeffer 1998, pp.189–92).

REDEPLOYMENT

Although employers' attempts to secure more flexible workforces have been subject to a great deal of debate of late, the concept of spatial flexibility and the redeployment of workers has received little attention. In the US redeployment – or 'inplacement' – is well established. In the recession of the mid-1970s, Japanese corporations maintained as many as 4 million permanent employees despite the lack of work for them to do, with redeployment made easier because of the tendency to straddle several industries (Hill 1989, p.51). Even in the 1990s, when Japanese weaknesses were identified, plant closure and sell-offs were rarely carried out, and while the Japanese method of labour handling during a recession makes it difficult to instigate quick turn-arounds, it also means that companies have resources at hand for a rapid expansion.

Redeployment is not an easy option for managers. It requires considerable cooperation between different divisions, plants and departments within a firm and brings a number of often costly implications. A common need is for redeployed workers to be retrained and reskilled. Relocation and/or travelling costs can be incurred. A key issue in supporting redeployment is the degree of pay protection given to such workers. The reality of redeployment is that most workers are redeployed to lower-graded posts. Many employers protect the existing income of redeployed workers for a specified period. Redeployment can also be problematic for the employee, and counselling, not least to help workers overcome a sense of loss, is helpful in such situations.

Box 16.2: HRM in practice

Redundant personalities

One controversial development in redundancy selection surrounds the use of psychometric tests, especially personality tests, in deciding who goes or stays. Tests have largely been used in redundancies involving white-collar jobs, for example at Anglian Water, Southwark and Brent Councils, Coventry Healthcare NHS Trust and Wyeth Laboratories. Their use has caused considerable concern among the employees and trade unions involved.

At Anglian Water around a third of the staff (around 900 employees) were to be made redundant. Instead of keeping the staff whose jobs remained, all employees undertook personality testing designed to measure conceptual thinking, innovation, teamwork, initiative, people-orientation and flexibility. The test was said to influence around 30 per cent of the final redundancy decision but the union believes it carried more weight. Whatever weight the tests were given in eventual termination decisions and despite their 'objective' nature, they became a focus of staff resentment. Unison claimed that the company determined the competencies to be tested before it identified what characteristics and skills were needed. Those dismissed felt unfairly deprived of their jobs and tribunal claims for unfair redundancy have ensued. Concerns about racial discrimination have also arisen with the use of tests for redundancy and downgrading. At the Coventry Healthcare NHS Trust five nurses won an out-of-court settlement from their employer on these grounds. A similar out-of-court settlement was also reached in the Brent case, where 53 workers lost their jobs after restructuring using aptitude tests. The particular tests used were found to be in error because they did not effectively take into account cultural differences.

A number of further concerns arise from the use of psychometric tests, which have been designed for other purposes, in downsizing decisions. Not least is the issue that effective testing relies on candidates behaving openly and honestly, and when some of the consequences of the test are redundancy and downgrading this is very difficult to achieve. Despite these problems, the use of tests for redundancy purposes is growing. It seems that managers like the idea of laying the blame for unpopular redundancy decisions on 'science' and the individual employee, rather than accepting responsibility themselves.

Sources: Rich and Donkin 1994; *Financial Times* 16 December, 1995: 13; Smith 1996

The redundancy process

Redundancy, despite the practice that managers have had in undertaking it of late, is often badly managed, with many negative consequences. In part this may stem from the rarity of formal redundancy procedures. The large majority of employers do not have an agreed and written redundancy procedure. Recent interest in notions of labour–management partnerships have begun to take on such concerns. Some have embodied no compulsory redundancy guarantees in such agreements.

There is much to be gained from a humane, planned and strategic approach to downsizing (Wilkinson 2004). According to Cameron (1994, 1998), the way downsizing is implemented is more important that the fact that it is implemented. He reports on three approaches to downsizing (see Table 16.1).

Workforce reduction strategies are focused primarily on reducing headcount and are usually implemented in a top-down, speedy way. However, the downside of such an approach is that it is seen as the 'equivalent to throwing a grenade into a crowded room, closing the door and expecting the explosion to eliminate a certain percentage of the workforce. It is difficult to predict exactly who will be eliminated and who will remain' (Cameron 1994, p.197), but it grabs the immediate attention of the workforce to the condition that exists. Because of the quick implementation associated with the workforce reduction strategy, management does not have time to think strategy through and communicate it properly to employees. This may result in a low 'perceived distributive fairness' (Brockner *et al.* 1987). As a result, employees may be negatively affected by the stress and uncertainty created by this type of downsizing and may react with reduced organisational commitment, less job involvement, and reduced work efforts.

Work redesign strategies are aimed at reducing work (in addition to, or instead of, reducing the number of workers) through redesigning tasks, reducing work hours, merging units, etc. However, these are difficult to implement swiftly and hence are seen as a medium-term strategy.

Systematic strategies focus more broadly on changing culture, attitude and values, not just changing workforce size. This involves 'redefining downsizing as an on-going process, as a basis for continuous improvement; rather than as a programme or a target. Downsizing is also equated with simplification of all aspects of the organisation – the entire system including supplies, inventories, design process, production methods, customer relations, marketing and sales support, and so on' (Cameron 1994, p.199). Again, this strategy requires longer-term perspectives than that of workforce reduction.

Table 16.1 Three types of downsizing strategies

	Workforce reduction	Work redesign	Systematic
Focus	Headcount	Jobs, levels, units	Culture
Eliminate	People	Work	Status quo
Implementation time	Quick	Moderate	Extended
Payoff target	Short-term payoff	Moderate-term payoff	Long-term payoff
Inhibits	Long-term adaptability	Quick payback	Short-term cost savings
Examples	Attrition	Combine functions	Involve everyone
	Layoffs	Merge units	Simplify everything
	Early retirement	Redesign jobs	Bottom-up change
	Buy-out packages	Eliminate layers	Target hidden costs

Source: Cameron 1994. Reprinted by permission of John Wiley & Sons, Inc. from *Human Resource Management*, Vol.33, No.2. Copyright © 1994 by John Wiley & Sons, Inc.

Box 16.3: HRM in practice

Best of a bad job

Nearly half of organisations that have carried out redundancies in the past 18 months plan to make further cuts, according to a CIPD/IRS report on redundancy workplace attitudes. The majority of organisations (52 per cent) also report a decline in employee morale in the aftermath of redundancies.

The main findings include:

- A large proportion of organisations (45 per cent) believed that they would need to make further redundancies over the next 12 months.
- Redundancies are concentrated in general manufacturing (17 per cent), engineering (10 per cent), retail (7 per cent) and financial services (5 per cent).
- 37 per cent of HR professionals said that organisations were too ready to make people redundant to meet short-term changes in demand.
- 53 per cent of HR professionals said that younger people were less worried about the prospect of redundancy, while 32 per cent said that employees do not see redundancy as the threat it used to be.
- 74 per cent of lay-offs were compulsory.
- The main criteria used by employers for selecting people to be made compulsorily redundant included (where three criteria were selected by respondents):
  1. the employee's role within the organisation (68 per cent);
  2. job performance (62 per cent);
  3. ability or flexibility (52 per cent).
- Most organisations (95 per cent) sought to minimise the number of redundancies. The main alternative measures used included:
  1. offering alternative employment to employees in affected posts (74 per cent);
  2. placing a freeze on recruitment (56 per cent);
  3. achieving workforce reduction through natural wastage (55 per cent).
- Employers reported that the most common reaction of employees to the announcement that they were to be made redundant was acceptance (49 per cent).
- The majority of employers (72 per cent) paid redundancy compensation above the statutory minimum. Fifty per cent of organisations provided counselling whereas 44 per cent provided access to a specialist outplacement agency/consultancy.
- HR professionals described the redundancy process as 'traumatic', although most considered the job cuts to be necessary.
- Organisational restructuring is the most common reason given by employers for making redundancies (66 per cent).

Source: This material is adapted from *Redundancy*, CIPD 2002, with permission of the publisher, the Chartered Institute of Personnel and Development, London

Sahdev (2003, p.72) suggests that the main focus of HR appears to be in implementing the procedural aspects of redundancy, including fair selection and provision of outplacement services for the leavers. While this is in keeping with the organisational justice approach, the contributions need to be directed towards managing the strategic aspects of decision-making processes with a view to managing survivors effectively. He suggests that HR practitioners need to be influential at both the strategic and operational levels, in order to manage survivors effectively and thereby enable the organisation to sustain competitiveness.

To what extent is such advice heeded in reality? Many problems relate to a low level of trust between those making decisions and those receiving them. A convincing rationale for downsizing is essential, as is a degree of planning. 'Good HR practice' suggests that three elements of the redundancy process are often critical: consultation with employees, the selection decision and pre/post-redundancy support for those made redundant as well as those who remain. We deal with each of these in turn.

CONSULTATION

Consultation with unions and employees is emphasised in most accounts of downsizing. Employees need to understand the rationale for downsizing and also how the process will be managed. Breaks in communication are seen as sinister and lead to rumours (Kettley 1995). Consultation with unions over redundancies can make a difference to the nature of the redundancy process used, and occasionally the numbers of jobs lost (Edwards and Hall 1999). The downsizing process is often characterised by secrecy and swiftness and is thus often poorly planned and executed with little scope for employee involvement. To some extent this reluctance to consult over workforce reduction stems from its being seen as part of a deeply entrenched managerial prerogative about the right to hire and fire and close down businesses. The case of the deputies, supervisors and correction officers dismissed by the newly elected sheriff at Clayton County, Georgia is fortunately not that common. Staff who thought they were being invited to a swearing-in ceremony had their badges, guns and car keys removed, were then dismissed and escorted to a ride home (in police vans) under the watchful eye of rooftop snipers who were there 'just in case someone got emotional' (Younge 2005).

Legislative restrictions on managerial prerogative in redundancy are extremely limited in the UK. First, the requirement is to consult rather than negotiate over redundancies (minimum of 30 days in cases of 20–99 redundancies and 90 days for greater than 100), although this should include examining ways of avoiding dismissal. Second, consultation was limited to recognised unions only and in the increasing non-union sector there was no such statutory requirement. However, following a ruling against the UK by the European Court of Justice in June 1994 under the Acquired Rights and the Collective Redundancies Directives, UK Regulations were issued in 1995 to provide for consultative mechanisms with 'appropriate' (employee) representatives in non-union organisations. The Collective Redundancies and Transfer of Undertakings (Protection of Employment) Regulations, which came into force in 1999, strengthened the 1995 regulations. The new regulations laid down specific requirements for electing employee representatives to be consulted in non-union organisations at times of redundancy. Third, redundancy consultation is often not complied with in practice, with managers choosing to make additional payments in lieu of notice so as to shed workers quickly via the short, sharp, shock approach of a sudden announcement and a quick layoff. Here the new regulations have buttressed and simplified the remedies that employees and their representatives may obtain in cases where employers fail to provide the required consultation. It remains to be seen how effective these new regulations are in practice. Most employers did not think the Information and Consultation Directive would have any effect on the way they currently consult with and inform staff in a redundancy situation (CIPD 2002).

Despite this lack of use, there is some evidence that extensive consultation and employee involvement, although it does little to reduce the stress caused by job loss, can help in its

Table 16.2 How employees were notified of potential redundancies

Means of notification	Employers using (n = 563)%
Individual meetings	80.5
Line manager notification	61.4
Individual letters	57.0
Collective meeting	47.6
Meeting with trade union representatives	30.3
Notice board	13.3
Circular letter	10.1
E-mail	5.1
Press or other media	2.1
Other means	5.1

Source: CIPD 2002

smooth implementation. US studies indicate that increased communication and participation of employees in the downsizing process were associated with improvement (Cameron 1994; DiFonzo and Bordia 1998).

SELECTION

Whatever methods are used to reach redundancy decisions, the notions of fairness and 'organisational justice' are key issues. Here the process of the decision making on redundancy is equally if not more important than the outcome. Research on the perception of organisational justice by employees has been found to be related to both how the decision was made and how much 'voice' they felt they had in the process. In general there are less negative attitudinal and behvaiours outcomes from employees when the decision to downsize is seen as more legitimate, e.g. because of a decline in sales, increased competition etc., compared to a desire to increase profits, cut costs etc. The other important factors in the selection process, which also help increase employees' perceptions of fairness, are that it should be clear and appropriate.

There are some noteworthy general trends within selection criteria. First is the distinct move away from seniority and the reduction of LIFO and towards selection based on an assessment of skills and performance (IRS 2004). Despite the advantages of LIFO, which according to ACAS are that it is an 'objective, easy to apply, readily understood, and widely accepted' criterion, it now tends to be used as a criterion of last resort when others fail to produce a clear-cut decision. An IRS report found that less than a quarter used LIFO, fewer than 2 per cent used length of service exclusively, with more than half using length of service as a factor alongside the job done by the employee or their level of skills and competencies. There can also be problems of unfair discrimination in its application. The issue of employers using sickness absences as a criterion for redundancy has caused much concern among unions, not least because of the worry that employees will now been frightened to take time off work when genuinely sick. In the IRS survey of those employers who use attendance as a criterion (60 per cent of the sample), certified absence appears to count against an employee in the selection process almost as much as unauthorised absence. Most employers (81 per cent) said that leave covered by a doctor's certificate would count against a worker, and 87 per cent said that self-certified leave would (IRS 2004).

Despite the outwardly 'objective' nature of many of these selection criteria and mechanisms, we can also find considerable evidence of subjective manipulation of a redundancy situation by managers. In the search for 'committed' workers, employers appear to use workforce reduction for a variety of ends. Often it seems a redundancy situation is used, or in some cases even engineered, to weed out 'troublemakers' and periodically get rid of 'deadwood'. Troublemakers are variously defined as the shirkers, union activists and the non-believers in new managerial philosophies and programmes. For example, the personnel director of Co-Steel Sheerness, a British-based but Canadian-owned steel mill, described how they dealt with employees who were unhappy with the new practices of 'total team culture' and union de-recognition thus:

> When it became clear that there were employees who became increasingly dissatisfied with our new philosophies. . . . we bit the bullet with those employees and put in place termination programmes. About 5 to 6 per cent of employees were terminated. (*The Guardian*, 6 September 1995, p.19)

EMPLOYEE SUPPORT

A wide variety of post-redundancy assistance can be offered to dismissed workers. There is considerable evidence to suggest that such help can have a very positive impact on the management of redundancy at a relatively low cost (e.g. Guest and Peccei 1992). The forms of support include redeployment centres, business start-up advice, training and loans, retraining, outplacement support, pre-retirement education, financial advice, job-search help, counselling, etc.

Redundancy counselling and stress management are emphasised to help employees overcome and come to terms with some of the intense feelings of damage to self-esteem, failure, loss of confidence, decreased morale, anxiety, bitter feelings of betrayal, debilitating shock and sense of loss that accompany downsizing. Real personal, social and financial problems also stem from redundancy situations. Studies of redundancy counselling and assistance programmes report it as being valued by the recipients but somewhat unproven in its actual benefits.

The availability of support is usually much greater the more senior the redundant employee is. Thus outplacement support is more often reserved for more senior grades, and where it is provided for all employees senior managers usually receive external specialist services while lower-grade employees have in-house services. Surveys of outplacement report its considerable growth in the UK since its import from the US in the mid-1970s (Doherty 1998). While most firms would claim expertise in wider career management advice, its main use is in downsizing situations. Its key aim is to help the redundant employee with the jobsearch process by providing practical services such as office support and specific counselling and advice. At more senior levels this is often provided on a one-to-one basis, involving psychometric tests and career counselling, while for other levels of employee, group programmes of CV construction and job-search strategies are provided.

The most common support for operatives is the statutorily supported one of time off to look for work. Some employers have even advertised the availability of redundant employees in national newspapers to facilitate their re-employment. The need for support in finding alternative work is a real one. Redundant workers suffer particularly in their search for a new job, the so called 'lemon effect' (Turnbull and Wass 1997). Here recruiters become concerned about hiring an employee who has been discarded by another employer. Employers assume that a redundant worker must be of poor quality and potential. The labelling of redundant employees as inferior may well increase in the future as employers move to more performance-oriented selection criteria and away from seniority. Thus those most likely to be made redundant are least likely to follow a smooth path to re-employment.

SEVERANCE PAY

Arguably the acid test of support for redundant employees is the level of compensatory financial support or 'severance' pay. The CIPD survey (2002) noted that three-quarters of employers provide redundancy compensation above that required by law. Some companies provide little else in the way of support for redundant workers. For example, the financially oriented

Hanson Trust did not use outplacement but were said to 'use pound notes to staunch the blood' with generous severance packages. Most employers offer better severance terms than the baseline required by statute, with the main exception being public sector employers, except for senior managers. In part this reflects the paternalistic nature of British employers but also the pragmatic need for a form of inducement to encourage employees to volunteer. Severance is usually paid in the form of a lump sum to facilitate a 'clean break' rather than staged payments.

SURVIVORS

The needs of those who remain post-downsizing appear to be often overlooked. For example, a survey of financial services found that 79 per cent of firms provided outplacement services for those employees who left but less than half gave support to the 'lucky' ones who remained (Doherty and Horsted 1995). Yet we have increasing evidence that such forgotten employees are often in need of support and counselling. For example, there is considerable evidence that remaining employees feel shocked, embittered towards management, fearful about their future and guilty about still having a job while colleagues have been laid off. The effects of such feelings are not difficult to predict. Such employees are more likely to have lower morale and increased stress levels, be less productive and less loyal, with increased quit levels. Sennett describes survivors as behaving as though 'they lived on borrowed time, feeling they had survived for no good reason' (1997, p.125). Indeed, the threat of further downsizing may create difficulties in that the most able seek alternative employment. Moreover, employees may be asked to do jobs they are untrained or ill-qualified to do.

A number of downsized companies have recognised such problems and have set up training courses for managers in how to deal with downsizing effects, and have provided counselling programmes and help lines. One study found that the response of survivors is closely linked to the treatment received by those laid off (Brockner et al. 1987). Survivors react most negatively when they perceive their colleagues to have been badly treated and poorly recompensed.

Devine et al. note that job control is important in terms of occupational stress and employee outcomes when dealing with downsizing (see also Niehoff et al. 2001; Spreitzer and Mishra 2002). Being laid off and having to attain new employment is not necessarily more negative than 'surviving' the downsizing as displaced individuals who gain new employment have a greater sense of control and, subsequently, fewer negative strains. Survivors feel less in control due to witnessing past layoffs and not knowing if they may be the next to go (Devine et al. 2003, p.121).

Conclusions: downsizing, rightsizing or dumbsizing?

The past decade or so has witnessed unmatched levels of workforce reduction in many industrialised countries. Few organisations have not undergone some form of downsizing. A number of key questions remain about downsizing. These are not so much about its nature or the effects on the redundant or surviving employees, rather they are centred on whether organisations, and in turn whole economies, are now in better shape post-downsizing. Are such organisations leaner and fitter or understaffed and anorexic? Has downsizing resulted in increased competitive advantage for those companies who have undergone it? What are the drivers of continuing downsizing?

An increasingly popular view is that the effects of downsizing are the equivalent of an industrial nuclear war:

> Below the chief executive and his cheer-leading human resources department, a number of companies resemble nothing so much as buildings blasted by a neutron bomb. The processes and structures are all there, but no human life to make them productive. (Caulkin 1995, p.19)

There is thus mounting evidence that all is not well in the downsized organisational form. As Pfeffer puts it: 'downsizing may cut labour costs in the short run, but it can erode both employee and eventually customer loyalty in the long run' (1998, p.192). As with all management tools, downsizing has unintended outcomes that could limit its presumed benefits such as cost reduction, removal of unnecessary layers of management, and better value for shareholders. Research has shown that downsizing has mixed effects on performance, Cascio (2002) showing no long-term financial payoff to downsizing, on average, and Hunter noting that while shares of downsizing companies have outperformed the stock market for six months there is little evidence to suggest that long-run performance or stock prices are improved by job cuts (Hunter 2000). A recent study by Said et al. (2007) called into question the economic legitimacy of major workforce reductions.

HRM clearly has an important role in the process. Indeed, Chadwick et al. (2004) confirm that downsizing is more likely to be effective in the longer term when accompanied by practices that reinforce the contribution of HR to financial success (e.g. extensive communication, respectful treatment of redundant employees and attention to survivors' concerns over job security). Trevor and Nyberg (2008) also find that supportive HRM practices buffer some of the negative employee attitudinal and behavioural consequences of downsizing.

A possible explanation for this increasingly reported negative relationship between downsizing and economic performance can be found in Hamel and Prahalad's (1993) analysis of competitive advantage via resource productivity, both capital and human. They suggest that there are two ways to achieve this. First, via downsizing, and second, by the strategic discipline of stretch and leverage. This latter approach seeks to get the most from existing resources. Their view is that leveraging is mostly energising while downsizing is essentially the reverse, resulting in demoralised managers and workforces. In the jargon, it appears that to achieve economic effectiveness downsizing is far from always 'rightsizing'. Strategic decision makers seem to have forgotten the benefits of growth strategies. Stephen Roach (chief economist, Morgan Stanley), the guru of downsizing business, has now disowned the practice of slash and burn restructuring (Carlin 1996). According to Roach, 'if you compete by building you have a future . . . if you compete by cutting you don't'.

There are undoubted variations across industries. Downsizing may be more damaging to R&D or knowledge-intensive industries where human capital is a very significant contributor to success.

Given such a grim picture of the effects of organisational downsizing, why then do managers persist in continuing with it? A number of explanations have been put forward. First, it is increasingly argued that managers have simply become addicted to downsizing because being lean and mean is now fashionable in itself. Downsizing, according to Brunning (1996), has become a corporate addiction and the 'cocaine of the boardroom'. Farrell and Mavondo (2004, p.396) suggest that:

> managers resort to downsizing because it is simple, generates considerable 'noise and attention' in the organisation, and may be viewed by some managers as tangible evidence of their 'strong leadership'. However, managers that pursue a reorientation strategy must necessarily engage in the much more difficult intellectual task of deciding how to reorient the organisation, combined with the associated challenges of building support, generating commitment and developing a shared vision.

Second, rather than a more 'acceptable' and appropriate use of downsizing because firms are now more productive or better organised or too bureaucratic and over-staffed, managers are often forced to do so by the market's demands for short-term boosts in profits. Depressingly, it seems that downsizing acts a reassuring signal to markets that managers are 'in control' and acting to put things right. Third, Hitt et al. (1994) suggest that the rage for 'mindless' downsizing (herd behaviour) is linked to the merger and acquisitions mania of the

An after-the-event review by senior management of the downsizing processes used in the two restructuring processes evidenced two major issues. The first was the realisation that much of what had transpired was based very much on a preoccupation with cost reduction. As one senior manager put it:

The consultants argued that the company needed to cut costs across the board and so we decided that the most expedient way of achieving this was to reduce the size of our workforce. We couldn't predict profits but it was obvious that we could control costs and downsizing immediately reduces costs. It wasn't so much a restructuring, as we wanted to cut our costs. Our costs were too high compared to our competitors. It is quite well known that, for example, our costs in mining are always going to be higher than some of our competitors because of the way our ore is structured. We have to move more waste than our competitors because our ore body, although it's a fine ore body has a lot more rubbish on it. So if you've got to move 3 tons of waste to get 1 ton of ore and your competitors have to move 1 ton or less than 1 ton, in some cases your costs are going to be higher. So the only way you can improve and be competitive is to make sure that your costs other than those uncontrolled ones are really spot on, and that's what we set out to do.

The second issue was based on negative feedback after the first restructuring from retrenched employees and survivors. The result of this was a rethinking of the idea of giving employees a minimal notification time for retrenchment, the establishment of a competence matrix to aid in the retrenchment selection process, and the establishment of an outplacement programme to assist retrenched employees in the search for new jobs.

The difficulty has been the fact that we've gone into this growth phase. Looking back now, we would've liked to have kept those people. Had we not had all this success this last year, had we had the same forward plans as when we went through the down-staffing, I don't think we would have been saying we'll let that person go.

Questions

1. What were the overriding issues that convinced International Mining it should restructure in each of the two episodes?
2. What was to be the desired outcome of the restructurings?
3. How did the company go about the process of downsizing in each of the two instances? How was the second restructuring different from the first?
4. What were the positive outcomes of the two restructurings? The negative ones?
5. What should the firm have done differently?

CASE STUDY 16.2

Downsizing down under: Perth and Western Bank

Allen Clabaugh

Perth and Western Bank is a regional bank founded in Western Australia. The bank was acquired by a nationally based organisation and was merged with the larger financial institution in 1996. The Western Australian organisation is self-contained within the larger

▶

corporate structure and maintains its own industrial relations, occupational health and safety, deployment, training, development, and finance functions. The organisational restructuring of Perth and Western Bank was precipitated by takeover by a larger, nationally based bank. The national bank had many branches in Western Australia, some of which were near those of Perth and Western Bank. The operation of the two systems side by side resulted in duplication of effort, administration and operations, so a rationalisation of the two operations was seen to be a logical business move. All the two sets of banks in Western Australia were to be fronted with the Perth and Western Bank name and logo, but some of both banks would be closed in order to avoid duplication. Perth and Western Bank was to function autonomously in the development of the amalgamation process for Western Australia and so it was decided that the national group would not participate in the integration process. An interviewee from Perth and Western Bank explained:

When the two organisations merged a lot of functions were actually duplicated and once we identified which functions were duplicated and once you merged or amalgamated them together there was a surplus of people actually required to do those functions. A good example of that is probably the Human Resource Department where [the parent company] in WA had 12 people and [the national partner] had 45 people. The reason why there was such a disparity of numbers was because [the local firm] actually ran their whole operation out of Perth whereas [the parent company] had some of their operations centralised in Sydney. So when you brought the two functions together we had quite a number of HR people which was a lot more than we really required to go forward.

Another issue to be taken under consideration by the strategic planners was the merging of the two organisational cultures. Three different cultural points of view coexisted in the merged banking system. There was the local (state-level) Perth and Western Bank culture, the national banking culture of the corporate group, and the local culture of the corporate group.

One of the things we did before we actually started the integration was that we did a cultural audit to actually see what makes up people from [Perth and Western Bank], and what makes up people from [the parent company]. Basically try and see where we can meld the two together. What we actually found is that there were three cultures running. There was the [Perth and Western Bank] culture, the [parent company]– Western Australia culture, and the [parent company]–Sydney culture operating in WA. People from Western Australia, their make-up is very different from people in the Eastern Seaboard and we discovered that Western Australians operate best in an atmosphere of going against the tide, a little adversity, and that if they can make their decisions locally they will do them quicker, and if they are a little more difficult, the task that you're asked to do, they will do it more vigorously, and so we unashamedly took as much as we could out of that culture in order to use it to our advantage during integration – and do so now. So the culture audit was probably one of the most important components that we did.

A survey of positions and jobs was undertaken in order to establish a baseline of integration between the two banking establishments:

The only jobs that were identified early on as being probably those that would go were those that were duplicated. We had two branches that were amalgamating and if they were duplicated at the branch next door then we decided that we would look at what the new branch would be, knowing that some jobs would go.

▶

A second aim of the restructuring was to be a flattening of the organisational structure. It was felt that the removal of some layers of the organisation's structure would result in a more efficient operation. As described by one of the senior HR managers.

We didn't want to have seven or eight layers between the person who starts on the front-line counter and [higher management].

Perth and Western Bank had learned from the downsizing pains of its parent company. The national organisation had recently restructured, and, in the process, provided attractive redundancy packages to its employees. As a result, the parent company lost a large number of high-performing workers. In addition, many employees perceived the use of redundancy packages as rewarding employees for leaving the organisation. The feeling at Perth and Western Bank was that the use of attractive early retirement and redundancy packages was not cost-effective over the longer term. Indeed, the company set a 'no-retrenchment policy' and actively communicated the message that no employees would be lost during the restructuring. Although some senior managers left the company, this was through resignation, rather than retrenchment or redundancy.

What happened during the last five or six years is that people, rather than resign because they want to go and do something different, will try their utmost to line up for a retrenchment. You get a maximum of 96 weeks payout which is quite a lot of money and this feeling was really running through the [Perth and Western Bank] network. During the integration we made a conscious decision to try and get a more community type atmosphere going, a community culture happening, that we would try to have a minimum amount of retrenchments as we possibly could and that we would actively as much as possible redeploy people to other areas. If you looked at it from a cost point of view, there is the cost of not only retrenching the person in the dollar and cent but it is also the cost of lost investment for the person walking out the door and there is also lost time from people then wondering, well this person's gone, I wonder if I can go. So we actually tried to look at how we could best change that and we had basically a no-retrenchment strategy happening since integration which really irked a lot of the more senior [Perth and Western Bank] managers who had been around for a long period of time. It now seems to have bitten, so to speak, and people now understand that there is no retrenchment, that if you do want to leave and look at a different lifestyle or a different job career then you make the decision to resign and go. What's helped us along on that is that [the parent company] has continued in other areas of the country to downsize using the retrenchment avenue whereas we have decided we won't do that. We've decided that when you look at the cost and the break-even points of where the cost is, there is a long time before you actually are starting to be in the red, so to speak. We've found that we have been able to downsize using that approach and it brings a better feel to what's actually happening in the branch within the network.

At the organisational level, the determination of redundant positions began with a functional analysis of the organisation's positions with the aim of targeting areas of functional duplication. At the individual level, the organisation developed a functional job analysis of all its positions that then produced job descriptions and a set of employee competencies for each position. Each employee was subject to a process of performance appraisal and competency analysis and was evaluated on the basis of job-competency performance matching. Once the organisation's functional analysis was completed, the redundant positions were publicised throughout the organisation. Staff reduction was accomplished primarily through attrition (the organisation normally has an attrition level of around 35 to 45 employees per month) and voluntary redundancy. All employees who left the company underwent an outplacement process, designed to smooth the transition out of the company.

▶

As described by the respondent:

> We did a job description of what we wanted the role to be, we looked at the competencies of what all the people had, we then ranked the people based on the competencies, ability to go forward, and past performance. We advised [the employees in those positions] that the positions which they were in had been made redundant, and [they were asked to decide who would like to stay and who would want to go].

Employee selection for retention and retrenchment at Perth and Western Bank, therefore, was a competitive process, not unlike that used by many firms when hiring new employees.

Despite all of these efforts, some senior managers suggested that the downsizing was not as successful as it could have been. During the transition to the amalgamated bank's new accounting system, some accounts were mismanaged because of computer software errors. As a result, some accounts were not credited with automatic deposits from the customers' employers, and many accounts were not properly audited. Because of this, the company lost quite a few customers to its competitors during the transition period. As outlined by the respondent:

> From a manpower point of view [the downsizing process] was successful. From a process point of view of profits and technology, it failed.

The company stated that it had lost some of its employees that it would rather have retained. As described by the respondent this was a result:

> . . . not of retrenchment though, [but] of resignation. There were some staff from the [organisation] that were in more senior positions that decided to go because they really weren't certain whether this was an organisation for which they would want to work in so they went. We never retrenched any person who we would, in hindsight, rather have kept.

Questions

1. How did Perth and Western go about restructuring?
2. How was the downsizing process at Perth and Western Bank different from that of International Mining?
3. What were the positive outcomes of the restructuring? And what were the negative ones?
4. What could Perth and Western Bank have done differently to ensure a more effective restructuring process?

Bibliography

Adams, S. (1996) *The Dilbert Principle*, London: Boxtree Press.

Ahmakjian, L.C. and Robinson, P. (2001) 'Safety in numbers: downsizing and the deinstitutionalization of permanent employment in Japan', *Administrative Science Quarterly*, Vol.46, No.4. pp.622–58.

Allen, T.D., Freeman, D.M., Russell, J.E.A., Reizenstein, R.C. and Rentz, J.O. (2001) 'Survivor reactions to organisational downsizing: does time ease the pain?', *Journal of Occupational and Organizational Psychology*, Vol.74, pp.145–64.

Amabile, T.M. and Conti, R. (1999) 'Changes in the work environment for creativity during downsizing', *Academy of Management Journal,* Vol.42, No.6, pp.630–40.

Anfunso, D. (1996) 'Strategies to stop the layoffs', *Personnel Journal,* June, pp.66–99.

Armour, J., Deakin, S. and Knozelmann, S. (2003) 'Shareholder primacy and the trajectory of UK corporate governance', *British Journal of Industrial Relations,* Vol.41, No.3, pp.531–55.

Barbee, G, (1986), 'Downsizing with dignity', *Retirement Planning,* Fall, pp.6–7.

*Baumol, J.W., Blinder, S.A. and Wolff, N.E. (2003) *Downsizing in America: Reality, Causes, and Consequences,* New York: Russell Sage Foundation Press.

Boone, J. (2000) 'Technological progress, downsizing and unemployment', *Economic Journal,* Vol.110, pp.581–600.

*Brockner, J. (1992) 'Managing the effects of lay-offs on survivors', *California Management Review,* Vol.34, No.2, pp.9–28.

Brockner, J., Grover, S., Reed, T., DeWitt, R. and O'Malley, M. (1987) 'Survivors' reactions to lay-offs: we get by with a little help from our friends', *Administrative Science Quarterly,* Vol.32, pp.526–41.

Brunning, F. (1996) 'Working at the office on borrowed time,' *Macleans,* February, pp.8–9.

Budros, A. (1999) 'A conceptual framework for analyzing why organizations downsize', *Organization Science,* Vol.10, No.1, pp.69–81.

Bulmer, M. (1971) 'Mining redundancy: a case study of the workings of the Redundancy Payments Act in the Durham coalfields', *Industrial Relations Journal,* Vol.26, No.15, pp.227–44.

Burke, W.W. (1997) 'The new agenda for organisation development', *Organizational Dynamics,* Vol.26, pp.6–20.

*Cameron, K.S. (1994) 'Strategies for successful organisational downsizing', *Human Resource Management,* Vol.33, No.2, pp.189–211.

Cameron, K.S. (1998) 'Downsizing', in M. Poole and M. Warner (eds) *The IEBM Handbook of Human Resource Management,* London: International Thomson Press.

Cameron, K.S., Freeman, S.J. and Mishra, A.K., (1991) 'Best practices in white collar downsizing: managing contradictions', *Academy of Management Executive,* Vol.5, No.3, pp.57–73.

Carlin, J. (1996) 'Guru of "downsizing" admits he got it all wrong', *The Independent on Sunday,* 12 May.

Cascio, F.W. (2002) 'Strategies for responsible restructuring', *Academy of Management Executive,* Vol.16, pp.80–91.

Cascio, W. (2008) 'Downsizing and redundancy', in A. Wilkinson, T. Redman, S. Snell and N. Bacon (eds) *The Sage Handbook of Human Resource Management,* London: Sage.

Cascio, F.W., Young, E.C. and Morris, J.R. (1997) 'Financial consequences of employment-change decisions in major U.S. corporations', *Academy of Management Journal,* Vol.40, pp.1175–89.

Caulkin, S. (1995) 'Take your partners', *Management Today,* February, pp.26–30.

Chadwick, C., Hunter, L. and Walston, S. (2004) 'Effects of downsizing practices on the performance of hospitals', *Strategic Management Journal,* Vol.25, No.5, pp.405–27.

Chorely, D. (2002) 'How to manage downsizing', *Financial Management,* May, p.6.

CIPD (2002) *Redundancy Survey Report,* May, Chartered Institute of Personnel and Development.

Clabaugh, A. (1997) 'Downsizing: implications for older employees', Working Paper, Perth, Australia: Edith Cowan University.

Cross, B. (2004) 'The times they are a-changing: who will stay and who will go in a downsizing organisation?', *Personnel Review,* Vol.33, No.3, pp.275–90.

Cully, M., Woodland, S., O'Reilly, A. and Dix, G. (1999) *Britain at Work,* London: Routledge.

De Meuse, K.P., Bergmann, T.J. and Vanderheiden, P.A. (1997) 'Corporate downsizing: separating myth from fact', *Journal of Management Inquiry,* Vol.6, No.2, pp.168–76.

Devine, K., Reay, T., Stainton, L. and Collins-Nakai, R. (2003) 'Downsizing outcomes: better a victim than a survivor?', *Human Resource Management,* Vol.42, No.2, pp.109–24.

Dewettinck, K. and Buyens, D. (2002) 'Downsizing: employee threat or opportunity? An empirical study on external and internal reorientation practices in Belgian companies', *Employee Relations,* Vol.24, No.4, pp.389–402.

DiFonzo, N. and Bordia, P. (1998) 'A tale of two corporations: managing uncertainty during organisational change', *Human Resource Management,* Vol.37, pp.295–303.

Doherty, N. (1998) 'The role of outplacement in redundancy management', *Personnel Review,* Vol.27, No.4, pp.343–51.

Doherty, N. and Horsted, J. (1995) 'Helping survivors to stay on board', *People Management*, 12 January, pp.26–31.

Edwards, P. and Hall, M. (1999) 'Remission: possible', *People Management*, 15 July, pp.44–6.

Farrell, M. and Mavondo, F. (2004) 'The effect of downsizing strategy and reorientation strategy on learning orientation', *Personnel Review*, Vol.33, No.4, pp.383–402.

Fisher, S.R. and White, M.A. (2000) 'Downsizing in a learning organisation: are there hidden costs?', *Academy of Management Review*, Vol.25, No.1, pp.244–51.

Garfield, A. (1999) 'Barclays shares soar as city welcomes job cuts', *The Independent*, 21 May.

Guest, D. and Peccei, R. (1992) 'Employee involvement: redundancy as a critical case', *Human Resource Management Journal*, Vol.2, No.3, pp.34–59.

Guthrie, J.P. and Datta, D.K. (2008) 'Dumb and dumber: the impact of downsizing on firm performance as moderated by industry conditions', *Organization Science*, Vol.19, pp.108–23.

Haigh, G. (2004) *Bad Company: The Strange Cult of the CEO*, London: Aurum.

Hamel, G. (2000) *Leading the Revolution*, New York: Harvard Business School Press.

Hamel, G. and Prahalad, C. K. (1993), 'Strategy as stretch and leverage', *Harvard Business Review*, March–April, pp.75–84.

Hancock, P. and Tyler, M. (2003) 'The tyranny of corporate slenderness: understanding organisations anorexically', Paper presented at SOCS 21: 'Organizational Wellness', Robinson College, University of Cambridge, 9–12 July 2003.

Hardy, C. (1987), 'Investing in retrenchment: avoiding the hidden costs', *California Management Review*, Vol.29, No.4, pp.111–25.

Hill, S. (1989) *Competition and Control at Work*, London: Heinemann.

Hitt, M.A., Hoskisson, R.E., Harrison, J.S. and Summers, T.P. (1994) 'Human capital and strategic competitiveness in the 1990s', *Journal of Management Development*, Vol.13, No.1, pp.35–46.

Hunter, L. (2000) 'Myths and methods of downsizing', *FT Mastering People Management*, 2000, pp.2–4.

Hutton, W. (1997) *The State to Come*, London: Vintage.

Inman, P. (2004) 'Flying right in the face of logic', *The Guardian*, 28 August.

IRS (1998a) 'The 1998 IRS Redundancy Survey Part 1', *Employment Trends*, No.658, pp.5–11.

IRS (1998b) 'The 1998 IRS Redundancy Survey Part 2', *Employment Trends*, No.659, pp.9–16.

IRS (2004) 'The changing shape of work: how organisations restructure', *Employment Review*, No.794.

Kersley, B., Alpin, C., Forth, J., Bryson, A., Bewley, H., Dix, G. and Oxenbridge, S. (2006) *Inside the Workplace: Findings from the 2004 Workplace Employment Relations Survey*, London: Routledge.

Kettley, P. (1995) *Employee Morale During Downsizing*, Brighton: Institute of Employment Studies, Report No.291.

Kivimaki, M, Vahtera, J, Pentti J and Ferrie, J (2000) 'Factors underlying the effect of organisational downsizing on health of employees: longitudinal cohort study', *British Medical Journal*, Vol.320, pp.971–75.

Lazonick, W. (2005) 'Corporate restructuring', in S. Ackroyd, R. Batt, P. Thompson and P. Tolbert (eds) *The Oxford Handbook of Work and Organization*, Oxford: Oxford University Press.

Littler, C. and Innes, P. (2003) 'Downsizing and deknowledging the firm', *Work, Employment and Society*, Vol.17, No.1, pp.73–100.

Mason, T. (2002) 'GSB top marketers exists as axe falls on budget', *Marketing*, Vol.31, p.6.

McCallister, T. (2001) 'Thomas Cook cuts jobs and pay', *The Guardian*, 1 November.

McGoldrick, A. and Cooper, C.L. (1989) *Early Retirement*, Aldershot: Gower.

McKinley, W., Zhao, J. and Rust, K.G. (2000) 'A sociocognitive interpretation of organisational downsizing', *Academy of Management Review*, Vol.25, pp.227–43.

Mellahi, K. and Wilkinson, A. (2004) *Downsizing and Innovation Output: A Review of Literature and Research Propositions*, BAM Paper 2004, British Academy of Management.

Mellahi, K. and Wilkinson, A. (2008) 'Slash and burn or nip and tuck: downsizing, innovation and human resources' (under review).

Moore, M. (1997) *Downsize This*, New York: Harper-Collins.

Mroczkowski, T. and Hanaoka, M. (1997), 'Effective downsizing strategies in Japan and America: is there a convergence of employment practices?', *Academy of Management Review*, Vol.22, No.1, pp.226–56.

Niehoff, B.P., Moorman, R.H., Blakely, G. and Fuller, J. (2001) 'The influence of empowerment and job enrichment on employee loyalty in a downsizing environment', *Group and Organization Management*, Vol.26, No.1, pp.93–113.

Peters, T. (1992) *Liberation Management*, London: Macmillan.

Pfeffer, J. (1998), *The Human Equation*, Boston, MA: Harvard Business School Press.

Priti, P.S. (2000) 'Network destruction: the structural implications of downsizing', *Academy of Management Journal*, Vol.43, pp.101–12.

Rogers, D. (2002) 'ITV digital culls staff to lure buyers', *Marketing*, 25 April, p.1.

*Sahdev, K. (2003) 'Survivors' reactions to downsizing: the importance of contextual factors', *Human Resource Management Journal*, Vol.13, No.4, pp.56–74.

Sahdev, K., Vinnicombe, S. and Tyson, S. (1999) 'Downsizing and the changing role of HR', *International Journal of Human Resource Management*, Vol.10, No.5, pp.906–23.

Said, T., Le Lovarn, Y. and Tremblay, M. (2007) 'The performance effects of major workforce reductions: longitudinal evidence from North America', *International Journal of Human Resource Management*, Vol.18, No.12, pp.2075–94.

Savery, L.K., Travaglione, A. and Firns, I.G.J. (1998) 'The links between absenteeism and commitment during downsizing', *Personnel Review*, Vol.27, No.4, pp.312–24.

Sennett, R. (1997) *The Corrosion of Character*, New York: Norton.

Sinclair, J., Seifert, R. and Ironside, M. (1995) 'Performance-related redundancy: school teacher lay-offs as management control strategy', Paper presented at BUIRA Annual Conference, Durham, July.

*Spreitzer, G. and Mishra, A.K. (2002) 'To stay or to go: voluntary survivor turnover following an organisational downsizing', *Journal of Organizational Behaviour*, Vol.26, No.6, pp.707–29.

Stebbins, M W, (1989) 'Downsizing with "mafia model" consultants', *Business Forum*, Winter, pp.45–7.

Sullivan, T. and Hogge, B. (1987) 'Instruments of adjustment in recession', *R & D Management*, Vol.17, No.4.

*Thornhill, A. and Saunders, M.N.K. (1998) 'The meanings, consequences and implications of the management of downsizing and redundancy: a review', *Personnel Review*, Vol.27, No.4, pp.271–95.

Torrington, D., Hall, L. and Taylor, S. (2005) *Human Resource Management*, London: FT/Prentice Hall.

Trevor, C and Nyberg, A (2008) 'Keeping your headcount when all about you are losing theirs: downsizing, voluntary turnover rates, and the moderating role of HR practices', *Academy of Management Journal*, Vol.51, No.2.

Turnbull, P. and Wass, V. (1997) 'Job insecurity and labour market lemons: the (mis)management of redundancy in steel making, coal mining, and port transport', *Journal of Management Studies*, Vol.34, No.1, pp.27–51.

Turnbull, P. and Wass, V. (2004) 'Job cuts and redundancy: managing the workforce complement', Paper presented at the BUIRA Annual Conference, University of Nottingham.

Wedderburn, D. (1965) *Redundancy and the Railwaymen*, Cambridge: Cambridge University Press.

Welch, J. (2001) *What I've Learned Leading a Great Company and Great People*, New York: Headline.

Weyer, M.V. (1994) 'The old men on the board', *Management Today*, October, pp.64–7.

Wilkinson, A. (2004) 'Downsizing, rightsizing and dumbsizing: quality, human resources and sustainability', Invited Keynote Paper presented at the 9th World Congress for Total Quality Management, Abu Dhabi, UAE, September 2004.

Wilkinson, A. and Tyler, M. (2007) 'The tyranny of corporate slenderness: understanding organizations anorexically', *Work, Employment and Society*, Vol.21, No.3, pp.537–49.

Worrall, L., Cooper, C. and Campbell, F. (2000) 'The impact of organisational change on UK managers' perceptions of their working lives', in R. Burke and C. Cooper (eds) *The Organization in Crisis*, Oxford: Blackwell.

Worrell, D.L., Davidson, W.N. and Sharma, V.M. (1991) 'Lay-off announcements and stockholder wealth', *Academy of Management Journal*, Vol.34, pp.662–78.

Younge, G. (2005) 'New black sheriff sacks opponents', *The Guardian*, 11 January.

*Useful reading

Chapter 17

EMPLOYEE PARTICIPATION

Tony Dundon and Adrian Wilkinson

Introduction

Employee participation has long been a central pillar of human resource management, with various practices often shaped by the different political, economic and legal climates found in different countries. These climates also influence the demand (among employees and unions) for participation as well as the desire (by managers and employers) for the types of mechanisms used. In different countries the terms 'employee participation' and 'involvement' can mean very different things, often with a lack of clarity surrounding the terms and practices used. The confusion of the terms 'involvement', 'participation' or 'communication' is made worse as some methods (such as team briefings or quality circles) tend to coexist and overlap with other techniques (such as joint union–management consultative committees or collective bargaining). In a European context, collective voice remains significant in certain countries, notably Germany and Sweden. However participation is not always exclusive to union-only channels in these countries and often includes works councils (Brewster *et al.* 2007). Moreover, employee participation is now set against an evolving regulatory (rather than voluntary) environment; in particular, the influence of both European policy and British legislation has added a new dimension to employee participation.

In considering these issues, this chapter is structured in a number of ways. First, we define participation and consider the context in which participation has changed over time. We then review a framework against which to evaluate employee participation, and this is followed by an explanation of the types of schemes used in practice. Fourth is a consideration of the meanings and possible impacts on organisational performance and employee well-being. Finally, we review some of the current influences and policy choices in the area of employee participation.

Defining participation

The literature surrounding participation can be confusing (Hyman and Mason 1995; Heller *et al.* 1998; Wilkinson 1998). Some authors refer to involvement as participation while others use empowerment or communications, often without fully extracting the key conceptual meanings or differences that are used in practice. For example, in one organisation the term 'involvement' may be used to identify certain practices that in another organisation are regarded as 'participatory'. There are further complications when considering employee participation in international terms. In European countries, for example, government policy and legislation provides for a statutory right to participation in certain areas, among both union and non-union establishments. In other countries, however, such as America or Australia, there is less emphasis on statutory provisions for employee involvement, with a greater tendency to rely on the preferences of managers and unions, resulting in a complex web of individual and collective participation in many organisations, while other employees lack the opportunity to express their voice. Differences can be further complicated depending on the presence or absence of a trade union. It is not uncommon for non-unionised companies to use the terms 'empowerment' or 'communications', even when they utilise representative forums such as European works councils (Benson 2000; Ackers *et al.* 2005). The WERS surveys have shown that the majority of managers (72 per cent) prefer to consult with workers directly (Cully *et al.* 1999, p.88), with less than half of all establishments using any form of representative participation, such as a union, joint-consultative committee or even non-union employee representative (Kersley *et al.* 2006, p.132).

One way of making sense of the elasticity of the terms is to see participation as an umbrella term covering all initiatives designed to engage employees. However, there are two separate underlying ideologies behind the nature of participation. First, the concept of industrial democracy (which draws from notions of industrial citizenship) sees participation as a fundamental democratic right for workers to extend a degree of control over managerial decision making in an organisation. Second, the economic efficiency model argues that it makes sense for companies to encourage greater participation. Allowing employees an input into work and business decisions can help create more understanding and hence commitment. Although these are two different perspectives towards employee participation, they are not polar opposites. As Cressey *et al.* (1985) usefully reminded us, no one wants a 'democratic bankruptcy'. This perspective is also useful in helping us chart the changing patterns and arrangements to do with participation over time. Much more important is what certain practices actually mean to the participants and whether such schemes can improve organisational effectiveness and employee well-being (Dundon *et al.* 2004). Brannen (1983, p.13) adopts a broad definition in this regard, defining participation as the processes by which 'individuals or groups may influence, control, be involved in, exercise power within, or be able to intervene in decision-making within organisations'. We define employee participation in a similarly broad way, following Boxall and Purcell (2003, p.162), as incorporating a range of mechanisms 'which enable, and at times empower employees, directly and indirectly, to contribute to decision-making in the firm'. As this chapter is also concerned with clarifying what is meant by different participation schemes, we will evaluate the extent to which various practices allow workers to have a say in organisational decisions. At times the extent of such a voice can be marginal, superficial and subject to managerial power; at other times it may be more extensive and embedded within an organisation.

The context for employee participation

Employee participation has a long history in most Westernised economies. Notwithstanding oversimplification, a number of distinct phases can be traced in Britain to help place the role of participation in a contemporary context. The 1960s was often preoccupied with a search for job enrichment and enhanced worker motivation. Managerial objectives tended to focus on employee skill acquisition and work enrichment. In the UK examples at ICI and British Coal included semi-autonomous workgroups to promote skill variety and job autonomy (Trist *et al.* 1963; Roeber 1975). In practice, these schemes were more concerned with employee motivation as an outcome rather than as a mechanism that allowed workers to have a say about organisational decisions.

The 1970s witnessed a shift in focus towards industrial democracy which emphasised worker rights to participate. Participation reached its high point in the UK with the 1977

Bullock Report on industrial democracy which addressed the question of how workers might be represented at board level (Bullock 1977). This report emerged in a period of strong union bargaining power and the Labour government's 'Social Contract' of inclusion. The Bullock Report was partly union-initiated, through the Labour party, and based on collectivist principles which saw trade unions playing a key role, although it was not without controversy (Brannen 1983); in particular, the general principle of employee rights established on a statutory basis (Ackers *et al.* 1992). Experiments with worker directors were initiated in the Post Office and the British Steel Corporation, although along with the Bullock Report itself, soon abandoned with the new neo-liberal agenda of the Thatcher government in 1979.

The 1980s saw a very different agenda for participation. Indeed, the vocabulary changed almost overnight. The term 'involvement' became more fashionable and associated with managerial initiatives designed to elicit employee commitment. During the 1980s the political climate was one of reducing union power and promoting more individualistic, anti-collectivist philosophies inspired by Thatcher's Conservative government. Out went statutory blueprints for greater industrial democracy such as the Bullock Report, and in came a new wave of financial deregulation and managerial self-confidence for employee rather than union-centred communication channels. Wedderburn summed up the general climate at the time:

> Those who opposed the new polices increasingly ran the risk of being seen not as critics with whom to debate and compromise (the supreme pluralist virtue), but as a domestic enemy within, which must be defeated ... [quoting government spokesman]. The mining dispute cannot be *settled*. It can only be *won*. (Wedderburn 1986, p.85)

From the 1980s onwards the context for participation changed significantly in Britain. The philosophy was much more managerialist and originated from outside the formal institutions of industrial relations (such as the Bullock Committee or union bodies). Second, the rationale for employee participation stressed direct communications with individual employees which, in turn, marginalised trade union influence. Third, the new agenda for participation was anchored on business improvements through employee commitment (Ackers *et al.* 1992, p.272). Unlike notions of industrial democracy, employee involvement during the 1980s stemmed from an economic efficiency argument. This new wave of involvement was neither interested in, nor allowed, employees to question managerial power (Marchington *et al.* 1992). In effect, this was a period of employee involvement on management's terms.

The 1990s saw a consolidation in the use of employee participation techniques. Tapping into employee ideas and drawing on their tacit knowledge was seen as one solution to the problems of managing in an increasingly competitive marketplace, in part due to globalisation and market liberalisation by governments, and also due to increasing customer demand for more choice, quality and design. The move to customised products with flexible specialisation, flatter and leaner structures was seen as the new route to competitive advantage, which focussed managerial attention on labour as a resource (Piore and Sabel 1983; Wilkinson 2002). Many of the specific mechanisms to tap into such a labour resource became crystallised in models of best-practice HRM and high-commitment management developed in the US in recent years (Huselid 1995; Becker and Huselid 1998; Pfeffer 1998). In the UK a series of studies sought to validate, in statistical terms, a link between a range of HR practices – including methods for employees to have a voice – and organisational performance (Patterson *et al.* 1997; Wood and De Menezes 1998). In this way the objectives for employee participation can be seen as unitarist in approach, often moralistic in tone, and predicated on the assumption that 'what is good for the business must be good for employees' (Claydon and Doyle 1996; Marchington and Wilkinson 2005).

The new millennium symbolised another phase towards employee participation. Alongside the 1990s flavour for managerial-led employee involvement, the twenty-first century also saw the emergence of increasing state regulation, particularly at a European level. According to Ackers *et al.* (2005), the significance of this has resulted in a continuing (and often complicated) policy dialectic that shapes management choice for employee participation. The broader environment now seems more sympathetic to trade union recognition, individual employment rights, as well as emergent collective-type regulations, such as the European Directive on Employee Information and Consultation (Ewing 2003). Arguably, the twenty-first century has ushered in a period of legal re-regulation, which can be divided between those policies that directly affect employee participation (European directives, for example) and those that indirectly alter the environment in which employee participation operates (the competitive environment and organisational strategies for HRM).

A framework for analysing employee participation

Before outlining various participation schemes, the purpose of this section is first to explain a framework that can be used to analyse the extent to which various schemes genuinely allow employees to have a say in matters that affect them at work. What is important here is to be able to unpick the purpose, meaning and subsequent impact of employee participation (Dundon *et al.* 2004). To this end a fourfold framework can be used: including the 'depth', 'level', 'scope' and 'form' of various participation schemes in actual practice (Marchington *et al.* 1992; Marchington and Wilkinson 2005).

First is the 'depth' to which employees have a say about organisational decisions (Marchington and Wilkinson 2005). A greater depth may be when employees, either directly or indirectly, can influence or control those decisions that are normally reserved for management. The other end of the continuum may be a shallow depth, evident when employees are simply informed of the decisions management have made (see Figure 17.1). Second is the 'level' at which participation takes place. This can be at a work-group, department, plant or corporate level. What is significant here is whether the schemes adopted by an organisation actually take place at an appropriate managerial level. For example, involvement in a team meeting over future strategy would in most instances be inappropriate, given that most team leaders would not have the authority to redesign organisational strategy. Third is the 'scope' of participation, that is, the topics on which employees can contribute. These range from relatively minor and insignificant matters, such as car-parking spaces, to more substantive issues, such as future investment strategies or plant relocation. Finally is the 'form' that participation takes, which may include a combination of both direct and indirect schemes. *Direct* employee participation, as noted earlier, has experienced a renewed focus since the 1980s and continued

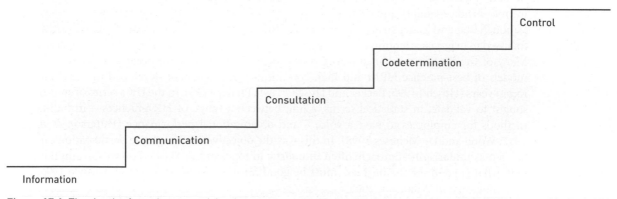

Figure 17.1 The depth of employee participation

Source: Marchington and Wilkinson 2005

through the 1990s. Direct schemes typically include individual techniques such as written and electronic communications, and face-to-face meetings between managers and employees (e.g. quality circles or team briefing). *Indirect* participation, in contrast, is via employee representatives, either union stewards or employee works council representatives in consultation with management. Another form of participation is task-based (or problem-solving) participation, where employees contribute directly to their job, either through focus groups or attitude surveys. There is also financial participation through variable pay and/or bonus schemes, such as profit sharing.

Taken together, this framework allows for a more accurate description not only of the type of involvement and participation schemes in use, but the extent to which they may or may not empower employees (Marchington and Wilkinson 2005). Figure 17.1 is more than a straightforward continuum from no involvement (information) to extensive worker participation (control). It illustrates the point that schemes can overlap and coexist. For example, the use of collective bargaining and joint consultation does not mean that management abandon communication techniques. Central to this understanding of participation is power within the employment relationship, differentiated by the methods used (direct or indirect classifications), the level at which participation takes place (individual to boardroom level), and the extent to which any particular technique is employee- or management-centred.

Employee participation in practice

The use of various employee involvement and participatory initiatives speeded up during the latter part of the 1980s and appears to have become more embedded and integrated with organisational practice during the 1990s (Table 17.1) (Marchington *et al.* 2001). A 'systematic use of the management chain' has been reported as one of the most frequent methods of communication between employer and employee (Millward *et al.* 1992, p.166). Regular meetings between managers and employees also grew, as did suggestions schemes and newsletters (Kersley *et al.* 2006). In the 2004 Workplace Employment Relations Survey (Kersley *et al.* 2006), direct employee involvement was evident through face-to-face meetings between management and employees (91 per cent of all workplaces), newsletters (45 per cent), suggestion schemes (30 per cent) and problem-solving groups such as quality circles

Table 17.1   Employee participation practices

	% of all workplaces	
	1998	2004
Face-to-face meetings between management and employees	85	91
Suggestion schemes	31	30
Regular newsletters	40	45
Problem-solving groups (e.g. quality circles)	28	36
Use of one or more employee share ownership scheme	15	21
Workplace-level joint consultative committee	28	14
Any form of representative voice[1]	57	49

Source: Kersley *et al.* 2006: 94; 127; 135; 191 (all workplaces with 10 or more employees). The advice of the WERS 2004 Information and Advice Service (www.wers2004.info) in the compilation of the above figures is acknowledged.

[1]Representative voice is defined as the existence of: a recognised trade union; any joint consultative committee; union or stand-alone non-union employee representatives (Kersley *et al.* 2006, p.132).

(36 per cent). Only 14 per cent of establishments had a workplace-level joint consultative committee (Kersley *et al.* 2006).

For the purpose of explanation and subsequent analysis, it is useful to break down the range of schemes in use into five broad classifications: communications, upward problem solving, task participation, teamworking, and representative participation.

Communication is a weak form of participation but is a means by which management share information with employees, ranging from written memos, e-mail or informal face-to-face communications. These have increased substantially in recent years, and are often regarded as a precursor to deeper forms of employee participation (Marchington and Wilkinson 2005). Of course, communication practices vary in frequency and intensity. Some companies rely on their own internal newsletter to report a range of issues, from profits and new products to in-house welfare and employee development topics. More sophisticated techniques found by Marchington *et al.* (2001) included the use of electronic media, such as e-mails, company intranets and senior management online discussion forums.

The main problem with communication as a form of participation is a lack of objectivity. Given that information is often political and power-centred, the messages managers seek to communicate to workers may be used to reinforce managerial prerogatives. The way information is communicated can also be ineffective, as many line managers responsible for disseminating corporate messages lack effective communication skills, or information is conveyed in an untimely manner (often when bad news has already passed to the media before employees are told).

Upward problem-solving techniques seek to go one step further than communication by tapping into employee ideas for improvements. As with communication methods, problem-solving practices have increased, often inspired by Japanese work systems which encourage employees to offer ideas (Wilkinson *et al.* 1998). Upward problem-solving practices are designed to increase the stock of ideas available to management as well as encourage a more cooperative industrial relations climate. Specific techniques can be either individual or collective, and range from employee suggestions schemes, focus groups or quality circles to workforce attitude surveys (Wilkinson 2002). The fundamental difference between these practices and communication methods is that they are upward (from employees to managers) rather than downward (managers disseminating information to workers).

In relation to the framework for analysing employee participation in the previous section, it is clear that upward problem-solving techniques do offer a greater degree of depth than managerial communications. However, they have also been highly criticised as being inherently unitarist in nature (Sewell and Wilkinson 1992). For example, the feedback given by workers in an attitude survey is essentially based on a managerial agenda as the information asked for tends to be set by employers. Furthermore, in organisations where quality circles have been introduced, the take-up and enthusiasm among employees have often been found wanting (Collard and Dale 1989).

The third category of practices is *task-based participation*. The objective here has been to focus attention on the actual job rather than the managerial processes for participation. These practices have a longer pedigree in seeking to counter the degradation of work and associated employee alienation (Proctor and Mueller 2000), and many schemes formed part of a series of work psychology experiments in the 1960s and 1970s (e.g. Tavistock Institute, Quality of WorkLife Programs in the USA and Sweden). More recently, task-based participation is celebrated as a root to sustained organisational performance via employee commitment and motivation (Patterson *et al.* 1997; Wood and De Menezes 1998). The types of practices include job enlargement and job enrichment, whereby employees perform a greater range of tasks with a greater degree of job autonomy. The criticisms levelled at task participation are that outcomes often result in work intensification rather than job enrichment. Arguably, devolving more and more responsibilities to employees can increase stress levels. In other words, employees simply work harder rather than smarter (Delbridge *et al.* 1992).

The fourth category is *teamworking*. Pfeffer's (1998) universal list of seven best practices includes, along other things, self-managed teams as integral to achieving better organisational performance through people. However, teamworking is one of the most imprecise of all the involvement and participation practices, and is often portrayed in an upbeat and uncritical way. For example, in the WERS 1998 survey, 65 per cent of managerial respondents indicated they have teamworking in their organisation, yet this figure reduced to 3 per cent when further questions probed the extent to which these teams were genuinely autonomous – such as deciding how tasks would be performed and appointing team leaders (Cully *et al.* 1999, p.43). Other commentators have reported a more subversive side to the effects of team-working that result in forms of peer surveillance and control (Sinclair 1992; Barker 1993). For example, the pressure to conform to group norms and meet production targets is often policed by co-workers while simultaneously monitored by management (Geary and Dobbins 2001).

The final category is *representative participation,* most typically via trade union representation, collective bargaining and/or joint consultation. This category has experienced the most significant decline in recent years. The proportion of establishments with a recognised union has declined considerably, with just 30 per cent of organisations recognising a trade union in 2004 (Kersley *et al.* 2006). The existence of joint consultation is even lower, with just 14 per cent of workplaces reporting the existence of a joint consultative committee (JCC) in 2004. However, the use of joint consultation varies by organisational size. For example, there are very few enterprises with fewer than 25 employees that have a workplace-level JCC, while around 59 per cent of those organisations with over 200 employees have in place some form of joint consultative forum (Kersley *et al.* 2006, p.126).

It is often acknowledged that collective bargaining indicates a deeper and broader level of participation in organisational decision making through the act of negotiation between management and employee (union) representatives (Pateman 1970). However, the reality can be very different, as British managers have involved unions less and less as a legitimate participatory channel (Geary 2003; Ackers *et al.* 2005). While collective bargaining covered 70 per cent of employees in 1984, this was down to 39 per cent by 2004 (Kersley *et al.* 2006, p.187).

This may indicate that representative participation is not necessarily dependent on the existence of a trade union, but mediated through newer forms of involvement such as European works councils and/or non-union company committees (Ackers *et al.* 2005). In Marchington *et al.*'s (2001) study into employee voice and management choice, it was found that non-union consultative committees were more common than a decade ago, and considered a range of organisational issues, including working conditions, capital investment expenditure and disciplinary procedures. At the same time, others have commented that non-union consultative committees are often weak on power and shallow in depth (Gollan 2002; Dundon and Rollinson 2004).

Inevitably, there are always dangers in seeking to locate discrete boundaries between certain practices. Some schemes are often unclear and ambiguous, ranging from the mechanistic descriptions of structures and procedures to more organic techniques that shape attitudes and behaviours. Other techniques limit participation to formal institutions and procedures, such as bargaining and joint consultation, while day-to-day interactions between employee and management may engender more informal dimensions to participation, particularly within the smaller workplace devoid of many formalised HR systems (Wilkinson *et al.* 2007). At the same time, there are questions about whether or not informality can survive as a viable mechanism for independent employee participation in the absence of formal structures, especially if market conditions or senior management philosophies change (Wilkinson *et al.* 2004). It is these dangers and uncertainties that warrant a consideration of the meanings and interpretations of how participation can impact organisational stakeholders.

The meanings and impact of participation

There are a number of problems with the meanings and definitions of the schemes outlined above. For example, in some organisations the full range of mechanisms – both direct and indirect – may be used simultaneously, while in other companies one or two techniques may be employed. There is no reason to assume that more is somehow better. It is also quite common for a particular label to be ascribed to very different practices (Wilkinson *et al.* 2004; Wilkinson 2008). For example, a joint consultative committee which takes place on a monthly basis at plant level, involving senior managers and shop stewards, may have a more significant impact on decision making than a European works council that meets once a year, even though both are consultative and indirect in nature. There is the possibility that the latter is regarded by participants as 'bolted-on' to other organisational practices, with little substance or meaning in reality (Marchington and Wilkinson 2005).

Arguably, the extrapolation of survey evidence about the use of various involvement and participation schemes tells us very little about the impact or extensiveness of such techniques within a particular organisation (Marchington 2005; Cox *et al.* 2006). Nor does this imply that certain schemes are an unwelcome intrusion into the lives of employees. For example, Geary and Dobbins (2001) suggest that while teamworking can lead to a reassertion of managerial authority, this is not always as a brutal form of coercion. Geary and Dobbins (2001) found that team participation can be accompanied by autonomy and freedom, which served as a more placid form of employee control by granting workers a degree of discretion which ultimately protected managerial interests. In a study by Diamond and Freeman (2001), while employees tended to express satisfaction with the extent of involvement on matters such as the pace of work, a much wider participation gap was evident on a range of substantive employment matters, such as working hours or overtime rates.

The ambiguity and lack of clarity about certain involvement and participation schemes is evident in relation to the impact such techniques are claimed to have on enhanced organisational performance (Dundon *et al.* 2004). First, it is practically impossible to isolate cause and effect and demonstrate that participation can lead to better organisational performance, given the whole range of other contextual influences. For example, labour turnover is likely to be influenced by the availability of other jobs, by relative pay levels and by the presence, absence or depth of particular participation schemes. Second is the unease associated with the reference to benchmarking: of assessing the date at which to start making 'before and after' comparisons. Should this be the date at which the new participative mechanism (say, a quality circle or consultative committee) is actually introduced into the organisation, or should it be some earlier or later date? For example, the claim that a quality circle saves money through a new work practice does not take into account that such ideas may have previously been channelled through a different and even better-established route. This also leads on to a third concern, that of evaluating the so-called impact and on whose terms. Should assessments be made in relation to workers having some voice (i.e. the process) or in terms of how things may be changed due to participation (i.e. the outcomes)? If it is the latter, then who gains? It remains the case that it is usually managers who decide what participation schemes to employ, at what level, depth and over what issues (Wilkinson *et al.* 2004).

Employee participation and the EU

A more recent issue with regard to employee participation is the influence of European social policy. As noted earlier, in Britain the trend has been predominantly for employer-led schemes of a 'direct' nature, particularly since the 1980s. However, the European Commission is beginning to promote what seems to be a favoured 'indirect' (i.e. more collectivist) route to employee participation. For example, the European Works Council Directive enables employee representatives in organisations of 1,000 or more employees (with 150 or more in two EU member countries) the right to consult with management and share information. Further, the European Company Statute (ECS) sets out a two-tier channel of participation for those companies that wish to avail themselves of the EU Statute (which grants companies tax advantages), including works-council-type forums along with employee representatives at board level. These are similar to a range of employee participation schemes that are currently more common in other EU countries such as Germany, Denmark, Sweden and the Netherlands. Of more immediate significance is the 2002 European Directive (2002/14/EC) on Employee Information and Consultation, transposed in Britain through the 2004 Information and Consultation of Employees (ICE) regulations. The remainder of this section will examine what these regulations mean for employee participation in Britain.

The directive set out the requirement for EU member countries to have in place a permanent and statutory framework for employee information and consultation. Because Britain and Ireland are the only two member states that did not already have a statutory system for involvement and participation, the effective full implementation date (for all establishments with 50 or more employees) was April 2008. The net effect is that British workers will have a legal right to be informed and consulted on a range of business and employment issues that may result in a significant departure from the traditional voluntarist system of British industrial relations (Gollan and Wilkinson 2007). The key caveat here is that the legal right is not automatic or universal. It excludes employees in establishments with fewer than 50 workers, and for those in defined organisations (e.g. 50+) employees have to trigger the mechanism by requesting that management implement an information and consultation system.

The scope of the directive defines 'information' as the transmission, by the employer to employee representatives, of data in order to enable them to acquaint themselves with the subject matter and to examine it. 'Consultation' means the exchange of views and establishment of dialogue between the employees' representatives and the employer, with a view to reaching agreement. Significantly, the explicit reference to 'employee representatives' in the directive is a clear indication of a preference for indirect (i.e. collectivist) forms of involvement and participation. However, the transposed ICE regulations allow for direct employee information and consultation practices, such as team meetings. Nor do the participation mechanisms have to incorporate or include unions, as the representative is defined as an 'employee' elected from and by the workforce (who may or may not be a union steward). Where the ICE regulations are likely to be contentious is among organisations that are either partly unionised, or have low union density levels. In all probability, companies that are highly unionised already have in place joint consultation arrangements that will suffice under the regulations. Similarly, in completely non-union companies management and employees have the scope to design and implement information and consultation mechanisms in line with the regulations without a union/non-union dichotomy. More problematic are organisations with partial union membership as it is unclear whether there have to be duplicate union and non-union employee forums, particularly if existing union representatives find it unacceptable to represent the interests of non-members. The regulations also state that organisations will have to inform and consult with employee representatives (whether union and/or non-union) on three general areas: the economic situation of the organisation; the structure and probable development of employment (including any threats to employment); and to inform and consult on decisions likely to lead to changes in work organisation or contractual relations (see Table 17.2 for a summary of the main features of the ICE regulations).

Table 17.2 Information and Consultation of Employees (ICE) Regulations 2004

- The regulations apply to undertakings in Great Britain with 50 or more employees. Equivalent legislation will be made in respect of Northern Ireland.
- The legal requirement to inform and consult employees is not automatic. A formal request has to be made by employees, or by an employer initiating the process (an employer notification).
- An employer must establish information and consultation procedures where a valid request has been made by employees.
- Such a request must be made in writing by 10 per cent of employees in an undertaking (subject to a minimum of 15 and a maximum of 2,500 employees).
- Where the employees making the request wish to remain anonymous, they can submit the request to an independent body (such as the Central Arbitration Committee (CAC)).
- The employer would have the opportunity to organise a ballot of employees to endorse or reject the initial request.
- An employer can continue with pre-existing information and consultation arrangements, provided that such arrangements have been agreed prior to an employee written request and:
  - (i)   the agreement is in writing, including any collective agreements with trade unions;
  - (ii) the agreement covers all employees in the undertaking;
  - (iii) the agreement sets out how the employer is to provide the information and seek employee views for consultation;
  - (iv) the arrangements have been agreed by the employees.
- If an employee request is to change a pre-existing agreement already in place in an undertaking, then 40 per cent plus a majority of those voting must endorse the request. The employer is then obliged to reach a negotiated agreement with genuine employee representatives.
- Where fewer than 40 per cent of employees endorse the request, the employer would be able to continue with pre-existing arrangements.
- The parties have six months to reach a negotiated agreement (extendable by agreement).
- Where a valid request (or employer notification) has been made, but no agreement reached, standard information and consultation provisions based on ICE Regulation 18 would apply.
- Where the standard information and consultation provisions apply, the employer shall arrange for a ballot to elect the employee representatives. Regulation 19 states that there shall be 1 representative per 50 employees, or part thereof, with a minimum of 2 and maximum of 25 representatives.
- Consultation should take place with a view to reaching agreement on decisions.
- Information must be given in such time, and in such fashion and with such content as is appropriate to enable the information and consultation representatives to conduct an adequate study and, where necessary, prepare for consultation.
- There are no prescriptive standard provisions and it is expected that these will vary from organisation to organisation. The standard provisions are based on Article 4 of the EU Directive. ICE Regulation 20 states that information and consultation (I&C) representatives, once elected, must have the opportunity to meet with the employer and give their opinion on matters subject to consultation, with a view to reaching agreement. The employer must give a reasoned response to I&C representatives' views.
- Enforcement regulations do not apply to pre-existing agreements.
- A complaint regarding a negotiated agreement, or a failure to comply with standard provisions, must be brought to the CAC within three months of the alleged failure.
- Where the CAC uphold a complaint for failure to comply, the complainant may make an application to the Employment Appeal Tribunal (EAT). An appeal must be made within 42 days of the date on which written notification of the CAC declaration is sent.
- The maximum penalty for failing to comply with a declaration made by the CAC is £75,000.
- ICE Regulations 25 and 26 provide for the confidentiality of sensitive information given to I&C representatives.
- I&C representatives, and employees making a request, are protected against discrimination/unfair dismissal for exercising their rights under the ICE Regulations.
- I&C representatives are to be afforded paid time off to carry out their duties.

Source: DTI 2005

There are currently a range of debates and issues associated with employee participation contained in the regulations (see, for example, Gollan and Wilkinson 2007). Article 6 (1) of the EU directive ensures confidentiality in that employee representatives (and experts that may assist them) cannot disclose commercially sensitive information provided to them. Article 7 stipulates that each of the EU countries has to ensure that employee representatives have adequate protection from managerial reprisals when carrying out their duties. This is likely to be particularly important given that employee representatives may not have the support and protection of a recognised trade union. Under the ICE regulations in Britain, the Central Arbitration Committee (CAC) is charged with ensuring company compliance and has powers to impose penalties for non-compliance, amounting to fines up to £75,000. Under the regulations, management and employee representatives have the opportunity to define and negotiate their own voluntary arrangements, which can vary from a statutory fall-back model; a principle that is not too dissimilar to voluntary arrangements contained in the European Works Council Directive.

The ICE regulations differ from the original EU directive in a number of fundamental respects (Rollinson and Dundon 2007). First, what the European directive defines as information and consultation is not the same as those contained in the ICE regulations. The former is a clearer indication for 'indirect' employee participation via elected employee representatives, whereas the language of the ICE regulations implies that direct information and communication channels are acceptable. Second, and referring back to the framework to analyse the depth of employee participation earlier in the chapter, the EU directive points towards a deeper and wider form of participation than the ICE regulations imply. It has been suggested that trade unions may become further marginalised because the ICE regulations apply to employee representatives, and consciously exclude any reference to recognised union officials (Gollan and Wilkinson 2007). Third, the trigger mechanism for employees to avail themselves of these new participation rights could result in fear or intimidation for those workers in non-union companies who do not have access to an independent trade union, employees who request these new rights could face managerial reprisals.

As a result of these issues and the newness of ICE regulations, it is difficult to predict any overall impact. However, one scenario is that these regulations may result in what has been termed 'legally-prompted' forms of employee participation (Hall and Terry 2004). In this scenario it is suggested that the law may encourage employers to be more creative by devising their own schemes for employee information and consultation, rather than rely on a legally imposed model of employee participation under the ICE regulations. A further possibility is that managers may seek to avoid an extension of employee participation by following a minimalist strategy, in which a compliance attitude is adopted and managers do little more than tick the required boxes (Dundon *et al.* 2006).

Conclusions

In this chapter we have outlined, briefly, the context of employee participation over the past few decades and pointed towards future directions through more recent European regulations. We have also considered the changing contours of management choice, public policy and that the adoption of various participation schemes is often uneven and complicated. In short, a range of schemes tend to coexist within an organisation. Moreover, we have sought to stress that the meanings and interpretations of such schemes are much more important than the type or number of techniques adopted. What is important is the depth to which participatory mechanisms are integrated with other organisational practices, the scope to which workers have a genuine say over matters that affect them, and the level at which participation occurs.

These factors are now influenced and shaped by a new British and European policy environment for employee participation. The case for industrial democracy in the 1960s and 1970s gave way to a neo-liberal climate in the 1980s and early 1990s, with an assumption that the state would remain largely absent from the employment relationship. Since 1997, British and EU initiatives have introduced a new policy framework which is having an impact on the approaches to participation (Ewing 2003). However, this impact is complex, belying simplistic dichotomies between state regulation and management choice for certain involvement schemes. Public policy represents neither a continuation of management-led involvement of the 1980s nor a rolling-back to the 1970s premise for industrial democracy. Instead, elements of a new regulatory dialectic are beginning to emerge with its own dynamics (Ackers *et al.* 2005).

At one level, the current practices of participation appear more embedded and less fragmented than they did in the early 1990s (Wilkinson *et al.* 2004). Attempts have been made to consolidate and integrate different involvement and participation mechanisms over time (Marchington *et al.* 2001). In some situations, the adversarial nature of shop-floor relations appears to have partially diminished, with a new generation of union representatives willing and able to sit alongside non-union employee representatives on joint consultative forums. The dualism in the 1980s, of separated direct (individual) and indirect (union) involvement channels, seems to be more intermingled with a range of schemes that overlap.

According to Willman *et al.* (2003), employers choosing voice regimes prior to 1960 did so in circumstances where union-based participation regimes were common exemplars and where there were normative and mimetic pressures to avoid non-union-only regimes. The risk-averse option was a dual-channel of voice. However, over time, with the shift from manufacturing to services and inward investments, non-union examples have become much more commonplace (Beardwell 1994; Millward *et al.* 1992, 2000). Where union participation exists it is highly likely to do so as part of a dual-channel voice regime (Bryson *et al.* 2007). In terms of choice, employers can 'make' voice through HR professionals or 'buy' voice through unions. As HRM professionals and the spread of HRM have become common, the default option in the choice of voice regime has shifted over time in the UK from union to non-union, from make to buy, or, in union-recognised establishments, negotiation has been relegated to consultation or communication (Marchington and Parker 1990). Switching costs, however, makes the options for participation 'sticky', with radical switching (from union to non-union and vice versa) rare (Willman *et al.* 2003).

Taken together, these developments suggest that the current policy environment holds better prospects for participation, partly as a result of greater EU regulation and partly because management has learned from the limitation of a weak form and a shallow depth to the participation initiatives of the 1980s. What remains problematic is that many managers find the European language of employment rights unpalatable and even alien to newer organisational cultures shaped by flatter and leaner market environments. This tension is significant as managers play a key part in interpreting legislative requirements in practice in the workplace. In this regard employee participation is best understood not in terms of particular techniques or discrete typologies located along a static either/or continuum, but rather as a set of complex and uneven meanings and interpretations shaped by external regulation as well as internal stakeholder expectations for greater choice and voice. The challenges that lie ahead are how such a dynamic will be played out in practice, and whether existing multiple schemes for participation will be integrated or the whether a new policy framework will result in another 'missed opportunity' for British managers (Wilkinson *et al.* 1992).

Employee voice at Compucom

Tony Dundon, Irena Grugulis and Adrian Wilkinson

Compucom is a small to medium-sized enterprise. It is non-unionised, though uses a variety of participation techniques that might be found in a more traditional unionised manufacturing facility, including a non-union employee–management consultative council. The company was founded on the principle of designing and manufacturing microcomputers for dedicated purposes. It was started in 1982 on a £6,000 overdraft by three friends, and now employs around 220 people in five different countries with a turnover in excess of £30 million per annum. About 90 technical and IT staff work at the head office in the UK, with 100 employees based at a manufacturing plant in Malta. Another 30 employees work in the distribution and sales offices in the US, Belgium, Asia and Australia.

There are two main ways in which employee participation occurs at Compucom. First, direct systems for employees to be able to articulate their voice are channelled through **monthly team briefings** and **informal day-to-day communications** between staff and team leaders. This is facilitated to a large extent by a **matrix teamworking** structure. Staff members from different functions in the company are established into one team to decide how to complete a task or develop a new product. The team is then disbanded once the task has been completed. Management prefer this direct employee-voice method, viewing it as appropriate where employees have a significant degree of professional freedom in their job. The second way employee voice is practised is indirect. Unlike most non-union companies, Compucom has a **works council** that meets on a bi-monthly basis (UK site only). There are 10 'elected' employee representatives and the personnel manager chairs the council. The council considers various work- and non-work-related matters, ranging from employee welfare programmes to staffing levels and health and safety. However, the council does not review pay or terms and conditions of employment. The personnel manager feels that the council is valuable in that it helps to reinforce company communications that add a degree of legitimacy to organisational change. For most of the time management regard the consultative council as a 'comfort blanket' for staff. Similarly, employees prefer to have the opportunity to express their concerns to management through a representative rather direct to their immediate supervisor on some occasions.

Compucom espouses the virtues of employee participation as a source of competitive advantage. There is a strong belief that obtaining employee views helps with product development, quality and better individual performance, while also promoting trust. Examples of employee-led new initiatives include a new flexi time attendance pattern, which corresponded to a reduction in absenteeism shortly after the introduction of flexi time working. The suggestion emerged from employees themselves and was endorsed by the works council.

Barriers to employee participation at Compucom seem to be minimal. Some line managers felt they were less 'people-centred' than the company now expected, and this caused some tension when communicating at a team level. In other areas employees lacked interest in the works council and some employee representative seats remained vacant. Overall, team briefings are central to employee participation, and actual decision making remains the prerogative of senior managers.

▶

Questions

1. In relation to the framework for analysing employee participation described earlier in the chapter, where would you locate Compucom in terms of the 'depth' and 'scope' of its participation practices?
2. Do you think the use of a non-union consultative council helps Compucom management remain union-free? Why/why not?
3. Do you think the size of the company is an important factor in the nature of employee participation practised at Compucom?
4. Why is it difficult to establish a relationship between employee voice and organisational performance?

CASE STUDY 17.2

Assessing participation

Tony Dundon

Debating the case for and against participation

In this chapter we reviewed the changing policy context for employee participation, in particular the ongoing tension between management choices for employee participation and recent regulations for consultation rights, such as the 2004 ICE regulations. Your task is to prepare an argument 'for' the legislation on employee information and consultation. You will be required to explain your argument in a class debate with co-students, who will speak 'against' your position.

Advising on employee participation

Imagine you are a management consultant. Your services have recently been retained by a large multinational company employing 7,000 people overall (2,800 in the UK; 3,200 in Germany; and 1,000 in Italy) to provide a report on the implications of the Information and Consultation of Employees (ICE) Regulations 2004. The company already has a European works council (EWC) and a union recognition agreement with AMICUS, the T&G and CWU. Union membership is currently 60 per cent for the UK site and a single table exists for collective negotiations. In particular, management would like:

(a) a brief explanation of what the ICE regulations mean;
(b) a timeframe for when the regulations are likely to affect the company;
(c) your considered opinion of any specific implications particular to this company.

Explain and justify the information you include in the report.

Beverage Co.: employee participation in an SME

Tony Dundon, Irena Grugulis and Adrian Wilkinson

Introduction

Employee participation (EP) has retained a central role in HRM over the past two decades (Marchington *et al.* 2001; Marchington and Wilkinson 2005). It can be seen as a key component of best-practice HRM or high-commitment management (Pfeffer 1998). However, much of the research on employee participation has focused on 'large' or 'mainstream' organisations where a combination of techniques tend to coexist (Marchington *et al.* 2001). Here we report on EP in a small organisation. Because of the apparent absence of formalised relations within many SMEs, the role of EP may be qualitatively different from that in larger firms (Wilkinson *et al.* 1999). It can be less formal, given the nature of communication flows together with the flexibility that is often associated with a small social setting (Scott *et al.* 1989; Dundon and Wilkinson 2003). While such informality has been a longstanding feature in the following case study, the range of EP techniques introduced was limited and at times problematic. In particular, the managerial motives for EP were not always understood among employees and the objective of greater employee commitment and loyalty was unsuccessful. The use of employee participation techniques tended to work against rather than with the informal character of relations that had existed previously in the company.

The company

Beverage Co. manufactures intermediary products for the food and drink industry. It employs 150 workers between its head office in Manchester and a manufacturing site in Cheshire. There is union recognition for around 65 process operatives based at the manufacturing plant. Here, the nature of work is organised around distinct production cells. Each production cell comprises approximately 10 employees, all of whom work on different production lines which make food and drink flavourings, including vanilla, coke, soup and meat additives. A similar team structure exists at the head office, with clerical workers engaged in administration, sales and marketing. There is no union recognition for these employees and, despite several requests from the GMB union, management has decided to keep this side of the business non-unionised.

In the late 1990s Beverage Co. experienced a period of commercial uncertainty. It faced increasing UK competition for food and drinks flavourings, lost a few export contracts and, in 1997, made 10 workers redundant. This was the first time that Beverage Co. had ever experienced any form of job losses. The company had been owned by members of the same family for more than a century and their management style was characterised by benevolent paternalism. However, with increased market competition, declining profits and redundancy, the company's owners decided to distance Beverage Co. from its informal industrial relations history. In its place they introduced a more strategic form of human resource management, much of which included several employee participation schemes.

EP techniques and management style at Beverage Co.

This new HR strategy had a profound impact on organisational culture and management style. In the past family owners were highly paternalist and the industrial relations procedures were informal. Indeed, the previous chairman and managing director, descendants of the founding owner, were known for stopping production quite regularly and asking

▶

Table 17.3 EP techniques introduced at Beverage Co.

EP category	EP technique introduced
Downward communication	Staff newsletter
	Notice boards
	Electronic message boards (manual staff only)
	E-mail communications (clerical staff only)
	Site-wide meetings by MD
	Team/cell briefings by team leaders
	Personnel management surgeries
	Individual performance reviews/appraisals
Upward problem-solving	Staff suggestion scheme
	Staff attitude surveys
Task participation	None
Financial involvement	Merit pay
Representative participation	Company joint consultative committee

manual employees to help repair the family Bentley, Jaguar and collection of classic sports cars. This all changed when non-family members were appointed to senior management and board-level positions. A personnel department was established with the aim of formalising HR policies and practices across the two sites. Key performance targets for profits, quality and customer satisfaction were linked to staff appraisals. Merit pay was introduced and based on individual outputs, monitored and assessed by team leaders. In describing this approach, the new MD regarded the strategy as 'a route to building a world class organisation'. The range of EP techniques that helped support this objective are summarised in Table 17.3.

'Downward communication' was the most extensive of all forms of EP at Beverage Co. These included a quarterly staff newsletter, monthly team briefings, formal presentations by the MD to the whole workforce (held twice a year in the staff canteen), e-mail communications and electronic message boards informing employees about new products, quality initiatives and conveying financial information. The company-wide presentations by the MD explained company objectives, profit details and more general developments to staff, such as the company's Investors in People (IiP) accreditation.

However, the introduction of these communication techniques was met with suspicion among some employees. Team leaders who held monthly briefings were regarded as 'supervisors on the cheap' by many staff. In effect, team leaders were the same grade as other workers but were also required to carry out briefing sessions without extra pay. The personnel manager compiled the information and team leaders then cascaded this down to shop-floor level. In addition, the site-wide meetings introduced by the new MD were also questioned. Several workers suggested that the information presented was often partial, with management controlling the agenda. One middle manager explained:

There's a reluctance to show the whole picture. We have canteen meetings but they're controlled, the information is very selective. That's a general feeling; that not all the info is given out.

Across the manufacturing plant, electronic notice boards would regularly 'flash' with messages from the personnel department. Typical examples included the latest figures for customer complaints, current absenteeism rates or the volume of products made hour by hour and compared against the expected target. As one process operator commented during his lunch in the canteen:

There's no getting away from them [i.e. management messages] here.

▶

Other EP mechanisms included a 'weekly surgery' held by the personnel manager. The aim was to allow employees to discuss issues of concern in private without appointment. In addition, a staff suggestion scheme was introduced to encourage workers to make improvements to product quality. A financial payment ranging from £10 to £1,000 was given for adopted suggestions. Individual staff appraisals were also introduced for supervisors and workers to discuss objectives for the coming months.

In practice, these EP techniques fell short of their intended objective, as few employees would attend such initiatives as the weekly surgery. According to the personnel manager, the time devoted to meeting staff in surgeries was often taken up discussing grievances with shop stewards. Several clerical employees were also critical of the staff suggestion scheme, especially the lack of any formal criteria for determining the amount of financial award. Further, employees at both sites commented that any 'discussion' about appraisal plans was a myth, as supervisors tended to 'inform' workers about new targets without any consultation. Overall, the range of EP at Beverage Co. can be seen to fit broadly those categories where management maintains greatest control, namely downward communication. Significantly, these 'newer' techniques tended to bureaucratise and formalise employee relations, as one production supervisor commented:

Too much communications in one sense – we've forgotten to use general conversation. They try and make things too formal, thinking it's a better way, which isn't always the case.

Indirect forms of EP were reduced at Beverage Co. in favour of the more direct techniques described above. Representative participation remained with the GMB union for manufacturing employees, although a former bi-monthly joint consultative committee (JCC) met on a quarterly basis, and its remit was restricted to heath and safety matters. Previously it had dealt with all employment terms and conditions. Similarly, collective bargaining became the responsibility of two local shop stewards, the MD and personnel manager. Previously a full-time regional official had negotiated pay with family-owners. The pay rise for non-union clerical employees was reviewed by the personnel manager, and usually set in accordance with the negotiated settlement for manual workers. In addition, merit pay accounted for up to 10 per cent of the gross salary for most staff, determined on the basis of targets set by supervisors.

Table 17.4 provides a summary of employee responses to a survey conducted at Beverage Co. by the authors. While workers confirmed that management pass on information (52 per cent) and encouraged staff to make suggestions (82 per cent), only 15 per cent of

Table 17.4 Employee responses (%) to EP at Beverage Co.

EP indicator	Agree	Not sure	Disagree
At Beverage Co. management regularly seek the views of employees	25	21	54
Employees are kept informed about changes at Beverage Co.	36	7	57
Management pass on information regularly	52	12	36
Management involve employees in decisions at Beverage Co.	9	10	81
Management encourage staff to make suggestions	82	13	5
Management at Beverage Co. act on staff suggestions	15	25	60

N = 67

▶

respondents said that management acted on such suggestions. Overall there were few positive responses to the range of EP techniques introduced. One-quarter of employees suggested that management sought their views while over 80 per cent disagreed with the statement that management involved them in decisions.

Workplace sabotage at Beverage Co.

Shortly after these EP techniques were introduced, a series of sabotage attacks were carried out at the manufacturing plant. The production unit in question manufactured food flavourings for a contract in the Far East. The company eventually lost the contract because of the sabotage incidents, which took a variety of forms. Flavouring products were labelled incorrectly, such that beef stocks were marked as vegetable soup ingredients and garlic batches packaged as cola additives. Other acts included racial and sexual graffiti written inside cartons. The commercial impact of these events was highly significant. Beverage Co. flavourings form essential ingredients for food and drinks made by other organisations. Not only did this sabotage damage Beverage Co.'s reputation, it also, owing to the intermediary character of the products, resulted in lost production of thousands of tonnes of food and drinks products. When incorrectly labelled food flavourings were used to produce final goods manufactured by Beverage Co.'s customers, these subsequently had to be destroyed.

Management were anxious to attribute these problems to the youth and immaturity of workers employed on the particular production line. One supervisor attributed the sabotage to the use of agency staff brought in to help meet sudden demand. For the shop steward, however, the sabotage was a form of resistance to increased supervisory pressures and poor working conditions. The nature of work was explained as dirty, dusty and intense. Interestingly, the system of cell working meant that management failed to identify the culprits. It was common for employees to work on several flavouring production lines simultaneously and switch to packaging duties during the same shift. As a result, management could not identify the employees who had been working on specific duties at the time of the sabotage.

Questions

1. What are the likely benefits for workers of employee participation as practised at Beverage Co.? Are these likely to differ in each of the union and non-union parts of the company? Why/why not?
2. The family owners of Beverage Co. have asked you to produce a report (or a short presentation) on the efficacy of EP in the company. Using the information in the case study, identify the main barriers to EP, and make recommendations to help the new management team gain the commitment of staff to these (or other) techniques.
3. What influence has the small firm context had on EP at Beverage Co.?
4. Should trade unions be worried about the introduction of EP techniques? Why/why not?
5. To what extent has the change in management style and HR strategy exacerbated the tensions and contradictions in the employment relationship at Beverage Co.?

▶

Bibliography

Ackers, P., Marchington, M., Wilkinson, A. and Goodman, J. (1992) 'The use of cycles? Explaining employee involvement in the 1990s', *Industrial Relations Journal,* Vol.23, No.4, pp.268–83.

*Ackers, P., Marchington, M., Wilkinson, A. and Dundon, T. (2005) 'Partnership and voice, with or without trade unions: changing UK management approaches to organisational participation', in M. Stuart and M. Martinez Lucio (eds) *Partnership and Modernisation in Employment Relations,* London: Routledge.

Barker, J. (1993) 'Tightening the iron cage: concertive control in self-managing teams', *Administrative Science Quarterly,* Vol.38, pp.408–37.

Beardwell, I. (1994) 'Managerial issues and the non-union firm', Paper presented to the Centre for Economic Performance Workshop, London School of Economics, April.

Becker, B.E. and Huselid, M.A. (1998) 'High performance work systems and firm performance synthesis of research and managerial implications', in G.R. Ferris (ed.) *Research in Personnel and Human Resources,* Vol.16, Stamford, CT: JAI Press.

Benson, J. (2000) 'Employee voice in union and non-union Australian workplaces', *British Journal of Industrial Relations.* Vol.38, No.3, pp.453–9.

Boxall, P. and Purcell, J. (2003) *Strategy and Human Resource Management,* London: Palgrave.

Brannen, P. (1983) *Authority and Participation in Industry,* London: Batsford.

Brewster, C., Croucher, R., Wood, G. and Brookes, M. (2007) 'Collective and individual voice: convergence in Europe?', *International Journal of Human Resource Management,* Vol.18, No.7, pp.1246–62.

Bryson, A., Willman, P., Gomez, R. and Kretchmer, T. (2007), 'Employee voice and human resource management: an empirical analysis using British data', *PSI Research Discussion Paper No 27,* Policy Studies Institute, London.

Bullock, A. (Lord) (1977) *Report of the Committee of Inquiry on Industrial Democracy,* London: HMSO (Cmnd. 6706).

Claydon, T. and Doyle, M. (1996) 'Trusting me, trusting you? The ethics of employee empowerment', *Personnel Review,* Vol.25, No.6, pp.13–25.

Collard, R. and Dale, B. (1989) 'Quality circles', in K. Sisson (ed.) *Personnel Management in Britain* (1st edn), Oxford: Blackwell.

Cox, A., Zagelmeyer, S. and Marchington, M. (2006) 'Embedding employee involvement and participation at work', *Human Resource Management Journal,* Vol.16, No.3, pp.250–67.

Cressey, P., Eldridge, J. and MacInnes, J. (1985) *Just Managing: Authority and Democracy in Industry,* Milton Keynes: Open University Press.

Cully M., O'Reilly A., Woodland, S. and Dix, G. (1999) *Britain at Work: As Depicted by the 1998 Workplace Employee Relations Survey,* London: Routledge.

Delbridge, R., Turnbull, P. and Wilkinson, B. (1992) 'Pushing back the frontiers: management control and work intensification under JIT/TQM factory regimes', *New Technology, Work and Employment,* Vol.7, No.2, pp.97–106.

Diamond, W. and Freeman, R. (2001) *What Workers Want from Workplace Organisations: Report to the TUC's Promoting Unionism Task Group,* London: Trades Union Congress.

*DTI (2005) *The Information and Consultation of Employees Regulations 2004: DTI Guidance,* January 2005, London: Department of Trade Industry, available at www.dti.gov.uk/er/consultation/ircrregsrguidance.pdf

Dundon, T. and Rollinson, D. (2004) *Employment Relations in Non-Union Firms,* London: Routledge.

Dundon, T. and Wilkinson, A. (2003) 'Employment relations in smaller firms', in B. Towers, *Handbook of Employment Relations, Law and Practice* (4th edn), London: Kogan Page.

*Dundon, T., Wilkinson, A., Marchington, M. and Ackers, P. (2004) 'The meanings and purpose of employee voice', *International Journal of Human Resource Management,* Vol.15, No.6, pp.1150–71.

*Dundon, T., Curran, D., Maloney, M. and Ryan, P. (2006) 'Conceptualising the dynamics of employee voice: evidence from the Republic of Ireland', *Industrial Relations Journal,* Vol.37, No.5, pp.492–512.

Ewing, K. (2003) 'Industrial relations and law', in P. Ackers and A. Wilkinson (eds) *Understanding Work and Employment: Industrial Relations in Transition*, Oxford: Oxford University Press.

*Geary, J. (2003) 'New Forms of work organizations: still limited, still controlled, but still welcome?', in P. Edwards (ed.) *Industrial Relations: Theory and Practice in Britain* (2nd edn), Oxford: Blackwell.

Geary, J. and Dobbins, A. (2001) 'Teamworking: a new dynamic in the pursuit of management control', *Human Resource Management Journal*, Vol.11, No.1, pp.3–23.

Gollan, P. (2002), 'So what's the news? Management strategies towards non-union employee representation at New International', *Industrial Relations Journal*, Vol.33, No.4, pp.316–31.

*Gollan, P. and Wilkinson, A. (2007), 'Implications of the EU Information and Consultation Directive and the Regulations in the UK – prospects for the future of employee representation', *International Journal of Human Resource Management*, Vol.18, No.7, pp.1145–58.

Goodman, J., Earnshaw, J., Marchington, M. and Harrison, R. (1998) 'Unfair dismissal cases, disciplinary procedures, recruitment methods and management style', *Employee Relations*, Vol.20, No.6, pp.536–50.

Hall, M. and Terry, M. (2004) 'The emerging system of statutory worker representation', in G. Healy, E. Heery, P. Taylor and W. Brown (eds), *The Future of Worker Representation*, Basingstoke: Palgrave Macmillan.

Heller, F., Pusic, E., Strauss, G. and Wilpert, B. (1998) *Organisational Participation: Myth and Reality*, Oxford: Oxford University Press.

Huselid, M. (1995), 'The impact of human resource management practices on turnover, production and corporate financial performance', *Academy of Management Journal*, Vol.38, No.3, pp.635–72.

Hyman, J. and Mason, B. (1995) *Managing Employee Involvement and Participation*, London: Sage.

Kersley, B., Alpin, C., Forth, J., Bryson, A., Bewley, H., Dix, J. and Oxenbridge, S. (2006) *Inside the Workplace: Findings from the 2004 Workplace Employment Relations Survey*, London: Routledge.

Lewis, P., Thornhill, A. and Saunders, M. (2003) *Employee Relations: Understanding the Employment Relationship*, London: Prentice Hall.

Marchington, M. (2005) 'Employee involvement: patterns and explanations', in B. Harley, J. Hyman and P. Thompson (eds) *Participation and Democracy at Work: Essays in Honour of Harvie Ramsay*, London: Palgrave.

Marchington, M. and Parker, P. (1990) *Changing Patterns of Employee Relations*, Hemel Hempstead: Harvester Wheatsheaf.

*Marchington, M. and Wilkinson, A. (2005) 'Direct participation', in S. Bach (ed.) *Personnel Management: A Comprehensive Guide to Theory and Practice* (4th edn), Oxford: Blackwell.

Marchington, M., Goodman, J. Wilkinson, A. and Ackers, P. (1992) *New Developments in Employee Involvement*, Research Paper No.2, London: Employment Department.

Marchington, M., Wilkinson, A., Ackers, P. and Dundon, T. (2001) *Management Choice and Employee Voice*, London: Chartered Institute of Personnel and Development.

Millward, N., Stevens, M., Smart, D. and Hawes, W (1992) *Workplace Industrial Relations in Transition*, Aldershot: Dartmouth.

Millward, N., Bryson, A. and Forth, J. (2000) *All Change at Work: British Employment Relations 1980–1998 as Portrayed by the Workplace Industrial Relations Survey Series*, London: Routledge.

Pateman, C. (1970) *Participation and Democratic Theory*, Cambridge: Cambridge University Press.

Patterson, M., West, M., Lawthorn, R. and Nickell, S. (1997) *Impact of People Management Practices on Business Performance*, London: Institute of Personnel and Development, Report No.22.

Pfeffer, J. (1998) *The Human Equation: Building Profits by Putting People First*, Boston, MA: Harvard Business School Press.

Piore, M. and Sabel, C. (1983) *The Second Industrial Divide*, New York: Basic Books.

Proctor, S. and Ackroyd, S. (2001) 'Flexibility', in T. Redman and A. Wilkinson (eds) *Contemporary Human Resource Management: Text and Cases*, London: Prentice Hall.

Proctor, S. and Mueller, F. (eds) (2000) *Teamworking*, London: Macmillan.

Roeber, J. (1975) *Social Change at Work*, London: Heinemann.

Rollinson, D and Dundon, T. (2007), *Understanding Employment Relations*, London: McGraw Hill.

Schuler, R., and Jackson, S. (1987) 'Linking competitive strategies with human resource management', *Academy of Management Executives,* Vol.1, No.3, pp.206–19.

Scott, M., Roberts, I., Holroyd, G. and Sawbridge, D. (1989) *Management and Industrial Relations in Small Firms,* Research Paper No.70, London: Department of Employment.

Sewell, G. and Wilkinson, B. (1992) 'Empowerment or emasculation? Shopfloor surveillance in a total quality organisation', in P. Blyton and P. Turnbull (eds) *Reassessing Human Resource Management,* London: Sage.

Sinclair, A. (1992) 'The tyranny of a team ideology', *Organization Studies,* Vol.13, No.4, pp.11–26.

Tebbutt, M. and Marchington, M. (1997) 'Look before you speak: gossip and the insecure workplace', *Work Employment and Society,* Vol.11, No.4, pp.713–35.

Trist, E., Higgin, G., Murray, H. and Pollock, A. (1963) *Organisational Choice: Capabilities of Groups at the Coalface Under Changing Technologies,* London: Tavistock Institute.

Wedderburn, K.W. (Lord) (1986) *The Worker and the Law* (3rd edn), Harmondsworth: Penguin.

Wilkinson, A. (1998) 'Empowerment: a review and a critique', *Personnel Review,* Vol.27, No.1, pp.40–56.

*Wilkinson, A. (2002) 'Empowerment', in M. Poole and M. Warner (eds) *International Encyclopaedia of Business and Management Handbook of Human Resource Management,* London: ITB Press.

Wilkinson, A. (2008) 'Empowerment,' in S. Clegg and J. Bailey (eds) *Encyclopaedia of Organizational Studies,* London: Sage.

Wilkinson, A., Marchington, M., Goodman, J. and Ackers, P. (1992) 'Total quality management and employee involvement', *Human Resource Management Journal,* Vol.2, No.4, pp.1–20.

Wilkinson, A., Redman, T., Snape, E. and Marchington, M. (1998) *Managing With TQM: Theory and Practice,* London: Macmillan.

Wilkinson, A., Dundon, T., Marchington, M. and Ackers, P. (2004) 'Changing patterns of employee voice', *Journal of Industrial Relations,* Vol.46, No.3, pp.298–322.

Wilkinson, A., Dundon T. and Grugulis, I. (2007), 'Information but not consultation: exploring employee involvement in SMEs', *International Journal of Human Resource Management,* Vol.18, No.7, pp.1279–97.

Willman, P., Bryson, A. and Gomez, R. (2003) 'Why do voice regimes differ?', Paper presented at International Industrial Relations Association (IIRA) 13th World Congress, Berlin, 8–12 September.

Wood, S. and De Menezes, L. (1998) 'High commitment management in the UK: evidence from the Workplace Industrial Relations Survey and Employers' Manpower Skills Survey', *Human Relations,* Vol.51, No.4, pp.485–515.

Chapter 18

KNOWLEDGE MANAGEMENT AND HUMAN RESOURCE MANAGEMENT

Donald Hislop

Introduction

The subject of knowledge management is relatively new, with interest in it initially starting in the mid-1990s. Despite the enormous amount of writing on the topic, there is still an enormous amount of debate on many key issues. Thus, there are still debates on topics such as whether knowledge can be codified, the extent to which knowledge can be managed, whether we live in a knowledge society and what the best methods of persuading workers to share their knowledge with each other are. One of the areas where understanding is still developing is in the linkages between knowledge management and the broad topic of human resource management. While the early knowledge management literature typically tended to ignore people-related issues (Hislop 2005), this is no longer the case, and a reasonable amount of writing now exists on the socio-cultural factors which shape workers' attitudes to knowledge management initiatives and how HRM practices can be utilised to encourage workers to share their knowledge and participate in knowledge management initiatives.

The objective of this chapter is to illustrate why HRM issues are of central importance to the topic of knowledge management, and to give an overview of the way that the topics have been linked thus far in the literature. In doing so, the chapter will give a flavour of the many active debates and disagreements which still exist. Before proceeding any further, however, it is necessary to define the term 'knowledge management'. At one level this is a simple task. Putting to the side the difficulties of defining such ambiguous terms as 'knowledge' and 'management' (Alvesson and Karreman 2001), knowledge management can be defined as the attempt by an organisation to explicitly manage and control the knowledge of its workforce. However, the issue becomes more complex when it is recognised that there are a myriad number of ways by which such a task can be attempted. This can be illustrated by the number of typologies of knowledge management strategies that have been developed. One of the simplest and most widely known is Hansen *et al.*'s (1999) distinction between personalisation and codification strategies, with a personalisation strategy focused on sharing knowledge between people, linked to a business strategy of knowledge creation. On the other hand, a codification strategy is focused on the codification of knowledge, linked to a business strategy of knowledge reuse. Hunter *et al.* (2002) and Alvesson and Karreman (2001) develop more complicated typologies, both of which produce four general knowledge management strategies. Of central significance to this chapter is that, as will be discussed in more detail later, the HRM implications of these different knowledge management strategies are quite distinctive.

The chapter begins by briefly examining the broad social context within which the growth of interest in knowledge management has occurred. Following this, subsequent sections consider how knowledge work is defined, why human motivation is key to making knowledge management initiatives successful, what general factors affect the willingness of workers to participate in knowledge management initiatives, and what specific HRM practices can be used to help persuade workers to participate in such initiatives.

Social context: the growing importance of knowledge

The growth of interest in knowledge management that occurred in the mid-1990s can be explained to some extent by the growing significance of knowledge in contemporary economies. This has led many, both within and without the knowledge management literature, to claim that we now live in a knowledge society (see for example Nonaka (1994), one of the 'gurus' of knowledge management). Thus, Littler and Innes (2003) suggest that the 'knowledge capitalism thesis' was one of the two dominant academic discourses during the 1990s and Tam *et al.* (2002) argue that such a belief has become 'conventional wisdom'. Bell's (1973) vision of a post-industrial service society with a workforce dominated by highly skilled knowledge workers thus, either explicitly or implicitly, casts a shadow over much of this writing.

Empirical evidence to some extent backs up this claim; however, as will be seen later, this is one area of debate. The growing importance of knowledge to contemporary economies and organisations can be illustrated in a number of ways. Firstly, since the 1950s there has been a growth in the proportion of knowledge workers in many economies. Reich (1991) showed that in the USA, between the 1950s and the 1990s, 'symbolic analysts' (his term for what contemporary writers call knowledge workers) grew from 8 to 20 per cent of the workforce. Contemporary evidence from other economies also supports this (Frenkel *et al.* 1999). Other claims that the knowledge intensity of all work has increased (see for example Harrison and Leitch 2000; Neef 1999) are supported by large-scale survey evidence which shows a general trajectory of upskilling to be evident (Gallie *et al.* 1998; Felstead *et al.* 2002).

Critics, however, suggest that such claims and evidence provide only a partial and distorted view of the changes in the nature of work, neglecting the extent to which there has been a simultaneous growth in low-skilled, routine service work, such as in call centres (Littler and Innes 2003; Mansell and Steinmueller 2000; Thompson *et al.* 2001). These writers suggest that it is more accurate to talk of a bi-modal trajectory in the contemporary evolution of work, with there being a simultaneous growth in highly skilled knowledge work and low-skilled, routine service work. Thus, even if a sceptical perspective to the 'knowledge society' rhetoric is taken, it is undeniable that, to some extent, there has been a growth in the importance of knowledge in contemporary economies.

Arguably, the enormous numbers of organisations which have been attempting to develop and implement knowledge management initiatives are inspired by the idea that their competitiveness and innovativeness are derived from and sustained by the way they manage, facilitate and control their knowledge base, and that neglecting to do so is likely to have some negative consequences for organisational performance.

Defining knowledge work

An enormous amount has been written on knowledge workers, and their growing importance is tied closely to the knowledge society perspective just discussed. Specifically, it is argued that for those societies that are evolving into knowledge societies, the number and importance of knowledge workers will increase significantly. Thus, as outlined, one of the key indicators used to establish whether a society can be characterised as being knowledge based is the proportion of knowledge workers employed in it. However, defining the types of work that can be considered to constitute knowledge work is by no means easy, to a large extent because there is an enormous debate on the question. This section therefore presents two contrasting definitions of the term.

The mainstream definition in the knowledge literature is that a knowledge worker is someone whose work is primarily intellectual in nature and which involves extensive and regular use of established bodies of formal, codified knowledge. From this perspective, knowledge workers represent an occupational elite: those workers who are in the vanguard of the knowledge economy, and whose work contributes significantly to the performance of their employers. Thus, as will be discussed later, they are typically regarded by their employers as workers who are worth retaining.

Based on such definitions, the range of occupations that are typically classified as knowledge work include:

■ lawyers (Hunter et al. 2002; Starbuck 1993);

■ consultants (Robertson and Swan 2003; Empson 2001; Morris 2001);

■ IT and software designers (Schulze 2000; Swart and Kinnie 2003; Horowitz *et al.* 2003);

■ advertising executives (Beaumont and Hunter 2002);

■ accountants (Morris and Empson 1998);

■ scientists and engineers (Beaumont and Hunter 2002; Benson and Brown 2007);

■ architects (Frenkel *et al.* 1995);

■ artists and art directors/producers (Beaumont and Hunter 2002).

Definitions of knowledge workers therefore overlap with, and include, the classical professions (such as lawyers, architects, etc.), but also extend beyond them to include a wide variety of other occupations (such as consultants, advertising executives, IT developers, etc.). Sometimes the term 'knowledge-intensive work' is used to refer to such occupations, owing to the extent to which they involve the creation and use of knowledge. However, the term 'knowledge intensive' has been criticised for being somewhat vague, making it open to interpretation as to which work constitutes knowledge-intensive work (Alvesson 2000).

However, embedded in such definitions of knowledge work is the privileging of certain forms of knowledge (abstract, theoretical, scientific knowledge) over other types of knowledge (tacit, contextual knowledge). Critics of the mainstream definition of knowledge workers, which ring-fences the term to refer to an elite range of occupations, argue that such definitions downplay, if not ignore, the extent to which all forms of work involve the application and use of knowledge to some extent (Allee 1997; Grant 2000; Thompson *et al.* 2001). Thus a second perspective on the definition of knowledge work is that in many ways all work can be defined as knowledge work.

Hislop (2008) outlines such a perspective through reconceptualising Frenkel *et al.*'s (1995) framework on knowledge work. Frenkel *et al.*'s (1995) framework provides a way of conceptualising all forms of work through taking account of three dimensions: knowledge, skills and level of creativity. The knowledge dimension takes account of the predominant form of knowledge used in work, with knowledge being characterised as being either theoretical or contextual, with theoretical knowledge representing codified concepts and principles, which have general relevance, whereas by contrast contextual knowledge is largely tacit and non-generalisible, being related to specific contexts of application. The skill dimension takes account of three types of skill: intellective, social and action based. Action-based skills relate to physical dexterity, social skills to the ability to motivate and manage others, while intellective skills are defined as the ability to undertake abstract reasoning and synthesise different ideas. Finally, the dimension of creativity (which is defined as a process of 'original problem solving', from which an original output is produced, Frenkel *et al.* 1995, p.779) considers the level of creativity in work as varying on a sliding scale from low to high.

Using these dimensions, Frenkel *et al.* (1995) define a knowledge worker as anyone who firstly has a high level of creativity in their work, secondly, makes extensive use of intellective skills, and finally, also makes use of theoretical rather than contextual knowledge. Thus conceptualised, this framework is compatible with the mainstream, elitist professional knowledge work perspective. However, Hislop (2008) suggests that because it takes account of both contextual and theoretical knowledge, as well as the skill involved in work, it can easily be reconceptualised to fit with the 'all work is knowledge work' perspective through defining knowledge work as any form of work involving the use of a reasonable amount of theoretical or contextual knowledge. This framework is illustrated at the end of the chapter in Case Study 18.2 through applying it to understand the character of two occupations, one of which fits the mainstream, elitist definition of knowledge work (management consultants) and one of which does not (office equipment service engineers).

Why worker motivation is key to achieving participation in knowledge management initiatives

As the knowledge management literature has evolved and developed there has been a growing awareness that socio-cultural factors are key to such initiatives. For example, survey evidence consistently reveals this:

■ KPMG (2003) conducted a survey of over 500 organisations in the UK, Germany, France and the Netherlands and found that some of the main implementation difficulties with knowledge management initiatives related to socio-cultural factors such as the lack of a knowledge-sharing culture, or workers not adequately prioritising knowledge management work.

■ Edwards *et al.* (2003), in a survey of 25 academics and knowledge management practitioners, identified 'people' and 'cultural' issues as the two key issues to be emphasised for knowledge management initiatives to be successful.

A plethora of case study evidence also reinforces this conclusion, with evidence of knowledge hoarding due to social factors not being uncommon (see Box 18.1, plus Hayes and Walsham 2000; Lam 2005; Newell *et al.* 2000).

Box 18.1: HRM in practice

Functional conflict and knowledge hoarding

UK-Pharm, a large, specialised UK-based pharmaceutical company with sites and business units spread throughout the UK, Europe and the USA, attempted to introduce a change programme in the late 1990s to encourage cross-functional knowledge sharing, as this was perceived as being a way to improve the effectiveness of its R&D efforts. However, the success of the project was inhibited by a general lack of willingness among staff from different functions to share knowledge with each other. A significant proportion of staff was unwilling to participate in the project to some extent because there had been a historical culture of inter-functional rivalry, which tended to make staff unwilling to cooperate with staff from outside their functional group, and also because many senior managers in certain functional areas felt that the change programme would reduce their level of autonomy and lead to greater levels of standardisation.

Source: Hislop 2003

Part of the explanation for why workers cannot be assumed to be automatically willing to participate in knowledge management initiatives is due to structural factors which transcend individual organisations, including the power and status that workers can typically derive from possessing specialist knowledge, the nature of the employment relationship, and the potential for interpersonal/group conflict that exists in all organisations. Firstly, not only is much organisational knowledge tacit and personal in character, being acquired and built up by workers over time, but the possession of knowledge can also be a significant source of power and status in organisations (Hislop 2005; Horowitz *et al.* 2003; Lam 2005). This fact alone means that workers may be unwilling to participate in organisational knowledge management initiatives if they feel this involves 'giving away' a source of their power and/or status (Martin 2006; Oltra 2005).

Another structural factor affecting the willingness of workers to participate in knowledge management initiatives is the nature of the employment relationship, which results in the interests of workers and management not always being totally compatible. Thus, in relation to knowledge workers, there is potential conflict between workers and their employers over both who owns the knowledge of the worker and how it is used (Scarbrough 1999). For example, Ciborra and Patriotta (1998) provide a clear example of such a conflict. Their research examined knowledge sharing among R&D staff in Unilever, via electronic discussion forums. When a very senior manager made a contribution to one particular forum, there was a 'panic reaction' (p.50) among the R&D staff using the forum, which contributed to staff not using the system for some months. This reaction was due to a sense of unease by the R&D staff that their privacy was being invaded by management, which made them reluctant to express opinions which did not comply with managerial perspectives.

The potential for conflict in organisations also emanates from another structural factor: the real (and/or perceived) differences of interests between different workers and groups within

Box 18.2: HRM in practice

An unwillingness to share knowledge in a post-merger environment: fear of exploitation and contamination

Empson (2001) conducted detailed studies into three separate mergers undertaken by two UK accounting firms, and two pairs of UK-based management consultants. Empson found that in the immediate post-merger period, in all three cases, staff were largely unwilling to share their knowledge with staff employed by the other partner to the merger. This unwillingness stemmed from the twin fears among workers of contamination and exploitation. The fear of exploitation stemmed from concerns related to perceptions that, owing to the knowledge possessed by the staff of their merger partners being of less value than their own, they would 'lose out' in any knowledge-sharing process. However, these fears were not based on any objective assessment of the value of the knowledge of those from the other organisation, and were more related to subjective, individual assessments. This is linked to the second fear, of contamination. As most staff in the mergers perceived the knowledge of staff from the organisation they were merging with to be of less value than their own, they were concerned not only that they would lose out in knowledge-sharing processes, but that their knowledge would also be contaminated and somehow devalued in the process. Thus, in all three cases, the integration of the knowledge bases of the merging partners was inhibited by the concerns staff had regarding the outcome of such processes, which itself stemmed from perceived differences of interest between staff.

organisations that inevitably exist (Marshall and Brady 2001). In relation to knowledge management initiatives, the fact that, as discussed above, power and knowledge are closely interrelated means that knowledge management initiatives can be used to play out what Storey and Barnett (2000) refer to as 'micro-political battles'. Thus, the attitudes towards, and participation (or not) by workers in, organisational knowledge management initiatives are shaped by the way such behaviours affect, and link into, the political battles that are a part of the fabric of organisations. For example, Storey and Barnett (2000) found that inter-functional battles to control a knowledge management initiative were key to the eventual failure of the project they studied.

This section therefore shows how the participation of workers in organisational knowledge management initiatives cannot be taken for granted. The following two sections look at more specific factors within organisations which affect the attitudes of workers to knowledge management initiatives, and consider what HRM policies can be utilised to encourage the participation of workers in such initiatives.

The organisational climate and workers' attitudes to knowledge management initiatives

This section continues with the themes discussed in the previous section: why human motivation is key to the success of knowledge management initiatives, and why the participation of workers in knowledge management initiatives cannot be guaranteed. However, the focus here shifts from structural factors, which are to some extent beyond the control of organisational management, to factors affecting the general climate within organisations that are within the control of management. As outlined earlier, a lot of survey and case study evidence has shown socio-cultural factors to be key in shaping the attitudes of workers to knowledge management initiatives. This section provides an abbreviated summary of this literature. While this literature identifies an enormous diversity of factors that influence workers' attitudes, these factors can be grouped into three general categories (see Table 18.1).

The overall, somewhat general conclusion from this evidence is that workers are most likely to be willing to participate in organisational knowledge management initiatives when the general organisational climate/culture is fair and positive, for example where people feel their efforts are fairly rewarded and interpersonal relations between workers, and also between workers and managers, are based on trust. The following section looks at the type of HRM practices which can be used to create such a climate, and which are thus likely to help facilitate organisational knowledge management initiatives.

HRM practices to support knowledge management initiatives

Before considering the way HRM practices can be used to help motivate workers to participate in organisational knowledge management initiatives, it is necessary to take account of the diversity of ways that organisations can manage their knowledge. As discussed earlier, a number of writers have developed typologies to categorise the range of knowledge management strategies that exist (Alvesson and Karreman 2001; Hansen *et al.* 1999; Hunter *et al.* 2002). Each particular approach to knowledge management requires different behaviours from workers. Thus, using Hansen *et al.*'s (1999) framework, a codification-based strategy requires workers to focus their knowledge management activities around the use of IT systems, where they should codify their own knowledge and use IT-based knowledge repositories (such as searchable databases) to search for any knowledge they do not possess. On the other hand, a personalisation strategy requires workers to be willing to share their tacit knowledge directly with other people. Therefore, as each knowledge management strategy requires different behaviours, their HRM implications are distinctive.

Table 18.1 Research data on organisational factors affecting the attitudes of workers to organisational knowledge management initiatives

Factor affecting workers' attitudes towards participation in knowledge processes	Supporting evidence/analysis	Conclusions/findings
The existence of interpersonal trust and good working relations among co-workers	Andrews and Delahaye 2000	Case study of knowledge sharing among scientists which showed trust to be necessary for knowledge sharing to occur.
	Storey and Barnett 2000	Case study of a single failed knowledge management project, with inter-group conflict being key to project's failure.
	Lam 2005	Case study of a failed knowledge management initiative in an Indian IT consultancy company which showed that workers were unwilling to codify and share knowledge owing to the competitive, individualistic culture which existed.
	Newell *et al.* 2000	Longitudinal case study of how inter-group conflict inhibited processes of knowledge sharing.
	Cabrera *et al.* 2006	Survey of a Spanish IT company which found that perceptions of support from colleagues was one of three key factors positively influencing workers' attitudes to knowledge sharing.
	De Long and Fahey 2000	Knowledge sharing between sub-cultures inhibited by differences in values, norms etc.
The existence of trust and good interpersonal relations between workers and their managers	MacNeil 2003	Suggests that the role of line managers in facilitating team/group-based knowledge sharing is key.
	Willman *et al.* 2001	Concerns that workers may be giving away key knowledge.
	Renzl 2008	Survey of two companies which found that levels of trust in management were positively related to workers' attitudes to knowledge sharing.

▶

Table 18.1   Continued

Factor affecting workers' attitudes towards participation in knowledge processes	Supporting evidence/analysis	Conclusions/findings
	Hayes and Walsham 2000	Concern by workers about expressing attitudes not deemed compatible with managerial perspectives in forums visible to management.
	Ribiere and Sitar 2003	The role of leaders key to success in developing appropriate knowledge cultures: leading by example, etc.
	Pan and Scarbrough 1999	The role of leaders key to success in developing appropriate knowledge cultures: leading by example, etc.
Proper recognition and reward for work efforts and use of individual knowledge	Cabrera and Cabrera 2005	Analysis suggests that one key way to develop a positive attitude to knowledge sharing is through developing a culture which regards knowledge sharing as a norm.
	Robertson and Swan 2003	Case study of a single consultancy showing how reward and recognition contribute to willingness by workers to participate in knowledge management initiatives.
	McDermott and O'Dell 2001	Knowledge management initiatives should be compatible with existing organisational culture.
	Hansen *et al.* 1999	Reward and recognition systems used must be compatible with, and reinforce, particular business strategy being pursued.
	Kim and Mauborgne 1998	Workers only likely to share their knowledge with others if they deem sense of 'procedural justice' to exist in decision-making processes.

The diversity of knowledge management strategies that exist means that it is impossible to develop a 'one best way' checklist of ways that HRM practices can be used to allow an organisation to manage its knowledge effectively. Ultimately, the way HRM practices are used requires account to be taken of the particular approach to knowledge management adopted by particular organisations (Haesli and Boxall 2005).

SHOULD DISTINCTIVE HRM PRACTICES BE USED FOR KNOWLEDGE WORKERS?

Another topic requiring discussion is the debate on whether knowledge workers require to be managed in a different way from other types of worker, which to some extent flows from the different ways that knowledge work is conceptualised that were outlined earlier.

One of the key ideas developed in the mainstream perspective on knowledge workers, which regards knowledge workers as a professional, elite and distinctive element of the workforce, is that such workers have a number of features which distinguish them from other types of worker, and that consequently they require to be managed in a fundamentally different way from other workers (Alvesson 2000; Horowitz *et al.* 2003; Robertson and O'Malley Hammersley 2000). A number of factors are argued to contribute to the distinctiveness of knowledge workers. Firstly, they typically require to be very highly qualified, and also require to continually develop their knowledge. For example, in the consultancy examined by Robertson and Swan (2003), one of the recruitment criteria was that prospective employees held doctorates. Secondly, their knowledge and expertise are typically of greater importance to their employers than those possessed by other workers. For example, in a law firm such as that examined by Starbuck (1993), the knowledge possessed by the firm's lawyers represents arguably the key organisational asset.

Thirdly, their knowledge and skills are typically highly tacit and difficult, if not impossible, to codify. For example, one of the main reasons why the consultants researched by Morris (2001) were happy to participate in their organisation's attempts to codify their knowledge was that they were confident that such efforts could be only partially successful, and would allow them to retain key aspects of their accumulated expertise. A further example of important tacit knowledge that knowledge workers can possess, but that is impossible to codify, is social capital: the possession of good working and personal relations with particular individuals in client organisations (Fosstenlokken *et al.* 2003). Fourthly, in labour market terms their knowledge is relatively scarce and simultaneously highly valued, which thus typically provides knowledge workers with extensive opportunities to change job. Fifthly, as discussed by Alvesson (2000), distinctive norms and expectations may have developed among knowledge workers with regard to factors such as pay, levels of autonomy, opportunities for development etc. Finally, their work tasks, focused centrally as they are on processes of knowledge creation, utilisation and application, are highly specialised in nature.

However, the argument that knowledge workers require to be treated in separate and distinct ways from other workers is criticised by those adopting the 'all work is knowledge work' perspective. The critique suggests that a potential problem with the 'distinctiveness' argument is that such approaches neglect the fact that if all workers are knowledge workers, then the knowledge of all workers is important to organisational performance (Allee 1997; Beaumont and Hunter 2002; Garvey and Williamson 2002). Further, organisations that utilise such an approach and treat knowledge workers as special and distinctive risk the development of a sense of resentment among the workforce that do not receive these favourable conditions, and that as a consequence these workers will potentially be less willing to participate in organisational knowledge management initiatives. In the following section on the way HRM practices can facilitate participation in knowledge management initiatives, no distinction is made between knowledge workers and other workers.

HRM PRACTICES TO FACILITATE KNOWLEDGE MANAGEMENT

Recruitment and selection

One way in which HRM practices can be used to underpin knowledge management initiatives is through using recruitment and selection processes to try to ensure that new staff have appropriate attitudes to organisational knowledge processes. The literature suggests that there are two ways in which this can be done. Firstly, recruitment and selection processes can be used to find people whose values and attitudes fit those of an organisation's existing culture and norms. For example, both Swart and Kinnie (2003) and Robertson and Swan (2003), whose analyses are focused on successful knowledge-intensive firms, suggested that the ability of the organisations they examined to recruit people who fitted in with the existing values of knowledge sharing and collegiality was a key element of their success. Achieving an effective people–organisation fit is also likely to help new workers develop a good sense of identity with their colleagues and their employer, which can facilitate positive attitudes to knowledge sharing.

How personality relates to knowledge-sharing attitudes is a topic that is significantly under-researched. However, a couple of studies in this area have concluded that certain personality traits did appear to be positively related to knowledge-sharing attitudes. Thus, the second way in which recruitment and selection processes could be used to facilitate organisational knowledge management efforts is through using personality tests to identify people who are likely to have positive attitudes to knowledge sharing. While both the studies in this area (Cabrera and Cabrera 2005; Mooradian *et al.* 2006) use the five-factor personality model, they come to different conclusions about which personality traits are related to positive knowledge-sharing attitudes. Thus, Cabrera and Cabrera's (2005) research, which is based on a survey of a single Spanish organisation, found that the 'openness to change' personality variable was related to a positive knowledge-sharing attitude. By contrast, Mooradian *et al.*'s (2006) study, which was also based on a survey of a single organisation, found a link between 'agreeableness' and positive knowledge-sharing attitudes. Thus, research in this area is in its infancy and does not come to firm and conclusive conclusions regarding how personality is related to knowledge-sharing attitudes. Therefore, using personality tests to identify positive knowledge-sharing attitudes is something that needs to be done with caution.

Creating/sustaining appropriate cultures

One of the most common ways the literature suggests that HRM practices can be used to support knowledge management initiatives is through creating, developing and supporting an organisational culture that is conducive to knowledge sharing/use/development (Cabrera and Cabrera 2005; Robertson and O'Malley Hammersley 2000; De Long and Fahey 2000; Ribiere and Sitar 2003; Pan and Scarbrough 1999). The general features of such a culture are that knowledge sharing is regarded as a norm and that people's knowledge-sharing efforts will be well supported by colleagues, that staff have a strong sense of collective identity, that organisational processes are regarded as fair, and finally, that staff have high levels of trust in, and commitment to, management. However, one of the weaknesses of much of this literature is that it is relatively vague on exactly what organisations have to do to achieve such cultures.

Further, within this literature there are debates which mirror those in the broader culture management literature (Ogbonna and Harris 1998). Firstly, there is disagreement on the extent to which organisations can create and manage such cultures. Thus while the mainstream position in the knowledge management literature is that organisational cultures can be changed and controlled by management, others suggest that the resilience of an organisation's culture means that unless its knowledge management initiative is designed to be compatible with the existing culture it is likely to fail (McDermott and O'Dell 2001; Schulze and Boland 2000).

Secondly, there is a growing acknowledgement that organisations may not have coherent and unitary cultures, and that distinctive sub-cultures may exist which shape the characteristics and dynamics of organisational knowledge-sharing processes. For example, Currie and Kerrin's (2003) study of knowledge sharing within the sales and marketing business of a UK pharmaceutical company found that the existence of strong subcultures within the sales and marketing divisions inhibited the sharing of knowledge between staff in them. Alavi *et al.* (2005–6), who examined how issues of culture shaped knowledge management practices in an American-based global IT company, found that some of the standard knowledge management tools utilised by the company were used differently within different subcultures. Thus, this research suggests that the utilisation of culture management practices to facilitate organisational knowledge management efforts must take account of any organisational subcultures that exist.

Job design

In the area of job design, there is virtual unanimity in the knowledge management literature about the best way to structure jobs to facilitate appropriate knowledge-sharing attitudes. Fundamentally, work should be challenging and fulfilling, providing opportunities for workers both to utilise existing skills and knowledge, and also to be able to continuously develop their knowledge and skills (Robertson and O'Malley Hammersley 2000; Swart and Kinnie 2003). Thus in Horowitz *et al.*'s (2003) survey of Singaporean knowledge workers and their managers, providing challenging work was ranked as the most important factor by managers for helping to retain their knowledge workers.

Further, as well as having work that is intrinsically interesting, the available evidence suggests that knowledge workers also typically regard having high levels of autonomy at work as important. For example, in the scientific consultancy examined by Robertson and Swan (2003), autonomy was found to be important to the consultants, and extended to areas as diverse as the projects they worked on (the consultants were free to pick and choose, so long as they reached their annual revenue targets), the selection of the training and development activities they undertook (it was the responsibility of the consultants to identify their own development needs, and funding was available to support this), and work clothing and work patterns (a wide diversity of work patterns, personalities and clothing styles were apparent, and a culture of heterogeneity rather than conformity was developed and encouraged).

Finally, Cabrera and Cabrera (2005) suggest that if work is designed to allow the development of social capital between colleagues (networks of relations with people which can provide access to resources such as skills and knowledge – see Nahapiet and Ghoshal 1998), this can provide another way to facilitate interpersonal knowledge-sharing within organisations. Two ways they suggest this can be done are through promoting and utilising team-based working (particularly cross-functional, interdisciplinary teams) and through encouraging the development of communities of practice.

Training

The previous section outlined the positive role that providing opportunities for self-development in work can play in motivating workers to participate in organisational knowledge management processes. While this can be done through the way jobs are organised, it can also be achieved through providing adequate and appropriate opportunities to undertake formal training. Research evidence suggests that knowledge workers regard the provision of such opportunities by their employers to be a crucially important way to help both motivate and retain them (Hunter *et al.* 2002; Robertson and O'Malley Hammersley 2000). While the provision of such opportunities is a potentially double-edged sword for employers (as supporting such activities potentially makes it easier for staff to leave), without supporting continuous development staff may be likely to leave anyway.

Various writers have suggested a number of more specific ways that particular types of training can facilitate appropriate knowledge behaviours. Thus, Hansen *et al.* (1999) suggest that the type of training provided should reflect the particular approach to knowledge management an organisation adopts, for example with IT-based training being suitable for those pursuing a codification-based strategy, and training to develop interpersonal skills and team-working being appropriate for organisations pursuing a personalisation knowledge management strategy. Further, Cabrera *et al.* (2006), whose study of a Spanish company found that self-efficacy (a person's belief in and confidence about their ability to perform a particular task) was related to positive knowledge-sharing attitudes, suggest that investments in training focused on developing workers' self-efficacy levels may also benefit their knowledge management efforts.

Finally, Garvey and Williamson (2002) suggest that the most useful sort of training to support and encourage a culture of learning and knowledge development is not investing in 'narrow' skills-based training, but training with a broader purpose to encourage reflexivity, learning through experimentation, and how to conduct critical dialogues with others.

Reward and performance appraisal

There is general agreement in the knowledge management literature that rewarding people for appropriate knowledge-related behaviours and embedding knowledge-related attitudes and behaviours in performance appraisal processes represents a potentially important way to use HRM practices to underpin organisational knowledge management efforts (Cabrera and Cabrera 2005; Oltra 2005). Further, it is also agreed that such reward systems should reflect the particular knowledge management strategy adopted by an organisation and the type of knowledge processes associated with it. For example, Hansen *et al.* (1999) argue that if a codification strategy is pursued, the pay and reward systems should acknowledge employee efforts to codify their knowledge and search for the knowledge of others, while with a personalisation strategy, pay and reward systems should recognise the efforts of workers to share their tacit knowledge with each other.

However, at a more detailed level there is disagreement about exactly how reward systems can be used to facilitate positive attitudes and behaviours with respect to knowledge processes. Some research suggests that individually focused financial rewards can play a positive role. For example, Horowitz *et al.*'s (2003) survey of Singaporean knowledge workers found that providing a 'highly competitive pay package' (p.32) was ranked as the second most effective way to help retain knowledge workers, with the lack of one being cited as the primary reason underlying the turnover of knowledge workers. Such findings reinforce Scarborough's (1999) assertion that knowledge workers are relatively instrumental in their outlook, with issues of pay being one of their primary concerns.

However, others suggest that such individually focused rewards can inhibit knowledge sharing through creating an instrumental attitude to it, and also through the way such reward mechanisms may undermine people's sense of team or community spirit and reduce the likelihood that people will share knowledge where the primary benefits of doing so are to the community or group (Fahey *et al.* 2007). Such writers thus suggest that the best way to develop group-focused knowledge sharing is through making knowledge-related rewards

Box 18.3: HRM in practice

Integrating HRM practices to facilitate knowledge management

Garvey and Williamson (2002) describe how an oil company, which they imaginatively title Oil Company Co., used its HRM practices to support its efforts in developing a culture of knowledge creation and knowledge sharing. In terms of pay, Oil Company Co. staff were rewarded both for meeting commercial performance targets and for undertaking and utilising self-development activities. To signal the importance of both these elements they were embedded in the annual appraisal/pay scheme and together constituted 30 per cent of a worker's pay. Development needs were an intrinsic part of the annual appraisal/review, and staff were expected to provide evidence of the self-development activities they had undertaken. Thus, Oil Company Co. linked the objectives of its pay, appraisal, and training and development systems together to create a coherent strategy for encouraging staff to take self-development and a culture of knowledge creation seriously. This scheme was successful, as it had a positive effect on the amount of time and effort staff devoted to development activities.

group, rather than individually, focused (Cabrera and Cabrera 2005; Lam 2005). Further, these writers suggest that non-financial rewards such as recognition can play an equally, if not more, important role in facilitating and encouraging appropriate knowledge behaviours in people (Robertson and O'Malley Hammersley 2000).

Finally, as illustrated in Box 18.3, HRM practices used to facilitate organisational knowledge management efforts must be integrated and complementary.

RETENTION: PREVENTING KNOWLEDGE LOSS THROUGH DEVELOPING LOYALTY

Developing the loyalty of workers to their organisations represents another potentially important way for organisations to facilitate their knowledge management efforts. Having a high turnover rate of knowledge workers is a potentially significant problem for the organisations that employ them, owing to some of the characteristics of knowledge workers outlined earlier (Alvesson 2000; Beaumont and Hunter 2002; Flood *et al.* 2000; Lee and Maurer 1997). Firstly, their knowledge is typically highly tacit. As outlined, one key source of knowledge possessed by knowledge workers is social capital: their knowledge of key individuals in client firms. Thus, when such workers leave, there is a risk for their employer that they will lose their clients as well. Secondly, low retention rates may be a problem for knowledge-intensive firms as the knowledge possessed by knowledge workers is often a crucial element in organisational performance. Thus, retaining workers who possess valuable knowledge should arguably be as important an element of an organisation's knowledge management strategy as motivating workers to participate in knowledge activities. This is because the tacit and embodied nature of much organisational knowledge means that when employees leave an organisation, they take their knowledge with them. As Byrne (2001, p.325) succinctly puts it, 'without loyalty knowledge is lost.'

Table 18.2 Reasons for knowledge worker turnover (adapted from Figure 1, Horowitz *et al.* 2003)

Reason for knowledge worker turnover	Percentage of organisations reporting this reason as most important
Better pay and prospects	39
Personal reasons	20
Career-related issues	13
Company-related issues	13
Market factors	10
Job-related issues	5

However, some analyses suggest that many organisations have high turnover rates and find retaining knowledge workers difficult. Benson and Brown (2007) present data from a counter-example where a large Australian research organisation did not suffer from such retention problems). This is to a large extent because labour market conditions, where the skills and knowledge of knowledge workers are typically relatively scarce, create conditions for knowledge workers which are favourable to their mobility (Flood *et al.* 2001; Horowitz *et al* 2003; Scarbrough 1999).

Horowitz *et al.*'s (2003) survey – the reasons knowledge workers gave their employers for leaving, and the proportion of cases where this was reported – is outlined in Table 18.2. Thus, this survey found that by far the most important reason for knowledge worker turnover levels was pay and conditions. This therefore suggests that the most effective way to deal with retention problems is through offering good systems of pay and reward.

Alvesson (2000) argues that one of the best ways to deal with the turnover problem is to create organisational loyalty in staff, particularly through developing their sense of organisational identity. Alvesson identifies two broad types of loyalty: instrumental-based loyalty and identification-based loyalty. Alvesson argues that the weakest form of loyalty is instrumental-based loyalty, which is when a worker remains loyal to their employer for as long as they receive specific personal benefits, with one of the most effective ways of developing such loyalty being through pay and working conditions. This conclusion is reinforced by the findings of Horowitz *et al.*, as outlined in Table 18.2, which appears to present a general picture of knowledge workers displaying limited levels of organisational loyalty and being motivated to move jobs primarily by pay-related factors.

For Alvesson, the second and stronger form of loyalty is identification-based loyalty, which is loyalty based on the worker having a strong sense of identity as being a member of the organisation, and where the worker identifies with the goals and objectives of the organisation. There are three strategies for developing identification-based loyalty. First, there is an institutionally based strategy, where the organisation develops a particular vision or set of values with which the knowledge worker identifies. Second is what Alvesson refers to as a communitarian-based strategy, where workers develop a strong sense of being part of a cohesive team, which is achieved partly through the use of social events which allow bonding and the development of good social relations between workers. Third is the socially integrative strategy, which is a combination of the institutionally based and communitarian strategies. Box 18.4 presents the case of a consultancy that primarily utilised a communitarian-based strategy.

A communitarian-based strategy for developing loyalty: an HR consultancy

Cheshire Consultants is an HR consultancy based in the northwest of England specialising in the areas of recruitment and selection and employee development. Research on it was conducted by this chapter's author and two colleagues from the Institute of Work Psychology at Sheffield. It is a small company, employing only 12 consultants plus some supporting administrative and management staff. The source of data on the company was based on interviews with one of its co-founders and seven of its consultants. Its consultants could be described as mobile teleworkers, as for much of their working week they are out of the office, visiting and working at various client locations. For example, one of their consultants described a typical week as involving two days based in the office and three days travelling to and visiting clients in different locations, spread throughout the UK. Thus extensive amounts of travelling were an intrinsic feature of their work. These work patterns therefore meant that during the course of their normal day-to-day work, most communication was via phone calls and e-mails, with opportunities for face-to-face communication between consultants typically occurring on a weekly or twice weekly, rather than a daily, basis.

To counteract the potential isolation and weakened sense of identity to the team that such working practices could produce, a communitarian-based strategy was utilised to reinforce social relations and sustain a sense of community identity among staff. This fits with the articulated culture of the company, which one of its founders argued was to 'create a sense of community . . . like being part of a team'. Two primary mechanisms were used to achieve this. Firstly, the managing director of the company (one of its co-founders) made efforts to maintain daily contact with all consultants. While such contacts had an element of surveillance to them, they also helped to support the work of the consultants through the provision of advice, and also simply to sustain social contacts with them. These contacts were regarded as typically positive and helpful by most consultants. The second strategy utilised was to have monthly meetings which were primarily social in purpose, and which were never cancelled or compromised by demands of work. While most consultants attended these events to some extent out of a sense of duty, they also found them useful as they helped them to sustain good social relations with colleagues, and reinforced their sense of organisational identity.

Domestic-Powerco: supporting knowledge sharing and use among distributed work teams

Donald Hislop

This case study examines the way management and HRM practices are used to support the work and knowledge activities in an organisation whose workers are geographically dispersed and isolated, with few opportunities to interact and meet on a face-to-face basis.

▶

Organisational context

Domestic-Powerco is a UK-wide company whose main business is installing, repairing and servicing heating equipment in the homes of private individuals. During the 1990s Domestic-Powerco management implemented a large-scale cost-cutting and restructuring programme, as such changes were believed necessary to allow the company to remain commercially competitive.

The research on which this case study is based was carried out during the first half of 2003, with two colleagues of the author from Sheffield's Institute of Work Psychology. The research was looking into the characteristics, knowledge sharing and communication dynamics of work that could be described as mobile telework, where people make extensive use of information and communication technologies as a central part of their work, and whose work requires geographic mobility between sites. The research study was small-scale and exploratory in nature, and in Domestic-Powerco involved extended, semi-structured interviews with six people who worked in the service, repair and installation division, in Lincolnshire and South Yorkshire.

Before the restructuring process it would have been inappropriate to describe the service engineers as mobile teleworkers, as while their work required them to be geographically mobile, the engineers were not required to use ICTs, and they all operated out of central depots, from which they started and finished their daily activities. During this period, while the engineers were required to work in customer's houses on their own, the fact that they began and finished work each day from a central depot, and had to return to the depot if they needed particular spare parts, meant that there were extensive opportunities to inter-act with, and share knowledge between, engineers. This can be illustrated by the following quotation, from one of the engineers interviewed:

I can remember just before the depot shut, we had some outside assessors come in to look at our training, and . . . the best training they saw was the informal training, with everyone stood around the locker, you know, and someone's got a part in their hand, and it's 'Oh don't take the right side off, do it from the left, it's a lot easier'.

The transformation of service engineers into mobile teleworkers

The changes involved in the restructuring project were extremely radical in nature, and involved reducing the workforce from approximately 10,000 to 4,000. Further, there was also a programme to close an enormous number of the 450 depots that existed in the UK at that time, with offices and depots being rationalised into regional centres. As part of this process the service engineers lost their bases in local depots. These workers no longer had any physical location from which they were based. While historically they had gone to the depot to be allocated jobs, under the new system this process was no longer necessary. Instead, each engineer, who had their own van and set of equipment, laptop and mobile phone, received their work instructions electronically. Thus, in terms of knowledge sharing, this change in working practices significantly reduced the opportunities for the type of interac-tion and knowledge sharing among peers illustrated by the first quote. This was summed up as follows by one of the engineers interviewed:

[Isolation] can be an issue. I think the one thing we have lost is the word of mouth to engineers, the group gathering in the morning. It is like taking a part of the social life off you. . . . A lot of the engineers would say the main thing they have lost is the contact with other engineers [about] this job.

As will be seen in the following section, Domestic-Powerco has recognised the conse-quences of these changes and has dealt with the loss of this informal means of knowledge

▶

sharing relatively successfully, through a number of mechanisms. However, among the engineers interviewed it was apparent that the organisational means to support interaction, communication and knowledge sharing did not totally satisfy their needs, and many of them developed their own informal means of doing this out of working hours, as illustrated in the following quotation:

We all go . . . to pick up our parts, and there's a canteen there and there's often four or five of us in the morning, so we'll go up and have a cup of tea and a chat, so we've gone together – we still do meet each other, you know, go in half an hour before the shift starts.

Managerial and HRM-related support for Domestic-Powerco's service engineers

Domestic-Powerco was relatively successful at providing support for its service engineers. Despite the fact that many of the engineers felt their work did not give them adequate formal opportunities to interact with colleagues, which were provided instead by the type of informal meeting described above, those interviewed were relatively happy with their work. Further, there was no evidence that they were unwilling to do their work, utilise their knowledge and share their knowledge with colleagues where appropriate.

Categorising Domestic-Powerco's strategy for managing the knowledge of its workers is difficult, as it does not fall neatly into any of the categories developed by the academic literature. For example, in terms of Hansen *et al.*'s (1999) framework, as will be seen, there are elements of both a codification-based strategy, where electronic means are used to collect and disseminate codified knowledge, and a personalisation-based strategy, where means are used to facilitate and encourage interpersonal knowledge sharing.

There are three broad knowledge processes that Domestic-Powerco's engineers must utilise in order to be able to do their job effectively. Firstly, they must utilise and apply their acquired knowledge. For example, the diagnosis of problems is one important task they carry out, going into customers' homes with a vague description of a problem, which requires them to identify the precise problem and sort it out. Secondly, they must continually acquire new knowledge, for example learning how to install and repair new types of equipment. Finally, as with the photocopy engineers studied by Orr (1996), there is a need for engineers to search for and share knowledge with their peers. The following subsection outlines the range of processes that Domestic-Powerco management utilised to facilitate and support these activities.

Training

There were a number of aspects to the training provided by Domestic-Powerco that supported the work activities and knowledge processes of its service engineers. Firstly, there was a formal apprenticeship scheme, which was the basic training programme that new recruits with no previous experience were put on to learn the basis skills and knowledge of the job. This programme ran for a year, with half of it being classroom based and half of it being on-the-job training in the region where the apprentices would finally be working. For the on-the-job part of the training, apprentices went out with specific engineers and learned both through observing the engineers at work and by being allowed to do some tasks themselves.

The second aspect of Domestic-Powerco's training scheme, a buddy system, followed immediately after the formal training programme, and was an extension and continuation of the engineers' on-the-job training, with new engineers working full time with experienced engineers. Thus, in this period, new engineers did not visit any customers' homes without a more senior engineer with them. This process served two purposes. Firstly, it helped the new engineers develop their diagnostic skills in applying their formal learning to specific domestic situations. Secondly, it allowed new engineers to develop good working and social

▶

relations with a number of more experienced engineers, which helped them develop a net-work of people they could contact if they required support and advice in the future, as most engineers do.

Thirdly, to provide the engineers with opportunities to update their skills and knowledge when necessary, there were a number of mobile training centres that toured the country, which groups of engineers took turns to go to. These centres were customised, articulated lorries, of which there were eight in the UK. For example, when a manufacturer launched a new piece of equipment, the mobile training centres might be used for this, as it allowed the engineers to get hands-on experience by looking at and working with the new equipment.

Finally, there was a system for providing staff with regular technical updates, in the form of codified knowledge and information that could be uploaded on to their laptops. This is discussed more below, in the section on codified knowledge.

Managerial support

An intrinsic and important element of the support system for the service engineers was provided by their managers. Groups of engineers were organised into geographically based teams of between 30 and 60, with one area manager being responsible for all the engi-neers in a particular area. For the 'small' areas that had only 30–40 engineers, the area manager was likely to have sole responsibility. For larger areas with over 50 engineers, the area managers would usually also have a supporting assistant manager working for them. With these supervisory ratios, the managers interviewed emphasised the importance of trust. Managers supported and supervised their engineers through a combination of phone calls, team meetings (see below) and face-to-face meetings (close to customers' homes, or when they were picking up parts from distribution depots). However, supervisory ratios mean that managers were typically only able to see and/or contact each of their engineers once per week. Therefore, a hands-off style of management was a necessity rather than a positive choice by managers. The day-to-day performance of engineers could be examined by managers via the performance management system that exists, which required engi-neers to complete weekly, electronic activity sheets detailing what jobs they have been working on (see below).

Team meetings/social events

Another mechanism used to bring teams of engineers together, which provided the manager an opportunity to interact with them face to face, allowed the engineers to share relevant knowledge and information and retained a sense of team spirit, were monthly team meetings. These were coordinated by the area manager and were typically relatively infor-mal and ad hoc in nature, providing engineers with a forum to raise and discuss issues they regarded as important. The staff interviewed also attended regular, team-based social events, organised outside working hours, but these were not a formal part of the manage-ment system and were organised at the discretion of area managers.

Codified knowledge

A lot of codified knowledge was also used to support the engineers in their work. For exam-ple, their laptops had extensive, step-by-step lists of instructions, supported by relevant dia-grams, for how to do most types of repair, on most types of equipment. Thus, theoretically, whatever model of equipment the customer had (with the exception of very old and outdated equipment), the engineer had, through their laptops, the resources to help them repair them. There were also regular (quarterly) updates of technical information sent to engi-neers on CD-ROMs. Finally, engineers also received some technical information as paper-work, via the postal system.

▶

Technical support

The final form of support provided to the engineers 'in the field' was access to a 'technical helpline', which they could call up at any time if they found problems with which they were unfamiliar, or their laptops did not have. Thus, a lot of formal mechanisms existed to support the service engineers in their work, which acknowledged the isolated nature of their work and provided mechanisms to search for and share knowledge and ideas when necessary.

Pay/performance management

The final issue examined is the pay and performance management system that the service engineers had. While searching for, sharing and utilising knowledge effectively were key aspects of their work, there were no direct pay-related incentives or rewards for doing so. These activities were assumed to be an intrinsic element of the engineers' work, and it was not therefore deemed appropriate to provide bonuses for conducting such activities. The main aspect of variability in pay that existed was where extra pay was available for working week-ends, or holidays, and where engineers had to work overtime. The main way their perfor-mance was measured and monitored was on the quality of their work, and on their work-rate. Thus, each engineer had to complete a weekly activity sheet detailing all the jobs they had done. Every type of job they could do was allocated an amount of time to complete, and engi-neers had to ensure that they carried out enough jobs so that the time allocated to the total number of jobs they had done added up to the amount of hours they were meant to work in a particular week.

Questions

1. Is there more that Domestic-Powerco could have done with its payment and reward system to encourage/reward appropriate knowledge-sharing behaviours among engineers?
2. What would be the benefits and disadvantages of Domestic-Powerco providing formal support, within work time, for the informal, pre-work meetings that many engineers used to organise? Is it better to leave these meetings to be managed by staff informally, or for management to organise them?
3. Is the ratio of managers to engineers adequate, or too high? Reflect on the benefits and disadvantages of either increasing or decreasing this ratio, for both managers and engi-neers. Is changing this ratio significantly likely to have any impact on the knowledge-sharing behaviours of the engineers?

CASE STUDY 18.2

Office equipment service engineers and consultants as knowledge workers

Donald Hislop

Introduction

Hislop (2008) reconceptualised Frenkel et al.'s knowledge work framework to make it compatible with the 'all work is knowledge work' perspective. The utility of the revised framework was illustrated by using it to describe and understand the skills and knowledge involved in two different jobs: management consultants and office equipment service

▶

Table 18.3 Characterising the work of management consultants and service engineers (from Hislop 2008, Table 2)

		Management consultant	Service engineer
Skills	Action based	Low	Medium
	Social (inc. aesthetic and emotional)	Medium	Medium
	Intellective	High	Medium
Knowledge	Contextual	Important	Medium–important
	Theoretical	Very important	Low
Degree of creativity		High	Low–medium

engineers.[1] Data on the engineers was collected via conducting interviews in three small office equipment servicing companies based in the same city in the English Midlands, while data on the consultants was collected via conducting interviews in two small HRM-focused management consultancies, from the northwest and southwest of England. Both these groups of workers were classified as knowledge workers, with the skills, knowledge and level of creativity involved in their work being summarised in Table 18.3.

Office equipment service engineers

The day-to-day work of the engineers involved visiting customers within a particular geographic area to repair, service and install office equipment such as copiers, fax machines, printers and scanners. The number of clients visited per day typically varied from between two and seven, depending on the complexity of particular jobs. For the service engineers the level of creativity typically involved in their work was relatively low. This was because the majority of the jobs they did were relatively repetitive and required little diagnostic analysis, with most repair and service work involving dealing with similar types of repairs and tasks. In terms of the skill dimension of the framework, there was a reasonable need to make use of all three skill types. Firstly, action-based skills were needed as most jobs involved some amount of physically disassembling and reassembling equipment. Thus one engineer compared such work to carrying out a routine service on a car. Social skills were also necessary to allow effective communication not only with clients, but also with colleagues. The individualised nature of their work, which involved travelling to clients and working alone, required much of this communication work to be done by mobile phone.

The apparent simplicity of most jobs undertaken by the engineers was a little deceptive as it disguised the extent to which intellective skills were used. This was largely because these skills were relatively tacit, being developed through experience. This process was summed up by one engineer as follows:

You do the training course and they show you how the machine works: you take it apart. But when you get to that machine [on a job] is when you start learning and obviously the first time you have a fault it might take you a couple of hours to figure out what it is and then the next time you go, because you have had it before, you are straight in and sort it.

[1]All the quotations presented in this case study are taken from Hislop (2008).

▶

In terms of knowledge, the engineers made little if any use of theoretical knowledge, but their work did involve developing and utilising contextual knowledge. This consisted of an understanding, developed over time, of what the business needs of their client's office equipment was (the engineers covered specific geographic areas and over time visited the same clients many times), and how this impacted on the type of problems that typically developed. One engineer described this as follows:

You get to know what they expect from the machine, which might be quite different from what someone else's identical machine expects.

Thus, the way their clients used their office equipment affected the type of faults that their equipment developed, and having an understanding of this constituted contextual knowledge for the engineers. They drew on this knowledge and combined it with the action-based and intellective skills they possessed in diagnosing and repairing these faults and carrying out their work.

Management consultants

In contrast to the engineers, the work of the consultants involved a high level of creativity. The consultancy firms that were examined provided HRM-related advice to clients, primarily in the area of recruitment and selection. In the consultant interviews, one of the features of their work that provided the most job satisfaction was the level of variety involved in their work. For the consultants, no two clients' needs and requirements were ever the same, thus every project the consultants worked on was different and involved developing a particular solution to the specific needs of each client.

In the skill dimension of the framework, while the consultants had negligible need to develop and use action-based skills, their work involved the frequent use of both social and intellective skills. As with the engineers, there were two features of their work which required them to use social skills, firstly in dealing with clients and secondly in dealing with colleagues. The consultants needed to spend a significant amount of their time interacting with clients, face to face, by phone and e-mail, as they needed first to work out what their requirements were, and then once they had developed a proposed solution they had to present it to their client, and if the client was happy with this, they would help implement their solution. As with the engineers, the consultants spent much of their working day away from colleagues, thus colleague-facing communication was mainly conducted by phone and e-mail.

In understanding the nature of their intellective skills and how the consultants drew on them in their work, it is useful to link them to the knowledge involved in their work. This is because all three were used simultaneously by the consultants in the key task their work involved: designing solutions to meet the specific needs of their various clients.

The work of the consultants involved the use of both theoretical and contextual knowledge. The need for theoretical knowledge and the intellectual character of the consultants' work is visible in the fact that all the consultants are educated to at least degree level, with most having post-graduate qualifications. The contextual knowledge developed and used by the consultants related to the needs and requirements of their clients. Each client was different, and typically had diverse needs, thus with each project that the consultants worked on they had to develop their contextual knowledge of their client, largely through speaking to them and reading relevant documentation. The need for intellective skills in the work of the consultants involved bringing together their theoretical knowledge with the contextual knowledge they had developed of their client's needs to design bespoke solutions for each client. Thus, intellective skills were required in synthesising these two types of knowledge. This practical application of theoretical knowledge was another feature of their work they

▶

typically found rewarding. This process of using intellective skills to apply theory to particular situations was described by one consultant as follows:

I believe abstract theories are all very well but actually, really what you want is something that applies. It's good to actually put into practice theory and hopefully make a difference to some people.

Conclusion

From the perspective of the mainstream, professionally focused definition of knowledge work outlined earlier, only the management consultants would be labelled as knowledge workers. However, by taking account of both the contextual knowledge and intellective skills involved in the work of the engineers, those adopting the 'all work is knowledge work' perspective consider it legitimate to label the work of both groups as constituting knowledge work.

Questions

1. Do you agree with the analysis that is presented, that due to the requirement of the service engineers to utilise contextual knowledge, they can be classified as knowledge workers?
2. If a knowledge worker is defined as anyone whose work involves the use of a reasonable amount of theoretical or contextual knowledge, can you think of any occupations that it is not appropriate to label knowledge work?

Bibliography

Alavi, M., Kayworth, T. and Leidner, D. (2005–6) 'An empirical examination of the influence of organizational culture on knowledge management practices', *Journal of Management Information Systems,* Vol.22, No.3, pp.191–224.

Allee, V. (1997) *The Knowledge Evolution: Expanding Organizational Intelligence,* Oxford: Butterworth-Heinemann.

Alvesson, M. (2000) 'Social identity and the problem of loyalty in knowledge-intensive companies', *Journal of Management Studies,* Vol.37, No.8, pp.1101–23.

Alvesson, M. and Karreman, D. (2001) 'Odd couple: making sense of the curious concept of knowledge management', *Journal of Management Studies,* Vol.38, No.7, pp.995–1018.

Andrews, K. and Delahaye, B. (2000) 'Influences on knowledge processes in organizational learning: the psychosocial filter', *Journal of Management Studies,* Vol.37, No.6, pp.797–810.

Beaumont, P. and Hunter, L. (2002) *Managing Knowledge Workers,* London: Chartered Institute of Personnel and Development.

Bell, D. (1973) *The Coming of Post-Industrial Society,* Harmondsworth: Penguin.

Benson, J. and Brown, M. (2007) 'Knowledge workers: what keeps them committed; what turns them away', *Work, Employment and Society,* Vol.21, No.1, pp.121–41.

Byrne, R. (2001) 'Employees: capital or commodity?' *Career Development International,* Vol.6, No.6, pp.324–30.

Cabrera, E. and Cabrera, A. (2005) 'Fostering knowledge sharing through people management practices', *International Journal of Human Resource Management,* Vol.16, No.5, pp.720–35.

Cabrera, A. Collins, W. and Salgado, J. (2006) 'Determinants of individual engagement in knowledge sharing', *International Journal of Human Resource Management,* Vol.17, No.2, pp.245–64.

Ciborra, C. and Patriotta, G. (1998) 'Groupware and teamwork in R&D: limits to learning and innovation', *R&D Management,* Vol.28, No.1, pp.1–10.

Currie, G. and Kerrin, M. (2003) 'Human resource management and knowledge management: enhancing knowledge sharing in a pharmaceutical company', *International Journal of Human Resource Management*, Vol.14, No.6, pp.1027–45.

De Long, D. and Fahey, L. (2000) 'Diagnosing cultural barriers to knowledge management', *Academy of Management Executive*, Vol.14, No.4, pp.113–27.

Edwards, J. Handzic, M. Carlsson, S. and Nissen, M. (2003) 'Knowledge management research and practice: visions and directions', *Knowledge Management Research and Practice*, Vol.1, No.1, pp.49–60.

Empson, L. (2001) 'Fear of exploitation and fear of contamination: impediments to knowledge transfer in mergers between professional service firms', *Human Relations*, Vol.54, No.7, pp.839–62.

Fahey, R., Vasconcelos, A. and Ellis, D. (2007) 'The impact of rewards within communities of practice: a study of the SAP online global community', *Knowledge Management Research and Practice*, Vol.5, pp.186–98.

Felstead, A., Gallie, D. and Green, F. (2002) *Work Skills in Britain 1986–2001*, Nottingham: DfES Publications.

Flood, P., Turner, T. and Hannaway, C. (2000). *Attracting and Retaining Knowledge Employees: Irish Knowledge Employees and the Psychological Contract*, Dublin: Blackhall.

Flood, P., Turner, T., Ramamoorthy, N. and Pearson, J. (2001) 'Causes and consequences of psychological contracts among knowledge workers in the high technology and financial services industry', *International Journal of Human Resource Management*, Vol.12, No.7, pp.1152–65.

Fosstenlokken, S., Lowendahl, B. and Revang, O. (2003) 'Knowledge development through client interaction: a comparative study', *Organization Studies*, Vol.24, No.6, pp.859–80.

Frenkel, S., Korczynski, M., Donohue, L. and Shire, K. (1995) 'Re-constituting work: trends towards knowledge work and info-normative control', *Work, Employment and Society*, Vol.9, pp.773–96.

Frenkel, S., Korczynski, M., Shire, K. and Tam, M. (1999) *On the Front Line: Organization of Work in the Information Economy*, London: Cornell University Press.

Gallie, D., White, M., Cheng, Y. and Tomlinson, M. (1998) *Restructuring the Employment Relationship*, Oxford: Clarendon Press.

Garvey, B. and Williamson, B. (2002) *Beyond Knowledge Management: Dialogue, Creativity and the Corporate Curriculum*, Harlow: Financial Times/Prentice Hall.

Grant, R. (2000) 'Shifts in the world economy: the drivers of knowledge management', in C. Despres and D. Chauvel (eds), *Knowledge Horizons: The Present and the Promise of Knowledge Management*, Oxford: Butterworth-Heinemann, pp.27–54.

Haesli, A. and Boxall, P. (2005). 'When knowledge management meets HR strategy: an exploration of personalization-retention and codification-recruitment configuration', *International Journal of Human Resource Management*, Vol.16, No.11, pp.1955–75.

Hansen, M., Nohria, N. and Tierney, T. (1999) 'What's your strategy for managing knowledge?', *Harvard Business Review*, Vol.77, No.2, p.106.

Harrison, R. and Leitch, C. (2000) 'Learning and organization in the knowledge-based information economy: initial findings from a participatory action research study', *British Journal of Management*, Vol.11, pp.103–19.

Hayes, N. and Walsham, G. (2000) 'Safe enclaves, political enclaves and knowledge working', in C. Prichard, R. Hull, M. Chumer and H. Willmott, (eds) *Managing Knowledge: Critical Investigations of Work and Learning*, London: Macmillan, pp.69–87.

Hislop, D. (2003) 'The complex relationship between communities of practice and the implementation of technological innovations', *International Journal of Innovation Management*, Vol.7, No.2, pp.163–88.

Hislop, D. (2005) *Knowledge Management in Organizations: A Critical Introduction*, Oxford: Oxford University Press.

Hislop, D. (2008) 'Conceptualizing knowledge work utilizing skill and knowledge-based concepts: the case of some consultants and service engineers', *Management Learning*, forthcoming.

Horowitz, F., Heng, C. and Quazi, H. (2003). 'Finders, keepers? Attracting, motivating and retaining knowledge workers', *Human Resource Management Journal*, Vol.13, No.4, pp.23–44.

Hunter, L., Beaumont, P. and Lee, M. (2002) 'Knowledge management practice in Scottish law firms,' *Human Resource Management Journal,* Vol.12, No.2, pp.4–21.

Kim, W. and Mauborgne, R. (1998). 'Procedural justice, strategic decision making, and the knowledge economy', *Strategic Management Journal,* Vol.19, pp.323–38.

KPMG (2003) *Insights from KPMG's European Knowledge Management Survey 2002/2003,* KPMG Knowledge Advisory Services, Netherlands.

Lam, W. (2005) 'Successful knowledge management requires a knowledge culture: a case study', *Knowledge Management Research and Practice,* Vol.3, pp.206–17.

Lee, T. and Maurer, S. (1997) 'The retention of knowledge workers with the unfolding model of voluntary turnover', *Human Resource Management Review,* Vol.7, No.3, pp.247–75.

Littler, C. and Innes, D. (2003) 'Downsizing and deknowledging the firm', *Work, Employment and Society,* Vol.17, No.1, pp.73–100.

MacNeil, C. (2003) 'Line managers: facilitators of knowledge sharing in teams', *Employee Relations,* Vol.25, No.3, pp.294–307.

Mansell, R. and Steinmueller, W. (2000) *Mobilizing the Information Society: Strategies for Growth and Opportunity,* Oxford: Oxford University Press.

Marshall, N. and Brady, T. (2001) 'Knowledge management and the politics of knowledge: illustrations from complex product systems', *European Journal of Information Systems,* Vol.10, pp.99–112.

Martin, J. (2006) 'Multiple intelligence theory, knowledge identification and trust', *Knowledge Management Research and Practice,* No.4, pp.207–15.

McDermott, R. and O'Dell, C. (2001) 'Overcoming cultural barriers to knowledge sharing', *Journal of Knowledge Management,* Vol.5, No.1, pp.76–85.

Mooradian, T., Renzl, B., Matzler, K. (2006) 'Who trusts? Personality trust and knowledge sharing', *Management Learning,* Vol.37, No.4, pp.523–40.

Morris, T. (2001) 'Asserting property rights: knowledge codification in the professional service firm', *Human Relations,* Vol.54, No.7, pp.819–38.

Morris, T. and Empson, L. (1998) 'Organization and expertise: an exploration of knowledge bases and the management of accounting and consulting firms', *Accounting, Organizations and Society,* Vol.23, No.5–6, pp.609–24.

Nahapiet, J. and Ghoshal, S. (1998) 'Social capital, intellectual capital and the organizational advantage', *Academy of Management Review,* Vol.23, No.2, pp.242–66.

Neef, D. (1999). 'Making the case for knowledge management: the bigger picture', *Management Decision,* Vol.37, No.1, pp.72–8.

Newell, S., Scarbrough, H., Swan, J. and Hislop, D. (2000) 'Intranets and knowledge management: de-centred technologies and the limits of technological discourse', in C. Prichard, R. Hull, M. Chumer and H. Willmott (eds) *Managing Knowledge: Critical Investigations of Work and Learning,* London: Macmillan, pp.88–106.

Nonaka, I. (1994) 'A dynamic theory of organizational knowledge creation', *Organization Science,* Vol.5, No.1, pp.14–37.

Ogbonna, E. and Harris, L. (1998) 'Managing organizational culture: compliance of genuine change', *British Journal of Management,* Vol.9, pp.273–88.

Oltra, V. (2005) 'Knowledge management effectiveness factors: the role of HRM', *Journal of Knowledge Management,* Vol.9, No.4, pp.70–86.

Orr, J. (1996) *Talking about Machines: An Ethnography of a Modern Job,* Ithaca, NY: ILR Press.

Pan, S. and Scarbrough, H. (1999) 'Knowledge management in practice: an exploratory case study'. *Technology Analysis and Strategic Management,* Vol.11, No.3, pp.359–74.

Reich, R. (1991) *The Work of Nations: Preparing Ourselves for 21st-Century Capitalism,* London: Simon & Schuster.

Ribiere, V. and Sitar, A. (2003) 'Critical role of leadership in nurturing a knowledge-supporting culture', *Knowledge Management Research and Practice,* Vol.1, No.1, pp.39–48.

Robertson, M. and O'Malley Hammersley, G. (2000) 'Knowledge management practices within a knowledge-intensive firm: the significance of the people management dimension', *Journal of European Industrial Training,* Vol.24, No.2–4, pp.241–53.

Robertson, M. and Swan, J. (2003) 'Control – what control?' Culture and ambiguity within a knowledge intensive firm', *Journal of Management Studies,* Vol.40, No.4, pp.831–58.

Scarbrough, H. (1999) 'Knowledge as work: conflicts in the management of knowledge workers', *Technology Analysis and Strategic Management,* Vol.11, No.1, pp.5–16.

Schultze, U. (2000) 'A confessional account of an ethnography about knowledge work', *MIS Quarterly,* Vol.24, No.1, pp.3–41.

Schulze, U. and Boland, R. (2000) 'Knowledge management technology and the reproduction of knowledge work practices', *Journal of Strategic Information Systems,* Vol.9, pp.193–212.

Starbuck, W. (1993) 'Keeping a butterfly and an elephant in a house of cards: the elements of exceptional success', *Journal of Management Studies,* Vol.30, No.6, pp.885–921.

Storey, J. and Barnett, E. (2000) 'Knowledge management initiatives: learning from failure', *Journal of Knowledge Management,* Vol.4, No.2, pp.145–56.

Swart, J. and Kinnie, N. (2003) 'Sharing knowledge in knowledge-intensive firms', *Human Resource Management Journal,* Vol.13, No.2, pp.60–75.

Tam, Y., Korczynski, M. and Frenkel, S. (2002) 'Organizational and occupational commitment: knowledge workers in large corporation', *Journal of Management Studies,* Vol.39, No.6, pp.775–801.

Thompson, P. Warhurst, C. and Callaghan, G. (2001) 'Ignorant theory and knowledgeable workers: interrogating the connections between knowledge, skills and services', *Journal of Management Studies,* Vol.38, No.7, pp.923–42.

Willman, P., Fenton O'Creevy, M., Nicholson, N. and Soane, E. (2001) 'Knowing the risks: theory and practice in financial market trading', *Human Relations,* Vol.54, No.7, pp.887–910.

Chapter 19

EMPLOYMENT ETHICS

Peter Ackers

> Ethics: The philosophical study of the moral value of human conduct and the rules and principles that *ought* to govern it. (*Collins Dictionary*, my emphasis)

Introduction

Employment ethics, as a subdivision of business ethics (see Chryssides and Kaler 1993; Crane and Matten 2004), involves the application of general moral principles to the management of employees' wages and conditions. In the same way as, say, sports or medical ethics, it begins with a concern about human relationships and how we treat other people. There are two dimensions to this: personal ethical issues at work; and broader questions of business social responsibility. The first addresses the way you or I should behave, as responsible individuals, towards other employees and our employer. This might include questions like personal honesty in completing expenses forms, using the work telephone or internet facilities (see Mars 1973), resisting the temptation of bribes, or simply kindness and consideration towards our workmates. Without a culture of personal ethics, high standards of business ethics are inconceivable. For this reason, many organisations now have an ethical code of practice to guide employee behaviour. The focus of this chapter, however, is on the second category, where you act as a management agent for the business organisation. In this case, while there is still scope for personal discretion, your approach to other employees will be heavily circumscribed by business policy. For instance, if 'the company' decides to close a factory – as Ford did at Dagenham – you will be left, as an individual manager, to implement a decision whether or not you agree with it.

In this light, the chapter aims to guide the student through employment ethics as it applies to real business management practice in the UK, past and present. Following some discussion of the complexities of applying ethics to business, various ethical theories are introduced by applying them to a real-life ethical problem. An employment ethics agenda is then established, contrasting a right-wing emphasis on the free market with left-wing social regulation. These are then linked to two competing unitarist and pluralist conceptions of management as an ethical agent in employment relations. The next section sketches the history of ethical employment management, followed by an assessment of a critical development of recent decades, the advent of HRM as a new way of talking about labour management. The chapter closes by advocating a left-wing, stakeholder view of employment ethics as an antidote to three fallacies of recent HRM theory and practice.

To begin with, however, the process of translating ethics from personal behaviour to business practice is not straightforward. As we have seen, one initial complication to business ethics is that decisions about right and wrong are made by an impersonal organisation, rather than a single identifiable individual, as in some other spheres of moral decision making. A further apparent difficulty, compared this time to other fields of management activity, is that ethics is about what ought to be, rather than what is. In short, it involves value judgements and differences of opinion rather than just technical decisions. In truth, the same is true of almost all organisational policy affecting human beings; only elsewhere these value-judgements are hidden behind technical-sounding words like 'efficiency'. As Fox (1966) has argued, employment relations are always viewed through competing frames of reference leading to different interpretations of the situation. In this sense, 'ethics' should be seen as part and parcel of everyday personnel policy, not some entirely different realm of activity.

Employment ethics is still a highly problematic issue, for two further reasons. While modern business seeks the moral high ground, often for public relations purposes, sceptics retort that business ethics in general is an oxymoron, a contradiction in terms. Is not the main goal of business, after all, to maximise profits, with all other considerations, such as the treatment of employees, coming a poor second? On the other hand, the employment relationship, between employer and employee, can become an especially deep-rooted and durable bond, evoking ethical notions of trust and loyalty. Paid work occupies many of our working hours and shapes our life chances, while HRM theory suggests that employees are a crucial resource to be nurtured, developed and retained by the business organisation (see Legge 2004). Some argue that good ethics is, in fact, good business and, therefore, that no serious conflict exists between doing the right thing towards employees and improving business performance. This may be true for some businesses, some of the time. But more often 'being ethical' involves making difficult choices between expedience and principle.

While all ethics starts with common-sense claims about what is 'right' and 'fair', we soon find there are very different views about what these words mean. For this reason, we cannot say whether some employment policy is ethical or unethical, without referring back to which ethical theory we are applying. One central employment issue is how much we pay people. Let me imagine for a moment that I am the main shareholder and senior manager of a business organisation. A group of manual workers have asked for a 20 per cent wages increase, to provide 'a fair day's pay for a fair day's work'. Their language asserts an ethical claim. I want to act 'ethically', but how can I decide whether their claim is a just one? To take the matter further, we must enter what is popularly known as a 'moral maze'. While the detailed facts of the case are always important, the way we interpret them will be shaped by which ethical theory we choose to follow as the road to truth (see Chryssides and Kaler 1993, pp.79–107; Winstanley and Woodall 1999).

Ethical theories: enter the moral maze

One common-sense starting point is to look to the costs and benefits of awarding a pay rise and to enter the passage to the maze marked 'Consequentialism'. Almost immediately, I begin to wonder how to weigh and measure these consequences. For instance, a pay increase will benefit these workers, but it will cut into my income as owner, perhaps reducing the amount I invest in new plant and machinery, spend on myself, or give to charity. How do I know which consequence is more beneficial? By now, however, my path has branched into another fairly wide thoroughfare entitled 'Utilitarianism', which claims to answer this question. Accordingly, whichever action gives the greatest happiness or utility is to be preferred. Since my employees are more numerous than me and on lower incomes, it may seem that a wage increase would be the most ethical course. But what of the broader consequences for happiness in society, if higher labour costs raise the cost of living for customers, or cut the incentive of entrepreneurs, like me, to establish business and create jobs? Another problem is that I do not know what the actual consequences will be, and can only guess. For instance, higher wages may benefit the business in the long run by improving employee performance and reducing labour turnover. Alternatively, higher labour costs may reduce competitiveness and lead to job loss. Thus, utilitarianism can nearly always provide good ammunition for both sides in an employment argument. More worrying, perhaps, it seems to provide a ready rationale for any employer seeking to wriggle out of any social responsibility – which, of course, I am not.

A little discouraged, I retrace my steps to another, narrower passage, with the strange offputting title of 'Deontology'. On closer inspection, however, we discover that this merely means that I should act out of duty and choose to 'do the right thing' irrespective of consequences. Indeed, this way purports to lead to a 'kingdom of ends' with two cardinal principles to guide my sense of duty. One is that I should be prepared to generalise or universalise my decision. So if I give these manual employees an increase, we will also have to consider the situation of office workers and whether they are being treated consistently. The second principle is that we must show a respect for persons, by treating them as an end in themselves and not a means to an end. In practical terms, this could mean that I should not sacrifice my present duty towards these employees – by rejecting their wage claim – in order to pursue the long-term best interests of my business and society. Indeed, one path branches off, called 'Human Rights', announcing that all employees have a 'right' to a decent living wage and so on. In this way, Kant's ethic of duty can appear so high-minded that it prevents business management from even considering economic factors, which may affect the long-term viability of the firm. Moreover, the assumption that we must act out of a sense of duty to be genuinely ethical appears to outlaw any considerations of economic self-interest. What happens, for instance, if my motive is disinterested, but I am also aware that granting an increase will solve the firm's labour turnover problems? Am I still acting ethically?

But how do I know that my primary duty lies towards these employees? Suddenly I notice two less obvious paths leading in diametrically opposite directions, each also departing from the deontological mainstream. The first states boldly, 'Your primary duty is to the shareholders who own and invest in the company'. Indeed, it turns out that their property rights can only be protected by keeping costs to a minimum, maximising profits and returning the best possible dividend. It is hard to see how a pay increase for employees can match these goals, unless it has a sound economic basis such as labour shortages or increased productivity. In this view, business efficiency must serve the shareholder, first and foremost. An alternative way, termed 'Stakeholding', argues that shareholders or investors are just one of several interest groups represented in the business corporation, including employees, customers, suppliers and the wider community. Accordingly, my ethical duty is to balance the needs of these different groups. Hence, if the pay and conditions of employees have been neglected in recent years, a pay award may be a justifiable piece of 'rebalancing'. On the other hand, if pay is already very high compared to elsewhere, and has been passed on in high prices to customers – as in Premier League football – it will not be the right thing to do. The general problem remains of how to adjudicate ethically between the claims of the competing stakeholders. By this point, many passages have begun to merge and overlap, as stakeholding and shareholding each blur into utilitarianism on the one side, and human rights on the other, at some point on the way.

Table 19.1 Fitting the ethical theories together

Consequentialist	Non-consequentialist
Utilitarianism	Kantianism
Happiness of the greatest number	Human dignity an end in itself
The end justifies the means	Universal moral rules
Language of economic utility	Language of human rights

At a clearing in the maze, however, a broad new passage begins, called 'Theories of Justice'. Yet within a few feet, this has divided in two completely different directions. The first route, 'Justice as Entitlement', eventually runs into the shareholder path on which we travelled earlier (see Nozick 1993). This argues that human beings have a right to acquire and transfer property freely, providing they follow due process and avoid fraud and theft. Neither the government, nor any other organised pressure group, has a right to interfere in this free, and therefore fair, exchange. Seen in this light, my employees should conclude individual deals with me over wages and conditions, and accept whatever is the commercial going rate. Although I may pay them more, through kindness and charity, this is an 'imperfect duty' or an act of gratuitous generosity and it remains quite just to pay them the bare market rate. If, by banding together in a trade union, my employees are trying to 'force' me to pay a higher rate than I would from free choice, this is unjust and I would be right to resist their efforts. This view of justice places little social responsibility on the business to protect the wages and conditions of employees and can lead to great economic inequality. It also demonstrates how far some ethical theories can depart from common-sense notions of fair treatment.

The other path, 'Justice as Fairness', leads to a table and chairs, where we all sit down, don blindfolds and think about what sort of society we would like to live in, without knowing what position we would occupy in it (see Rawls 1993). The conclusion drawn is that we would choose equal treatment except where differences work to the benefit of the worst off. We would not choose 'justice as entitlement' for fear that we might be born without talent or resources, and end up penniless and sleeping in the streets. Applied to my situation, this suggests that if the claimants are substantially poorer than I, or other shareholders and white-collar employees, I must either demonstrate that they benefit from these inequalities, or allow the pay claim. In defence, my unique skill and responsibility may be an adequate justification. Maybe to stay within the spirit of this social contract, I should give employees some say in the running of the business. This might involve establishing a consultation committee, including union representatives, having 'worker directors' or even turning the business into some sort of cooperative owned by the entire workforce, similar to the John Lewis Partnership. These options, if taken, lead into a common passage, shared with 'Stakeholding'. One linking way is 'Communitarianism' (see Etzioni 1995), whereby we ponder not just the distribution of economic resources in terms of poverty and inequality, but also the impact on social cohesion. In short, will high manual pay contribute to a more tightly knit workforce and community?

After all this wandering in the moral maze, it is easy to become confused and disheartened. And there are three wide avenues radiating from a clearing, each promising a quick route to a satisfactory ethical conclusion. One, termed 'Divine Judgement', invites us to abandon all this confusion and buy a tried-and-tested set of moral rules off the religious shelf. My problem is that rules like the Ten Commandments were devised long before the genesis of modern business, and are too general to tell me what to do in this precise situation. In addition, many of my employees already have alternative sets of rules – which will make them hard to convince. Another path, 'Ethical Relativism', runs in precisely the opposite direction, reassuring me that such diversity of opinion is unavoidable in our postmodern society, and recommending that I avoid the sort of universal claims made by the deontologists earlier (see Smith and Johnson 1996). Far better, this approach suggests, to follow the shared opinion of my particular subculture. I belong, however, to many social circles each with different ethical views, while my business friends simply press a shareholder view that is quite unacceptable to my employees. Finally, I encounter 'Enlightened Self-Interest', a way that reassures me that I worry too much (see Pearson 1995). In the long term, good wages and conditions create loyal, productive, well-trained trustworthy employees, who, in turn, produce great rewards for all the stakeholders at the same time. This is the familiar human resource management (HRM) theory to which we return below. Yet still I wonder, how does this pay award help or hinder and what about the short term?

An employment ethics agenda

While the various ethical theories offer plenty of clues for what an ethical employment policy might look like, there are no straightforward and easy solutions that can be drawn from them. Moreover, most general ethical theories can be interpreted in very divergent ways. This said, the big debate in employment ethics concerns how far the state and social agencies, like trade unions, should be allowed to regulate the free market in order to protect workers' wages and conditions. And we can quickly see two main sides lining up and drawing together different elements from the above ethical theories. In general terms, this division bears an uncanny resemblance to the right–left political divide in Britain and America, between conservatives on one side and liberals or social democrats on the other. The right wing stresses the utilitarian benefits of free-market capitalism, duty to the shareholder, justice as the entitlement to own and freely dispose of property, and a paternalist version of enlightened self-interest which renders state intervention unnecessary. The left wing emphasises the disutilities of short-term, free-market capitalism for society, employee rights, stakeholding, justice as fairness and a sceptical view of enlightened self-interest which presupposes the need for substantial state regulation to ensure good employment practices. In these terms, the question of what is ethical employment practice transmutes into the question: how should employment be regulated and to what ends? But first, what sort of employment issues are we talking about?

Business ethics in general is already a major preoccupation of most large companies. Many corporate mission statements and ethical codes pay lip service to virtues such as integrity, fairness and loyalty and envision a variety of stakeholders, including employees. In some cases, this enthusiasm for ethics has been prompted by a scandal, which damaged a company's or industry's reputation, as with criticism of the banks for mis-selling pensions in the 1990s, the Enron case in the USA, or Shell's bad publicity over human rights in Nigeria. In other cases, ethics has been used as a marketing tool in a more proactive way. Hence, the Body Shop launched itself around a strong opposition to testing on animals for cosmetic purposes and has campaigned for fair trade with the Third World, while the Co-operative Bank has responded to customer objections to fur farming and investment in oppressive regimes (see Burchill 1994). By and large, these companies have concentrated their attention on external public relations and the customer as a stakeholder, with the often undeclared assumption that stakeholding will work directly to improve the position of the shareholder. In all this, employees often appear as a poor relation in the family of stakeholders, such that companies can flaunt their ethics to customers while making thousands of workers redundant. Any distinctively employment ethics agenda will revolve around the damage caused to workers' wages and conditions by unregulated, flexible, free-market capitalism. In so far as customers and shareholders benefit from this regime – high dividends and low prices at the expense of low wages, for instance – it may reflect a clash of stakeholder interests. As a consequence, employment ethics tends to deploy left-wing ethical arguments against free-market capitalism. Let us briefly rehearse four of these.

One points to just pay and the enormous gap that has opened up between executive pay and perks, on the one hand, and those of people in low-paid, temporary jobs on the other. In

Table 19.2 Capitalism and theories of justice – an interpretation

	Theory of justice	Corporate responsibility	Employment policies
Right wing	Nozick (entitlement)	Shareholder (unitarist)	Free market
Left wing	Rawls (fairness)	Stakeholder (pluralist)	Regulated market

deciding whether these are 'just' rewards we can apply Rawls' test – for example, senior management rewards are much lower in Europe and Japan than in Britain and the USA – and explore issues of 'merit' and 'need'. The national minimum wage is prompted by an ethical assessment that the 'market rate' is not always a fair rate and that the state has to intervene to regulate bad employers. Another issue related to the flexible labour market concerns individual and family welfare associated with working time. Some workers today are trapped in such sporadic, part-time and temporary work that they find it hard to support themselves, let alone a family. Other, better-paid salaried workers find it hard to draw boundaries between their work and home lives, such that they suffer stress and their relationships and children suffer neglect. In all these cases, as communitarians argue, the price for society may be family and community breakdown (see Ackers 2002). Once more, the European Union (EU) Working Time Directive, laying down a maximum 48-hour working week and minimum holiday provisions, rests on the assumption that in certain circumstances the free market can fail employees and society.

Two other issues are less directly economic in character. The first regards the right to employee participation, or the entitlement of workers (and the local community in cases of major plant closure) to have some say in the running of their business organisation. This relates to broader issues of corporate governance, and whose interests the business organisation should serve. Full-blown stakeholding or organisational pluralism demands some sort of representative structure by which workers can influence company decision making (see Ackers *et al.* 2005). In the past, trade unions played this role, and in many cases they still do. Legislation on statutory trade union recognition offers to bolster this union role. But this still begs the question of what happens across more than half of the economy where trade unions are completely absent. The European Social Chapter included a right to worker participation and European works councils already provide for this in large companies.

In addition to such positive rights, there is the issue of negative rights or civil liberties. For public sector workers these are now enshrined in the Human Rights Act. If left-wing thinking has often underestimated the threat of the state to individual freedom, right-wing thinkers are equally blind to the threat posed by the large business. Equal opportunities issues around race, gender, disability and sexuality are already established in law and public policy. Measures against age discrimination have followed. But can an employer dismiss someone because they are fat, smoke, wear an earring or tattoo, or have eccentric religious or political views? In short, how far can a business, seeking to mould corporate culture, invade the private self of the individual employee or potential employee? This conundrum links to the question of whistleblowers or workers who expose unethical practices in their company. Does the business own their conscience because it pays the wages, or do they have a higher obligation to society?

Here again, a pluralist or stakeholding view of the corporation demands forms of external regulation to underpin these rights. Enlightened companies may address these issues of their own accord, through voluntary agreements, procedures and codes of practice. But, from this perspective, business as a whole cannot be trusted to do so. And firms with bad employment practices may gain short-term cost advantages and undermine the high standards elsewhere. In several of the above examples, recent British government or EU regulation has been prompted by the decline of trade unions and collective bargaining, leaving many employees exposed to the full power of the employer. Moreover, as we shall see below, employers in general have failed to fill this 'ethical gap' by voluntary action. This said, the state can only secure minimum standards, leaving great scope for companies and managers to establish exemplary wages and conditions. Today, these may also include well-resourced efforts to train and involve workers, as well as 'family-friendly' policies such as extended maternity and paternity provision, flexitime or nursery facilities.

Shaping an ethical workplace

If employment ethics is to mean anything in practice, we need to identify institutions or agencies capable of implementing it. Individual virtue is necessary, but not sufficient. Rarely does one person have the capacity to resolve a moral dilemma, as in the wages scenario earlier. Economic life is highly complex and beyond the scope of personal acts of goodwill. Only the state or substantial social institutions can impress some ethical pattern on the relationships that ensue. As Clegg's (1979) rule-making framework for employment relations suggests, three agencies can help to build an ethical approach into the very structure and process of economic life: from above, companies and their managers; from below, workers' own self-help organisations, most notably trade unions; and, finally, from without, the state as an expression of society's collective moral conscience.

Let us turn now to the most pervasive rule-making agent in most contemporary employment relationships: employers and the professional managers who act on their behalf. Even where the state and trade unions play a central part in framing the employment relationship, the chosen style of employers and managers is crucial in defining the experience of work. While some good practices can be imposed from outside – as with racial and sexual discrimination or minimum wages – the devil is in the detail, and management culture may become a major obstacle to the full realisation of an ethical workplace. In order to understand what role management can play, I will sketch the historical evolution of management practice, particularly in relation to the personnel function, and then look more closely at the experience of HRM since 1979. First, though, we need to understand what management is and how this shapes the ethical tone of the enterprise.

Today, employer regulation is only rarely exercised by the single owner in person, except in the small business. Management is the collective name for those specialist, technical workers who act as the employer's agents in day-to-day dealings with the workforce. As businesses grow in size, and as the personality of the individual owner fragments into the thousands of anonymous individual and institutional shareholders of the modern public limited company, managers become the visible hands and face of employer power. In line with modern rational-legal authority and scientific management, the extensive and ill-defined prerogatives of the individual master are broken down into a specialist management hierarchy. In large, complex organisations, this managerial division of labour is characterised by horizontal layers according to seniority, and vertical lines of function. At the apex, there are senior managers, headed by the managing director, who concentrate on business strategy; while, at the base, are line managers or supervisors who deal directly and regularly with ordinary workers. In between, lie various strata of middle managers who connect the two types of activity. Those at the two opposite ends of the management ladder tend to be general managers, but most of the intermediaries are allocated some specialist function, such as marketing, production or personnel. This management specialism is reinforced by some professional organisation and identity as is the case with groups like accountants, or more pertinently for us, HRM or personnel managers.

While few would dispute this general description of management, there is far greater controversy over who exactly managers are answerable to, and what their social responsibilities are. What we expect of managers in the business organisation depends largely on our chosen frame of reference and this is likely to dovetail with one of the competing ethical theories discussed above. For the unitarists, differences of management function and level are a purely technical issue, subordinate to their single purpose as the unquestioning agents of the shareholder owners. This 'stockholder' conception is enshrined in Anglo-American company law, though not in continental European stakeholder traditions. As the right-wing economist Milton Friedman (1993) argues, once managers or companies take on goals and responsibilities which do not serve their ultimate aim of higher profits, they betray their ultimate employers and endanger the whole future of the enterprise, indeed of capitalism itself. In short, absolute adherence to market principles outside the business, and to the single line of authoritarian command within it, are but two sides of the same unitarist coin.

By contrast, pluralists are likely to perceive and welcome much greater diversity of allegiance and objectives among modern managers, for two main reasons. First, from a purely sociological point of view, this conforms to their image of the business as fractured by competing interest groups, including various management levels and functions. Thus, senior company directors often belong to the Institute of Directors, while line managers join supervisory trade unions. Personnel specialists seek professional status and accreditation through the Chartered Institute of Personnel and Development (CIPD) courses and exams – modelled on other professional bodies such as the British Medical Association and the Law Society. Second, from a more normative perspective, this view of managers also provides them with some scope to exercise independent ethical action, as is implied in the ethical codes of bodies like the CIPD. They are no longer just servants of the shareholders, at their every beck and call. Rather, they hold responsibilities to all the stakeholders in the organisation, including workers, customers and the local community, and to society as a whole. As always, observed fact and value judgement become intertwined. Post-war pluralist industrial relations thinkers like Flanders (1974) found hope in the growing separation between the ownership and control of large public limited companies, precisely because it created new scope for professional managers to exercise a more spacious and socially responsible role. For them formal ownership no longer mattered, since *de facto* pluralism reigned even where, as in Britain, company law did not provide for this. In this they have been proved mistaken, for under Margaret Thatcher a free-market government rolled back the blanket of state protection and trade union influence to reveal the short-term shareholder model beneath. For these reasons, the ethical role of management must be closely related to the responsibilities of business and the way in which society defines these.

The greatest burden of pluralist hope lay upon the shoulders of personnel, the company function and department that specialises in dealing with employees and their representatives. This aspiring management profession seemed to personify the broader social concerns of management, as in the old conception of personnel managers as enlightened umpires, bringing management and workers together, and creating industrial relations concord. As we shall see, the history of personnel management has parallels with the growth of social work, beginning as a predominately female caring profession concerned with people. Below, I ponder whether the new title of HRM marks a rediscovery of this ethical mission, as some suggest, or an irrevocable break from any emphasis on workers as social beings, towards a calculating image of them as mere economic counters. But the management of people has never been the exclusive mandate of personnel. So it is important to set personnel's fluctuating role in the broader context of the overall management style adopted by the business towards employees, from the senior managers who attempt to shape the culture of the organisation, down to the line managers who actually conduct most relations between management and ordinary workers (see Fox 1974).

The history of ethical employment management

In *History and Heritage* (1985, pp.1–30), Alan Fox identifies two competing systems of labour control as, from the eighteenth century onwards, British society adjusted to the modern, capitalist employment relationship. Each operated at the level of state policy and law and through the strategies of individual business units. In this, there is much that is familiar today. The first strategy, paternalism, was carried over from the pre-industrial past, and combined notions of worker deference and a rigid social hierarchy with a sense of ruling-class social responsibility. Hence, for many years, wage levels and customary rights were underwritten by law, partly for fear that a desperate and dispossessed poor would prove dangerous to the rich and powerful. The second strategy, market individualism, was informed by the new capitalist economic order that was breaking free of these semi-feudal bonds. This challenged the notion of a fixed social order and focused on the rights of individuals in politics, while reinterpreting the employment relationship as a private economic contract. Either approach was a mixed blessing for ordinary working people. While paternalism locked workers into a position of permanent subordination, as a price for some moral concern and social protection, market individualism threatened to cast them adrift with no reliable source of income or living, in exchange for the opportunity to freely sell their labour at the best price and better themselves.

Today, the balance between these two strategies has been largely reversed, at least at the level of the firm, with market individualism being regarded as the normal economic relationship and paternalism a noteworthy and deviant one (see Ackers 1998, 2001). Nonetheless, the same tension in management strategy continues and connects with the central rightwing–left-wing ethical divide outlined above. Should the business manage labour as an economic commodity, to be bought on the market at the cheapest possible price, or seek a long-term social relationship with their employees that transcends instant economic calculation? In most cases, the solution is a compromise between market and managerial relations, for, while labour may be hired in an outside marketplace, it can only be put to work in the social context of the workplace. For these reasons, though market individualism may be in the driving seat, it can rarely control the vehicle without some element of paternalism seated alongside. The development of management in general, and personnel management in particular, reflects this need to control and motivate the workforce as a social group, and passed through two main stages prior to 1979.

Stage one, roughly from 1850 to 1945 in most large companies, saw a new social hybrid, paternalist capitalism, emerge from the antisocial anarchy of early capitalism (see Joyce 1980; Ackers and Black 1991; Greene *et al.* 2001). It is not surprising, therefore, that the birth of personnel management, as a distinctive profession, with its own authoritative body, code of practice and range of qualifications, coincided with the late Victorian movement towards a more socially conscious, if paternalist, employer style of management. As Britain settled down into more stable work communities, some large employers, influenced by Christian ideas about social responsibility, sought to shape a stronger social dimension to their businesses and the communities in which they operated. Many work towns of the early industrial revolution were merely factories surrounded by cheap housing for their workers. They lacked the most basic facilities, such as schools and sewage systems. To a large extent, the new working classes began to create their own civilisation through self-help bodies like trade unions, local religious congregations and cooperative societies. However, enlightened employers also played an important part, for a mixture of motives including disinterested public service, personal self-aggrandisement, and a concern for work discipline and social cohesion. Through involvement in local government or by personal direct donations, they sponsored the creation of social and cultural amenities like parks, chapels and libraries. At the turn of the century, the Quaker George Cadbury built the chocolate factory and garden city of Bournville, Birmingham for his workers and the local community, and it remains an impressive spectacle today. In the midst of acres of pleasant houses with large gardens stood the model factory, with its exemplary working conditions, splendid playing fields and welfare facilities.

Personnel management emerged from large-scale Victorian paternalist capitalism, as direct personal contact between master and servant declined, and the employer families sought more institutional expressions of their ethical calling. According to Torrington and Hall's (1991) rather idealised seven-stage taxonomy, social reformers were the first on the scene, notably the Quaker chocolate manufacturer's wife, Elizabeth Fry, who conducted social work outside the factory and campaigned for legislation to protect health and safety. Next, during the full flowering of Christian paternalism, on the Bournville scale, came the welfare officer, again usually a woman, who conducted industrial social work within the workplace. This brought social concern in line with the modern management division of labour then emerging in large factories. Thus, in 1913, the Institute of Welfare Officers was formed at Rowntree's York chocolate factory. In this respect, personnel began with the same high ideals of caring for employees as the best representatives of paternalist capitalism, and travelled with them from a personal to a professional and institutional expression of these values.

However, a number of factors began to unpick the fabric of paternalist capitalism, so that from the 1930s onwards a new modern bureaucratic company emerged associated with a more scientific and less moralistic personnel outlook (Kynaston 2008). By 1945 the sense of religious mission had entered into decline, as part of the general secularisation of mid-twentieth-century Britain. Trade unions had advanced during 'the people's war', which itself had eroded the spirit of worker deference. A comprehensive welfare state, meanwhile, superseded many company provisions. Otherwise, the main reason for the retreat of religious paternalism was the demise of the owner-manager and the private family company. This presents something of a paradox for pluralist advocates of social responsibility, since the growing separation of ownership and control destroyed the personal moral responsibility of individual or family ownership. Business owners moved away from the dirty towns they had created to live as country gentlemen, passed the running of the business completely to professional managers, and, ultimately, sold their shares to the highest bidder. Their children were educated at exclusive schools, and most preferred a genteel lifestyle to managing an ugly factory or busy store. As ownership of the new joint stock companies devolved to a multitude of passive shareholders and pension funds, only interested in a return on their investment, the guiding hand of employer paternalism slipped from view. To many employees this was welcome, since company beneficence had often gone hand in hand with a desire to interfere in and shape their private lives outside work.

In this new era of rational-legal authority, when professional career managers ran business and trade unions represented workers' interests, the religious language of calling and service appeared condescending and redundant. The emerging professions of teaching, social work and personnel reflected a new spirit of value-free social engineering. At work, social science theories of behaviour, such as scientific management and human relations, supplanted ethical idealism. During this phase, most employers withdrew from an active ethical role in both their business and the local community, as the welfare state and local government supplanted many of their earlier roles. Workers became more independent of their employers, preferring higher pay to cricket pitches, sermons and company picnics, and trade unions to consultative arrangements. In the long run, however, there would be a price to pay for this, as the business corporation was able to divest itself of any social responsibility beyond the efficient pursuit of profit.

Torrington and Hall (1991) identify four new and overlapping personnel roles which arose in this second period. The humane bureaucrat, a management specialist with skills in selection and training, first appeared during the inter-war years at public limited companies like the chemical giant, ICI. Later, after the Second World War, a company-level industrial relations role gained increasing importance. From the 1950s onwards, collective bargaining with trade unions was pulled down to the workplace, calling for negotiating expertise at that level. This saw the arrival of the consensus negotiator, or contracts manager, a tough masculine role, involving new skills of conflict resolution. At the same time, the organisation person was concerned with the effectiveness of the whole organisation, and not just employee welfare, linking together other management activities through their role in management development. Meanwhile, the manpower analyst set about quantifying human resources, for instance by measuring the cost of labour turnover and planning the labour supply. A concern for workers still lingered on in these roles, though not as an end in itself, even in theory. Even the consensus negotiators restricted their relations with employees to the arm's-length, institutionalised relationship with trade union representatives. If the soul had gone out of personnel management, it seemed that at least a disinterested profession had been created, with an apparently social scientific knowledge base linked to practical skills.

Before turning to contemporary developments associated with HRM, it is important to qualify this generalised image of British business. Sophisticated modern companies, such as Cadbury's, were far from the norm in the history of British industrial relations. What we have seen so far is the best parts of British business putting their best face forward. For, as Fox (1985) argues, market individualism remained the dominant preference of British employers, tempered only by the often uninvited presence of trade unions that forced businesses to confront the collective nature of the employment relationship through detailed personnel policies. These standard modern employers embraced trade unions as a short-term and pragmatic response to organised labour, rather than as a principled, long-term social vision of the employment relationship (Fox 1974). Most industrial relations commentators see this dual view of labour – a commodity in the external market and a cost within the firm – as conducive to a relatively low-skilled, low-waged and poorly trained labour force, in contrast to the best continental practice in economies like Germany. Arguably, too, this mentality has denied personnel its proper status in the business organisation, creating a ragbag of low-status administrators and industrial relations firefighters, rather than a cohesive profession of influential employment architects (see Sisson 1994). This, in turn, has stymied the development of distinctively ethical employment policies.

The advent of HRM

The third period, from 1979 to 1997, presented a remarkable opportunity for business to demonstrate its concern for employees, unhindered by state or trade union regulation. For two decades, the right-wing ethical perspective reigned supreme. During these years, management was cast as the principal agent of social change, and the rhetoric of the enterprise culture spoke eloquently of employee involvement and commitment, while remaining strangely silent about justice and rights at work (see Ackers 1994). For personnel, HRM was the big new theme in management thinking that tied together these various initiatives, and promised a new constructive role for people management in the workplace. It is to this that we now turn. Hitherto, the academic debate over HRM has revolved around the poles of 'rhetoric' and 'reality' (Legge 1995). In other words, has business lived up to the promises it has made? We begin, therefore, with the claims of HRM in theory and then turn to what this has meant for the employment relationship in practice.

The ethical rhetoric of HRM is everywhere in contemporary business and society. Some variation on the phrase – 'this business regards employees as its number one resource' – has become part of the ritual of company reports and briefings, tripping easily from the lips of chief executives. The CIPD's magazine, *People Management,* is now subtitled '*the magazine for human resources professionals*'. The sleek new HRM model is boldly contrasted with the 'bad old days' of personnel past, much as a born-again Christian celebrates their new creation by darkening their own past (see Clark 1993; Ackers and Preston 1997). Before, labour was a cost to be controlled; now, a resource to be nurtured. Before, personnel was a routine administrative activity; now, a strategic champion of people management for heightened business performance. Before, industrial relations was adversarial and arm's length; now, founded on consensus and employee consent. Before, personnel coveted people management; now, a human relations gospel for all. Rather than chase all these hares, as so many others have already, let us concentrate, first, on HRM's central claim – to have made human resources more central to today's businesses than they were a generation ago. This, after all, is one key test of the ethical employment credentials of contemporary business.

Sisson's (1994, p.42) authoritative summary of the survey and case study evidence on the free-market experiment in Britain concludes that 'personnel management in many organisations in

Britain is locked into a vicious circle of low pay, low skill, and low productivity'. This is surprising, as he recognises, since HRM had promised exactly the opposite, arguing that people are the key to competitive advantage for Western economies where Third World low-cost labour is not an option. Old, rigid and authoritarian forms of management control were supposed to yield to 'the development of a highly committed and adaptable workforce willing and able to learn new skills and take on new tasks'. At face value, British business appeared to be placing a new stress on human resources, and this is the conventional wisdom taught in many business schools. However, the research paints a much more depressing picture. Following Fox (1985) and MacInnes (1987), this suggests that the enterprise culture has exacerbated the laissez-faire, short-term, cost-reduction employer attitudes to labour, endemic in the British employment relations tradition. Moreover, the definitive Workplace Industrial Relations Surveys suggest that HRM in practice has been largely a chimera (Millward *et al.* 1992; Cully *et al.* 1999; Kersley *et al.* 2004). Yes, some HRM techniques, like employee involvement, are widespread in mainstream companies where trade unions remain a factor; no doubt partly as a means of countering their influence. Yet, where management has a free hand, in the now majority non-union sector, there is little evidence of a new 'ethical' HRM approach to managing labour.

The obvious conclusion is that union representation and effective joint consultation was replaced, not by a new enlightened HRM, but by a tough 'Bleak House' hire-and-fire employment policy. Overall, the evidence supports the view of labour as a disposable commodity, a cost to be controlled rather than a resource to be developed. At this level, employment ethics is mainly about good public relations towards customers and staying on the right side of the law. Accordingly, this Anglo-American share or 'stockholder' model concentrates on short-term costs, profits and dividends, dictated by city and financial markets. As in the past, British capital is short-term and cost-minimising in outlook, and has failed to invest in labour as a resource, while management remains attached to crude, cost-effective, payment-by-results systems. Within this framework, there is very little space for active employment ethics. For this to change, Sisson (1994, pp.42–44) argues,

> There would have to be a fundamental reappraisal of the way in which British companies are run . . . A policy of laissez-faire not only sends the wrong signals, above all to small and medium-sized businesses, it also fails to take into account that, left to their own devices, many UK companies will find the 'high pay, high skill, high productivity' route quite simply beyond them.

Writing before the 1997 general election, when the prospects were 'extremely remote', Sisson (1994) proposed the following stakeholding initiatives:

> overhauling the regulatory framework of companies and their relationships with the city; developing an appropriate training system; and introducing a legal framework of rights and obligations that would help to raise standards . . . the kind of framework that our partners in Europe are anxious to introduce in the form of the Social Charter.

Since then, New Labour has made some modest but significant moves in this direction. Overall, though, HRM rhetoric still has to translate into a management approach that values people, even in its own economic terms, as a resource. If the reality of HRM has proved a disappointment so far, maybe the idea at least is worthwhile. It is to this that we now turn.

Conclusion: three fallacies of HRM ethics

Much of this analysis presupposes that HRM has failed because British institutions have frustrated the managerial reforms that could have made it a reality, not that HRM itself presents a positive barrier to any progress towards a more 'ethical' workplace. Only rarely has anyone asked whether the rhetoric, let alone the practice, offers an attractive and credible vision of the world of work and management's place in this (see Hart 1993; Torrington 1993). We might, for instance, regard HRM as some do as organised religion, and conclude that, despite all the bad things done in its name, there remains a valuable ethical essence that is worth retaining. Some academics and trade unionists have approached HRM in this spirit, arguing that we can 'play back' promises about 'people being our number one resource' and ask management to live up to these. In purely pragmatic terms, there is much to be said for this approach in a business environment where HRM is unlikely to go away, as I have argued elsewhere (see Ackers and Payne 1998; Ackers and Wilkinson 2003). On the other hand, if we do not go beyond such necessary opportunism, there is a danger of becoming ensnared within the HRM worldview. For once we peel away the layers of HRM hyperbole, we reach a hollow core: an impoverished ethical vision of the employment relationship. This rests upon three ethical fallacies, which I will term 'golden calf', 'enlightened self-interest' and 'happy family'.

The golden calf fallacy assumes that all human values should be subordinated to business considerations and calculations. At the heart of the HRM worldview stands the claim that the human resource is a business's most valued asset. This appears, at first glance, a noble belief, even if it flies in the face of the manner in which many employers actually treat their workers. In particular, it suggests a culture in which companies invest in workers' long-term development, instead of regarding them as merely costs, to be cut and controlled. Yet, there is a dangerous flaw in this ethical vision, and this relates to the broader stream of right-wing ethical thinking, which redefines human beings, with their complex social, spiritual and material needs, as mere rational economic categories, be these consumers or human resources. Such language assumes that business and its economic terminology should shape human aspirations, and not the other way round. From a practical management point of view, enlightened employment policies will always require a business case. Ethics should not be a recipe for economic suicide or ridicule. But to have a long-term competitive advantage at the back of your mind is not to subordinate every decision to short-term economic calculus, as HRM implies. For workers, the choice is between being a most valued economic asset and being a rounded human being whose dignity should be respected by all – in Kant's terms, a subject that should never become an object. This has grave implications for the role of managers, since they are asked to lead the worship at the altar of false values. They too are required to treat their subordinates as merely a means to economic ends, to count the cost of every act of kindness. To personnel management in particular, HRM offers a Faustian pact within the enterprise culture. The prize advertised is an ever-growing personnel influence inside the business organisation; the price is personnel's professional soul and its total commitment to goals defined by senior executives and large shareholders, over and above all other stakeholders.

The enlightened self-interest fallacy takes the heresy a stage further, by pretending that business considerations alone are sufficient for companies to look after their employees, without outside regulation from the state or trade unions. As Pearson (1995) argues, a business needs to build long-term trust relationships with employees, customers and other companies in order to thrive, and therefore it needs to behave with integrity towards all these groups. Thus HRM theory fosters the seductive idea that it is in the self-interest of business to treat workers well, and that, for this reason alone, they no longer need to fear for their own protection. Yet numerous businesses, large and small, thrive on short-term, one-sided relationships, as the evidence for the failure of HRM shows. Perhaps, as Sisson suggests, this is against the long-term interests of Great Britain PLC, but there is little reason why that thought should detain for long the mobile, well-rewarded, modern business executive. The significance for workers' pay and conditions is that their entitlements are entirely contingent upon what makes business successful. If profitability demands investment in the human resource, employers will undertake this; if it entails exploiting cheap disposable labour, and breaking trade unions to this end, they will do the same. Once more, an economic theory that makes human rights entirely conditional on business convenience, and puts a price on human dignity, lies at the heartless centre of HRM's view of the world.

The happy family fallacy assumes that the state and trade unions are unwelcome intrusions into a fundamentally harmonious, unitarist employment relationship. Most American-style HRM theory is unitarist in outlook and either silent about or actively hostile to trade unions as representative bodies (Guest 1989). This approach to HRM claims to place this happy paternalist conjunction of self-interest and employee well-being on a new, harder, more calculative footing. However, it does so against all the evidence that the tradition went into decline long ago, and has collapsed in the post-war period. The way we live now, in post-modern Britain, talk of company loyalty is as specious and insincere as easy appeals to 'community' and calls for street parties to mark national anniversaries. The break-up of occupational communities, founded on steel, coal, cotton, tin, fishing or carpets, where large extended families all worked for the same firm, has created a much greater occupational and social fragmentation and a far more mobile workforce. When the HRM 'good news' hit British business in the early 1980s, most large companies had already shed their family bene-factors, faded out the welfare provisions, sold off their leafy garden villages to middle-class professionals, turned their consultative committees into a branch line on which hardly any-one travelled, and begun building on their playing fields. Like the Cheshire Cat, too often all that remains of paternalism is the smile. Management can still make a central contribution in the creation of a more cooperative and cohesive employment system. However, it will not do so by pretending that one exists already, if only we could see it.

The sheer ambiguity of HRM may pose the biggest ethical problem, leading to charges of misrepresentation and bad faith. What so often sounds like a species of left-wing ethical thinking, promising something extra for employees, turns out on closer examination to be a sugar-coated edition of right-wing moral and economic philosophy. Milton Friedman (1993), from the latter perspective, suggests that such spurious claims to added 'social responsibility' are better left unsaid and merely detract from the strong, unvarnished case for capitalism. And it is true that right-wing ethical thinking has a firm grounding in certain business, economic and social realities. Most of us recognise, to some degree, the utilitarian benefits of a capitalist economic system, wherein countless selfish, individual market trans-actions produce unprecedented living standards for most people. In our personal lives, we expect this 'hidden hand' (Smith 1993 [1776]) to be allowed considerable freedom, in order to ensure that our pensions keep pace with inflation and our supermarket groceries are as cheap as possible. We also want to be free to use our own money and property as freely as possible without undue interference from the state. We probably regard this economic free-dom from state control (including the freedom to change job when we wish) as one essential freedom in a liberal democratic society. For all these reasons, any framework of employment ethics which, like full-blooded socialism in the past, threatened to 'kill the goose that laid the golden egg' is likely to be unacceptable to us. The problem with right-wing ethical thinking is that it forces these genuine concerns to an extreme, so that only the most minimal, indi-vidual ethics, such as honesty and trust in contracts, is deemed either necessary or possible. By denying the reality of a long-term employment relationship and presenting the labour contract as a spot-market transaction, like buying a bag of apples, right-wing ethics sends HRM managers into the workplace naked. They either have to imagine new clothes, like the emperor, and hope their employees will believe them, or else they have to look elsewhere.

Perhaps the crucial distinction here, then, is between employment ethics as a public rela-tions façade and rationalisation for what business already does out of short-term economic self-interest, and employment ethics as an active commitment to employees above and beyond this. For managers can and should play a crucial role in constructing socially respon-sible business organisations at the heart of a decent society. This would require, however, a pluralist institutional framework which placed the long-term employment relationship and the wages and conditions of employees, alongside other stakeholders, at the heart of the business organisation. In these circumstances, we could speak meaningfully of social partnership, loyalty and commitment. Within a framework of relationship capitalism, managers could regain their professional autonomy and integrity, as public servants with a stakeholder ethos, rather than the handmaidens of private capital (see Hutton 1995). In communitarian language, the workplace would become a genuine 'moral community' responsive to society as a whole. HRM presents us with a paradox, because it talks of developing people, while considering its subjects as human resources. The reversion to economic language, and the lack of evidence for modern welfare capitalism (see Jacoby 1997), leads to the suspicion that when push comes to shove, the calculator will always take priority over the human being. Although the rhetoric of HRM contains elements that appeal to ethical employment principles, it fails to meet its promises on two counts. First, it bears little relation to the main developments in British employment relations, and thus presents itself as a mystifying ideology, a false promise of a better life in another world which will never arrive. Second, it abdicates any autonomous, ethical role for management, beyond doing whatever makes large shareholders and senior executives richer.

CASE STUDY 19.1

Employment ethics at A&B stores

Peter Ackers

Introduction

A&B is a chain of department stores, selling clothes, food and hardware. It employs 10,000 UK workers in retail, distribution and office positions, mostly on permanent, full-time contracts. In addition, around 1,000 manufacturing workers, employed by its main subcontractor, are highly dependent on A&B's success and employment policy. This case study presents an opportunity to assess the ethics of the business at all stages in its development (was it doing the 'right thing' towards employees?), and to address a major contemporary dilemma between remaining competitive as a business and retaining a reputation as an ethical employer. It allows you to explore various ethical theories and to consider this business dilemma as a choice between different ethical frames of reference.

In the beginning

A&B was founded in 1900 as a small store in a medium-sized Scottish town by an austere, very religious Presbyterian (with his elder brother as a 'sleeping partner'). In the early days, the founder knew all his employees by their first name and exercised a strong 'fatherly' influence over their lives in and out of work. This had both benign and harsh aspects. The company was generous at times of family sickness, with the founder often visiting in person, though sometimes employees wondered if he was really checking up on them. And any employees who were caught with the smell of alcohol on their breath at work, or even drunk outside work, were summarily dismissed. The founder also promoted a strong sense of family values, organising (alcohol-free) works picnics and providing a free hamper every Christmas and at the birth of any child (up to three in number) and 200 cigarettes to the 'employee of the month'. Christian prayers were compulsory before each morning's work began. He also initiated and contributed towards various 'self-help' savings and mortgage schemes. Wages were generally slightly above the industry norm, according to the discretion of the founder, who liked to quote the parable of 'The Workers in the Vineyard' and reward those whom he thought deserved and needed most. Women employees who married

▶

were required to leave, in order to fulfil their family duties, and all managerial positions were reserved for men with families. The firm promised lifetime job security for male employees and encouraged children to follow their parents into the trade. For many years, jobs were only rarely advertised externally.

Growth

The founder died in 1940 and ownership and control passed completely into the hands of his two sons. The boys had been educated at an English public school and lived in the Home Counties. But the founder's personal control had declined long before, as the company grew first into a Scottish chain in the 1920s, and then a nationwide chain during the Second World War. The founder had always strongly opposed trade unions as inimical to the family atmos-phere of the firm, and in 1923 the firm fought off an organising campaign by the shop workers' union which was already well established in the stores of the strong Scottish co-operative movement. As a result, 20 'ringleaders' were dismissed. During the 'hungry thirties' A&B gained a good reputation for maintaining employment when other businesses were laying people off. This was partly due to good business performance, but it was also widely believed that the owning family accepted lower profits in order to continue both to keep the loyal workforce and invest in the expansion of the firm.

The workforce was now counted in thousands rather than tens, so it was impossible for senior managers to retain personal, face-to-face contact – though local store managers were encouraged to do so. In response, the company developed a professional personnel department to create a more systematic set of provisions and policies. These included a non-union, representative company council that operated monthly at store level, and bian-nually across the whole company. Representatives were elected from every work group, and both negotiated with management over wages and consulted over any issues affecting the welfare of the workforce. There was also a welfare and sports society, which was heavily subsidised by the company and provided local A&B social clubs – initially on a strict tem-perance basis. These organised competitions for football, cricket, ballroom dancing and so on. Company developments and these social activities were reported in *Voice of A&B,* a monthly company newspaper produced by the personnel department. The firm also pio-neered a number of other welfare benefits, including a contributory pension scheme for all employees, and a seniority and promotion system called 'Growing Our Own', which meant that nearly all middle and senior managers were recruited from the shop floor. Following one year's service, all employees joined the company profit-sharing scheme, which, in most years, added a further 10 per cent to their income.

PLC

In 1965, A&B became a public limited company (PLC), and within a few years family shareholdings had been dwarfed by those of pension funds and other outside investors. No senior managers now belonged to the original family, and many were being recruited from outside the business, rather than rising through its lower ranks as they had in the past. A new graduate recruitment programme had short-circuited the old seniority sys-tems, though most middle managers had still risen from below. The business had also had to adapt to outside social trends, such as legislation for sexual and racial equality, and relaxed social mores – leading, among other things, to the serving of alcohol in A&B clubs. A&B was still perceived by workers, customers and the general public as a family-run business with a strong ethical commitment to fair play. This was reflected in the trust and loyalty of long-service employees (and very low labour turnover), and of customers who repeatedly told surveys that they would not buy their clothes anywhere else. A&B contin-ued to play a high-profile public charitable role, both in the town of its origin, where the

▶

head office remains, and in the wider community. In the latter case, the company sponsored a City Technology College in inner-city Glasgow during the 1980s and actively supported 'Business in the Community'. It also funded the first professorship in Business
Ethics at a leading British business school.

The company had developed another long-term business relationship since its first
major expansion in 1920, with a large clothing manufacturing firm situated in the town
where the founder was born and A&B originated. Although Smiths & Co. is an independent
firm, 70 per cent of its output is contracted to A&B – whose letters also prefix the name of
the local football team. Company head office and the local store employ between them 750
people, while the founder had presented to the town a park and art gallery, as well as a row
of cottages for long-service company pensioners. The founder's wife had played a prominent charitable role in the inter-war town, including organising youth clubs and holidays for
children of the local poor and unemployed.

Today

A&B's personnel policy has remained fairly stable since the main structures were set in
place in the 1930s. In line with 1960s and 1970s labour law and 'best practice', however, the
company council system has been supplemented by a more formal (but still non-union)
grievance and disciplinary procedure. Employees have shown no further interest in union
membership, partly because wages and conditions are as good as those of most comparable unionised firms, and partly because they know A&B senior management are strongly
anti-union and fear they might lose existing benefits if they push the issue. A new company
interest in equal opportunities for women was partly inspired by the national policy mood,
but also by labour shortages and recruitment difficulties in the post-war retail labour
market. As a result, there has been a small influx of women graduates into managerial and
supervisory roles, and the old distinction between 'men's' and 'women's' jobs has been
replaced by a formally nondiscriminatory, A–G grading system. Equally, criticism that
internal recruitment reproduced an 'all white' workforce, even in cities with large ethnic
minorities, has led the company to advertise all vacancies in job centres and local newspapers, followed by a formal interview. Once again, outside policy influences have dovetailed
with business concerns that its workforce should reflect the stores' potential customer
base. Notwithstanding these developments, personnel policy still cultivates a long-term
relationship with both the directly employed workforce and the manufacturing subcontractor. In the latter case, A&B has insisted on exercising substantial 'quality control' over the
subcontractor's production process, while offering Smith & Co. employees access to its
social clubs and welfare provisions (though wages and conditions are handled separately).
The company's commitment to high-quality, British-made products is a major attraction for
its traditional customer base.

Until recently, A&B has interpreted the new wave of HRM thinking as largely an extension of its existing personnel practices. For instance, it has added team briefing, quality
circles and a modest element of performance-related pay to its existing communications,
consultation and reward structures. In some respects, like profit sharing, the firm was
already a pioneer. Today, however, major changes in the retail market are forcing the
company to reassess all elements of its activities. After years as a market leader, with
steadily rising profits, A&B is now in some commercial difficulty. In particular, it faces
competition from a new generation of fashion shops, which threaten its core clothing
market. These firms source their products from low-cost Third World suppliers and are
happy to switch these where and when the market justifies. They also employ a raw, if
enthusiastic UK workforce of students and young people, almost entirely on short-term
and temporary contracts. Their wages are close to the national minimum, often about
25 per cent less than A&B, and they spend far less on training and welfare. A&B has

▶

already responded to this threat by shedding 10 per cent of its workforce through natural wastage, early retirement and voluntary redundancy, while terminating one major contract with Smith & Co.

The ethical and business dilemma

A new managing director has been appointed to 'turn around' A&B. He has asked all the main functional directors to present a root-and-branch analysis of how the business can regain its market position and restore stock market confidence. These papers will be presented to and discussed at a 'Retail 2050: Future Directions' seminar, the outcome of which will determine the new business strategy to be presented to the next company Annual General Meeting.

The recently appointed head of marketing has already stolen a march on the others by circulating radical plans for a new, marketing-led, customer-focused, flexible firm that breaks almost completely with the traditional shape of the business, including its much-vaunted ethical employment policies. She proposes a new 'culture of entrepreneurship' which will withdraw the 'comfort zone' and 'time-serving' of current employment practices. Using a cricket metaphor, she argues that the point is 'not to occupy the crease but to score runs'. This will include establishing specialist boutiques and other facilities (including restaurants) within the stores, run on a franchise basis, using external subcontractors wherever possible, transferring all remaining direct employees to part-time contracts, except for a core of 'enterprise managers and supervisors' who, in future, will be paid largely according to performance. In addition, she moots the closure of the Scottish company headquarters and complete withdrawal from the town to smaller, more convenient facilities in an English new town; and the ending of the contract with Smith & Co. to enable A&B to buy on the open market and benefit from low labour costs in southeast Asia. In the marketing director's view, the traditional paternalist approach is now completely archaic and untenable in the fast-moving retail market.

To further complicate matters, a whistleblower, within either senior management or the marketing department, has leaked these plans to the media. Rumours are circulating that A&B has been negotiating with a military dictatorship in the Far East for access to its labour force. Concerns about the abandonment of existing employees and the exploitation of Third World 'cheap labour' have been tabled by the founder's family for the company AGM. There have been demonstrations by employees in the original 'company town', addressed by outside trade union leaders, who called for union recognition for A&B employees under the new legislation and an effective European works council. A petition has been presented to the Scottish Assembly by local MPs and church leaders, describing A&B as 'the unacceptable face of capitalism' and urging a consumer boycott of stores nationwide.

Historically, the personnel function, now renamed HRM, has been seen as the custodian of the company's ethical employment policies. As we have seen, these centre on a long-term relationship with a stable workforce. Concerned at the bad publicity the business is attracting, the managing director has asked you, as personnel director, to frame an explicitly ethical employment policy which overcomes the difficulties you are facing and draws on some of the business' existing strengths. There are signs that the adverse publicity is affecting customers and undermining their trust and loyalty towards the company. No options are barred, but the managing director has asked you to consider specifically the following questions.

Note: While A&B is a fictional ideal-type company, it incorporates many real-life elements from a number of leading British manufacturing and retail organisations. These all began as paternalist family firms with their own ethical ideas about how employment should be managed and adapted, and developed these as they grew into large, modern businesses.

▶

Questions

1. How far was A&B's original employment policy 'ethical' in modern terms? What sort of ethical principles did it draw upon? Which elements would be acceptable today, and which would not?

2. How justified was the decision to prevent trade union organisation and is it still appropriate today? Consider the arguments *for* and *against* and the principles involved.

3. Construct an ethical case in favour of the flexible firm solution proposed by the director of marketing, explaining which principles you draw on.

4. Devise an alternative, HRM-driven business and ethical case for maintaining the existing long-term relationship with employees, customers and subcontractors.

5. Which stakeholder groups should take priority when push comes to shove? What duty, if any, does the company owe to its employees and shareholders in a modern free-market society?

6. Design an up-to-date and realistic, *ethical employment code of practice*, consistent with your answers to the above questions, which can be issued by the personnel department to all employees and used for external public relations purposes. Begin with some general principles and then identify key areas of business and employee rights and responsibilities.

CASE STUDY 19.2

Applying the 'veil of ignorance'

Peter Ackers

1. In the spirit of Rawls' 'veil of ignorance', imagine how it would feel to occupy someone else's role in society. Consider the following roles:

   (a) Carworker

   (b) black civil servant

   (c) hospital cleaner

   (d) female junior doctor

   (e) supermarket manager

   (f) social worker.

2. What workplace issues might concern you? What would justice mean to you? Think of both issues specific to your new situation, and more general issues affecting workers and employees.

Bibliography

Ackers, P. (1994) 'Back to basics: industrial relations and the enterprise culture', *Employee Relations*, Vol.16, No.8, pp.32–47.

Ackers, P. (1998) 'On paternalism: seven observations on the uses and abuses of the concept in industrial relations, past and present', *Historical Studies in Industrial Relations*, Vol.6, pp.173–93.

*Ackers, P. (2001) 'Paternalism, participation and partnership: rethinking the employment relationship', *Human Relations*, Vol.54, No.3, pp.373–84.

*Ackers, P. (2002) 'Reframing employment relations: the case for neo-pluralism', *Industrial Relations Journal,* Vol.33, No.1, pp.2–19.

Ackers, P. and Black, J. (1991) 'Paternalist capitalism: an organisation culture in transition', in M. Cross and G. Payne (eds) *Work and the Enterprise Culture,* London: Falmer.

Ackers, P. and Payne, J. (1998) 'British trade unions and social partnership: rhetoric, reality and strategy', *International Journal of Human Resource Management,* Vol.9, No.3, pp.529–50.

Ackers, P. and Preston, D. (1997) 'Born again? The ethics and efficacy of the conversion experience in contemporary management development', *Journal of Management Studies,* Vol.34, No.5, pp.677–701.

Ackers, P. and Wilkinson, A.J. (2003) 'Introduction: the British industrial relations tradition – formation, breakdown and salvage', in P. Ackers and A.J. Wilkinson (eds) *Understanding Work and Employment: Industrial Relations in Transition,* Oxford: Oxford University Press, pp.1–27.

Ackers, P., Smith, C. and Smith, P. (eds) (1996) *The New Workplace and Trade Unionism,* London: Routledge.

Ackers, P., Marchington, M., Wilkinson, A.J. and Dundon, T. (2005) 'Partnership and voice: with or without trade unions – changing UK management approaches to organisational participation', in M. Stuart and M.M. Lucio (eds) *Partnership and Modernisation in Employment Relations,* London: Routledge, pp.23–45.

Armstrong, P. (1989) 'Limits and possibilities for HRM in an age of management accountancy', in J. Storey (ed.) *New Perspectives on Human Resource Management,* London: Routledge.

Burchill, J. (1994) *Co-op: The People's Business,* Manchester: Manchester University Press. (Reviewed by this author in *Review of Employment Topics,* Vol.5, No.1 (1997), pp.206–9.)

Carroll, S.J. and Gannon, M.J. (1997) *Ethical Dimensions of International Management,* London: Sage. (Reviewed by this author in *Human Resource Management Journal,* Vol.9, No.1 (1999), pp.89–91).

*Chryssides, G.D. and Kaler, J.H. (eds) (1993) *An Introduction to Business Ethics,* London: Chapman & Hall. (Reviewed by this author in *Human Resource Management Journal,* Vol.5, No.1, pp.103–5.)

Clark, J. (1993) 'Procedures and consistency versus flexibility and commitment in employee relations: a comment on Storey', *Human Resource Management Journal,* Vol.3, No.4, p.79.

Clegg, H.A. (1979) *The Changing System of Industrial Relations in Great Britain,* Oxford: Blackwell.

Crane, A. and Matten, D. (2004) *Business Ethics,* Oxford: Oxford University Press.

Cully, M., Woodland, S., O'Reilly, A. and Dix, G. (1999) *Britain at Work, As Depicted By the 1998 Workplace Employee Relations Survey,* London: Routledge.

*Etzioni, A. (1995) *The Spirit of Community: Rights, Responsibilities and the Communitarian Agenda,* London: Fontana.

Flanders, A. (1974) *Management and Unions: The Theory and Reform of Industrial Relations,* London: Faber.

Fox, A. (1966) 'Industrial sociology and industrial relations', Royal Commission on Trade Unions and Employers' Associations, Research Paper No.3, London: HMSO.

Fox, A. (1974) *Beyond Contract: Work, Power and Trust Relations,* London: Faber.

Fox, A. (1985) *History and Heritage: The Social Origins of the British Industrial Relations System,* London: Allen & Unwin.

Friedman, M. (1993) 'The social responsibility of business is to increase its profits', reprint of 1973 article in G.D. Chryssides and J.H. Kaler (eds) *An Introduction to Business Ethics,* London: Chapman & Hall.

Greene, A.M., Ackers, P. and Black, J. (2001) 'Lost narratives? From paternalism to team working in a lock manufacturing firm', *Economic and Industrial Democracy,* Vol.22, No.2, pp.211–37.

Guest, D. (1989) 'HRM: its implications for industrial relations and trade unions', in J. Storey (ed.) *New Perspectives on Human Resource Management,* London: Routledge.

Guest, D. (1999) 'Human resource management: the workers' verdict', *Human Resource Management Journal,* Vol.9, No.3, pp.5–25.

*Hart, T.J. (1993) 'Human resource management: time to exorcise the militant tendency', *Employee Relations,* Vol.15, No.3, pp.29–36.

Hutton, W. (1995) *The State We're In,* London: Cape.

Jacoby, S.M. (1997) *Modern Manors: Welfare Capitalism Since the New Deal,* Princeton, NJ: Princeton University Press. (Reviewed by this author in *Historical Studies in Industrial Relations,* Vol.8, pp.188–94.)

Joyce, P. (1980) *Work, Society and Politics: The Culture of the Factory in Later Victorian England,* Brighton: Harvester.

Kersley, B., Alpin, C., Forth, J., Bryson, A., Bewley, H. and Dix Goxenbridge, S. (2004) *Inside the Workplace,* London: ACAS.

Kynaston, D. (2008) *Austerity Britain 1945–51,* London: Bloomsbury.

*Legge, K. (1995) 'Morality bound', *People Management,* 19 December, pp.34–6.

Legge, K. (2004) *Human Resource Management: Rhetorics and Reality,* London: Macmillan.

MacInnes, J. (1987) *Thatcherism at Work: Industrial Relations and Economic Change,* Milton Keynes: Open University Press.

Marchington, M. and Wilkinson, A. (1996) *Core Personnel and Development,* London: Institute of Personnel and Development.

Mars, G. (1973) 'Hotel pilferage: a case study in occupational theft', in M. Warner (ed.) *The Sociology of the Workplace: An Interdisciplinary Approach,* London: Allen & Unwin.

Millward, N., Stevens, M., Smart, D. and Hawes, W.R. (1992) *Workplace Industrial Relations in Transition: The ED/ESRC/PSI/ACAS Surveys,* Aldershot: Dartmouth.

Nozick, R. (1993) 'Anarchy, state and utopia', (extract), in G.D. Chryssides and J.H. Kaler (eds) *An Introduction to Business Ethics,* London: Chapman and Hall.

Pearson, G. (1995) *Integrity in Organisations: An Alternative Business Ethic,* London: McGraw-Hill. (Reviewed by this author in *Employee Relations,* Vol.18, No.6 (1996), pp.97–98.)

Priestley, J.B. (1934, 1977) *English Journey,* London: Penguin.

Rawls, J. (1993) 'A theory of justice' (extract), in G.D. Chryssides and J.H. Kaler (eds) *An Introduction to Business Ethics,* London: Chapman & Hall.

Sisson, K. (ed.) (1989) *Personnel Management,* Oxford: Blackwell.

Sisson, K. (ed.) (1994) *Personnel Management* (2nd edn), Oxford: Blackwell.

Smith, A. (1993 [1776]) 'The wealth of nations' (extract), in G.D. Chryssides and J.H. Kaler (eds) *An Introduction to Business Ethics,* London: Chapman & Hall.

Smith, K. and Johnson, P. (eds) (1996) *Business Ethics and Business Behaviour,* London: International Thomson. (Reviewed by this author in *Human Resource Management Journal,* Vol.8, No.2 (1998), pp.97–98).

Storey, J. (ed.) (1989) *New Perspectives on Human Resource Management,* London: Routledge.

Storey, J. and Sisson, K. (1993) *Managing Human Resources and Industrial Relations,* Milton Keynes: Open University Press.

*Torrington, D. (1993) 'How dangerous is human resource management?: A reply to Tim Hart', *Employee Relations,* Vol.15, No.5, pp.40–53.

Torrington, D. and Hall, L. (1991) *Personnel Management: A New Approach,* Hemel Hempstead: Prentice Hall.

Warren, R.C. (1999) 'Against paternalism in human resource management', *Business Ethics,* Vol.8, No.1, pp.50–60.

*Winstanley, D. and Woodall, J. (eds) (1999) *Ethical Issues in Contemporary Human Resource Management,* London: Macmillan.

*Useful reading

Chapter 20

EMOTION AT WORK

Philip Hancock and Melissa Tyler

> Commit to your business. Believe in it more than anybody else. I think I overcame every single one of my personal shortcomings by the sheer passion I brought to my work. I don't know if you're born with this kind of passion, or if you can learn it. But I do know you need it. If you love your work, you'll be out there every day trying to do it the best you possibly can, and pretty soon everybody around will catch the passion from you – like a fever. (Walton, 1992 p.3)

Introduction

Consider the following extract from a recent job advertisement:

> You will need to be full of energy and want to add to the fun . . . if you want to start work with a great cast of characters then telephone . . .

You might be forgiven for assuming that this advert is for a job in what Robin Leidner (1993) calls 'interactive service provision' – work involving direct contact with customers or clients. In fact it is advertising vacancies for warehouse staff at a European distribution centre; for workers who handle 'things' rather than 'people'. Why is it important, then, for applicants to want to 'add to the fun', and why are potential colleagues and co-workers described as 'a great cast of characters'? Emotion is now thought of as central to business success, whether that business is selling fast food or sorting boxes. As management writers such as Robert Cooper (1998, p.48) have argued:

> Emotion has been rejected for many years as the messy, effeminate counterpoint to masculine logic and objectivity, but now it has become the latest business buzzword.

This raises the questions, then, why emotion, and why now? And of course, what exactly are emotions? Can they be managed, and if so, how and with what consequences? As sociologist Simon Williams (2001, p.132) has observed, 'emotion is a moving and slippery target'. As he goes on to note:

> The very term emotion, it seems, is far from settled (being many things to many people); a trend exacerbated perhaps, by the recent upsurge of interest in this domain. What is fair to say, given these differing viewpoints, is that emotion is a complex, *multidimensional, multifaceted human compound*, including *irreducible* biological and cultural components, which arise or emerge in various socio-relationship contexts [original emphasis].

Broadly speaking, emotions are human responses to a whole range of socio-relational events relating to how we feel and how we express and make sense of those feelings, either individually or socially. Emotions are largely intersubjective (experienced or made sense of with reference to others) and communicative (used to convey how we feel – see Crossley 1998). They are often complex and contradictory – we might hear people saying that they have 'laughed until they cried' or 'wept tears of joy', for instance. As sources of (sometimes simultaneous) pleasure and pain, they are clearly central to who and what we are. Emotions can operate at many different levels, and can be highly reflexive or calculated strategies; they can be habitual or routine practices, as well as unconscious or involuntary responses, varying across time, place and culture (Lupton 1998).

Traditionally the province of psychology – with its emphasis on studying emotions largely as psychosomatic responses – it has increasingly been sociology that has dominated debates on the social nature of emotions, considering their expression and function, and also the way in which socio-cultural milieux shape the experience of emotion. In this sense, sociologists have argued that no emotion is ever an 'entirely unlearnt response' (Elias 1991), and that the emotional experiences of individuals – our ability to think about, feel and express emotions (relating to what sociologists call 'agency') – are linked to enduring social institutions and arrangements such as power and status (what sociologists call 'structure'). In this sense, as Peter Freund (1990, p.453) has put it, '*emotions represent a juncture between society and the most personal realms of an individual's experiences*. They also straddle both the mental and physical aspects of our being' (emphasis added). That emotions act as something of a 'pivot' in this respect, between the individual and the structural or the personal and the social, explains, at least in part, why management theorists and practitioners alike have begun to take an interest in emotions, focusing (at least relatively recently) on emotion as central to understanding and controlling organisations.

To complicate matters further, emotions are often thought about and expressed metaphorically – as if they were fluids in a container that might spill out or overflow at any moment. This fluid metaphor has been a strong theme in organisation and management studies, in which the workplace is often talked about as if it were an 'emotional cauldron' (Albrow 1992) beneath the surface of which a toxic brew is thought to bubble away. Others have thought of emotions with reference to a weaving metaphor, arguing that emotions are 'woven' into the very fabric of organisational life (Fineman 1994). For Fineman, the centrality of emotions is reflected, for instance, in the evocation of work organisations as families, communities or social groups; ideas perpetuated by managerial attempts to conflate formal and informal aspects of organisational culture, so that 'stage-managed meetings and reward ceremonies, "graduation" ceremonies and "away days" all have *a distinct evangelical tone, intended "to keep spirits high"*' (Fineman 1993, p.20, emphasis added).

Not that such allusions to the spiritual needs of employees are always entirely metaphorical, however. Many organisations are increasingly supporting employees' participation in real spiritually oriented programmes and events as a means of encouraging personal well-being and emotional contentment (Bell and Taylor 2003). This is a trend which itself is likely to continue as more and more organisations embrace the idea that valuing employees' spirituality and the emotional benefits that this brings can also provide a powerful impetus to workplace productivity (Konz and Ryan 1999; Neck and Milliman 1994).

Significantly, many such emotional and spiritual events occur outside normal working hours and so blur the boundaries between work and non-work, between who and what 'belongs' to the organisation and what does not, and hence, many would argue, extends the scope of HRM into relatively uncharted territories. Obligations on organisational members to participate in social events, outside the organisation's normal time and space, are often seen as opportunities to share 'real' (disorganised, unmanaged) feelings safely within a receptive audience of peers. Thus, 'apart from being individually cathartic, the social sharing of normally hidden feelings creates a subculture through which organisational members can emotionally bond and feel at one' (Fineman 1993, p.21) – a central theme in contemporary HRM. In this sense, potentially anti-organisational emotions become subject to 'strategic renegotiations' (1993, p.22) so that the possibility for emotional leakage (to continue the 'fluid' metaphor) *within* the organisation's time and space is minimised. For Fineman (1994), then, by effectively organising out 'bad' (unprofitable) feelings, by implication, the productive energy associated with 'good' feelings can be channelled into the labour process – a theme that has underpinned the turn to emotion in HRM.

The emotional turn: key concepts and issues

Although the presence of emotion and its organisation has long since been recognised by management practitioners and academics, it seems to be only relatively recently (in the last two decades or so) that specific and sustained attention has been paid to the emotional aspects of organisations and their management; it is only relatively recently that emotion has become both an academic and a practitioner 'buzzword'. As Sharon Bolton (2000) has noted, emotions now seem to be 'here, there and everywhere'. Several reasons can perhaps be identified for this relatively recent turn to emotion in organisation and management studies.

Much of the academic interest in emotion was inspired by US sociologist Arlie Russell Hochschild's book *The Managed Heart,* published in 1983. As Bolton and Boyd (2003, p.292) have put it, 'there is little that has been written concerning the subject of emotions and organizations in the last 20 years that does not take *The Managed Heart* as a reference point'. Hochschild's introduction of the term 'emotional labour' to describe the ways in which emotions are incorporated into the labour process illuminated an aspect of paid work that has since beeen recognised as central to the lived experience of many workers, particularly those employed in the service sector, but that had been relatively obscured by dominant theoretical approaches both to management and to the study of management. Conceptualising some of the distinctive aspects of work in this way opened up fruitful avenues of investigation and analysis, and facilitated the ongoing reformulation of both academic and managerial conceptions of work necessary to keep pace with transformations in the nature of work, and in the economy in general.

One such transformation is that increasingly 'people's working lives are shaped overwhelmingly by the experience of delivering a service' (Allen and Du Gay 1994, p.255). This increase, over the past few decades, in the proportion of jobs in which people are employed specifically to work as front-line, customer-facing service providers has meant that sustained managerial attention has been paid to customer relations as a vital contributor to competitive advantage and hence particularly to the stage management of what Jan Carlzon (1987) called 'moments of truth': when customers interact with organisations through interpersonal encounters with sales-service providers. This recognition has increased the importance accorded to emotion and its management, particularly for those employees in direct contact with customers; those 'making a difference at the margins' (Peters and Austin 1985, p.45). Consequently, 'a key component of the work performed by many workers has become the presentation of emotions that are specified and desired by their organisations' (Morris and Feldman 1997, p.987).

Certainly in contemporary (what we might call 'post-Excellence') managerial discourse – that is, managerialism inspired largely by Peters and Waterman's (1982) *In Search of Excellence* and concerned particularly with the management of the cultural and subjective aspects of work – emotion has come to be viewed as an important resource that managers should harness in the service of organisational performance. In their book *A Passion For Excellence,* Peters and Austin (1985, p.287) argue that organisational emotions (the feelings, sensations and affective responses to organisation) 'must come from the market and the soul simultaneously'. In later work (Peters 1989, p.457), managers themselves are called upon to harness their own emotional energies by developing a 'passionate public hatred for bureaucracy'.

The turn to emotion, in management and organisation theory particularly, has also been fuelled by something of a challenge, brought about by the impact of postmodern, feminist and post-structuralist ideas, to the dominant, disengaged and largely disembodied traditions of Western thought and practice that have traditionally neglected emotion in favour of reason (Dale 2001; Williams 2001; Wolkowitz 2006). This development relates, broadly speaking, to a revived interest in the body brought about, in part, by recent developments in the biological and human sciences – in genetic engineering and reproductive technologies, for instance (Martin 1994; Hancock *et al.* 2000). It has also been fuelled by the expansion of consumer culture in most market societies (Falk 1994), and by the increasing organisational commodification of various forms of emotional experience, ranging from new-age spirituality to Holocaust museums and theme parks (Bryman 2004). As Lupton (1998) notes, ours is an era characterised by an intense, voyeuristic and largely commercial interest in how others experience and express emotion.

In sum, the turn to emotion has been fuelled by various recent developments, including:

■ *conceptual developments* in the way in which we describe and understand the emotional aspects of work organisations and their management;

■ *empirical changes* in the way in which we experience work;

■ *theoretical trends* in the way in which ideal forms of management are defined, largely in managerial texts and 'how to' guides, as well as in the ways in which social scientists and management academics have tried to make sense of contemporary organisational life.

Cumulatively, each of these developments has amounted to something of a 'challenge' to rationality in Western thought (including managerialism), involving a renewed preoccupation with the body in management theory and practice, a concern with consumer culture and emotional labour (a concept to which we return below), and a largely commercial and mediated interest in emotions and their expression. As we will now reflect, however, it is not the case that management and emotion have always been seen as ideal business partners.

Emotion in management theory and practice

EMOTION, BUREAUCRACY AND SCIENTIFIC MANAGEMENT

Modern organisations have been hailed since their inception as incarnations of rationality and instruments of rationalisation. Bureaucracy – as the typically modern (advanced) mode of organising – has been defined largely according to an autonomous, impersonal, procedural rationality that has no place for emotion. What Rosabeth Moss Kanter (1977, p.22) in her now classic critique of bureaucracy refers to as 'the passionless organisation', one that strives to exclude emotion from its boundaries, is an organisation that believes that efficiency should not be sullied by the 'irrationality' of personal feelings.

In her account of the development of this modern, bureaucratic organisation, Kanter (1977) argues that the 'corporation' began to emerge as the dominant organisational form in the late nineteenth century, when what she calls the 'administrative revolution' (the successor to the industrial revolution) took place. By this she means that an increasing number of organisational functions were brought together and merged into a single corporate administration in order to gain control over a range of disparate activities that would otherwise have continued to be subject to a high degree of uncertainty. Hence, the need to coordinate complex operations made management a specialised occupation and, as she notes, managerial skills began to be more rewarded in business than technical ones. However, as managers were neither owners nor a traditional 'ruling class', they were required to establish their legitimacy and did so through the language of rationality and efficiency.

Control by managers was therefore presented as the most 'rational' way to run a corporate enterprise. Early twentieth-century management theory – such as Taylor's (1911) 'principles of scientific management' – therefore enshrined rationality as the central ideal of organisation, and defined it as the special province of managers. As Kanter (1977, p.22) notes in this respect, 'the very design of organisations thus was oriented toward and assumed to be capable of suppressing irrationality, personality and emotionality'.

For Max Weber, whose sociological analysis focused largely on the rationalisation of Western societies, the suppression of emotion gave bureaucracies their advantage over other organisational forms. Indeed, Weber built his critique of the spirit of capitalism – 'that attitude which seeks profit rationally and systematically' (Weber 1989 [1921], p.64) – on the belief that it is anchored in deeply held religious and emotional attitudes of affect control; in other words, on the exclusion of emotions from organisational life. Thus, as contemporary commentators have noted, privileging rationality and marginalising or excluding emotion 'means that bureaucracy perpetuates the belief that rationality and the control of emotions are not only inseparable but also necessary for effective organisational life' (Putnam and Mumby 1993, p.41).

Returning to Weber for a moment, it would be incorrect to say that his ideal type of bureaucracy is based on a total exclusion of emotion, however (Albrow 1992). As the following passage from his book *Economy and Society* indicates, Weber's account does allow for emotions within modern organisations, but only in so far as their rational calculation is perceived as an intrinsic aspect of their constitution; it is not emotion per se that Weber admits into the organisation, then, but rationalised emotion, ensuring

> First, that everything is rationally calculated, especially those seemingly imponderable and irrational, emotional factors – in principle, at least, calculable in the same manner as the yields of coal and iron deposits. Secondly, devotion is normally impersonal, oriented towards a purpose, a common cause, a rationally intended. (Weber 1978 [1921], p.1150)

In sum, then, emotion was seen as irrational and unreasonable in Taylorism and bureaucracy, as the antithesis of organisation and in need either of exclusion or rational calculation.

EMOTION AND HUMAN RELATIONS

Yet, from the 1930s onwards management theorists and practitioners had begun to realise that even within the confines of organisational life, emotions cannot be excluded or ordered in any meaningful way. In management terms, this meant a significant shift from a view of 'ideal' organisations as based on the exclusion or rational calculation of emotion to an emphasis on the idea that work is meaningful and motivating only if it offers security and opportunities for achievement and self-actualisation (Herzberg 1974; Maslow 1943). In what came to be known as the human relations school of management, emotion therefore became 'in', so to speak, as affectivity began to be recognised as being of central importance to the pursuit of organisational performance. It became increasingly emphasised, therefore, that the management of work organisations should be based on 'articulating and incorporating *the logic* of sentiments' (Roethlisberger and Dickson 1939, p.462, emphasis added).

Elaborating on this recognition of emotions within organisational life, Chester Barnard (1938, p.235) argued that 'feeling', 'judgement', a 'sense of proportion', 'balance' and 'appropriateness' are all vital attributes of the executive. Participative styles of management, deemed to engender loyalty and commitment and so increase worker satisfaction and productivity, increasingly perceived emotion as an important aspect of organisational life.

Elton Mayo (1933), for instance, emphasised the importance for productivity of primary, informal relations among workers and developed the concept of the 'informal organisation' to include the emotional, non-rational and sentimental aspects of organisational behaviour. In Mayo's view, workers were controlled by their sentiments, emotions and social instincts – a phenomenon that he argued needed to be taken into account when devising, executing and evaluating management strategies. As Kanter (1977) notes in her critique, however, in emotional management terms human relations continued to rely on a relatively simplistic formula according to which managers were viewed as those who were able to control their own emotions as well as those of their workers, but not vice versa. According to a management training manual written in 1947 for instance,

> He [the manager] knows that the master of men [sic] has physical energies and skills and intellectual abilities, vision and integrity, and he knows that, above all, the leader must have emotional balance and control. The great leader is even-tempered when others rage, brave when others fear, calm when others are excited, self-controlled when others indulge. (Cited in Bendix 1956, p.332)

While the human relations emphasis on informal social factors may appear to diverge from those organisational traits considered important by scientific management, therefore, both approaches shared in common a similar (Kipling-esque) conception of the role of in the HR movement management heroism vis-à-vis emotion. This meant that in the HR movement management education continued to be thought of largely as a vehicle for learning how to master, not unleash, emotional factors counter-productive to the organisation. In other words, human relations may have 'modified the idea of rationality but preserved its flavour' (Kanter 1977, p.22), often in highly gendered terms. As feminist writer Rosemary Pringle notes in this respect,

> While the Human Relations theorists added an informal dimension, they did not challenge the theorising of the formal bureaucratic structures. In some ways they reinforced the idea of managerial rationality: while *workers* might be controlled by sentiment and emotion, *managers* were supposed to be rational, logical and able to control their emotions. The division between reason and emotion was tightened in a way that marked off managers from the rest. (Pringle 1989, p.87, original emphasis)

HRM: MANAGEMENT GETS EMOTIONAL?

More recently, management practitioners and theorists have begun to emphasize that effective emotional management is a prerequisite for successful organisational interaction. Consequently, recent managerial accounts of the importance of, say, successful service interaction place a considerable premium on the role of emotion and its contribution to organisational success. Many such approaches advocate the use of techniques that manage the emotions of service providers and consumers simultaneously, through the use, for instance, of particular aesthetic techniques such as corporate slogans. Take, for example, the McDonald's 'I'm lovin' it' advertising campaign. Launched in 2003, it represents perhaps the organisation's first truly global tagline, one that has been translated into several languages across the world. The aim of the campaign, according to material on the McDonald's website, was to focus on the whole McDonald's 'experience' rather than simply its product range, and in doing so, to convey 'warmth' and 'passion'.

Examples such as these suggest that while broadly modernist approaches to management, including Taylorism, bureaucracy and human relations, were concerned largely with the *organisation of emotion*, more contemporary managerial orientations are more preoccupied with the reverse, that is, with the *emotion of organisation*.

Hence, management writers, consultants and practitioners have begun to advocate a less 'rationalistic' approach to the management of emotion and have emphasised instead the extent to which

> emotions, properly managed, can drive trust, loyalty and commitment and many of the greatest productivity gains, innovations and accomplishments of individuals, teams and organisations. (Cooper 1998, p.48)

According to Cooper 'the ability to sense, understand and effectively apply the power and acumen of emotions as a source of human energy, information, trust, creativity, connection and influence' (Cooper 1998, p.48) represents that 'really crucial ingredient' for organisational success in the contemporary era, or as Jack Welch (former chair of General Electric), has put it, 'soft stuff with hard results' (cited in Cooper 1998). The 'proper' management of emotions, in this context, is often framed in terms of the deployment of *emotional intelligence*.

The term 'emotional intelligence' (EQ) is associated most notably with the work of Harvard psychologist Daniel Goleman (1997, 1999) and his colleagues (Goleman *et al.* 2002) who have argued that the effective management of EQ involves:

- knowing one's emotions (emotional self-awareness);
- controlling one's emotions (emotional self-regulation);
- recognising emotions in others (social awareness);
- controlling emotions in others (relationship management);
- self-motivation.

Goleman (1996) argues that emotions play a far greater role in decision making and individual success than is commonly recognised. In his best-selling book *Emotional Intelligence* (which, he claims, can be read as an update on Aristotle's *Nicomachean Ethics*), he argues that *the* contemporary challenge is to manage our emotional life with intelligence. In other words, our emotions:

> when well exercised, have wisdom; they guide our thinking, our values, our survival. But they can easily go awry, and do so all too often. As Aristotle saw, the problem is not with emotionality, but with the appropriateness of emotion and its expression. The question is, how can we bring intelligence to our emotions – and civility to our streets and caring to our communal life? (Goleman 1996, p.xiv; cited in Williams 2001)

The answer, for Goleman, lies in effective emotional management. With the right training and development, he argues (1998, p.24), emotionally intelligent managers can achieve a high level of *emotional competence* which he defines as 'a learned capability based on emotional intelligence that results in outstanding performance at work'. Goleman argues that EQ matters more to organisational performance than cognitive abilities or technical skills and impacts particularly, he argues, at the top of the 'leadership pyramid'.

In *Primal Leadership: Realizing the Power of Emotional Intelligence* (Goleman *et al.* 2002, p.3) the authors emphasis that 'great leadership works through the emotions'. Echoing particularly Mayo's earlier work on the importance of managing the informal organisation, he distinguishes between leaders who drive emotions positively (achieving *resonance*) and those who spawn emotional *dissonance,* 'undermining the emotional foundations that let people shine'. Here management is redefined as 'the emotional art of leadership' (ibid., p.13) and emotionally intelligent management is deemed to make effective use of the EQ competencies outlined above.

In a similar (albeit more collective) vein, Thomson (1997), then chair of the UK Marketing and Communication Agency, argues that an organisation's most important asset is its *emotional capital:* 'the combination of emotions, feelings, beliefs and values that are held around an organisation'. Management writers Kandola and Fullerton (1995), known for their conception of the contemporary organisation as a 'mosaic', have also highlighted the organisational benefits of incorporating emotions into the management of diversity, including improved access to talent, enhanced organisational flexibility, promotion of team creativity and innovation, improved customer services, the fostering of satisfying work environments, enhanced morale and job satisfaction, greater productivity and sustained competitive advantage.

Not that such strategies are entirely without risk, however. Peter Frost (2003), for instance, has warned of the dangers of what he terms 'toxic emotions' and, in particular, the threat they pose to emotionally engaged managers whom he refers to as 'toxin handlers'. This refers to those managers (and other employees) who possess high levels of EQ, and are able to 'recognize the emotional pain in other people and in a situation' and as a result either absorb or deflect it 'so that people can get back to their work' (Frost 2003, p.1). Yet while the endeavours of such figures are often vital to the success of an organisation, such individuals can themselves suffer from the absence of adequate support mechanisms or organisational recognition. Thus, as Frost (2003) observes, they are highly vulnerable to personal burnout unless they develop their own coping strategies or are provided with appropriate support from those within the organisation responsible for the well-being of its employees.

This concern notwithstanding, however, underpinning the championing of EQ is the broader perception that 'without an actively engaged heart, excellence is impossible' (Harris 1996, p.18). In this respect, contemporary approaches share much in common with the earlier advocates of human relations and their concern to conflate what are perceived as artificial (and unprofitable) boundaries between the corporation and the individual. They have emphasised, perhaps most notably, that organisational stability comes at the price of losing originality, flexibility and creativity. The identification of innovative solutions that might emerge from processes that mediate and negotiate between diverse groups is thought to be foreclosed in more bureaucratic or scientific approaches to management that prioritise rationality over emotion. Organisational input that might come from valuing diversity is also thought to be denied. Passionate commitment to organisational goals, to co-workers and to the organisation itself is also seen to be lost in the unemotional organisation. In her critical account of recent attempts to 'refashion' management as a passionate enterprise, Caroline Hatcher (2003, p.391) notes, for instance, that:

> Despite what has traditionally been historically recognized as the masculinity of the credentials required for successful business life, contemporary managers now face new challenges. They are required to be caring and relationship-oriented. The traditional masculine/feminine hierarchy of logic/emotion is being reshaped by the imperative to be 'passionate' about work.

The deployment of emotional intelligence competencies has also come to be seen as central to management consultancy. The role of intuition has been highlighted, for example, by recent research focusing on the change management process. In their account of the knowledge and facilitation conceptions held by operational research (OR) consultants at British Airways in supporting the decisions and management processes of their internal 'clients', Yeoman *et al.* (2000, p.121), for instance, found that:

> While the fundamental ethos of analytical rigour characterises the world-view that the OR consultants adopt, it may be the modifications to techniques and practices that consultants make in *intuitive and creative ways* that secure their effectiveness [emphasis added].

Critical perspectives on emotion

More critical perspectives on emotion have emerged primarily from the Marxist-inspired critique of capitalism and, particularly since the 1980s and inspired largely by Hochschild's *The Managed Heart*, out of attempts to synthesise elements of labour process theory, feminism and organisational sociology. Such approaches tend to emphasise that employees are increasingly required to personify an emotional ethos prescribed by their employing organisation and have drawn attention largely to the alienating, degrading and objectifying consequences of this, particularly in relation to the control mechanisms and surveillance techniques used by organisations to prescribe and monitor the expression of emotion.

EMOTIONAL LABOUR

Coined initially by Hochschild (1979, 1983, 1990), the phrase 'emotional labour' refers, broadly speaking, to the commodification of emotions within the labour process. In *The Managed Heart*, Hochschild (1983) made a fundamental distinction between two conceptually different if empirically related ways of managing emotions; namely, emotion work and emotional labour. *Emotion work* describes the act of attempting to change an emotion and how it is displayed in everyday life. In everyday social interaction emotions are thought to be governed by what Hochschild termed 'feeling rules' – 'a set of shared albeit often latent, rules' (Hochschild 1983, p.268) that define what is emotionally appropriate in any given situation. The effort involved in conforming to these rules is what she means by emotion work. So when we laugh at someone's unfunny joke, or express gratitude for an unwanted gift, we are engaging in 'emotion work', in Hochschild's terms. *Emotional labour,* however, is what occurs when a profit motive underpins the performance of emotion work within the labour process – when someone pays us to manage our own emotions and those of others. As she puts it,

> by 'emotion work' I refer to the emotion management we do in private life; by 'emotional labour' I refer to the emotion management we do for a wage. (Hochschild, 1990, p.118)

According to Hochschild, emotional labour 'requires one to induce or suppress feeling in order to sustain the outward countenance that produces the proper state of mind in others' (1983, p.7). Drawing on the work of sociologist Erving Goffman (1959), Hochschild argues that producing the 'proper state of mind in others' involves techniques she describes as 'surface' and 'deep' acting. *Surface acting* involves pretending to experience emotions that are not genuine; 'faking it', in other words. *Deep acting* involves something more sustained and potentially intrusive – actually changing what, or rather, how we feel.

Hochschild argues that 'just as we may become alienated from our physical labour in a goods-producing society, so we may become alienated from our emotional labour in a service-producing society' (1979, p.571). This sense of alienation may cause emotional labourers to feel false and estranged from their own 'real' feelings, an experience Hochschild (1983, p.90) terms 'emotive dissonance'.

Example In her account of the emotional labour undertaken by hospice nurses, Nicky James (1989) outlines the various skills involved in the performance of emotional labour. These include:

- being able to understand and interpret the needs of others;

- being able to provide a personal response to those needs;

- being able to juggle the delicate balance of individual and group needs;

- being able to pace work, and take account of other responsibilities.

Try to list other occupations in which these skills might be particularly important. Why might these occupations (and the skills they require) result in what Hochschild calls 'emotional dissonance'?

Research suggests that a wide range of organisational contexts exist in which employees are required to manage their own emotions and those of others in the service of an employing organisation. Empirical studies of emotional labour have appeared in a range of sociology and management journals in recent years. In sociology, the emphasis has primarily been on documenting the content of emotional labour, and to a large extent, noting its gendered aspects. Studies have also emphasised the impact of emotional labour on job satisfaction, and have drawn attention to the negative effects of performing work that involves managing one's own and others' feelings and to the ethical issues this raises. Such accounts have tended to examine jobs with the most obvious emotional labour content, particularly in interactive service work. These include studies of fast-food workers at McDonald's (Leidner 1993, 1999), flight attendants (Hochschild 1983; Tyler and Abbott 1998), nurses (James 1989; O'Brien 1994), waiters and waitresses (Hall 1993; Paules 1996), hair stylists (Parkinson 1991), sex workers (Sanders 2004) and many others (see Fineman, 2008).

In management journals the concern has largely been with highlighting the importance of managing emotion through effective recruitment, selection, socialisation and supervision in order to increase product or service quality and hence, raise profitability. Notable examples include studies of supermarket and convenience store cashiers (Sutton and Rafaeli 1988; Rafaeli 1989) and of ride operators at Disneyland (Van Maanen and Kunda 1989). These studies emphasise that the successful performance of emotional labour typically requires 'a complex combination of facial expression, body language, spoken words and tone of voice' (Rafaeli and Sutton 1987, p.33). This combination seems to be achieved through a range of human resource management techniques, including recruitment and selection, training, supervision and monitoring of employee presentation and performance.

MANAGING EMOTIONAL LABOUR

The importance accorded to emotion and particularly to emotional labour in recent years means that considerable efforts have been made to control both its experience and expression. Hence, whereas what Hochschild termed 'emotion work' is governed largely according to an informal network of rules, including social values, attitudes and expectations, emotional labour is subject to a complex range of direct and indirect management control techniques. The importance of recruitment and selection of individuals of appropriate emotional dispositions has been highlighted (Ashforth and Humphrey 1995), as has the role of induction and training in establishing group norms of emotional expression (Willetts and Leff 2003). The importance of increasing group solidarity by creating opportunities for shared emotion during communal activities has also been emphasised (Morris and Feldman 1997). In particular, the rationalisation of emotion has been highlighted, particularly through the use of managerial attempts to introduce an element of routine and uniformity into the performance of emotional labour (Leidner 1993, 1999).

Leidner's research suggests that employers introduce a variety of strategies intended to reduce unpredictable elements, in order to standardise the behaviour of workers and service recipients. Also, to overcome resistance to mass-produced service, employees are often required to find ways to personalise routines, or to appear to do so. Further, where too much unpredictability remains to make it possible to dispense with worker flexibility entirely, employers often undertake what Leidner (1993) calls 'routinization by transformation' – changing workers into the kinds of people who will make decisions and interact with customers in ways that management desire and approve of. Indeed, the organisations in her research (McDonald's and Combined Insurance) paid 'close attention to how their workers looked, spoke, and felt, rather than limiting standardization to the performance of physical tasks' (Leidner 1993, p.18).

Management writers Ashforth and Humphrey (1995 p.104) identify four overlapping mechanisms for the management of emotion. These involve: *neutralising, buffering, prescribing* and *normalising* emotion:

> 'neutralizing' is used to prevent the emergence of socially unacceptable emotions, while the remaining means are used to regulate emotions that are either unavoidable or inherent in role performance; 'buffering' is used to encapsulate and segregate potentially disruptive emotions from ongoing activities; 'prescribing' is used to specify socially acceptable means of experiencing and expressing emotions; and 'normalizing' is used to diffuse or reframe acceptable emotions to preserve the status quo.

In her recent account of stories collected from members of various organisations in the US following terrorist attacks on 11 September 2001, Michaela Driver (2003) found that all

Control behaviour:	Neutralise	Normalise	Buffer	Prescribe
Reaction:	negative	neutral		positive

Figure 20.1
Source: Driver 2003, p.542, figure 1. Republished with permission, Emerald Group Publishing Limited (www.emeraldinsight.com)

four of Ashforth and Humphrey's measures were deployed as behavioural controls governing the expression of emotion. While buffering, prescribing and normalising seemed to have a positive effect on employee morale, the use of neutralising controls appeared to be somewhat damaging to employee commitment. Driver argues that it is useful to think of the range of reactions to organisational control attempts along a continuum (Figure 20.1).

In her research, buffering controls seemed to result in fairly positive reactions, somewhat above those that attempted to normalise emotion. Prescriptive controls, which 'refocused emotional expression from the horror of the events to acts of caring, seemed to result in the most positive reaction' (Driver 2003, p.542), as many employees were 'elated by how humane or family-like their organization appeared to be'. By the same token, employees perceived organisations that sought to neutralise or suppress emotional expression largely negatively, primarily because 'they would not grant space to express emotion but instead sought to return to business as usual'.

Driver's (2003) account highlights several themes in the management and study of emotion. First, it emphasises the importance of employee perceptions of the relationship between emotional control and organisational culture. As she puts it,

> if organizational members view organizational control behaviours as indicators of their organization's culture, then the selection of control behaviours may be a critical process. (Driver 2003, p.543)

Furthermore, such measures may be an important means by which employees assess whether they 'fit' with the values and culture of the organisation, and hence are important in terms of recruitment, selection and retention (this illustrates the point made above that emotions often act as a 'pivot' between the individual and the social or organisational).

Second, employees seemed not only to accept but to expect some level of organisational control of emotional expression – 'none of the stories indicated that the storytellers resented their organizations for attempting to control their emotions' (Driver 2003, p.544). Finally, her analysis emphasised the importance of developing a contingency approach to understanding the ways in which different employees respond to varying types of organisational controls on emotional expression in different circumstances and across different levels of organisational and occupational hierarchies.

Developing this contingency theme, Sloan (2004) has recently highlighted the importance of occupational status for those who experience workplace frustration, noting how individuals working in highly esteemed occupations are more likely than lower-status workers to deal with anger directly, and hence experience less anger-induced, work-related stress. A similar finding has emerged from recent research on the relationship between emotion, management and learning which has emphasised the tensions that can exist between individual and organisational learning. Vince and Saleem (2004), for example, have highlighted the tensions created through repeated patterns of caution and blame within organisations. Their study shows how these tensions actually inhibit emotional processes of reflection and communication, undermining the implementation and further development of strategies explicitly designed for organisational learning.

Such contingencies, status inequalities and tensions are relatively neglected themes in the highly functionalist literature on emotional intelligence, which tends to emphasise that the successful harnessing of emotion leads unproblematically to increased identification, commitment, productivity and manageability. Yet recent research on service work has suggested that managerial efforts to secure employee identification and commitment through training, in the use of scripted and set-piece dialogue techniques for example, can actually have the opposite effect, engendering emotional dissonance and disharmony (Lashley 2002).

To avoid such 'emotional dissonance' and 'synthetic compassion', Ashforth and Humphrey (1993, p.108), in their account of what they term *bounded emotionality* (rationalised emotion), advocate 'job involvement and identification with the role and organisation'. An interesting issue, in this respect, is the considerable emphasis that they suggest should be placed on recruiting and selecting individuals predisposed to a particular emotional orientation as opposed to socialising and rewarding employees who appear to internalise an empathic approach. Similarly, Sutton (1991) has suggested that to the extent that emotional expression is 'dependent upon enduring dispositional factors', effective recruitment and selection is preferable to socialisation and reward.

Many of the studies of emotional labour also highlight the ways in which it is managed through the design of systems and routines ('scripts', for instance – see Leidner 1993), and through particular supervisory practices (Van Maanen and Kunda 1989), often involving self-and peer surveillance (Tyler and Abbott 1998).

Example   Consider the following instructions, given to flight attendants during a training course at an international airline:

Always walk softly through the cabin, always make eye contact with each and every passenger, and always smile at them. This makes for a much more personal service, and is what First Class travel and [we] as a company are all about. It's what we're here for. (Cited in Hancock and Tyler 2001b, p.31)

Why might these instructions have been given – what were the management team and the trainers trying to achieve?

How might the performance of emotional labour (through making eye contact, smiling and so on) have conflicted with other aspects of the flight attendant's job?

How might the flight attendants manage (or avoid) this potential conflict?

When combined with the various demands of the work involved, techniques used to manage emotional labour can result in its performance becoming especially problematic for the individual. Such demands can involve, for instance, the requirement that a particular emotional display – such as smiling for the entire duration of a long flight – be maintained over long periods of time, often in working environments that are entirely unconducive to maintaining such displays (Bain and Boyd 1998). Similarly, emotional labourers tend to be required to maintain an appropriate emotional display to customers who are being rude or offensive (Hochschild 1983; Filby 1992; Adkins 1995), resulting in many emotional labourers experiencing difficulties in performing this aspect of their work and, as such, devising various coping strategies.

COPING STRATEGIES

At their simplest, coping strategies may involve employees making use of 'back stage' areas (where customers and possibly co-workers are not present) to let off steam or simply 'switch off' (Van Maanen and Kunda 1989, p.67). Respondents in Bolton and Boyd's (2003, p.298) study emphasised the importance of camaraderie. According to one flight attendant:

The other crew are the best thing about this job and the only thing that keeps me going. We always manage to have a laugh during flights and that's what makes the long hours, annoying passengers and terrible working conditions bearable.

Indeed, humour appears to be a particularly important mechanism for diffusing the potentially negative aspects of emotional labour – when police officers have to deal with major disasters, for instance (Alexander and Wells 1991). In her account of humour as a coping strategy in the sex industry, for example, Teela Sanders (2004) argues that sex workers consciously manipulate humour as a social and psychological distancing technique; humour contributes to a range of defence mechanisms that are necessary to protect the personal and emotional well-being of sex workers. She identifies six types of humour among sex workers that probably apply to many other forms of interactive service work that require a range of emotional management skills and coping strategies. These are:

- private jokes used to ridicule clients;

- coded jokes that flow between sex workers in the presence of clients;

- stories and anecdotes of personal disclosure framed in terms of jocularity and jest;

- humour as a strategy to resist harassment and verbal aggression from community harassers and protesters;

- humour as a source of communication with professionals (healthcare workers and police officers, for instance);

- humour as a signifier of conflict and group membership.

An alternative strategy is to retreat into the routine. Leidner (1993, 1999) suggests that sales-service workers resort to their scripts as a way of separation and that scripting is not more alienating therefore, but less so, because 'routines may actually offer interactive service workers some protection from assaults on their selves' (Leidner 1993, p.14). Another strategy identified involves a more empathetic form of deflection. For instance, in dealing with situations involving emotional conflict, Hochschild (1983, pp.105–8) reports that flight attendants are trained to perceive difficult or offensive passengers as people who are experiencing problems in their personal lives or who are afraid of flying, and to manage their emotions accordingly. Underlying this aspect of their training, however, is the requirement for attendants to respond positively to emotional conflicts and to manage them in such a way as to always 'think sales' and so, essentially, to rationalise an otherwise 'irrational' organisational interaction.

EMOTIONAL LABOUR: A CRITIQUE

In her critique of Hochschild's use of the term emotional labour – a concept she suggests 'has now been stretched to its very limits' – Sharon Bolton (2000) has offered a typology that distinguishes four distinct types of emotion management:

- *presentational* (emotion management according to general, social 'rules' – Hochschild's (1983) 'emotion work', see Bolton and Boyd 2003);

- *philanthropic* (emotion management given as a 'gift');

- *prescriptive* (emotion management according to organisational/professional rules of conduct, but not necessarily in the pursuit of profit);

- *pecuniary* (emotion management for commercial gain – Hochschild's 'emotional labour', see Bolton and Boyd 2003).

Bolton emphasises that emotional labour can be a source of pleasure as well as pain, and that many opportunities exist to engage in what Ackroyd and Thompson (1999) have called 'organisational misbehaviour'. For Yiannis Gabriel (1995), affective aspects of work are a fundamental part of what he calls 'the unmanaged organisation' – those spaces for resistance that are ultimately beyond the reach of managerial control. This may suggest, as Bolton argues, that an over-concentration on the 'pecuniary' category of emotional labour can lead to the neglect of vital parts of organisational life, in particular of 'the emotional management skills organizational actors possess' (Bolton and Boyd 2003, p.289), and of the potential for pleasure and job satisfaction in the performance of emotional labour.

Hence, despite its widespread and enduring influence, Bolton and Boyd (2003) note three central weaknesses in Hochschild's account of emotional labour. First, they argue, Hochschild over-emphasises the divide between public and private performances of emotional self-management, and tends to use the terms 'public' and 'commercial' interchangeably, creating an oversimplified dichotomy. Bolton and Boyd argue that here (and elsewhere) Hochschild operates according to the assumption that there is no room for 'emotion work' within organisational life.

Second, they argue that Hochschild mistakenly equates a physical labour process with an emotional one. However, Bolton and Boyd argue that unlike the factory worker in Marx's analysis, for instance, interactive service workers such as airline cabin crew 'own' the means of production (their bodies and emotions) and, therefore, ultimately control the capacity to present a 'sincere' or 'cynical' performance. What Hochschild fails to recognise, they argue, is that the indeterminacy of labour, and of managerial attempts to control it, is further exacerbated within the contested terrain of the emotional labour process as a result.

Third, Bolton and Boyd argue that 'Hochschild's concern with management attempts to seduce employees into "loving" the company, its product and its customers, creates an illusion of emotionally crippled actors' (Bolton and Boyd 2003, p.290). In contrast, they conclude that emotional labourers such as airline cabin crew demonstrate high levels of emotional dexterity as they are able to draw on different sets of feeling rules (commercial, professional, organisational and social) in order to match feeling to situation, thus rendering them multi-skilled emotional managers who are able to 'balance conflicting demands and still . . . effect polished performances' (Bolton and Boyd 2003, p.295).

Despite the efficaciousness of Bolton's critique, however, what remains the case is that emotional labour is relatively low-paid, low-status work. One of the main reasons for this is that it is predominantly carried out by women because women are deemed to be inherently skilled in its performance; in other words, the skill involved is 'essentialised'. In O'Brien's study of the UK nursing profession for instance, he argued that the skills possessed by nurses are often thought to derive 'not from the qualities of being a nurse, but from the qualities of being a woman' (O'Brien 1994, p.399).

Furthermore, work roles involving the performance of emotional labour may also include a sexual, component itself often referred to as 'sexual labour' (Hall 1993; Adkins 1995). Secretaries, receptionists and waitresses are often expected, as part of the informal, everyday aspects of their jobs, to be flirtatious and to look sexually attractive, an aspect of the job that may result in sexual harassment – unwanted and unwelcome sexual attention from clients, customers or co-workers. In her study of restaurant employees for example, Elaine Hall found that management encouraged waitresses to smile, defer and flirt with male customers, carefully monitoring their body language and (sexual) displays of emotion.

Conclusions

In discussing emotion in organisations we have endeavoured to identify the various factors underpinning its emergence as an increasingly significant concern within HRM theory and practice. In sum, while traditionally emotion has largely been perceived as a relatively undesirable appendage to organisational rationality and, as such, to be excluded from organised life, in more recent approaches, particularly those associated with HRM, emotions have become increasingly valued as organisational resources in themselves. A prime example of this can be found in the idea of 'emotional intelligence'. Yet, as Fineman has noted, although

HRM 'aims to harness positive emotion as a "success" ingredient' (1994, p.86), emotion is still regarded as being in need of careful managerial rationalisation. As Fineman (1994, p.545) has put it, the dominant belief continues to be that

> Cool, clear, strategic thinking is not to be too sullied by messy feelings. Efficient thought and behaviour tame emotion. Accordingly, good organisations are places where feelings are managed, designed out or removed.

In the latter part of the chapter, however, we also outlined the insights of a range of more critical approaches to understanding organisations as 'emotional arenas' that demand the performance of emotional labour. Here, we drew largely on the work of those who have sought to understand organisational emotions in terms of their commodification. This approach has emphasised the extent to which the emotions of employees are considered fair game for employer intervention when self-presentation and interactive service style are integral parts of the labour process. As Simon Williams (2001, p.112) has put it, the contemporary era is one in which emotions appear to be 'managed if not manipulated, and marketed if not manufactured, to an unprecedented degree'. Hence, the '(re)discovery' of the emotional has provided an important lever in terms of management practice and critique.

This led us to pay particular attention to the idea of emotional labour. While the definition first proposed by Hochschild over 20 years ago has endured, we acknowledged how subsequent research has not only demonstrated how the contours and experiences of emotional labour are now thought to be more complex than those described in her account, but how much more widespread it is becoming across the contemporary organisational landscape. For as Steinberg and Figart (1999, p.23) have noted in this regard,

> As our economy moves increasingly toward the provision of services and as the public–private distinction further blurs, the skills, effort and responsibilities associated with emotional labour will become more central to our understanding of what it means to work.

In this chapter, then, we have tried to think critically about emotion in work organisations in terms of the management of emotion and the performance of emotional labour. In Case Study 20.1 (based on Russell and Tyler 2002), we consider some of the concepts, ideas and debates introduced here with reference to the lived experience of emotion in the workplace, and reflect on some of the issues this raises for HRM theory and practice.

CASE STUDY 20.1

Emotion management at Girlie Glitter Co.

Melissa Tyler and Philip Hancock

The Girlie Glitter Co. concept and design

Girlie Glitter Co. is a UK-based chain of retail outlets whose products and services are marketed primarily at 3–13-year-old girls. The team who designed the concept took the theme of 'girl power' as their starting point, and aimed to create a retail format catering specifically for young girls. The idea was to develop a retail store that stocked not only a range of (largely dressing up and party) clothes, hair-styling products, cosmetics and fashion accessories, but also that provided the opportunity for girls to have a 'make-over' in store. The aim, as one of the co-founders of the company described it, was to create 'a girl friendly . . . pleasurable space . . . in which young girls could enjoy shopping together, and . . . mothers could enjoy shopping with their daughters'. In short, as the design team put it, the idea was to develop a retail experience that 'lets little girls live a dream'.

▶

The format that was developed reflects a broader evolution in retail marketing towards stores as places to do more than just shop. With this in mind, a distinct design was developed – the stores are loud, bright and have a discernible colour and style theme that clearly differentiates them from other retail outlets in the shopping centres in which they are located. Indeed, colour was considered to be a vital component of their aesthetic and the design team decided that everything should be 'pink ... and glittery, with lots of hearts'. This provided the style theme throughout the project and helped to bring to life the idea that the presentation of the products and services on offer should be a 'magical experience'. Much like other retail outlets and theme parks marketed particularly at children and families, the emphasis was upon the creation of an atmosphere of 'clean, wholesome, family fun'.

The Girlie Glitter Co. experience

Customers are enticed into the stores largely by the theatricality of what they have to offer. This is experienced through a combination of music, abundant use of glitter, bright lighting and white flooring, combined with distinctive chrome fittings, pink lettering and iconography (hearts and stars), as well as rows of sparkly costumes and make-up. Sales staff perform dance routines at the front of stores at regular intervals throughout the day creating 'an atmosphere of excitement', as one store manager put it. This reflects a broader performance ethos throughout the company that, at least in part, differentiates Girlie Glitter Co. from other retail outlets selling similar products. It has important implications for the recruitment, selection, training and monitoring of sales staff. As one of the co-founders of the company put it, 'staff don't see themselves as sales assistants but as performers'. Store managers are encouraged think of themselves as 'co-ordinators of a leisure experience'.

In this respect, the marketing team developed a number of other features designed to differentiate the Girlie Glitter brand from other retail 'experiences'. As the store's publicity puts it, 'not only does Girlie Glitter stock all things feminine and girlie, it provides its young customers with the opportunity to be transformed into a fairy princess in store'. At the front of the stores are located spaces called 'Princess Studios'. These are hair-styling and make-up areas where customers can have their hair and nails done, as well as a range of themed make-overs.

Because of this aspect of their work, sales assistants (or 'performers') function not only as dancers but also as hairdressers, make-up artists and nail technicians. Instructed to 'have fun while thinking sales' on the shop floor, they are also told to just 'do what comes naturally' as one sales assistant put it. This means that sales assistants 'need to look right because we are there for the girls [customers] to copy'. In this sense, 'standard presentation is important because they are like role models, they influence the kids, much like characters in kids' cartoons or TV programmes, really', as one area sales manager said.

Aware of the potential pitfalls of standardisation and thematic repetition, however, the aim was to 'customise' the service provided, and to recruit staff capable of making individual customers feel special. Crucially, as the Girlie Glitter Co. marketing officer put it, 'this shop was not to be seen as an exploitation of children: it had to represent their dreams, and every girl who visited Girlie Glitter had to feel as though she had walked into a shop that was there just for her'. He goes on to say that this is because 'customers are no longer willing to accept that the shops they visit are just places to buy goods. They demand drama and deserve to be delighted by the experience. Shops have become destinations in themselves – not only a place to purchase, but as a place to be entertained, inspired and, in the case of Girlie Glitter Co., to have loads of fun. This means that the staff we select to work here, particularly on the shop floor, are absolutely crucial.'

▶

Recruitment, selection and training at Girlie Glitter Co.

Recruitment at Girlie Glitter Co. can be likened to the formation of an all-girl pop group; potential employees are asked to sing and dance. Recruitment sessions are described not as interviews but as auditions. When a number of sales staff are being recruited for a new store, group interviews (or 'auditions') are held, followed by individual ones. As the HR officer responsible for recruitment and selection put it, 'group auditions allow you to see who shines through above the rest . . . and that's what we're looking for, people who really shine through and have that extra special something to offer'. Applicants, even those with relevant work experience, are often rejected because they do not look, sound or perform right. This is largely because 'personality is so important to what we do. It is vital for staff to really believe in the concept, so we recruit the personality not just the person.'

There is no specific training as such for sales staff, more an informal process of socialisation that involves, for those not skilled in hairstyling and make-up techniques, learning largely from each other. The make-overs are taught and practised much like 'painting by numbers', according to colour-coded charts and a pre-determined make-up palette. Dance routines are taught by store managers who act as choreographers, and are practised by staff mainly before and after store opening hours. All staff are encouraged to socialise together and it is routine practice for staff at new stores or new staff at established ones to be taken out to a local bar by the store or area manager on group social events. There is a lot of informal pressure to attend these social gatherings and anyone who does not go along is thought to be 'not much fun' and so not really a Girlie Glitter person.

The sales and marketing director at Girlie Glitter Co. likens her role to that of a theatre director or a stage manager: 'responsible for managing the performers who work together like a cast'. She also suggested that she sees herself very much as a script writer, involved in the production of Girlie Glitter Co. as a performance. This theatre metaphor carried through into other aspects of the format – store managers were likened to floor or 'front of house' managers, whose primary role is to stage manage those aspects of the store that are visible to the 'audience' [customers]; the till area was referred to by experienced staff as the 'box office', and the storerooms were described as 'backstage'. The opening of the store each day was called 'curtain call', and sales staff reported feeling 'stage fright' before the store opened and the 'performance' became subject to public scrutiny.

Emotional labour at Girlie Glitter Co.

Despite their nerves, staff were told it was 'more important to smile, and to look happy, than to be step perfect' in the dance routines. As one sales assistant put it, 'We're told it's more important to *look* happy than to *be* happy.' For many staff, this meant either faking it or as one described it, 'going into robot':

Sometimes I just look in the mirror, smile, and remind myself to hold that position during the day. At other times, when we've got the music on and we're dancing, I start thinking about messing around with my mates the night before and then I start to smile anyway. So I daydream quite a lot. It looks like I am really enjoying myself there and then, and the customers don't know any different, so there's no harm done really. At other times you don't really have to try, because it is such good fun. You see these really cute little girls come in and do their hair and make-up and they look so pretty, really cute and it's just great. I think how much I would've loved that when I was their age, all the dressing up and stuff. Some days I really love it here. Other days, if we're busy, or there are kids that are playing up, or older girls are in here just messing about and being a pain then it's not so great and you have to just put it on because that's what we're being paid for . . . that's what we're selling, big smiles and loads of fun.

▶

Some sales assistants coped with the embarrassment or 'stage fright' of the dance routines by relying on each other, and by 'having a laugh': 'It is scary when you're out there and it's a really busy day and you maybe see someone you know going by, or people are pointing and laughing and you just look at each other and giggle. I couldn't do it out there on my own, but at least together we can have a bit of a laugh, and I mean, to be dancing about with your mates and getting paid for it, you can't really complain can you?' New recruits particularly tended to feel anxious about performing in front of a crowd, however: 'I get very nervous before curtain call. But afterwards I get that coming off stage feeling and think, "Thank God, I did it", until the next time.'

Many of the staff are conscious that they are role models for their young customers, and realise the extent to which their uniform appearance (all shop floor staff wear fitted pink T-shirts with the Girlie Glitter logo on them – for sale in children's sizes in store, and black trousers) helped them to identify together as a group. The uniform appearance of staff is thought to be particularly important by the Girlie Glitter management team. One of the area sales managers (the only male employed by the company at the time of the research) also wore black trousers and a pink company T-shirt. He reflected 'I could wear a traditional suit and tie, but choose to wear the pink to fit in. It's not glittery and tight-fitting like theirs [the all-female sales staff], but at least we all look the same and that's important . . . so that we all fit in.'

Music is also particularly important to the management of Girlie Glitter Co., especially in terms of fostering employee and customer identification. Particular types of music (mainly by all-girl pop groups) or even specific songs come to be associated with the store, and these tend to provide a continuous soundtrack to the 'front stage' areas and, of course, to the dance routines performed at the store entrances. One particular store manager summed up the general effect of this when she said: 'Every time I hear one of the songs we play, I am immediately reminded of the company, wherever I am or whatever I'm doing'.

Some sales assistants had experienced really rude or aggressive customers – either children playing up, or their parents shouting and being abusive. When this happens 'you just think, "Oh well they're paying for it I suppose". It's their kid's birthday or whatever, or maybe they're divorced Dads and this is their only day with the children and so you think, "Just let them get on with it". But it can be hard, sometimes. Some days when I've finished work all I can hear is the same music over and over in my head, and screaming, whining children saying "I want this. . . ." I don't think I'll ever have kids of my own, thanks very much. I've seen enough tantrums to last me a lifetime!'

Questions

1. In what ways is gender relevant to the performance and management of emotional labour at Girlie Glitter Co.?
2. How might the concepts of 'surface acting' and 'deep acting' (Hochschild 1983) be applied to the experiences of sales assistants?
3. Drawing on Bolton and Boyd's (2003) typology, identify the different types of emotion management performed by sales assistants at Girlie Glitter Co.
4. What techniques have the management team devised to encourage sales assistants to perform emotional labour?
5. What coping strategies do staff implement to alleviate the negative consequences of the emotional labour aspects of their work?
6. Draft a recruitment advertisement for sales assistants at Girlie Glitter Co. What key issues might you need to consider in recruiting, selecting and training new staff?

Managing family fun at Theme Park Co.

Peter Ackers

Jason is a section manager at Theme Park Co. He is responsible for managing 8 full-time and 14 part-time, largely seasonally employed workers, who work in the family section of a major theme park. This particular area of the park includes rides specifically designed for children who are under the minimum height requirement for the 'thrill' rides (the roller-coasters and so on), and many of the rides are based on familiar children's characters from television pro-grammes, films and children's books. This section of the park has been experiencing recur-ring problems with unacceptably high levels of voluntary staff turnover, as well as escalating reports of customer dissatisfaction. The latter have been revealed as a result of verbal reports both to Jason himself, and to members of his team, as well as through customer exit surveys. These have suggested that both adult and child customers are particularly unhappy about excessively long waiting times, rides not functioning correctly and disappointment when children are refused entrance to a ride or attraction because it is being serviced or cleaned. The most stressful side of the job for Jason is balancing the need for 'throughput' (processing customers through the rides and attractions as efficiently as possible) with the demand for customer satisfaction, and the need to provide a quality, personalised service to children and their families. As he puts it, 'It's, you know, pushing people through but with a smile, so we do actually have to spend some time, to keep them coming back'. Through their staff develop-ment mechanisms, Jason and his line manager have reached the conclusion that while Jason is coping extremely well with the logistical aspects of his role, he would benefit from develop-ing his skills in coping with the emotional side of the job, and in particular the competing demands placed upon him. They have identified a training consultancy that runs courses on emotional intelligence and need to outline what Jason feels he needs and how he is likely to benefit through developing his emotional intelligence.

Questions

1. Clarify what the term 'emotional intelligence' means and outline the kind of skills and abilities that Jason might improve as a result of developing his emotional intelligence.
2. What might be the main benefits of providing Jason with an opportunity to develop his emotional intelligence – for Jason, for Theme Park Co. as an employer, and for customers?
3. With reference to this particular example, what criticisms might be made of this approach, and of the concept of 'emotional intelligence'?

Change and emotion at Hotel Co.

Melissa Tyler and Philip Hancock

The senior management at Hotel Co., a large hotel in Singapore employing some 243 people at any one time, have recently introduced a computerised system that has fully integrated all aspects of customer service. The hotel's clientele are primarily Western business travellers and their families, and many of these are now able to make their own hotel

▶

bookings online. While all customer-facing and support staff have been fully trained in the more technical aspects of accessing and operating the system, this major change has impacted on staff in a number of ways that senior managers had not anticipated. First, staff who previously worked closely together even though they were formally part of different teams no longer have any reason to work together or to interact during the normal course of their work. This has caused a degree of disharmony and disappointment among some members of staff, particularly those who have been employed by the hotel for some time. Newer members of staff are also finding little reason to engage with their colleagues in any sustained way, as most forms of interaction and communication can be carried out electronically. Second, members of staff who have worked for the hotel for some time and had been happy with the old ways of working have resented not only the change itself, but also the way in which it has been introduced, with limited communication, consultation or explanation from senior management before, during or after the introduction of the new system. Third, the electronic booking system means that hotel guests can now book direct and request specific items for their room such as a room-service meal or even a particular type of pillow on their bed upon their arrival. However, as the system is relatively new and in the early stages of implementation, the hotel's staff are finding that they often have to intervene to correct or amend particular arrangements. Hotel guests are reporting that their rooms are not entirely what they expected when they booked and particularly front-line reception staff are finding that they have to increase the effort they put into providing a high-quality customer service. In recognition of some of the difficulties they face, the hotel's senior management team have enforced strict guidelines on uniform and grooming in order to convey a professional image of the hotel at all times. All staff have also been required to attend a one-day training course at which the '3 S's' of effective customer interaction are reinforced: 'smiling, sincerity and service'.

Questions

1. Why might Hotel Co., following the introduction of the new ICT system, be described as an 'emotional cauldron'? What does this mean – for staff, for senior managers and for customers?
2. What key aspects of managing change at Hotel Co. did senior management overlook?
3. What impact has this had on staff, and on customers?
4. In addition to the additional training courses they are offering, what measures might be introduced to address some of the difficulties the organisation faces in this current situation?

Bibliography

Ackroyd, S. and Thompson, P. (1999) *Organizational Misbehaviour*, London: Sage.

Adkins, L. (1995) *Gendered Work: Sexuality, Family and the Labour Market*, Milton Keynes: Open University Press.

Albrow, M. (1992) '*Sine ira et studio* – or do organizations have feelings?', *Organization Studies*, Vol.13, No.3, pp.313–29.

Alexander, D. and Wells, W. (1991) 'Reactions of police officers to body handling after a major disaster', *British Journal of Psychiatry*, Vol.159, pp.547–55.

Allen, J. and Du Gay, P. (1994) 'Industry and the rest: the economic identity of services', *Work, Employment and Society*, Vol.8, No.2, pp.255–71.

*Ashforth, B. and Humphrey, R. (1993) 'Emotional labour in service roles: the influence of identity', *Academy of Management Review*, Vol.18, No.1, pp.18–115.

*Ashforth, B. and Humphrey, R. (1995) 'Emotion in the workplace: a reappraisal', *Human Relations*, Vol.48, No.2, pp.97–121.

Bain, P. and Boyd, C. (1998) 'Once I get you up there where the air is rarefied: health, safety and the working conditions of airline cabin crews', *New Technology, Work and Employment*, Vol.13, No.1, pp.16–28.

Barnard, C. (1938) *The Functions of the Executive*, Cambridge, MA: Harvard University Press.

Bell, E. and Taylor, S. (2003) 'The elevation of work: pastoral power and the new age work ethic', *Organization*, Vol.10, No.2, pp.329–49.

Bendix, R. (1956) *Work and Authority in Industry: Ideologies of Management in the Course of Industrialization*, New York: Wiley.

*Bolton, S. (2000) 'Emotion here, emotion there, emotional organizations everywhere', *Critical Perspectives on Accounting*, Vol.11, pp.155–71.

Bolton, S. and Boyd, C. (2003) 'Trolley dolly or skilled emotion manager? Moving on from Hochschild's managed heart', *Work, Employment and Society*, Vol.17, No.2, pp.289–308.

Bryman, A. (2004) *The Disneyization of Society*, London: Sage.

Carlzon, J. (1987) *Moments of Truth*, New York: Harper Row.

Cooper, R. (1998) 'Sentimental value', *People Management*, April, pp.48–50.

Crossley, N. (1998) 'Emotions and communicative action', in G. Bendelow and S. Williams (eds) *Emotions in Social Life: Critical Themes and Contemporary Issues*, London: Routledge.

Dale, K. (2001) *Anatomising Embodiment and Organisation Theory*, London: Palgrave.

Driver, M. (2003) 'United we stand, or else? Exploring organizational attempts to control emotional expression by employees on September 11, 2001', *Journal of Organizational Change Management*, Vol.16, No.5, pp.534–46.

Elias, N. (1991) 'On human beings and their emotions: a process sociological essay', in M. Featherstone, M. Hepworth and B.S. Turner (eds) *The Body: Social Process and Cultural Theory*, London: Sage.

Falk, P. (1994) *The Consuming Body*, London: Sage.

Filby, M. (1992) 'The figures, the personality and the bums: service work and sexuality', *Work, Employment and Society*, Vol.6, No.1, pp.23–42.

*Fineman, S. (ed.) (1993) *Emotion in Organizations*, London: Sage.

Fineman, S. (1994) 'Organizing and emotion: towards a social construction', in J. Hassard and M. Parker (eds) *Towards a New Theory of Organizations*, London: Routledge.

Fineman, S. (ed.) (2008) *The Emotional Organization: Passions and Power*, Oxford: Blackwell.

Freund, P. (1990) 'The expressive body: a common ground for the sociology of emotions and health and illness', *Sociology of Health and Illness*, Vol.12, No.4, pp.452–77.

Frost, P. (2003) *Toxic Emotions at Work: How Compassionate Managers Handle Pain and Conflict*, Boston, MA: Harvard Business School Press.

Gabriel, Y. (1995) 'The unmanaged organization: stories, fantasies and subjectivity', *Organization Studies*, Vol.16, pp.477–502.

Gabriel, Y. (2000) *Storytelling in Organizations*, London: Sage.

Goffman, E. (1959) *The Presentation of Self in Everyday Life*, Harmondsworth: Penguin.

Goleman, D. (1996) *Emotional Intelligence: Why It Can Matter More Than IQ*, London: Bloomsbury.

Goleman, D. (1997) *Working with Emotional Intelligence*, New York: Bantam Books.

Goleman, D. (1998) *Emotional Intelligence: Why It Can Matter More Than IQ*, London: Bloomsbury.

Goleman, D. (1999) *Working with Emotional Intelligence*, London, Bloomsbury.

Goleman, D., Boyatzis, R. and McKee, A. (2002) *Primal Leadership: Realizing the Power of Emotional Intelligence*, Boston, MA: Harvard Business School Press.

Hall, E.J. (1993) 'Waitering/waitressing: engendering the work of table servers', *Gender and Society*, Vol.17, No.3, pp.329–46.

Hancock, P. and Tyler, M. (2001a) *Work, Postmodernism and Organization: A Critical Introduction*, London: Sage.

Hancock, P. and Tyler, M. (2001b) 'The look of love: gender and the organization of aesthetics', in J. Hassard, R. Holliday and H. Willmott (eds) *Body and Organization*, London: Sage.

Hancock, P., Hughes, B., Jagger, E., Paterson, K., Russell, R., Tulle, E. and Tyler, M. (2000) *The Body, Culture and Society: An Introduction,* Milton Keynes: Open University Press.

Harris, J. (1996) *Getting Employees to Fall in Love With Your Company,* New York: Amacom.

Hatcher, C. (2003) 'Refashioning a passionate manager: gender at work', *Gender, Work and Organization,* Vol.10, No.4, pp.391–412.

Herzberg, F. (1974) *Work and the Nature of Man,* London: Crosby Lockwood Staples.

Hochschild, A.R. (1979) 'Emotion work, feeling rules and social structure', *American Journal of Sociology,* Vol.85, No.3, pp.551–75.

*Hochschild, A.R. (1983) *The Managed Heart: Commercialization of Human Feeling,* Berkeley, CA: University of California Press.

Hochschild, A.R. (1990) 'Ideology and emotion management: a perspective and path for future research', in T. Kemper (ed.) *Research Agendas in the Sociology of Emotions,* New York: SUNY Press.

James, N. (1989) 'Emotional labour: skill and work in the social regulation of human feeling', *Sociological Review,* Vol.37, No.1, pp.15–42.

Kandola, R. and Fullerton, J. (1995) *Managing the Mosaic: Diversity in Action,* London: Institute of Personnel Development.

Kanter, R.M. (1977) *Men and Women of the Corporation,* New York: Basic Books.

Konz, G.N.P. and Ryan, F.X. (1999) 'Maintaining an organizational spirituality: no easy task', *Journal of Organizational Change Management,* Vol.12, No.3, pp.200–10.

Lashley, C. (2002) 'Emotional harmony, dissonance and deviance at work', *International Journal of Contemporary Hospitality Management,* Vol.14, No.5, pp.255–57.

Leidner, R. (1993) *Fast Food, Fast Talk: Service Work and the Routinization of Everyday Life,* Berkeley, CA: University of California Press.

Leidner, R. (1999) 'Emotional labour in service work', *Annals of the American Academy of Political and Social Sciences,* No.561, pp.81–95.

Lupton, D. (1998) *The Emotional Self,* London: Sage.

Martin, E. (1994) *Flexible Bodies,* Boston, MA: Beacon Press.

Maslow, A.H. (1943) 'A theory of human motivation', *Psychological Review,* Vol.50, pp.372–96.

Mayo, E. (1933) *The Human Problems of Industrial Civilization,* New York: Macmillan.

Morris, J. and Feldman, D. (1997) 'Managing emotions in the workplace', *Journal of Management Issues,* Vol.9, No.3, pp.257–75.

Neck, C.P. and Milliman, J.F. (1994) 'Thought self-leadership: finding spiritual fulfillment in organizational life', *Journal of Managerial Psychology,* Vol.9, No.6, pp.9–16.

O'Brien, M. (1994) 'The managed heart revisited: health and social control', *Sociological Review,* Vol.42, No.3, pp.393–413.

Parkinson, B. (1991) 'Emotional stylists: strategies of expressive management among trainee hairdressers', *Cognition and Emotion,* Vol.5, pp.419–34.

Paules, G. (1996) 'Resisting the symbolism of service', in C. Macdonald and C. Sirianni (eds) *Working in the Service Society,* Philadelphia, PA: Temple University Press.

Peters, T. (1989) *Thriving on Chaos,* London: Pan Books.

Peters, T. and Austin, N. (1985) *A Passion For Excellence,* New York: Random House.

Peters, T. and Waterman, R. (1982) *In Search of Excellence,* New York: Harper & Row.

Pringle, R. (1989) 'Bureaucracy, rationality and sexuality: the case of secretaries', in J. Hearn, D. Sheppard, P. Tancred-Sheriff and G. Burrell (eds) *The Sexuality of Organization,* London: Sage.

Putnam, L. and Mumby, D. (1993) 'Organizations, emotion and the myth of rationality', in S. Fineman (ed.) *Emotion in Organizations,* London: Sage.

Rafaeli, A. (1989) 'When cashiers meet customers: an analysis of the role of supermarket cashiers', *Academy of Management Journal,* Vol.32, No.2, pp.245–73.

*Rafaeli, A. and Sutton, R. (1987) 'Expression of emotion as part of the work role', *Academy of Management Review,* Vol.12, pp.23–37.

Roethlisberger, F.J. and Dickson, W.J. (1939) *Management and the Worker,* Cambridge, MA: Harvard University Press.

Russell, R. and Tyler, M. (2002) 'Thank heaven for little girls: "Girl Heaven" and the commercial context of feminine childhood', *Sociology,* Vol.36, No.3, pp.619–37.

Sanders, T. (2004) 'Controllable laughter: managing sex work through humour', *Sociology,* Vol.38, No.2, pp.273–91.

Sloan, M. (2004) 'The effects of occupational characteristics on the experience and expression of anger in the workplace', *Work and Occupations,* Vol.31, No.1, pp.38–72.

Steinberg, R. and Figart, D. (1999) 'Emotional labour since the managed heart', *Annals of the American Academy of Political and Social Sciences,* No.561, pp.8–26.

Sutton, R. (1991) 'Maintaining norms about expressed emotions: the case of bill collectors', *Administrative Science Quarterly,* Vol.36, pp.245–68.

Sutton, R. and Rafaeli, A. (1988) 'Untangling the relationship between displayed emotions and organizational sales: the case of convenience stores', *Academy of Management Journal,* Vol.31, No.3, pp.461–87.

Taylor, F.W. (1911) *Principles of Scientific Management,* New York: Harper & Row.

Thomson, K. (1997) *Emotional Capital: Capturing Hearts and Minds to Create Lasting Business Success,* London: Carstone.

Tyler, M. and Abbott, P. (1998) 'Chocs away: weight watching in the contemporary airline industry', *Sociology,* Vol.32, No.3, pp.433–50.

Van Maanen, J. and Kunda, G. (1989) 'Real feelings: emotional expression and organizational culture', in L.L. Cummings and B. Straw (eds) *Research in Organizational Behaviour,* Vol.11. Greenwich, CT: JAI Press.

Vince, R. and Saleem, T. (2004) 'The impact of caution and blame on organizational learning', *Management Learning,* Vol.35, No.2, pp.133–54.

Walton, S. (1992) *Made in America,* New York: Bantham.

Weber, M. (1978 [1921]) *Economy and Society,* Berkeley, CA: University of California Press.

Weber, M. (1989 [1904]) *The Protestant Ethic and the Spirit of Capitalism,* London: Unwin Hyman.

Willetts, L. and Leff, J. (2003) 'Improving the knowledge and skills of psychiatric nurses: efficacy of a staff training programme', *Journal of Advanced Nursing,* Vol.42, No.3, pp.237–43.

Williams, S. (2001) *Emotion and Social Theory,* London: Sage.

Wolkowitz, C. (2006) *Bodies at Work,* London: Sage.

Yeoman, I., Sparrow, J. and McGunnigle, F. (2000) 'Accessing knowledge at British Airways: the impact of soft OR', *Journal of Organizational Change Management,* Vol.13, No.2, pp.121–39.

*Useful reading

Chapter 21

FLEXIBILITY

Stephen Procter and Stephen Ackroyd

Introduction: what do we mean by flexibility?

Flexibility is a concept that can be understood in many different ways and at many different levels. At its broadest it is perhaps best understood as the quality by which an entity adapts itself to a change in the demands made upon it. The appeal of flexibility as a concept can be seen by a consideration of its opposites – inflexibility, rigidity, etc. – all of which carry a quite negative connotation. Before portraying flexibility as something which in all cases should be welcomed, however, we need to raise two simple questions: flexibility of what and flexibility for whom?

In answer to the first question, we can identify four basic areas in which the idea of flexibility has been applied:

- **Flexibility of labour:** this in turn can be understood in two different ways: as the ability and willingness of individual workers to perform a wider range of tasks, jobs or skills; and as the ability of organisations to vary the amount of labour they use in accordance with fluctuations in demand.

- **Flexibility of technology:** technology here can include both physical technology and the broader ideas of technique and know-how; flexibility refers to both the range of things technology can do and the ease with which it can move between them.

- **Flexibility of organisations:** this might include the flexibility of both labour and technology, but refers to the more general ability of organisations to adapt themselves to the demands made upon them.

- **Flexibility of systems:** at a broader level still, we are concerned with the systems within which organisations operate. A system might thus be a national economy, a region or even the world economy as a whole. Again, to understand what form this might take, we must take into account the other forms of flexibility.

The nature of the present volume means that our focus is on the flexibility of labour. As we shall see, however, it is impossible to understand this in isolation from the other types of flexibility we have described. What we shall also see is that – in answer to our second basic question – flexibility is defined from the point of view of those who run and those who own organisations. In terms of the employment relationship, it is flexibility *for* the employer, which, in all likelihood, is likely to mean flexibility *of* the employee. The nature of the employment relationship means that, while in some circumstances this will mean flexibility *for* the employee, the fact that the interests of employee and employer will not always coincide means that from the point of view of the employee, flexibility cannot unequivocally be seen as a good thing (see also Legge 1998).

The rest of the chapter is structured as follows. We look first at flexibility in historical perspective, showing how the idea of flexibility needs to be understood against the background of longer-term trends in how work is organised. We turn then to how labour and organisational flexibility have been conceptualised in recent and current debates. We shall see that although the so-called 'flexible firm' model has much to commend it, it cannot offer a full explanation of the developments we observe. The idea of flexible specialisation also has its drawbacks, and we shall see how this leads us on to the 'new flexible firm' model, which combines labour, technological and organisational flexibility in a way which offers us much greater insight. The new flexible firm is then compared to a rival configuration which is based on the idea that British organisations have attempted to achieve flexibility through the emulation of their Japanese counterparts. We turn finally to the area on which much current interest in flexibility is focused: the public sector, in which the idea of 'skills mix' provides a powerful example of how management in organisations both conceives of and pursues flexibility in its labour force.

Flexibility in historical perspective

Our understanding of flexibility can also be enhanced by understanding its historical context. Although we can trace the history of job or work design back to Adam Smith's (1776) enunciation of the benefits of a highly developed division of labour, it is only really since the end of the nineteenth century that these and other ideas have been applied systematically in organisations. According to Buchanan's (1994) account, the period from then until around 1980 can be divided into two: the move towards work based on the principles of scientific management; and the subsequent reversal of this trend as its negative effects on workers became apparent (for a fuller account, see Buchanan 1994; Parker and Wall 1998; Parker *et al.* 2001).

The period of scientific management centres on the development and influence of the ideas of Frederick Taylor (1856–1917; see Taylor 1911). Taylor's concern was to eliminate what he saw as systematic inefficiencies in the manner in which work was organised and managed. This implied that work was to be fragmented into its most basic components, each of which would be undertaken in a manner deemed to the most efficient. There was, in short, a 'one best way' of organising work (see Kanigel 1997), and achieving this, it was argued, would benefit both workers and employers. Just as important was the idea that the organising of work was to be the exclusive responsibility of managers: there was thus a separation between those who did the work – the workers – and those who determined how it should be done – the managers.

The extent to which these ideas were used, and the nature of their impact on people's work and lives, are issues which have generated a great deal of research and discussion. Much of this derives from Harry Braverman's (1974) 'deskilling thesis', which was based on Marxist ideas of the 'labour process'. In Braverman's account, Taylor's ideas had proved to be overwhelmingly the dominant force in the organisation and control of work. The fragmentation of work and the removal of worker responsibility for its organisation had thus led to its being progressively deskilled or degraded (see, for example, Noble 1977). Subsequent research has sought to modify Braverman's basic thesis (see, for example, Littler 1982; McIvor 2001). Important here is Friedman's (1977) distinction between 'direct control' and 'responsible autonomy'. His argument was that management interests would not in all cases be best served by the 'direct control' of the workforce which scientific management involved. Where workers were skilled and work more complex, it might be better to acknowledge and exploit this through pursuit of a more trust-based strategy of 'responsible autonomy'.

New developments in thinking on how work should be organised were in any case already well established by the mid-1970s. Problems associated with the simplified and repetitive nature of work under scientific management had from an early stage led to such measures as job rotation – the movement of workers between tasks – and job enlargement – the creation of jobs combining larger numbers of tasks (Parker and Wall 1998). From the 1950s onwards more fundamental concerns began to be addressed, as the design of jobs began more systematically to take into account the motivation and satisfaction of employees (Parker and Wall 1998) through ideas such as job enrichment (Herzberg 1966) and the job characteristics model (Hackman and Oldham 1976). Also influential was the sociotechnical systems approach. Trist and Bamforth's (1951) study of the post-war British coal-mining industry showed how automation had brought with it the introduction of a version of scientific management, the 'longwall' method, which displaced the autonomous multi-skilled groups which had operated under the old 'hand-got' system. Later work (Trist *et al.* 1963) revealed the development of a compromise 'composite shortwall' method, based on multi-skilled, self-selecting groups, responsible on one shift for the whole of the coal-getting cycle. Sociotechnical ideas were picked up in several countries, most notably in Scandinavia (Benders and Van Hootegem 1999).

From the mid-/late 1970s onwards, however, we see a more fundamental challenge to the principle that the division of labour should be extended as far as possible. From this time onwards we see debate coalescing around the idea that work was undergoing a basic restructuring. What in many ways was the central theme running through these debates was that work was becoming more flexible. In the following sections we look at the main models advanced both to explain and to encourage these developments.

The flexible firm

In the period since the early 1980s, debates on the flexibility of work and organisation began with the model of the flexible firm. Put forward by Atkinson and others (Atkinson 1984; Atkinson and Meager 1986; NEDO 1986), it claimed that firms were increasingly seeking and achieving greater flexibility from their workforce. This flexibility was of two main kinds:

■ **numerical:** the ability of firms to adjust numbers employed and hours worked;

■ **functional:** the ability of firms to match the skills profiles of their workforces to changing patterns of demand.

As part of these developments, it was argued, the workforce was being divided into two basic groups. Represented diagrammatically in Figure 21.1, the two groups are:

■ **core workers:** workers expected to display functional flexibility in return for security of employment;

■ **peripheral workers:** workers expected to provide the firm with the numerical flexibility it requires. This group would include part-time workers, contract workers, and so on.

The idea of the flexible firm model gave rise to an extensive and often heated debate. There certainly was enough evidence to offer the model at least *prima facie* support. With regard to numerical flexibility, besides the NEDO (1986) study itself, the work of Hakim (1990), Casey (1991), Marginson (1991) and Penn (1992) all contributed to establishing its continued importance. Evidence for functional flexibility was less easy to identify from survey data, but there was support for the idea that it was on the increase (Daniel 1987; Cross 1988; Elger 1991). Although applied originally to the UK, moreover, evidence pointed to the increasing use

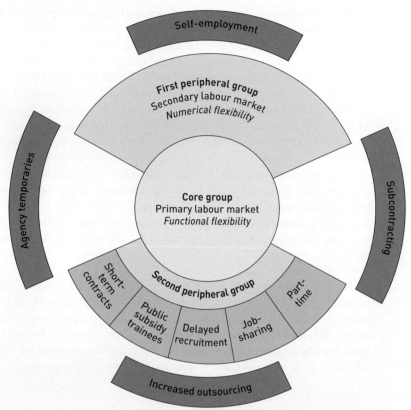

Figure 21.1 The flexible firm
Source: Atkinson 1984

of flexible working practices across a range of countries (see Brewster *et al.* 1994). Although critics of the flexible firm took issue with the idea that these developments were part of a deliberate or 'strategic' move on the part of employers (see Mayne *et al.* 1996; Friedrich *et al.* 1998; Wood and Smith 1989), Procter *et al.* (1994) demonstrated that such arguments were based on a rather restricted view of what 'strategy' is. In more recent conceptions of strategy, in which it seen is a 'pattern' rather a 'plan', account can be taken of its 'emergent' as well as its 'deliberate' aspects (see, for example, Mintzberg 1978).

Patterns of flexibility

Looking first at patterns of functional flexibility, we can see that it was wildly optimistic to take the view that this would involve the development of a core group of polyvalent super-craftspersons. Functional flexibility in the UK has had two main characteristics:

- **negative in nature:** it involves the breaking down of lines of demarcation rather than the more positive development of multi-skilled workers;

- **limited in degree:** the most important thing from the employer's point of view is not that individual workers are fully flexible but that the workforce taken as a whole is flexible enough.

The negative nature of flexibility is shown in studies undertaken largely in manufacturing settings (Cross 1988; Daniel 1987). In this context, the employers' major concern has been to

Box 21.1: HRM in practice

Limits to flexibility: why full flexibility might not be a good idea

In his book, *Managing Innovation and Change* (1995), Jon Clark looks at the creation and operation by Pirelli of a cable manufacturing plant in Aberdare, South Wales over the period 1984–92. Work within the plant was divided into 'skill modules', each of which set out the skills and knowledge required to perform an activity. It was envisaged that each worker would acquire between six and ten of these modules, each attracting a supplement of 4 per cent on basic pay. Workers were divided into three main groups – producers, maintainers and administrators – and it was expected that they would acquire at least one module from outside their own area.

Responsibility for developing and awarding the modules passed eventually to line managers, but the inconsistencies this generated became a serious source of dissatisfaction among employees. Wide disparities became evident between the three main groups of workers, and eventually separate settlements had to be arrived at with each of them. For producers, this involved 'capping' or limiting the number of modules employees could acquire and allocating them 'primary' and 'secondary' work areas.

Thus the 'full flexibility' of employees to which Pirelli had aspired was not achieved. In fact, the 'full flexibility' of employees was considered unnecessary. As Clark expresses it, Pirelli 'achieved what they set out to achieve, namely full flexibility to do what they wanted. In practice, however, to do what they wanted they did not need full flexibility' (1995, p.153).

Source: Clark 1995

---

break down demarcations between production and maintenance work or between different areas of maintenance responsibility. The direct evidence on the nature of functional flexibility is consistent with other evidence on trends in training and skill (see Gallie 1991; Gospel 1995). As for the limited degree of flexibility, this in many cases is linked to its negative nature (Cross 1988). But even when flexibility is associated with a more positive attitude towards multi-skilling, its extent depends on the requirements of the employer rather than those of the employee. This is brought out clearly by Clark's study of Pirelli (see Box 21.1). As Clark expresses it, Pirelli 'achieved what they set out to achieve, namely full flexibility to do what they wanted. In practice, however, to do what they wanted they did not need full flexibility' (1995, p.153).

Turning now to patterns in numerical flexibility, we need to look at recent developments in the context of long-term labour market trends. The fourth Workplace Employee Relations Survey (WERS) showed part-timers to account for around 25 per cent of all UK employment in 1998 (Cully *et al.* 1999, p.32). The recent *growth rate* in part-time employment, however, has been nothing like that recorded in the 1960s and 1970s, and a large part of the growth can in any case be accounted for by changes in the sectoral composition of the economy (Emmott and Hutchinson 1998, pp.232–33). The use of temporary workers did increase markedly in the 1990s, as employers moved out of the recession of the early part of the decade. Although the Labour Force Survey showed temporary workers to account for only around 7 per cent of the workforce by 1996, what was more significant was that temporary jobs accounted for almost one-third of all engagements since 1984 (Emmott and Hutchinson 1998, p.234).

Taken together with trends in functional flexibility, this could be regarded as at least *prima facie* evidence of the establishment of the flexible firm model. What the model is based on, however, is the association of each of the forms of flexibility with a particular group of employees: the protected core exhibits functional flexibility in return for employment security, while the peripheral workforce provides the necessary numerical flexibility. The difficulties involved in taking this line of argument are illustrated most clearly by the findings of WERS. 'It appears,' Cully *et al.* (1999, p.38) conclude, 'that the use of the non-standard forms of labour is more closely related to employment *within* the core than outside it' (emphasis in original). Again, this is paralleled by developments elsewhere. Cappelli's (1995, p.591) review shows there is little sign of a core–periphery strategy being adopted in the US: 'there is no evidence that the current changes in the employment relationship in the USA are driven by an interest in buffering core employees'. In other words, the boundaries between 'core' and 'peripheral' workers, in so far as they ever existed, are being broken down, and all workers are being made subject to a greater degree of insecurity.

Flexible specialisation

One of the most important attempts to conceptualise and explain the restructuring of work and production was Piore and Sabel's 'flexible specialisation' thesis. As the title of their book, *The Second Industrial Divide* (1984), suggests, they argued that the capitalist world faced a fundamental choice between persisting with an economy based on mass production and returning to one based on craft production. In this account, the system of mass production which had established itself as dominant by the early part of the twentieth century had, from the end of the 1960s, found its existence under threat. It was at this point that craft production, in the shape of flexible specialisation, presented itself as the alternative.

Under flexible specialisation, production was based on flexible networks of technologically sophisticated manufacturing firms. The networks were situated in certain geographical areas, in which firms did not compete directly with each other on the basis of cost, and where industry was able to develop and draw on regional institutions. In some areas, argued Piore and Sabel, these arrangements were already emerging to challenge the dominance of mass production. The three most prominent and widely cited were the so-called 'Third Italy', the area around the city of Salzburg, and the Baden-Württemberg region of Germany. Although flexible specialisation is portrayed as the revival of craft production, Piore and Sabel did not explore in any real depth its implications for the nature of work. The assumption was that the use of more flexible capital equipment would be associated with the development of a highly flexible, multi-skilled workforce.

The flexible specialisation thesis was at the centre of many of the debates concerning the restructuring of work and production in the 1980s and 1990s. Partly as a result of its appeal from a policy point of view, it did attract a number of adherents (e.g. Hirst and Zeitlin 1989). A substantial part of the reaction it generated, however, was either sceptical or actively hostile (Amin 1994; Tomaney 1994; Williams *et al.* 1987). Among the concerns was the question of whether flexible specialisation was being put forward as a description of what was happening, a prediction of what was going to happen, or a prescription of what should happen. Added to the conceptual difficulties are the more prosaic problems of lack of evidence. Even if taken as prediction rather than description, it is difficult to find examples of UK industries that have been restructured along the lines of flexible specialisation. This applies even in industries like ceramics, where the conditions for such a restructuring might be considered to be the most conducive (Rowley 1996).

The new flexible firm

As the previous section showed, there is very little evidence to suggest that flexibility in British industry is based on technologically sophisticated, flexible production systems. What has emerged instead is a system of cell- or group-based production, in which, rather than on functional lines, production is organised so as to bring together in one place the people and equipment needed to produce a certain range of goods. Particularly in manufacturing industry, cellular working has quite quickly become widespread (Ingersoll Engineers 1994). Cellular production will often be introduced on the initiative of production managers and for what seem largely technical reasons. Nonetheless, the implications or associations from a human resource management point of view are likely to be profound. For one thing, the operation of cellular production will both encourage and be encouraged by the kind of flexibility in labour we explored in the previous sections. The introduction of a product 'focus' to the organisation of work will militate against too strong a reliance on functional specialisation, especially if, as in a number of cases, the reorganisation of production is accompanied by reduction in workforce numbers, thus effectively forcing functional flexibility on to those remaining (Turnbull 1988).

If we broaden our perspective we can observe in other sectors the reorganisation of production on the basis of product or customer. In the case of business process re-engineering (BPR), this would involve restructuring work so as to group together all the tasks necessary to satisfy a particular group of customers (Hammer and Champy 1993). The survey undertaken by Willcocks and Grint (1997) found nearly 60 per cent of large and medium-sized UK companies either planning or actually undertaking some BPR activity. In sectors involving direct 'front-line' contact with customers, a similar reorganisation might be based on the 'strategic segmentation' of customers into different 'revenue streams' (Batt 2000; Frenkel *et al.* 1999).

What is common to all these developments is that work design has come to be central to the way organisations deal with their customers and competitors (Buchanan 1994). As Buchanan (1994: 86) expresses it, 'It has . . . become increasingly unrealistic to distinguish between work design on the one hand and organizational design on the other. The former now typically implies the latter.'

How, then, is flexibility managed and organised? The short answer is that this takes the form not of direct control based on high levels of surveillance – a line of argument to which we return below – but of indirect control based on the allocation of costs. From the second Company-level Industrial Relations Survey (CLIRS) we get some idea of how large British firms use a range of budgetary controls in the relationship between the corporate centre and the operating or business units (Armstrong *et al.* 1996). Perhaps most important for our purposes is the relationship Armstrong *et al.* establish between the use of budgetary controls based on labour cost and the extent of labour flexibility. Using the original flexible firm model, Armstrong *et al.* argue that because of the relative ease with which it is possible to change the numbers or tasks of these 'flexible' workers, labour cost budgets were more likely to be used.

But how do these corporate-level strategies translate into workplace-level decisions? Here, although the evidence is less systematic, a pattern can tentatively be identified. The survey data of Armstrong *et al.* (1996) shows a definite association between the use of labour cost targets and the declaration of redundancies in operating units which fail to meet them. Other evidence is provided by Hunter *et al.* (1993), whose analysis of the flexible firm concluded that there was no tendency on the part of employers to effect horizontal segmentation by levels of skill. What we have instead is a vertical segmentation on the basis of the team or a group of teams. For each of these product-focused segments a calculation of costs and benefits can be made, and this allows firms to make decisions about discrete areas of activities. In other words, a form of numerical flexibility is achieved by taking on and dispensing with not sections of a peripheral workforce but sections of the workforce as a whole.

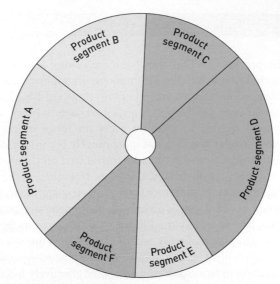

Figure 21.2 The new flexible firm
Source: Based on Ackroyd and Procter 1998

We can combine all these elements – labour, technology, management, organisation – into a model of the 'new flexible firm' (Ackroyd and Procter 1998). This is represented in diagrammatic form in Figure 21.2, which should be compared directly with the original flexible firm model portrayed in Figure 21.1. In the terms of the original flexible firm, the core of the new flexible firm is of almost negligible proportions; the distinction between core and periphery has disappeared; and flexibility is achieved through the manipulation of product-focused segments of activity.

The high-surveillance firm and lean production

Although the flexible firm model and flexible specialisation have been the focuses of debate, and although the 'new flexible firm' appears to offer a better way of conceptualising the changes that have been taking place, we also need to look at other attempts to describe and explain the restructuring of work and organisation. One very popular idea is that organisations in Western Europe and the US have been restructuring themselves along the lines of their Japanese counterparts – a process known as Japanisation, perhaps the best-known exponents of which are Oliver and Wilkinson (1992).

What the focus on Japanese investment and Japanese practice have given rise to is a model of organisation and management we can call the high-surveillance firm. In this model, emphasis is put on the ability of specific procedures and techniques to secure increased quality and variety of production (Conti and Warner 1993; Delbridge *et al.* 1992; Sewell and Wilkinson 1992). Control is exerted over individuals and groups by constantly monitoring, measuring and reporting their performance. This is achieved in part through the discipline imposed by such techniques as just-in-time production (JIT) and total quality management (TQM), but supplementing these are more recent developments which make use of the ability of IT-based systems to record and provide information on work performance. At the extreme, such systems are held to exercise an absolute control over employees, thus representing the modern-day application of the 'panopticon', the principles

Box 21.2: HRM in practice

Flexibility, surveillance and resistance: working in a call centre

Phil Taylor and Peter Bain's study of work in Scottish call centres set out to test the idea that the centres allowed management to exercise absolute control over employees. Their description of work in call centres is worth quoting in full (Taylor and Bain 1999, p.115):

The typical call centre operator is young, female and works in a large open plan office or fabricated building, which may well justify the white-collar factory description. Although probably full-time, she is increasingly likely to be a part-time permanent employee, working complex shift patterns which correspond to peaks of customer demand. Promotion prospects and career advancement are limited so that the attraction of better pay and conditions in another call centre may prove irresistible. In all probability, work consists of an uninterrupted and endless sequence of similar conversations with customers she never meets. She has to concentrate hard on what is being said, jump from page to page on a screen, making sure that the details entered are accurate and that she has said the right things in a pleasant manner. The conversation ends and as she tidies up the loose ends there is another voice in her headset. The pressure is intense because she knows her work is being measured, her speech monitored, and it often leaves her mentally, physically and emotionally exhausted.

As Taylor and Bain make clear, however, all this does not mean that work in call centres is best understood as the application of a modern form of panoptical control. As well as being able to exert collective resistance through their membership of trade unions, workers have open to them a number of less formal, more individual courses of action. They find ways of removing themselves from waiting queues of calls, for example, or can merely pretend to be involved in making a call. Management, say Taylor and Bain, 'would certainly be surprised to discover that they exercise total control over the workforce' (1999, p.115). What the enhanced means of surveillance offers management is not a solution but a dilemma: while it cannot be abandoned altogether, 'intense surveillance can be counterproductive, costly in terms of work-force motivation and commitment' 1999, p.116.

Source: Taylor and Bain 1999. For a fictional account of work in a call centre see Matt Thorne's novel, *Eight Minutes Idle* (Sceptre, 1999).

---

underlying which had previously applied to the design of prisons (Sewell and Wilkinson 1992). These ideas have been developed most recently in attempts to describe and understand the operation of telephone call centres. These have been portrayed as the apotheosis of panoptical control, the success of which is achieved ultimately by its 'internalisation' by workers as a result of its ubiquitous nature (Fernie and Metcalf 1997). There are, however, a number of reasons to cast doubt on such conclusions. Perhaps more importantly, the idea of absolute control assumes away the notion of worker resistance, the different forms such resistance can take, and the effects it can have (Thompson and Ackroyd 1995; Taylor and Bain 1999).

Perhaps the grandest claims made for a Japanese model of production and work are those made on behalf of 'lean production' . This term arose from the US-based International Motor Vehicle Program, a $5M, 14-country project which resulted in the publication of *The Machine that Changed the World* (Womack *et al.* 1990). Lean production, it was claimed, 'uses less of everything compared with mass production' (1990, p.13). Lean production had its origins in the system first developed in Toyota in the 1950s. Although mass production was at its zenith at this time, the argument runs that Toyota management did not consider it suitable for the conditions then prevailing in Japan. In particular, production volumes were not considered large enough to justify the use of dedicated machine tools. Instead, emphasis was placed on simplifying tool changes, with the responsibility given to production workers. This in turn reduced stocks and forced attention on improving product quality.

Womack *et al.* (1990) present the results of lean production in dramatic fashion. Taking the Toyota plant in Takaoka as representative of lean production and the GM plant in Framingham as representative of mass production, their comparison showed the former to have twice the level of productivity (or 'half the human effort'). The claims made by *The Machine that Changed the World* have been subject to challenge on a variety of grounds. Prime amongst the critics are Williams *et al.* (1992), who question almost all aspects of the Womack *et al.* thesis. In particular, the claim that lean production requires 'half the human effort' is based, argue Williams *et al.*, on focusing on parts of the manufacturing process that together account for less than 15 per cent of the total value of the labour involved in making a car.

Two aspects of the claims made by the advocates of lean production are of particular interest to us here. The first is that the organisation of work – rather than the management of production – is placed centre-stage. A lean plant, it was claimed (Womack *et al.* 1990, p.99), 'transfers the maximum number of tasks and responsibilities to those workers actually adding value to the car on the line, and it has in place a system for detecting defects that quickly traces every problem . . . to its ultimate cause'. But what kind of work team would operate under lean production? The idea of teamworking is usually associated with a group's ability to act with some degree of autonomy, but any control over the pace of production would be severely circumscribed by the removal of buffer stocks which lean production implies (Klein 1989). Delbridge *et al.*'s (2000) examination of teams in 'lean' plants in the automotive components sector found that the role of production workers was quite limited in the areas of maintenance and production management. More generally, Benders and Van Hootegem (2000) focus on the use of continuous improvement (*kaizen*) techniques to effect marginal improvement in firms' standard operating procedures. Comparing this with the idea of scientific management that we examined earlier in this chapter, we see that while both might be based on a tightly defined division of labour, the main difference arises in the allocation of responsibility for changing the way in which work is organised. It is with this in mind that Kenney and Florida (1993) refer to the Japanese system as 'innovation-mediated Taylorism'.

The second main aspect of lean production that we need to consider here is the claim that its principles are of universal application. Womack *et al.* (1990, p.88) maintain that 'lean production can be introduced anywhere in the world'. The claims of universalism made by the original advocates of lean production have also been the subject of research work. In particular, MacDuffie and Pil (1997) were keen to see if practice across a range of countries was converging on the lean production model. Although their study does stress the idea of convergence, it recognises also that powerful forces were at work in the opposite direction. Thus although some – mainly European – automotive plants were classified as 'rapid move to lean', others were included under the headings of 'hybrid' and 'sticking with tradition'.

Box 21.3: HRM in practice

Flexibility through lean production: can its principles be applied anywhere?

Following on from the International Motor Vehicle Program, the Arthur Andersen 'Worldwide Manufacturing Competitiveness Survey' looked at the use of the principles of lean production by companies in the automotive components industry. Taking three areas – seats, exhausts and brakes – they explored what they defined as 'world-class performance' in terms of both productivity and quality. The key factor, it was argued, was whether a company was located in a supply chain that was operated in a disciplined manner. The study found no convincing evidence of the universal applicability and superiority of any particular systems of work organisation and human resource management. Although some of the world-class performers were operating under lean production principles, these were largely Japanese companies in Japan, and there were other world-class performers who were operating in quite different ways.

The Arthur Andersen study could thus not be used to support the universalist hypothesis. In the UK automotive components sector, for example, support was found for the idea that it was the supply chain that was the most important factor: significant differences were found between those supplying Japanese car assemblers and those not. Inventories were found to be high relative to those in Japan but there was some evidence of the adoption of the 'softer' aspects of the lean production model. At the same time, Japanese plants tended to follow the lean production model regardless of any linkage with performance. What all this suggested was that location and ownership were important explanatory factors in both performance and management practice. Oliver *et al.*'s (1996, p.S43) conclusion about the UK automotive components sector is quite stark: 'we are pessimistic about the prospects for building world-class manufacturing facilities in what may be basically a non-world-class economy'.

Sources: Lowe *et al.* 1997; Oliver *et al.* 1996

Although the ideas underlying lean production and the high-surveillance firm deserve to be treated with respect, they offer little insight into the way British organisations are restructuring work and technology in order to achieve an enhanced flexibility of operation. A summary of the high-surveillance firm and our other two models of flexibility is presented in Table 21.1. As we have argued, the original model of the flexible firm is useful to the extent that it focuses attention on labour as the main route through which flexibility is achieved; less useful is its neglect of technology and its division of the workforce into core and peripheral elements. The new flexible firm attempts to overcome some of these deficiencies. Although still focusing on the role of labour, this is combined with a low-technology, product-based organisational restructuring and an indirect, cost-based form of control. The high-surveillance firm shares some of this concern with technique and organisation, but stresses also the ability of high-technology IT systems to effect direct control over the workforce.

Table 21.1 Dimensions of the three models: original flexible firm, high-surveillance firm and new flexible firm

	Labour	Technology in use	Sources of flexibility	Management	Network	Problems/sector
Original flexible firm (OFF)	*Requirements:* High-skill and low-skill groups *Policy:* Segmentation	Little or nothing specified	Labour	*Objective:* Rapid changes in direction and scale of production *Strategy:* Labour segmentation	Little or nothing specified; independent producer	Does it exist anywhere?
High-surveillance firm (HSF)	*Requirements:* Semi-skilled *Policy:* Progressive training	Medium to high investment in productive technology	Mix of technical and labour flexibility	*Objective:* Medium to large batch production *Strategy:* High quality/low price	Japanese parent	Electronics and automotives
New flexible firm (NFF)	*Requirements:* Mostly unskilled/ semi-skilled *Policy:* Limited on-the-job training	Low to medium technology; cell-working	Labour and selection of product markets	*Objective:* Medium batches of related products for specific niches *Strategy:* Short-term profit	Specialist provider to supply chains	General manufacturing

Flexibility in the public services

As we have seen in the course of this chapter, many of the important studies of flexibility (as of work and organisation more generally) have been conducted in the manufacturing sector of the economy. In this respect, academic work has failed to keep pace with the restructuring of the economy, which has seen the proportion of activity accounted for by the manufacturing sector decline. We have seen the growth in importance of services and, in particular, public services, and it is this sector that now provide the main focus for developments in both the management of, and research in, the area of flexibility.

Within the public sector, a key focus has been healthcare and, more specifically, the work of nurses. Flexibility in this area is often expressed by the term 'skills mix' . Like 'flexibility' itself, this is a term that benefits from being defined rather loosely. It arises from the general concern that an organisation requires a certain mix of skills in order to meet the demands made upon it; beyond this, there is the requirement that the mix can be changed in response to any changes in these demands. A more specific concern is that the necessary skills are not being provided at too great a cost. In the healthcare context a typical concern would thus be whether certain tasks undertaken by doctors could in fact be undertaken by nurses and, in turn, whether some of the nurses' work could be done by healthcare assistants. To echo Clark's (1995) insight, the basic issue from a management perspective is whether the workforce as a whole has the right skills mix or is flexible enough. This does not necessarily imply that individual workers themselves are flexible or have the right mix of skills.

As Buchan and Dal Paz's (2002) review of the largely US-based work on skills mix makes clear, in the key subsector of healthcare the role of nurses is pivotal. These issues have also been examined in a series of UK-based studies. Bolton's (2004) longitudinal study of nurses working in an NHS hospital paints a broadly positive picture of their experiences of change, arguing that the professional autonomy they have traditionally enjoyed has allowed them both to resist and accommodate changes in their working practices. Adams *et al.*'s (2000) examination of skills-mix changes across eight NHS Trusts, on the other hand, stressed the negative effects. These included the expanded managerial roles that more senior nurses were expected to take on; and the nurses' concerns that the quality of patient care was being affected and that their working relationships with doctors and other professional groups were coming under increased strain.

Perhaps the most in-depth study of this question has been undertaken by Grimshaw (1999), who examined the impact on skills mix and pay determination of the recruitment of healthcare assistants in NHS Trusts. As part of reforms introduced in the 1990s, Trusts were given the discretion to hire nursing or healthcare assistants on locally determined pay scales. To examine the effect on the work and pay of qualified nurses, Grimshaw looked at two Trusts, one of which had taken full advantage of its new powers to recruit new staff and to encourage existing staff to move over to new pay scales, while the other recruited few healthcare assistants and retained the national pay scales. Grimshaw's analysis showed how the differences in pay across staff groups were much greater in the former Trust. This was partly because the expense incurred in encouraging higher-paid staff to transfer to the new, local pay scales was offset by restricting the rates at which staff at lower grades could be hired and also by making it more difficult to progress through the new pay scales. In terms of the composition of the workforce in the two cases, Grimshaw found clear differences emerging in the overall skills mix as represented by the ratio of qualified to unqualified nursing staff – an outcome which from the point of view of the qualified staff could appear as skill or grade 'dilution' .

Issues of skills mix have not been restricted to the nursing workforce. Desombre *et al.* (2006) examined the introduction of functional flexibility in a number of healthcare settings, concluding on a positive note that 'These case studies indicate that functional flexibility does work and that it is accepted by the majority of staff' (p.147). Hyde *et al.* (2005) undertook an evaluation of the NHS's 'Changing Workforce Programme', which piloted what it called 'role

Box 21.4: HRM in practice

Flexibility in public services: professionals and assistants in teaching and social work

Stephen Bach, Ian Kessler and Paul Heron have examined the impact of the 'assistant' role in the areas of teaching and social work. Unlike a number of other researchers they did not just study how the role affected the work of the professionals being assisted (teachers and social workers in this case) but looked also at the experiences of the assistants themselves. Using Gospel's (1992) distinction, they looked at both the work-centred and the employment-centred dimensions of the role – the former covering the actual tasks undertaken, and the latter the role's wider setting in terms of such things as career prospects. In these dimensions, argue Bach *et al.*, work might be seen as being either degraded or empowered. From the point of view of the professional worker – the teacher or the social worker – the employment of an assistant could represent the opportunity to relieve themselves of some of the more mundane aspects of their work or it could be seen as the 'dilution' of their work and the undermining of their status. Looked at from the assistant's perspective, their role might be seen as either giving them the opportunity to be involved in worthwhile and satisfying work or being the repository of those tasks unwanted by the professionals. In the longer term, moreover, it might be seen as being the first step on a career path towards professional status or a way of confining certain workers in an employment 'ghetto'. All eight possible outcomes are set out in tabular form below (see Bach *et al.* 2007, p.1275).

	Assistant		Professional	
	Degradation	**Empowerment**	**Degradation**	**Empowerment**
Work-centred	Intensification	Enrichment	Dilution	Relief
Employment-centred	Ghetto	Opportunity	Responsibility	Complementarity

Bach *et al.*'s (2007) study in fact finds support for the idea that 'both occupations are empowered by the emergence of the assistant role' (p.1288) – the outcomes located in the second and fourth columns of the table.

Sources: Bach *et al.* 2007; Gospel 1992

redesign' across a number of occupational areas. The concerns picked up by Hyde *et al.* (2005) were largely those related to the broader HR strategies of organisations. The remuneration of the redesigned roles was particularly important, with local pay seen as a way of addressing it that might in fact cause greater problems in the longer term. The roles also raised issues of management and accountability, particularly when they cut across well-established professional – and sometimes organisational – boundaries.

An important study has looked at these issues in the context of social work and education (Bach *et al.* 2007; Kessler *et al.* 2006). Although the term 'skills mix' is not used in these areas, both have been characterised by the development of the role of 'assistant'. So just as in the health service the employment of healthcare assistants has implications for nurses, the increasing use of teaching and social work assistants has implications for teachers and social workers respectively. The situation to which this has given rise in examined in Box 21.4.

Also important for this study were the differences between sectors, with teaching assistants being less satisfied with their work and career opportunities than their counterparts in social work. This is explored in more depth by Kessler *et al.* (2006). Focusing on the social work assistants, they show how the nature of the assistant role is shaped not just at this sub-sectoral level but at the organisational and workplace levels as well. Significant differences could exist, for example, between the motivations of the local authorities who employed the assistants, with some seeing it as a role entailing significant responsibility and the possibility of career progression. Even within a single local authority, the role could vary according to the area in which the assistant was working and even the experience and capabilities of the assistants themselves.

Conclusions

This chapter carries a mixed message for specialist HR managers and general managers with HR responsibilities. On the one hand, there exist severe constraints within which they have to operate. This means that with regard to flexibility – as with other issues – some courses of action are more likely to be taken than others. Thus in their pursuit of flexibility, organisations are likely to place the emphasis on the flexibility of labour. The type of flexibility required of labour may be of a negative form: we are much less likely to see securely employed, highly trained, multi-skilled workers than we are their insecure, semi-trained, multi-tasked counterparts. At the level of the individual manager or the individual organisation, there is little opportunity to change the conditions which bring this situation about. This is not to say, however, that there is nothing at all that can be done. HR managers might at least be able to shift the emphasis of the employment relationship from areas in which the interests of employers conflict with the interests of employees, to areas in which the interests of the two coincide.

CASE STUDY 21.1

Managing flexibility: the Theatres Project in Midland City Hospital NHS Trust

Stephen Procter and Graeme Currie

Organisational setting

Our case study organisation, Midland City Hospital NHS Trust is an acute NHS hospital based in a city in the English Midlands. It has an annual budget of over £100 million and employs around 5,000 staff. Within the hospital, our main focus is the Theatres Directorate, which consists of a total of 15 operating theatres. Over 200 people were employed in the directorate. Its annual budget was over £6 million, of which around half was accounted for by pay. Head of the directorate was the clinical director. Two other key members of staff were the theatre manager and the specialty manager. The former, a senior nurse, had joined the hospital in the early 1970s, and her chief concern was staff management within the directorate. The specialty manager had been in the job eight years. His own role he described as 'really processes, money, ensuring things happen'. Head of the Human Resources Department was the Director of Human Resources, who sits on the Trust's board. Among those reporting to the director were the management development manager and the personnel manager.

▶

Background to change

Although the Trust had earlier attempted to introduce a system of local pay in response to central government requirements, the impetus for the Theatres Project came very much from within. 'From there [theatres],' as the HR director expressed it, 'the managers were screaming.' The problems faced by the Theatres Directorate arose from the coexistence of two groups of staff – nurses and operational department practitioners or assistants [ODPs/ODAs] – who worked very closely together and who, in some aspects of work, were interchangeable, but who were trained, paid, progressed, managed and organised quite separately from each other. The reason for this was that the nurses' role had been to assist the surgeons, and the ODPs' to assist the anaesthetist. The two groups of staffs each had their own management and organisation within the directorate, had different duty rosters, and were employed on different terms and conditions. A number of ad hoc ways had been found of dealing with this situation. Because the ODPs were the less well-paid group, for example, it was felt they should be given greater opportunity to work at overtime rates of pay – something which generated conflict between them and the nurses. It was the harmonisation of terms and conditions between these two groups that the Theatres Project set out to introduce.

The Theatres Project

The provision of a common pay scale and common terms and conditions would, claimed the official Trust line, have the following advantages:

- increase in flexibility of relevant staff;
- enable a positive movement to equal pay for equal contribution to the service;
- encourage the development of knowledge and skills among theatre staff;
- ensure the most effective and efficient provision of cover at particular times during the week.

The project's concern for flexibility was made clear in interviews with the directorate's managers. In reference to the nurses and ODPs, the clinical director said, 'We wanted to get them multi-skilled for flexibility'. 'The purpose of doing it,' said the specialty manager, 'was so that we could use the staff interchangeably . . . and so that we could make savings.'

The terms of the agreement eventually arrived at came into effect on 1 January 1998. The clinical director described its essence: 'We call everybody a theatre practitioner now; you're not a nurse, you're a theatre practitioner.' Its chief elements were:

- single pay spine for nurses and ODPs;
- new seven-day single duty rota;
- common 37.5 hour week;
- pay enhancements for commitment to working 'non-core' hours;
- managers encouraged to avoid use of overtime;
- overtime rate of time-and-a-third;
- competence-based system of progression.

What did these changes imply for the two groups of workers? The 37.5-hour week, although leaving the hours of nurses unchanged, meant an increase in hours for the ODPs. At the same time, unsocial hours pay was abolished, managers were encouraged to avoid using overtime, and the overtime rate was cut from the previous standard rate of time-and-a-half. As we saw above, it was the ODPs who had the most to lose in these respects as well.

The competence-based system of progression was designed to replace a system in which progression had been based largely on time served. For movement within the new Grade 6,

▶

for example, the general principles upon which the first bar could be crossed meant the new theatre practitioners would have to 'demonstrate competency in both areas of work – anaesthesia and surgery – and willingness to work flexibly in both'.

The Trust, said the personnel manager, was under great pressure to break even financially. In these circumstances, he argued, it could be very difficult to make a case for this kind of flexibility agreement. Nonetheless, it was felt that a longer-term, more strategic view should be taken:

For me, the benefits of harmonised terms and conditions . . . are lost in the 'let's look at the bottom line cost' issue, are lost to a certain extent in the wider strategic view of what are the long-term benefits of actually doing certain things within the organisation. [Personnel manager]

The change process

We thus have some idea of what flexibility looks like in this case. But what was the process of change? Once the unified terms and conditions had come into effect, all new staff in the Theatres Directorate were appointed on that basis. For the directorate and Trust management, the main problem was how existing staff could be moved across. This was to be achieved through a process of consultation and negotiation.

The Theatres Project had begun with the establishment of a working group. Consisting of representatives of the Human Resources Department and both management and staff of the Theatres Directorate, compromises had to be made. In particular, there was the issue of to what extent a scheme designed for the hospital as a whole should be modified so as better to fit the conditions in theatres. '[Other directorates] don't have a similar situation,' said the clinical director, 'they have wards that are staffed by nurses. They don't have two separate groups of people working side by side on different conditions.' Another issue was the harmonisation of night-time breaks. Under the existing terms and conditions, both groups of workers had one hour's break but, while ODPs were paid for theirs, nurses were not. The original proposal was that there would be an hour's break, half of which would be paid and half unpaid. The initial reaction from staff was that they would make themselves unavailable for the half-hour for which they were not being paid, but in the end agreement was reached.

The proposed changes were then put into booklet form and submitted to the theatres staff as a whole. This was done in three stages, the first being a series of meetings – 16 in number, according to the specialty manager – which were open to all staff. The meetings continued until it was felt that demand for them had been satisfied. The second stage was the drawing-up of each individual's terms and conditions. Because nobody was being forced to move on to the new terms and conditions, said the specialty manager, 'everybody was made an offer that actually was slightly better or considerably better for them'. In the third stage, the offers were discussed in individual interviews with all staff. 'We interviewed about 240 people at 20 minutes a time,' said the theatre manager. The interviews could be quite fraught, with staff anxious to ensure that they were not being disadvantaged by the move.

Evaluating the project

As a first consideration, the project was judged to have been successful because of the proportion of theatres staff that had elected to take up the new terms and conditions. It was estimated that over 70 per cent of existing staff had moved over. A 100 per cent take-up had

▶

not been expected. More important to the Trust and directorate management was what the Theatres Project implied for the way in which work was organised. The creation of the new position of theatre practitioner was seen by some to have facilitated a great improvement. Under the new structure, the ODP manager had disappeared, and the teams of theatre practitioners were each responsible to a team leader, who in turn reported to the theatre manager. What the changes had allowed was the much more effective operation of these teams:

Before the changes we would often have the right number of staff, but not the right mix of skills, so we had to cancel operations. Now it is a lot easier to fill gaps and we don't cancel lists as often because we can find someone either to scrub or to assist the anaesthetist, as staff do both on a regular basis. Throughput is smoother, there is more flexibility, we have better motivated teams and lower staff turnover. [Clinical director, professional journal]

From the perspective of some of those working in the teams, the changes in working arrangements had been welcomed or at least accepted. In particular, it was felt that the distinction between the two main groups of staff was beginning to be broken down in practice:

Certainly now we've got more nurses doing anaesthetics as well as the scrub side; and a lot more technicians working the scrub side. So, certainly, there's been a lot more of interchange between the roles . . . There was always . . . this 'them and us' scenario. It's still there to a certain extent but not as much as it was before. [Team leader]

It was recognised that not all had welcomed the new arrangements. According to the clinical director, some of the senior nurses had regarded it as a 'levelling down' or re-grading exercise designed simply to cut costs. Interviews with staff revealed that, for some, the divides were still important. This seemed to be felt particularly strongly by the former nurses:

ODAs and nurses do exactly the same job now but with different training. And nurses are . . . I can't really explain it, but it's because we're no longer classed as nurses, morale has plummeted and that's the main thing. [Theatre practitioner]

As we have already noted, the new, unified pay spine was to be supplemented by a competence-based system of progression. For the management development manager, the system provided the incentive to staff to be able to do a number of jobs, thus allowing management to deploy staff more efficiently. Opinions were divided among those working in the new system. Some welcomed it as providing clear and achievable targets. Others felt it had made little difference or even that it served to disadvantage those who could do the job but who were not skilled enough academically to be able to demonstrate their abilities.

As well as management in theatres considering the project a success in terms of their ability to manage and deploy staff, the HR Department was keen to exploit its wider implications. The personnel manager said that it was now planned to apply the principles of the project in other areas of the Trust. Managers now saw, he said, that this corporate-level project could meet their operational needs.

▶

Questions

1. From where did the Theatres Project emerge? What issues did it address? If you had been looking at the project at the time of its emergence, would you have said that it was likely to be a success?

2. How is flexibility understood by, respectively, the management of the Theatres Directorate, Theatres Directorate staff and the Human Resources Department?

3. What does the harmonisation agreement imply for the terms and conditions of the two main groups of staff involved? Would you welcome the new terms and conditions if you were formerly (a) a nurse and (b) an ODP?

4. How well was the process of change managed?

5. On what criteria would you judge the Theatres Project? Would you say that it has been successful? Are there any lessons that might be learned by other NHS Trusts and other organisations more generally?

Bibliography

Ackroyd, S. and Procter, S. (1998) 'British manufacturing organization and workplace industrial relations: some attributes of the new flexible firm', *British Journal of Industrial Relations,* Vol.36, No.2, pp.163–83.

Adams, A., Lugsden, E., Chase, J., Arber, S. and Bond, S. (2000) 'Skill-mix changes and work intensification in nursing', *Work, Employment and Society,* Vol.14, No.3, pp.541–55.

Amin, A. (1994) (ed.) *Post-Fordism: a Reader,* Oxford: Blackwell, pp.43–70.

Atkinson, J. (1984) 'Manpower strategies for flexible organizations', *Personnel Management,* August, pp.28–31.

Atkinson, J. and Meager, N. (1986) 'Is flexibility just a flash in the pan?', *Personnel Management,* September, pp.26–9.

Armstrong, P., Marginson, P., Edwards, P. and Purcell, J. (1996) 'Budgetary control and the labour force: findings from a survey of large British companies', *Management Accounting Research,* Vol.7, No.1, pp.1–23.

Bach, S., Kessler, I. and Heron, P. (2007) 'The consequences of assistant roles in the public services: degradation or empowerment?', *Human Relations,* Vol.60, No.9, pp.1267–92.

Batt, R. (2000) 'Strategic segmentation in front-line services: matching customers, employees and human resource systems', *International Journal of Human Resource Management,* Vol.11, No.3.

Benders, J. and Van Hootegem, G. (1999) 'Teams and their context: moving the team discussion beyond dichotomies', *Journal of Management Studies,* Vol.36, No.5, pp.609–28.

Benders, J. and Van Hootegem, G. (2000) 'How the Japanese got teams', in S. Procter and F. Mueller (eds) *Teamworking,* London: Macmillan, pp.43–59.

Bolton, S. (2004) 'A simple matter of control? NHS hospital nurses and new management', *Journal of Management Studies,* Vol.41, No.2, pp.317–33.

Braverman, H. (1974) *Labor and Monopoly Capital: The Degradation of Work in the Twentieth Century,* New York: Monthly Review Press.

Brewster, C., Hegewisch, A. and Mayne, L. (1994) 'Flexible working practices: the controversy and the evidence', in C. Brewster and A. Hegewisch (eds) *Policy and Practice in European Human Resource Management,* London: Routledge, pp.168–93.

Buchan, J. and Dal Poz, M. (2002) 'Skill mix in the healthcare workforce: reviewing the evidence', *Bulletin of the World Health Organization,* Vol.80, No.7, pp.575–80.

Buchanan, D. (1994) 'Principles and practice in work design', in K. Sisson (ed.) *Personnel Management: A Comprehensive Guide to Theory and Practice in Britain* (2nd edn), Oxford: Blackwell.

Cappelli, P. (1995) 'Rethinking employment', *British Journal of Industrial Relations*, Vol.33, No.4, pp.563–602.

Casey, B. (1991) 'Survey evidence on trends in "non-standard" employment', in A. Pollert (ed.) *Farewell to Flexibility?*, Oxford: Blackwell, pp.171–99.

Clark, J. (1995) *Managing Innovation and Change: People, Technology and Strategy*, London: Sage.

Conti, R. and Warner, M. (1993) 'Taylorism, teams and technology in "Re-engineering" work-organization', *New Technology, Work and Employment*, Vol.8, No.1, pp.31–46.

Cross, M. (1988) 'Changes in working practices in UK manufacturing 1981–88', *Industrial Relations Review and Report 415*, pp.2–10.

Cully, M., Woodland, S., O'Reilly, A. and Dix, G. (1999) *Britain at Work: as Depicted by the 1998 Workplace Employee Relations Survey*, London/New York: Routledge.

Daniel, W. (1987) *Workplace Industrial Relations and Technical Change*, London: Pinter.

Delbridge, R., Turnbull, P. and Wilkinson, B. (1992) 'Pushing back the frontiers: management control and work intensification under JIT/TQM factory regimes', *New Technology, Work and Employment*, Vol.7, No.2, pp.97–106.

Delbridge, R., Lowe, J. and Oliver, N. (2000) 'Worker autonomy in lean teams: evidence from the world automotive components industry', in S. Procter and F. Mueller (eds) *Teamworking*, London: Macmillan, pp.125–42.

Desombre, T., Kelliher, C., McFarlane, F. and Ozbilgin, M. (2006) 'Reorganizing work roles in health care: evidence from the implementation of functional flexibility', *British Journal of Management*, Vol.17, pp.139–51.

Elam, M. (1990) 'Puzzling out the post-Fordist debate: technology, markets and institutions', *Economic and Industrial Democracy*, Vol.11, No.3, pp.9–37. Reprinted in A. Amin (ed.) (1994) *Post-Fordism: A Reader*, Oxford: Blackwell, pp.43–70.

Elger, T. (1991) 'Task flexibility and the intensification of labour in UK manufacturing in the 1980s', in A. Pollert (ed.) *Farewell to Flexibility?*, Oxford: Blackwell, pp.46–66.

Emmott, M. and Hutchinson, S. (1998) 'Employment flexibility: threat or promise?', in P. Sparrow and M. Marchington (eds) *Human Resource Management: The New Agenda*, London: Financial Times Pitman, pp.229–44.

Fernie, S. and Metcalf, D. (1997) '(Not) hanging on the telephone: payment systems in the new sweatshops', Centre for Economic Performance, London School of Economics.

Friedman, A. (1977) *Industry and Labour*, London: Macmillan.

Friedrich, A., Kabst, R., Weber, W. and Rodehuth, M. (1998) 'Functional flexibility: merely reacting or acting strategically?', *Employee Relations*, Vol.20, No.5, pp.504–23.

Frenkel, S., Korczynski, M., Shire, K. and Tam, M. (1999) *On the Front Line: Organization of Work in the Information Economy*, New York: Cornell University Press.

Gallie, D. (1991) 'Patterns of skill change: upskilling, deskilling or the polarization of skills', *Work, Employment and Society*, Vol.5, No.3, pp.319–51.

Gospel, H. (1992) *Markets, Firms and the Management of Labour in Modern Britain*, Cambridge: Cambridge University Press.

Gospel, H. (1995) 'The decline in apprenticeship training in Britain', *Industrial Relations Journal*, Vol.26, pp.32–44.

Gregg, P. and Wadsworth, J. (1999) 'Job tenure, 1975–98', in P. Gregg and J. Wadsworth (eds) *The State of Working Britain*, Manchester: Manchester University Press, pp.109–26.

Grimshaw, D. (1999) 'Changes in skills-mix and pay determination among the nursing workforce in the UK', *Work, Employment and Society*, Vol.13, No.2, pp.295–328.

Hackman, J. and Oldham, G. (1976) 'Motivation through the design of work: test of a theory', *Organizational Behaviour and Performance*, Vol.16, pp.250–79.

Hakim, C. (1990) 'Core and periphery in employers' workplace strategies: evidence from the 1987 ELUS Survey', *Work, Employment and Society*, Vol.4, No.2, pp.157–88.

Hammer, M. and Champy, J. (1993) *Reorganizing the Corporation*, New York: Harper Business.

Herzberg, F. (1966) *Work and the Nature of Man*, Cleveland, OH: World Publishing.

Hirst, P. and Zeitlin, J. (1989) 'Flexible specialisation and the competitive failure of UK manufacturing', *Political Quarterly*, Vol.60, No.2, pp.164–78.

Hunter, L., McGregor, A., MacInnes, J. and Sproull, A. (1993) 'The "flexible firm": strategy and segmentation', *British Journal of Industrial Relations*, Vol.31, No.3, pp.383–407.

Hutton, W. (1995) *The State We're In*, London: Jonathan Cape.

Hyde, P., McBride, A., Young, R. and Walshe, K. (2005) 'Role redesign: new ways of working in the NHS', *Personnel Review*, Vol.34, No.6, pp.697–712.

Hyman, R. (1987) 'Strategy or structure? Capital, labour and control', *Work, Employment and Society*, Vol.1, No.1, pp.25–55.

Ingersoll Engineers. (1994) *The Quiet Revolution Continues*, Rugby: Ingersoll Engineers.

Jenkins, A. (1994) 'Teams: from "ideology" to analysis', *Organization Studies*, Vol.15, No.6, pp.849–60.

Kalleberg, A. (2001) 'Organizing flexibility: the flexible firm in the new century', *British Journal of Industrial Relations*, Vol.39, No.4, pp.479–504.

Kanigel, R. (1997) *The One Best Way: Frederick Winslow Taylor and the Enigma of Efficiency*, London: Little, Brown.

Kenney, M. and Florida, R. (1993) *Beyond Mass Production: the Japanese System and its Transfer to the United States*, New York: Oxford University Press.

Klein, J. (1989) 'The human costs of manufacturing reform', *Harvard Business Review*, March–April, pp.60–66.

Kessler, I., Bach, S. and Heron, P. (2006) 'Understanding assistant roles in social care', *Work, Employment and Society*, Vol.20, No.4, pp.667–85.

Legge, K. (1998) 'Flexibility: the gift-wrapping on employment degradation?', in P. Sparrow and M. Marchington (eds) *Human Resource Management: The New Agenda*, London: Financial Times Pitman, pp.286–95.

Littler, C. (1982) *The Development of the Labour Process in Capitalist Societies*, London: Heinemann.

Lowe, J., Delbridge, R. and Oliver, N. (1997) 'High-performance manufacturing: evidence from the automotive components industry', *Organization Studies*, Vol.18, No.5, pp.783–98.

MacDuffie, J. and Pil, F. (1997) 'Changes in auto industry employment practices: an international overview', in T. Kochan, R. Lansbury and J. MacDuffie (eds) *After Lean Production*, New York: Cornell University Press, pp.9–42.

Marginson, P. (1991) 'Change and continuity in the employment structure of large companies', in A. Pollert (ed.) *Farewell to Flexibility?*, Oxford: Blackwell, pp.32–45.

Mayne, L. (1996) 'A comparative analysis of the link between flexibility and HRM strategy', *Employee Relations*, Vol.18, No.3, pp.5–24.

McIvor, A. (2001) *A History of Work in Britain, 1880–1950*, London: Palgrave.

Mintzberg, H. (1978) 'Patterns in strategy formation', *Management Science*, Vol.24, No.9, pp.934–48.

Munday, M. and Peel, M. (1998) 'An analysis of the performance of Japanese, US and domestic manufacturing firms in the UK electronics/electrical sector', in R. Delbridge and J. Lowe (eds) *Manufacturing in Transition*, London: Routledge, pp.53–78.

NEDO (1986) *Changing Working Patterns: How Companies Achieve Flexibility to Meet New Needs*, London: National Economic Development Office.

Noble, D. (1977) 'Social choice in machine design: the case of automatically controlled machine tools', in A. Zimbalist (ed.) *Case Studies in the Labour Process*, London: Monthly Review Press, pp.18–50.

Oliver, N. and Wilkinson, B. (1992) *The Japanization of British Industry* (2nd edn), Oxford: Blackwell.

Oliver, N., Delbridge, R. and Lowe, J. (1996) 'Lean production practices: international comparisons in the auto components industry', *British Journal of Management*, Vol.7, special issue, pp.29–44.

O'Reilly, J. (1992) 'Where do you draw the line? Functional flexibility, training and skill in Britain and France', *Work, Employment and Society*, Vol.6, No.3, pp.369–96.

Parker, S. and Wall, T. (1998) *Job and Work Design: Organizing Work to Promote Well-being and Effectiveness*, London: Sage.

Parker, S., Wall, T. and Cordery, J. (2001) 'Future work design research and practice: towards an elaborated model of work design', *Journal of Occupational and Organizational Psychology*, Vol.74, No.4, pp.413–40.

Penn, R. (1992) 'Flexibility in Britain during the 1980s: recent empirical evidence', in N. Gilbert, R. Burrows and A. Pollert (eds) *Fordism and Flexibility: Divisions and Change*, London: Macmillan, pp.66–86.

Pil, F. and MacDuffie, J. (1996) 'The adoption of high-involvement work practices', *Industrial Relations*, Vol.35, No.3.

Piore, M. and Sabel, C. (1984) *The Second Industrial Divide: Possibilities for Prosperity*, New York: Basic Books.

Procter, S. and Ackroyd, S. (1998) 'Against Japanization: understanding the reorganization of British manufacturing', *Employee Relations*, Vol.20, No.3, pp.237–47.

Procter, S., Rowlinson, M., McArdle, L., Hassard, J. and Forrester, P. (1994), 'Flexibility, politics and strategy: in defence of the model of the flexible firm', *Work, Employment and Society*, Vol.8, pp.221–42.

Rowley, C. (1996) 'Flexible specialisation: some comparative dimensions and evidence from the ceramic tile industry', *New Technology, Work and Employment*, Vol.11, No.2, pp.125–36.

Sewell, G. and Wilkinson, B. (1992) 'Someone to watch over me: surveillance, discipline and the just in time labour process', *Sociology*, Vol.26, No.2, pp.271–89.

Smith, A. (1986 [1776]) *The Wealth of Nations*, Books 1–3, London: Penguin.

Taylor, F.W. (1911) *The Principles of Scientific Management*, New York: Harper.

Taylor, P. and Bain, P. (1999) '"An assembly line in the head": work and employee relations in the call centre', *Industrial Relations Journal*, Vol.30, No.2, pp.101–17.

Thompson, P. and Ackroyd, S. (1995) 'All quiet on the workplace front? A critique of recent trends in British industrial sociology', *Sociology*, Vol.29, No.4, pp.615–33.

Tomaney, J. (1994) 'A new paradigm of work organisation and technology?', in A. Amin (ed.) *Post-Fordism: A Reader*, Oxford: Blackwell, pp.157–94.

Trist, E. and Bamforth, K. (1951) 'Some social and psychological consequences of the longwall method of coal-getting', *Human Relations*, Vol.4, No.1, pp.3–38.

Trist, E., Higgin, G., Murray, H. and Pollock, A. (1963) *Organizational Choice: Capabilities of Groups at the Coal Face under Changing Technologies: The Loss, Rediscovery and Transformation of a Work Tradition*, London: Tavistock.

Turnbull, P. (1988) 'The limits to "Japanization": just-in-time, labour relations and the UK automotive industry', *Industrial Relations Journal*, Vol.17, No.3, pp.193–206.

Willcocks, L. and Grint, K. (1997) 'Reinventing the organization? Towards a critique of business process re-engineering', in I. McLoughlin and M. Harris (eds) *Innovation, Organizational Change and Technology*, International Thomson, pp.87–110.

Williams, K., Cutler, T., Williams, J. and Haslam, C. (1987) 'The end of mass production?', *Economy and Society*, Vol.16, No.3, pp.405–39.

Williams, K., Haslam, C., Williams, J. and Cutler, T. (1992) 'Against lean production', *Economy and Society*, Vol.21, No.3, pp.321–54.

Womack, J., Jones, D. and Roos, D. (1990) *The Machine that Changed the World*, Rawson Associates.

Wood, D. and Smith, P. (1989) 'Employers' labour use strategies: first report of the 1987 survey', Department of Employment Research Paper No.63, London: Department of Employment.

Chapter 22

WORKPLACE BULLYING

Sara Branch, Sheryl Ramsay and Michelle Barker

Introduction

Understanding workplace bullying is of great importance to managers, who have an important part to play in the development and maintenance of vital, diverse and productive workplaces. As a complex phenomenon, workplace bullying presents significant challenges, including its theoretical conceptualisation, the identification of bullying behaviours, and practical strategies for preventing and reducing its many negative facets. This chapter offers a comprehensive insight into each of these areas.

Described recently as a serious wrongdoing (Brown 2007), research consistently shows that workplace bullying is a significant issue for organisations because of its relatively high rate of occurrence or prevalence (e.g. Brown 2007). In the management field, workplace bullying has been presented as an 'alarming issue' (De Cieri and Kramar 2005, p.576) that requires comprehensive understanding and management with effective organisational processes, if the costs to individuals and organisations are to be alleviated. These costs include the significantly high emotional impacts on people and the associated economic losses that mount up (e.g. McCarthy and Mayhew 2004). This chapter aims firstly to present a conceptual overview of workplace bullying, including its associated behaviours, impacts, risks and antecedents, and secondly a discussion of prevention and management strategies of relevance to the field of management. It includes examples of research findings (based largely on quantitative studies) to help explain particular points and also to demonstrate the type of research being conducted in the area.

Research into workplace bullying began in the late 1970s (Smith and Brain 2000), largely growing out of Scandinavian investigations into schoolyard bullying (McCarthy and Mayhew 2004). Indeed, links between schoolyard and workplace bullying are evident. For instance, a study of 5,288 adults in Great Britain found that children who had been targets or perpetrators of schoolyard bullying were more likely to be targets of workplace bullying (Smith *et al.* 2003). Moreover, the nature of bullying is similar across school and work. For instance, verbal abuse and harassment represent the most common types of schoolyard bullying, followed by exclusion and social manipulation (Rigby 2001), which is similar to the type of bullying behaviours identified in workplace bullying research (Bjorkqvist *et al.* 1994; Einarsen *et al.* 2003; O'Moore *et al.* 1998; Zapf *et al.* 1996). However, the formal power of the bully presents an interesting difference between schoolyard and workplace bullying because 'children are bullied for the most part by peers who have no formal organizational power over them, whereas adults are at least as likely to be bullied by managers and supervisors as by others who are lacking such authority' (Rigby 2001, p.5). Interestingly, recent research into upwards bullying (i.e. staff member bullying a supervisor or manager) supports the notion that those

Figure 22.1 Poster highlighting workplace bullying

Source: Overcome Bullying Canada: www.mobbing.ca; acknowledgements: Bobbie Osborne (photographer) and Anton Hout (designer)

who lack formal sources of power within the workplace can bully individuals in positions of authority (Branch *et al.* 2007a, 2007b).

Throughout the world a range of terms have been used in reference to negative social behaviour at work, including mobbing, workplace bullying, workplace aggression, workplace incivility, workplace harassment, workplace deviance, social undermining, emotional abuse, abusive supervision and antisocial behaviour (Zapf 2004). The term 'workplace bullying' has been described as an umbrella term, as it can incorporate harassing, intimidating, and aggressive or violent behaviours (Fox and Stallworth 2004). In Scandinavia (the source of considerable research in this area), the term 'mobbing' was introduced by the late Heinz Leymann (1990), who referred to mobbing as a psychological phenomenon where repeated incidents, which are often minor, result in significant negative impacts for the target. As a result, the term 'mobbing' is commonly used within Scandinavian countries in place of workplace bullying (Einarsen 2000; Rylance 2001). In the US researchers often encompass bullying behaviours in the term 'emotional abuse' (Keashly 1998, 2001), which is often characterised as a persistent and enduring form of 'workplace aggression' (Baron and Neuman, 1996, 1998). Researchers within Australia and Great Britain (namely, Hoel and Cooper 2001; Rayner and Cooper 2003; Sheehan *et al.* 2004) tend to use the term 'workplace bullying', which is used throughout this chapter.

How is workplace bullying defined?

Despite increased research focus on workplace bullying in recent decades, considerable confusion exists as to what workplace bullying is and how it differs from, or is similar to, other forms of counter-productive behaviours in the workplace (e.g. harassment; see Figure 22.1). Indeed, given the complexity of workplace bullying incidents, some researchers question whether it is even possible to achieve a uniform definition of workplace bullying (Rayner *et al.* 2002). Despite differences, agreement generally exists about the inclusion of and importance placed on several characteristics within the definition of workplace bullying (see Figure 22.2).

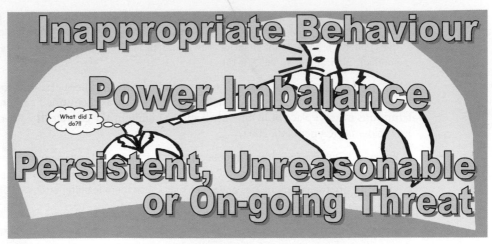

Figure 22.2 Components of workplace bullying

First, workplace bullying behaviours are often defined as *inappropriate* or *unreasonable behaviours* (Einarsen and Raknes 1997; Gorman 1999; Hoel and Cooper 2001; McCarthy 1996; McCarthy *et al.* 1995). Examples of such behaviours include ridiculing people, keeping a constant eye on another's work, questioning another's professional ability, spreading damaging rumours, and explosive outbursts and threats (Bassman 1992; Rayner and Hoel 1997; Zapf and Einarsen 2001).

Second, definitions of workplace bullying emphasise that inappropriate *behaviours occur persistently or regularly over a period of time* (Einarsen 2000; Einarsen *et al.* 2003; Einarsen and Mikkelsen 2003; Hoel 1997; Smith 1997). According to Hoel and Cooper (2001), 'the long-term nature of the phenomenon is one of the most salient features of the problem' (p.4). In fact, some researchers have explained workplace bullying as a form of conflict escalation in which the intensity of the attacks escalates, with increasingly negative effects on the target (Einarsen and Skogstad 1996; Leymann and Gustafsson 1996). An important variation to the concept of persistent and possibly escalating behaviour is the notion of 'ongoing threat' (Zapf 2004). For example, a verbal attack on someone may induce a long-lasting fear that it could recur.

Third, the existence of a *power imbalance* between the two parties (Keashly and Jagatic 2003) is often regarded as an essential definitional component. Thus, when the two parties have an equal balance of power, the conflict would not be considered workplace bullying (Hoel and Cooper 2001; Rayner *et al.* 2002). Commonly, dependency on the part of the target is cited as a prime reason for a power imbalance developing, and for targets of workplace bullying being unable to defend themselves (e.g. because another person possesses greater formal, hierarchical power and/or informal power such as access to information or influence). Importantly, it is the power imbalance between the two parties that makes it difficult for targets of workplace bullying to defend themselves and is therefore an essential characteristic of the definition of workplace bullying (Einarsen 2000).

In summary, the important defining characteristics of workplace bullying appear to be the persistent use of inappropriate behaviours (be it regular use of these behaviours, or an ongoing threat as a result of a single event), coupled with the inability of the target to defend themselves owing to a power imbalance (Einarsen 2000). Elements of these characteristics can be seen in the following, widely accepted academic definition:

> Bullying at work means harassing, offending, socially excluding someone or negatively affecting someone's work tasks. In order for the label bullying (or mobbing) to be applied to a particular activity, interaction or process it has to occur repeatedly and regularly (e.g. weekly) and over a period of time (e.g. about six months). Bullying is an escalating

process in the course of which the person confronted ends up in an inferior position and becomes the target of systematic negative social acts. A conflict cannot be called bullying if the incident is an isolated event or if two parties of approximately equal 'strength' are in conflict. (Einarsen et al. 2003, p.15)

Furthermore, the concepts of power and inappropriate–persistent behaviours are included in the following practical definition. However, as mentioned earlier, differences in definitions of workplace bullying only begin to highlight the complexity of workplace bullying incidents (Rayner *et al.* 2002).

Workplace Bullying is 'persistent unacceptable "offensive, intimidating, malicious, insulting or humiliating behaviour, abuse of power or authority which attempts to undermine an individual or group of employees and which may cause them to suffer stress"'. (UNISON 2003)

You might like to explore the workplace bullying definition used by the university at which you are studying or organisation in which you are working and, to see how their definition of workplace bullying is similar or different to the definitions provided here, and what elements are included in the definition.

The importance of power and dependency in workplace bullying

Power relationships within organisations have gained importance recently as work environments have become increasingly complex and unpredictable (Asch and Salaman 2002). Power and how it is used constitutes a central concept when discussing relationships in organisations. Indeed power is especially relevant to any discussion of workplace bullying (Hoel and Salin 2003), which often focuses on an imbalance of power between those involved and the defencelessness of the recipients (Keashly and Jagatic 2003). As introduced earlier, one concept closely related to power is *dependency*. Importantly, it is the target's dependency on the offender that produces the power imbalance necessary for bullying to occur (Einarsen *et al.* 2003; Keashly and Jagatic 2003). Bassman (1992) even states, 'one common thread in all abusive relationships is the element of dependency. The abuser controls some important resources in the [target's] life, the [target] is dependent on the abuser' (p.2). For example, staff rely on managers for direction, resources and rewards, while managers are dependent on staff to be productive and fulfil the goals of the organisation (Cook *et al.* 1997). If however, either party denies or hinders the other person in achieving their goals then power can be derived (Emerson 1962).

Group processes may also play a role in the occurrence of workplace bullying (Zapf and Einarsen 2003). Einarsen and his colleagues (2003), for example, suggest that being a member of a group which is considered to be outside the accepted dominant culture may be the only reason some people are bullied. Indeed, Zapf (1999) proposed that some group processes (e.g. scapegoating) are also related to workplace bullying. Group characteristics such as ethnicity (Fox and Stallworth 2004; Rayner and Hoel, 1997), gender (Djurkovic *et al.* 2004), age (Zapf, cited in Zapf and Einarsen 2003), and organisational status differences (Hoel *et al.* 2001), such as the division between management and staff (Jablin, 1986), have been found to be related to workplace bullying.

Identifying workplace bullying behaviours

A number of the specific behaviours that constitute bullying in the workplace have been identified and are summarised in Figure 22.3.

However, another demonstration of the complexity of workplace bullying research is that within different work environments patterns of bullying behaviours appear to differ.

Figure 22.3 Behaviours that may constitute bullying
Source: Bassman 1992; Rayner and Hoel 1997; Zapf and Einarsen 2001

For example, Djurkovic and colleagues' (2004) study of 150 undergraduate students found that the most common bullying behaviours experienced were unjustified criticism, monitoring of performance, unfair pressure and comments or sarcasm. Alternatively, in an academic institution, Pietersen (2007) found isolating the target or obstructing their work, as well as blocking career advancement, to be the most common bullying behaviours. There is also an indication that work-related bullying behaviours (e.g. withholding of information) are more common than non-work-related behaviours (e.g. insulting remarks) in managerial ranks, where greater competition and significant work pressures may prevail (Salin 2001). These differences in bullying behaviours may reflect the particular culture within different workplaces or environments.

There are, however, a number of difficulties with looking at the different behaviours that can constitute bullying in the workplace. Although some are observable and easy to label as bullying (such as irrational outbursts), other behaviours may be more covert and difficult to observe or describe. In fact, despite the assumption that bullying is physical in nature (Rigby 2001), it has been recognised that most bullying behaviour tends to be psychologically based (Bjorkqvist *et al.* 1994; Einarsen *et al.* 2003; O'Moore *et al.* 1998; Zapf *et al.* 1996), as can be seen in Figure 22.3. For instance, in a study of 460 male shipyard workers in Norway, threats of physical abuse and actual physical abuse were rarely reported (2.4 per cent), while the more covert behaviours of withdrawal of information (51.7 per cent) and dismissing a person's opinion (53.6 per cent) were reported more often (Einarsen and Raknes 1997). Moreover, workplace bullying is not only about what someone does to another, but can also include what is not done (Rayner *et al.* 2002), for example the withholding of information or excluding the target from a social event (Einarsen and Raknes 1997). As a result, workplace bullying behaviours are not always easy to recognise or identify. Again, this highlights the complexity of workplace bullying.

Identifying bullying behaviours is also complicated by the fact that recipients of workplace bullying may not label it as such, often selecting other terms, such as aggression, harassment and intimidation (Hadikin and O'Driscoll 2000). Moreover, the lack of recognition of particular behaviours as bullying may be the result of bullying behaviours becoming normalised in some workplaces (Archer 1999; Hadikin and O'Driscoll 2000; Rayner 1997, 1999). This conclusion was reached by Lewis (2004) in relation to his interview study within the UK further and higher education context, where bullying was sometimes difficult to identify as it appeared to have become a behavioural norm.

Reporting of frequency of workplace bullying behaviours and risk groups

Research indicates that a significant number of people are exposed to persistent abusive treatment within the workplace (Keashly and Harvey 2006). However, statistics on the frequency of workplace bullying can vary quite dramatically owing to different definitions of workplace bullying and various approaches to measuring it. To demonstrate, Hoel and Cooper's (2000) questionnaire study of 5,288 individuals from 70 different organisations within the UK found that 10.6 per cent of respondents reported being bullied within the last six months, and 24.7 per cent of respondents reporting being bullied within the last five years. Notably, 46.5 per cent reported witnessing bullying within the last five years. However, consistent with other Scandinavian studies, Mikkelsen and Einarsen (2001) found lower levels of bullying (between 2.7 and 8 per cent) in their research, which may be due to their use of a strict criterion of experiencing two negative acts per week during a six-month period. In addition, they found that 17.7 per cent of respondents stated that they had witnessed bullying acts within the workplace. The authors concluded that the higher rates of witnessing may indicate that 'the real prevalence of bullying is higher than shown by the data' (Mikkelsen and Einarsen 2001, p.404).

You might like to consider if a strict criterion of experiencing two bullying behaviours twice a week for six months is a practical criterion for organisations to adopt.

Frequency studies may also enable researchers to identify particular traits of targets and perpetrators. Accordingly, Zapf and Einarsen (2005) suggest most studies indicate that, of those targeted, the majority are women. For example, Lewis and Gunn (2007) found that women in the public sector (24 per cent) were bullied more than men (17 per cent). By contrast, Djurkovic *et al.*'s (2004) study of 150 undergraduate students found that women and men were equally likely to be perpetrators of workplace bullying. Interestingly, they also found that the gender of the target and perpetrator often matched, suggesting that 'same-gender bullying occurs more frequently than between-gender bullying' (Djurkovic *et al.* 2004, p.487). The authors indicate that this may explain the concentration of bullying in either male- or female-dominated industries (Djurkovic *et al.* 2004), such as in nursing (e.g. Quine 2001) and the fire service (e.g. Archer 1999).

While workplace bullying can be found in most organisations (Lewis and Gunn 2007), research suggests that particular groups and industries may be more vulnerable. For instance, Lewis and Gunn (2007) found a higher occurrence of workplace bullying among non-white groups in the public sector in South Wales. Indeed, 35 per cent of non-white respondents indicated an experience of workplace bullying, compared with only 9 per cent of white respondents. This research may reflect the group processes that occur in workplace bullying (as introduced earlier). That is, it may be that the only reason some people are bullied is that they belong to a group which is considered to be outside the accepted dominant culture (Einarsen *et al.* 2003).

Predominantly, research has examined downwards bullying (as perpetrated by a manager(s) against staff) and, more recently, horizontal bullying (one colleague bullying another) (Lewis and Sheehan 2003). Notably, however, the voice of managers who feel they have been bullied by a staff member(s) has rarely been heard in this research data. Until recently, cases of upwards bullying have been reported rarely in the literature (Rayner and Cooper 2003) and are often presented anecdotally or as a single instance (see Braverman 1999 for example). Similarly, Scandinavian, UK and European research has identified the occurrence of upwards bullying as being between 2 and 27 per cent, with a mean of 11 per cent (figures obtained from a table presented in Zapf *et al.* 2003, p.116). Furthermore, Salin (2001) found that one-sixth of self-identified managerial targets of workplace bullying reported being bullied by a staff member. This led Salin to conclude that the power imbalance necessary for workplace bullying to occur can be created via means other than formal position, suggesting that it would be of interest to study further 'how superiors can be put into a position in which they cannot defend themselves and how bullying alters power relations' (Salin 2001, p.435).

Indeed, a recent doctoral study by Branch (2006) into upwards bullying found that power and dependency appeared to play a role in the occurrence of upwards bullying. For instance, in an interview study it was found that managers (in discussing either their managerial work environment or a more direct experience of upwards bullying) were able to identify factors that could play a part in reducing a manager's positional power; factors such as lack of support and resources from upper management and particular dependency on the staff member(s). For instance, a number of managers interviewed indicated how a staff member being critical to the functioning of the workplace (e.g. highly advanced IT skills) created a dependency on that staff member which resulted in the manager being reluctant, at first, to take any action when the staff member demonstrated inappropriate behaviour. Interestingly, the majority of those who discussed dependency on a staff member were managers who reported a direct experience of upwards bullying (Branch 2006). Further research into upwards bullying is needed to clarify this aspect but it again highlights the complexity of workplace bullying.

Impact on targets

Although some bullying behaviours occur relatively frequently within the workplace and are manageable, they have the ability to negatively affect a person's health (Mikkelsen and Einarsen 2002) and ability to cope (Leymann 1990), especially when they occur regularly over a period of time. The consequences of bullying at work can range from physical harm through to an increase in psychological stress for the recipient (Hadikin and O'Driscoll 2000). In a study that demonstrates the severe impact that workplace bullying can have on an individual, Mikkelsen and Einarsen (2002) found that 80.5 per cent of participants reported that 'no other event in their life affected them more negatively than the bullying' (p.98). This was despite the reporting of experiences such as accidents, divorce, bereavement and serious illness (Mikkelsen and Einarsen 2002). Furthermore, in a unique study into the metaphors that self-identified targets of workplace bullying use to describe their experience, Tracy *et al.* (2006) described targets' feelings of vulnerability and degradation (e.g. feeling like a slave or a prisoner isolated from others; being degraded like an animal; or being treated like a child). Indeed, for the individual experiencing workplace bullying, the impacts can be so pervasive that they may negatively affect not only their ability to function at work but other areas of life as well (Keashly and Harvey 2006).

Examples of the wide-ranging impact that workplace bullying can have on a person's life is demonstrated in its links to the occurrence of stress-related symptoms (Mikkelsen and Einarsen 2001), depression (Niedhammer *et al.* 2006) and post-traumatic stress disorder (PTSD) (Bjorkqvist *et al.* 1994; Matthiesen and Einarsen 2004, 2002; Tehrani 2004). For instance, researchers found that as exposure to bullying increased, so too did the risk of depressive symptoms (Niedhammer *et al.* 2006). Of further concern, researchers found that 76 per cent of 118 targets of workplace bullying displayed PTSD symptoms, with 29 per cent fulfilling the full diagnostic criteria of PTSD (Mikkelsen and Einarsen 2002). Workplace bullying has also been associated with other psychological symptoms such as a higher risk of suicide attempts (O'Moore *et al.* 1998) and clinical levels of anxiety (Quine 1999). Finally, workplace bullying has been linked to greater long-term health risks through an increase in stress-related behaviours such as smoking, drinking, and excessive eating (Quine 1999; Savva and Alexandrou 1998). Therefore, bullying in the workplace can have severe and enduring physical and psychological health consequences for those who experience it.

Impact on witnesses

The complexity of workplace bullying can also be seen in the web of those drawn into incidents of bullying. For example, co-workers of those who experience workplace bullying have reported that workplace bullying impacts on them in a number of ways. In a British study of 761 public sector trade union members, 73 per cent of witnesses of workplace bullying reported an increase in their stress levels, and 44 per cent of respondents were concerned about being the next target (Rayner 1999). In fact, it was found that those who witness workplace bullying and violence can be affected almost as severely as the actual target (Mayhew *et al.* 2004), which has vital implications for the loyalty of staff and productivity of organisations (Mayhew *et al.* 2004). Understandably, such a climate of fear (Rayner 1999) could flow on to an increase in absenteeism (Kivimaki *et al.* 2000) which could place additional work demands on those who remain. Lowered work morale, increases in workplace conflict, and stress generated as a direct consequence of workplace bullying are also seen as impacting on others' well-being through the creation of an abusive work environment and culture (Einarsen and Mikkelsen 2003). Thus, workplace bullying can have direct and indirect impacts on those who witness it, as well as others (who are not direct targets or witnesses) within the workplace who experience the culture more generally, magnifying the impact on the organisation.

You might like to think of how you would react if you witnessed a colleague of yours being bullied keeping in mind the climate of fear that can be created when bullying occurs.

Impact on the organisation

As would be expected, when the physical and psychological health impacts begin to be felt by targets and witnesses of workplace bullying, an individual's ability to function at work will also be affected (Einarsen 2000). In general, bullying in the workplace can affect an organisation through loss of productivity, an increase in absenteeism and intention to leave, as well as the cost of intervention programmes (Einarsen 2000; McCarthy and Barker 2000; McCarthy *et al.* 1995). For instance, a questionnaire study of 1,100 employees of a National Health Service Community Trust in the UK revealed that targets of workplace bullying not only had higher levels of job-induced stress, including higher levels of depression and anxiety, but also had lower levels of job satisfaction and higher intention to leave than other workers (Quine 1999). In addition, workplace bullying has also been linked to absenteeism within the workplace. Kivimaki *et al.*'s (2000) study of 5,655 hospital employees found a link between workplace bullying and an increase in sick leave taken. As well as the direct costs to the hospital, the financial impacts of lower motivation, impaired patient care and the potential of staff leaving the workplace show the ongoing negative impact of workplace bullying (Kivimaki *et al.* 2000). Indeed, the cost of workplace bullying to organisations is staggering. In the UK alone, it is estimated that workplace bullying costs organisations £2 billion in lost revenue

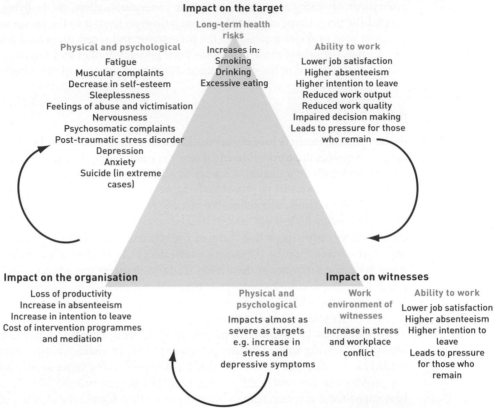

Impact on the target

Long-term health risks

Physical and psychological

Fatigue
Muscular complaints
Decrease in self-esteem
Sleeplessness
Feelings of abuse and victimisation
Nervousness
Psychosomatic complaints
Post-traumatic stress disorder
Depression
Anxiety
Suicide (in extreme cases)

Increases in:
Smoking
Drinking
Excessive eating

Ability to work

Lower job satisfaction
Higher absenteeism
Higher intention to leave
Reduced work output
Reduced work quality
Impaired decision making
Leads to pressure for those who remain

Impact on the organisation

Loss of productivity
Increase in absenteeism
Increase in intention to leave
Cost of intervention programmes and mediation

Physical and psychological

Impacts almost as severe as targets e.g. increase in stress and depressive symptoms

Work environment of witnesses

Increase in stress and workplace conflict

Impact on witnesses

Ability to work

Lower job satisfaction
Higher absenteeism
Higher intention to leave
Leads to pressure for those who remain

Figure 22.4 The impacts of workplace bullying

and 80 million lost working days (Health and Safety Executive 2006). In conclusion, workplace bullying can have severe impacts on targets, witnesses and the organisation as a whole, as summarised in Figure 22.4.

Antecedents of workplace bullying

In an attempt to examine how the impacts of workplace bullying could be reduced for individuals and organisations, researchers have explored the antecedents of workplace bullying. Research has examined individual factors, such as personality traits of the target or the bully (Ashforth 1997; Coyne *et al.* 2000; Douglas and Martinko 2001; Zapf 1999) and bullying as an interpersonal conflict (Einarsen *et al.* 2003). In addition, others have emphasised that bullying is a multi-faceted and complex phenomenon and, as such, multiple causes, including organisational and group-related factors, need to be considered along with individual factors (Zapf 1999). For instance, Hoel and Salin (2003) suggest that, owing to the complexity of workplace bullying, the actions and reactions of the target and perpetrator can only be understood within the context in which they occur.

In a further demonstration of the complexity of workplace bullying, Harvey *et al.* (2006) suggest that the characteristics of the perpetrator, target and environment all need to be considered and that for bullying to occur all three elements need to be present. That is, if the environment does not support bullying behaviours, or if bullies do not have access to potential targets, then bullying will not occur. This interplay between these three elements is further explained by Heames and Harvey (2006) in their recent proposal of a cross-level assessment of workplace bullying. In their conceptualisation, the bullying event stretches beyond the perpetrator and target and has a flow-on impact to the group and organisation, which in turn provides feedback to the perpetrator and target that could potentially perpetuate or halt the behaviour. Thus, interactions between bullies and targets, and the environment are all involved in the occurrence and continuation of workplace bullying.

INDIVIDUAL LEVEL

In the main, researchers have conceptualised and investigated workplace bullying as an individual phenomenon, through research into the personality of targets and perpetrators, or as an interpersonal phenomenon (Einarsen *et al.* 2003). For instance, an Irish study into workplace bullying found that targets of bullying were identified by the researchers as introverted, conscientious, neurotic and submissive (Coyne *et al.* 2000). Indeed, it is commonly suggested that individuals with low self-esteem may be more often targeted. Harvey *et al.* (2006), however, very elegantly suggest that there are five elements to an individual's self-esteem at work, any of which may increase the target's vulnerability in that the bully can direct their energies towards one or a number of these areas. The five elements include an individual's: 1) cognitive ability; 2) emotional maturity; 3) personal and professional achievements; 4) organisational network (i.e. if the person is well liked) and the individual's character; and 5) physical characteristics (Harvey *et al.* 2006).

Caution must be taken, however, when considering results that indicate that targets of workplace bullying have particular personality traits or characteristics (Rayner *et al.* 2002). Some researchers argue that results that identify personality traits could actually be describing profiles that have occurred as a result of the bullying process (see Quine 1999). Others have suggested that researching the target's personality 'blames the victim', rather than reflecting a more balanced approach to understanding the circumstances of the situation. However, Keashly and Harvey (2006) suggest that because conflicts like workplace bullying can be defined as a hostile relationship between target and perpetrator, exploring individual factors, including those of the target, is a valid approach in some circumstances.

In addition to research which has focused on the targets of workplace bullying, the personality of the perpetrator has also been investigated (Einarsen *et al.* 2003). Counter to the common assumption that low self-esteem leads to aggression and violence, Baumeister *et al.* (1996), in a theoretical review of research into aggression, proposed that high self-esteem combined with ego threat is a major cause of aggression and violence. In a study that tested Baumeister *et al.*'s (1996) conceptualisation, Stucke and Sporer (2002) explored the relationship between narcissism (individuals with an inflated but unstable self-esteem), self-concept clarity and aggression. The authors found that 'high narcissists, with low self-concept clarity reacted with anger and aggression', while less narcissistic participants displayed no aggression (Stucke and Sporer 2002, p.309). Despite the body of research into the personality of workplace bullying targets and perpetrators, Rayner and her colleagues (2002) suggest that using personality screening would not be useful in identifying potential targets and bullies. This is mainly due to the difficulty of identifying whether personality traits were a cause or effect of bullying and that factors other than personality alone appear to influence the occurrence of workplace bullying.

INTERACTIONS BETWEEN BULLIES AND TARGETS

As a further demonstration of the complexity of workplace bullying, recent research suggests that the reactions of targets may also play a part in the occurrence of workplace bullying (Keashly and Harvey 2006). For instance, Zapf and Gross (2001) argue that the response of targets may further escalate the conflict between the perpetrator and themselves. Indeed, they found that targets who successfully coped with workplace bullying were better at recognising and avoiding escalating behaviour by using less active direct strategies to de-escalate the situation (Zapf and Gross 2001). Moreover, supporting the argument that workplace bullying incidents are complex, Tehrani (2003) suggests that the target–perpetrator relationship is not always simple to define, and that instead, an accusation of bullying is often 'triggered by the individual's responses to a series of interactions that are built up over a period of time' (Tehrani 2003, p. 280). In fact, Tehrani (2003) proposes that during times of high stress and when a relationship is perceived as negative, small issues such as not saying hello in the morning may be interpreted as an aggressive act. Alternatively, Einarsen (1999) suggests that some bullying cases may be predatory bullying, that is, the target has done nothing to provoke the perpetrator (Zapf and Einarsen 2005). In this case, targets may be persecuted for no other reason than turning up to work or being a member of a minority group, as noted earlier (Einarsen *et al.* 2003).

ENVIRONMENTAL LEVEL

There have also been calls for researchers to move beyond the individual and dyadic levels of analysis and to consider group (previously discussed) and organisational factors in workplace bullying (Einarsen *et al.* 2003; Liefooghe and Davey 2001; Rayner *et al.* 2002). Indeed, organisational factors, such as a negative social environment, poor job design, leadership style and role conflict, have been associated with the occurrence of workplace bullying (Einarsen *et al.* 2003; Leymann 1996; Rayner *et al.* 2002; Skogstad *et al.* 2007). In a recent analysis, Harvey *et al.* (2006) proposed a number of environmental factors, which they link to the increase in workplace bullying (see Table 22.1).

Perhaps reflecting current work environments, research suggests that workplace bullying is associated with highly competitive workplaces (O'Moore *et al.* 1998; Salin 2003). For instance, Salin's (2003) study of 385 members of the Finnish Association of Graduates in Economics and Business Administration found a strong link between perceived organisational politics and workplace bullying. It was proposed that within the current organisational climate of increased organisational pressures, bullying may be a rational response to the level of competition and 'need for survival' (Salin 2003). Salin concluded that, in some cases, workplace bullying may be perpetrated in order to promote some people's own self-interest, which is in turn rewarded by the organisation (e.g. given a promotion).

Branch and her colleagues (2007a), in a unique study into upwards bullying, found that work environments characterised by high workloads, workgroup disharmony and acceptance of inappropriate behaviours appeared to contribute to upwards bullying. Indeed, it has been suggested that when stress in the workplace and interpersonal tension are not dealt with, they

Table 22.1 Organisational factors likely to be related to the increase in workplace bullying

Rate of change resulting in a high levels of uncertainty in the workplace
Lack of time to achieve tasks
Growing rate of diversity in the workplace
Downsizing/rightsizing resulting in concern for future longevity of survivors
Reduction of middle management resulting in an increased gap between management and workers
Lack of clearly outlined cultural norms within today's organisations

Source: Harvey *et al.* 2006, p.4

can eventually lead to workplace bullying (Skogstad *et al.* 2007). Furthermore, Branch *et al.* (2007a) found that change (e.g. an organisational restructure) appeared to play an important role in contributing to workplace pressures. In addition, it has been suggested that in a work environment of 'continuous change the potential for employees to project their fears and resentments into the construction of managers as bullies, whether deservedly or not, is high' (McCarthy *et al.* 2002, p.536). In other words, a 'victim-mentality' environment is created (McCarthy 1999). Interestingly, it has even been proposed that staff may actually be using the term 'bullying' as a way of voicing their dissatisfaction with organisational issues (Liefooghe and Davey 2001). Similarly, McCarthy (2004) suggests that the term '"bullying at work" has become a new signifier of distress that has acted as a solar collector of resentments' (p.xv). Perhaps this demonstrates more than ever the complexity of workplace bullying and how a number of factors all work towards the occurrence of bullying in the workplace.

Prevention and management of workplace bullying

As noted by De Cieri and Kramar (2005), it is vital that the field of management comprehends and addresses the 'alarming issue' of bullying (p.576). In light of 'the emotional, physical, legal, reputational and financial costs' of bullying and its impact on individuals, unions and employers, they recommend a comprehensive approach whereby organisations articulate their stance on preventing and eliminating bullying and then develop and maintain appropriate processes to support this stance (De Cieri and Kramar 2005, p.577). However, given the complex and multidimensional nature of workplace bullying, no single approach is likely to provide organisations with the answer to solving 'workplace bullying' problems. As such, a number of researchers and practitioners have suggested a range of responses to prevent and manage bullying in the workplace. McCarthy and his colleagues (2002) suggested that any effective response to workplace bullying needs to include 'prevention, redress/resolution, and support' (McCarthy *et al.* 2002, p.528). However, until recently the effectiveness of proposed interventions to address workplace bullying has been under-researched (Einarsen 2000; see Raver 2005 for recent research into interventions). This may be due to a lack of a suitable theoretical model explaining workplace bullying (Einarsen 2000), or due to the complexity of the phenomenon. Nonetheless, the lack of research into this area means that relatively little is known about the success of proposed interventions. With this limitation in mind, the following section will now expand upon the framework proposed by McCarthy and colleagues (2002).

PREVENTION

Policy

Typical methods of preventing workplace bullying include a clearly articulated 'no bullying' policy; training, which includes knowledge of responsibilities and obligations of employers and employees alike; as well as an effective risk identification and system for complaints (McCarthy *et al.* 2002; Vartia *et al.* 2003). When respondents were asked about how to deter workplace bullying in a questionnaire study of 512 Chartered Management Institute members in the UK, four strategies were rated highly: training, a contact point for advice, the provision of an internal confidential counselling service, and external mediation (Woodman and Cook 2005).

Furthermore, Woodman and Cook (2005) provide additional insight into the use and possible importance of a workplace bullying policy. When asked to rate their organisation's ability to deter bullying, 70 per cent of respondents from organisations that had a formal policy addressing workplace bullying felt their organisation was quite effective or very effective at

Figure 22.5 Poster encouraging the prevention of workplace bullying

Source: Workplace Mobbing Australia: www.workplacemobbing.com/mobbing.html; acknowledgements: Linda Shallcross (designer)

deterring bullying. The percentage of respondents rating the organisation as favourable was reduced considerably when the organisation had no formal policy (Woodman and Cook 2005). Therefore, the provision of a workplace bullying policy appears to be a potentially effective method by which organisations may begin to prevent workplace bullying. Participants in the Woodman and Cook (2005) study identified the need to involve a wide range of stakeholders, including line managers and employees, in the development and implementation of the policy. It is recommended that a workplace bullying policy should be widely available and include clearly defined terms (Richards and Daley 2003).

Training

As suggested by McCarthy *et al.* (2002), a training programme that includes information on the responsibilities and obligations of employers and employees is one measure to prevent workplace bullying (see example in Figure 22.5). Awareness-raising about what constitutes workplace bullying, its impacts, and what interventions can occur are vital steps in preventing workplace bullying and should take place throughout the whole organisation (McCarthy *et al.* 2002). Training about workplace bullying should outline the importance of clear objectives, roles and processes within the workplace, as well as the causes, impacts and how workplace bullying is handled in the workplace (Vartia *et al.* 2003). It is suggested that training should also be provided to managers on how to manage cases of bullying (McCarthy *et al.* 2002; Richards and Daley 2003).

Coping skills and resilience

The promotion of coping skills and resilience is also suggested as essential to assist targets to handle workplace bullying experiences (McCarthy *et al.* 2002). In an earlier study, McCarthy *et al.* (1995) found that training in interpersonal skills, conflict resolution and stress management assisted in helping targets of workplace bullying manage the behaviours of perpetrators better. Dispelling the myths of workplace bullying through awareness training may also assist in increasing targets' and potential targets' resilience to workplace bullying (McCarthy *et al.* 2002).

REDRESS OR RESOLUTION

Owing to the potential of workplace bullying to intensify if not dealt with early, the provision of early intervention measures is vital (McCarthy *et al.* 2002). Early intervention is important not just in terms of assisting the target, but also in sending a clear message that inappropriate behaviours will actually be addressed within the organisation (McCarthy *et al.* 2002). Redress can include informal (e.g. a contact officers' network to provide advice) and formal measures (e.g. a timely investigation process) (Richards and Daley 2003). Similarly, an appropriate grievance procedure should include both informal and formal measures, such as informal mediation processes, disciplinary action, the provision of information about internal and external opportunities for redress, and compensation (McCarthy *et al.* 2002). However, evidence suggests that informal discussions may make the situation worse for some targets because further retaliatory actions may occur (Woodman and Cook 2005), indicating the need for great sensitivity and skill in these areas.

According to McCarthy and his colleagues (2002), it is crucial that perpetrators of workplace bullying, whether their behaviour is intentional or unintentional, are made aware of their inappropriate behaviours. This can occur, if suitable, at the point of the inappropriate behaviour, or through a performance review. Importantly, it has been suggested that when approaching the perpetrator, managers should take a problem-solving approach, rather than adopt a punitive framework (McCarthy *et al.* 2002).

If a formal complaint is lodged, Richards and Daley (2003) advise that clear and specific information be provided within the complaint. This should include information as to the 'dates, times, and witnesses to incidents with direct quotes; factual description of events; indication of how each incident made the complainant feel; documentary evidence; details of any action the complainant or others have already taken' (Richards and Daley 2003, p.254). Complaints of workplace bullying should be treated seriously and investigated in a timely manner while maintaining confidentiality (Victorian WorkCover Authority, cited in McCarthy *et al.* 2002). However, owing to the subtle nature of workplace bullying, a no-blame resolution approach is recommended as a first intervention, when appropriate (McCarthy *et al.* 2002).

If an investigation is necessary, it should be fair and impartial (Richards and Daley 2003). In cases where a serious allegation has been made, where the target does not want to work with the perpetrator or pressure may be placed on witnesses, it is recommended that the alleged perpetrator (and target) be suspended with pay (Merchant and Hoel 2003; Rayner *et al.* 2002). Furthermore, the organisation should ensure that the complainant is protected from reprisals (Richards and Daley 2003). In cases where the organisation does not have the capacity to investigate claims of workplace bullying, or if the alleged perpetrator is a senior manager, an external investigator is recommended (Merchant and Hoel 2003). Confidentiality throughout the investigation process should be maintained; however, it is recognised that it is difficult to stop the informal 'rumour mill' . Once the investigation has been finalised, discussions with members of the workgroup as to the outcome and reasons for the final decision may be necessary (Richards and Daley 2003).

At the end of the investigation, a report should be provided to all parties, with the right to appeal for either party (Richards and Daley 2003). Provision to manage malicious complaints, which can be related to revenge, should also be made within the procedure (Richards and Daley 2003). In the case of a suspected malicious complaint, a motive must be shown (Merchant and Hoel 2003). Referring to a policy from a local council, Richards and Daley (2003) indicate that if the investigator considers the complaint to be malicious, then disciplinary action should be taken. Similarly, disciplinary action should be taken in cases of substantiated complaints (McCarthy *et al.* 2002). Despite the suitability of relocating the perpetrator in cases of substantiated bullying, often relocation of the target is the normal course of action, owing to the willingness of the target to transfer (Richards and Daley 2003).

SUPPORT

It is recommended that support via employee assistance schemes and human relations systems, such as counselling, be provided to both parties (McCarthy *et al.* 2002; Richards and Daley 2003; Tehrani 2003). Indeed, 'support at work may function as a buffer against stress by providing resources to enable [targets] to cope' (Quine 1999, p.231). Conversely, it has been suggested that the lack of support is central to the ability or inability of targets to cope (Lewis and Orford 2005; Leymann and Gustafsson 1996; Matthiesen *et al.* 2003). Seeking support, however, is proactive and is not a behaviour someone who is feeling helpless and victimised would be likely to perform, especially if they feel it could damage their position further (Lee 1997). For instance, by seeking help individuals may be concerned that they will appear incompetent (Lee 1997). In an important interview study of 15 college and university lecturers who had experienced workplace bullying, Lewis (2004) found that targets experience profound feelings of shame. Furthermore, despite the recognition that the provision of support is important in assisting targets to cope with workplace bullying (Lewis and Orford 2005; Leymann and Gustafsson 1996; Matthiesen *et al.* 2003), research indicates that targets are reluctant to seek support from an organisation that is perceived to be ineffective in addressing workplace bullying (Ferris 2004; Hoel and Cooper 2000).

Conclusion

Workplace bullying is a complex phenomenon which has increasingly become the focus of global research. Research, mainly using quantitative approaches, has explored the behaviours, prevalence, groups within workplaces who are most vulnerable, and the factors that contribute to the occurrence of workplace bullying. Research has consistently found that workplace bullying can have detrimental impacts upon those who are targeted, those who witness it, and the organisations in which it occurs. Management processes are of utmost importance in articulating and managing workplace bullying issues. Commonly, a 'no bullying' policy, training and support are considered useful interventions in deterring and managing bullying in the workplace. Clearly, this is an area which demands urgent attention by researchers and practitioners alike.

CASE STUDY 22.1

Managing in the short and longer term at GDB: a section of the public service

Sara Branch, Sheryl Ramsay and Michelle Barker

Two years ago GDB had a major restructure. The Client Relations Section, however, seemed to fall into the 'too-hard basket' and was never assigned a permanent manager. The section has had to make do with temporary managers who tend to stay for only a couple of months. However, for the last four months Chris (who has worked in client relations for a long time and for GDB for 30 years) has been taking on the temporary manager's role.

4. What impact is Lee's behaviour having on you in your manager role and your ability to do your job?
5. What impact do you think that Lee's behaviour is having (or could have) on the members of the group?
6. How do you think you, as the manager, could have handled the situation differently?
7. How do you think Robin, the senior manager, could have handled the situation differently?
8. Taking a strategic perspective, how could these types of situations be minimised or avoided in the future?

Epilogue

It has been eight months and although a lot has happened you seem to be in the same position, trying to get Lee to follow your directions and requests.

Since the meeting with Lee and Chris where they stated they would file a grievance against you, accusing you of bullying Lee, there has been an investigation. It took all of seven months to finalise! Lee's grievance was lengthy, outlining a number of incidents that, while they occurred, were inaccurate with regard to the detail. There was, of course, no mention of Lee's snide comments in meetings. This grievance took you a week to respond to: more time away from your real job!

You were interviewed, by the independent investigator, at least three times for about two hours each time. About seven other people within the team and workplace were also interviewed over the grievance, which caused a lot of disruption in the workplace, took others away from their job, and worst of all upset a number of those who were interviewed. It seemed to you that the grievance process divided the workgroup into those who supported Lee and those who supported you.

Throughout this whole time you felt that you were unsupported by your manager. You understand that he had to be seen to be impartial but you really had no one at work you could talk to. You felt very isolated at work. The only support you really felt was forthcoming was from home.

In the end you were cleared of all of Lee's accusations but your concerns about Lee's behaviour were not addressed by the organisation as too much time had passed since they had occurred. The outcome of the investigation was that you and Lee attend mediation together. You thought this was a good idea and might help you get to a point where the two of you could work effectively together. However, although you have attended three mediation sessions Lee only attended the first session. Lee made it very clear in this session that you are the one who needs the help. So it would seem that Lee still thinks the problem is yours and that there remains a lack of respect for your position and authority from Lee.

The crazy thing about the grievance investigation was that you were expected to manage Lee during the investigation! At issue here is the protection of all involved in the grievance investigation. If Lee's claims were legitimate, you could have very easily retaliated against Lee. Alternatively, as in this case, where the accusations were either malicious or frivolous, it placed you as the manager in a situation of limited power in terms of managing Lee, especially until the investigation was concluded. It would seem that for the safety of all parties involved in the grievance, there was a need to separate you and Lee or, if this was not possible, implement safeguards until an outcome had been reached.

Questions

1. What disruptions did the grievance have on the workplace?
2. What would you do differently if you were the senior manager overseeing the investigation?
3. Did the investigation resolve the conflict that existed between Lee and yourself?

CASE STUDY 22.2

Is this a case of peer bullying?

Sara Branch, Sheryl Ramsay and Michelle Barker

Ingrid's story: I cannot believe it has been a month since I took sick leave from Triple A. I am feeling so much better now but the thought of going back to work and working with Carmel terrifies me. Why, just the other day I had to go in and submit my doctor's certificate to HR and as I got closer to work I started shaking and crying uncontrollably and had to get off the train and go home. I ended up mailing the doctor's certificate. When I went to see the doctor she was really concerned for my well-being. The headaches, not sleeping and panic attacks seem to be getting worse, not better!

I really don't understand what went wrong. Work used to be a great place, full of inter-esting people and projects that engaged and challenged me. But that all changed when Carmel arrived and started bossing everyone around, but more so me.

In the beginning I really liked Carmel and I thought she liked me. I thought, here we go, she will fit in really well here and spice up the place a bit. How wrong was I! She was employed at the same level as me, in the same role, but seemed to think she knew it all and that I knew nothing. After about three months she really started to boss me around, almost using me as her own private slave. It started with 'Can you get me that information?', using the excuse that she was new to Triple A, and progressed to 'Where is that information I wanted? Why are you so useless?'

Everything I did was wrong, even the clothes that I wore to work she didn't like. It all came to a head when a report I was working on was sabotaged, making me look foolish and humili-ating me in front of my manager and the client. What she did was take the report on the pre-tence of editing it and made changes that were not accurate. Why am I such a fool for trusting her? After that I really felt like I was being set up all the time and strange things started hap-pening. Nothing I could put my finger on, but things like messages not being passed on to me, things going missing from my desk and then reappearing a day later. It wouldn't have been so bad if my colleagues had supported me but unfortunately most of them seem to have been talking to Carmel and think I am useless. I really feel as if I have been bullied.

Questions

1. Do you have the full picture?
2. What else would help you to have greater understanding of the case?

What other people in the workplace think

Jen – 'OK, Carmel sets high standards but what is wrong with that? Ingrid just needs to pull up her socks and get to work and stop worrying about Carmel. I really don't think that Carmel has been bullying Ingrid, I haven't seen her yell at her or anything like that; isn't that bullying?'

Ross – 'Really Ingrid is just too sensitive. Carmel does a great job and helps out around the place a lot. She really seems to fit in nicely. If Ingrid has a problem with that then maybe she should not come back to Triple A.'

Kate – 'Ingrid has had a difficult time lately. I know everybody around here seems to think that Carmel is great, and she is, as long as she likes you. I have been lucky and she seems to like me but I have noticed how she bosses Ingrid around. I tried talking to Ingrid on the

▶

side but she said that it was OK and that it would work out. Well it hasn't. I cannot say for sure if Carmel has been bullying Ingrid as I don't know what has been happening but I have worked with Ingrid for a long time and it is not like her to make mistakes such as the ones that were in the report.'

Paul – 'As Ingrid's boss I take her accusations of bullying seriously but Ingrid didn't want to have a mediation session to try to get back to a working relationship. When I talked to Carmel about it she didn't seem to know what Ingrid was talking about. It is hard to know which way to go with this type of stuff: in a way you are damned if you do something and damned if you do nothing.'

Questions

Imagine you are an HR professional employed by this organisation. You have been asked to provide a development programme for staff (in relation to the above scenario).

1. Where would you start?
2. What are the main issues you need to clarify before getting started?
3. Indicate the aims of such a programme and outline the most important elements that need to be addressed within the programme.
4. How would you evaluate such a programme?

CASE STUDY 22.3

Workplace bullying: reflective exercises

Sara Branch, Sheryl Ramsay and Michelle Barker

Exercise a

1. In pairs reflect on the interpersonal conflicts you may have experienced, witnessed or heard about in the workplace and make a list of antisocial behaviours that occur in the workplace.

2. Consider if gender contributed to this conflict.

3. Consider if power played a role in the conflict. If yes, then what power sources were being used?

4. What is the potential impact on witnesses and what could they say or do?

Exercise b

Within small groups reflect on the factors contributing to workplace bullying and brainstorm three strategies at each level (i.e. individual, group and organisational) that you could use to address, and potentially reduce or prevent, workplace bullying.

Exercise c

Judy receives a call from her old university friend Jan, who is now working as a support worker. Jan, in tears, relates to Judy the mean things her boss has been doing to her. He was nice enough when she first arrived at her job last year, but now he has become

▶

unbearable. Jan listed some of the things he had done that week: 'On Monday, he came in to work and told me in front of everyone that I was too slow and that I dragged down the whole department. The rest of the week he spent glaring at me each time he passed me in the hall. He threw a huge temper tantrum when I did not have a report ready two days before it was due. I snapped back and unfortunately that seemed to inflame the situation. I later found out that there had been a meeting involving all the support workers that he failed to tell me about. I even heard a rumour that I was sleeping with a client, and I am certain he started it. I just don't know what to do and who to turn to, especially as those around me just seem to keep their heads down. What do you think, Judy?'

Discuss how the issues raised in this scenario could be addressed using the strategies discussed in the previous exercise (Exercise b).

Bibliography

Archer, D. (1999) 'Exploring "bullying" culture in the para-military organisation', *International Journal of Manpower*, Vol.20, No.1/2, pp.94–105.

Asch, D. and Salaman, G. (2002) 'The challenge of change', *European Business Journal*, Vol.14, No.3, pp.133–43.

Ashforth, B. (1997) 'Petty tyranny in organizations: a preliminary examination of antecedents and consequences', *Canadian Journal of Administrative Sciences*, Vol.14, No.2, pp.126–40.

Baron, R. and Neuman, J. (1996) 'Workplace violence and workplace aggression: evidence on their relative frequency and potential causes', *Aggressive Behavior*, Vol.22, No.3, pp.161–73.

Baron, R. and Neuman, J. (1998) 'Workplace aggression – the iceberg beneath the tip of workplace violence: evidence on its forms, frequency, and targets', *Public Administration Quarterly*, Vol.21, No.4, pp.446–64.

Bassman, E. (1992) *Abuse in the Workplace*, Westport, CT: Quorum Books.

Baumeister, R., Smart, L. and Boden, J. (1996) 'Relation of threatened egotism to violence and aggression: the dark side of high self-esteem', *Psychological Review*, Vol.103, No.1, pp.5–33.

Bjorkqvist, K., Osterman, K. and Hjelt-Back, M. (1994) 'Aggression among university employees', *Aggressive Behavior*, Vol.20, pp.173–84.

Branch, S. (2006) 'Upwards bullying: an exploratory study of power, dependency and the work environment for Australian Managers, unpublished doctoral thesis, Griffith University, Brisbane.

Branch, S., Ramsay, C. and Barker, M. (2007a) 'Managers in the firing line: contributing factors to workplace bullying by staff – an interview study', *Journal of Management and Organization*, Vol.13, pp.264–81.

Branch, S., Ramsay, S. and Barker, M. (2007b) 'The bullied boss: a conceptual exploration of upwards bullying', in A. I. Glendon, B. M. Thompson and B. Myors (eds), *Advances in Organisational Psychology*, Bowen Hills, Qld: Australian Academic Press, pp.93–112.

Braverman, M. (1999) *Preventing Workplace Violence: A Guide for Employers and Practitioners*, London: Sage Publications.

Brown, A. J. (ed.) (2007) *Whistling While They Work: Enhancing the Theory and Practice of Internal Witness Management in Public Sector Organisations – Draft Report*, Socio-Legal Research Centre, Griffith Law School.

Cook, K., Yamagishi, T. and Donnelly, S. (1997) 'Power and dependence in exchange networks: a comment on structural measures of power', in J. Szmatka, J. Skvoretz and J. Berger (eds) *Status, Network, and Structure: Theory Development in Group Processes*, Stanford, CA: Stanford University Press.

Coyne, I., Seigne, E. and Randall, P. (2000) 'Predicting workplace victim status from personality', *European Journal of Work and Organizational Psychology*, Vol.9, No.3, pp.335–49.

De Cieri, H. and Kramar, R. (2005) *Human Resource Management in Australia*, North Ryde, NSW: McGraw Hill Irwin.

Djurkovic, N., McCormack, D. and Casimir, G. (2004) 'The physical and psychological effects of workplace bullying and their relationship to intention to leave: a test of the psychosomatic and disability hypotheses', *International Journal of Organization Theory and Behavior,* Vol.7, No.4, pp.469–97.

Douglas, S. and Martinko, M. (2001) 'Exploring the role of individual differences in the prediction of workplace aggression', *Journal of Applied Psychology,* Vol.86, No.4, pp.547–59.

Einarsen, S. (1999) 'The nature and causes of bullying at work', *International Journal of Manpower,* Vol.20, No.1/2, pp.16–27.

Einarsen, S. (2000) 'Harassment and bullying at work: a review of the Scandinavian approach', *Aggression and Violent Behavior,* Vol.5, No.4, pp.379–401.

Einarsen, S. and Mikkelsen, G. (2003) 'Individual effects of exposure to bullying at work', in S. Einarsen, H. Hoel, D. Zapf and C. L. Cooper (eds) *Bullying and Emotional Abuse in the Workplace: International Perspectives in Research and Practice* (pp.127–44), London: Taylor & Francis Books.

Einarsen, S. and Raknes, B. (1997) 'Harassment in the workplace and the victimization of men', *Violence and Victims,* Vol.12, No.3, pp.247–63.

Einarsen, S. and Skogstad, A. (1996) 'Bullying at work: epidemiological findings in public and private organizations', *European Journal of Work and Organizational Psychology,* Vol.5, No.2, pp.185–201.

Einarsen, S., Hoel, H., Zapf, D. and Cooper, C. (2003) 'The concept of bullying at work: the European tradition', in S. Einarsen, H. Hoel, D. Zapf and C. Cooper (eds) *Bullying and Emotional Abuse in the Workplace: International Perspectives in Research and Practice,* London: Taylor and Francis, pp.1–30.

Emerson, R. M. (1962) 'Power-ependence relations', *American Sociological Review,* Vol.27, No.1, pp.31–41.

Ferris, P. (2004) 'A preliminary typology of organisational response to allegations of workplace bullying: see no evil, hear no evil, speak no evil', *British Journal of Guidance and Counselling,* Vol.32, No.3, pp.389–95.

Fox, S. and Stallworth, L. (2004) 'Racial/ethnic bullying: exploring links between bullying and racism in the US workforce', *Journal of Vocational Behavior,* Vol.66, pp.438–56.

Gorman, P. (1999, 2–3 July) *Bullying of victims by the present injustices in the system,* Paper presented at the Beyond Bullying Association Responding to Professional Abuse Conference, St Johns College, University of Queensland.

Hadikin, R. and O'Driscoll, M. (2000) *The Bullying Culture: Cause, Effect, Harm Reduction,* Melbourne: Books for Midwives.

Harvey, M. G., Heames, J. T., Richey, R. G. and Leonard, N. (2006) 'Bullying: from the playground to the boardroom', *Journal of Leadership and Organizational Studies,* Vol.12, No.4, pp.1–11.

Health and Safety Executive (2006) 'Bullying, bullying its way to the workplace', available at www.hse.gov.uk, accessed March 2008.

Heames, J. and Harvey, M. (2006) 'Workplace bullying: a cross-level assessment', *Management Decision,* Vol.44, No.9, pp.1214–30.

Hoel, H. (1997) 'Bullying at work: a Scandinavian perspective', *Journal of the Institution of Occupational Safety and Health,* Vol.1, pp.51–9.

Hoel, H. and Cooper, C. (2000) *Destructive Conflict and Bullying at Work,* Manchester, UK: School of Management, University of Manchester, Institute of Science and Technology.

Hoel, H. and Cooper, C. (2001) 'Origins of bullying: theoretical frameworks for explaining workplace bullying', in N. Tehrani (ed.) *Building a Culture of respect: Managing Bullying at Work,* London: Taylor & Francis, pp.3–20.

Hoel, H. and Salin, D. (2003) 'Organisational antecedents of workplace bullying', in S. Einarsen, H. Hoel, D. Zapf and C. Cooper (eds) *Bullying and Emotional Abuse in the Workplace: International Perspectives in Research and Practice,* London: Taylor and Francis, pp.203–18.

Hoel, H., Cooper, C. and Faragher, B. (2001) 'The experience of bullying in Great Britain: the impact of organizational status', *European Journal of Work and Organizational Psychology,* Vol.10, No.4, pp.443–65.

Jablin, F. (1986) 'Superior-subordinate communication: the state of the art', *Psychological Bulletin,* Vol.86, pp.1201–22.

Keashly, L. (1998) 'Emotional abuse in the workplace: conceptual and empirical issues', *Journal of Emotional Abuse*, Vol.1, pp.85–116.

Keashly, L. (2001) 'Interpersonal and systemic aspects of emotional abuse at work: the target's perspective', *Violence and Victims*, Vol.16, No.3, pp.233–68.

Keashly, L. and Harvey, S. (2006). 'Workplace emotional abuse', in E. Kelloway, J. Barling and J. Hurrell Jr. (eds) *Handbook of Workplace Violence*, Thousand Oaks: Sage Publications, pp.95–120.

Keashly, L. and Jagatic, K. (2003) 'By any other name: American perspectives on workplace bullying', in S. Einarsen, H. Hoel, D. Zapf and C. Cooper (eds) *Bullying and Emotional Abuse in the Workplace: International Perspectives in Research and Practice*, London: Taylor and Francis, pp.31–61.

Kivimaki, M., Elovainio, M. and Vahtera, J. (2000) 'Workplace bullying and sickness absence in hospital staff', *Occupational and Environmental Medicine*, Vol.57, No.10, pp.656–60.

Lee, F. (1997) 'When the going gets tough, do the tough ask for help? Help seeking and power motivation in organizations', *Organizational Behavior and Human Decision Processes*, Vol.72, No.3, pp.336–63.

Lewis, D. (2004) 'Bullying at work: the impact of shame among university and college lecturers', *British Journal of Guidance and Counselling*, Vol.32, No.3, pp.281–99.

Lewis, D. and Gunn, R. (2007) 'Workplace bullying in the public sector: understanding the racial dimension', *Public Administration*, Vol.83, No.3, pp.641–65.

Lewis, S. and Orford, J. (2005) 'Women's experiences of workplace bullying: changes in social relationships', *Journal of Community and Applied Social Psychology*, Vol.15, pp.29–47.

Lewis, D. and Sheehan, M. (2003) 'Introduction: workplace bullying: theoretical and practical approaches to a management challenge', *International Journal of Management and Decision Making*, Vol.4, No.1, pp.1–10.

Leymann, H. (1990) 'Mobbing and psychological terror at workplaces', *Violence and Victims*, Vol.5, pp.119–26.

Leymann, H. (1996) 'The content and development of mobbing at work', *European Journal of Work and Organizational Psychology*, Vol.5, No.2, pp.165–84.

Leymann, H. and Gustafsson, A. (1996) 'Mobbing at work and the development of post-traumatic stress disorders', *European Journal of Work and Organizational Psychology*, Vol.5, No.2, pp.251–75.

Liefooghe, A. and Davey, K. (2001) 'Accounts of workplace bullying: the role of the organization', *European Journal of Work and Organizational Psychology*, Vol.10, No.4, pp.375–92.

Matthiesen, S. and Einarsen, S. (2004) 'Psychiatric distress and symptoms of PTSD among victims of bullying at work', *British Journal of Guidance and Counselling*, Vol.32, No.3, pp.335–56.

Matthiesen, S., Aasen, E., Holst, G., Wie, K. and Einarsen, S. (2003) 'The escalation of conflict: a case study of bullying at work', *International Journal of Management and Decision Making*, Vol.4, No.1, pp.96–112.

Mayhew, C., McCarthy, P., Chappell, D., Quinlan, M., Barker, M. and Sheehan, M. (2004) 'Measuring the extent of impact from occupational violence and bullying on traumatised workers', *Employee Responsibilities and Rights Journal*, Vol.16, No.3, pp.117–34.

McCarthy, P. (1996) 'When the mask slips: inappropriate coercion in organisations undergoing restructuring', in P. McCarthy, M. Sheehan and W. Wilkie (eds) *Bullying: From Backyard to Boardroom*, Alexandria: Millennium Books, pp.47–66.

McCarthy, P. (1999) 'Strategies between managementality and victimmentality in the pressures of continuous change', in C. Fraser, M. Barker and A. Martin (eds) *Organisations Looking Ahead: Challenges and Directions*, Logan Campus, Queensland: Griffith University, pp.22–3.

McCarthy, P. (2004) 'Costs of occupational violence and bullying', in P. McCarthy and C. Mayhew (eds) *Safeguarding the Organization against Violence and Bullying*, Basingstoke, UK: Palgrave Macmillan.

McCarthy, P. and Barker, M. (2000) 'Workplace bullying risk audit', *The Journal of Occupational Health and Safety – Australia and New Zealand*, Vol.16, pp.409–18.

McCarthy, P. and Mayhew, C. (2004) *Safeguarding the Organization against Violence and Bullying*, New York: Palgrave Macmillan.

McCarthy, P., Sheehan, M. and Kearns, D. (1995) *Managerial Styles and Their Effects on Employees' Health and Well-being in Organisations Undergoing Restructuring*, Brisbane: School of Organisational Behaviour and Human Resource Management.

McCarthy, P., Henderson, M., Sheehan, M. and Barker, M. (2002) 'Workplace bullying: its management and prevention', in *Australian Master OHS and Environment Guide 2003*, Sydney: CCH Australia Limited, pp.519–49.

Merchant, V. and Hoel, H. (2003) 'Investigating complaints of bullying', in S. Einarsen, H. Hoel, D. Zapf and C. Cooper (eds) *Bullying and Emotional Abuse in the Workplace: International Perspectives in Research and Practice*, London: Taylor and Francis.

Mikkelsen, E. and Einarsen, S. (2001) 'Bullying in Danish work-life: prevalence and health correlates', *European Journal of Work and Organizational Psychology*, Vol.10, No.4, pp.393–413.

Mikkelsen, E. and Einarsen, S. (2002) 'Basic assumptions and symptoms of post-traumatic stress among victims of bullying at work', *European Journal of Work and Organizational Psychology*, Vol.11, No.1, pp.87–111.

Niedhammer, I., David, S., Degioanni, S. and 143 occupational physicians (2006) 'Association between workplace bullying and depressive symptoms in the French working population', *Journal of Psychosomatic Research*, Vol.61, No.5, pp.251–59.

O'Moore, M., Seigne, E., McGuire, L. and Smith, M. (1998) 'Victims of bullying at work in Ireland', *The Journal of Occupational Health and Safety – Australia and New Zealand*, Vol.14, pp.569–74.

Pietersen, C. (2007) 'Interpersonal bullying behaviours in the workplace', *SA Journal of Industrial Psychology*, Vol.33, No.1, pp.59–66.

Quine, L. (1999) 'Workplace bullying in NHS community trust: staff questionnaire survey', *British Medical Journal*, Vol.318, No.7178, pp.228–32.

Quine, L. (2001) 'Workplace Bullying in nurses', *Journal of Health Psychology*, Vol.6, No.1, pp.73–84.

Raver, J. (2005) *Workplace Bullying: International Perspectives on Moving from Research to Practice*, Symposium presented at the Academy of Management, Honolulu, HI.

Rayner, C. (1997) 'The incidence of workplace bullying', *Journal of Community and Applied Social Psychology*, Vol.7, pp.199–208.

Rayner, C. (1999) 'From research to implementation: finding leverage for prevention', *International Journal of Manpower*, Vol.20, No.1/2, pp.28–38.

Rayner, C. and Cooper, C. (2003) 'The black hole in "bullying at work" research', *International Journal of Management and Decision Making*, Vol.4 No.1, pp.47–64.

Rayner, C. and Hoel, H. (1997) 'A summary review of literature relating to workplace bullying', *Journal of Community and Applied Social Psychology*, Vol.7, pp.181–81.

Rayner, C., Hoel, H. and Cooper, C. (2002) *Workplace Bullying: What We Know, Who is to Blame, and What Can We Do?* London: Taylor and Francis.

Richards, J. and Daley, H. (2003) 'Bullying policy: development, implementation and monitoring', in S. Einarsen, H. Hoel, D. Zapf and C. Cooper (eds) *Bullying and Emotional Abuse in the Workplace: International Perspectives in Research and Practice*, London: Taylor and Francis.

Rigby, K. (2001) 'Bullying in schools and in the workplace', in P. McCarthy, J. Rylance, R. Bennett and H. Zimmermann (eds) *Bullying: From Backyard to Boardroom* (2nd edn), Sydney: The Federation Press, pp.1–10.

Rylance, J. (2001) 'Bullying in the helping professions', in P. McCarthy, J. Rylance, R. Bennett and H. Zimmermann (eds) *Bullying: From Backyard to Boardroom* (2nd edn), Sydney: The Federation Press, pp.23–33.

Salin, D. (2001) 'Prevalence and forms of bullying among business professionals: a comparison of two different strategies for measuring bullying', *European Journal of Work and Organizational Psychology*, Vol.10, No.4, pp.425–41.

Salin, D. (2003) 'Bullying and organisational politics in competitive and rapidly changing work environments', *International Journal of Management and Decision Making*, Vol.4, No.1, pp.35–46.

Savva, C. and Alexandrou, A. (1998) *The Impact of Bullying in Further and Higher Education*, Paper presented at the Bullying at Work: 1998 Research Update Conference, Staffordshire University Business School.

Sheehan, M., Barker, M. and McCarthy, P. (2004) 'Analysing metaphors used by victims of workplace bullying', *International Journal of Management and Decision Making*, Vol.5, No.1, pp.21–34.

Skogstad, A., Einarsen, S., Torsheim, T., Aasland, M. and Hetland, J. (2007) 'The destructiveness of laissez-faire leadership behavior', *Journal of Occupational Health Psychology*, Vol.12, No.1, pp.80–92.

Smith, P. (1997) 'Commentary III', *Journal of Community and Applied Social Psychology*, Vol.7, pp.249–55.

Smith, P. and Brain, P. (2000) 'Bullying in schools: lessons from two decades of research', *Aggressive Behavior*, Vol.26, pp.1–9.

Smith, P., Singer, M., Hoel, H. and Cooper, C. (2003) 'Victimization in the school and the workplace: are there any links?' *British Journal of Psychology*, Vol.94, pp.175–88.

Stucke, T. and Sporer, S. (2002) 'When a grandiose self-image is threatened: narcissism and self-concept clarity as predictors of negative emotions and aggression following ego-threat', *Journal of Personality*, Vol.70, No.4, pp.509–32.

Tehrani, N. (2003) 'Counselling and rehabilitating employees involved with bullying', in S. Einarsen, H. Hoel, D. Zapf and C. Cooper (eds) *Bullying and Emotional Abuse in the Workplace: International Perspectives in Research and Practice*, London: Taylor and Francis.

Tehrani, N. (2004) 'Bullying: a source of chronic post traumatic stress?', *British Journal of Guidance and Counselling*, Vol.32, No.3, pp.357–66.

Tracy, S., Lutgen-Sandvik, P. and Alberts, J. (2006) 'Nightmares, demons, and slaves: exploring the painful metaphors or workplace bullying', *Management Communication Quarterly*, Vol.20, No.2, pp.148–85.

UNISON (2003) *Bullying at Work: Guidelines for UNISON Branches, Stewards and Safety Representatives*, London: UNISON.

Vartia, M., Korppoo, L., Fallenius, S. and Mattila, M. (2003) 'Workplace bullying: the role of occupational health services', in S. Einarsen, H. Hoel, D. Zapf and C. Cooper (eds) *Bullying and Emotional Abuse in the Workplace: International Perspectives in Research and Practice*, London: Taylor and Francis.

Woodman, P. and Cook, P. (2005) *Bullying at Work: The Experience of Managers*, London: Chartered Management Institute.

Zapf, D. (1999) 'Organisational, work group related and personal causes of mobbing/bullying at work', *International Journal of Manpower*, Vol.20, No.1/2, pp.70–85.

Zapf, D. (2004) *Negative Social Behaviour at Work and Workplace Bullying*, Paper presented at the Fourth International Conference on Bullying and Harassment in the Workplace, Bergen, Norway.

Zapf, D. and Einarsen, S. (2001) 'Bullying in the workplace: recent trends in research and practice: an introduction', *European Journal of Work and Organizational Psychology*, Vol.10, No.4, pp.369–73.

Zapf, D. and Einarsen, S. (2003) 'Individual antecedents of bullying: victims and perpetrators', in S. Einarsen, H. Hoel, D. Zapf and C. Cooper (eds) *Bullying and Emotional Abuse in the Workplace: International Perspectives in Research and Practice*, London: Taylor and Francis, pp.165–84.

Zapf, D. and Einarsen, S. (2005) 'Mobbing at work: escalated conflicts in organizations', in S. Fox and P. Spector (eds) *Counterproductive Work Behavior: Investigations of Actors and Targets*, Washington, DC: American Psychological Association.

Zapf, D. and Gross, C. (2001) 'Conflict escalation and coping with workplace bullying: a replication and extension', *European Journal of Work and Organizational Psychology*, Vol.10, No.4, pp.497–522.

Zapf, D., Knorz, C. and Kulla, M. (1996) 'On the relationship between mobbing factors, and job content, social work environment, and health outcomes', *European Journal of Work and Organizational Psychology*, Vol.5, No.2, pp.215–37.

Zapf, D., Einarsen, S., Hoel, H. and Vartia, M. (2003) 'Empirical findings on bullying in the workplace', in S. Einarsen, H. Hoel, D. Zapf and C. Cooper (eds) *Bullying and Emotional Abuse in the Workplace: International Perspectives in Research and Practice*, London: Taylor and Francis, pp.103–26.

INDEX